select material from

The McGraw-Hill Reader

Issues Across the Disciplines

Eleventh Edition

Gilbert Muller
The City University of New York
LaGuardia College

custom edition for

Wake Tech Community College

 Learning Solutions

Boston   Burr Ridge, IL   Dubuque, IA   New York   San Francisco   St. Louis
Bangkok   Bogotá   Caracas   Lisbon   London   Madrid
Mexico City   Milan   New Delhi   Seoul   Singapore   Sydney   Taipei   Toronto

Select Material from
The McGraw-Hill Reader: Issues Across the Disciplines, Eleventh Edition
Custom Edition for Wake Tech Community College

3 4 5 6 7 8 9 0 QTN QTN 14 13

ISBN-13: 978-0-07-767840-1
ISBN-10: 0-07-767840-0

Learning Solutions Consultant: Lauren Langley
Learning Solutions Representative: Nikki Schmitt
Production Editor: Heather Willison
Cover Designer: Lou Civitello
Printer/Binder: Quad/Graphics
Cover Photo Credits: © 2012 JupiterImages Corporation

About the Author

GILBERT H. MULLER is professor emeritus of English at the LaGuardia campus of the City University of New York. He has also taught at Stanford University, where he received a PhD in English and American Literature; Vassar College; and several universities overseas. Dr. Muller is the author of the award-winning *Nightmares and Visions: Flannery O'Connor and the Catholic Grotesque; Chester Himes; New Strangers in Paradise: The Immigrant Experience and Contemporary American Fiction; William Cullen Bryant: Author of America*, and other critical studies. His essays and reviews have appeared in *The New York Times, The New Republic, The Nation, The Sewanee Review, The Georgia Review*, and elsewhere. He has written and edited best-selling textbooks in English and composition, including McGraw-Hill's *The Short Prose Reader*, with Harvey Wiener, now in its twelfth edition. Among Dr. Muller's awards are fellowships from the National Endowment for the Humanities, the Fulbright Commission, the Ford Foundation, and the Mellon Foundation.

To Parisa and Darius
My favorite readers

Brief Contents

PART 2
ISSUES ACROSS THE DISCIPLINES

From WAKE TECH CC, 3rd Party Readings, Author Original

Contents

PART 2
ISSUES ACROSS THE DISCIPLINES

From WAKE TECH CC, 3rd Party Readings, Author Original

Contents of Essays by Rhetorical Mode

NARRATION

DESCRIPTION

ILLUSTRATION

COMPARISON AND CONTRAST

ANALOGY

DEFINITION

CLASSIFICATION

PROCESS ANALYSIS

CAUSAL ANALYSIS

ARGUMENTATION AND PERSUASION

HUMOR, IRONY, AND SATIRE

Networking Assignments

Preface

ISSUES ACROSS DISCIPLINES, LITERACIES ACROSS MEDIA

The eleventh edition of *The McGraw-Hill Reader* is a textbook for twenty-first century composition classrooms. Like its previous bestselling editions, this reader continues to engage students with the finest classic and contemporary essays—works that span myriad ages, cultures, and disciplines—and in this latest version, it also prompts students to read, watch, research, listen to, interact with, and compose in multiple media. Recognizing that digital technologies and the Internet have had a revolutionary impact on conventional concepts of composition, *The McGraw-Hill Reader* now prepares students for an expanded universe of literacies. In today's college classrooms, this means fluency with print, audio, visual, digital, electronic, interactive, and hybrid texts.

Eudora Welty (whose work appears in this collection) speaks of reading as "a sweet devouring," and *The McGraw-Hill Reader* invites students to participate in—and enjoy—the vast and varied pleasures of responding to texts in any form; additionally, this book's approach affords opportunities to experiment with numerous contexts for academic discourse. Addressing the abiding national interest in core liberal arts programs, interdisciplinary issues, and multicultural perspectives, the eleventh edition offers students and instructors a full range of quality prose models important to writing courses, reading sequences, and key undergraduate disciplines. All of the selections have been chosen for their significance, vitality, and stylistic precision. With the high quality of its essays, its consistent humanistic emphases, its clear organization, and its new focus on the importance of 21st-century literacies, *The McGraw-Hill Reader* offers instructors a lively, sophisticated, and eminently flexible text for college composition programs.

Organization

Composed of two parts and 15 chapters, *The McGraw-Hill Reader* covers the major modes of writing and many of the disciplines that college students will encounter as undergraduates. In Part 1, a new Chapter 1 presents an overview of the ways we read and respond to texts today. Chapter 2 focuses on strategies for critical thinking, reading, and writing, emphasizing multiple 21st-century electronic options. Chapter 3 provides extensive coverage of argument and persuasion. Chapter 4 provides an updated tour of research, research writing, and MLA/APA documentation in this age of new media.

In Part 2, Chapters 5–15 explore core liberal arts disciplines, including education, the social sciences, business and economics, the humanities, and the sciences. Each chapter asks a key question, drawn from the disciplines it represents, designed to elicit constructive class discussion and sound critical writing. These disciplinary chapters offer prose models that encourage students to practice skills they will need throughout college—including analysis, criticism, argumentation, as well as facility with digital texts.

Highlights of the Eleventh Edition

Informed by the comments and suggestions of instructors from across the country who reviewed the previous edition and provided useful advice for the eleventh, *The McGraw-Hill Reader* offers several new and significant features:

- **Thirty-four new selections.** Fresh essays appear on topics of current and enduring interest. Topics like the Obama generation, marriage equality, global climate change, online social networking, swine flu, the legacy of Michael Jackson, the appeal of *Mad Men*, the wars in Iraq and Afghanistan, globalization, torture, and medical breakthroughs should elicit lively student response and effective writing. Several longer, more demanding selections have been included, as well as readings that contain visuals. New readings to this edition include essays by Julia Alvarez, Jamaica Kincaid, Paul Krugman, Woody Allen, John Updike, Atul Gawande, Nora Ephron, Barry Lopez, and other established and emerging writers.
- **New Chapter 1 and integrated coverage of 21st-century literacies throughout Part 1.** These sections introduce students to 21st-century (as well as traditional) literacies, composition practices, and communication strategies. This chapter—like each chapter in the eleventh edition—examines the nature of different writing environments and ways to utilize various communication technologies spanning textual, visual, and technological realms. Chapter 2 now focuses on writing processes, offering enhanced coverage of tone relating to texts across media.
- **New "Networking: Applying 21st-Century Literacies " assignments.** A new category of question has been added to *every reading*. Designed to foster digital, multimedia, and real-world literacy skills, these new assignments send students online; to video, audio, or interactive sources; or away from their desks to create visual texts or conduct primary research. These assignments may provide opportunities for collaborative work, enhanced research projects, or composition in different genres or across media. For easy reference, these are listed on page xxxiii.
- **Two new case studies for synthesis on themes of multimodal communication and composition.** *Classic and Contemporary: The Impulse to Compose* (Chapter 1) features selections by Henry David Thoreau and comedian Steve Martin. *Social Networking: Friend or Foe?* (Chapter 3), inspired by the 10th edition's focus on MySpace, examines what online relationships mean in many contexts—from following a celebrity on Twitter, to meeting a future spouse on OKCupid, to figuring out how one's identity and place in the actual community might be enhanced or challenged by virtual spaces.
- **New Research Project Casebook.** In Chapter 4, this new feature walks through one student's process in finding, evaluating, and working with sources to craft a research essay. The casebook examines how to choose, research, synthesize, and document sources in five widely used media: a print book, a scholarly journal article accessed through a library database, a popular magazine article accessed online, a Web site, and an image.
- **Revised and enhanced Chapter 4 on 21st-century research practices.** In addition to its new casebook, this chapter now offers guidance on the most current research

writing processes and the documentation styles recommended and recently updated by the Modern Language Association (2009) and the American Psychological Association (2010). This new edition offers an array of new model entries from new media sources. Students are encouraged to use multiple communications technologies to develop complex research-based texts.

- **New visuals.** Throughout the text, provocative images with accompanying apparatus add insight into essays and engage students while encouraging critical thought. These include **seven new images** in the **full-color insert on advertising and culture,** which encourages students to respond to advertisements as visual texts. Select images from the book will be available for viewing (or linked to) in a full-color gallery on this text's Web site.

Proven Features

Throughout many editions, instructors and students have found the following features of *The McGraw-Hill Reader* useful:

- **A rich selection of readings.** A distinct strength of *The McGraw-Hill Reader*—perhaps the primary one for teachers who prefer to create their own approaches to composition and reading courses—is the wide range of material and the varied constituencies represented in the text. The essays in this book have been selected carefully to embrace a rich assortment of authors, to achieve balance among constituencies, to cover major historical periods, and to provide prose models and styles for class analysis, discussion, and imitation. The authors in this text—from Plato to Nora Ephron, Jonathan Swift to Amy Tan—all have high visibility as writers and thinkers of value. Some of these authors are represented by more than one essay. All the authors—writing from such vantage points as literature, journalism, anthropology, sociology, art history, biology, and philosophy—start from the perspective that ideas exist in the world, that we should be alert to them, and that we should be able to deal with them in our own discourse.

- **A text that works with a wide variety of levels and approaches.** Because the selections range from very simple essays to more abstract and complex modes of discourse, teachers and students will be able to use *The McGraw-Hill Reader* at virtually all levels of a program. Containing more than one hundred complete essays, *The McGraw-Hill Reader* is thus a flexible companion for composition courses. It can be used with any of the major pedagogical perspectives common to the practice of composition today: as a writing-across-the-curricula text, as the basis for a rhetorically focused course, as a thematic reader, as a multicultural anthology, or as an in-depth reader. An alternate table of contents, listing carefully selected essays in eleven rhetorical categories, also makes *The McGraw-Hill Reader* adaptable to an approach based on the rhetorical patterns. Above all, teachers can develop their own sequences of essays that will contribute not only to their students' reading and writing proficiency but also to their growing intellectual power.

- **Chapter introductions that encourage students to reflect on major issues in the discipline.** The introduction to each disciplinary chapter gives students a broad perspective on the field at hand by putting major issues and concerns in context. Each introduction ends with a previewing section that alerts students to strategies for reading, discussion, and writing.

- **Integrated and focused treatment of argument, plagiarism, summary and précis, and research.** The chapters in Part 1 provide integrated guidelines on these topics. Additionally, argumentation is stressed throughout the text, with a writing assignment following all selections asking students to compose an argumentative essay.
- **Uniform apparatus that reinforces critical reading and writing.** Another major strength of *The McGraw-Hill Reader* is in the uniform apparatus that accompanies every essay. Much can be learned from any well-written essay, especially if the apparatus is systematic in design. Each selection in this text is preceded by a brief introduction that offers biographical information about the author. The questions that follow each essay are organized in a consistent format created to reinforce essential reading, writing, and oral communication skills. Now arranged in four categories—Comprehension, Rhetoric, Writing, and Networking: Applying 21st-Century Literacies—these questions reflect current compositional theory as they move students from audience analysis to various modes, processes, and media of composition. Specialized terms used in the questions are defined in an extensive Glossary of Terms at the end of the text. The integrated design of these questions makes each essay—simple or complex, short or long, old or new—accessible to college students who possess varied reading and writing abilities.
- **"Synthesis: Connections for Critical Thinking" sections.** The topics listed at the end of each chapter help students to gain practice in synthesis and critique, and make comparative assessments of various groups of essays. Many of these question sets now conclude with Networking: Applying 21st-Century Literacies questions.
- **Classic and Contemporary Images.** These paired visuals appear at the beginning of each chapter. These photographs, paintings, cartoons, and other visual texts, along with the accompanying "Using a Critical Perspective" questions, serve to interest students in the chapter's central topics and get them thinking and writing.

USEFUL SUPPLEMENTS

The following supplements are designed to help instructors and students derive the full benefit from *The McGraw-Hill Reader*:

- **Enhanced online component (*www.mhhe.com/mhreader11e*).** This reader's Web site features launch pages for Networking assignments; bibliographical, biographical, and cultural links; and additional readings—as well as access to Connect Composition's extensive additional resources: electronic peer review utilities; a database of sample student projects; tutorials on avoiding plagiarism, using document design, and understanding visual rhetoric; over 4,500 exercises with feedback on grammar, punctuation, and usage; and more.
- **A *Guide to the McGraw-Hill Reader*.** This supplement—revised by Jim Iddings, Karen Laing-Urbina, and Christian Clark (all of the College of Southern Nevada)—offers well-considered strategies for teaching individual essays, sample rhetorical analyses, answers to questions, additional thought-provoking questions, comparative essay discussion formats, and tips for prewriting and guided writing activities. There is also a bibliography of criticism and research on the teaching of composition. This guide is available for instructors on the Online Learning Center at *www.mhhe.com/mhreader11e*.

ACKNOWLEDGMENTS

It is a pleasure to acknowledge the support, assistance, and guidance of numerous individuals who helped create *The McGraw-Hill Reader*. I want to thank the excellent McGraw-Hill family of assistants, editors, and executives who participated enthusiastically in the project from the outset and who encouraged me at every step. My editors, Christopher Bennem and John Kindler, have been loyal, enthusiastic supporters of *The McGraw-Hill Reader* for many years. Thanks, too, to others on the McGraw-Hill editorial team who have made valuable contributions to this edition: Dawn Groundwater, Zachary Norton, and Jesse Hassenger. Cleatta Morris from Louisiana State University in Shreveport has done a first-rate job revising and enhancing the chapter on research writing to reflect 21st-century practices. Thanks to Jim Iddings, Karen Laing-Urbina, and Christian Clark (all from the College of Southern Nevada) for their excellent revisions of the *Guide to The McGraw-Hill Reader*. I also want to thank Judith Brown, my astute copyeditor, and Holly Paulsen, my superlative production editor. Above all, I offer sincere thanks to Anne Stameshkin, my development editor, who in countless ways helped make this revision fresh and exciting.

The final content and design of *The McGraw-Hill Reader,* Eleventh Edition, reflects the expertise and advice offered by college instructors across the country who gave generously of their time when asked to review the text:

Brenda Hardin Abbott, Bay Path College
Jacob Agatucci, Central Oregon Community College
Gillian F. Anderson, Eastern New Mexico University
Rebecca Babcock, The University of Texas of the Permian Basin
Christine Barkley, Palomar College
Laurel Bollinger, University of Alabama in Huntsville
Jay T. Dolmage, West Virginia University
Tom Flanigan, Idaho State University
Kimberly Greenfield, Lorain County Community College
Randolph Handel, Santa Fe College
Rebecca M. Heintz, Polk Community College
Bev Hogue, Marietta College
Jennifer Kaufman, State University of New York in Ulster
Alicia Leopold, Community College of Allegheny County
Miles McCrimmon, J. Sargent Reynolds Community College
Mark Meritt, University of San Francisco
Cleatta Morris, Louisiana State University in Shreveport
Rebecca J. Neagle, Wake Technical Community College
Jane Rosencrans, J. Sargeant Reynolds Community College
Doug Swartz, Indiana University Northwest
Kathleen G. White, Bellevue College

I am pleased to acknowledge support from the Mellon Foundation, the Graduate Center of The City University of New York, and the United States Department of Education (Title III and Title IV) that enabled me to develop this text.

Gilbert H. Muller

part 2

Issues across
the Disciplines

chapter **5**

Education and Society
How, What, and Why Do We Learn?

In "Learning to Read and Write," a chapter from his autobiography, Frederick Douglass offers a spirited affirmation of the rights we all should have to pursue an education. For Douglass, who was born into slavery, knowledge began not only with experience but also with the need to articulate that experience through literacy. The ability to read and write should be the possession of all human beings, and Douglass was willing to risk punishment—even death—to gain that ability. Today, all over the globe, as ethnic and political conflicts arise, men and women face the same challenge of expressing themselves. For even with a tool like the Internet, if one does not have the tools to express oneself or if the expression of thought is suppressed, the vehicle for conveying ideas, no matter how powerful, is rendered useless.

Perhaps the struggle for an education always involves a certain amount of effort and risk, but the struggle also conveys excitement and the deep, abiding satisfaction that derives from achieving knowledge of oneself and of the world. Time and again in the essays in this chapter, we discover that there is always a price to be paid for acquiring knowledge, developing intellectual skills, and attaining wisdom. However, numerous task forces and national commissions tell us that students today are not willing to pay this price and that, as a consequence, we have become academically mediocre. Is it true that we no longer delight in educating ourselves through reading, as Richard Rodriguez recounts in "The Lonely, Good Company of Books"? Is it true that we take libraries for granted—we expect them to be available but never visit them? A democratic society requires an educated citizenry, people who refuse to commit intellectual suicide or self-neglect. The writers in this chapter, who take many pathways to understanding, remind us that we cannot afford to be passive or compliant when our right to an education is challenged.

Today we are in an era of dynamic change in attitudes toward education. Such issues as sex education, multiculturalism, racism, sexism, and immigration suggest the liveliness of the educational debate on campus. Any debate over contemporary education touches on the themes of politics, economics, religion, or the social agenda, forcing us to recognize that configurations of power are at the heart of virtually all educational issues in society today.

Without education, many of our ideas and opinions can be stereotyped or prejudiced, bearing no relationship to the truth. It is easy to understand how such views can arise if we are merely passive vessels for others' uninformed opinions rather than active learners who seek true knowledge. If we judge the tenor of the essayists in this section, we discover that many of them are subversives, waging war against both ignorance *and* received dogma. These writers treat education as the key to upsetting the status quo and effecting change. Operating from diverse backgrounds, they challenge many assumptions about our educational system and invite us to think critically about its purpose.

PREVIEWING THE CHAPTER

As you read the essays in this chapter and respond to them in discussion and writing, consider the following questions:

- What is the main educational issue that the author deals with?
- What tone does the author establish in treating the subject? Does the author take a positive or a negative position?
- Does the author define *education*? If so, how? If not, does the author suggest what he or she means by it?
- What is the impact of society at large on how education is perceived?
- What forms of evidence do the authors use to support their views on education?
- How do the rhetorical features of the essays that focus on personal experience differ from those of the essays that examine education from a more global perspective?
- What have you learned about the value of education from reading these selections?
- Which essays persuaded you the most? Which the least? Why?

Classic and Contemporary Images

DOES EDUCATION CHANGE OVER TIME?

Using a Critical Perspective   Consider these two photographs of students in science laboratories, the first from the 19th century and the second from the present. What is the setting of each laboratory like? Who are the people? What does each photographer frame and leave out of the scene? Which educational setting seems more conducive to scientific or educational inquiry? Why?

Founded in 1833, Oberlin College in Ohio was the first U.S. college
to grant undergraduate degrees to women. The photograph reprinted
here shows both male and female students in a zoology lab
at Oberlin sometime during the 1890s.

At the beginning of the 21st century, most colleges and universities in the United States are coeducational, and it is no longer unusual to see both male and female students in a laboratory setting, as shown in this contemporary photo of a biology lab at the University of Maine.

Classic and Contemporary Essays
WHAT IS THE VALUE OF EDUCATION?

A famous adage proclaims that "the pen is mightier than the sword." In Frederick Douglass's narrative and the excerpt from the work of Richard Rodriguez, we get two portraits that demonstrate the truth of the adage. Douglass's efforts at becoming fully literate freed him from what would have been a life of slavery. No weapon could have done that for him. It is obvious that Douglass learned his lesson well, for his prose is stately, clear, direct, and precise. His story speaks of a determined youth and man who had a powerful motivation in learning to read and write. Would he have done so without this motivation? Perhaps, because he seems to be a very self-directed individual, as is evident from the anecdotes he relates. Rodriguez, too, has a strong motivation to master, and even to excel at, reading and writing. Writing nearly 150 years after Douglass, and at a time when he needn't fear slavery looming over him, Rodriguez nevertheless perceived that by emulating his teachers, who promoted book reading, his own reading would make him a better person. He, like Douglass, sensed that there was something about acquiring knowledge and about expanding one's view of the world by learning how others viewed it that would provide him with a certain amount of independence. As you read the following two essays, you may wish to consider whether the quiet, modest tone each author projects may have something to do with the subject matter. For reading, although active and mind-opening, is still a private and "lonely" activity.

Learning to Read and Write

Frederick Douglass

Frederick Douglass (1817–1895) was an American abolitionist, orator, and journalist. Born of the union between a slave and a white man, Douglass later escaped to Massachusetts. An impassioned antislavery speech brought him recognition as a powerful orator; thereafter he was much in demand for speaking engagements. He described his experience as a black man in America in Narrative of the Life of Frederick Douglass *(1845). After managing to buy his freedom, Douglass founded the* North Star, *a newspaper he published for the next 17 years. In the following excerpt from his stirring autobiography, Douglass recounts the tremendous obstacles he overcame in his efforts to become literate.*

1   I lived in Master Hugh's family about seven years. During this time, I succeeded in learning to read and write. In accomplishing this, I was compelled to resort to

various stratagems. I had no regular teacher. My mistress, who had kindly commenced to instruct me, had, in compliance with the advice and direction of her husband, not only ceased to instruct, but had set her face against my being instructed by any one else. It is due, however, to my mistress to say of her, that she did not adopt this course of treatment immediately. She at first lacked the depravity indispensable to shutting me up in mental darkness. It was at least necessary for her to have some training in the exercise of irresponsible power, to make her equal to the task of treating me as though I were a brute.

My mistress was, as I have said, a kind and tender-hearted woman; and in 2 the simplicity of her soul she commenced, when I first went to live with her, to treat me as she supposed one human being ought to treat another. In entering upon the duties of a slaveholder, she did not seem to perceive that I sustained to her the relation of a mere chattel, and that for her to treat me as a human being was not only wrong, but dangerously so. Slavery proved as injurious to her as it did to me. When I went there, she was a pious, warm, and tender-hearted woman. There was no sorrow or suffering for which she had not a tear. She had bread for the hungry, clothes for the naked, and comfort for every mourner that came within her reach. Slavery soon proved its ability to divest her of these heavenly qualities. Under its influence, the tender heart became stone, and the lamb-like disposition gave way to one of tiger-like fierceness. The first step in her downward course was in her ceasing to instruct me. She now commenced to practise her husband's precepts. She finally became even more violent in her opposition than her husband himself. She was not satisfied with simply doing as well as he had commanded; she seemed anxious to do better. Nothing seemed to make her more angry than to see me with a newspaper. She seemed to think that here lay the danger. I have had her rush at me with a face made all up of fury, and snatch from me a newspaper, in a manner that fully revealed her apprehension. She was an apt woman; and a little experience soon demonstrated, to her satisfaction, that education and slavery were incompatible with each other.

From this time I was most narrowly watched. If I was in a separate room 3 any considerable length of time, I was sure to be suspected of having a book, and was at once called to give an account of myself. All this, however, was too late. The first step had been taken. Mistress, in teaching me the alphabet, had given me the *inch*, and no precaution could prevent me from taking the *ell*.

The plan which I adopted, and the one by which I was most successful, 4 was that of making friends of all the little white boys whom I met in the street. As many of these as I could, I converted into teachers. With their kindly aid, obtained at different times and in different places, I finally succeeded in learning to read. When I was sent on errands, I always took my book with me, and by doing one part of my errand quickly, I found time to get a lesson before my return. I used also to carry bread with me, enough of which was always in the house, and to which I was always welcome; for I was much better off in this regard than many of the poor white children in our neighborhood. This bread I used to bestow upon the hungry little urchins, who, in return, would give me that more valuable bread of knowledge. I am strongly tempted to give the names of two or three of those little boys, a testimonial of the gratitude and affection I bear them; but prudence forbids—not that it would injure me, but it might embarrass them; for it is almost an unpardonable offence to teach slaves to read in this Christian country. It is enough to say of the dear little fellows, that they lived on Philpot Street, very near Durgin and Bailey's shipyard. I used to talk this matter of slavery over with them. I would sometimes say to them, I wished I could be as free as they would be when they got to be men. "You will be free as soon as you are twenty-one, *but I am a slave for life!* Have not I as good a right to be free as you have?" These words used to trouble them; they would express for me the liveliest sympathy, and console me with the hope that something would occur by which I might be free.

5   I was now about twelve years old, and the thought of being a *slave for life* began to bear heavily upon my heart. Just about this time, I got hold of a book entitled "The Colombian Orator." Every opportunity I got, I used to read this book. Among much of other interesting matter, I found in it a dialogue between a master and his slave. The slave was represented as having run away from his master three times. The dialogue represented the conversation which took place between them, when the slave was retaken the third time. In this dialogue, the whole argument in behalf of slavery was brought forward by the master, all of which was disposed of by the slave. The slave was made to say some very smart as well as impressive things in reply to his master—things which had the desired though unexpected effect; for the conversation resulted in the voluntary emancipation of the slave on the part of the master.

6   In the same book, I met with one of Sheridan's mighty speeches on and in behalf of Catholic emancipation. These were choice documents to me. I read them over and over again with unabated interest. They gave tongue to interesting thoughts of my own soul, which had frequently flashed through my mind, and died away for want of utterance. The moral which I gained from the dialogue was the power of truth over the conscience of even a slaveholder. What I got from Sheridan was a bold denunciation of slavery, and a powerful vindication of human rights. The reading of these documents enabled me to utter my thoughts, and to meet the arguments brought forward to sustain slavery; but while they relieved me of one difficulty, they brought on another even more painful than the one of which I was relieved. The more I read, the more I was led to abhor and detest my enslavers. I could regard them in no other light than a band of successful robbers, who had left their homes, and gone to Africa, and stolen us from our homes, and in a strange land reduced us to slavery. I loathed them as being the meanest as well as the most wicked of men. As I read and contemplated the subject, behold! that very discontentment which Master Hugh had predicted would follow my learning to read had already come, to torment and sting my soul to unutterable anguish. As I writhed under it, I would at times feel that learning to read had been a curse rather than a blessing. It had given me a view of my wretched condition,

without the remedy. It opened my eyes to the horrible pit, but to no ladder upon which to get out. In moments of agony, I envied my fellow-slaves for their stupidity. I have often wished myself a beast. I preferred the condition of the meanest reptile to my own. Any thing, no matter what, to get rid of thinking! It was this everlasting thinking of my condition that tormented me. There was no getting rid of it. It was pressed upon me by every object within sight or hearing, animate or inanimate. The silver trump of freedom had roused my soul to eternal wakefulness. Freedom now appeared, to disappear no more forever. It was heard in every sound, and seen in every thing. It was ever present to torment me with a sense of my wretched condition. I saw nothing without seeing it, I heard nothing without hearing it, and felt nothing without feeling it. It looked from every star, it smiled in every calm, breathed in every wind, and moved in every storm.

I often found myself regretting my own existence, and wishing myself 7 dead; and but for the hope of being free, I have no doubt but that I should have killed myself, or done something for which I should have been killed. While in this state of mind, I was eager to hear anyone speak of slavery. I was a ready listener. Every little while, I could hear something about the abolitionists. It was some time before I found what the word meant. It was always used in such connections as to make it an interesting word to me. If a slave ran away and succeeded in getting clear, or if a slave killed his master, set fire to a barn, or did any thing very wrong in the mind of a slaveholder, it was spoken of as the fruit of *abolition.* Hearing the word in this connection very often, I set about learning what it meant. The dictionary afforded me little or no help. I found it was "the act of abolishing"; but then I did not know what was to be abolished. Here I was perplexed. I did not dare to ask any one about its meaning, for I was satisfied that it was something they wanted me to know very little about. After a patient waiting, I got one of our city papers, containing an account of the number of petitions from the north, praying for the abolition of slavery in the District of Columbia, and of the slave trade between the States. From this time I understood the words *abolition* and *abolitionist,* and always drew near when that word was spoken, expecting to hear something of importance to myself and fellow-slaves. The light broke in upon me by degrees. I went one day down on the wharf of Mr. Waters; and seeing two Irishmen unloading a scow of stone, I went, unasked, and helped them. When we had finished, one of them came to me and asked me if I were a slave. I told him I was. He asked, "Are ye a slave for life?" I told him that I was. The good Irishman seemed to be deeply affected by the statement. He said to the other that it was a pity so fine a little fellow as myself should be a slave for life. He said it was a shame to hold me. They both advised me to run away to the north; that I should find friends there, and that I should be free. I pretended not to be interested in what they said, and treated them as if I did not understand them; for I feared they might be treacherous. White men have been known to encourage slaves to escape, and then, to get the reward, catch them and return them to their masters. I was afraid that these seemingly good men might use me so; but I nevertheless remembered their advice, and from that time I resolved to run away. I looked forward to a time at which it would be safe for me to escape. I was too young to think of doing so immediately; besides, I wished to learn how to write, as I might have occasion to write my own pass. I consoled myself with the hope that I should one day find a good chance. Meanwhile, I would learn to write.

8   The idea as to how I might learn to write was suggested to me by being in Durgin and Bailey's ship-yard, and frequently seeing the ship carpenters, after hewing, and getting a piece of timber ready for use, write on the timber the name of that part of the ship for which it was intended. When a piece of timber was intended for the larboard side, it would be marked thus—"L." When a piece was for the starboard side, it would be marked thus—"S." A piece for the larboard side forward, would be marked thus—"L. F." When a piece was for starboard side forward, it would be marked thus—"S. F." For larboard aft, it would be marked thus—"L. A." For starboard aft, it would be marked thus— "S. A." I soon learned the names of these letters, and for what they were intended when placed upon a piece of timber in the ship-yard. I immediately commenced copying them, and in a short time was able to make the four letters named. After that, when I met with any boy who I knew could write, I would tell him I could write as well as he. The next word would be, "I don't believe you. Let me see you try it." I would then make the letters which I had been so fortunate as to learn, and ask him to beat that. In this way I got a good many lessons in writing, which it is quite possible I should never have gotten in any other way. During this time, my copy-book was the board fence, brick wall, and pavement; my pen and ink was a lump of chalk. With these, I learned mainly how to write. I then commenced and continued copying the Italics in Webster's Spelling Book, until I could make them all without looking on the book. By this time, my little Master Thomas had gone to school, and learned how to write, and had written over a number of copy-books. These had been brought home, and shown to some of our near neighbors, and then laid aside. My mistress used to go to class meeting at the Wilk Street meetinghouse every Monday afternoon, and leave me to take care of the house. When left thus, I used to spend the time in writing in the spaces left in Master Thomas's copy-book, copying what he had written. I continued to do this until I could write a hand very similar to that of Master Thomas. Thus, after a long, tedious effort for years, I finally succeeded in learning how to write.

COMPREHENSION

1. What strategies does Douglass use to continue his education after his mistress's abandonment?
2. Why did the author's mistress find his reading newspapers particularly threatening?
3. Why does Douglass call learning to read "a curse rather than a blessing" (paragraph 6)?

RHETORIC

1. What is the thesis of Douglass's narration? How well is it supported and developed by the body paragraphs? Explain.
2. The first couple of sentences in the story, though simple, are very powerful. How do they serve to set up the mood of the piece and the reader's expectations?
3. Cite examples of Douglass's use of metaphors, and discuss why they work in those paragraphs.
4. How would you describe Douglass's writing style and level of language? Does it reveal anything about his character? Justify your response.
5. Explain the way in which the author uses comparison and contrast.
6. What is Douglass's definition of *abolition*, and how does he help the reader define it? How does this method contribute to the reader's understanding of the learning process?

WRITING

1. What does Douglass mean when he writes that "education and slavery were incompatible with each other" (paragraph 2)? Write an essay in which you consider the relationship between the two.
2. Both Douglass and his mistress were in inferior positions to Master Hugh. Write an essay in which you compare and contrast their positions in society at the time.
3. Illiteracy is still a major problem in the United States. Write an account of what your day-to-day life would be like if you couldn't write or read. What impact would this deficiency have on your life? Use concrete examples to illustrate your narrative.
4. **Writing an Argument:** Write an essay in which you argue for or against the proposition that American education continues to discriminate against minority groups.

NETWORKING
Applying 21st-Century Literacies

Analyzing a News Report on 21st-Century Illiteracy: On the Chapter 5 Networking page (at *www.mhhe.com/mhreader11e*), link to and watch this 2009 CBS report on adult illiteracy in the United States. What challenges has John Jones faced because of his illiteracy? Why do you think the report chose to focus not only on larger statistics, such as results from the Board of Education's report, but also on illiteracy's effects on an individual? How does John Jones's story contribute to the report's purpose and argument? How does the report make use of its medium (television) to convey its message?

The Lonely, Good Company
of Books

Richard Rodriguez

Richard Rodriguez (b. 1944) was born in San Francisco and received degrees from Stanford University and Columbia University. He also did graduate study at the University of California, Berkeley, and at the Warburg Institute, London. Rodriguez became a nationally known writer with the publication of his autobiography, Hunger of Memory: The Education of Richard Rodriguez *(1982). In it, he describes the struggles of growing up biculturally—feeling alienated from his Spanish-speaking parents yet not wholly comfortable in the dominant culture of the United States. He opposes bilingualism and affirmative action as they are now practiced in the United States, and his stance has caused much controversy in educational and intellectual circles. Rodriguez continues to write about social issues such as acculturation, education, and language in* Days of Obligation: An Argument with My Mexican Father *(1992) and* Brown: The Last Discovery of America *(2002). In the following essay, Rodriguez records his childhood passion for reading.*

1   From an early age I knew that my mother and father could read and write both Spanish and English. I had observed my father making his way through what, I now suppose, must have been income tax forms. On other occasions I waited apprehensively while my mother read onion-paper letters air-mailed from Mexico with news of a relative's illness or death. For both my parents, however, reading was something done out of necessity and as quickly as possible. Never did I see either of them read an entire book. Nor did I see them read for pleasure. Their reading consisted of work manuals, prayer books, newspapers, recipes. . . .

2   In our house each school year would begin with my mother's careful instruction: "Don't write in your books so we can sell them at the end of the year." The remark was echoed in public by my teachers, but only in part: "Boys and girls, don't write in your books. You must learn to treat them with great care and respect."

3   OPEN THE DOORS OF YOUR MIND WITH BOOKS, read the red and white poster over the nun's desk in early September. It soon was apparent to me that reading was the classroom's central activity. Each course had its own book. And the information gathered from a book was unquestioned. READ TO LEARN, the sign on the wall advised in December. I privately wondered: What was the connection between reading and learning? Did one learn something only by reading it? Was an idea only an idea if it could be written down? In June, CONSIDER BOOKS YOUR BEST FRIENDS. Friends? Reading was, at best, only a chore. I needed to look up whole paragraphs of words in a dictionary. Lines of type were dizzying, the eye having

to move slowly across the page, then down, and across. . . . The sentences of the first books I read were coolly impersonal. Toned hard. What most bothered me, however, was the isolation reading required. To console myself for the loneliness I'd feel when I read, I tried reading in a very soft voice. Until: "Who is doing all that talking to his neighbor?" Shortly after, remedial reading classes were arranged for me with a very old nun.

At the end of each school day, for nearly six months, I would meet with her 4
in the tiny room that served as the school's library but was actually only a store-room for used textbooks and a vast collection of *National Geographics.* Everything about our sessions pleased me: the smallness of the room; the noise of the janitor's broom hitting the edge of the long hallway outside the door; the green of the sun, lighting the wall; and the old woman's face blurred white with a beard. Most of the time we took turns. I began with my elementary text. Sentences of astonishing simplicity seemed to me lifeless and drab: "The boys ran from the rain. . . . She wanted to sing. . . . The kite rose in the blue." Then the old nun would read from her favorite books, usually biographies of early American presidents. Playfully she ran through complex sentences, calling the words alive with her voice, making it seem that the author somehow was speaking directly to me. I smiled just to listen to her. I sat there and sensed for the very first time some possibility of fellowship between a reader and a writer, a communication, never *intimate* like that I heard spoken words at home convey, but one nonetheless *personal.*

One day the nun concluded a session by asking me why I was so reluctant 5
to read by myself. I tried to explain; said something about the way written words made me feel all alone—almost, I wanted to add but didn't, as when I spoke to myself in a room just emptied of furniture. She studied my face as I spoke; she seemed to be watching more than listening. In an uneventful voice she replied that I had nothing to fear. Didn't I realize that reading would open up whole new worlds? A book could open doors for me. It could introduce me to people and show me places I never imagined existed. She gestured toward the bookshelves. (Bare-breasted African women danced, and the shiny hubcaps of automobiles on the back covers of the *Geographic* gleamed in my mind.) I listened with respect. But her words were not very influential. I was thinking then of another consequence of literacy, one I was too shy to admit but nonetheless trusted. Books were going to make me "educated." *That* confidence enabled me, several months later, to overcome my fear of the silence.

In fourth grade I embarked upon a grandiose reading program. "Give me 6
the names of important books," I would say to startled teachers. They soon found out that I had in mind "adult books." I ignored their suggestion of anything I suspected was written for children. (Not until I was in college, as a result, did I read *Huckleberry Finn* or *Alice's Adventures in Wonderland.*) Instead, I read *The Scarlet Letter* and Franklin's *Autobiography.* And whatever I read I read for extra credit. Each time I finished a book, I reported the achievement to a teacher and basked in the praise my effort earned. Despite my best efforts, however, there seemed to be more and more books I needed to read. At the library I would literally tremble as I came upon whole shelves of books I hadn't

read. So I read and I read and I read: *Great Expectations;* all the short stories of Kipling; *The Babe Ruth Story;* the entire first volume of the *Encyclopaedia Britannica* (A–ANSTEY); the *Iliad; Moby Dick; Gone with the Wind; The Good Earth; Ramona; Forever Amber; The Lives of the Saints; Crime and Punishment; The Pearl.* . . . Librarians who initially frowned when I checked out the maximum ten books at a time started saving books they thought I might like. Teachers would say to the rest of the class, "I only wish the rest of you took reading as seriously as Richard obviously does."

7   But at home I would hear my mother wondering, "What do you see in your books?" (Was reading a hobby like her knitting? Was so much reading even healthy for a boy? Was it the sign of "brains"? Or was it just a convenient excuse for not helping around the house on Saturday mornings?) Always, "What do you see . . . ?"

8   What *did* I see in my books? I had the idea that they were crucial for my academic success, though I couldn't have said exactly how or why. In the sixth grade I simply concluded that what gave a book its value was some major idea or theme it contained. If that core essence could be mined and memorized, I would become learned like my teachers. I decided to record in a notebook the themes of the books that I read. After reading *Robinson Crusoe,* I wrote that its theme was "the value of learning to live by oneself." When I completed *Wuthering Heights,* I noted the danger of "letting emotions get out of control." Rereading these brief moralistic appraisals usually left me disheartened. I couldn't believe that they were really the source of reading's value. But for many years, they constituted the only means I had of describing to myself the educational value of books.

9   In spite of my earnestness, I found reading a pleasurable activity. I came to enjoy the lonely, good company of books. Early on weekday mornings, I'd read in my bed. I'd feel a mysterious comfort then, reading in the dawn quiet—the blue-gray silence interrupted by the occasional churning of the refrigerator motor a few rooms away or the more distant sounds of a city bus beginning its run. On weekends I'd go to the public library to read, surrounded by old men and women. Or, if the weather was fine, I would take my books to the park and read in the shade of a tree. Neighbors would leave for vacation and I would water their lawns. I would sit through the twilight on the front porches or in backyards, reading to the cool, whirling sounds of the sprinklers.

10   I also had favorite writers. But often those writers I enjoyed most I was least able to value. When I read William Saroyan's *The Human Comedy,* I was immediately pleased by the narrator's warmth and the charm of his story. But as quickly I became suspicious. A book so enjoyable to read couldn't be very "important." Another summer I determined to read all the novels of Dickens. Reading his fat novels, I loved the feeling I got—after the first hundred pages—of being at home in a fictional world where I knew the names of the characters and cared about was going to happen to them. And it bothered me that I was forced away at the conclusion, when the fiction closed tight, like a fortune-teller's fist—the futures of all the major characters neatly resolved. I never knew how to take such feelings seriously, however. Nor did I suspect that these experiences could be part

of a novel's meaning. Still, there were pleasures to sustain me after I'd finish my books. Carrying a volume back to the library, I would be pleased by its weight. I'd run my fingers along the edge of the pages and marvel at the breadth of my achievement. Around my room, growing stacks of paperback books reinforced my assurance.

I entered high school having read hundreds of books. My habit of reading 11 made me a confident speaker and writer of English. Reading also enabled me to sense something of the shape, the major concerns, of Western thought. (I was able to say something about Dante and Descartes and Engels and James Baldwin in my high school term papers.) In these various ways, books brought me academic success as I hoped that they would. But I was not a good reader. Merely bookish, I lacked a point of view when I read. Rather, I read in order to acquire a point of view. I vacuumed books for epigrams, scraps of information, ideas, themes—anything to fill the hollow within me and make me feel educated. When one of my teachers suggested to his drowsy tenth-grade English class that a person could not have a "complicated idea" until he had read at least two thousand books, I heard the remark without detecting either its irony or its very complicated truth. I merely determined to compile a list of all the books I had ever read. Harsh with myself, I included only once a title I might have read several times. (How, after all, could one read a book more than once?) And I included only those books over a hundred pages in length. (Could anything shorter be a book?)

There was yet another high school list I compiled. One day I came across a 12 newspaper article about the retirement of an English professor at a nearby state college. The article was accompanied by a list of the "hundred most important books of Western Civilization." "More than anything else in my life," the professor told the reporter with finality, "these books have made me all that I am." That was the kind of remark I couldn't ignore. I clipped out the list and kept it for the several months it took me to read all of the titles. Most books, of course, I barely understood. While reading Plato's *Republic,* for instance, I needed to keep looking at the book jacket comments to remind myself what the text was about. Nevertheless, with the special patience and superstition of a scholarship boy, I looked at every word of the text. And by the time I reached the last word, relieved, I convinced myself that I had read *The Republic.* In a ceremony of great pride, I solemnly crossed Plato off my list.

COMPREHENSION

1. What was Rodriguez's parents' attitude toward reading? Did it influence his attitude? Cite examples from the essay that support your opinion.
2. What does Rodriguez mean by the "fellowship between a reader and a writer" (paragraph 4)? Why does he differentiate between "intimate" and "personal" forms of communication?
3. Rodriguez hoped that reading would fill "the hollow" inside him. What was the cause of his emptiness? Did he succeed in filling the void? Why did he find reading a lonely experience? Did reading fulfill any of his expectations?

RHETORIC

1. What is the thesis of Rodriguez's essay? Is it stated or implied? Explain.
2. How does the author's use of narrative advance his views on reading and education?
3. What is the writer's tone? How effective is it in conveying his point of view?
4. Rodriguez uses uppercase letters (small capitals) when referring to signs advocating reading. Why does he use this device? How does it support his point of view?
5. The essay ends with an ironic anecdote. Why did Rodriguez choose to conclude this way? Does it satisfactorily illustrate his attitude?
6. What words or phrases imply that there is an ethnic component in Rodriguez's conflict? Is the subtlety effective? Justify your response.

WRITING

1. Rodriguez's parents had a pragmatic attitude toward reading. What was the attitude in your home as you were growing up? Did your parents encourage your interest in reading? Did they read themselves? What is the first book you remember reading by yourself? Write an essay in which you describe your reading history.
2. Is reading still a significant source of information and entertainment, or has it been usurped by television? Is it important (or necessary) to be a reader today?
3. **Writing an Argument:** Rodriguez believed reading would make him "educated." Do you agree or disagree? Is reading vital to a person's education? How do you define *education?* Can it be acquired only through reading, or are there other contributing factors? Write an argumentative essay on this topic.

NETWORKING
Applying 21st-Century Literacies

Considering the Impact of e-Books: From the Chapter 5 Networking page (at *www.mhhe.com/mhreader11e*), link to and read "How the e-Book Will Change the Way We Read and Write" from the *Wall Street Journal.* In this article, Steven Johnson argues that the advent of e-readers and online books means that soon reading will be no longer be something people do in isolation. "As you read," Johnson predicts, "you will know that at any given moment, a conversation is available about the paragraph or even *sentence* you are reading. Nobody will read alone anymore. Reading books will go from being a fundamentally private activity—a direct exchange between author and reader—to a community event, with every isolated paragraph the launching pad for a conversation with strangers around the world."

If Richard Rodriguez had embarked on reading in a world like the one Johnson describes, how might his experience with books have been different? In what ways do you think it would have been less, or more, rewarding? What do you see as some advantages of reading offline, alone, and what are some advantages of reading online, in a network?

Synthesis: Classic and Contemporary Questions for Comparison

1. Both Rodriguez and Douglass were motivated to educate themselves in a society inimical to this achievement. Compare and contrast their struggles and attitudes in their quests for knowledge.
2. Pretend you are Rodriguez, and write a letter to Douglass addressing the issues of minorities and education in present-day America. What would Rodriguez say about the progress of minorities in our society?
3. Although Rodriguez and Douglass treat a similar theme, they communicate their messages differently. Which narration do you consider more powerful, and why?
4. Rodriguez explores the theme of isolation in his story. Is there any evidence that this feeling was shared by Douglass in his efforts to learn how to read? Use proof from both narratives to support your view.
5. Slavery was an obvious obstacle to Douglass's attempt to educate himself. What impeded Rodriguez's progress? Were similar forces at work? Cite examples from Rodriguez's narrative to prove your point.

The Graduates

Louis Menand

Louis Menand (b. 1951) is an influential contemporary educator and writer. He has degrees from Pomona College (BA, 1973; MA, 1975) and Columbia University (PhD, 1980), and he is a professor of English and American literature at Harvard. Menand has written and edited books on modernism, academic freedom, and pragmatism, receiving the Pulitzer Prize in history for The Metaphysical Club: A Story of Ideas in America *(2001). Menand has also been a contributing editor to* New Republic *and* New York Review of Books *and a staff writer for the* New Yorker. *"I don't think of there being any division between my academic career and my career in journalism," he writes; "it happens that some of my interests are relatively scholarly and some are not." In the following "unscholarly," or popular essay, published in the* New Yorker *in 2007, Menand offers a dissenting opinion on the value of a college education.*

On your first sleepover, your best friend's mother asks if you would like a tuna-fish-salad sandwich. Your own mother gives you tuna-fish-salad sandwiches all the time, so you say, "Sure." When you bite into the sandwich, though, you realize, too late, that your best friend's mother's tuna-fish salad tastes nothing like the tuna-fish salad your mother makes. You never dreamed that it was possible for there to be more than one way to prepare tuna-fish salad. And what's 1 with the bread? It's brown, and appears to have tiny seeds in it. What is more unnerving is the fact that your best friend obviously considers his mother's tuna-fish salad to be perfectly normal and has been eating it with enjoyment all his life. Later on, you discover that the pillows in your best friend's house are filled with some kind of foam-rubber stuff instead of feathers. The toilet paper is pink. What kind of human beings are these? At two o'clock in the morning, you throw up, and your mother comes and takes you home.

2   College, from which some 1.5 million people will graduate this year, is, basically, a sleepover with grades. In college, it is not so cool to throw up or for your mother to come and take you home. But plenty of students do throw up, and undergo other forms of mental and bodily distress, and plenty take time off from school or drop out. Almost half the people who go to college never graduate. Except in the case of a few highfliers and a somewhat larger number of inveterate slackers, college is a stressful experience.

3   American colleges notoriously inflate grades, but they can never inflate them enough, because education in the United States has become hypercompetitive and every little difference matters. In 1960, Harvard College had around five thousand applicants and accepted roughly thirty percent; this year, it had almost twenty-three thousand applicants and accepted nine percent. And the narrower the funnel, the finer applicants grind themselves in order to squeeze through it. Perversely, though, the competitiveness is a sign that the system is doing what Americans want it to be doing. Americans want education to be two things, universal and meritocratic. They want everyone to have a slot who wants one, and they want the slots to be awarded according to merit. The system is not perfect: Children from higher-income families enjoy an advantage in competing for the top slots. But there are lots of slots. There are more than four thousand institutions of higher education in the United States, enrolling more than seventeen million students. Can you name fifty colleges? Even if you could name a thousand, there would be three thousand you hadn't heard of. Most of these schools accept virtually all qualified applicants.

4   What makes for the stress is meritocracy. Meritocratic systems are democratic (since, in theory, everyone gets a place at the starting line) and efficient (since resources are not wasted on the unqualified), but they are huge engines of anxiety. The more purely meritocratic the system—the more open, the more efficient, the fairer—the more anxiety it produces, because there is no haven from competition. Your mother can't come over and help you out—that would be cheating! You're on your own. Everything you do in a meritocratic society is some kind of test, and there is never a final exam. There is only another test. People seem to pick up on this earlier and earlier in their lives, and at some point it starts to get in the way of their becoming educated. You can't learn when you're afraid of being wrong.

5   The biggest undergraduate major by far in the United States today is business. Twenty-two per cent of bachelor's degrees are awarded in that field. Eight percent are awarded in education, five percent in the health professions. By

contrast, fewer than four percent of college graduates major in English, and only two percent major in history. There are more bachelor's degrees awarded every year in Parks, Recreation, Leisure, and Fitness Studies than in all foreign languages and literatures combined. The Carnegie Foundation for the Advancement of Teaching, which classifies institutions of higher education, no longer uses the concept "liberal arts" in making its distinctions. This makes the obsession of some critics of American higher education with things like whether Shakespeare is being required of English majors beside the point. The question isn't what the English majors aren't taking; the question is what everyone else isn't taking.

More than fifty percent of Americans spend some time in college, and 6 American higher education is the most expensive in the world. The average annual tuition at a four-year private college is more than twenty-two thousand dollars. What do we want from college, though? It is hard to imagine that there could be one answer that was right for each of the 1.5 million or so people graduating this year, one part of the college experience they all must have had. Any prescription that had to spread itself across that many institutions would not be very deep. One thing that might be hoped for, though, is that, somewhere along the way, every student had a moment of vertigo (without unpleasant side effects). In commencement speeches and the like, people say that education is all about opportunity and expanding your horizons. But some part of it is about shrinking people, about teaching them that they are not the measure of everything. College should give them the intellectual equivalent of their childhood sleepover experience. We want to give graduates confidence to face the world, but we also want to protect the world a little from their confidence. Humility is good. There is not enough of it these days.

COMPREHENSION

1. What is Menand's opinion of the American system of education? Do you think he is biased? Why or why not?
2. According to Menand, what are some of the reasons why a college education has become devalued?
3. Explain what Menand means by *meritocracy*. Would you say that the fact that he teaches at Harvard and refers to this institution in his essay explains his focus on this concept? Justify your response by referring to the text.

RHETORIC

1. Menand wrote this brief essay for a well-known and decidedly urbane publication. How does he address his audience? What elements of Menand's style would appeal to *New Yorker* readers?
2. What is Menand's purpose in creating an analogy in his introductory paragraph? Do you find this strategy effective? Why or why not?

3. Where does Menand state his claim? What are his main supporting points, and what types of evidence does he present?
4. Does Menand rely largely on appeals to reason, emotion, or ethics, or does he combine these approaches? Justify your response.
5. How does Menand link his opening and concluding paragraphs? Why does he use the word *vertigo* in the last paragraph?

WRITING

1. Write a causal essay in which you analyze the reasons why college can be a stressful experience.
2. Compose your own extended definition of meritocracy and how this relates to the American educational system.
3. **Writing an Argument:** Write a rebuttal to Menand, arguing that a college education is in no way comparable to one's first sleepover.

NETWORKING
Applying 21st-Century Literacies

Examining a Mission Statement: Look up your college's or university's mission statement on its Web site's home page. Is the statement relevant? Is it truthful? Why or why not? Use personal observation and experience to support your view.

America, Still on Top

Vartan Gregorian

Vartan Gregorian (b. 1934), a celebrated educator, foundation head, and public intellectual, was born in Tabriz, Iran. He immigrated with his parents to the United States in 1956 and studied at Stanford University (BA, 1958; PhD, 1964), majoring in history. Gregorian was a popular professor of history at San Francisco State University, the University of Texas, the University of Pennsylvania, and several other institutions before embarking on a distinguished career as an administrator. Known for his fund-raising prowess, Gregorian has been provost of the University of Pennsylvania, president of the New York Public Library in the 1980s, president of Brown University in the 1990s, and since 1997 president of the Carnegie Corporation of New York. He has written several books, including The Emergence of Modern Afghanistan, 1880–1946 *(1969),* Islam: A Mosaic, Not a Monolith *(2003), and* The Road to Home: My Life and Times *(2003). In this essay, which appeared in* Newsweek International *in 2007, Gregorian compares American colleges with competing educational systems abroad.*

One of the great strengths of U.S. higher education is that it grew by informal 1
design. Following the 1862 Morrill Act, which gave federal land to the states to
found colleges, the states created not only universities but also state, junior,
city and county colleges, some of them two-year. Without a formal national
plan, there emerged a template for public higher education—affordable schooling for all, close to home, paid for by both state and federal governments.
Today American higher education is a more than $200 billion enterprise, en-
rolling nearly 18 million students in almost 4,000 public and private colleges
and universities.

Elsewhere, higher education grew in a much more top-down manner. In 2
communist societies from the Soviet Union to China and throughout most of
Asia and Latin America, a central bureaucracy ran universities, and often still
does. Typically, these systems have been unprepared for changing expectations,
as even the most remote and repressed populations have begun to develop—via
the media and the Internet—a perception of how the other half lives. Many view
education as a way to get their fair share. When they see countrymen returning
with degrees from the United States or Europe and getting the best jobs, they
begin to demand quality improvements in their own universities, for which resources are often lacking. The result is a growing gap between expectations and
reality. That's one reason that after a falloff following 9/11, the United States has
regained its status as the destination of choice for international students.

To catch up, countries in Europe—not to mention Asia, Africa and Latin 3
America—have welcomed a proliferation of private universities, including
"virtual" online entities. But many of these institutions are of questionable legitimacy. In the central Indian state of Chattisgarh, private colleges are spring-
ing up rapidly, but most are "universities only in name," run out of flats and
thus quite literally "a cottage industry," reported the local Tribune newspaper.
Faculty is also an issue: in many countries, professors are poorly paid and institutions rely on temporary adjuncts, lecturers and part-timers.

Providing poor-quality schools will likely backfire, because students are in- 4
creasingly unwilling to accept substandard fare. In an era of global brand
awareness, everyone wants the "right name" on clothes, cars and diplomas,
too. In China, students at second-tier schools have been known to pay extra to
have their diplomas bear the name of a better university—and to riot if that
promise is not met.

Many universities are looking to America as a model for how to survive. That 5
means raising or introducing tuition, increasing enrollment (including the number of foreign students who pay full fare) and boosting endowments through
fund-raising. Money, however, is not enough to build a quality university.
In many countries, for example, professors are members of the civil service and
do not enjoy the status, or salary, that will draw the best talent. In centralized

systems like China's, authorities can order up any number of engineers or scientists, but that does not mean they will be any good. Other nations are expanding bureaucracies to accommodate unemployed graduates, especially in the humanities and social science—an obvious recipe for disaster.

6   Today, free markets are on a collision course with state ownership or sponsorship of universities. The main challenge for each nation is to meet not only the aspirations of its citizens but the demands of its job markets as well. Countries that fail will face a debilitating brain drain. Even America is not immune. In the past, the United States relied on the many international students who came to study—especially science, math and technology—and then stayed. It also gave preferential treatment to immigrants with specialized skills. Today, as many societies advance economically, they are better able to retain talent and even attract professionals from the United States. Now America must increasingly rely on its own population to produce the necessary engineers, teachers, scientists and other professionals. It can no longer afford, for example, to accept the fact that last year, Maryland's entire 11-campus university system produced only 46 secondary math and science teachers. Or that the proportion of foreign-born doctoral students in engineering at U.S. universities is close to 60 percent.

7   The United States needs to redouble its efforts, particularly by investing more to improve education in the K-through-12 years and at the university level, too. There is no room for complacency in the global competition, even though America's diverse and hybrid system of public and private schools has solved the challenges of higher education better than most.

COMPREHENSION

1. According to Gregorian, what are the strengths of American higher education? What are the weaknesses?
2. Why is American higher education, on balance, superior to those in Europe, Asia, Africa, and Latin America?
3. Explain the "collision course" that Gregorian mentions in this essay.

RHETORIC

1. What is the purpose of Gregorian's introductory paragraph? How effective do you find this strategy? Justify your response with reference to the text.
2. What is Gregorian's claim, and where does he present it most clearly?
3. How does Gregorian use comparison and contrast to structure this essay? What points of comparison does he develop?
4. What types of evidence does Gregorian provide to support his argument? Do you find this evidence to be sufficient? Why or why not?
5. What is Gregorian's purpose in referring to the post-9/11 and increasingly globalized world? Does this motif reinforce his argument or detract from it? Explain.

WRITING

1. Write a brief essay on what you perceive as the strengths of American higher education.
2. Compare and contrast Gregorian's essay with the previous one, Louis Menand's "The Graduates."
3. **Writing an Argument:** Argue for or against the proposition that in a globalized world foreign educational systems will ultimately catch up with American higher education.

NETWORKING
Applying 21st-Century Literacies

Composing a Persuasive Photo Essay: Create a photo essay, complete with a paragraph-long introduction and short captions, to convey a specific argument about the state of higher education in America. Whether you want to raise concerns about, argue the strengths of, or portray a complex view of American higher education, be sure you have a specific point to make and that the photos work together (or in purposeful opposition) to convey this point. Use photographs of your own and/or images from other sources; if the latter, make sure to credit your sources properly and to treat them fairly. Consider responding to a specific quotation or idea from Gregorian's essay, or from Menand's (p. 269).

Sex Ed

Anna Quindlen

Anna Quindlen (b. 1953) was born in Philadelphia and educated at Barnard College (BA, 1974). A journalist and novelist, she began her writing career as a reporter for the New York Post *and later moved on to the* New York Times, *where she was a syndicated columnist. Quindlen has written a number of books, including* Living Out Loud *(1986),* Object Lessons *(1991),* One True Thing *(1994),* Blessings *(2002),* Being Perfect *(2005), and* Rise and Shine *(2006). Quindlen received the Pulitzer Prize for Commentary in 1992. She is currently a columnist for* Newsweek *magazine. In this essay, Quindlen focuses on the problem of teenage pregnancy and suggests that children be given more than textbook information to help them cope with their sexuality.*

Several years ago I spent the day at a family planning clinic in one of New York   1
City's poorest neighborhoods. I sat around a Formica table with a half-dozen sixteen-year-old girls and listened with some amazement as they showed off their knowledge of human sexuality.

2   They knew how long sperm lived inside the body, how many women out of a hundred using a diaphragm were statistically likely to get pregnant and the medical term for the mouth of the cervix. One girl pointed out all the parts of the female reproductive system on a placard; another recited the stages of the ovulation cycle from day one to twenty-eight. There was just one problem with this performance: Although the results of their laboratory tests would not be available for fifteen more minutes, every last one of them was pregnant.

3   I always think of that day when someone suggests that sex education at school is a big part of the answer to the problem of teenage pregnancy. I happen to be a proponent of such programs; I think human sexuality is a subject for dispassionate study, like civics and ethics and dozens of other topics that have a moral component. I'd like my sons to know as much as possible about how someone gets pregnant, how pregnancy can be avoided, and what it means when avoidance techniques have failed.

4   I remember adolescence about as vividly as I remember anything, however, and I am not in the least convinced that that information alone will significantly alter the rate of teenage pregnancy. It seemed to me that day in the clinic, and on days I spent at schools and on street corners, that teenage pregnancy has a lot more to do with what it means to be a teenager than with how someone gets pregnant. When I was in high school, at the tail end of the sixties, there was a straightforward line on sex among my friends. Boys could have it; girls couldn't. A girl who was not a virgin pretended she was. A girl who was sleeping with her boyfriend, no matter how long-playing the relationship, pretended she was not.

5   It is the nature of adolescence that there is no past and no future, only the present, burning as fierce, bright, and merciless as a bare light bulb. Girls had sex with boys because nothing seemed to matter except right now, not pregnancy, not parental disapprobation, nothing but those minutes, this dance, that face, those words. Most of them knew that pregnancy could result, but they assured themselves that they would be the lucky ones who would not get caught. Naturally, some of them were wrong, and in my experience they did one of three things: They went to Puerto Rico for a mysterious weekend trip; visited an aunt in some faraway state for three months and came back with empty eyes and a vague reputation; or got married, quickly, in Empire-waist dresses.

6   What seems to have changed most since then is that there is little philosophical counterpoint, hypocritical or not, to the raging hormones of adolescence, and that so many of the once-hidden pregnancies are hidden no more.

7   Not long after the day at the family planning clinic, I went to a public high school in the suburbs. In the girl's room was this graffito: Jennifer Is a Virgin. I asked the kids about it and they said it was shorthand for geek, nerd, weirdo, somebody who was so incredibly out of it that they were in high school and still hadn't had sex. If you were a virgin, they told me, you just lied about it so that no one would think you were that immature. The girls in the family planning clinic told me much the same thing—that everyone did it, that the boys wanted it, that not doing it made them seem out of it. The only difference, really, was that the girls in the clinic were poor and would have their babies, and the girls

in the high school were well-to-do and would have abortions. Pleasure didn't seem to have very much to do with sex for either group. After she learned she was pregnant, one of the girls at the clinic said, without a trace of irony, that she hoped childbirth didn't hurt as much as sex had. Birth control was easily disposed of in both cases. The pill, the youngsters said, could give you a stroke; the IUD could make you sterile. A diaphragm was disgusting.

One girl told me the funniest thing her boyfriend—a real original thinker—   8 had told her: They couldn't use condoms because it was like taking a shower with a raincoat on. She was a smart girl and pretty, and I wanted to tell her that it sounded as if she was sleeping with a jerk who didn't deserve her. But that is the kind of basic fact of life that must be taught not in the classroom, not by a stranger, but at home by the family. It is this that, finally, I will try to teach my sons about sex, after I've explained fertile periods and birth control and all the other mechanics that are important to understand but never really go to the heart of the matter: I believe I will say that when you sleep with someone you take off a lot more than your clothes.

COMPREHENSION

1. Does Quindlen approve of sex education? Explain.
2. How does the writer characterize the attitude of adolescents regarding sex and pregnancy?
3. What advice or information about sex will the writer give her sons? Why?

RHETORIC

1. Why did Quindlen choose "Sex Ed" as a title? What is its significance in relation to the thesis?
2. What is Quindlen's thesis? Where is it contained in the essay? Is it directly stated or implied?
3. Is Quindlen's writing an argumentative essay? Support your position with citations from the text.
4. What point is the writer making through use of accumulated details in paragraph 2?
5. What does Quindlen mean by the term "moral component" in paragraph 3? Where else in the essay does she allude to it? How does she employ definition in this essay?
6. What does Quindlen mean by her final statement that "when you sleep with someone you take off a lot more than your clothes"? How does this ending serve to underscore the thesis of the essay?

WRITING

1. Write a paper analyzing the most common forms of birth control available and listing the advantages and disadvantages of each.

2. In an essay, consider possible solutions to the problem of teenage pregnancy. What role do you think sex education has in ameliorating the problem? Use support from the Quindlen essay if applicable.

3. **Writing an Argument:** Quindlen claims that sex education is like "civics" and "ethics" and should be taught in schools. Do you agree or disagree? Write an essay defending your position.

NETWORKING
Applying 21st-Century Literacies

Interpreting Advocacy Group Web Sites: The Chapter 5 Networking page (at *www.mhhe.com/mhreader11e*) links to several Web sites, each of which is published by an advocacy group dedicated to preventing teen pregnancy. For each, sum up (in 1–2 sentences) its position on educating teens about sex. How do the Web site's various features, as well as its design; organization; and use of images, video, and links, contribute to its message?

Unplugged: The Myth of Computers in the Classroom

David Gelernter

David Gelernter (b. 1955) is a professor of computer science at Yale University. He is a leading figure in the field of human cognition and a seminal thinker in the field known as parallel computing. Gelernter, who was injured by a package sent by the Unabomber in 1993, is the author of Mirror Worlds *(1991),* The Muse in the Machine *(1994),* 1939: The Lost World of the Fair *(1995), and* Machine Beauty *(1998). In the following essay, published in the* New Republic *in 1994, Gelernter offers a cogent analysis of the limits of technology in the classroom.*

1   Over the last decade an estimated $2 billion has been spent on more than 2 million computers for America's classrooms. That's not surprising. We constantly hear from Washington that the schools are in trouble and that computers are a godsend. Within the education establishment, in poor as well as rich schools, the machines are awaited with nearly religious awe. An inner-city principal bragged to a teacher friend of mine recently that his school "has a computer in every classroom . . . despite being in a bad neighborhood!"

2   Computers should be in the schools. They have the potential to accomplish great things. With the right software, they could help make science tangible or teach neglected topics like art and music. They help students form a concrete idea of society by displaying onscreen a version of the city in which they live—a picture that tracks real life moment by moment.

In practice, however, computers make our worst educational nightmares 3
come true. While we bemoan the decline of literacy, computers discount
words in favor of pictures and pictures in favor of video. While we fret about
the decreasing cogency of public debate, computers dismiss linear argument
and promote fast, shallow romps across the information landscape. While we
worry about basic skills, we allow into the classroom software that will do a
student's arithmetic or correct his spelling.

Take multimedia. The idea of multimedia is to combine text, sound and pic- 4
tures in a single package that you browse on screen. You don't just *read* Shakespeare; you watch actors performing, listen to songs, view Elizabethan
buildings. What's wrong with that? By offering children candy-coated books,
multimedia is guaranteed to sour them on unsweetened reading. It makes the
printed page look even more boring than it used to look. Sure, books will be
available in the classroom, too—but they'll have all the appeal of a dusty piano
to a teen who has a Walkman handy.

So what if the little nippers don't read? If they're watching Olivier instead, 5
what do they lose? The text, the written word along with all of its attendant pleasures. Besides, a book is more portable than a computer, has a higher-resolution
display, can be written on and dog-eared and is comparatively dirt cheap.

Hypermedia, multimedia's comrade in the struggle for a brave new class- 6
room, is just as troubling. It's a way of presenting documents on screen without
imposing a linear start-to-finish order. Disembodied paragraphs are linked by
theme; after reading one about the First World War, for example, you might be
able to choose another about the technology of battleships, or the life of Wood-
row Wilson, or hemlines in the '20s. This is another cute idea that is good in minor ways and terrible in major ones. Teaching children to understand the orderly
unfolding of a plot or a logical argument is a crucial part of education. Authors
don't merely agglomerate paragraphs; they work hard to make the narrative
read a certain way, prove a particular point. To turn a book or a document into
hypertext is to invite readers to ignore exactly what counts—the story.

The real problem, again, is the accentuation of already bad habits. Dynamit- 7
ing documents into disjointed paragraphs is one more expression of the sorry
fact that sustained argument is not our style. If you're a newspaper or magazine
editor and your readership is dwindling, what's the solution? Shorter pieces. If
you're a politician and you want to get elected, what do you need? Tasty sound
bites. Logical presentation be damned.

Another software species, "allow me" programs, is not much better. These 8
programs correct spelling and, by applying canned grammatical and stylistic
rules, fix prose. In terms of promoting basic skills, though, they have all the
virtues of a pocket calculator.

In Kentucky, as *The Wall Street Journal* recently reported, students in grades 9
K–3 are mixed together regardless of age in a relaxed environment. It works
great, the *Journal* says. Yes, scores on computation tests have dropped 10 percent at one school, but not to worry: "Drilling addition and subtraction in an
age of calculators is a waste of time," the principal reassures us. Meanwhile, a

Japanese educator informs University of Wisconsin mathematician Richard Akey that in his country, "calculators are not used in elementary or junior high school because the primary emphasis is on helping students develop their mental abilities." No wonder Japanese kids blow the pants off American kids in math. Do we really think "drilling addition and subtraction in an age of calculators is a waste of time"? If we do, then "drilling reading in an age of multimedia is a waste of time" can't be far behind.

10   Prose-correcting programs are also a little ghoulish, like asking a computer for tips on improving your personality. On the other hand, I ran this article through a spell-checker, so how can I ban the use of such programs in schools? Because to misspell is human; to have no idea of correct spelling is to be semiliterate.

11 There's no denying that computers have the potential to perform inspiring feats in the classroom. If we are ever to see that potential realized, however, we ought to agree on three conditions. First, there should be a completely new crop of children's software. Most of today's offerings show no imagination. There are hundreds of similar reading and geography and arithmetic programs, but almost nothing on electricity or physics or architecture. Also, they abuse the technical capacities of new media to glitz up old forms instead of creating new ones. Why not build a time-travel program that gives kids a feel for how history is structured by zooming you backward? A spectrum program that lets users twirl a frequency knob to see what happens?

12   Second, computers should be used only during recess or relaxation periods. Treat them as fillips, not as surrogate teachers. When I was in school in the '60s, we all loved educational films. When we saw a movie in class, everybody won: Teachers didn't have to teach, and pupils didn't have to learn. I suspect that classroom computers are popular today for the same reasons.

13   Most important, educators should learn what parents and most teachers already know: You cannot teach a child anything unless you look him in the face. We should not forget what computers are. Like books—better in some ways, worse in others—they are devices that help children mobilize their own resources and learn for themselves. The computer's potential to do good is modestly greater than a book's in some areas. Its potential to do harm is vastly greater, across the board.

COMPREHENSION

1. State Gelernter's thesis or claim in one sentence.
2. In the final paragraph, Gelernter defines what he believes to be the most important shortcoming of the computer as a teaching tool. Explain the reason why this weakness is so significant.
3. In your own words, explain the author's dislike of hypermedia as a pedagogic tool (as expressed in paragraph 6) and why the orderly arrangement of paragraphs in a book is superior to this newer technological capability.

RHETORIC

1. The introductory paragraph goes from a general fact to a specific quotation. What is the effect of this method of paragraph patterning?

2. Much of Gelernter's argument hinges on providing evidence that one medium is superior to another. Explain terms such as *linear argument* (paragraph 3), *agglomerate paragraphs* (paragraph 6), and *"allow me" programs* (paragraph 8). How do these terms help Gelernter prove his point?

3. The essay has a three-part structure, each section divided by space. How would you characterize the purpose of each section? How does the author use transitions to move from one section to the next?

4. Gelernter states that the overuse of computers in the classroom can hinder the development of clear thinking and reasoned argument. How clearly written is *his* essay? How reasoned is his argument? Gather evidence for your answer by reviewing the essay and determining whether each sentence seems to flow logically to the next and whether each paragraph seems to move reasonably to the next.

5. The author uses metaphors, similes, and other rhetorical devices. Explain the effectiveness of expressions such as "have all the appeal of a dusty piano to a teen who has a Walkman handy" (paragraph 4), "dynamiting documents" (paragraph 7), and "software species" (paragraph 8). Locate other unconventional descriptions.

6. Who is the intended audience for this essay? Educators? Parents? Students? Politicians? What evidence can you cite to back up your view?

7. What rhetorical device is Gelernter using in his title? What is the implicit meaning of the title?

WRITING

1. Visit the writing or reading computer lab in your school. As an objective observer, study the interaction of student and computer. Write a descriptive essay focusing on the demeanor and behavior of the student and the atmosphere of the classroom. If you wish, compare it to a traditional classroom.

2. Copy a paragraph from the essay, and enter it into a word-processing program that has a grammar-check function. Record any comments that the program makes in response to its evaluation of the writing. Do the computer's responses to the author's sentence structure make sense?

NETWORKING
Applying 21st-Century Literacies

WRITING AN ARGUMENT>Weighing the Potential of Smart Classrooms: Select one of the teaching capabilities of modern computers—multimedia, hypertext, or spell- and grammar-check programs. Argue for the benefits of one of these features, noting how it could be used effectively in a smart classroom. Consider at least one counterargument to your position, and describe how you would rebut it.

When Bright Girls Decide That
Math Is "a Waste of Time"

Susan Jacoby

Susan Jacoby (b. 1945) has worked as an educator and as a reporter for the Washington Post *and a columnist for the* New York Times. *As a freelance journalist in
the former Soviet Union (from 1969 to 1971), she produced two books about her
experiences. Jacoby now contributes to the* Nation *and* McCall's; *her books include*
The Possible She *(1979), a collection of autobiographical essays;* Wild Justice:
The Evolution of Revenge *(1983);* Half-Jew: A Daughter's Search for Her
Buried Past *(2000); and* The Age of American Unreason *(2008). In this essay
from the* New York Times, *Jacoby examines the reasons girls are often deficient in
math and science.*

1   Susannah, a 16-year-old who has always been an A student in every subject
from algebra to English, recently informed her parents that she intended to
drop physics and calculus in her senior year of high school and replace them
with a drama seminar and a work-study program. She expects a major in art or
history in college, she explained, and "any more science or math will just be a
waste of my time."

2   Her parents were neither concerned by nor opposed to her decision. "Fine,
dear," they said. Their daughter is, after all, an outstanding student. What does
it matter if, at age 16, she has taken a step that may limit her understanding of
both machines and the natural world for the rest of her life?

3   This kind of decision, in which girls turn away from studies that would give
them a sure footing in the world of science and technology, is a self-inflicted female disability that is, regrettably, almost as common today as it was when I
was in high school. If Susannah had announced that she had decided to stop
taking English in her senior year, her mother and father would have been horrified. I also think they would have been a good deal less sanguine about her
decision if she were a boy.

4   In saying that scientific and mathematical ignorance is a self-inflicted female wound, I do not, obviously, mean that cultural expectations play no role in
the process. But the world does not conspire to deprive modern women of access to science as it did in the 1930s, when Rosalyn S. Yalow, the Nobel Prize–
winning physicist, graduated from Hunter College and was advised to go to
work as a secretary because no graduate school would admit her to its physics
department. The current generation of adolescent girls—and their parents, bred
on old expectations about women's interests—are active conspirators in limiting their own intellectual development.

It is true that the proportion of young women in science-related graduate 5 and professional schools, most notably medical schools, has increased significantly in the past decade. It is also true that so few women were studying advanced science and mathematics before the early 1970s that the percentage increase in female enrollment does not yet translate into large numbers of women actually working in science.

The real problem is that so many girls eliminate themselves from any serious possibility of studying science as a result of decisions made during the vulnerable period of midadolescence, when they are most likely to be influenced—on both conscious and subconscious levels—by the traditional belief that math and science are "masculine" subjects.

During the teen-age years the well-documented phenomenon of "math anxiety" strikes girls who never had any problem handling numbers during earlier schooling. Some men, too, experience this syndrome—a form of panic, akin to a phobia, at any task involving numbers—but women constitute the overwhelming majority of sufferers. The onset of acute math anxiety during the teen-age years is, as Stalin was fond of saying, "not by accident."

In adolescence girls begin to fear that they will be unattractive to boys if they are typed as "brains." Science and math epitomize unfeminine braininess in a way that, say, foreign languages do not. High-school girls who pursue an advanced interest in science and math (unless they are students at special institutions like the Bronx High School of Science where everyone is a brain) usually find that they are greatly outnumbered by boys in their classes. They are, therefore, intruding on male turf at a time when their sexual confidence, as well as that of the boys, is most fragile.

A 1981 assessment of female achievement in mathematics, based on research conducted under a National Institute for Education grant, found significant differences in the mathematical achievements of 9th and 12th graders. At age 13 girls were equal to or slightly better than boys in tests involving algebra, problem solving and spatial ability; four years later the boys had outstripped the girls.

It is not mysterious that some very bright high-school girls suddenly decide that math is "too hard" and "a waste of time." In my experience, self-sabotage of mathematical and scientific ability is often a conscious process. I remember deliberately pretending to be puzzled by geometry problems in my sophomore year in high school. A male teacher called me in after class and said, in a baffled tone, "I don't see how you can be having so much trouble when you got straight A's last year in my algebra class."

The decision to avoid advanced biology, chemistry, physics and calculus in high school automatically restricts academic and professional choices that ought to be wide open to anyone beginning college. At all coeducational universities women are overwhelmingly concentrated in the fine arts, social sciences and traditionally female departments like education. Courses leading to degrees in science- and technology-related fields are filled mainly by men.

In my generation, the practical consequences of mathematical and scientific illiteracy are visible in the large number of special programs to help professional women overcome the anxiety they feel when they are promoted into jobs that require them to handle statistics.

13   The consequences of this syndrome should not, however, be viewed in narrowly professional terms. Competence in science and math does not mean one is going to become a scientist or mathematician any more than competence in writing English means one is going to become a professional writer. Scientific and mathematical illiteracy—which has been cited in several recent critiques by panels studying American education from kindergarten through college—produces an incalculably impoverished vision of human experience.

14   Scientific illiteracy is not, of course, the exclusive province of women. In certain intellectual circles it has become fashionable to proclaim a willed, aggressive ignorance about science and technology. Some female writers specialize in ominous, uninformed diatribes against genetic research as a plot to remove control of childbearing from women, while some well-known men of letters proudly announce that they understand absolutely nothing about computers, or, for that matter, about electricity. This lack of understanding is nothing in which women or men ought to take pride.

15   Failure to comprehend either computers or chromosomes leads to a terrible sense of helplessness, because the profound impact of science on everyday life is evident even to those who insist they don't, won't, can't understand why the changes are taking place. At this stage of history women are more prone to such feelings of helplessness than men because the culture judges their ignorance less harshly and because women themselves acquiesce in that indulgence.

16   Since there is ample evidence of such feelings in adolescence, it is up to parents to see that their daughters do not accede to the old stereotypes about "masculine" and "feminine" knowledge. Unless we want our daughters to share our intellectual handicaps, we had better tell them no, they can't stop taking mathematics and science at the ripe old age of 16.

COMPREHENSION

1. What reasons does Jacoby give for girls' deficiency in math and science?
2. Why does Jacoby call it a "self-inflicted female disability" (paragraph 3)?
3. What are the consequences of being math- and science-illiterate?

RHETORIC

1. Explain the main idea of Jacoby's essay in your own words.
2. Does the writer use abstract or concrete language in her essay? Cite examples to support your response.
3. What technique does Jacoby use in paragraphs 1 and 2? How does it aid in setting up her argument?
4. What rhetorical strategies does the writer use in her essay?

5. How does the use of dialogue aid in developing paragraph 10? What effect does the general use of dialogue have on Jacoby's point?
6. How is Jacoby's conclusion consistent in tone with the rest of the essay? Does it supply a sense of unity? Why or why not?

WRITING

1. Write an essay describing a school-related phobia you once had or continue to have (for example, in math, writing, physical education, or biology). Explain where you think that fear came from, how it affected your performance in school, and what you did (or are doing) to cope with the problem.
2. Write an essay about the need for math and science literacy in today's world. Use support from Jacoby's essay.
3. **Writing an Argument:** Write an argumentation essay proposing that math and science phobia is not "self-inflicted" but is caused primarily by the continued presence of sexism in society.

NETWORKING
Applying 21st-Century Literacies

Analyzing How Design Informs a Web Site's Purpose: Via the Chapter 5 Networking page (at *www.mhhe.com/mhreader11e*), link to *BrainCake*, the Web site of the Girls' Math and Science Partnership. Watch the whole opening video, and then explore the site itself. How might an organization like this one address the issues Susan Jacoby raises in her essay? How does this Web site aim to make science and math (and the Carnegie Science Center's programs) seem appealing and important to girls ages 11–17—and to their parents? What questions might Jacoby have for its organizers?

Two Cheers for *Brown v. Board of Education*

Clayborne Carson

Clayborne Carson (b. 1944) is professor of history and director of the Martin Luther King Jr. Papers Project at Stanford University. He was born in Buffalo, New York, and educated at the University of California at Los Angeles, where he received his BA (1967), MA (1968), and PhD (1977). A specialist in African-American and civil rights history, Carson has written and edited numerous books, including

In Struggle: SNCC and the Black Awakening of the 1960s *(1981, rev. ed. 1995), which received the Frederick Jackson Turner Award;* Eyes on the Prize: America's Civil Rights Years *(1987); and* The Malcolm X File *(1991). Asked by Coretta Scott King to handle her late husband's literary estate, Carson is the lead editor of* The Papers of Martin Luther King Jr. *(University of California Press). "It was a job you couldn't say no to," Carson said. In this essay, published in the* Journal of American History *in 2004, Carson offers an evaluation of the impact of a major Supreme Court decision on school segregation.*

1   My gratuitous opinion of *Brown v. Board of Education* (1954) is somewhat ambivalent and certainly arrives too late to alter the racial policies of the past fifty years. But for those of us who practice history, hindsight offers a far more reliable kind of wisdom than does foresight. We see clearly now that while the *Brown* decision informed the attitudes that have shaped contemporary American race relations, it did not resolve persistent disputes about the nation's civil rights policies. The Supreme Court's unanimous opinion in *Brown* broke decisively with the racist interpretations of traditional American values set forth in *Scott v. Sandford* (1857) and *Plessy v. Ferguson* (1896), offering instead the optimistic "American Creed" that Gunnar Myrdal saw as the solution to "the Negro problem."[1] Like the two earlier landmark decisions, *Brown* overestimated the extent of ideological consensus among Americans and soon exacerbated racial and regional conflicts instead of resolving them. The Court's ruling against school segregation encouraged African Americans to believe that the entire structure of white supremacy was illegitimate and legally vulnerable. But the civil rights struggles *Brown* inspired sought broader goals than the decision could deliver, and that gap fostered frustration and resentment among many black Americans. In short, the decision's virtues and limitations reflect both the achievements and the failures of the efforts made in the last half century to solve America's racial dilemma and to realize the nation's egalitarian ideals.

2   That the *Brown* decision spurred subsequent civil rights progress seems apparent, but its impact and its significance as a source of inspiration are difficult to measure.[2] Although the Court's initial unwillingness to set firm timetables for school desegregation undercut *Brown*'s immediate impact, African Americans expanded the limited scope of the decision by individual and collective challenges to the Jim Crow system. Small-scale protests escalated during the decade after 1954, becoming a sustained mass movement against all facets of segregation and discrimination in the North as well as the South. Civil rights protests and litigation prompted Congress to pass the Civil Rights Act of 1964 and the

---

[1]*Scott v. Sandford,* 19 How. 393 (1857); *Plessy v. Ferguson,* 163 U.S. 537 (1896); *Brown v. Board of Education,* 347 U.S. 483 (1954); Gunnar Myrdal, *An American Dilemma: The Negro Problem and Modern Democracy* (2 vols., New York, 1944).

[2]On *Brown*'s direct and indirect consequences, see, for example, Michael J. Klarman, "How *Brown* Changed Race Relations: The Backlash Thesis," *Journal of American History,* 81 (June 1994), 81–118. Klarman correctly points out that *Brown* had limited impact on school desegregation, especially in the Deep South, and stimulated southern white resistance to racial reform. He concludes that the contributions of *Brown* to the broader civil rights struggle were mostly indirect.

Voting Rights Act of 1965, both of which extended the *Brown* decision's egalitarian principles well beyond education. The historic mass struggle that followed *Brown* ultimately destroyed the legal foundations of the Jim Crow system, and their destruction prepared the way for a still more far-reaching expansion of prevailing American conceptions of civil rights and of the role of government in protecting those rights. During the past forty years, women and many minority groups, including immigrants and people with disabilities, have gained new legal protections modeled on the civil rights gains of African Americans.[3]

But the *Brown* decision also created racial aspirations that remain unrealized. Although the decision may have been predicated on the notion of a shared American creed, most white Americans were unwilling to risk their own racial privileges to bring about racial equality. The decision was neither universally accepted nor consistently enforced. "Instead, it provoked overwhelming resistance in the South and only tepid interest in the North," the historian John Higham insisted. "In the South the decision released a tidal wave of racial hysteria that swept moderates out of office or turned them into demagogues. State and local officials declined to obstruct a revival of the Ku Klux Klan. Instead, they employed every conceivable device to maintain segregation, including harassment and dissolution of NAACP chapters."[4] By the 1970s, resistance to school desegregation had become national. Northern whites in Boston and elsewhere demonstrated their unwillingness to send their children to predominantly black schools or to allow large-scale desegregation that would drastically alter the racial composition of "their" schools in "their" neighborhoods. Voters in the states of Washington and California passed initiatives to restrict the right of school boards (Washington) and state courts (California) to order busing to achieve school desegregation (the Supreme Court later held the Washington initiative unconstitutional). Nationwide, white racial resentments encouraged an enduring shift of white voters from the Democratic to the Republican party. The 1964 election would be the last presidential contest in which the majority of black voters and of white voters backed the same candidate. Since 1974, when the Supreme Court's *Milliken v. Bradley* decision set limits on busing, the legal meaning of desegregation has been scaled back to conform to American racial and political realities.[5]

3

[3]Cf. Hugh Davis Graham, *The Civil Rights Era: Origins and Development of National Policy, 1960–1972* (New York, 1990); Hugh Davis Graham, *Collision Course: The Strange Convergence of Affirmative Action and Immigration Policy in America* (New York, 2002); and John D. Skrentny, *The Minority Rights Revolution* (Cambridge, Mass., 2002).

[4]John Higham, "Introduction: A Historical Perspective," in *Civil Rights and Civil Wrongs: Black-White Relations since World War II*, ed. John Higham (University Park, 1997), 4. See also Klarman, "How *Brown* Changed Race Relations"; Numan V. Bartley, *The Rise of Massive Resistance: Race and Politics in the South in the 1950s* (Baton Rouge, 1969); and Neil McMillen, *The Citizens' Council: Organized Resistance to the Second Reconstruction, 1954–1964* (Urbana, 1971).

[5]See Ronald P. Formisano, *Boston against Busing: Race, Class, and Ethnicity in the 1960s and 1970s* (Chapel Hill, 1991); and J. Anthony Lukas, *Common Ground: A Turbulent Decade in the Lives of Three American Families* (New York, 1985). *Washington v. Seattle School District*, 458 U.S. 457 (1982); *Crawford v. Los Angeles Board of Education*, 458 U.S. 527 (1982); *Milliken v. Bradley*, 418 U.S. 717 (1974). See Gary Orfield and Susan E. Eaton, *Dismantling Desegregation: The Quiet Reversal of* Brown v. Board of Education (New York, 1996).

4   African Americans generally applauded the *Brown* decision when it was announced, but the Court's failure to realize *Brown's* bold affirmation of egalitarian ideals fueled subsequent black discontent and disillusionment. *Brown* cited studies that demonstrated the harmful psychological impact of enforced segregation on black students, reporting, "To separate them from others of similar age and qualifications solely because of their race generates a feeling of inferiority as to their status in the community that may affect their hearts and minds in a way unlikely ever to be undone." Yet the Court did not offer an effective means to correct the problem it had identified. During the decades after *Brown,* most southern black children continued to suffer the psychological consequences of segregation, while a small minority assumed the often considerable psychological and physical risks of attending newly integrated public schools. Rather than bringing large numbers of black and white students together in public schools, the *Brown* decision—and the subsequent years of litigation and social conflict—enabled a minority of black students to attend predominantly white schools. Ten years after the *Brown* decision, according to data compiled by the U.S. Department of Education, almost 98 percent of southern black students still attended predominantly black schools. Now, at the beginning of the twenty-first century, the Court's ideal of educational opportunity as "a right which must be made available to all on equal terms" is still far from being realized. American schools, both public and private, are still highly segregated. According to a recent study, the typical Latino or black student in the United States still attends a school where members of minority groups are predominant.[6]

5   Certainly, the *Brown* decision's most significant deficiency is its failure to address the concerns of the majority of African American students who have been unable or unwilling to seek better educational opportunities by leaving predominantly black schools for predominantly white ones. While it opened the door for the Little Rock Nine, who desegregated Central High School in 1957, the *Brown* decision offered little solace to the hundreds of students who remained at Little Rock's all-black Horace Mann High School. When Arkansas officials reacted to desegregation by closing all of Little Rock's high schools, those students were denied even segregated educational opportunities.[7] With the encouragement of the lawyers for the National Association for the Advancement of Colored People's (NAACP) Legal Defense and Education Fund, the Supreme Court largely abandoned previous efforts to enforce the separate but equal mandate in order to adopt a narrowly conceived strategy for achieving

---

[6]*Brown v. Board of Education,* 347 U.S. at 494, 493; Gary Orfield and Chungmei Lee, "*Brown* at Fifty: King's Dream or Plessy's Nightmare?" Jan. 17, 2004, *The Civil Rights Project, Harvard University* <http://www.civilrightsproject.harvard.edu/research/reseg04/resegregation04.php> (April 4, 2004). In every region of the nation, at least 30% of black students still attend schools with less than 10% white enrollment. *Ibid.*

[7]Cf. Melba Beals, *Warriors Don't Cry: A Searing Memoir of the Battle to Integrate Little Rock's Central High* (New York, 1995); and Melba Beals, *White Is a State of Mind: A Memoir* (New York, 1995).

equal educational opportunity through desegregation. The pre-*Brown* equaliza-
tion effort had encouraged social scientists to develop increasingly sophisticated ways of measuring differences in the quality of schools. But during the
1950s, pro–civil rights scholars shifted their focus from the educational environment of black students in black schools to the psychological state of black students experiencing desegregation. The NAACP's initial strategy of forcing
southern states to equalize facilities at all-black schools had resulted in tangible
improvements, whereas the removal of racial barriers in public schools was advertised as offering intangible psychological gains.

For Thurgood Marshall, who headed the NAACP legal staff, the equaliza- 6
tion effort had always been a means of achieving the ultimate goal of desegregation. After the Supreme Court decided in *Sweatt v. Painter* (1950) that a
makeshift segregated law school at a black college could not provide educational opportunities equal to those offered by the University of Texas Law
School, Marshall exulted, "The complete destruction of *all* enforced segregation
is now in sight." Despite having attended predominantly black schools at every
stage of his academic career, he saw segregation as a racial stigma that could
not be removed by increased state appropriations for Jim Crow schools. In the
early 1950s he noted that social scientists were "almost in universal agreement
that segregated education produces inequality." He therefore concluded "that
segregated schools, perhaps more than any other single factor, are of major concern to the individual of public school age and contribute greatly to the un-
wholesomeness and unhappy development of the personality of Negroes
which the color caste system in the United States has produced."[8]

Few African Americans would wish to return to the pre-*Brown* world of 7
legally enforced segregation, but in the half century since 1954, only a minority
of Americans has experienced the promised land of truly integrated public education. By the mid-1960s, with dual school systems still in place in many areas
of the Deep South, and with de facto segregation a recognized reality in urban
areas, the limitations of *Brown* had become evident to many of those who had
spearheaded previous civil rights struggles. The ideological gulf that appeared
in African American politics during the period was largely the result of efforts
to draw attention to the predominantly black institutions neglected in the drive
for racial integration. The black power movement arose in part as an effort by
African Americans to control and improve such institutions. Some black power
proponents exaggerated the benefits of racial separatism, but their extremism
can be best understood as a reaction against the unbalanced post-*Brown* strategy of seeking racial advancement solely through integration. Although James
S. Coleman's landmark 1966 study of equality of educational opportunity
found that black children attending integrated schools did better than students

[8]*Sweatt v. Painter,* 339 U.S. 629 (1950); *Baltimore Afro-American,* June 17, 1950, quoted in Juan
Williams, *Thurgood Marshall: American Revolutionary* (New York, 1998), 195; Thurgood Marshall,
"An Evaluation of Recent Efforts to Achieve Racial Integration in Education through Resort to
the Courts," *Journal of Negro Education,* 21 (Summer 1952), 316–27, esp. 322.

attending predominantly black schools, it was by no means clear that the gap was the result of interracial interactions rather than of differences in the socioeconomic backgrounds of the students involved. By the late 1960s, growing numbers of black leaders had concluded that improvement of black schools should take priority over school desegregation. In 1967, shortly before the National Advisory Commission on Civil Disorders warned that the United States was "moving toward two societies, one white, one black—separate and unequal," Martin Luther King Jr. acknowledged the need to refocus attention, at least in the short run, on "schools in ghetto areas." He also insisted that "the drive for immediate improvements in segregated schools should not retard progress toward integrated education later." Even veterans of the NAACP's legal campaign had second thoughts. "*Brown* has little practical relevance to central city blacks," Constance Baker Motley commented in 1974. "Its psychological and legal relevance has already had its effect."[9]

8   Black power advocates sometimes sought to replace the narrow strategy of achieving racial advancement through integration with the equally narrow strategy of achieving it through racial separatism. In both instances, claims of psychological gains often substituted for measurable racial advancements, but the continued popularity of Afrocentric educational experiments indicates that many African Americans now see voluntary segregation as psychologically uplifting. Having personally experienced the burden of desegregating numerous classrooms and having watched my son move with great success from a predominantly black college to a predominantly white law school, I am skeptical of sweeping claims about the impact of racial environment on learning. While believing that debates among African Americans during the last half century about their destiny have been useful, I regret that those debates have often exacerbated ideological conflict rather than encouraging us toward collective action. Rather than having to choose between overcoming racial barriers and improving black community institutions, we should be able to choose both.

9   In hindsight, the nation would have been better served if the *Brown* decision had evinced a more realistic understanding of the deep historical roots of America's racial problems—perhaps a little more familiarity with the writings of W. E. B. DuBois and Carter C. Woodson as well as those of Myrdal and his colleagues. Rather than blandly advising that desegregation of public schools be achieved with "all deliberate speed," the Supreme Court—and the NAACP lawyers who argued before it—should have launched a two-pronged attack, not only against racial segregation but also against inferior schools, whatever their racial composition. Such an attack would have heeded the admonition

[9]J. S. Coleman et al., *Equality of Educational Opportunity* (Washington, 1966), *passim; Report of the National Advisory Commission on Civil Disorders* (New York, 1968), 1; Martin Luther King Jr., *Where Do We Go from Here: Chaos or Community?* (New York, 1967), 228. For Constance Baker Motley's statement (quoted from the *New York Times,* May 13, 1974), see James T. Patterson, Brown v. Board of Education: *A Civil Rights Milestone and Its Troubled Legacy* (New York, 2001), 168.

that DuBois offered in 1935, soon after his forced resignation as editor of the NAACP's journal, the *Crisis:*

> Theoretically, the Negro needs neither segregated schools nor mixed schools. What he needs is Education. . . . Other things being equal, the mixed school is the broader, more natural basis for the education of all youth. It gives wider contacts; it inspires great self-confidence; and suppresses the inferiority complex. But other things seldom are equal, and in that case, Sympathy, Knowledge, and the Truth, outweigh all that the mixed school can offer.[10]

Because the *Brown* decision was a decisive departure from *Plessy's* separate   10
but equal principle, it was an important turning point in African American history. Nevertheless, fifty years later the Court's assumptions about the psychological consequences of legally enforced segregation seem dated. The Jim Crow system no longer exists, but most black American schoolchildren still attend predominantly black public schools that offer fewer opportunities for advancement than typical predominantly white public schools. Moreover, there is no contemporary civil rights movement able to alter that fact. Yet, if *Brown* represents a failed attempt to achieve comprehensive racial advancement, the opinion nonetheless still challenges us by affirming egalitarian ideals that remain relevant: "In these days, it is doubtful that any child may reasonably be expected to succeed in life if he is denied the opportunity of an education. Such an opportunity, where the state has undertaken to provide it, is a right which must be made available to all on equal terms."[11]

COMPREHENSION

1. According to Carson, what are the benefits and shortcomings of the *Brown v. Board of Education* decision? Why does he give two cheers (instead of the traditional three cheers) for the Supreme Court's 1954 verdict?
2. What are the psychological effects of both segregation and desegregation on black students?
3. Why does Carson say that the impact of the *Brown* decision is difficult to measure? What evidence does he provide to support this assessment?

RHETORIC

1. Who is Carson's audience for this essay? How does he fit his style to the expectations he holds for this specific audience? Provide examples of vocabulary, syntax,

---

[10]*Brown v. Board of Education,* 349 U.S. 294 (1955); W. E. B. DuBois, "Does the Negro Need Separate Schools?" *Journal of Negro Education,* 4 (July 1935), in The *Oxford W. E. B. DuBois Reader,* ed. Eric J. Sundquist (New York, 1996), 431.
[11]*Brown v. Board of Education of Topeka:* Opinion on Segregation Laws," in *Civil Rights and African Americans: A Documentary History,* ed. Albert P. Blaustein and Robert I. Zangrando (Evanston, 1991), 436.

and abstract language to support your response. Why would the article also be of interest to a more general audience?

2. Carson lays out a well-informed argument. What is his claim or major proposition? What are his warrants? What is his support? How does he deal with opposing viewpoints? What conclusions does he draw to convince the reader of his position?

3. Analyze the pattern of cause and effect that Carson presents in this essay.

4. Carson has very strong topic sentences at the start of virtually every paragraph. List these topic sentences, and then show how they control the flow of his thoughts within paragraphs while at the same time advancing his argument.

5. Examine the writer's footnotes. What are his sources? What range and variety of evidence do these notes suggest?

WRITING

1. Using Carson's article as a reference point, write an essay describing the ethnic and racial composition of your former high school or the college you now attend. How does this demographic profile support some of Carson's key insights into *Brown v. Board of Education?*

2. Write an essay in which you offer your own analysis of the ways in which varieties of discrimination you encounter in education can have psychological consequences. Feel free to offer personal experience to support your analysis.

3. **Writing an Argument:** Unlike Carson, who argues both sides of the *Brown* decision in terms of the historical aftermath, write an argumentative essay in which you defend or criticize the results of *Brown* since 1954. Conduct research and collaborate with class members if you wish.

NETWORKING
Applying 21st-Century Literacies

Supporting an Argument with Visuals: Enhance your response to the Writing an Argument assignment above by incorporating three images from the electronic exhibit *In Pursuit of Freedom & Equality: Kansas and the African American Public School Experience, 1855–1955* (see the Chapter 5 Networking page at *www.mhhe .com/mhreader11e*). Be sure to credit your sources and not to misuse the images; that said, you can certainly debate what they *mean* in this argument and either draw on or argue with the way they are portrayed in the exhibit.

Synthesis: Connections for Critical Thinking

1. Compare and contrast the rhetoric of the personal essay as it is represented in Rodriguez's "The Lonely, Good Company of Books" with the rhetoric of such expository and argumentative essays as Quindlen's "Sex Ed" or Carson's "Two Cheers for *Brown v. Board of Education.*"

2. Analyze an event in your education when you had a disagreement with a teacher or administrator. Explain and explore whether the differences in viewpoint were based on emotional perspective, intellectual perspective, or both.
3. Select the essay in this chapter you find most pertinent to your life as a student. Explain why you selected the essay, and explore your intellectual and emotional responses to it.
4. Does your college seem to support Jacoby's views regarding the educational lives of women? Explain why or why not.
5. Argue for or against the view that the publicized sexual activity of politicians and other celebrities makes the decision whether to keep sex education out of the schools entirely moot.
6. It is 2050. Write an essay in which you explore the demographics of a typical college classroom. Refer to the ideas contained in the Gregorian, Jacoby, and Carson essays.
7. Write an essay that classifies at least three educational issues that the authors in this chapter examine. Establish a clear thesis to unify the categories you establish.
8. Analyze the patterns and techniques used by Menand, Gelernter, and Jacoby to advance their claims about education today.

NETWORKING

Applying 21st-Century Literacies

1. Do an online search for *sex education* and *France* (or another country of your choice). Write an essay describing the policies of your chosen country on the topic.
2. Argue for or against the proposition that despite Gelernter's warnings about the purported shortcomings of computers in the classroom, in the future many students will prefer to obtain a degree completely via computer and the Internet. To support your viewpoint, research and report on at least three online sites that offer college degrees.

CH 5   www.mhhe.com/**mhreader11e**

- *Image Gallery:* Chapter images in color
- *Education:* Information on the authors in this chapter
- *Ch. 5 Networking*

chapter *6*

Family Life and Gender Roles
How Do We Become Who We Are?

Every culture has its own ideas about what identity is, how it is formed, and where it comes from. What is the influence of family, of environment, of gender, and, as we saw in Chapter 5, of education on the creation of identity? Although it is challenging to reconcile these various cross-cultural ideas, the writers in this chapter attempt to make sense of identity from the perspectives of family and gender, and they invite readers to liberate themselves from the tyranny of stereotyping.

Families nourish us during childhood, and the values our families seek to maintain usually affect our identities in powerful ways, whether we adopt them wholly, modify them, or reject them outright. Writers have always been aware of the importance of the family in human development and behavior, and have written about it from various perspectives, using narration, sociological and psychological analysis, and cultural criticism, among other approaches. Tolstoy wrote that "happy families are all alike; every unhappy family is unhappy in its own way." But we shall discover that Tolstoy had a limited view of family life and its values—probably circumscribed by the mores of the time he lived in. Some of our finest essayists and observers of social life today demonstrate in this chapter that what constitutes the definition of a family is up for grabs as we begin the new millennium.

The family is one of the few institutions that we find in every society throughout the world, at least every thriving society. Anthropologists, sociologists, and psychologists tell us that family patterns are exceedingly diverse even in the same societies. In the past and even more so today, children grow up in many ways: in nuclear and in nontraditional households; in single-parent and in dual-parent arrangements; in extended families and in blended families; and in patriarchal and matriarchal, heterosexual and homosexual, monogamous and polygamous situations. And the dynamics of family life assume added dimension as we move across cultures, studying European families, African American families, Hispanic families, Asian families, and so forth. Even within these groups, we find variables that affect family life and values, such as economic class, social class, and educational levels.

Unlike in previous periods in our history, Americans today seem to be groping for a definition of what constitutes the happy family. With the influences of the media and of peer pressure on children, the rise in the number of latchkey children, and the fact that there is a growing diversity of cultures in America owing to the new wave of immigration, the family appears to be less of a traditional haven than it was even a generation ago. This chapter contains vivid accounts of the long-standing bonds within the family that have been treasured for their capacity to build values of love and sharing. It also contains essays that demonstrate how family life is filled with emotional complexities and conflicts that the child must negotiate as she or he finds meaning and attempts to construct an identity. Each writer, whether writing narration, exposition, or argumentation, shows how signifi-cant the family is for the development of our values, personalities, and lifestyles.

As much as our identities are shaped by powerful institutional forces like the family, what we are might be even more powerfully determined by the forces of sexuality and gender. Freud asserted that human behavior is rooted in sexuality, that gender (rather than family or school or any social institution) is destiny. Clearly, notions of what it means to be a man or a woman have an impact on the construction of our identities.

The identity issues discussed in this chapter might prove to be controversial, but they will encourage you to confront your sense of identity. These essays are like a mirror in which you can see and evaluate what you really are.

PREVIEWING THE CHAPTER

As you read the essays in this chapter and respond to them in discussion and writing, consider the following questions:

- What form of rhetoric is the author using: narration, exposition, or argumentation? Why is this form appropriate for the author's purpose?
- What perspective does the writer take on the subject of identity formation? Is the writer optimistic, pessimistic, or something else?
- What are the cultural, social, and economic issues addressed in the essay?
- How do you regard the authority of the author? Does she or he seem to be speaking from experience and knowledge? In essays that explain or argue, does the evidence appear substantial or questionable? Explain.
- What stylistic devices does the author employ to re-create a memory, explain a function, or argue a stance regarding an issue of identity?
- Which essays appear alike in purpose and method, and why?
- What have you learned or discovered about your own identity from reading these essays?
- Do you prefer one rhetorical form over another—for example, personal narration over argumentation? If so, why?

Classic and Contemporary Images

HOW DO WE RESPOND TO MARRIAGE?

Using a Critical Perspective   What was your first impression of Brueghel's *Rustic Wedding* and Elise Amendola's *Gay Marriage?* What details do you see? What senses do the artist and the photographer draw on to convey the atmosphere of the wedding? What does each want to say about the institution of marriage? How do you know?

The Flemish artist Pieter Brueghel the Elder (1525–1569) was one of the greatest painters of the 16th century and was renowned for his exuberant depictions of peasant life. His son Pieter Brueghel the Younger (1564–1638) copied many of his father's works and also painted religious subjects. He was responsible for *Rustic Wedding,* shown here.

Hillary, left, and Julie Goodridge, lead plaintiffs in the landmark Massachusetts gay marriage lawsuit, receive their wedding rings from their daughter, Annie, 8, as Unitarian Reverend William Sinkford presides over their marriage ceremony in Boston during the first day of state-sanctioned gay marriage in the United States on May 17, 2004.

Classic and Contemporary Essays
HOW MUCH DO FAMILIES MATTER?

E. B. White and Barbara Kingsolver represent two generations, each raised with different values regarding the function, structure, and role of the family. Both authors are master stylists, but each reflects a style of writing, an intellectual universe, and an external world that views the healthy family differently. White writes in clear, concise, elegiac prose. It marches on in a quiet, evenly patterned rhythm. Perhaps it is a metaphor of his view of life in general and family life in particular. Tradition is to be treasured; continuity is to be celebrated. He attends to the details of a nature outing and suggests that the sights, sounds, and smells that imbue the events he and his son experience are the same as those he experienced years before with his own father. For White, it seems, pleasure is derived from connectivity and permanence.

Kingsolver is passionate about her perspective on what constitutes a healthy family structure, but it is a family transformed, reconfigured, and rearranged by contemporary events and values. Kingsolver's notion of family is various while White's view is archetypal. Kingsolver seems to believe that change in families creates security, particularly if one is moving from a dysfunctional environment to a more coherent one. Is White conservative in his views? Is Kingsolver a liberal? Perhaps a better way to get a sense of their differences is to inquire whether our amorphous contemporary world requires us to be more flexible and critical. And, of course, we must consider that Kingsolver adds a woman's voice to the conversation about family, a voice that was not as frequently heard by the members of White's generation.

Once More to the Lake

E. B. White

E(lwyn) B(rooks) White (1899–1985), perhaps the finest American essayist of the 20th century, was at his most distinctive in his treatments of people and nature. A recipient of the National Medal for Literature, and associated for years with the New Yorker, *White is the author of* One Man's Meat *(1942),* Here Is New York *(1949), and* The Second Tree from the Corner *(1954), among numerous other works. He was also one of the most talented writers of literature for children, the author of* Stuart Little *(1945),* Charlotte's Web *(1952), and* The Trumpet of the Swan *(1970). In this essay, White combines narration and description to make a poignant and vivid statement about past and present, youth and age, life and death.*

One summer, along about 1904, my father rented a camp on a lake in Maine and ₁
took us all there for the month of August. We all got ringworm from some kit-
tens and had to rub Pond's Extract on our arms and legs night and morning, and
my father rolled over in a canoe with all his clothes on; but outside of that the
vacation was a success and from then on none of us ever thought there was any
place in the world like that lake in Maine. We returned summer after summer—
always on August 1st for one month. I have since become a saltwater man, but
sometimes in summer there are days when the restlessness of the tides and the
fearful cold of the sea water and the incessant wind which blows across the afternoon and into the evening make me wish for the placidity of a lake in the woods.
A few weeks ago this feeling got so strong I bought myself a couple of bass
hooks and a spinner and returned to the lake where we used to go, for a week's
fishing and to revisit old haunts.

I took along my son, who had never had any fresh water up his nose and ₂
who had seen lily pads only from train windows. On the journey over to the lake
I began to wonder what it would be like. I wondered how time would have
marred this unique, this holy spot—the coves and streams, the hills that the sun
set behind, the camps and the paths behind the camps. I was sure the tarred road
would have found it out and I wondered in what other ways it would be deso-
lated. It is strange how much you can remember about places like that once you
allow your mind to return into the grooves which lead back. You remember one
thing, and that suddenly reminds you of another thing. I guess I remembered
clearest of all the early mornings, when the lake was cool and motionless, remembered how the bedroom smelled of the lumber it was made of and of the wet
woods whose scent entered through the screen. The partitions in the camp were
thin and did not extend clear to the top of the rooms, and as I was always the first
up I would dress softly so as not to wake the others, and sneak out into the sweet
outdoors and start out in the canoe, keeping close along the shore in the long
shadows of the pines. I remembered being very careful never to rub my paddle
against the gunwale for fear of disturbing the stillness of the cathedral.

The lake had never been what you would call a wild lake. There were cot- ₃
tages sprinkled around the shores, and it was in farming country although the
shores of the lake were quite heavily wooded. Some of the cottages were owned
by nearby farmers, and you would live at the shore and eat your meals at the
farmhouse. That's what our family did. But although it wasn't wild, it was a
fairly large and undisturbed lake and there were places in it which, to a child at
least, seemed infinitely remote and primeval.

I was right about the tar: It led to within half a mile of the shore. But when I ₄
got back there, with my boy, and we settled into a camp near a farmhouse and
into the kind of summertime I had known, I could tell that it was going to be
pretty much the same as it had been before—I knew it, lying in bed the first
morning, smelling the bedroom, and hearing the boy sneak quietly out and go
off along the shore in a boat. I began to sustain the illusion that he was I, and
therefore, by simple transposition, that I was my father. This sensation persisted,

kept cropping up all the time we were there. It was not an entirely new feeling, but in this setting it grew much stronger. I seemed to be living a dual existence. I would be in the middle of some simple act, I would be picking up a bait box or laying down a table fork, or I would be saying something, and suddenly it would be not I but my father who was saying the words or making the gesture. It gave me a creepy sensation.

5   We went fishing the first morning. I felt the same damp moss covering the worms in the bait can, and saw the dragonfly alight on the tip of my rod as it hovered a few inches from the surface of the water. It was the arrival of this fly that convinced me beyond any doubt that everything was as it always had been, that the years were a mirage and there had been no years. The small waves were the same, chucking the rowboat under the chin as we fished at anchor, and the boat was the same boat, the same color green and the ribs broken in the same place, and under the floor-boards the same fresh-water leavings and débris—the dead hellgrammite, the wisps of moss, the rusty discarded fishhook, the dried blood from yesterday's catch. We stared silently at the tips of our rods, at the dragonflies that came and went. I lowered the tip of mine into the water, tentatively, pensively dislodging the fly, which darted two feet away, poised, darted two feet back, and came to rest again a little farther up the rod. There had been no years between the ducking of this dragonfly and the other one—the one that was part of memory. I looked at the boy, who was silently watching his fly, and it was my hands that held his rod, my eyes watching. I felt dizzy and didn't know which rod I was at the end of.

6   We caught two bass, hauling them in briskly as though they were mackerel, pulling them over the side of the boat in a businesslike manner without any landing net, and stunning them with a blow on the back of the head. When we got back for a swim before lunch, the lake was exactly where we had left it, the same number of inches from the dock, and there was only the merest suggestion of a breeze. This seemed an utterly enchanted sea, this lake you could leave to its own devices for a few hours and come back to, and find that it had not stirred, this constant and trustworthy body of water. In the shallows, the dark, water-soaked sticks and twigs, smooth and old, were undulating in clusters on the bottom against the clean ribbed sand, and the track of the mussel was plain. A school of minnows swam by, each minnow with its small individual shadow, doubling the attendance, so clear and sharp in the sunlight. Some of the other campers were in swimming, along the shore, one of them with a cake of soap, and the water felt thin and clear and unsubstantial. Over the years there had been this person with the cake of soap, this cultist, and here he was. There had been no years.

7   Up to the farmhouse to dinner through the teeming, dusty field, the road under our sneakers was only a two-track road. The middle track was missing, the one with the marks of the hooves and the splotches of dried, flaky manure. There had always been three tracks to choose from in choosing which track to walk in; now the choice was narrowed down to two. For a moment I missed terribly the middle alternative. But the way led past the tennis court, and something about the way it lay there in the sun reassured me; the tape had loosened

along the backline, the alleys were green with plantains and other weeds, and the net (installed in June and removed in September) sagged in the dry noon, and the whole place steamed with midday heat and hunger and emptiness. There was a choice of pie for dessert, and one was blueberry and one was apple, and the waitresses were the same country girls, there having been no passage of time, only the illusion of it as in a dropped curtain—the waitresses were still fifteen; their hair had been washed, that was the only difference—they had been to the movies and seen the pretty girls with the clean hair.

Summertime, oh summertime, pattern of life indelible, the fade-proof lake, 8 the woods unshatterable, the pasture with the sweetfern and the juniper forever and ever, summer without end; this was the background, and the life along the shore was the design, the cottagers with their innocent and tranquil design, their tiny docks with the flagpole and the American flag floating against the white clouds in the blue sky, the little paths over the roots of the trees leading from camp to camp and the paths leading back to the outhouses and the can of lime for sprinkling, and at the souvenir counters at the store the miniature birch-bark canoes and the post cards that showed things looking a little better than they looked. This was the American family at play, escaping the city heat, wondering whether the newcomers in the camp at the head of the cove were "common" or "nice," wondering whether it was true that the people who drove up for Sunday dinner at the farmhouse were turned away because there wasn't enough chicken.

It seemed to me, as I kept remembering all this, that those times and those 9 summers had been infinitely precious and worth saving. There had been jollity and peace and goodness. The arriving (at the beginning of August) had been so big a business in itself, at the railway station the farm wagon drawn up, the first smell of the pine-laden air, the first glimpse of the smiling farmer, and the great importance of the trunks and your father's enormous authority in such matters, and the feel of the wagon under you for the long ten-mile haul, and at the top of the last long hill catching the first view of the lake after eleven months of not seeing this cherished body of water. The shouts and cries of the other campers when they saw you, and the trunks to be unpacked, to give up their rich burden. (Arriving was less exciting nowadays, when you sneaked up in your car and parked it under a tree near the camp and took out the bags and in five minutes it was all over, no fuss, no loud wonderful fuss about trunks.)

Peace and goodness and jollity. The only thing that was wrong now, really, 10 was the sound of the place, an unfamiliar nervous sound of the outboard motors. This was the note that jarred, the one thing that would sometimes break the illusion and set the years moving. In those other summertimes all motors were inboard; and when they were at a little distance, the noise they made was a sedative, an ingredient of summer sleep. They were one-cylinder and two-cylinder engines, and some were make-and-break and some were jump-spark, but they all made a sleepy sound across the lake. The one-lungers throbbed and fluttered, and the twin-cylinder ones purred and purred, and that was a quiet sound too. But now the campers all had outboards. In the daytime, in the hot mornings, these motors made a petulant, irritable sound; at night, in the still evening when the afterglow lit the water, they whined about one's ears like mosquitoes. My boy loved our rented outboard, and his great desire was to achieve singlehanded mastery over it, and authority, and he soon learned the trick of choking it a little (but not too much), and the adjustment of the needle valve. Watching him I would remember the things you could do with the old one-cylinder engine with the heavy flywheel, how you could have it eating out of your hand if you got really close to it spiritually. Motor boats in those days didn't have clutches, and you would make a landing by shutting off the motor at the proper time and coasting in with a dead rudder. But there was a way of reversing them, if you learned the trick, by cutting the switch and putting it on again ex- actly on the final dying revolution of the flywheel, so that it would kick back against compression and begin reversing. Approaching a dock in a strong follow- ing breeze, it was difficult to slow up sufficiently by the ordinary coasting method, and if a boy felt he had complete mastery over his motor, he was tempted to keep it running beyond its time and then reverse it a few feet from the dock. It took a cool nerve, because if you threw the switch a twentieth of a second too soon you would catch the flywheel when it still had speed enough to go up past center, and the boat would leap ahead, charging bull-fashion at the dock.

11   We had a good week at the camp. The bass were biting well and the sun shone endlessly, day after day. We would be tired at night and lie down in the accumulated heat of the little bedrooms after the long hot day and the breeze would stir almost imperceptibly outside and the smell of the swamp drift in through the rusty screens. Sleep would come easily and in the morning the red squirrel would be on the roof, tapping out his gay routine. I kept remembering everything, lying in bed in the mornings—the small steamboat that had a long rounded stern like the lip of a Ubangi, and how quietly she ran on the moon- light sails, when the older boys played their mandolins and the girls sang and we ate doughnuts dipped in sugar, and how sweet the music was on the water in the shining night, and what it had felt like to think about girls then. After breakfast we would go up to the store and the things were in the same place— minnows in a bottle, the plugs and spinners disarranged and pawed over by the youngsters from the boys' camp, the fig newtons and the Beeman's gum. Outside, the road was tarred and cars stood in front of the store. Inside, all was just as it had always been, except there was more Coca-Cola and not so much Moxie and root beer and birch beer and sarsaparilla. We would walk out with a bottle of pop apiece and sometimes the pop would backfire up our noses and hurt. We explored the streams, quietly, where the turtles slid off the sunny logs and dug their way into the soft bottom, and we lay on the town wharf and fed worms to the tame bass. Everywhere we went I had trouble making out which was I, the one walking at my side, the one walking in my pants.

12   One afternoon while we were there at that lake a thunderstorm came up. It was like the revival of an old melodrama that I had seen long ago with childish awe. The second-act climax of the drama of the electrical disturbance over a lake in America had not changed in any important respect. This was the big scene, still the big scene. The whole thing was so familiar, the first feeling of oppression

and heat and a general air around camp of not wanting to go very far away. In midafternoon (it was all the same) a curious darkening of the sky, and a lull in everything that had made life tick; and then the way the boats suddenly swung the other way at their moorings with the coming of a breeze out of the new quarter, and the premonitory rumble. Then the kettle drum, then the snare, then the bass drum and cymbals, then crackling light against the dark, and the gods grinning and licking their chops in the hills. Afterward the calm, the rain steadily rustling in the calm lake, the return of light and hope and spirits, and the campers running out in joy and relief to go swimming in the rain, their bright cries perpetuating the deathless joke about how they were getting simply drenched, and the children screaming with delight at the new sensation of bathing in the rain, and the joke about getting drenched linking the generations in a strong indestructible chain. And the comedian who waded in carrying an umbrella.

When the others went swimming my son said he was going in too. He 13 pulled his dripping trunks from the line where they had hung all through the shower, and wrung them out. Languidly, and with no thought of going in, I watched him, his hard little body, skinny and bare, saw him wince slightly as he pulled up around his vitals the small, soggy, icy garment. As he buckled the swollen belt suddenly my groin felt the chill of death.

COMPREHENSION

1. At what point in the essay do you begin to sense White's main purpose? What is his purpose? What type of reader might his purpose appeal to?
2. What motivates White to return to the lake in Maine? Explain the "simple transposition" that he mentions in paragraph 4. List the illustrations that he gives of this phenomenon. What change does he detect in the lake?
3. Explain the significance of White's last sentence. Where are there foreshadowings of this statement?

RHETORIC

1. Describe White's use of figurative language in paragraphs 2, 10, and 12.
2. Identify those words and phrases that White invokes to establish the sense of mystery about the lake. Why are these words and their connotations important to the nature of the illusion that he describes?
3. Explain the organization of the essay in terms of the following paragraph units: 1–4, 5–7, 8–10, and 11–13. Explain the function of paragraphs 8 and 12.
4. There are many vivid and unusual descriptive details in this essay—for example, the dragonfly in paragraph 5 and the two-track road in paragraph 7. How does White create symbolic overtones for these descriptive details and others? Why is the lake itself a complex symbol? Explain with reference to paragraph 6.
5. Describe the persona that White creates for himself in the essay. How does this persona function?
6. What is the relation between the introductory and concluding paragraphs, specifically in terms of irony of statement?

WRITING

1. Explore in an essay the theme of nostalgia in "Once More to the Lake." What are the beauties and the dangers of nostalgia? Can the past ever be recaptured or relived? Justify your answer.
2. Referring to revisiting a site on the lake that he had visited years before with his father, White remarks in paragraph 4, "I could tell that it was going to be pretty much the same as it had been before." How does this observation reflect the general sentiment White has about the role and function of the family? Respond to the question in an analytical essay.
3. **Writing an Argument:** Argue for or against the proposition that nostalgia can obscure the true nature of family relationships and even suppress painful memories that should be confronted.

NETWORKING
Applying 21st-Century Literacies

Alluding to Print on the Web: Do a Google Images search for *once more to the lake.* Explore how various people around the world used this caption or description with their own photographs, blog entries, or professional articles. Choose three or four examples and discuss how they use this allusion to the E. B. White essay. Do they mention the piece itself, or only its title? What power of nostalgia might this essay possess in and of itself, for readers who have known it for years? What books, poems, stories, or songs make you nostalgic—for family, friends, a particular time in your life? How does thinking about these specific examples influence your response to question 3 under Writing?

Stone Soup

Barbara Kingsolver

Barbara Kingsolver (b. 1955) was born in Annapolis, Maryland; grew up in rural Kentucky, and was educated at DePauw University and the University of Arizona. Her fiction includes The Bean Trees *(1988);* Homeland *(1990);* Animal Dreams *(1991), for which she won a PEN fiction prize and an Edward Abbey Ecofiction Award;* Pigs in Heaven *(1993), which won a Los Angeles Times Book Award for Fiction; and* The Poisonwood Bible *(1998). Kingsolver's nonfiction includes* High Tide in Tusson: Essays from Now or Never *(1995),* Last Stand: America's Virgin Lands *(2002), and* Animal, Vegetable, Miracle: A Year of Food Life *(2007). She has also worked as a biologist, is active in the field of human rights, and plays keyboard with an amateur rock 'n' roll band. The following essay, first published in the January 1995 issue of* Parenting, *eschews the idea of the nuclear family as the standard by which the healthy family should be judged.*

In the catalog of family values, where do we rank an occasion like this? A curly- 1
haired boy who wanted to run before he walked, age seven now, a soccer player
scoring a winning goal. He turns to the bleachers with his fists in the air and a
smile wide as a gap-toothed galaxy. His own cheering section of grown-ups and
kids all leap to their feet and hug each other, delirious with love for this boy.
He's Andy, my best friend's son. The cheering section includes his mother and
her friends, his brother, his father and stepmother, a stepbrother and stepsister,
and a grandparent. Lucky is the child with this many relatives on hand to hail a
proud accomplishment. I'm there too, witnessing a family fortune. But in spite
of myself, defensive words take shape in my head. I am thinking: I dare *anybody*
to call this a broken home.

Families change, and remain the same. Why are our names for home so 2
slow to catch up to the truth of where we live?

When I was a child, I had two parents who loved me without cease. One of 3
them attended every excuse for attention I ever contrived, and the other made
it to the ones with higher production values, like piano recitals and appendicitis.
So I was a lucky child too. I played with a set of paper dolls called "The Family
of Dolls," four in number, who came with the factory-assigned names of Dad,
Mom, Sis, and Junior. I think you know what they looked like, at least before I
loved them to death and their heads fell off.

Now I've replaced the dolls with a life. I knit my days around my daugh- 4
ter's survival and happiness, and am proud to say her head is still on. But we
aren't the Family of Dolls. Maybe you're not, either. And if not, even though
you are statistically no oddity, it's probably been suggested to you in a hundred
ways that yours isn't exactly a real family, but an impostor family, a harbinger
of cultural ruin, a slapdash substitute—something like counterfeit money. Here
at the tail end of our century, most of us are up to our ears in the noisy business
of trying to support and love a thing called family. But there's a current in the
air with ferocious moral force that finds its way even into political campaigns,
claiming there is only one right way to do it, the Way It Has Always Been.

In the face of a thriving, particolored world, this narrow view is so pickled 5
and absurd I'm astonished that it gets airplay. And I'm astonished that it still
stings.

Every parent has endured the arrogance of a child-unfriendly grump sit- 6
ting in judgment, explaining what those kids of ours really need (for example,
"a good licking"). If we're polite, we move our crew to another bench in the
park. If we're forthright (as I am in my mind, only, for the rest of the day), we
fix them with a sweet imperious stare and say, "Come back and let's talk about
it after you've changed a thousand diapers."

But it's harder somehow to shrug off the Family-of-Dolls Family Values 7
crew when they judge (from their safe distance) that divorced people, blended
families, gay families, and single parents are failures. That our children are at

risk, and the whole arrangement is messy and embarrassing. A marriage that ends is not called "finished," it's called *failed*. The children of this family may have been born to a happy union, but now they are called *the children of divorce.*

8   I had no idea how thoroughly these assumptions overlaid my culture until I went through divorce myself. I wrote to a friend: "This might be worse than being widowed. Overnight I've suffered the same losses—companionship, financial and practical support, my identity as a wife and partner, the future I'd taken for granted. I am lonely, grieving, and hard-pressed to take care of my household alone. But instead of bringing casseroles, people are acting like I had a fit and broke up the family china."

9   Once upon a time I held these beliefs about divorce: that everyone who does it could have chosen not to do it. That it's a lazy way out of marital problems. That it selfishly puts personal happiness ahead of family integrity. Now I tremble for my ignorance. It's easy, in fortunate times, to forget about the ambush that could leave your head reeling: serious mental or physical illness, death in the family, abandonment, financial calamity, humiliation, violence, despair.

10   I started out like any child, intent on being the Family of Dolls. I set upon young womanhood believing in most of the doctrines of my generation: I wore my skirts four inches above the knee. I had that Barbie with her zebra-striped swimsuit and a figure unlike anything found in nature. And I understood the Prince Charming Theory of Marriage, a quest for Mr. Right that ends smack dab where you find him. I did not completely understand that another whole story *begins* there, and no fairy tale prepared me for the combination of bad luck and persistent hope that would interrupt my dream and lead me to other arrangements. Like a cancer diagnosis, a dying marriage is a thing to fight, to deny, and finally, when there's no choice left, to dig in and survive. Casseroles would help. Likewise, I imagine it must be a painful reckoning in adolescence (or later on) to realize one's own true love will never look like the soft-focus fragrance ads because Prince Charming (surprise!) is a princess. Or vice versa. Or has skin the color your parents didn't want you messing with, except in the Crayola box.

11   It's awfully easy to hold in contempt the straw broken home, and that mythical category of persons who toss away nuclear family for the sheer fun of it. Even the legal terms we use have a suggestion of caprice. I resent the phrase "irreconcilable differences," which suggests a stubborn refusal to accept a spouse's little quirks. This is specious. Every happily married couple I know has loads of irreconcilable differences. Negotiating where to set the thermostat is not the point. A nonfunctioning marriage is a slow asphyxiation. It is waking up despised each morning, listening to the pulse of your own loneliness before the radio begins to blare its raucous gospel that you're nothing if you aren't loved. It is sharing your airless house with the threat of suicide or other kinds of violence, while the ghost that whispers, "Leave here and destroy your children," has passed over every door and nailed it shut. Disassembling a marriage in these circumstances is as much *fun* as amputating your own gangrenous leg. You do it, if you can, to save a life—or two, or more.

I know of no one who really went looking to hoe the harder row, especially 12 the daunting one of single parenthood. Yet it seems to be the most American of customs to blame the burdened for their destiny. We'd like so desperately to believe in freedom and justice for all, we can hardly name that rogue bad luck, even when he's a close enough snake to bite us. In the wake of my divorce, some friends (even a few close ones) chose to vanish, rather than linger within striking distance of misfortune.

But most stuck around, bless their hearts, and if I'm any the wiser for my 13 trials, it's from having learned the worth of steadfast friendship. And also, what not to say. The least helpful question is: "Did you want the divorce, or didn't you?" Did I want to keep that gangrenous leg, or not? How to explain, in a culture that venerates choice: two terrifying options are much worse than none at all. Give me any day the quick hand of cruel fate that will leave me scarred but blameless. As it was, I kept thinking of that wicked third-grade joke in which some boy comes up behind you and grabs your ear, starts in with a prolonged tug, and asks, "Do you want this ear any longer?"

Still, the friend who holds your hand and says the wrong thing is made of 14 dearer stuff than the one who stays away. And generally, through all of it, you live. My favorite fictional character, Kate Vaiden (in the novel by Reynolds Price), advises: "Strength just comes in one brand—you stand up at sunrise and meet what they send you and keep your hair combed."

Once you've weathered the straits, you get to cross the tricky juncture from 15 casualty to survivor. If you're on your feet at the end of a year or two, and have begun putting together a happy new existence, those friends who were kind enough to feel sorry for you when you needed it must now accept you back to the ranks of the living. If you're truly blessed, they will dance at your second wedding. Everybody else, for heavens sake, should stop throwing stones.

Arguing about whether nontraditional families deserve pity or tolerance is a 16 little like the medieval debate about left-handedness as a mark of the devil. Divorce, remarriage, single parenthood, gay parents, and blended families simply are. They're facts of our time. Some of the reasons listed by sociologists for these family reconstructions are: the idea of marriage as a romantic partnership rather than a pragmatic one; a shift in women's expectations, from servility to self-respect and independence; and longevity (prior to antibiotics no marriage was expected to last many decades—in Colonial days the average couple lived to be married less than twelve years). Add to all this, our growing sense of entitlement to happiness and safety from abuse. Most would agree these are all good things. Yet their result—a culture in which serial monogamy and the consequent reshaping of families are the norm—gets diagnosed as "failing."

For many of us, once we have put ourselves Humpty-Dumpty–wise back 17 together again, the main problem with our reorganized family is that other people think we have a problem. My daughter tells me the only time she's uncomfortable about being the child of divorced parents is when her friends say they feel sorry for her. It's a bizarre sympathy, given that half the kids in her school and nation are in the same boat, pursuing childish happiness with the same energy as their married-parent peers. When anyone asks how she feels about it, she spontaneously lists the benefits: our house is in the country and we have a dog, but she can go to her dad's neighborhood for the urban thrills of a pool and sidewalks for roller-skating. What's more, she has three sets of grandparents!

18   Why is it surprising that a child would revel in a widened family and the right to feel at home in more than one house? Isn't it the opposite that should worry us—a child with no home at all, or too few resources to feel safe? The child at risk is the one whose parents are too immature themselves to guide wisely; too diminished by poverty to nurture; too far from opportunity to offer hope. The number of children in the U.S. living in poverty at this moment is almost unfathomably large: twenty percent. There are families among us that need help all right, and by no means are they new on the landscape. The rate at which teenage girls had babies in 1957 (ninety-six per thousand) was twice what it is now. That remarkable statistic is ignored by the religious right—probably because the teen birth rate was cut in half mainly by legalized abortion. In fact, the policy gatekeepers who coined the phrase "family values" have steadfastly ignored the desperation of too-small families, and since 1979 have steadily reduced the amount of financial support available to a single parent. But, this camp's most outspoken attacks seem aimed at the notion of families getting too complex, with add-ons and extras such as a gay parent's partner, or a remarried mother's new husband and his children.

19   To judge a family's value by its tidy symmetry is to purchase a book for its cover. There's no moral authority there. The famous family comprised by Dad, Mom, Sis, and Junior living as an isolated economic unit is not built on historical bedrock. In *The Way We Never Were*, Stephanie Coontz writes, "Whenever people propose that we go back to the traditional family, I always suggest that they pick a ballpark date for the family they have in mind." Colonial families were tidily disciplined, but their members (meaning everyone but infants) labored incessantly and died young. Then the Victorian family adopted a new division of labor, in which women's role was domestic and children were allowed time for study and play, but this was an upper-class construct supported by myriad slaves. Coontz writes, "For every nineteenth-century middle-class family that protected its wife and child within the family circle, there was an Irish or German girl scrubbing floors . . . a Welsh boy mining coal to keep the home-baked goodies warm, a black girl doing the family laundry, a black mother and child picking cotton to be made into clothes for the family, and a Jewish or an Italian daughter in a sweatshop making 'ladies' dresses or artificial flowers for the family to purchase."

20   The abolition of slavery brought slightly more democratic arrangements, in which extended families were harnessed together in cottage industries; at the turn of the century came a steep rise in child labor in mines and sweat-shops. Twenty percent of American children lived in orphanages at the time; their parents were not necessarily dead, but couldn't afford to keep them.

21   During the Depression and up to the end of World War II, many millions of U.S. households were more multigenerational than nuclear. Women my

grandmother's age were likely to live with a fluid assortment of elderly relatives, in-laws, siblings, and children. In many cases they spent virtually every
waking hour working in the company of other women—a companionable scenario in which it would be easier, I imagine, to tolerate an estranged or difficult
spouse. I'm reluctant to idealize a life of so much hard work and so little spousal
intimacy, but its advantage may have been resilience. A family so large and
varied would not easily be brought down by a single blow: It could absorb a
death, long-illness, an abandonment here or there, and any number of irreconcilable differences.

The Family of Dolls came along midcentury as a great American experi- 22
ment. A booming economy required a mobile labor force and demanded that
women surrender jobs to returning soldiers. Families came to be defined by a
single breadwinner. They struck out for single-family homes at an earlier age
than ever before, and in unprecedented numbers they raised children in suburban isolation. The nuclear family was launched to sink or swim.

More than a few sank. Social historians corroborate that the suburban fam- 23
ily of the postwar economic boom, which we have recently selected as our definition of "traditional," was no panacea. Twenty-five percent of Americans were
poor in the mid-1950s, and as yet there were no food stamps. Sixty percent of
the elderly lived on less than $1,000 a year, and most had no medical insurance.
In the sequestered suburbs, alcoholism and sexual abuse of children were far
more widespread than anyone imagined.

Expectations soared, and the economy sagged. It's hard to depend on one 24
other adult for everything, come what may. In the last three decades, that amorphous, adaptable structure we call "family" has been reshaped once more by
economic tides. Compared with fifties families, mothers are far more likely now
to be employed. We are statistically more likely to divorce, and to live in
blended families or other extranuclear arrangements. We are also more likely to
plan and space our children, and to rate our marriages as "happy." We are less
likely to suffer abuse without recourse, or to stare out at our lives through a
glaze of prescription tranquilizers. Our aged parents are less likely to be desti-
tute, and we're half as likely to have a teenage daughter turn up a mother herself. All in all, I would say that if "intact" in modern family-values jargon means
living quietly desperate in the bell jar, then hip-hip-hooray for "broken." A neat
family model constructed to service the Baby Boom economy seems to be returning gradually to a grand, lumpy shape that human families apparently
have tended toward since they first took root in the Olduvai Gorge. We're social
animals, deeply fond of companionship, and children love best to run in packs.
If there is a *normal* for humans, at all, I expect it looks like two or three Families
of Dolls, connected variously by kinship and passion, shuffled like cards and
strewn over several shoeboxes.

The sooner we can let go the fairy tale of families functioning perfectly in 25
isolation, the better we might embrace the relief of community. Even the admirable parents who've stayed married through thick and thin are very likely, at
present, to incorporate other adults into their families—household help and

baby-sitters if they can afford them or neighbors and grandparents if they can't. For single parents, this support is the rock-bottom definition of family. And most parents who have split apart, however painfully, still manage to maintain family continuity for their children, creating in many cases a boisterous phenomenon that Constance Ahrons in her book *The Good Divorce* calls the "binuclear family." Call it what you will—when ex-spouses beat swords into plowshares and jump up and down at a soccer game together, it makes for happy kids.

26   Cinderella, look, who needs her? All those evil stepsisters? That story always seemed like too much cotton-picking fuss over clothes. A childhood tale that fascinated me more was the one called "Stone Soup," and the gist of it is this: Once upon a time, a pair of beleaguered soldiers straggled home to a village empty-handed, in a land ruined by war. They were famished, but the villagers had so little they shouted evil words and slammed their doors. So the soldiers dragged out a big kettle, filled it with water, and put it on a fire to boil. They rolled a clean round stone into the pot, while the villagers peered through their curtains in amazement.

27   "What kind of soup is that?" they hooted.

28   "Stone soup," the soldiers replied. "Everybody can have some when it's done."

29   "Well, thanks," one matron grumbled, coming out with a shriveled carrot. "But it'd be better if you threw this in."

30   And so on, of course, a vegetable at a time, until the whole suspicious village managed to feed itself grandly.

31   Any family is a big empty pot, save for what gets thrown in. Each stew turns out different. Generosity, a resolve to turn bad luck into good, and respect for variety—these things will nourish a nation of children. Name-calling and suspicion will not. My soup contains a rock or two of hard times, and maybe yours does too. I expect it's a heck of a bouillabaisse.

COMPREHENSION

1. What is the essay's thesis?
2. According to Kingsolver, why is our society so apt to condemn divorce?
3. What is the author's view of family symmetry (paragraph 19)?

RHETORIC

1. What rhetorical function does the opening anecdote serve in introducing the essay's subject matter?
2. What is Kingsolver's purpose in capitalizing, italicizing, and placing quotation marks around certain phrases—for example, the Way It Has Always Been (paragraph 4), *failed* and *the children of divorce* (paragraph 7), and "family values" (paragraph 18)?
3. What is the author's purpose in creating a gap between paragraphs 15 and 16? What is the focus of her argument after this break?

4. Compare the introductory paragraph with the concluding one. How do they differ? How are they similar? How do they help set the boundaries of the essay?

5. This essay contains personal observations, personal experiences, historical data, and anecdotes. How would you describe the author's overall method to a person who has not read the essay?

6. Unlike the titles of most essays, the title "Stone Soup" gives no hint at the essay's content. What is the rhetorical purpose in keeping the meaning of the title a mystery until the very end?

7. In paragraph 2, Kingsolver asks the question, "Why are our names for home so slow to catch up to the truth of where we live?" Does the author suggest an answer to this question either implicitly or explicitly during the course of the essay? If so, where?

WRITING

1. Interview two individuals at least 25 years apart in age. Compare and contrast their views on divorce.

2. Describe the dynamics of a blended family with which you are familiar. It may be your own or a friend's.

3. **Writing an Argument:** Write an essay arguing that some negative outcomes could occur in the type of family the author celebrates.

NETWORKING
Applying 21st-Century Literacies

Using Keyword Searches to Find Articles: Do a keyword search in your library's online databases for popular or scholarly articles about *Family Values*. Write an extended analysis about the results of this initial search. Which databases did you search? What kinds of sources did they (and these keywords) lead you to? If the term *Family Values* is defined in any of the abstracts you encountered, compile a few of these definitions and compare them.

Synthesis: Classic and Contemporary Questions for Comparison

1. Compare and contrast the tone of each writer. How does tone affect purpose? How does it affect mood? Select at least three passages from White and three from Kingsolver that demonstrate how their tones differ. Do they offer any hints as to the "voice" or personality of the writers? Why or why not?

2. What contemporary issues does Kingsolver address that White either ignores or is unaware of? Consider that White was born 58 years before Kingsolver, so his world was quite a different one. Are there other variables that might help us distinguish their concerns and outlooks—for example, gender, class, and environment?

3. What central values does each author have regarding the family? How are they similar? How do they differ? How do their values reflect their times?

An American Childhood

Annie Dillard

Annie Dillard (b. 1945 in Pittsburgh) received her BA and MA degrees from Hollins College. Her first book, Pilgrim at Tinker Creek *(1975), won the Pulitzer Prize for general nonfiction. Her other published works of nonfiction include* Teaching a Stone to Talk *(1982) and* An American Childhood *(1987). Dillard expanded her range of writing with the publication of her first novel,* The Living *(1992), and her latest novel,* The Maytrees *(2007). She has received awards from the National Endowment for the Arts and the Guggenheim Foundation as well as many other sources. As an essayist, poet, memoirist, and literary critic, she focuses her themes on the relationships among the self, nature, religion, and faith. Her writing is recognizable by its observations of the minutiae of life and its search for meaning in unlikely places, such as a stone or an insect. In this passage from* An American Childhood, *the author gives us a portrait of her mother by focusing on her small idiosyncrasies of speech, gesture, and attitude.*

1   One Sunday afternoon Mother wandered through our kitchen, where Father was making a sandwich and listening to the ball game. The Pirates were play-ing the New York Giants at Forbes Field. In those days, the Giants had a utility infielder named Wayne Terwilliger. Just as Mother passed through, the radio announcer cried—with undue drama—"Terwilliger bunts one!"

2   "Terwilliger bunts one?" Mother cried back, stopped short. She turned. "Is that English?"

3   "The player's name is Terwilliger," Father said. "He bunted."

4   "That's marvelous," Mother said. "'Terwilliger bunts one.' No wonder you listen to baseball. 'Terwilliger bunts one.'"

5   For the next seven or eight years, Mother made this surprising string of syl-lables her own. Testing a microphone, she repeated, "Terwilliger bunts one"; testing a pen or a typewriter, she wrote it. If, as happened surprisingly often in the course of various improvised gags, she pretended to whisper something else in my ear, she actually whispered, "Terwilliger bunts one." Whenever someone used a French phrase, or a Latin one, she answered solemnly, "Terwil-liger bunts one." If Mother had had, like Andrew Carnegie, the opportunity to cook up a motto for a coat of arms, hers would have read simply and tellingly, "Terwilliger bunts one." (Carnegie's was "Death to Privilege.")

6   She served us with other words and phrases. On a Florida trip, she repeated tremulously, "That . . . is a royal poinciana." I don't remember the tree; I re-member the thrill in her voice. She pronounced it carefully, and spelled it. She also liked to say "portulaca."

7   The drama of the words "Tamiami Trail" stirred her, we learned on the same Florida trip. People built Tampa on one coast, and they built Miami on

another. Then—the height of visionary ambition and folly—they piled a slow, tremendous road through the terrible Everglades to connect them. To build the road, men stood sunk in muck to their armpits. They fought off cottonmouth moccasins and six-foot alligators. They slept in boats, wet. They blasted muck with dynamite, cut jungle with machetes; they laid logs, dragged drilling machines, hauled dredges, heaped limestone. The road took fourteen years to build up by the shovelful, a Panama Canal in reverse, and cost hundreds of lives from tropical, mosquito-carried diseases. Then, capping it all, some genius thought of the word Tamiami: they called the road from Tampa to Miami, this very road under our spinning wheels, the Tamiami Trail. Some called it Alligator Alley. Anyone could drive over this road without a thought.

Hearing this, moved, I thought all the suffering of road building was worth it (it wasn't my suffering), now that we had this new thing to hang these new words on—Alligator Alley for those who liked things cute, and, for connoisseurs like Mother, for lovers of the human drama in all its boldness and terror, the Tamiami Trail. 8

Back home, Mother cut clips from reels of talk, as it were, and played them back at leisure. She noticed that many Pittsburghers confuse "leave" and "let." One kind relative brightened our morning by mentioning why she'd brought her son to visit: "He wanted to come with me, so I left him." Mother filled in Amy and me on locutions we missed. "I can't do it on Friday," her pretty sister told a crowded dinner party, "because Friday's the day I lay in the stores." 9

(All unconsciously, though, we ourselves used some pure Pittsburghisms. We said "tele pole," pronounced "telly pole," for that splintery sidewalk post I loved to climb. We said "slippy"—the sidewalks are "slippy." We said, "That's all the farther I could go." And we said, as Pittsburghers do say, "This glass needs washed," or "The dog needs walked"—a usage our father eschewed; he knew it was not standard English, nor even comprehensible English, but he never let on.) 10

"Spell 'poinsettia,'" Mother would throw out at me, smiling with pleasure. "Spell 'sherbet.'" The idea was not to make us whizzes, but, quite the contrary, to remind us—and I, especially, needed reminding—that we didn't know it all just yet. 11

"There's a deer standing in the front hall," she told me one quiet evening in the country. 12

"Really?" 13

"No. I just wanted to tell you something once without your saying, 'I know.'" 14

Supermarkets in the middle 1950s began luring, or bothering, customers by giving out Top Value Stamps or Green Stamps. When, shopping with Mother, we got to the head of the checkout line, the checker, always a young man, asked, "Save stamps?" 15

"No," Mother replied genially, week after week, "I build model airplanes." I believe she originated this line. It took me years to determine where the joke lay. 16

Anyone who met her verbal challenges she adored. She had surgery on one of her eyes. On the operating table, just before she conked out, she appealed 17 feelingly to the surgeon, saying, as she had been planning to say for weeks, "Will I be able to play the piano?" "Not on me," the surgeon said. "You won't pull that old one on me."

18   It was, indeed, an old one. The surgeon was supposed to answer, "Yes, my dear, brave woman, you will be able to play the piano after this operation," to which Mother intended to reply, "Oh, good, I've always wanted to play the piano." This pat scenario bored her; she loved having it interrupted. It must have galled her that usually her acquaintances were so predictably unalert; it must have galled her that, for the length of her life, she could surprise everyone so continually, so easily, when she had been the same all along. At any rate, she loved anyone who, as she put it, saw it coming, and called her on it.

19   She regarded the instructions on bureaucratic forms as straight lines. "Do you advocate the overthrow of the United States government by force or violence?" After some thought she wrote, "Force." She regarded children, even babies, as straight men. When Molly learned to crawl, Mother delighted in buying her gowns with drawstrings at the bottom, like Swee'pea's, because, as she explained energetically, you could easily step on the drawstring without the baby's noticing, so that she crawled and crawled and crawled and never got anywhere except into a small ball at the gown's top.

20 When we children were young, she mothered us tenderly and dependably; as we got older, she resumed her career of anarchism. She collared us into her gags. If she answered the phone on a wrong number, she told the caller, "Just a minute," and dragged the receiver to Amy or me, saying, "Here, take this, your name is Cecile," or, worse, just, "It's for you." You had to think on your feet. But did you want to perform well as Cecile, or did you want to take pity on the wretched caller?

21   During a family trip to the Highland Park Zoo, Mother and I were alone for a minute. She approached a young couple holding hands on a bench by the seals, and addressed the young man in dripping tones: "Where have you been? Still got those baby-blue eyes; always did slay me. And this"—a swift nod at the dumbstruck young woman, who had removed her hand from the man's— "must be the one you were telling me about. She's not so bad, really, as you used to make out. But listen, you know how I miss you, you know where to reach me, same old place. And there's Ann over there—see how she's grown? See the blue eyes?"

22   And off she sashayed, taking me firmly by the hand, and leading us around briskly past the monkey house and away. She cocked an ear back, and both of us heard the desperate man begin, in a high-pitched wail, "I swear, I never saw her before in my life . . ."

23 On a long, sloping beach by the ocean, she lay stretched out sunning with Father and friends, until the conversation gradually grew tedious, when without forethought she gave a little push with her heel and rolled away. People were stunned. She rolled deadpan and apparently effortlessly, arms and legs

extended and tidy, down the beach to the distant water's edge, where she lay at ease just as she had been, but half in the surf, and well out of earshot.

She dearly loved to fluster people by throwing out a game's rules at a 24 whim—when she was getting bored, losing in a dull sort of way, and when everybody else was taking it too seriously. If you turned your back, she moved the checkers around on the board. When you got them all straightened out, she denied she'd touched them; the next time you turned your back, she lined them up on the rug or hid them under your chair. In a betting rummy game called Michigan, she routinely played out of turn, or called out a card she didn't hold, or counted backward, simply to amuse herself by causing an uproar and watching the rest of us do double-takes and have fits. (Much later, when serious suitors came to call, Mother subjected them to this fast card game as a trial by ordeal; she used it as an intelligence test and a measure of spirit. If the poor man could stay a round without breaking down or running out, he got to marry one of us, if he still wanted to.)

She excelled at bridge, playing fast and boldly, but when the stakes were 25 low and the hands dull, she bid slams for the devilment of it, or raised her opponents' suit to bug them, or showed her hand, or tossed her cards in a handful behind her back in a characteristic swift motion accompanied by a vibrantly innocent look. It drove our stolid father crazy. The hand was over before it began, and the guests were appalled. How do you score it, who deals now, what do you do with a crazy person who is having so much fun? Or they were down seven, and the guests were appalled. "Pam!" "Dammit, Pam!" He groaned. What ails such people? What on earth possesses them? He rubbed his face.

She was an unstoppable force; she never let go. When we moved across 26 town, she persuaded the U.S. Post Office to let her keep her old address— forever—because she'd had stationery printed. I don't know how she did it. Every new post office worker, over decades, needed to learn that although the Doaks' mail is addressed to here, it is delivered to there.

Mother's energy and intelligence suited her for a greater role in a larger 27 arena—mayor of New York, say—than the one she had. She followed American politics closely; she had been known to vote for Democrats. She saw how things should be run, but she had nothing to run but our household. Even there, small minds bugged her; she was smarter than the people who designed the things she had to use all day for the length of her life.

"Look," she said. "Whoever designed this corkscrew never used one. Why 28 would anyone sell it without trying it out?" So she invented a better one. She showed me a drawing of it. The spirit of American enterprise never faded in Mother. If capitalizing and tooling up had been as interesting as theorizing and thinking up, she would have fired up a new factory every week, and chaired several hundred corporations.

"It grieves me," she would say, "it grieves my heart," that the company that 29 made one superior product packaged it poorly, or took the wrong tack in its advertising. She knew, as she held the thing mournfully in her two hands, that she'd never find another. She was right. We children wholly sympathized, and so did Father; what could she do, what could anyone do, about it? She was Samson in chains. She paced.

30   She didn't like the taste of stamps so she didn't lick stamps; she licked the corner of the envelope instead. She glued sandpaper to the sides of kitchen drawers, and under kitchen cabinets, so she always had a handy place to strike a match. She designed, and hounded workmen to build against all norms, doubly wide kitchen counters and elevated bathroom sinks. To splint a finger, she stuck it in a lightweight cigar tube. Conversely, to protect a pack of ciga-rettes, she carried it in a Band-Aid box. She drew plans for an over-the-finger toothbrush for babies, an oven rack that slid up and down, and—the family favorite—Lendalarm. Lendalarm was a beeper you attached to books (or tools) you loaned friends. After ten days, the beeper sounded. Only the rightful owner could silence it.

31   She repeatedly reminded us of P. T. Barnum's dictum: You could sell any-thing to anybody if you marketed it right. The adman who thought of making Americans believe they needed underarm deodorant was a visionary. So, too, was the hero who made a success of a new product, Ivory soap. The executives were horrified, Mother told me, that a cake of this stuff floated. Soap wasn't supposed to float. Anyone would be able to tell it was mostly whipped-up air. Then some inspired adman made a leap: Advertise that it floats. Flaunt it. The rest is history.

32   She respected the rare few who broke through to new ways. "Look," she'd say, "here's an intelligent apron." She called upon us to admire intelligent control knobs and intelligent pan handles, intelligent andirons and picture frames and knife sharpeners. She questioned everything, every pair of scissors, every knit-ting needle, gardening glove, tape dispenser. Hers was a restless mental vigor that just about ignited the dumb household objects with its force.

33   Torpid conformity was a kind of sin; it was stupidity itself, the mighty stream against which Mother would never cease to struggle. If you held no minority opinions, or if you failed to risk total ostracism for them daily, the world would be a better place without you.

34   Always I heard Mother's emotional voice asking Amy and me the same few questions: "Is that your own idea? Or somebody else's?" "*Giant* is a good movie," I pronounced to the family at dinner. "Oh, really?" Mother warmed to these occasions. She all but rolled up her sleeves. She knew I hadn't seen it. "Is that your considered opinion?"

35   She herself held many unpopular, even fantastic, positions. She was scath-ingly sarcastic about the McCarthy hearings while they took place, right on our living-room television; she frantically opposed Father's wait-and-see calm. "We don't know enough about it," he said. "I do," she said. "I know all I need to know."

36   She asserted, against all opposition, that people who lived in trailer parks were not bad but simply poor, and had as much right to settle on beautiful land, such as rural Ligonier, Pennsylvania, as did the oldest of families in the

finest of hidden houses. Therefore, the people who owned trailer parks, and sought zoning changes to permit trailer parks, needed our help. Her profound belief that the country-club pool sweeper was a person, and that the department-store saleslady, the bus driver, telephone operator, and house-painter were people, and even in groups the steelworkers who carried pickets and the Christmas shoppers who clogged intersections were people—this was a conviction common enough in democratic Pittsburgh, but not altogether common among our friends' parents, or even, perhaps, among our parents' friends.

Opposition emboldened Mother, and she would take on anybody on any 37 issue—the chairman of the board, at a cocktail party, on the current strike; she would fly at him in a flurry of passion, as a songbird selflessly attacks a big hawk.

"Eisenhower's going to win," I announced after school. She lowered her 38 magazine and looked me in the eyes: "How do you know?" I was doomed. It was fatal to say, "Everyone says so." We all knew well what happened. "Do you consult this Everyone before you make your decisions? What if Everyone decided to round up all the Jews?" Mother knew there was no danger of cowing me. She simply tried to keep us all awake. And in fact it was always clear to Amy and me, and to Molly when she grew old enough to listen, that if our classmates came to cruelty, just as much as if the neighborhood or the nation came to madness, we were expected to take, and would be each separately capable of taking, a stand.

COMPREHENSION

1. Dillard creates a picture of her mother's personality through a number of anecdotes and explanations. How would you sum up the mother's personality?
2. Dillard's mother appears to have a special appreciation for words and language. To what purpose does she apply this appreciation? What effect does it have on her family and acquaintances?
3. What values does the mother hold? What behaviors and attitudes does she abhor and discourage?

RHETORIC

1. In paragraph 7, Dillard explains that the highway from Tampa to Miami is referred to either as "Tamiami Trail" or "Alligator Alley." What is the connotation of each of these terms? Why does her mother prefer to call it "Tamiami Trail"?
2. The author herself seems to have inherited a special fascination for language. Study her use of dashes and semicolons in paragraphs 26 and 27. How do they help contribute to energetic writing?
3. What are the functions of the spaces between paragraphs 19 and 20, 22 and 23, and 32 and 33? How do these divisions contribute to the structure of the essay as a whole?
4. How does Dillard use her writing talents to create paragraph 8 out of one long sentence? What other examples can you provide of long sentences in the essay? How do they contribute to the overall style of the writing?

5. What is the overall emotional "tone" of the writer toward her subject—admiring, or loving, or cautionary? What adjectives does she use in describing her mother that provides the reader with clues to the tone?
6. Dillard quotes her mother directly on several occasions. Can we assume that she is quoting precisely, given that the essay was written years after the incidents described? Does it matter?
7. The final paragraph not only provides closure to the essay but transmits a lesson the mother wants her family to learn. How do the style and structure of this paragraph contribute to the ultimate message of the essay? In other words, how does the form help convey the meaning?

WRITING

1. Write a descriptive essay about someone you know very well, using at least five anecdotes from that person's life, so that by the end of the essay, we have a mental picture of your subject's personality, values, and attitudes. This could be someone in your biological family, or someone else you are or were very close to.
2. Describe an incident in your life when the unexpected taught you an important lesson.
3. **Writing an Argument:** Argue for or against the proposition that an effective parent should have—at least—a touch of unconventionality.

NETWORKING
Applying 21st-Century Literacies

Creating a Playlist Narrative: Enhance your response to question 1 under Writing by creating a playlist of five songs that contribute to your description of that person you are or were close to. For each song, write a short paragraph about what it says about either this person or your relationship with him or her. The specific song might have a story behind it—if so, tell it—or it might describe (literally or figuratively) some aspect or quality of that person's character, appearance, beliefs, experiences, interests, location, talents, regrets, or hopes. What is the music capable of describing about this person that words couldn't?

Love, Internet Style

David Brooks

David Brooks (b. 1961) is a columnist for the op-ed page of the New York Times. *Prior to joining the* Times, *he was a senior editor at the* Weekly Standard, *an op-ed page editor at the* Wall Street Journal, *and a contributing editor to* Newsweek. *He is also a weekly guest on the* PBS NewsHour. *A graduate of the University of Chicago, Brooks writes on a wide range of topics, often from a conservative perspective; he has edited* Backward and Upward: The New Conservative Writing. *Brooks's recent books* Bobos in Paradise: The New Upper Class and How They Got There *(2000) and* On Paradise Drive *(2004), which explores the lives of people living in the suburbs, offer fascinating and often amusing insights into contemporary American culture. In this essay, which appeared in the* New York Times *in 2003, Brooks examines the ways in which the Internet facilitates personal relationships.*

The Internet slows things down.   1

If you're dating in the Age of the Hook-Up, sex is this looming possibility 2
from the first moment you meet a prospective partner. But couples who meet through online dating services tend to exchange e-mail for weeks or months. Then they'll progress to phone conversations for a few more weeks. Only then will there be a face-to-face meeting, almost always at some public place early in the evening, and the first date will often be tentative and Dutch.

Online dating puts structure back into courtship. For generations Americans 3
had certain courtship rituals. The boy would call the girl and ask her to the movies. He might come in and meet the father. After a few dates he might ask her to go steady. Sex would progress gradually from kissing to petting and beyond.

But over the past few decades that structure dissolved. And human beings, 4
who are really good at adapting, found that the Internet, of all places, imposes the restraints they need to let relationships develop gradually. So now 40 million Americans look at online dating sites each month, and we are seeing a revolution in the way people meet and court one another.

The new restraints are not like the old restraints. The online dating scene is 5
like a real estate market where people go to fulfill their most sensitive needs. It is at once ruthlessly transactional and strangely tender.

It begins with sorting. Online daters can scan through millions of possible 6
partners in an evening and select for age, education, height, politics, religion and ethnic background. JDate is a popular site for Jews. EHarmony insists that members fill out a long, introspective questionnaire, and thus is one of the few sites where most members are women. Vanity Date is for the South Beach crowd. "At Vanity Date," the Web site declares, "we have a vision of creating the largest database of the world's most good-looking, rich and superficial people."

Most of the sites have programs that link you up with people like yourself. 7
One of the side effects of online dating is that it is bound to accelerate social stratification, as highly educated people become more efficient at finding and marrying one another.

Each member at a dating site creates his or her own Web page. The most 8
important feature on the page is the photo; studies show that looks are twice as powerful as income in attracting mates.

9   But there are also autobiographical essays. If you judge by these essays, skinny-dipping with intellectuals is the most popular activity in America. All the writers try to show they are sensual yet smart.

10   The women on these sites are, or project themselves as being, incredibly self-confident. "I am a vivacious, intelligent, warm-hearted, attractive, cool chick, with a sharp, witty, and effervescent personality," writes one on Match .com. Another says: "I am a slender, radiantly beautiful woman on fire with passion and enthusiasm for life. I am articulate, intelligent and routinely given the accolade of being brilliant."

11   Still, men almost always make the first contact. Prospective partners begin a long series of e-mail interviews. Internet exchanges encourage both extreme honesty (the strangers-on-a-train phenomenon) and extreme dishonesty, as people lie about their ages, their jobs, whether they have kids and, most often, whether they are married. (About a fifth of online daters are married men.)

12   Whatever else has changed, men are more likely to be predators looking for sex, while women try to hold back. Men will ask women for more photos "from different angles." A woman, wanting to be reassured that this guy is not some rapist, will shut off anyone who calls her "hottie" or who mentions sex first. Women generally control the pace of the relationship.

13   But despite all the crass competition, all the marketing, all the shopping around, people connect. Studies by Katelyn McKenna at N.Y.U. and others indicate that Internet relationships are at least as powerful as relationships that begin face to face. Many people are better at revealing their true selves through the keyboard than through conversation. And couples who slow down and prolong the e-mail phase have a better chance of seeing their relationships last than people who get together more quickly.

14   The online dating world is superficially cynical. The word "love" will almost never appear on a member's page, because it is so heavy and intimidating. But love is what this is all about. And the heart, even in this commercial age, finds a way.

COMPREHENSION

1. How does Brooks describe Internet "love"? What does he mean by his opening sentence, "The Internet slows things down"?
2. What features of Internet culture does the writer identify as facilitating human relationships?
3. According to Brooks, how do men and women differ in their approach to online relationships?

RHETORIC

1. What is Brooks's purpose in beginning his essay with a single-sentence paragraph? Is this sentence the thesis? Why or why not?
2. How would you describe the writer's stance? What is his attitude toward his subject? Offer examples to support your answer.

3. What are Brooks's main reasons in support of his thesis or claim? What forms of evidence does he offer to support his claim?
4. How does the writer develop an extended definition of Internet "love"?
5. Brooks frequently structures his essay by means of comparison and contrast. Why do you think he uses this strategy? Do you find the method effective? Why or why not?
6. Does the final paragraph provide a solid conclusion? Justify your answer.

WRITING

1. Write a definition essay on "Internet love." Be certain to provide examples and utilize other rhetorical strategies like comparison and contrast to develop this extended definition.
2. **Writing an Argument:** Write a persuasive essay arguing that online dating is either dangerous or harmless. Provide at least three minor propositions and sufficient evidence to support your position.

NETWORKING
Applying 21st-Century Literacies

Reflecting on Online Relationships: Narrate and describe your own experience with Internet-based relationships or online dating. Explain why the Internet has helped or hindered your relationships.

Family Values
Richard Rodriguez

Richard Rodriguez (b. 1944) received degrees from Stanford University and Columbia University. He also did graduate study at the University of California, Berkeley, and at the Warburg Institute in London. He is a writer and editor for Pacifica News Service *and a contributing editor and writer for many major American magazines and journals including* Harper's *and the* Los Angeles Times. *His books include* Hunger of Memory: The Education of Richard Rodriguez *(1982) and* Days of Obligation: An Argument with My Mexican Father *(1992). Both books have been profoundly influential in the public discussion on race, bilingualism, affirmative action, and biculturalism. He has also made many appearances as a commentator on the* PBS News-Hour. *In the following essay, originally published in the Sunday "Opinion" section of the* Los Angeles Times *in 1992, he addresses the concept of "family values" and focuses on the controversial thesis that homosexuality—rather than being a threat to family values—is actually a buttress against their dissolution.*

1   I am sitting alone in my car, in front of my parents' house—a middle-aged man with a boy's secret to tell. What words will I use to tell them? I hate the word *gay*, find its little affirming sparkle more pathetic than assertive. I am happier with the less polite *queer*. But to my parents I would say *homosexual*, avoiding the Mexican slang *joto* (I had always heard it said in our house with hints of condescension), though *joto* is less mocking than the sissy-boy *maricon*.

2   The buzz on everyone's lips now: Family values. The other night on TV, the vice president of the United States, his arm around his wife, smiled into the camera and described homosexuality as "mostly a choice." But how would he know? Homosexuality never felt like a choice to me.

3   A few minutes ago Rush Limbaugh, the radio guy with a voice that reminds me, for some reason, of a butcher's arms, was banging his console and booming a near-reasonable polemic about family values. Limbaugh was not very clear about which values exactly he considers to be family values. A divorced man who lives alone in New York?

4   My parents live on a gray, treeless street in San Francisco not far from the ocean. Probably more than half of the neighborhood is immigrant. India lives next door to Greece, who lives next door to Russia. I wonder what the Chinese lady next door to my parents makes of the politicians' phrase *family values.*

5   What immigrants know, what my parents certainly know, is that when you come to this country, you risk losing your children. The assurance of family—continuity, inevitability—is precisely what America encourages its children to overturn. *Become your own man.* We who are native to this country know this too, of course, though we are likely to deny it. Only a society so guilty about its betrayal of family would tolerate the pieties of politicians regarding family values.

6   On the same summer day that Republicans were swarming in Houston (buzzing about family values), a friend of mine who escaped family values awhile back and who now wears earrings resembling intrauterine devices, was complaining to me over coffee about the Chinese. The Chinese will never take over San Francisco, my friend said, because the Chinese do not want to take over San Francisco. The Chinese do not even see San Francisco! All they care about is their damn families. All they care about is double-parking smack in front of the restaurant on Clement Street and pulling granny out of the car—and damn anyone who happens to be in the car behind them or the next or the next.

7   Politicians would be horrified by such an American opinion, of course. But then, what do politicians, Republicans or Democrats, really know of our family life? Or what are they willing to admit? Even in that area where they could reasonably be expected to have something to say—regarding the relationship of family life to our economic system—the politicians say nothing. Republicans celebrate American economic freedom, but Republicans don't seem to connect

that economic freedom to the social breakdown they find appalling. Democrats, on the other hand, if more tolerant of the drift from familial tradition, are suspicious of the very capitalism that creates social freedom.

How you become free in America: Consider the immigrant. He gets a job. 8 Soon he is earning more money than his father ever made (his father's authority is thereby subtly undermined). The immigrant begins living a life his father never knew. The immigrant moves from one job to another, changes houses. His economic choices determine his home address—not the other way around. The immigrant is on his way to becoming his own man.

When I was broke a few years ago and trying to finish a book, I lived with 9 my parents. What a thing to do! A major theme of America is leaving home. We trust the child who forsakes family connections to make it on his own. We call that the making of a man.

Let's talk about this man stuff for a minute. America's ethos is anti-domestic. 10 We may be intrigued by blood that runs through wealth—the Kennedys or the Rockefellers—but they seem European to us. Which is to say, they are movies. They are Corleones. Our real pledge of allegiance: We say in America that nothing about your family—your class, your race, your pedigree—should be as important as what you yourself achieve. We end up in 1992 introducing ourselves by first names.

What authority can Papa have in a country that formed its identity in an act 11 of Oedipal rebellion against a mad British king? Papa is a joke in America, a stock sitcom figure—Archie Bunker or Homer Simpson. But my Mexican father went to work every morning, and he stood in a white smock, making false teeth, oblivious of the shelves of grinning false teeth mocking his devotion.

The nuns in grammar school—my wonderful Irish nuns—used to push 12 Mark Twain on me. I distrusted Huck Finn, he seemed like a gringo kid I would steer clear of in the schoolyard. (He was too confident.) I realize now, of course, that Huck is the closest we have to a national hero. We trust the story of a boy who has no home and is restless for the river. (Huck's Pap is drunk.) Americans are more forgiving of Huck's wildness than of the sweetness of the Chinese boy who walks to school with his mama or grandma. (There is no worse thing in America than to be a mama's boy, nothing better than to be a real boy—all boy—like Huck, who eludes Aunt Sally, and is eager for the world of men.)

There's a bent old woman coming up the street. She glances nervously as she 13 passes my car. What would you tell us, old lady, of family values in America?

America is an immigrant country, we say. Motherhood—parenthood—is 14 less our point than adoption. If I had to assign gender to America, I would note the consensus of the rest of the world. When America is burned in effigy, a male is burned. Americans themselves speak of Uncle Sam.

Like the Goddess of Liberty, Uncle Sam has no children of his own. He 15 steals children to make men of them, mocks all reticence, all modesty, all memory. Uncle Sam is a hectoring Yankee, a skinflint uncle, gaunt, uncouth, unloved. He is the American Savonarola—hater of moonshine, destroyer of stills, burner of cocaine. Sam has no patience with mamas' boys.

16   You betray Uncle Sam by favoring private over public life, by seeking to exempt yourself, by cheating on your income taxes, by avoiding jury duty, by trying to keep your boy on the farm.

17   Mothers are traditionally the guardians of the family against America—though even Mom may side with America against queers and deserters, at least when the Old Man is around. Premature gray hair. Arthritis in her shoulders. Bowlegged with time, red hands. In their fiercely flowered housedresses, mothers are always smarter than fathers in America. But in reality they are betrayed by their children who leave. In a thousand ways. They end up alone.

18   We kind of like the daughter who was a tomboy. Remember her? It was always easier to be a tomboy in America than a sissy. Americans admired Annie Oakley more than they admired Liberace (who, nevertheless, always remembered his mother). But today we do not admire Annie Oakley when we see Mom becoming Annie Oakley.

19   The American household now needs two incomes, everyone says. Meaning: Mom is *forced* to leave home out of economic necessity. But lots of us know lots of moms who are sick and tired of being mom, or only mom. It's like the nuns getting fed up, teaching kids for all those years and having those kids grow up telling stories of how awful Catholic school was! Not every woman in America wants her life's work to be forgiveness. Today there are moms who don't want their husbands' names. And the most disturbing possibility: What happens when Mom doesn't want to be Mom at all? Refuses pregnancy?

20   Mom is only becoming an American like the rest of us. Certainly, people all over the world are going to describe the influence of feminism on women (all over the world) as their "Americanization." And rightly so.

21   Nothing of this, of course, will the politician's wife tell you. The politician's wife is careful to follow her husband's sentimental reassurances that nothing has changed about America except perhaps for the sinister influence of deviants. Like myself.

22   I contain within myself an anomaly at least as interesting as the Republican Party's version of family values. I am a homosexual Catholic, a communicant in a tradition that rejects even as it upholds me.

23   I do not count myself among those Christians who proclaim themselves protectors of family values. They regard me as no less an enemy of the family than the "radical feminists." But the joke about families that all homosexuals know is that we are the ones who stick around and make families possible. Call on us. I can think of 20 or 30 examples. A gay son or daughter is the only one who is "free" (married brothers and sisters are too busy). And, indeed, because we have admitted the inadmissible about ourselves (that we are queer)—we are adepts at imagination—we can even imagine those who refuse to imagine us. We can imagine Mom's loneliness, for example. If Mom needs to be taken to church or to the doctor or ferried between Christmas dinners, depend on the gay son or lesbian daughter.

24   I won't deny that the so-called gay liberation movement, along with feminism, undermined the heterosexual household, if that's what politicians mean

when they say family values. Against churchly reminders that sex was for pro-creation, the gay bar as much as the birth-control pill taught Americans not to fear sexual pleasure. In the past two decades—and, not coincidentally, parallel to the feminist movement—the gay liberation movement moved a generation of Americans toward the idea of a childless adulthood. If the women's move-ment was ultimately more concerned about getting out of the house and into the workplace, the gay movement was in its way more subversive to puritan America because it stressed the importance of play.

Several months ago, the society editor of the morning paper in San Francisco 25 suggested (on a list of "must haves") that every society dame must have at least one gay male friend. A ballet companion. A lunch date. The remark was glib and incorrect enough to beg complaints from homosexual readers, but there was a truth about it as well. Homosexual men have provided women with an alternate model of masculinity. And the truth: The Old Man, God bless him, is a bore. Thus are we seen as preserving marriages? Even Republican marriages?

For myself, homosexuality is a deep brotherhood but does not involve do- 26 mestic life. Which is why, my married sisters will tell you, I can afford the time to be a writer. And why are so many homosexuals such wonderful teachers and priests and favorite aunts, if not because we are freed from the house? On the other hand, I know lots of homosexual couples (male and female) who model their lives on the traditional heterosexual version of domesticity and marriage. Republican politicians mock the notion of a homosexual marriage, but ironi-cally such marriages honor the heterosexual marriage by imitating it.

"The only loving couples I know," a friend of mine recently remarked, "are 27 all gay couples."

This woman was not saying that she does not love her children or that she 28 is planning a divorce. But she was saying something about the sadness of American domestic life: the fact that there is so little joy in family intimacy. Which is perhaps why gossip (public intrusion into the private) has become a national industry. All day long, in forlorn houses, the television lights up a freakish parade of husbands and mothers-in-law and children upon the stage of Sally or Oprah or Phil. They tell on each other. The audience ooohhhs. Then a psychiatrist-shaman appears at the end to dispense prescriptions—the impor-tance of family members granting one another more "space."

The question I desperately need to ask you is whether we Americans have 29 ever truly valued the family. We are famous, or our immigrant ancestors were fa-mous, for the willingness to leave home. And it is ironic that a crusade under the banner of family values has been taken up by those who would otherwise pass themselves off as patriots. For they seem not to understand America, nor do I think they love the freedoms America grants. Do they understand why, in a country that prizes individuality and is suspicious of authority, children are disin-clined to submit to their parents? You cannot celebrate American values in the public realm without expecting them to touch our private lives. As Barbara Bush remarked recently, family values are also neighborhood values. It may be harm-less enough for Barbara Bush to recall a sweeter America—Midland, Texas, in the

1950s. But the question left begging is why we chose to leave Midland, Texas. Americans like to say that we can't go home again. The truth is that we don't want to go home again, don't want to be known, recognized. Don't want to respond in the same old ways. (And you know you will if you go back there.)

30   Little 10-year-old girls know that there are reasons for getting away from the family. They learn to keep their secrets—under lock and key—addressed to Dear Diary. Growing up queer, you learn to keep secrets as well. In no place are those secrets more firmly held than within the family house. You learn to live in closets. I know a Chinese man who arrived in America about 10 years ago. He got a job and made some money. And during that time he came to confront his homosexuality. And then his family arrived. I do not yet know the end of this story.

31   The genius of America is that it permits children to leave home, it permits us to become different from our parents. But the sadness, the loneliness of America, is clear too.

32   Listen to the way Americans talk about immigrants. If, on the one hand, there is impatience when today's immigrants do not seem to give up their family, there is also a fascination with this reluctance. In Los Angeles, Hispanics are considered people of family. Hispanic women are hired to be at the center of the American family—to babysit and diaper, to cook and to clean and to ease the dying. Hispanic attachment to family is seen by many Americans, I think, as the reason why Hispanics don't get ahead. But if Asians privately annoy us for being so family oriented, they are also stereotypically celebrated as the new "whiz kids" in school. Don't Asians go to college, after all, to honor their parents?

33   More important still is the technological and economic ascendancy of Asia, particularly Japan, on the American imagination. Americans are starting to wonder whether perhaps the family values of Asia put the United States at a disadvantage. The old platitude had it that ours is a vibrant, robust society for being a society of individuals. Now we look to Asia and see team effort paying off.

34   In this time of national homesickness, of nostalgia, for how we imagine America used to be, there are obvious dangers. We are going to start blaming each other for the loss. Since we are inclined, as Americans, to think of ourselves individually, we are disinclined to think of ourselves as creating one another or influencing one another.

35   But it is not the politician or any political debate about family values that has brought me here on a gray morning to my parents' house. It is some payment I owe to my youth and to my parents' youth. I imagine us sitting in the living room, amid my mother's sentimental doilies and the family photographs, trying to take the measure of the people we have turned out to be in America.

36   A San Francisco poet, when he was in the hospital and dying, called a priest to his bedside. The old poet wanted to make his peace with Mother Church. He wanted baptism. The priest asked why. "Because the Catholic Church has to accept me," said the poet. "Because I am a sinner."

37   Isn't willy-nilly inclusiveness the point, the only possible point to be derived from the concept of family? Curiously, both President Bush and Vice President Quayle got in trouble with their constituents recently for expressing a real

family value. Both men said that they would try to dissuade a daughter or granddaughter from having an abortion. But, finally, they said they would support her decision, continue to love her, never abandon her.

There are families that do not accept. There are children who are forced to 38 leave home because of abortions or homosexuality. There are family secrets that Papa never hears. Which is to say there are families that never learn the point of families.

But there she is at the window. My mother has seen me and she waves me 39 in. Her face asks: Why am I sitting outside? (Have they, after all, known my secret for years and kept it, out of embarrassment, not knowing what to say?) Families accept, often by silence. My father opens the door to welcome me in.

COMPREHENSION

1. The title of this essay is "Family Values." What does Rodriguez mean by *family values*? According to the author, do Americans respect family values as they claim? Why or why not?

2. According to Rodriguez, do immigrants newly arrived to the United States possess a traditional allegiance to family values? Explain your answer.

3. In the conclusion, the author reflects—regarding his homosexuality—that "families accept, often in silence." Is this an aspect of traditional family values? Why or why not?

4. Why does Rodriguez think that gay men and women are often the primary upholders of family values within their families?

5. What is the thesis of the essay? Is it implicit or explicit? Explain.

RHETORIC

1. Although much of this essay is expository, Rodriguez begins and ends with an event—that is, visiting his family to announce his homosexuality. Why has he shaped his essay in this way? What is problematic about his relationship to the gay community? Why does he feel uncomfortable with the term *gay* to denote homosexual?

2. Rodriguez employs considerable irony in his essay. For example, in paragraph 15, he notes that two icons of American democracy, the Goddess of Liberty and Uncle Sam, are childless. Select two other ironic statements he makes in order to point out the contradiction between the idea of family values in America and the actual state of family values.

3. In paragraph 20, Rodriguez uses the term "Americanization." What does he mean by this term? How is it central to his thesis?

4. Does Rodriguez suggest that much of what is said in public regarding "family values" in America is hypocritical? If so, what group or groups does he focus on? How does he support his argument?

5. Explain the meaning of the following stylistic flourishes: "the word *gay* . . . [is a] little affirming sparkle more pathetic than assertive" (paragraph 1), "America's ethos is anti-domestic" (paragraph 10), "Oedipal rebellion" (paragraph 11), "American

Savonarola" (paragraph 15), "psychiatrist-shaman" (paragraph 28), "national homesickness" (paragraph 34), and "willy-nilly inclusiveness" (paragraph 37).

6. In paragraph 10, Rodriguez states that the Kennedys and Rockefellers "are movies." What does he mean?
7. Describe the emotional tone of this essay, considering that it is written by a man who is openly gay and understands that he is considered suspect and outside the mainstream of the American "value" system. Is it angry? Thoughtful? Defiant? Sympathetic? Select three or four passages that led you to your conclusion regarding tone.

WRITING

1. Interview a member of your grandparents' generation, a member of your parents' generation, and a member of your own generation regarding their views on family values. Write an essay summarizing the similarities and differences among the three views.
2. Interview a counselor at your college or university. Ask the counselor to explain the various issues surrounding family conflict he or she comes across in the course of his or her job. Write an essay exploring your interview findings. Be sure to obtain permission from your interviewee and follow appropriate guidelines for protecting his or her anonymity.
3. **Writing an Argument:** Argue for or against the proposition that American society today is more tolerant of homosexuals than when Rodriguez published this essay in 1992.

NETWORKING
Applying 21st-Century Literacies

Synthesizing Blog Entries: Read these two recent entries from author/blogger Andrew Sullivan's *The Daily Dish* and Sullivan's 1987 essay "Here Comes the Groom" (from the *New Republic*). (Links are available on the Chapter 6 Networking page at *www.mhhe.com/mhreader11e.*) From these sources, what do you make of Sullivan's relationship with the gay community? With the right? With the left? How do these relationships influence his take on family values?

Once Upon a Quinceañera

Julia Alvarez

Julia Alvarez (b. 1950), a novelist, poet, and nonfiction writer, was born in New York City but raised until age 10 in the Dominican Republic. She was forced to flee with her family after her father, a physician, was implicated in a plot to overthrow

the dictator Rafael Trujillo, an event alluded to in her semiautobiographical novel,
How the Garcia Girls Lost Their Accents *(1991). (A second novel,* Yo!, *which
continues the Garcia/Alvarez family saga, appeared in 1997.) Alvarez attended Middlebury College (BA, 1971) and Syracuse University (MFA, 1975), and she is currently on the English faculty at Middlebury. In addition to her fiction, Alvarez has
published several volumes of poetry, books for children, a collection of essays, and
numerous articles for major magazines. One of her latest books is* Saving the World
*(2006), in which Alvarez examines the global attempt to eradicate smallpox. In this
selection from* Once Upon a Quinceañera *(2007), Alvarez provides readers with
insight into one of the most common and compelling rituals that frame the lives of
young Latinas.*

I'm sitting in my room at the Pan American Hotel feeling pretty much like 1
Cinderella before her fairy godmother shows up. I drove down from Vermont
early this morning, a five-hour drive that had taken me six hours since I'm not
used to finding my way through the urban labyrinths of parkways and expressways with exits popping up out of nowhere to this multicultural, multilingual,
multimulti area of Queens where forty years ago my own immigrant adolescence was spent.

I've driven down here to attend Monica Ramos's quinceañera. The plan 2
was that I would phone the Ramoses as soon as I arrived and they would come
and get me so I could follow the quinceañera in the last few hours of her preparations. But I've been calling the family home number and Monica's father's
cell number for the last half hour and nobody answers. Maybe it's the busy
floral pattern of the hotel bedspread or the scented air freshener recently
sprayed in the room, but I'm beginning to feel lightheaded with misgivings.
Did I come this far just to spend a night in my overpriced room at the Pan
American, only to have to turn around tomorrow morning and drive back to
Vermont without even a glimpse of this Queens quinceañera?

Like many USA-born Latinas, Monica, whose parents were both born in 3
the Dominican Republic, is actually celebrating her quinceañera on her sixteenth birthday. This is just one more adaptation of the old-country tradition
which has now survived more than four decades on American soil. But with a
persistence unique to this immigrant group that seems to retain at least some
of its Spanish and its feeling that "home" is still south of the Rio Grande even
into a second and third generation, Monica calls her sweet sixteen a "quinceañera sort of."

Monica's quinceañera had sounded great over the phone. It was going to be 4
so special, she told me during several long-distance conversations. Open,
friendly, easy to talk to, Monica was one of the most verbal and forthcoming
quinceañeras I interviewed. She didn't want a party at first, but she was finally
won over by two things: the chance to dress up in a beautiful princess gown
and the opportunity to give a speech in front of her whole family and all her
friends. Monica's party will include the lighting of seventeen candles, each one
dedicated to a special person with a little speech about why this person is so
special to her.

5   "There's always an added candle, dedicated to someone absent," Monica explains about the extra candle. "Mine's going to be dedicated to God for giving me such a special life."

6   Monica has told me that she is a devoted Catholic. I have to bite my tongue so as not to point out that a candle meant for someone absent is perhaps not the best category for a God who I'm sure Monica believes is everywhere. But it's hard enough to get these young ladies to confide in a virtual stranger without peppering them with prickly questions. As one young lady told me when I pursued a line of questioning about how exactly she thought she was going to go from being a girl to being a woman by having a quinceañera, "This is becoming annoying."

7   Instead I asked Monica if her quinceañera was going to have a theme. Themes are popular: The quinceañera is a butterfly, emerging from a flower. The quinceañera is a princess, sitting on a throne. The quinceañera is a cowgirl, with a court of boys sporting lassos. The quinceañera, like a magician's trick, rises up out of a trapdoor in a puff of smoke.

8   "Mine is all based on Disney characters," Monica announced excitedly. The girlfriends in her court were going to be Sleeping Beauty, Snow White, Jasmine, Belle . . . "We're going to do like a little play where my prince is going to find my heels on the dance floor and bring them to my dad to put on my feet," Monica gushed on.

9   Before hanging up, I asked Monica what her quinceañera meant to her. Although she had been quite garrulous about the party details, Monica seemed stumped by the question. Every quinceañera I've asked has given me the same pat answer. Claudia in Lawrence, Massachusetts, a short, stocky girl in sweat pants, pressured by her mami to have a quince party; Ashley in San Antonio, a popular, petite girl with a string of girlfriends who had celebrated or were in line to celebrate their quinces; Leticia in East L.A., who ran off with her chambelán seven months later—all of them echoed Monica as if reciting the mantra of quinceañeras: "I'm going from being a girl to being a woman." When I pressed Monica about what this meant, she answered vaguely: "It's like part of my culture."

10   "So, did your mother have a quinceañera back in the D.R.?" I wondered.

11   Monica wasn't sure. "Mami!" she called out from her end of the phone. "Did you have a quinceañera?" The answer came back, "A quinceañera, no, mi'ja."

12   I found out about Monica's quinceañera only four days ago in that word-of-mouth way so reminiscent of our home cultures. A Dominican student's Colombian friend has a mother who owns a flower shop in Queens that does a lot of quinceañeras, and she (the mother) was doing Monica's flowers and also providing some of the props, and she told the Ramoses about me. By the time I got word back that the Ramoses would be happy to have me attend Monica's party and, phone number in hand, I called them, they were into that forty-eight-hour countdown usually associated with weddings in which everyone is racing around, hyperventilating, arguing, bursting into tears, and the bride is

threatening to call the whole thing off. In fact, Monica's party is taking place soon after the headline story about the runaway bride, Jennifer Wilbanks, who disappeared days before her wedding in Duluth, Georgia. As I sit in my hotel room, waiting to get through to the Ramoses, I wonder if no one is answering because Monica has run off. Perhaps she will be the first runaway quinceañera to get national media attention.

On the phone, a very generous Mr. Ramos ("José, por favor!") had offered   13
to pick me up at the airport should I come by plane. "I wouldn't think of it with as much as you have to do," I declined. In part, I thought it wise to have a way to get from the church, where a Mass or blessing would precede the party, to the Dance Club, where the ceremony, supper, and dance would take place, and back to the hotel at a reasonable hour, as these parties tend to go on past the Cinderella stroke of midnight. Bringing my own wheels will turn out to be an inspired decision in more ways than I would ever have anticipated. But at the moment, I am wondering if the long drive has been in vain as none of the messages I've left on Mr. Ramos's cell phone or home phone have been returned. Foolishly, I have no address, no other way to contact the family. I look out the grimy picture window of the Pan American past the back parking lot toward street after street of fenced-in row houses, and I know, with a sinking heart, that this is not the kind of neighborhood where everyone knows everybody else.

An hour goes by. It's Friday, so back in Vermont, my husband is still at   14
work. I had suggested we both fly down, wimpy city driver that I am, and make a weekend of it, but before I could finish outlining the fun of two nights at the Pan American Hotel, my husband was shaking his head. He'd had enough of quinceañeras, thank you. "You've only been to a few," I argued, feeling vaguely wounded at his obvious disenchantment with one of *my* cultural traditions. "I've been to four and that's three too many," he countered. I don't know if it's his thrifty German-Lutheran roots, but from the beginning he has looked askance at these over the top celebrations, many of them costing much more than working-class families can afford.

His skepticism about this tradition is also my own. The incredible expense;   15
a girl encouraged in the dubious fantasy of being a princess as if news of feminism had never reached her mami; the marketing of a young lady as attractive, marriageable goods. Why not save the money for education? I've snuck in that question in all of my interviews. Why not have coming-of-age celebrations for boys as well as girls? But still, every time the young lady makes an entrance through her archway, or curtains part and there she is, sitting on her swing or a throne or a carousel horse, while the whole familia and roomful of friends applaud her, my eyes tear up and my throat catches. The tradition, whatever its trappings, is homing in on a need to acknowledge and celebrate these new arrivals in the field of time. From my spot in the crowd I am torn between optimism for this tender, young being emerging from the cocoon of her childhood and a sense of dread that the world she is entering, unlike the fantasy she is enjoying this one night, will not allow for such winged flight.

COMPREHENSION

1. Why does Alvarez inject herself into this story? What is her purpose?
2. Why, according to Alvarez, is quinceañera so important in Latino/Hispanic culture? Do you think she makes a convincing case for its importance? Why or why not?
3. What, ultimately, is Alvarez's attitude toward quinceañera? How do you know? Why doesn't Alvarez's husband want to accompany her as she attends the Ramos's quinceañera?

RHETORIC

1. Although she writes in various literary modes, Alvarez is best known as a novelist. What elements of fiction do you detect in this essay? Identify specific passages to support your analysis. How effective are these strategies, and why?
2. How would you describe Alvarez's audience for this essay? How successful is she in tailoring the tone and content of the selection to this audience? Does she present herself as an authority on the subject or an investigator, and what is the importance of this stance?
3. Does Alvarez establish a thesis or claim about quinceañeras? Why or why not?
4. Alvarez gradually establishes an extended or working definition of quinceañera. Locate passages where the reader receives information about this custom or ritual.
5. How does Alvarez link her introductory and concluding paragraphs? How do these two paragraphs serve as a framing device for the body of the selection?

WRITING

1. Write a narrative essay in which you tell about a ritual, custom, or celebration that is important to your family or culture.
2. Compose a comparative essay on quinceañeras and sweet sixteen celebrations, bar/bat mitzvahs, or other coming-of-age celebrations.
3. **Writing an Argument:** Argue for or against the proposition that coming-of-age celebrations have become too expensive and ostentatious in contemporary American culture.

NETWORKING
Applying 21st-Century Literacies

Shooting a Video Essay or Documentary: Approach question 1 under Writing as a video essay/documentary. If you don't own camera equipment borrow some from the school. Shoot and narrate a video documenting a ritual, custom, holiday, or other type of celebration important to your family or culture. To make your video especially engaging, before you begin the actual shooting, think of questions to ask participants, and write yourself at least the outline of a script. You can also edit sound in later for the main narration. You might focus on something specific, like the preparation of a particular type of dish, or show a broader overview of the events that make up the tradition.

The Estrangement

Jamaica Kincaid

Jamaica Kincaid (b. 1949) was born Elaine Potter Richardson in St. John's, Antigua. She came to the United States at age 16 and attended the New School for Social Research and Franconia College. In time she became a staff writer for the New Yorker *and started to publish her fiction in* Rolling Stone, *the* Paris Review, *and elsewhere. She has taught at several colleges, including Harvard University and currently Claremont-McKenna College, while compiling a distinguished body of fiction and nonfiction. Among her notable works are* Annie John *(1985),* A Small Place *(1988),* Lucy *(1991),* The Autobiography of My Mother *(1996), and* Among Flowers: A Walk in the Himalaya *(2005). In "The Estrangement," which appeared originally in a 2008 issue of* AARP Magazine, *Kincaid offers an account of the complicated relationship with her mother.*

Three years before my mother died, I decided not to speak to her again. And 1 why? During a conversation over the telephone, she had once again let me know that my accomplishments—becoming a responsible and independent woman— did not amount to very much, that the life I lived was nothing more than a silly show, that she truly wished me dead. I didn't disagree. I didn't tell her that it would be just about the best thing in the world not to hear this from her.

And so, after that conversation, I never spoke to her, said a word to her of 2 any kind, and then she died, and her death was a shock to me, not because I would miss her presence and long for it but because I could not believe that such a presence could ever be stilled.

For many years and many a time, her children, of which I was the only fe- 3 male, wondered what would happen to her, as we wondered what would happen to us; because she seemed to us not a mother at all but a God, not a Goddess but a God.

How to explain in this brief space what I mean? When we were children 4 and in need of a mother's love and care, there was no better mother to provide such an ideal entity. When we were adolescents, and embracing with adolescent certainty our various incarnations, she could see through the thinness of our efforts, she could see through the emptiness of our aspirations; when we fell apart, there she was, bringing us dinner in jail or in a hospital ward, cold compresses for our temples, or just standing above us as we lay flat on our backs in bed. That sort of mother is God.

I am the oldest, by nine, eleven, and thirteen years, of four children. My three 5 brothers and I share only our mother; they have the same father, I have a different one. I knew their father very well, better than they did, but I did not know my own. (When I was seven months in her womb, my mother quarreled with the man with whom she had conceived me and then ran away with the money he had been saving up to establish a little business for himself. He never forgave her.) I didn't mind not knowing my real father because in the place I am from, Antigua, when people love you, your blood relationship to them is not necessarily the most important component. My mother's husband, the father of my brothers, loved me, and his love took on the shape of a father's love: He told me about himself when he was a boy and the things he loved to do and the ways in which his life changed for better and worse, giving me some idea about how he came to be himself, my father, the father of my brothers, the person married to my mother.

6   She was a very nice person, apparently; that is what everybody said about her at her funeral. There were descriptions of her good and selfless deeds, kindnesses, generosity, testaments of her love expressed in humor. We, her children, looked at one another in wonder then, for such a person as described was not at all known to us. The person we knew, our Mother, said horrible things to us more often than not.

7   The youngest of my three brothers died of AIDS when he was thirty-three years of age. In the years he spent actively dying, our mother tended to him with the greatest tenderness, a tenderness that was absent all the time before he was dying. Before he got sick, before he became afflicted with that disease, his mother, my mother too, quarreled with him and disparaged him. This was enabled by the fact that he did not know how to go off somewhere and make a home of any kind for himself. Yes, he had been unable to move out into the world, away from this woman, his mother, and become the sole possessor of his own destiny, with all the loss and gain that this implies.

8   The two remaining brothers and I buried her right next to him, and we were not sure we should have done that: For we didn't know then, and still don't know even now, if he wanted to spend eternity lying beside her, since we were sure we would rather be dead than spend eternity lying next to her.

9   Is this clear? It is to me right now as I write it: I would rather be dead than spend eternity with our mother! And do I really mean that when I say it? Yes, I really mean just that: After being my mother's daughter, I would rather be dead than spend eternity with her.

10   By the time my mother died, I was not only one of her four children, I had become the mother of two children: a girl and then a boy. This was bliss, my two children in love with me, and I with them. Nothing has gone wrong, as far as I can see, but tears have been shed over my not being completely enthusiastic about going to a final basketball game in a snowstorm, or my saying something I should have kept in my mind's mouth. A particularly unforgivable act in my children's eyes is a book's dedication I made to them; it read: "With blind, instinctive, and confused love to Annie and Harold, who from time to time are furiously certain that the only thing standing between them and a perfect union with their mother is the garden, and from time to time, they are correct."

11   I wrote this with a feeling of overbrimming love for them, my children. I was not thinking of my own mother directly, not thinking of her at all consciously at

that exact time, but then again, I am always thinking of my mother; I believe every action of a certain kind that I make is completely influenced by her, completely infused with her realness, her existence in my life.

I am now middle-aged (fifty-nine years of age); I not only hope to live for a very long time after this, I will be angry in eternity if this turns out not be the case. And so in eternity will my children want to be with me? And in eternity will I, their mother, want to be with them?   12

In regard to my children, eternity is right now, and I always want to be with them. In regard to my mother, my progenitor, eternity is beyond now, and is that not forever? I will not speak to her again in person, of that I am certain, but I am not sure that I will never speak to her again. For in eternity is she in me, and are even my children speaking to her? I do not know, I do not know.   13

COMPREHENSION

1. How does Kincaid describe her mother? Do you think she is fair-minded or biased in her perceptions? Explain.
2. In what ways does Kincaid resemble her mother? In what ways is she unlike this "God"? Is she aware of the complexities in this mother-daughter relationship? Why or why not? How does her mother's death alter her perception of this relationship?
3. Kincaid offers a brief, concentrated portrait of her family. Who are its members? Do you find this family to be traditional or atypical? Justify your response.

RHETORIC

1. What is the significance of Kincaid's title? What are its possible meanings? Does the title capture the complete meaning of the essay? Why or why not?
2. Does this essay have a thesis or claim? Justify your response by careful reference to the text.
3. Locate the details of her mother's life that Kincaid presents, and explain why the writer has selected these details. What tone emerges from these details?
4. This essay has three parts. What is the relationship among them?
5. Why does Kincaid pose a series of questions in the last two paragraphs? What is the final effect?

WRITING

1. Compose an honest and revealing appraisal of your relationship with your mother or another family member.
2. Write an essay in which you consider the roles that mothers play in various cultures. Base this essay on your own background and personal knowledge.
3. **Writing an Argument:** Can we ever escape or distance ourselves from the influence of our parents in our lives? Is such an escape even necessary or desirable? Write an argumentative essay in response to these questions.

NETWORKING
Applying 21st-Century Literacies

Negotiating Parents, Privacy, and Technology: How do relatively recent innovations, like the wide use of personal cell phones and of social networking sites, influence your relationship with parents or guardians? Is your mother your Facebook friend? Is it harder to become independent and distance yourself from family when you can reach each other anywhere, anytime? In an essay, explore how parents or guardians and their adult children can create boundaries while staying connected in a 21st-century family.

Digital Scheherazades in the Arab World

Fatema Mernissi

Fatema Mernissi (b. 1940), a contemporary sociologist, university professor, and feminist scholar, was born in Fez, Morocco. She received a degree in political science at Mohammad V University and a degree in sociology at the Sorbonne in Paris. In 1973, she earned a PhD in sociology at Brandeis University. At present, she is a research scholar at the University Institute for Scientific Research in Rabat. Mernissi's work focuses on the intersection of gender and religion in Muslim society. Among her numerous publications are The Veil and the Male Elite *(1975),* Islam and Democracy *(1992), and* Scheherazade Goes West *(2001). Two memoirs,* Dreams of Trespass *(1994) and* Harem Days *(1999), recount her life growing up as Muslim, Moroccan, and female. In this essay, published in* Current History *in 2006, Mernissi assesses the changing roles of women in the Arab Gulf as technology influences the thinking of a previously all-male elite.*

1   In May 2005, I listened attentively to the questions of the 30 journalists my Spanish publisher had scheduled to meet with me in Madrid to promote the translation of my book, *Les Sindbads marocains: Voyage dans le Maroc civique (Moroccan Sinbads: Travels through Civic Morocco).* From their questions, which all dealt with the veil and terrorism, it was clear that they had no clue about the strategic issue mobilizing the Arab world: *alfitna raqmiya* (digital chaos), the destruction of space frontiers by information technology.

2   The key problem that makes everyone anxious today in the Arab world— elites and masses, heads of state and street vendors, men and women—is the digital chaos induced by information technologies such as the Internet. These new technologies have destroyed the *hudud,* the frontier that divided the

universe into a sheltered private arena, where women and children were supposed to be protected, and a public one where adult males exercised their presumed problem-solving authority.

Now, according to a best-selling book, *The Internet and Love (Al Internet Wa* 3
I-Hub), by Imam Qaradawi, a star host on the Arab television network Al
Jazeera, the satellite and the Internet have spawned apocalyptic chaos in Arab
civilization by destroying that division of spheres. The imam's book, which is
advertised on the popular IslamOnline website, is alerting crowds to the fact
that Arab women and youth now navigate freely on the web and communicate
intimately with strangers, escaping religious and parental censorship.

"Since the World Wide Web invaded our lives," explains Qaradawi, "we 4
have been going through nonstop transformations. . . . The faraway has become
nearer with a simple push on the keyboard. This has deeply affected our societies,
which have suffered from a lack of communication and the lack of educational
quality entertainment. . . . Suddenly, the new technologies have provided opportunities to communicate and entertain oneself, and this without the supervision
of a censoring authority or a controller to whom you are accountable. . . . This
leaves individual responsibility as the sole controlling agency. And unfortunately, we have never cared to develop an educational system which focused
on developing individual responsibility."

But what is also new is that even imams suggest we stop thinking about 5
static solutions like strengthening authority and reinforcing hudud and focus
instead on inventing strategies that nurture a civilization of ethical nomadism,
where individual responsibility creates order. The Arab world is a besieged
place, but in many quarters the response to chaos is quietly shifting from crying
to action. This shift helps explain the emergence of what I call "digital Scheherazades," after the fictional storyteller of *1,001 Nights.* Her successors are
Arab women who take advantage of new communication strategies as the only
initiatives likely to liberate both themselves and their countries.

Digital Chaos

Imagine the anxiety of a parent reading "The Electronic Disfiguration of Our 6
Children," an article by an Egyptian psychoanalyst, Dr. Khalil Fadel, that appeared in the Kuwait-based *Al Arabi,* one of the most widely circulated cultural
magazines in the region. Fadel identifies the child as the most vulnerable victim
of the Western-made electronic war games that invade "our children's rooms
and are available in the cyber-cafés which now exist on every street corner." According to Fadel, these war games are responsible for inciting violent behavior
among Arab youth because they glorify "solitude, narcissism, and hatred of the
other," all of which reflect the cultural choices of the Westerners who produce
these games.

But if electronic war games are bad enough, sex is worse, according to an 7
article—"Electronic Sex Attack on the Arab World"—by Ahmed Mohamed Ali
in the Saudi-based magazine *Al Majalla.* Ali, who believes this attack was first

launched in 1999, describes "the unimaginable profit made from selling virtual prostitution or electronic sex on the Internet" to Arabs. Parents, he says, quoting Al-Hami Abdelaziz, an Egyptian psychology professor, are totally at a loss about what to do: "They know that the future of their children depends on their mastering such technologies, but they are afraid they will slip into these pornographic websites. The fact is that the parents are totally unarmed and ill-equipped to protect their children from such dangers."

8   Add to this the booming Arab satellite industry of erotic video-clips targeting youth. These clips constitute a terrifying challenge to the Islamic vision of the world, where sex belongs exclusively to the private sphere (which explains why no straightforward pornographic films are to be found on Arab satellite stations such as Arabsat and Nilesat). The video-clip is a tricky phenomenon, since its official objective is entertainment through music and songs. For Arabs, music and songs, just like poetry, have been regarded, even before Islam and since, as important sources of licit pleasure. Now they must confront the digital chaos induced by music video-clips that slip into explicit sex between unmarried people surrounding the singer. As Patricia Kabala has written, the video-clip "has without doubt become a symbol of access via satellite television stations and the Internet to the previously inaccessible sexually explicit material that state-controlled television channels in the Middle East censored and continue to censor."

9   Yet what is interesting once again is that instead of wasting time in complaints as Arabs usually do, a new attitude has appeared, the desire to invent solutions. Some ethically minded operators are trying to exploit that very video-clip technology to spread Islamic values among the youth. To counteract the sexual flood, investing in video-clips to promote young attractive religious singers as role models—such as Sami Yusuf Yusu, a British-born Muslim of Azeri origin—is one of the emerging positive responses to the previously frightening new information technologies. The lesson one gets from reading about the video-clip debate is that either you transform yourself into an agile digital surfer or you fade away.

10   It is this kind of immense civilizational shift in the Arab world, where men are finally embarking on becoming skilled digital nomads instead of decrying the frontier's collapse and dreaming of harems for their wives, that I tried to share with the Spanish journalists obsessed by the veil and terrorism during my Madrid encounter in May 2005. Although the Spanish city of Gibraltar is just 13 kilometers from the Moroccan port of Tangiers, I realized that Spaniards had no idea about the revolution that information technologies have produced in our part of the world. And one reason for this is the fact that in Madrid's plush hotel, which advertised itself as satellite-connected, I could not connect to my favorite, Al Jazeera, or to any one of the two hundred pan-Arab satellite channels beaming now in the Mediterranean.

11   At one point, I tried to illustrate this change by sharing with them the extraordinary emergence of women I saw in the Arab Gulf during a visit to Bahrain in March 2005. I tried to describe to them Mai al-Khalifa, a historian who in less

than a decade has created modern spaces such as museums and cultural centers that encourage dialogue between the sexes and the generations. I tried to explain that this unexpected emergence of women in the oil-rich Arab Gulf is more significant than the question of the veil in the Muslim migrant community, but the Spanish journalists were trapped in their own veils and terror.

I left Madrid feeling guilty and helpless, an intellectual unable to carry out 12 her job of facilitating dialogue. The journalists continued to haunt me after my return to Morocco, and when I saw al-Khalifa on a pan-Arab satellite television one day, I caught myself wishing they could share that experience with me.

The Historian on TV

The café near University Mohamed V in Rabat was full of young students and 13 teachers when al-Khalifa appeared on Al Arabia, a new rival of Al Jazeera that is financed by the Saudis. The manager of the café automatically turned up the television's volume because he was a fan of Turki al-Dakhil, the show's anchor, an electrifying young man who appears on the screen dressed in the Gulf region's traditional white robes just to surprise you by his insolent remarks toward all kinds of authorities.

At this moment, I noticed a striking change in the café: Conversations 14 came to a halt even though al-Khalifa was dressed like a professional woman in a white suit and looked very much on guard, unlike belly dancers who blink their eyes and sway hands and buttocks. The dynamics of what occurred in my Rabat café were as important for me as what was happening on the television screen. (When I was a child, the only women one could see in my hometown, Fez, in movies or on television when it made its appearance in Morocco in the 1960s, were belly dancers and singers; intellectual women were not part of the fare.)

It was by chance that I was in the café, because I am a rather homebound 15 creature. I was invited there by Kamal, one of my favorite colleagues, who is a *1,001 Nights* expert. He was intrigued by what I had told him about my March 2005 Bahrain trip because there is very little cultural exchange between North Africa and the Gulf. The gender ratio in the café was typical of Morocco: 10 women among 40 or so customers. Moroccan women, starting with myself, are so exhausted by their daily chores that they rarely think about going out in the evening.

One of al-Khalifa's best-known books deals with the Qarmatians, a contro- 16 versial group of Shiites who rebelled in the tenth century against the Sunni Abbasid caliphs, described as terrorists by some historians and as the founders of the first republic in Islam by others. I thought this would be the topic al-Dakhil, the Al Arabia host, would start with. To my great surprise, he opted for a very personal angle instead: Why was al-Khalifa so controversial in her own country? One has to realize that the title of the show is *Idaat,* which literally means "Flashes." The host is supposed to help the viewer discover some secret corner of those he invites to his show.

17   Why, wondered al-Dakhil, was al-Khalifa generating so much debate in Bahrain concerning the projects she promoted as one of the first women to hold an official position? (Al-Khalifa was the first woman to be appointed in Bahrain as assistant undersecretary for culture and national heritage.) Was it because she was a woman, or because she was incompetent, coming from an academic background and being thus unfit for practical work? Some people at the Ministry of Information, al-Dakhil argued, were saying that academics are too isolated in their ivory towers to be effective cultural operators.

18   "That intellectuals are unable to invent effective cultural strategies is a totally wrong assumption," al-Khalifa responded brusquely, brushing her black hair away from her face. Such statements, she added, are typical of bureaucrats who are in fact totally unfit to design the dynamic cultural strategies the Arab world needs to face the challenges posed by new technologies, and this for the simple reason that they lack vision. "I am an intellectual who has both a clear vision (*ruya*) of the future and the capacity to go ahead and act by undertaking successful innovative projects." Only intellectuals, she stressed, have *ruya*, a precious gift amid today's global chaos.

19   The reaction to al-Khalifa's response in the café was amazing. The crowd laughed merrily. One of the students stood up to declaim the Palestinian Mahmoud Darwish's poem about his compatriot Edward Said, in which he celebrates a strong vision rooted in one's reading of the past as the key allowing the Palestinian diaspora to survive and thrive: "If your past is a tough experience, make your future meaningful by developing a vision. . . . My dream directs my steps. And my vision places my dream in my lap like a friendly cat."

The Vision Thing

20 The absence of a clear vision of the future has been identified by Arab intellectuals as a contributor to the dangerous political disengagement of Arab youth and their confusion, which makes them vulnerable to the violence spread on the Internet. The new voices of the Arab diaspora include the Palestinian Khaled Hroub, who lives in London but is extremely influential among young Arabs because he hosts a show on Al Jazeera. He argues in his recent book on Hamas that the generational gap is particularly explosive in Arab society.

21   Indeed, one of the causes of terrorism is the demographic split between the aging minority of decision makers and the youthful majority they are supposed to represent. In a burlesque article published in the very academic journal of the Arab League, Hroub notices that being "decadently old" (*chaykhoukha*) does not help Arab leaders design pertinent strategies for the majority of the population, which is young. The tiny minority that monopolizes political decisions, he says, "operates on a set of concepts and reasoning frameworks that have very little relevancy to the youth's own problems." It is this politico-demographic divide, he concludes, that explains "the disastrous scorn of our younger generations for politics." And this brings us to the enigma of why the café youth reacted so strongly when the word *ruya* came up on the television show.

To stop terrorism, Arab leaders have to provide Arab youth with a vision of 22 a future in which they have a role to play as defenders of an ethical planet, explains Nabil Abdel-Fattah of the Al Ahram Center for Political and Strategic Studies in Egypt. The frustration of Arab youth results from the elite's failure to articulate a clear ethical view of a future in which every individual has a mission and a purpose. It is this emergence of the *ruya* as the antidote to terrorism that explains the café crowd's response to al-Khalifa's defiant answer to her television host. She was reminding him that her *ruya* is the likely reason why some Bahrain government bureaucrats were angered by her audacious cultural projects such as museums and cultural centers that teach children to understand that diversity is the root of their identity.

Because Arabs in general and youth in particular are fed up with fanaticism 23 and censorship, neighborhood cafés are turning, thanks to the new culture-focus satellite television outlets such as Al Jazeera and Al Arabia, to debates over *ruya*, visions of the future as the key to empowerment.

Many men in the café followed the rough exchange between al-Dakhil and 24 his guest with beaming smiles, including my colleague Kamal. I asked him why he was smiling and he said because al-Khalifa's quick response to al-Dakhil was so spontaneous: "I think Arab intellectuals should create a fund to support this lady," he said, "because she is creating fantastic publicity for us. If she continues appearing on television shows making such statements, we, the poor marginalized intellectuals, will soon be receiving well-paid job offers to replace our vision-blind bureaucrats in all the 22 Arab states!"

Kamal was right, because very few Arab male intellectuals would have 25 dared to declare with so much self-confidence, as al-Khalifa did on television, that they are visionaries and that only far-sighted thinkers can invent futuristic strategies for an Arab world doubly assaulted by both new information technologies and the powerful American military. Yet one of the positive changes initiated by these assaults is that people have stopped complaining and are going one step further toward identifying concrete solutions: first defeat the bureaucrats who have monopolized power for decades.

It is a daring message that increasingly bold women, making use of the new 26 information technologies, are proclaiming to fellow Arabs. In the Arab Gulf, the amazing thing about this new breed of women is that growing numbers of them, like al-Khalifa, do not limit themselves to writing but manage to jump into action as well. "She, like Sheikha Hussa Al-Sabah from Kuwait, builds museums and cultural centers like other women turn out couscous tagines!" remarked my colleague, who always condemned my decision not to get involved in politics. For Kamal, who, unlike me, became involved in politics and paid for it by having trouble with the Moroccan police, it is clear that now only intellectuals can help rulers to engineer power and engage the future.

The challenge for the intellectuals is to help rulers equip the youth to navi- 27 gate responsibly on the Internet. In particular, these solutions must help young people navigate not only in space but also in time. In a globalized planet where meeting strangers daily is the only way to make a living, mastering time is the secret of graceful navigation. To travel in the past, that is, to navigate in time, is the best way to teach oneself tolerance and respect for diversity.

28   Mobility is the name of the game, be they men or women, local or exiled, Sunni or Shiite, upper-class or from modest backgrounds. We are seeing a sudden shift from complaining about the West and its technological superiority to deciding to begin using the new information technologies to protect ourselves by participating in building a more just and humanist planet. Oil wealth, which makes it easy for visionaries to step quickly from vision to realization, has helped fuel this shift in the Arab Gulf. But so has the emergence of women in a region supposedly condemned to archaic conservatism.

Women Can Play Too

29 Is it because the threats of destabilization and terrorism are so great in the oil-rich Arab Gulf that emirs and sheikhs are keen on promoting e-government and women as information technology and financial allies? Or is it because the new information technologies are perceived by them as a fantastic opportunity to get rid of American domination and empower themselves to become global cybersurfers? What is certain is that electronic surfing has become a favorite sport of the Gulf rulers, and they are discovering a secret rule of this game: that it is essential for women to join in.

30   Al-Khalifa's emergence in Bahrain is impossible to understand if you do not realize that Bahrain is one of the first Arab countries to invest in e-government. The first step was the creation of an electronic visa system—an e-visa service—that went into operation in mid-2004. The second was reported on the front page of the *Bahrain Tribune* on March 9, 2005: "King Stresses Larger Role for Women." The story explained that "His Majesty the King, Hamad bin Isa al-Khalifa, yesterday requested all government and civil administrations and organizations to help implement the National Strategy for the Advancement of Bahraini Women."

31   To make sure that his routine-inclined bureaucrats grasped what he meant, the king provided a detailed description: "The implementation of the National Strategy, the first of its type in the country, will help us achieve our objective, which is to see women assume their roles fully as dependable partners to men and fully capable of contributing to building the family, the society, and the state, and eventually, to be involved in making decisions in modern Bahrain."

32   It is important to note, in this context, that the number of women employed in Bahrain has risen from just over 5 percent in 1971 to more than 40 percent today. Now how can you explain this strange coincidence between the onset of e-government and women's invasion of the labor force and their promotion as public actors if not by a cataclysmic shift in the region's ideological references? Is there not a repudiation of fanatic conservatism to embark on new horizons where power implies feminization of decision making?

33   In a humorous 2004 article entitled "The 50 Most Powerful Arab Women," which appeared in the Dubai-based Arabic version of *Forbes* magazine, the editor,

A woman in charge: Sheikha Lubna
al-Qasimi, minister of economy and
planning for the UAE, speaks
during a meeting in Abu Dhabi.

Rasha Owais, and her team undertook a survey to answer that question. They
came to the conclusion that, beyond the traditional profile of the wives and
daughters of heads of state, a new breed of digitally literate and financially
skilled women has emerged on the Arab scene.

Some of them do fit the profile of wives of leaders, but—unlike, say, Egypt's   34
Suzan Mubarak or Queen Rania of Jordan—the new Digital Scheherazades are
themselves communication wizards. For example, Sheikha Muza, the wife of
the emir of Qatar, the man who financed Al Jazeera, launched in September
2005 the first Arab children's channel. The ambitious objective, financed by a
foundation she controls, is to snatch Arab kids from the foreign television influence by providing them with a new ethical content where education and entertainment mix.

Being from a royal family helps, of course, but not automatically: I know   35
many wives of powerful, rich men who spend their time swallowing antide-
pression pills. Self-confidence and ability seem to be key characteristics of the
new Digital Scheherazades.

When you start looking for them instead of focusing on the veiled women,   36
as many Europeans do, you are amazed by their rapidly growing number. The
minister of economy and planning for the United Arab Emirates, for example,
is a woman: Lubna al-Qasimi. Before assuming this post, al-Qasimi, who has a
computer science degree from the University of California, was a senior manager of the Information Systems department of the Dubai Port Authority and
participated in the launch of her country as a planetary digital hub.

Investing in Female Brains

Did al-Qasimi owe her success to her being the niece of Sheikh Sultan bin   37
Mohammed al-Qasimi, the ruler of Sharjah, one of the United Arab Emirate
kingdoms? There are numerous nieces of powerful emirs and sheikhs in the

Gulf who never manage to emerge as top players in the power game. One of her favorite slogans is "I have earned my desk."

38   Indeed, those who still identify the region with veiling women and traditional archaism miss the essential point: the Arab Gulf's previously all-male ruling elite is investing in female brains as the winning card for information-fueled power. "We have a system for our children whereby we encourage them to gain experience outside the group first," says Muhamed al-Sayer, the billionaire chairman of a Kuwait-based group of companies. "For example, my daughter Lulwa spent eight years with Gulf Bank and is its head of Treasury. Male and female family members are offered the same opportunities."

39   It is this fascinating paradox that explains the emergence of Digital Scheherazades. Because men in the Arab Gulf have chosen to invest in communication as a power base, we can understand why one of the most important modern museum initiatives in Kuwait was that of Hussa al-Sabah, who forced Saddam Hussein to give back the cultural heritage pieces stolen from Kuwait after Iraq's invasion, and whose main supporter was her husband. Kuwait is also home to the very young Maha al-Ghunaim, the vice chairwoman and managing director of Global Investment House, which had net profits of $73 million in 2004.

40   In Qatar, where the clever emir propelled his tiny capital of Doha into a global player by financing Al Jazeera, one would expect to find Digital Scheherazades taking advantage of the kingdom's new information technologies. Such is the case with Hanadi Nasser, a businesswoman who has become a key player as the managing director of Amwal, a well-funded Qatari investment company.

The Caliph's Partner

41 According to my friend Kamal, Caliph Harun al-Rashid, who took power in Baghdad in 786 AD, is the key to elucidating the enigma of the Digital Scheherazades. The caliph's wife, Zubaida, made herself famous by digging wells along the Baghdad-Mecca road she had built to transform Muslims' yearly hajj into a comfortable and engaging trip.

42   Both Harun and Zubaida were heroes of the *1,001 Nights*, invented by eighth- and ninth-century Baghdad male street-storytellers who mirrored in their tales the fascination of Muslim elites and crowds with strangers as a source of magic diversity. And the primary fascinating strangers for men are indeed women. So, although Scheherazade, the storyteller of the *1,001 Nights*, was supposed to be Persian, it was Arab women like Princess Zubaida—who managed to seduce the Caliph Harun while digging wells and building walls to provide creature comforts during the hajj—who inspired our Baghdad storytellers.

43   These male storytellers forbade in their fiction the imaginary Scheherazade to speak during the day and condemned her to limit her activity to the night only, but modern historians are discovering that Zubaida exercised her power 24 hours a day.

44   Limiting women's power to the night while forbidding them from exercising authority during daylight—the monopoly of males—is a deep-seated reflex

that goes back far into history. It is well condensed in the slogan-like sentence that ends mechanically each of the 1,001 stories: "When dawn overtook Scheherazade, she lapsed into silence." But limiting women's power to the private sphere has always been a male fiction. And the defensive fear of the feminine has always gone together with the fear of strangers. When the leaders of a nation embark on communication as their way to glory, welcoming the different other as a partner is the magic shift that explains their success.

To understand why modern Arab Gulf emirs are suddenly investing in information technology as their power base and promoting women as their partners, we must go back to Harun, who did the same when he decided to invest in the paper industry to launch Islam as a communication-powered civilization whose main weapon was the Arabic language. Just as today, Arabs were scientifically backward in the eighth century, but their switch to communication enabled them to catch up with other nations by using language to navigate and conduct dialogue. Arabic, the language of illiterate pagans, was transformed into a medium of religion, the law, and sciences, promoting the Arabs to global prominence. 45

Are we witnessing once again the emergence of women as brainy allies when men opt for communication as their power base? Just to make sure you do not take me to be blindly optimistic, let me tell you that Western television companies such as the BBC and CBC are worried about competition in the United States from Al Jazeera, which has decided to launch an English language channel. As a woman, I will be more than thrilled if the competition between East and West switches from bombs and armies to communication strategies. 46

COMPREHENSION

1. Who is Scheherazade? (If necessary, check Google or another site for information.) Where does she (or the connotations she evokes) appear in the essay?
2. What does Mernissi mean by "digital chaos"? What examples does she provide to illuminate this idea?
3. Explain the connections between digital chaos and the changing roles of women in Muslim society.

RHETORIC

1. Is Mernissi's purpose to inform or to argue—or perhaps both? Justify your response by citing specific sentences and passages.
2. Mernissi's essay appeared in the journal *Current History*. What assumptions does she make about her primary audience? How does she establish her authority for this audience? How might the article appeal to a broader audience?
3. What is the effect of Mernissi's dividing the essay into sections? How does she manage transitions?
4. Analyze the ways in which Scheherazade serves as both symbol and organizing strategy in the essay.

5. Mernissi uses several forms of evidence to support her key ideas. Identify these various strategies of exemplification, and cite specific passages reflecting them.
6. The author is a noted feminist scholar. How do her feminist assumptions affect the tone of the essay? Where does she inject personal opinion? Where, if anywhere, does she make ethical and emotional appeals?

WRITING

1. Although Mernissi writes about a part of the world that might not be familiar, she raises issues that have not just regional but global implications. Write an analytical essay in which you examine the ways in which "digital chaos" is changing gender relationships in the United States or elsewhere.
2. Write a comparative essay linking the articles by David Brooks and Fatema Mernissi appearing in this chapter.

NETWORKING
Applying 21st-Century Literacies

WRITING AN ARGUMENT>Exploring the Effectiveness of New Communication Strategies: Do you believe that "new communication strategies," as Mernissi terms it, can actually liberate women and reform society? Argue for or against this proposition.

Synthesis: Connections for Critical Thinking

1. Both Annie Dillard's "An American Childhood" and E. B. White's "Once More to the Lake" explore the experience of childhood from a different perspective. Do they share a common voice or mood? What is distinctive about each essay? Which essay do you prefer, and why? Consider the style and emotional impact of the writing.
2. Both Barbara Kingsolver's "Stone Soup" and Richard Rodriguez's "Family Values" attempt to alter stereotypes commonly held about contemporary families. What type of family does each author address? How do the authors differ in their rhetorical strategies and their use of supporting points to buttress their arguments? Who is the implied audience for each of the essays? How did you reach your conclusion?
3. Argue for or against the claim that Alvarez's portrayal of a quinceañera and Mernissi's analysis of Arab men are biased.
4. Argue for or against the idea that descriptions of the relatively new types of family relationships described by Kingsolver in "Stone Soup" or in Rodriguez's "Family Values" are presented in a biased, romanticized manner.
5. Argue for or against the view that changes in society and its norms—specifically, increased geographical mobility, an evolving workplace, ideas about economic class, individual liberties, and sexual preference—have resulted in new forms of identity. Use examples from the work of Brooks, Mernissi, and Rodriguez.

6. Select the two more substantially argued essays in this chapter, Mernissi's "Digital Scheherazades in the Arab World," and Rodriguez's "Family Values." Compare and contrast their methods of argumentation.
7. Establish your own definition of what it means to be a male or a female. Refer to the essays of Alvarez, Kincaid, Mernissi, and Rodriguez.

NETWORKING
Applying 21st-Century Literacies

1. Join several newsgroups or chat rooms that focus on online dating. Compare and contrast the ideological focus of the conversations among members.
2. Create your own blog, and post a selected quote regarding the family taken from one of your essays. Enable comments so fellow students can respond regarding the quotation. At the end of the semester, write a report and summary of the responses you received. You may ask students to include their country of origin or their ethnicity to help you find possible connections between these factors and the responses.

CH 6   **www.mhhe.com/mhreader11e**

- *Image Gallery:* Chapter images in color
- *Family and Gender:* Information on the authors in this chapter
- *Ch. 6 Networking*

chapter 7

History, Culture, and Civilization

Are We Citizens of the World?

In the 21st century, the paroxysms caused by conflicts among peoples, nations, ethnic groups, and cultures continue to shake continents. The United States might have emerged from the cold war as the dominant superpower, but numerous local and global challenges remain. We seem to be at a crossroads in history, culture, and civilization, but does the future hold great promise or equally great danger—or both?

The future assuredly holds significant peril as well as promise. History tells us that while there has never been complete absence of barbarism and nonrational behavior in human affairs, there have been societies, cultures, and nations committed to harmonious, or civil, conduct within various social realms. While it is clear that we have not attained an ideal state of cultural or world development, at the same time, we have advanced beyond the point in primitive civilization at which someone chipped at a stone in order to make a better tool.

As we consider the course of contemporary civilization, we must contend with our own personal histories and cultures as well as with the interplay of contradictory global forces. We have become increasingly concerned with finding a purpose beyond the parameters of our very limiting personal and nationalistic identities, something that the Czech writer and statesman Václav Havel calls the "divine revolution." Indeed, we have entered an era of renewed ethnic strife, in which a preoccupation with cultural difference seems stronger than the desire for universal civilization. The writers assembled here grapple with these contradictions; they search for those constituents of history and culture that might hasten the advent of a civilized world.

The idea of civilization suggests a pluralistic ethos whereby people of diverse histories and backgrounds can maintain cultural identities but also coexist with other cultural representatives in a spirit of tolerance and mutual respect. The wars, upheavals, and catastrophes of the 20th century were spawned by a narrow consciousness. Hopefully, in the new century, all of us can advance the goal of a universal civilization based on the best that we have been able to create for humankind.

PREVIEWING THE CHAPTER

As you read the essays in this chapter and respond to them in discussion and writing, consider the following questions:

- How does the author define *culture, history,* or *civilization?* Is this definition stated or implied? Is it broad or narrow? Explain.
- Is the writer hopeful or pessimistic about the state of culture and history?
- What values does the author seem to think are necessary to advance the idea of history and culture?
- Is the author's tone objective or subjective? What is his or her purpose? Does the author have a personal motive in addressing the topic in the way he or she does?
- Which areas of knowledge—for example, history, philosophy, and political science—does the author bring to bear on the subject?
- Do you agree or disagree with the author's view of the contemporary state of civilization?
- What cultural problems and historical conflicts are raised by the author in his or her treatment of the subject?
- Does the author have a narrow or a broad focus on the relationship of history and culture to the larger society?
- How does the medium the author writes in contribute to his or her perspective on culture, history, or civilization?
- Which authors altered your perspective on a topic, and why?
- Based on your reading of these essays, how would you define *civilization?* Are you hopeful about the current state of civilization?

Classic and Contemporary Images

HOW DO WE BECOME AMERICANS?

Using a Critical Perspective   Compare the scene of early-20th-century immigrants at New York City's Ellis Island with the March 1999 X-ray photo taken by Mexican authorities of human forms and cargo in a truck. What mood is conveyed by each representation? Does each photograph have a thesis or argument? Explain. Which photo do you find more engaging and provocative, and why?

From the time of the first European settlers, the North American continent has experienced wave after wave of immigration from every part of the world. One period of heavy immigration occurred in the late 19th and early 20th centuries, when millions of people from eastern and southern Europe entered the United States through Ellis Island in New York City, as shown in this classic photograph.

More recently, immigrants continue to come from all over the world, often entering the country illegally. The X-ray photo shows a wide shot and a close-up image of people being smuggled across Mexico's border with Guatemala.

Classic and Contemporary Essays
ARE WE MOVING TOWARD A WORLD CULTURE?

Both of these essays address the issues of national and global identification. As you read them, consider not only the differing styles and strategies of discourse of their authors, but also their common themes and claims. In addition, consider that J. B. Priestley writes from a classically British experience of the nation-state, while Ishmael Reed is writing as a representative of a racial and (to his mind) cultural minority. Both, however, write within the context of the modern democratic state. And both are forthright and direct in their arguments, offering cultural analysis, appeals to authority, and historical evidence. As keen observers of the modern political scene, Priestley and Reed examine the very contours of civilization. But Priestley, a more traditional or classical writer than Reed, operates from a uniquely English perspective rooted in a clear sense of region. On the other hand, Reed, whose style is more informal, operates from an African American perspective rooted in an understanding that much of Western civilization draws its roots from a multiplicity of sources, not just European. We might be examining the reflections of two different personalities, but consider also the ways in which their agendas overlap.

Wrong Ism

J. B. Priestley

John Boynton Priestley (1894–1984), best-selling English novelist and popular dramatist, was also a prolific writer of essays, many of them involving social and political criticism. His work includes The English Novel *(1927),* The Good Companions *(1929),* Time and the Conways *(1937),* An Inspector Calls *(1946), and* The English *(1973). This selection from* Essays of Five Decades *(1968) offers an astute analysis of contemporary political habits.*

1   There are three isms that we ought to consider very carefully—regionalism, nationalism, internationalism. Of these three the one there is most fuss about, the one that starts men shouting and marching and shooting, the one that seems to have all the depth and thrust and fire, is of course nationalism. Nine people out of ten, I fancy, would say that of this trio it is the one that really counts, the big boss. Regionalism and internationalism, they would add, are comparatively small, shadowy, rather cranky. And I believe all this to be quite wrong. Like

many another big boss, nationalism is largely bogus. It is like a bunch of flowers made of plastics.

The real flowers belong to regionalism. The mass of people everywhere 2 may never have used the term. They are probably regionalists without knowing it. Because they have been brought up in a certain part of the world, they have formed perhaps quite unconsciously a deep attachment to its landscape and speech, its traditional customs, its food and drink, its songs and jokes. (There are of course always the rebels, often intellectuals and writers, but they are not the mass of people.) They are rooted in their region. Indeed, without this attachment a man can have no roots.

So much of people's lives, from earliest childhood onwards, is deeply inter- 3 twined with the common life of the region, they cannot help feeling strongly about it. A threat to it is a knife pointing at the heart. How can life ever be the same if bullying strangers come to change everything? The form and colour, the very taste and smell of dear familiar things will be different, alien, life-destroying. It would be better to die fighting. And it is precisely this, the nourishing life of the region, for which common men have so often fought and died.

This attachment to the region exists on a level far deeper than that of any 4 political hocus-pocus. When a man says "my country" with real feeling, he is thinking about his region, all that has made up his life, and not about that political entity, the nation. There can be some confusion here simply because some countries are so small—and ours is one of them—and so old, again like ours, that much of what is national is also regional. Down the centuries, the nation, itself, so comparatively small, has been able to attach to itself the feeling really created by the region. (Even so there is something left over, as most people in Yorkshire or Devon, for example, would tell you.) This probably explains the fervent patriotism developed early in small countries. The English were announcing that they were English in the Middle Ages, before nationalism had arrived elsewhere.

If we deduct from nationalism all that it has borrowed or stolen from re- 5 gionalism, what remains is mostly rubbish. The nation, as distinct from the region, is largely the creation of power-men and political manipulators. Almost all nationalist movements are led by ambitious frustrated men determined to hold office. I am not blaming them. I would do the same if I were in their place and wanted power so badly. But nearly always they make use of the rich warm regional feeling, the emotional dynamo of the movement, while being almost untouched by it themselves. This is because they are not as a rule deeply loyal to any region themselves. Ambition and a love of power can eat like acid into the tissues of regional loyalty. It is hard, if not impossible, to retain a natural piety and yet be for ever playing both ends against the middle.

Being itself a power structure, devised by men of power, the nation tends to 6 think and act in terms of power. What would benefit the real life of the region, where men, women and children actually live, is soon sacrificed for the power and prestige of the nation. (And the personal vanity of presidents and ministers themselves, which historians too often disregard.) Among the new nations of

our time innumerable peasants and labourers must have found themselves being cut down from five square meals a week to three in order to provide unnecessary airlines, military forces that can only be used against them and nobody
else, great conference halls and official yachts and the rest. The last traces of
imperialism and colonialism may have to be removed from Asia and Africa,
where men can no longer endure being condemned to a permanent inferiority
by the colour of their skins; but even so, the modern world, the real world of
our time, does not want and would be far better without more and more nations, busy creating for themselves the very paraphernalia that western Europe
is now trying to abolish. You are compelled to answer more questions when
trying to spend half a day in Cambodia than you are now travelling from the
Hook of Holland to Syracuse.

7   This brings me to internationalism. I dislike this term, which I used only to
complete the isms. It suggests financiers and dubious promoters living nowhere but in luxury hotels; a shallow world of entrepreneurs and impresarios.
(Was it Sacha Guitry who said that impresarios were men who spoke many
languages but all with a foreign accent?) The internationalism I have in mind
here is best described as world civilisation. It is life considered on a global scale.
Most of our communications and transport already exist on this high wide
level. So do many other things from medicine to meteorology. Our astronomers
and physicists (except where they have allowed themselves to be hush-hushed)
work here. The UN special agencies, about which we hear far too little, have
contributed more and more to this world civilisation. All the arts, when they are
arts and not chunks of nationalist propaganda, naturally take their place in it.
And it grows, widens, deepens, in spite of the fact that for every dollar, ruble,
pound or franc spent in explaining and praising it, a thousand are spent by the
nations explaining and praising themselves.

8   This world civilisation and regionalism can get along together, especially if
we keep ourselves sharply aware of their quite different but equally important
values and rewards. A man can make his contribution to world civilisation and
yet remain strongly regional in feeling: I know several men of this sort. There is of
course the danger—it is with us now—of the global style flattening out the regional, taking local form, colour, flavour, away for ever, disinheriting future generations, threatening them with sensuous poverty and a huge boredom. But to
understand and appreciate regionalism is to be on guard against this danger. And
we must therefore make a clear distinction between regionalism and nationalism.

9   It is nationalism that tries to check the growth of world civilisation. And
nationalism, when taken on a global scale, is more aggressive and demanding
now than it has ever been before. This in the giant powers is largely disguised
by the endless fuss in public about rival ideologies, now a largely unreal quar-
rel. What is intensely real is the glaring nationalism. Even the desire to police
the world is nationalistic in origin. (Only the world can police the world.) Moreover, the nation-states of today are for the most part far narrower in their out-
look, far more inclined to allow prejudice against the foreigner to impoverish
their own style of living, than the old imperial states were. It should be part of

world civilisation that men with particular skills, perhaps the product of the very regionalism they are rebelling against, should be able to move easily from country to country, to exercise those skills, in anything from teaching the violin to running a new type of factory to managing an old hotel. But nationalism, especially of the newer sort, would rather see everything done badly than allow a few non-nationals to get to work. And people face a barrage of passports, visas, immigration controls, labour permits; and in this respect are worse off than they were in 1900. But even so, in spite of all that nationalism can do—so long as it keeps its nuclear bombs to itself—the internationalism I have in mind, slowly creating a world civilisation, cannot be checked.

Nevertheless, we are still backing the wrong ism. Almost all our money 10 goes on the middle one, nationalism, the rotten meat between the two healthy slices of bread. We need regionalism to give us roots and that very depth of feeling which nationalism unjustly and greedily claims for itself. We need internationalism to save the world and to broaden and heighten our civilisation. While regional man enriches the lives that international man is already working to keep secure and healthy, national man, drunk with power, demands our loyalty, money and applause, and poisons the very air with his dangerous nonsense.

COMPREHENSION

1. What thesis does Priestley present? State the thesis in your own words.
2. Define *regionalism, nationalism,* and *internationalism* as Priestley presents these terms.
3. Explain Priestley's objections to nationalism. Where does he state these objections in the essay? What alternative does he propose?

RHETORIC

1. What striking metaphor does the author develop to capture the essence of nationalism? What is its sensory impact? Analyze another example of metaphorical language in the essay.
2. How does the suffix *-ism* function stylistically in the essay?
3. What is Priestley's principle of classification in this essay? How does he maintain proportion in the presentation of categories?
4. Analyze the relationship between definition and classification in the essay.
5. Examine Priestley's use of comparison and contrast.
6. Explain the connection between the introductory and concluding paragraphs.

WRITING

1. Priestley makes many assumptions about regionalism, nationalism, and internationalism. Which assumptions do you accept? Which assumptions do you reject? Explain in an essay.

2. Write a classification essay on at least three related isms: capitalism, socialism, and communism; Protestantism, Catholicism, and Judaism; or regionalism, nationalism, and internationalism.

3. **Writing an Argument:** Take issue with Priestley's assertion that the "real flowers belong to regionalism," and argue that regionalism today is a destructive force in world affairs.

NETWORKING
Applying 21st-Century Literacies

Considering the Isms of Online Communities: Write an essay arguing that a particular online community—such as a social networking site (Facebook, Twitter, Meetup, Craigslist), a virtual community like Second Life, a gaming site or subscription (such as X-Box Live), or similar—contributes primarily to a sense of internationalism, nationalism, regionalism, and/or isolationism. Use specific evidence to support your argument.

America: The Multinational Society

Ishmael Reed

Ishmael Reed (b. 1938), an American novelist, poet, and essayist, is the founder and editor (along with Al Young) of Quilt *magazine, begun in 1981. In his writing, Reed uses a combination of standard English, black dialect, and slang to interrogate American society. He believes that African Americans must move away from identification with Europe in order to rediscover their African qualities. Reed's books include* Flight to Canada *(1976),* The Terrible Twos *(1982),* The Terrible Threes *(1989),* Japanese by Spring *(1993), and* The Reed Reader *(2000). In addition, he has written volumes of verse, including* A Secretary to the Spirits *(1975), and has published collections of his essays, including* Airing Dirty Laundry *(1993). In the following essay from* Writin' Is Fightin' *(1990), Reed seeks to debunk the myth of the European ideal and argues for a universal definition of culture.*

At the annual Lower East Side Jewish Festival yesterday, a Chinese woman ate a pizza slice in front of Ty Thuan Duc's Vietnamese grocery store. Beside her a Spanish-speaking family patronized a cart with two signs: "Italian Ices" and "Kosher by Rabbi Alper." And after the pastrami ran out, everybody ate knishes.

—New York Times, June 23, 1983

1 On the day before Memorial Day, 1983, a poet called me to describe a city he had just visited. He said that one section included mosques, built by the Islamic

people who dwelled there. Attending his reading, he said, were large numbers of Hispanic people, forty thousand of whom lived in the same city. He was not talking about a fabled city located in some mysterious region of the world. The city he'd visited was Detroit.

A few months before, as I was leaving Houston, Texas, I heard it announced 2 on the radio that Texas's largest minority was Mexican American, and though a foundation recently issued a report critical of bilingual education, the taped voice used to guide the passengers on the air trams connecting terminals in Dallas Airport is in both Spanish and English. If the trend continues, a day will come when it will be difficult to travel through some sections of the country without hearing commands in both English and Spanish; after all, for some western states, Spanish was the first written language and the Spanish style lives on in the western way of life.

Shortly after my Texas trip, I sat in an auditorium located on the campus of 3 the University of Wisconsin at Milwaukee as a Yale professor—whose original work on the influence of African cultures upon those of the Americas has led to his ostracism from some monocultural intellectual circles—walked up and down the aisle, like an old-time southern evangelist, dancing and drumming the top of the lectern, illustrating his points before some serious Afro-American intellectuals and artists who cheered and applauded his performance and his mastery of information. The professor was "white." After his lecture, he joined a group of Milwaukeeans in a conversation. All of the participants spoke Yoruban, though only the professor had ever traveled to Africa.

One of the artists told me that his paintings, which included African and 4 Afro-American mythological symbols and imagery, were hanging in the local McDonald's restaurant. The next day I went to McDonald's and snapped pictures of smiling youngsters eating hamburgers below paintings that could grace the walls of any of the country's leading museums. The manager of the local McDonald's said, "I don't know what you boys are doing, but I like it," as he commissioned the local painters to exhibit in his restaurant.

Such blurring of cultural styles occurs in everyday life in the United States 5 to a greater extent than anyone can imagine and is probably more prevalent than the sensational conflict between people of different backgrounds that is played up and often encouraged by the media. The result is what the Yale professor, Robert Thompson, referred to as a cultural bouillabaisse, yet members of the nation's present educational and cultural Elect still cling to the notion that the United States belongs to some vaguely defined entity they refer to as "Western civilization," by which they mean, presumably, a civilization created by the people of Europe, as if Europe can be viewed in monolithic terms. Is Beethoven's Ninth Symphony, which includes Turkish marches, a part of Western civilization, or the late nineteenth- and twentieth-century French paintings, whose creators were influenced by Japanese art? And what of the cubists, through whom the influence of African art changed modern painting, or the surrealists, who were so impressed with the art of the Pacific Northwest Indians that, in their map of North America, Alaska dwarfs the lower forty-eight in size?

6   Are the Russians, who are often criticized for their adoption of "Western" ways by Tsarist dissidents in exile, members of Western civilization? And what of the millions of Europeans who have black African and Asian ancestry, black Africans having occupied several countries for hundreds of years? Are these "Europeans" members of Western civilization, or the Hungarians, who originated across the Urals in a place called Greater Hungary, or the Irish, who came from the Iberian Peninsula?

7   Even the notion that North America is part of Western civilization because our "system of government" is derived from Europe is being challenged by Native American historians who say that the founding fathers, Benjamin Franklin especially, were actually influenced by the system of government that had been adopted by the Iroquois hundreds of years prior to the arrival of large numbers of Europeans.

8   Western civilization, then, becomes another confusing category like Third World, or Judeo-Christian culture, as man attempts to impose his small-screen view of political and cultural reality upon a complex world. Our most publicized novelist recently said that Western civilization was the greatest achievement of mankind, an attitude that flourishes on the street level as scribbles in public restrooms: "White Power," "Niggers and Spics Suck," or "Hitler was a prophet," the latter being the most telling, for wasn't Adolph [sic] Hitler the archetypal monoculturalist who, in his pigheaded arrogance, believed that one way and one blood was so pure that it had to be protected from alien strains at all costs? Where did such an attitude, which has caused so much misery and depression in our national life, which has tainted even our noblest achievements, begin? An attitude that caused the incarceration of Japanese-American citizens during World War II, the persecution of Chicanos and Chinese Americans, the near-extermination of the Indians, and the murder and lynchings of thousands of Afro-Americans.

9   Virtuous, hardworking, pious, even though they occasionally would wander off after some fancy clothes, or rendezvous in the woods with the town prostitute, the Puritans are idealized in our schoolbooks as "a hardy band" of no-nonsense patriarchs whose discipline razed the forest and brought order to the New World (a term that annoys Native American historians). Industrious, responsible, it was their "Yankee ingenuity" and practicality that created the work ethic. They were simple folk who produced a number of good poets, and they set the tone for the American writing style, of lean and spare lines, long before Hemingway. They worshiped in churches whose colors blended in with the New England snow, churches with simple structures and ornate lecterns.

10   The Puritans were a daring lot, but they had a mean streak. They hated the theater and banned Christmas. They punished people in a cruel and inhuman manner. They killed children who disobeyed their parents. When they came in contact with those whom they considered heathens or aliens, they behaved in such a bizarre and irrational manner that this chapter in the American history comes down to us as a late-movie horror film. They exterminated the Indians,

who taught them how to survive in a world unknown to them, and their encounter with the calypso culture of Barbados resulted in what the tourist guide in Salem's Witches' House refers to as the Witchcraft Hysteria.

The Puritan legacy of hard work and meticulous accounting led to the 11 establishment of a great industrial society; it is no wonder that the American industrial revolution began in Lowell, Massachusetts, but there was the other side, the strange and paranoid attitudes toward those different from the Elect.

The cultural attitudes of that early Elect continue to be voiced in everyday 12 life in the United States: the president of a distinguished university, writing a letter to the *Times*, belittling the study of African civilizations; the television network that promoted its show on the Vatican art with the boast that this art represented "the finest achievements of the human spirit." A modern up-tempo state of complex rhythms that depends upon contacts with an international community can no longer behave as if it dwelled in a "Zion Wilderness" surrounded by beasts and pagans.

When I heard a schoolteacher warn the other night about the invasion of 13 the American educational system by foreign curriculums, I wanted to yell at the television set, "Lady, they're already here." It has already begun because the world is here. The world has been arriving at these shores for at least ten thousand years from Europe, Africa, and Asia. In the late nineteenth and early twentieth centuries, large numbers of Europeans arrived, adding their cultures to those of the European, African, and Asian settlers who were already here, and recently millions have been entering the country from South America and the Caribbean, making Yale Professor Bob Thompson's bouillabaisse richer and thicker.

One of our most visionary politicians said that he envisioned a time when 14 the United States could become the brain of the world, by which he meant the repository of all of the latest advanced information systems. I thought of that remark when an enterprising poet friend of mine called to say that he had just sold a poem to a computer magazine and that the editors were delighted to get it because they didn't carry fiction or poetry. Is that the kind of world we desire? A humdrum homogeneous world of all brains but no heart, no fiction, no poetry; a world of robots with human attendants bereft of imagination, of culture? Or does North America deserve a more exciting destiny? To become a place where the cultures of the world crisscross. This is possible because the United States is unique in the world: The world is here.

COMPREHENSION

1. Why does Reed believe that the conventional notion of Western or European civilization is misleading when applied to the American experience?
2. According to Reed, what are the origins of our monoculturalist view?
3. What are the dangers of such a narrow view? What historical examples does Reed allude to?

RHETORIC

1. How do paragraphs 1–4 help set the stage for Reed's discourse? Does this section contain his thesis?
2. Does the computer analogy in Reed's conclusion work? Do his rhetorical questions underscore the thesis?
3. Comment on the author's extensive use of details and examples. How do they serve to support his point? Which examples are especially illuminating, and why?
4. What kind of humor does Reed use in his essay? Does its use contribute to the force of his essay? Why or why not?
5. Is Reed's reasoning inductive or deductive? Justify your answer.
6. How does Reed employ definitions to structure his essay?

WRITING

1. How does America's insistence that it "belongs to . . . 'Western Civilization'" affect its dealings with other nations? How does it influence the way it treats its own citizens? Explore these questions in a causal-analysis essay, using support from Reed.
2. Write an essay in which you consider how a multinational United States affects you on a day-to-day basis. How does it enrich your life or the life of the country? Use specific examples and details to support your opinion.
3. **Writing an Argument:** Write an essay arguing that a multinational society is often riddled with complex problems. What are some of the drawbacks or disadvantages of such a society? What causes these conflicts? Explore these issues in your writing.

NETWORKING
Applying 21st-Century Literacies

Comparing Style across Media: On the Chapter 7 Networking page (at *www .mhhe.com/mhreader11e*), click on the link to watch Ishmael Reed discuss the concept of being an "ethnic gate-crasher," an advocate of transnationalism. How does this brief video influence your reading of "America: The Multinational Society"? What does Reed convey through his physical presence and voice? Discuss the advantages and disadvantages of this conversational style of conveying ideas, as opposed to the formal but text-only presentation of a polished essay.

Synthesis: Classic and Contemporary Questions for Comparison

1. How do the respective tones of Priestley's and Reed's essays differ? What clues are contained in the texts that make this difference evident? Use examples from both.
2. In his essay, Priestley argues against nationalism and professes to be a proponent of regionalism and internationalism. Compare Priestley's view with Reed's argument that to be an "American" means to accept the variety of influences that have converged into a "multinational society." How do these arguments differ? How are they similar?

3. Discuss both Priestley's and Reed's essays in terms of formality of voice. Does one author speak with more authority than the other? Or are they equally authoritative, but employing the stylistic modes of their times? Use examples from both essays.

1776 and All That: America after September 11

Edward Hoagland

Edward Hoagland (b. 1932) is an acknowledged American master of both fiction and nonfiction; he is especially adept in the art of nature writing. Hoagland had published his first award-winning novel, Cat Man *(1956), before he graduated from Harvard University, and in the following decades he wrote 16 additional books, including* Walking the Dead Diamond River *(1973),* African Calliope *(1976),* Tigers and Ice *(1999), and a memoir,* Compass Points *(2001). Among his honors are a Guggenheim Fellowship, an O. Henry Award, and an award from the American Academy of Arts and Letters. Hoagland, a world traveler constantly in search of raw personal experience set against natural backdrops and ecological crises, taught at Bennington College for two decades before retiring in 2005. In the essay that follows, which appeared in* the Nation *shortly after the events of 9/11, Hoagland warns us about the dangers awaiting a nation forgetful of its revolutionary origins.*

The country is riven and ailing, with a guns-plus-butter nuttiness in some of its 1 governing echelons and the sort of lapsed logic implicit in the collapse of trust in money-center capitalism, which has been an undergirding theory of a good deal of the work that many people do. The tallest buildings, real profit centers, fall, as "wogs" and "ragheads" defy us, perhaps comparably to how the "gooks" in Vietnam did (from whose example Osama bin Laden may have learned that we could be defeated). But that was on foreign soil, and we believed that we had pulled our punches and beaten ourselves, and so remained triumphalist for the remainder of the twentieth century, as we had been practically since Reconstruction.

Now we're not so sure. For the first time since the War of 1812 we have 2 been damaged in continental America by foreigners, having made other people hate us, though we had never needed to pay attention to such matters before. Proxies could fight the malcontents for us in places like Central America, and the Japanese and Germans, would-be conquerors, had not felt much real animus, becoming close, amicable allies after the war. Our first World War II hero, Colin Kelly, three days after Pearl Harbor, flew his B-17 bomber (as media myth had it) in kamikaze fashion to hit a Japanese cruiser, before the Japanese made a practice of it. To give your life for your country, like Nathan Hale, is an ideal that's since evaporated.

3   Obese individually and as a nation, and trying to stall the aging process, we talk instead of cars and taxes, sports and movies, cancer and entitlements, but with a half-unmentioned inkling too of what more ominously may be in store— a premonition that our righteous confidence might have served us just a bit too well. We never agonized a lot about killing off the Indians, or our slaving history either, once that was over, or being the only nuclear power ever to incinerate multitudes of people. We've hardly seemed to notice when free enterprise segues into simple greed, because our religious beginnings countenanced rapacity, as long as you tithed. Settling the seaboard in official belts of piety, whether Puritan, Anglican, Quaker or Dutch Reformed (only the frontier tended to be atheistic), we seized land and water with abandon, joined by Catholics, Lutherans, Methodists and what have you, westward ho. Each group encouraged its rich men to creep like a camel through the eye of the needle, and political freedoms were gradually canted away from the pure ballot box toward influence-buying.

4   We swallowed all of that because the New World dream envisioned everybody working hard and getting fairly rich, except when undertows of doubt pervaded our prosperity, as in the 1930s and 1960s; or now when, feeling gridlocked, we wonder if we haven't gone too far and used the whole place up. We seem to need some kind of condom invented just for greed—a latex sac where spasms of that particular vice can be ejaculated, captured and contained. Like lust, it's not going to go away. Nor will Monopoly games do the trick, any more than pornographic videos erase impulses that might result in harm. The old phrase patrons of prostitutes used to use—"getting your ashes hauled"—said it pretty well, and if we could persuade people to think of greed, as well, that way and expel its destructiveness perhaps into a computer screen, trapping the piggishness in cyberspace might save a bit of Earth. The greediest guys would not be satisfied, but greed might be looked on as slightly outre.

5   Some vertigo or "near death" experience of global warming may be required to trip the necessary degree of alarm. The droughts and water wars, a polar meltdown and pelagic crisis—too much saltwater and insufficient fresh. In the meantime, dried-up high plains agriculture and Sunbelt golf greens in the Republicans' heartlands will help because African famines are never enough. We need a surge of altruism, artesian decency. The oddity of greed nowadays is that it is so often solo—in the service of one ego—not ducal or kingly, as the apparatus of an unjust state. Overweening possession, such as McMansions and so on, will be loony in the century we are entering upon— ecologically, economically, morally, commonsensically. But how will we realize this, short of disastrous procrastination? Hurricanes and centrifugal violence on the home front, not to mention angry Arabs flying into the World Trade Center? That astounded us: both the anger and the technological savvy. These camel-herding primitives whom we had manipulated, fleeced, romanticized and

patronized for generations, while pumping out their oil and bottling them up in monarchies and emirates that we cultivated and maintained, while jeering at them with casual racism in the meantime, when we thought of it, for not having democracies like ours. To discover that satellite TV, the Internet and some subversive preaching should suddenly provide them access to divergent opinions disconcerts if it doesn't frighten us, as does their willingness to counterpose rudimentary suicide missions to the helicopter gunships and F-16s we provide the Israelis. "Don't they value life?"

They won't be the last. The Vietcong were as culturally different from the 6 Palestinians as we are and yet succeeded in winning a country for themselves, at a tremendous but bearable cost, which the Palestinians will also undoubtedly do. Self-sacrifice can be a match for weaponry, not because the Americans or Israelis value Asian or Arab life—at key junctures and for essentially racist reasons they have not—but because of the value they place on their own citizenry. As many as fifty Vietnamese lives were lost for every American's, but that was not a high enough ratio for us, even though, unlike some Israelis, we don't ascribe to ourselves a biblical imprimatur. So we let them have their land, and the domino calamities that had been famously predicted did not result.

To equate our own revolution with anybody else's is quite offensive to us. 7 Mostly, in fact, we prefer to forget that we had a revolutionary past and kicked thousands of wealthy Tories into Canada, seizing their property. We were slow to condemn apartheid in South Africa, having scarcely finished abolishing our own at the time, and have been slow in general to support self-governance in the warmer climates or to acknowledge suffering among people whose skins are beiger than ours. And if our income per capita is sixty or eighty times theirs, that doesn't strike us as strange. We are a bootstrap country, after all. They should pay us heed. And the whole United Nations is "a cesspool," according to a recent New York City mayor.

But primitive notions like those of Ed Koch invite a primitive response. 8 And box-cutters in the hands of Taliban fundamentalists are not our main problem. We have gratuitously destroyed so much of nature that the Taliban's smashing up of Buddhist statues, as comparative vandalism, will someday seem quite minuscule. We have also denatured our own nominal religions: that is, taken the bite of authenticity out of Christianity, for instance. Our real problem, I think, is a centrifugal disorientation and disbelief. There is a cost to cynicism (as in our previous activities in Afghanistan), and the systematic demonizing of communitarianism during the cold war made it harder afterward for us to reject as perverse the double-talking profiteering implicit in phenomena like Enron, when we had thought that anything was better than collective regulation and planning.

But ceasing to believe in revolutionary democracy—whether of the secular 9 or Christian (or Emersonian) variety—has proven costly. A decent regard for the welfare of other people, in international as well as local life, is going to be more than just a matter of private virtue. In a shrinking world it may be a survival tool. Fanaticism doesn't carry as far unless catastrophic economic conditions lurk in the background, as we learned in the case of Germany between the two world wars but then, when non-Caucasians were involved, forgot. Our foreign aid budget, once the cold war ended, collapsed into spectacular stinginess, and our sole response to September 11 has been police work. This can probably erase Al Qaeda—which became after its instant victory that one morning quite superfluous anyway—but not the knowledge of our vulnerability to any handful of smart and angry plotters in this technological age. We might see an explosion of those.

10   Our national self-absorption (in which the focus seems more on trying to stay young than helping the young) may give capitalism a bad name. Simple hedonism and materialism was not the point of crossing the ocean. Our revolution was better than that. It was to paint the world anew.

COMPREHENSION

1. According to Hoagland, what are the main reasons that America "is riven and ailing" (paragraph 1)? How has the 9/11 disaster served to highlight this national malaise?
2. What does Hoagland mean by "obesity," and how does this term illuminate certain national problems?
3. Explain Hoagland's assessment of America's role in world affairs. Do you agree or disagree with his critique, and why?

RHETORIC

1. What is Hoagland's claim, and where does he state his main proposition most clearly? What are his minor propositions, and what forms of evidence does he provide to support his admittedly complex argument?
2. What assumptions does Hoagland make about the audience for this essay? How do you know?
3. Explain the tone of this essay. Point to specific aspects of style that reinforce this tone. For example, what is the effect of the extended metaphor, "We seem to need some kind of condom invented just for greed . . ." (paragraph 4)? What other types of figurative language does Hoagland employ?
4. What allusions to American history does Hoagland make, and what is his purpose?
5. How do comparison and contrast, causal analysis, and definition serve to structure this essay?

WRITING

1. Write an essay of causal analysis in which you explain why international terrorists would want to inflict harm on America.
2. Take one of Hoagland's assertions (for example, that we are "[o]bese individually and as a nation"), and write your own analysis of this idea.

3. **Writing an Argument:** Argue for or against Hoagland's claim that Americans have forgotten their revolutionary origins and no longer have a "decent regard for the welfare of other people, in international as well as local life" (paragraph 9).

NETWORKING
Applying 21st-Century Literacies

Using Visuals in Argument: In your argument paper for question 3 under Writing, find and integrate two or three images to support and enhance your position. Be sure to correctly document and provide captions for the visuals you use (see Chapter 4).

The Myth of the Latin Woman: I Just Met a Girl Named María

Judith Ortiz Cofer

Judith Ortiz Cofer (b. 1952) was born in Puerto Rico and immigrated to the United States in 1956. Once a bilingual teacher in Florida public schools, Cofer has written several books of poetry; plays; a novel, The Line of the Sun *(1989); an award-winning collection of essays and poems,* Silent Dancing: A Partial Remembrance of a Puerto Rican Childhood *(1990); and a collection of short stories,* An Island Like You: Stories of the Barrio *(1995). Her more recent books include* Woman in Front of the Sun: On Becoming a Writer *(2000),* The Meaning of Consuelo *(2003), and* A Love Story Beginning in Spanish *(2005). She is a professor of English and creative writing at the University of Georgia. In the following essay, she offers both personal insight and philosophical reflection on the theme of ethnic stereotyping.*

On a bus trip to London from Oxford University where I was earning some   1
graduate credits one summer, a young man, obviously fresh from a pub, spotted me and as if struck by inspiration went down on his knees in the aisle. With both hands over his heart he broke into an Irish tenor's rendition of "María" from *West Side Story.* My politely amused fellow passengers gave his lovely voice the round of gentle applause it deserved. Though I was not quite as amused, I managed my version of an English smile: no show of teeth, no extreme contortions of the facial muscles—I was at this time of my life practicing

reserve and cool. Oh, that British control, how I coveted it. But "María" had followed me to London, reminding me of a prime fact of my life: You can leave the island, master the English language, and travel as far as you can, but if you are a Latina, especially one like me who so obviously belongs to Rita Moreno's gene pool, the island travels with you.

2   This is sometimes a very good thing. It may win you that extra minute of someone's attention. But with some people, the same things can make *you* an island—not a tropical paradise but an Alcatraz, a place nobody wants to visit. As a Puerto Rican girl living in the United States and wanting like most children to "belong," I resented the stereotype that my Hispanic appearance called forth from many people I met.

3   Growing up in a large urban center in New Jersey during the 1960s, I suffered from what I think of as "cultural schizophrenia." Our life was designed by my parents as a microcosm of their *casas* on the island. We spoke in Spanish, ate Puerto Rican food bought at the *bodega,* and practiced strict Catholicism at a church that allotted us a one-hour slot each week for mass, performed in Spanish by a Chinese priest trained as a missionary for Latin America.

4   As a girl I was kept under strict surveillance by my parents, since my virtue and modesty were, by their cultural equation, the same as their honor. As a teenager I was lectured constantly on how to behave as a proper *senorita.* But it was a conflicting message I received, since the Puerto Rican mothers also encouraged their daughters to look and act like women and to dress in clothes our Anglo friends and their mothers found too "mature" and flashy. The difference was, and is, cultural; yet I often felt humiliated when I appeared at an American friend's party wearing a dress more suitable to a semiformal than to a playroom birthday celebration. At Puerto Rican festivities, neither the music nor the colors we wore could be too loud.

5   I remember Career Day in our high school, when teachers told us to come dressed as if for a job interview. It quickly became obvious that to the Puerto Rican girls "dressing up" meant wearing their mother's ornate jewelry and clothing, more appropriate (by mainstream standards) for the company Christmas party than as daily office attire. That morning I had agonized in front of my closet, trying to figure out what a "career girl" would wear. I knew how to dress for school (at the Catholic school I attended, we all wore uniforms), I knew how to dress for Sunday mass, and I knew what dresses to wear for parties at my relatives' homes. Though I do not recall the precise details of my Career Day outfit, it must have been a composite of these choices. But I remember a comment my friend (an Italian American) made in later years that coalesced my impressions of that day. She said that at the business school she was attending, the Puerto Rican girls always stood out for wearing "everything at once." She meant, of course, too much jewelry, too many accessories. On that day at school we were simply made the negative models by the nuns, who were themselves not credible fashion experts to any of us. But it was painfully obvious to me that to the others, in their tailored skirts and silk blouses, we must have seemed "hopeless" and "vulgar." Though I now know that most adolescents feel out of

step much of the time, I also know that for the Puerto Rican girls of my generation that sense was intensified. The way our teachers and classmates looked at
us that day in school was just a taste of the cultural clash that awaited us in the
real world, where prospective employers and men on the street would often
misinterpret our tight skirts and jingling bracelets as a "come-on."

Mixed cultural signals have perpetuated certain stereotypes—for example, 6
that of the Hispanic woman as the "hot tamale" or sexual firebrand. It is a one-
dimensional view that the media have found easy to promote. In their special
vocabulary, advertisers have designated "sizzling" and "smoldering" as the adjectives of choice for describing not only the foods but also the women of Latin
America. From conversations in my house I recall hearing about the harassment that Puerto Rican women endured in factories where the "boss-men"
talked to them as if sexual innuendo was all they understood, and worse, often
gave them the choice of submitting to their advances or being fired.

It is custom, however, not chromosomes, that leads us to choose scarlet 7
over pale pink. As young girls it was our mothers who influenced our decisions
about clothes and colors—mothers who had grown up on a tropical island
where the natural environment was a riot of primary colors, where showing
your skin was one way to keep cool as well as to look sexy. Most important of
all, on the island, women perhaps felt freer to dress and move more provoca-
tively since, in most cases, they were protected by the traditions, mores, and
laws of a Spanish/Catholic system of morality and machismo whose main rule
was: *You may look at my sister, but if you touch her I will kill you.* The extended family
and church structure could provide a young woman with a circle of safety in her
small pueblo on the island; if a man "wronged" a girl, everyone would close in to
save her family honor.

My mother has told me about dressing in her best party clothes on Saturday 8
nights and going to the town's plaza to promenade with her girlfriends in front
of the boys they liked. The males were thus given an opportunity to admire the
women and to express their admiration in the form of *piropos:* erotically charged
street poems they composed on the spot. (I have myself been subjected to a few
piropos while visiting the island, and they can be outrageous, although custom
dictates that they must never cross into obscenity.) This ritual, as I understand it,
also entails a show of studied indifference on the woman's part; if she is "decent," she must not acknowledge the man's impassioned words. So I do understand how things can be lost in translation. When a Puerto Rican girl dressed in
her idea of what is attractive meets a man from the mainstream culture who has
been trained to react to certain types of clothing as a sexual signal, a clash is
likely to take place. I remember the boy who took me to my first formal dance
leaning over to plant a sloppy, overeager kiss painfully on my mouth; when I
didn't respond with sufficient passion, he remarked resentfully: "I thought you
Latin girls were supposed to mature early," as if I were expected to *ripen* like a
fruit or vegetable, not just grow into womanhood like other girls.

It is surprising to my professional friends that even today some people, 9
including those who should know better, still put others "in their place." It

happened to me most recently during a stay at a classy metropolitan hotel favored by young professional couples for weddings. Late one evening after the theater, as I walked toward my room with a colleague (a woman with whom I was coordinating an arts program), a middle-aged man in a tuxedo, with a young girl in satin and lace on his arm, stepped directly into our path. With his champagne glass extended toward me, he exclaimed "Evita!"

10   Our way blocked, my companion and I listened as the man half-recited, half-bellowed "Don't Cry for Me, Argentina." When he finished, the young girl said: "How about a round of applause for my daddy?" We complied, hoping this would bring the silly spectacle to a close. I was becoming aware that our little group was attracting the attention of the other guests. "Daddy" must have perceived this too, and he once more barred the way as we tried to walk past him. He began to shout-sing a ditty to the tune of "La Bamba"—except the lyrics were about a girl named María whose exploits rhymed with her name and gonorrhea. The girl kept saying "Oh, Daddy" and looking at me with pleading eyes. She wanted me to laugh along with the others. My companion and I stood silently waiting for the man to end his offensive song. When he finished, I looked not at him but at his daughter. I advised her calmly never to ask her father what he had done in the army. Then I walked between them and to my room. My friend complimented me on my cool handling of the situation, but I confessed that I had really wanted to push the jerk into the swimming pool. This same man—probably a corporate executive, well-educated, even worldly by most standards—would not have been likely to regale an Anglo woman with a dirty song in public. He might have checked his impulse by assuming that she could be somebody's wife or mother, or at least *somebody* who might take offense. But, to him, I was just an Evita or a María: merely a character in his cartoon-populated universe.

11   Another facet of the myth of the Latin woman in the United States is the menial, the domestic—María the housemaid or countergirl. It's true that work as domestics, as waitresses, and in factories is all that's available to women with little English and few skills. But the myth of the Hispanic menial—the funny maid, mispronouncing words and cooking up a spicy storm in a shiny California kitchen—has been perpetuated by the media in the same way that "Mammy" from *Gone with the Wind* became America's idea of the black woman for generations. Since I do not wear my diplomas around my neck for all to see, I have on occasion been sent to that "kitchen" where some think I obviously belong.

12   One incident has stayed with me, though I recognize it as a minor offense. My first public poetry reading took place in Miami, at a restaurant where a luncheon was being held before the event. I was nervous and excited as I walked in with notebook in hand. An older woman motioned me to her table, and thinking (foolish me) that she wanted me to autograph a copy of my newly published slender volume of verse, I went over. She ordered a cup of coffee from me, assuming that I was the waitress. (Easy enough to mistake my poems for menus, I suppose.) I know it wasn't an intentional act of cruelty. Yet of all the

good things that happened later, I remember that scene most clearly, because it reminded me of what I had to overcome before anyone would take me seriously. In retrospect I understand that my anger gave my reading fire. In fact, I have almost always taken any doubt in my abilities as a challenge, the result most often being the satisfaction of winning a convert, of seeing the cold, appraising eyes warm to my words, the body language change, the smile that indicates I have opened some avenue for communication. So that day as I read, I looked directly at that woman. Her lowered eyes told me she was embarrassed at her faux pas, and when I willed her to look up at me, she graciously allowed me to punish her with my full attention. We shook hands at the end of the reading and I never saw her again. She has probably forgotten the entire incident, but maybe not.

Yet I am one of the lucky ones. There are thousands of Latinas without the 13 privilege of an education or the entrees into society that I have. For them life is a constant struggle against the misconceptions perpetuated by the myth of the Latina. My goal is to try to replace the old stereotypes with a much more interesting set of realities. Every time I give a reading, I hope the stories I tell, the dreams and fears I examine in my work, can achieve some universal truth that will get my audience past the particulars of my skin color, my accent, or my clothes.

I once wrote a poem in which I called all Latinas "God's brown daugh- 14 ters." This poem is really a prayer of sorts, offered upward, but also, through the human-to-human channel of art, outward. It is a prayer for communication and for respect. In it, Latin women pray "in Spanish to an Anglo God/with a Jewish heritage," and they are "fervently hoping/that if not omnipotent,/at least He be bilingual."

COMPREHENSION

1. What is the thesis of the essay?
2. What does Cofer mean by the expression "cultural schizophrenia" (paragraph 3)?
3. Define the following words: *coveted* (paragraph 1), *Anglo* (paragraph 4), *coalesced* (paragraph 5), *machismo* (paragraph 7), and *entrees* (paragraph 13).

RHETORIC

1. Cofer uses many anecdotes in her discussion of stereotyping. How does this affect the tone of the essay?
2. Who is the implied audience for this essay? What aspects of the writing led you to your conclusion?
3. This essay is written in the first person, which tends to reveal a lot about the writer's personality. What adjectives come to mind when you think of the writer's singular voice?
4. Although this essay has a sociological theme, Cofer demonstrates that she has a poet's sensitivity toward language. What in the following sentence from paragraph 7

demonstrates this poetic style: "It is custom, however, not chromosomes, that leads us to choose scarlet over pale pink"? Select two other sentences from the essay that demonstrate Cofer's stylistic talent, and explain why they, too, are poetic.

5. In paragraph 8, Cofer contrasts cultural perceptions related to Hispanic and Anglo behavior. How is the paragraph structured so that this difference is demonstrated dramatically?

6. Cofer uses quotation marks to emphasize the connotation of certain words. Explain the significance of the following words: *mature* (paragraph 4), *hopeless* (paragraph 5), *hot tamale* (paragraph 6), *wronged* (paragraph 7), and *decent* (paragraph 8).

WRITING

1. Write a problem-solution essay in which you discuss the reasons behind cultural stereotyping and provide suggestions on how to overcome stereotyped thinking.

2. **Writing an Argument:** In an essay, argue for or against the proposition that stereotyping is excusable because it often is based on learned assumptions about which an individual cannot be expected to have knowledge.

NETWORKING
Applying 21st-Century Literacies

Examining Stereotypes in Television Shows and Commercials: Select an ethnic, racial, or cultural group, and explain how group members undergo stereotyping through their depiction in the media, particularly television shows or commercials. Use specific examples from specific programs or commercials to support your claims.

We Are the World

William Ecenbarger

William Ecenbarger, *who graduated from Susquehanna University (BA, 1961) and lives in Lancaster, Pennsylvania, has had a distinguished career as a freelance writer and journalist, contributing to the* Philadelphia Inquirer, Reader's Digest, Smithsonian, *and many other publications. He received a Pulitzer Prize in 1979 for his role in covering the Three Mile Island nuclear accident for the* Inquirer. *An inveterate traveler who has visited more than 40 countries and written about many of them, Ecenbarger is the author of* Walkin' the Line: A Journey from Past to Present Along the Mason-Dixon *(2000). He received the Travel Journalist of the Year award from the Society of American Travel Writers in 1996. In the following essay, which appeared* *in the* Times-Picayune *of New Orleans in 2003, Ecenbarger offers snapshots from his travels that reveal the impact of American popular culture on even the most remote parts of the world.*

At 5 a.m. I am awakened by the voice of the pilot, who delivers his words as 1
though they were oracular. The gist is that the No. 3 engine is leaking oil, we're
going out to sea to dump most of our fuel, and then we're going to make an
emergency landing in Asuncion, Paraguay. I have an appointment at 10 a.m. in
Buenos Aires, but that doesn't seem important now.

The cabin is prickly with tension, but we land without incident. Shaken 2
passengers on the DC-10 begin filing off the plane. The heat slams into me as I
step down to the runway and think that Paraguay brings to my mind a Banana
Republic dictatorship peopled by unrepentant Nazis. I will learn later that the
nation recently became democratized, but right now I'm looking at a line of
khaki-clad soldiers with slung carbines, standing as though glued to the tarmac
by their shadows, glowering like sullen watchdogs.

The leader of these carabineros, a balding man with a face like a pallbearer, 3
is checking passports and furrowing his brow with self-importance. He returns
mine with a look Patton might direct toward a deserter. I am wondering
whether anyone ever tries to sneak IN to Paraguay.

There are vintage DC-3s parked all over the airport, their tails low to the 4
ground and their fuselages tilted at 30 degrees, just like in Terry and the Pirates
or Steve Canyon. The airport access road is lined with billboards for Coca Cola
and Kent cigarettes. The latter shows two tanned Americans, Ken and Barbie,
smoking as they lean on a white convertible parked at a palm-fringed lagoon in
which is moored a yacht flying Old Glory.

There are a few places on Earth where an American can get away from 5
America, but I haven't been to any of them recently.

Most of the world has literally become a Mickey Mouse operation. The USA 6
reigns supreme as the exporter of music, film, television, sports, food and hundreds of consumer products ranging form Levis to Pampers to Barbie dolls.

American travelers are discovering that the sun never sets on the U.S. pop- 7
ular culture empire. Madonna writhes and jiggles and kisses Britney Spears on
MTV from Rangoon to Rio de Janeiro. I visited a Burger King in Kuala Lumpur,
a Pizza Hut on Fiji and a McDonald's in Buenos Aires. I turned on my hotel
television in Taipei to find Geraldo interviewing Elvis impersonators.

In Hanoi, I saw former Viet Cong soldiers standing in line wearing New 8
York Yankee baseball caps waiting to see movies such as "Platoon" and "Apocalypse Now." From my hotel room in Manila, I watched protesters against
American policies burning the Stars and Stripes while wearing Nikes and Levis,
righteously indignant right down to their Calvin Klein underwear . . .

In many Asian and Latin American cities, hanging out at the local Amer- 9
ican fast-food restaurant is part of the trendy youth lifestyle. Conspicuous

consumption takes on a new meaning in Bangkok, where the McDonald's restaurants have floor-to-ceiling windows. The better, I was advised by a local doctor, to be seen.

10   Unlike their U.S. counterparts, Dunkin' Donut stores in Asia do the bulk of their business at night. They are a gathering place for young professional men to impress their dates. Meanwhile, Coke and Pepsi are slugging it out on the Serengeti Plain and in the tin-roofed kampungs of Malaysia.

11   I was in a cab whiz-banging from the airport into downtown Bangkok, and it was a real white-knuckler. I peeked at the speedometer and tried to convert 127 kilometers into miles per hour. The driver didn't speak English, but nevertheless he lip-synched along with Ray Charles, whose voice was coming from a speaker inches behind my right ear . . . "just an old sweet song keeps Georgia on my mind."

12   We stopped for a red light and I saw two young Thai boys, wearing Mohawk haircuts and Guns N' Roses T-shirts, standing in front of a Pizza Hut, bartering with tourists in English over pirated music cassettes. Paula Abdul was going for $1. The driver pointed across the street to a long line waiting to get into the latest Sylvester Stallone epic. He shrugged philosophically, lit a Marlboro and hooked up with Simon and Garfunkel, "What's that you say, Mrs. Robinson . . . ?"

13   MTV, with all its nymphets in underwear, screaming guitars, and guys with earrings and gold chains, is wrapped around the globe like an extension cord, and it is nothing less than the defining influence of a new international youth culture. These days a 17-year-old Malaysian has more in common with a 17-year-old Chilean than with a 40-year-old Malaysian.

14   The emphasis on American music can turn wretched at times. In Suva, capital of Fiji, I watched four perfectly talented local doctors make fools of themselves trying to play light jazz for the Americans in the audience; I've heard various versions of "Feelings" played in Manila, Bangkok and Nairobi—and heard it sung over and over at a karaoke bar in Santiago.

15   From Togo to Tegucigalpa, people are doing the same thing: sitting in front of their televisions watching American programs and American commercials. Couch potatoes are sprouting up along the Amazon, the Nile and the Ganges.

16   Even local TV takes its cues from the Americans. The local news in Taipei is delivered by blow-dried mannequins who confuse the substantive with the merely photogenic. Just like the Americans on action news, they exchange quips, give the temperature at the airport (the last place anyone needs to know the temperature) and at the sign-off, pound their stack of 8-by-11-inch papers endlessly into the table.

17   In Taipei, I had some time on my hands and felt like a bit of the National Pastime. So I plunked down and watched the Weichuan Dragons battle the Brother Hotel Elephants in an important Taiwan Professional Baseball League contest.

18   "Play ball" is now a global cry, and they're tying on the spikes from Australia to Zaire. About 100 million people are playing organized baseball—and

only about one in every five is an American. Baseball is now the International Pastime.

Baseball isn't the only American game gone global. Some 300 million Chi- 19 nese watched the 1992 Super Bowl, and National Basketball Association games are telecast to 90 nations, including Reykjavik, Iceland, where they love the Boston Celtics.

Some American advertisers don't even bother to dub their spots in the local 20 language, figuring that English is understood in many places, and even if it's not, it carries a certain snob appeal. In fact, the sun never sets on the English language.

English has long been spoken in cockpits and control towers the world 21 over, and now it is becoming a language for universal communication, because of the dominance of American popular culture.

With 700 million people using it, English ranks second only to Chinese in 22 number of speakers, but it is spoken commonly in more countries than any other language. Indeed, the number of non-native users of the English language now outnumber those who were born into it.

Perhaps *New York Times* columnist Thomas Friedman summed it up best in 23 his book, "The Lexus and the Olive Tree: Understanding Globalization." He wrote, "On top of it all, globalization has a distinctly American face. It wears Mickey Mouse ears, it eats Big Macs, it drinks Coke or Pepsi and it does its computing on an IBM or Apple laptop, using Windows 98. . . . In most societies, most people cannot distinguish anymore between American power, American exports, American cultural assaults, American cultural exports and plain vanilla globalization. They are now all wrapped into one."

I have just flown over the Rift Valley, where Darwinists believe mankind be- 24 gan at least 2.7 million years ago, and now I sit in an outdoor restaurant in a small market town near Nairobi, sampling grilled wildebeest and smoked impala with my Kenyan host.

Around us the market throbs like a helicopter. It is a thicket of humanity, 25 and everyone is talking earnestly, rapidly, as though if they stop for an instant they will crumble to dust in the red clay ground. The cacophony is like an over-populated marsh. We are interrupted by a young boy, who seems to have stepped off a page of National Geographic. He extends toward me a wood-carving of a tribal mask.

"He wants to trade you," says my companion. 26

"What does he want?" 27

He talks to the boy in Swahili and then answers. "He wants anything from 28 America. A T-shirt, a cassette, a baseball cap. As long as it's from America." In my bag I find a gray sweatshirt that says "New York Giants."

The boy's eyes widen in appreciation, and we make a deal. Later the boy 29 comes back and takes my picture with a Polaroid camera. And then he offers to come to the United States and work as my "assistant."

30   "Our young people are absolutely daft about America," says my host, a
Kenyan of English ancestry. "It is said that Kenyan children hope for two
things—to go to heaven, and to go to America. . . ."

COMPREHENSION

1. What are the major popular culture references that Ecenbarger mentions in his
   essay? What is his attitude toward these manifestations of American culture?
2. What does Ecenbarger mean when he writes, "Most of the world has literally become a Mickey Mouse operation" (paragraph 6)? What common saying does he
   seem to be invoking, and why?
3. What nations, regions, and continents does Ecenbarger touch on? What is his purpose in creating this panorama of places?

RHETORIC

1. How does Ecenbarger's introductory section (paragraphs 1–4) help to establish his
   claim? What is his claim, and where does he state it?
2. What tone does Ecenbarger establish in this essay? What aspects of his style reinforce this tone?
3. What grounds or types of support does Ecenbarger provide to reinforce his claim?
4. How does Ecenbarger employ narration and description to support his argument?
   How effective do you find these strategies, and why?
5. Why does Ecenbarger divide this essay into sections? Do you sense a progression,
   or could these units be reorganized without damaging the essay's unity and coherence? Justify your response.

WRITING

1. Write an essay analyzing the reasons why American popular culture is so popular
   overseas. Refer to at least three varieties of popular culture to develop your thesis.
2. Write an extended definition of *cultural imperialism,* and explain the role of the
   United States in perpetuating his phenomenon.
3. **Writing an Argument:** Compose an argumentative essay in which you attempt to
   persuade readers that American popular culture is actually good for people around
   the world.

NETWORKING
Applying 21st-Century Literacies

Composing a Hyperlinked Essay: Format your essay for question 3 under Writing as an electronic or online text: Use hyperlinks to enhance your content and
take readers to relevant sites that support your argument or help refute specific
counterarguments to your case for American popular culture. Use at least six
hyperlinks in your essay.

Yellow Woman and a Beauty of the Spirit

Leslie Marmon Silko

Leslie Marmon Silko (b. 1948) was born in Albuquerque, New Mexico, and grew up on the Laguna Pueblo Reservation on the Rio Grande plateau. Of mixed Laguna, Mexican, and European American ancestry, Silko attended the University of New Mexico (BA, 1969) and briefly enrolled in law school before deciding to pursue a career as a writer. Associated with the Native American Renaissance, Silko has written stories, novels, essays, and poetry exploring Native American myths and traditions as well as the relationship of the tribes to contemporary culture. Silko has taught at the University of New Mexico and the University of Arizona, and has received numerous awards, including a prestigious five-year MacArthur Foundation grant. Her best-known work includes the novels Ceremony *(1977) and* Gardens in the Dunes *(1999); a collection of poetry,* Laguna Woman *(1974); a collection of short stories,* Storyteller *(1981); and an autobiography,* Sacred Water *(1993). Silko has also published a collection of essays,* Yellow Woman and a Beauty of the Spirit *(1996); in the title essay from this collection, Silko examines her mixed ancestry and explains traditional Pueblo culture.*

From the time I was a small child, I was aware that I was different. I looked different from my playmates. My two sisters looked different too. We didn't look quite like the other Laguna Pueblo children, but we didn't look quite white either. In the 1880s, my great-grandfather had followed his older brother west from Ohio to the New Mexico Territory to survey the land for the U.S. government. The two Marmon brothers came to the Laguna Pueblo reservation because they had an Ohio cousin who already lived there. The Ohio cousin was involved in sending Indian children thousands of miles away from their families to the War Department's big Indian boarding school in Carlisle, Pennsylvania. Both brothers married full-blood Laguna Pueblo women. My great-grandfather had first married my great-grandmother's older sister, but she died in childbirth and left two small children. My great-grandmother was fifteen or twenty years younger than my great-grandfather. She had attended Carlisle Indian School and spoke and wrote English beautifully. 1

I called her Grandma A'mooh because that's what I heard her say whenever she saw me. *A'mooh* means "granddaughter" in the Laguna language. I remember this word because her love and her acceptance of me as a small child were so important. I had sensed immediately that something about my appearance was 2 not acceptable to some people, white and Indian. But I did not see any signs of that strain or anxiety in the face of my beloved Grandma A'mooh.

3   Younger people, people my parents' age, seemed to look at the world in a more modern way. The modern way included racism. My physical appearance seemed not to matter to the old-time people. They looked at the world very differently; a person's appearance and possessions did not matter nearly as much as a person's behavior. For them, a person's value lies in how that person interacts with other people, how that person behaves toward the animals and the earth. That is what matters most to the old-time people. The Pueblo people believed this long before the Puritans arrived with their notions of sin and damnation, and racism. The old-time beliefs persist today; thus I will refer to the old-time people in the present tense as well as the past. Many worlds may coexist here.

4   I spent a great deal of time with my great-grandmother. Her house was next to our house, and I used to wake up at dawn, hours before my parents or younger sisters, and I'd go wait on the porch swing or on the back steps by her kitchen door. She got up at dawn, but she was more than eighty years old, so she needed a little while to get dressed and to get the fire going in the cookstove. I had been carefully instructed by my parents not to bother her and to behave, and to try to help her any way I could. I always loved the early mornings when the air was so cool with a hint of rain smell in the breeze. In the dry New Mexico air, the least hint of dampness smells sweet.

5   My great-grandmother's yard was planted with lilac bushes and iris; there were four o'clocks, cosmos, morning glories, and hollyhocks, and old-fashioned rosebushes that I helped her water. If the garden hose got stuck on one of the big rocks that lined the path in the yard, I ran and pulled it free. That's what I came to do early every morning: to help Grandma water the plants before the heat of the day arrived.

6   Grandma A'mooh would tell about the old days, family stories about relatives who had been killed by Apache raiders who stole the sheep our relatives had been herding near Swahnee. Sometimes she read Bible stories that we kids liked because of the illustrations of Jonah in the mouth of a whale and Daniel surrounded by lions. Grandma A'mooh would send me home when she took her nap, but when the sun got low and the afternoon began to cool off, I would be back on the porch swing, waiting for her to come out to water the plants and to haul in firewood for the evening. When Grandma was eighty-five, she still chopped her own kindling. She used to let me carry in the coal bucket for her, but she would not allow me to use the ax. I carried armloads of kindling too, and I learned to be proud of my strength.

7   I was allowed to listen quietly when Aunt Susie or Aunt Alice came to visit Grandma. When I got old enough to cross the road alone, I went and visited them almost daily. They were vigorous women who valued books and writing. They were usually busy chopping wood or cooking but never hesitated to take time to answer my questions. Best of all they told me the *hummah-hah* stories, about an earlier time when animals and humans shared a common language. In the old days, the Pueblo people had educated their children in this manner;

adults took time out to talk to and teach young people. Everyone was a teacher, and every activity had the potential to teach the child.

But as soon as I started kindergarten at the Bureau of Indian Affairs day 8 school, I began to learn more about the differences between the Laguna Pueblo world and the outside world. It was at school that I learned just how different I looked from my classmates. Sometimes tourists driving past on Route 66 would stop by Laguna Day School at recess time to take photographs of us kids. One day, when I was in the first grade, we all crowded around the smiling white tourists, who peered at our faces. We all wanted to be in the picture because afterward the tourists sometimes gave us each a penny. Just as we were all posed and ready to have our picture taken, the tourist man looked at me. "Not you," he said and motioned for me to step away from my classmates. I felt so embarrassed that I wanted to disappear. My classmates were puzzled by the tourists' behavior, but I knew the tourists didn't want me in their snapshot because I looked different, because I was part white.

In the view of the old-time people, we are all sisters and brothers because the 9 Mother Creator made all of us—all colors and all sizes. We are sisters and brothers, clanspeople of all the living beings around us. The plants, the birds, fish, clouds, water, even the clay—they are all related to us. The old-time people believe that all things, even rocks and water, have spirit and being. They understood that all things want only to continue being as they are; they need only to be left as they are. Thus the old folks used to tell us kids not to disturb the earth unnecessarily. All things as they were created exist already in harmony with one another as long as we do not disturb them.

As the old story tells us, Tse'itsi'nako, Thought Woman, the Spider, thought 10 of her three sisters, and as she thought of them, they came into being. Together with Thought Woman, they thought of the sun and the stars and the moon. The Mother Creators imagined the earth and the oceans, the animals and the people, and the *ka'tsina* spirits that reside in the mountains. The Mother Creators imagined all the plants that flower and the trees that bear fruit. As Thought Woman and her sisters thought of it, the whole universe came into being. In this universe, there is no absolute good or absolute bad; they are only balances and harmonies that ebb and flow. Some years the desert receives abundant rain, other years there is too little rain, and sometimes there is so much rain that floods cause destruction. But rain itself is neither innocent nor guilty. The rain is simply itself.

My great-grandmother was dark and handsome. Her expression in photo- 11 graphs is one of confidence and strength. I do not know if white people then or now would consider her beautiful. I do not know if the old-time Laguna Pueblo people considered her beautiful or if the old-time people even thought in those terms. To the Pueblo way of thinking, the act of comparing one living being with another was silly, because each being or thing is unique and therefore incomparably valuable because it is the only one of its kind. The old-time people thought it was crazy to attach such importance to a person's appearance. I understood very early that there were two distinct ways of interpreting the world. There was the white people's way and there was the Laguna way. In the Laguna way, it was bad manners to make comparisons that might hurt another person's feelings.

12   In everyday Pueblo life, not much attention was paid to one's physical appearance or clothing. Ceremonial clothing was quite elaborate but was used only for the sacred dances. The traditional Pueblo societies were communal and strictly egalitarian, which means that no matter how well or how poorly one might have dressed, there was no social ladder to fall from. All food and other resources were strictly shared so that no one person or group had more than another. I mention social status because it seems to me that most of the definitions of beauty in contemporary Western culture are really codes for determining social status. People no longer hide their face-lifts and they discuss their liposuctions because the point of the procedures isn't just cosmetic, it is social. It says to the world, "I have enough spare cash that I can afford surgery for cosmetic purposes."

13   In the old-time Pueblo world, beauty was manifested in behavior and in one's relationships with other living beings. Beauty was as much a feeling of harmony as it was a visual, aural, or sensual effect. The whole person had to be beautiful, not just the face or the body; faces and bodies could not be separated from hearts and souls. Health was foremost in achieving this sense of well-being and harmony; in the old-time Pueblo world, a person who did not look healthy inspired feelings of worry and anxiety, not feelings of well-being. A healthy person, of course, is in harmony with the world around her; she is at peace with herself too. Thus an unhappy person or spiteful person would not be considered beautiful.

14   In the old days, strong, sturdy women were most admired. One of my most vivid preschool memories is of the crew of Laguna women, in their forties and fifties, who came to cover our house with adobe plaster. They handled the ladders with great ease, and while two women ground the adobe mud on stones and added straw, another woman loaded the hod with mud and passed it up to the two women on ladders, who were smoothing the plaster on the wall with their hands. Since women owned the houses, they did the plastering. At Laguna, men did the basket making and the weaving of fine textiles; men helped a great deal with the child care too. Because the Creator is female, there is no stigma on being female; gender is not used to control behavior. No job was a man's job or a woman's job; the most able person did the work.

15   My Grandma Lily had been a Ford Model A mechanic when she was a teenager. I remember when I was young, she was always fixing broken lamps and appliances. She was small and wiry, but she could lift her weight in rolled roofing or boxes of nails. When she was seventy-five, she was still repairing washing machines in my uncle's coin-operated laundry.

16   The old-time people paid no attention to birthdays. When a person was ready to do something, she did it. When she no longer was able, she stopped.

Thus the traditional Pueblo people did not worry about aging or about looking old because there were no social boundaries drawn by the passage of years. It was not remarkable for young men to marry women as old as their mothers. I never heard anyone talk about "women's work" until after I left Laguna for college. Work was there to be done by any able-bodied person who wanted to do it. At the same time, in the old-time Pueblo world, identity was acknowledged to be always in a flux; in the old stories, one minute Spider Woman is a little spider under a yucca plant, and the next instant she is a sprightly grandmother walking down the road.

When I was growing up, there was a young man from a nearby village who 17 wore nail polish and women's blouses and permed his hair. People paid little attention to his appearance; he was always part of a group of other young men from his village. No one ever made fun of him. Pueblo communities were and still are very independent, but they also have to be tolerant of individual eccentricities because survival of the group means everyone has to cooperate.

In the old Pueblo world, differences were celebrated as signs of the Mother 18 Creator's grace. Persons born with exceptional physical or sexual differences were highly respected and honored because their physical differences gave them special positions as mediators between this world and the spirit world. The great Navajo medicine man of the 1920s, the Crawler, had a hunchback and could not walk upright, but he was able to heal even the most difficult cases.

Before the arrival of Christian missionaries, a man could dress as a woman 19 and work with the women and even marry a man without any fanfare. Likewise, a woman was free to dress like a man, to hunt and go to war with the men, and to marry a woman. In the old Pueblo worldview, we are all a mixture of male and female, and this sexual identity is changing constantly. Sexual inhibition did not begin until the Christian missionaries arrived. For the old-time people, marriage was about teamwork and social relationships, not about sexual excitement. In the days before the Puritans came, marriage did not mean an end to sex with people other than your spouse. Women were just as likely as men to have a *si'ash*, or lover.

New life was so precious that pregnancy was always appropriate, and 20 pregnancy before marriage was celebrated as a good sign. Since the children belonged to the mother and her clan, and women owned and bequeathed the houses and farmland, the exact determination of paternity wasn't critical. Although fertility was prized, infertility was no problem because mothers with unplanned pregnancies gave their babies to childless couples within the clan in open adoption arrangements. Children called their mother's sisters "mother" as well, and a child became attached to a number of parent figures.

In the sacred kiva ceremonies, men mask and dress as women to pay hom- 21 age and to be possessed by the female energies of the spirit beings. Because differences in physical appearance were so highly valued, surgery to change one's face and body to resemble a model's face and body would be unimaginable. To be different, to be unique was blessed and was best of all.

22   The traditional clothing of Pueblo women emphasized a woman's sturdiness. Buckskin leggings wrapped around the legs protected her from scratches and injuries while she worked. The more layers of buckskin, the better. All those layers gave her legs the appearance of strength, like sturdy tree trunks. To demonstrate sisterhood and brotherhood with the plants and animals, the old-time people make masks and costumes that transform the human figures of the dancers into the animal beings they portray. Dancers paint their exposed skin; their postures and motions are adapted from their observations. But the motions are stylized. The observer sees not an actual eagle or actual deer dancing, but witnesses a human being, a dancer, gradually changing into a woman/buffalo or a man/deer. Every impulse is to reaffirm the urgent relationships that human beings have with the plant and animal world.

23   In the high desert plateau country, all vegetation, even weeds and thorns, becomes special, and all life is precious and beautiful because without the plants, the insects, and the animals, human beings living here cannot survive. Perhaps human beings long ago noticed the devastating impact human activity can have on the plants and animals; maybe this is why tribal cultures devised the stories about humans and animals intermarrying, and the clans that bind humans to animals and plants through a whole complex of duties.

24   We children were always warned not to harm frogs or toads, the beloved children of the rain clouds, because terrible floods would occur. I remember in the summer the old folks used to stick bog bolls of cotton on the outside of their screen doors as bait to keep the flies from going in the house when the door was opened. The old folks staunchly resisted the killing of flies because once, long, long ago, when human beings were in a great deal of trouble, a Green Bottle Fly carried the desperate messages of human beings to the Mother Creator in the Fourth World, below this one. Human beings had outraged the Mother Creator by neglecting the Mother Corn altar while they dabbled with sorcery and magic. The Mother Creator disappeared, and with her disappeared the rain clouds, and the plants and the animals too. The people began to starve, and they had no way of reaching the Mother Creator down below. Green Bottle Fly took the message to the Mother Creator, and the people were saved. To show their gratitude, the old folks refused to kill any flies.

25   The old stories demonstrate the interrelationships that the Pueblo people have maintained with their plant and animal clanspeople. Kochininako, Yellow Woman, represents all women in the old stories. Her deeds span the spectrum of human behavior and are mostly heroic acts, though in at least one story, she chooses to join the secret Destroyer Clan, which worships destruction and death. Because Laguna Pueblo cosmology features a female Creator, the status of women is equal with the status of men, and women appear as often as men in the old stories as hero figures. Yellow Woman is my favorite because she dares to cross traditional boundaries of ordinary behavior during times of crisis in order to save the Pueblo; her power lies in her courage and in her

uninhibited sexuality, which the old-time Pueblo stories celebrate again and again because fertility was so highly valued.

The old stories always say that Yellow Woman was beautiful, but remember 26 that the old-time people were not so much thinking about physical appearances. In each story, the beauty that Yellow Woman possesses is the beauty of her passion, her daring, and her sheer strength to act when catastrophe is imminent.

In one story, the people are suffering during a great drought and accompa- 27 nying famine. Each day, Kochininako has to walk farther and farther from the village to find fresh water for her husband and children. One day she travels far, far to the east, to the plains, and she finally locates a freshwater spring. But when she reaches the pool, the water is churning violently as if something large had just gotten out of the pool, Kochininako does not want to see what huge creature had been at the pool, but just as she fills her water jar and turns to hurry away, a strong, sexy man in buffalo skin leggings appears by the pool. Little drops of water glisten on his chest. She cannot help but look at him because he is so strong and so good to look at. Able to transform himself from human to buffalo in the wink of an eye, Buffalo Man gallops away with her on his back. Kochininako falls in love with Buffalo Man, and because of this liaison, the Buffalo People agree to give their bodies to the hunters to feed the starving Pueblo. Thus Kochininako's fearless sensuality results in the salvation of the people of her village, who are saved by the meat the Buffalo People "give" to them.

My father taught me and my sisters to shoot .22 rifles when we were seven; 28 I went hunting with my father when I was eight, and I killed my first mule deer buck when I was thirteen. The Kochininako stories were always my favorite because Yellow Woman had so many adventures. In one story, as she hunts rabbits to feed her family, a giant monster pursues her, but she has the courage and presence of mind to outwit it.

In another story, Kochininako has a fling with Whirlwind Man and returns 29 to her husband ten months later with twin baby boys. The twin boys grow up to be great heroes of the people. Once again, Kochininako's vibrant sexuality benefits her people.

The stories about Kochininako made me aware that sometimes an individ- 30 ual must act despite disapproval, or concern for appearances or what others may say. From Yellow Woman's adventures, I learned to be comfortable with my differences. I even imagined that Yellow Woman had yellow skin, brown hair, and green eyes like mine, although her name does not refer to her color, but rather to the ritual color of the east.

There have been many other moments like the one with the camera-toting 31 tourist in the schoolyard. But the old-time people always say, remember the stories, the stories will help you be strong. So all these years I have depended on Kochininako and the stories of her adventures.

Kochininako is beautiful because she has the courage to act in times of great 32 peril, and her triumph is achieved by her sensuality, not through violence and destruction. For these qualities of the spirit, Yellow Woman and all women are beautiful.

COMPREHENSION

1. Silko devotes part of this essay to recollections of her great-grandmother, Grandma A'mooh. What is her great-grandmother like? What does the writer learn from Grandma A'mooh? Why is the essay more about Pueblo women than men?
2. Explain what you learned about traditional Pueblo culture from this essay. What values does the writer associate with this "old-time" culture? According to Silko, how does this culture contrast both explicitly and implicitly with modern Anglo culture? How did this traditional culture sustain her as a young girl?
3. Silko summarizes several Pueblo stories. What are the main ones? Why does she especially like the story of Kochininako, or Yellow Woman?

RHETORIC

1. What is Silko's thesis? Does this thesis appear in a single sentence? If so, what is it? If not, what is the implied thesis?
2. What strategy does the writer use to both start and conclude this essay? Is this strategy effective? Justify your response.
3. Silko provides an extended definition of Pueblo culture in this selection. Explain how she uses description, narration, comparison and contrast, and analysis to develop this definition.
4. While Silko's primary purpose is to define or explain Pueblo culture, she also provides several supporting definitions. Identify them, and explain how they contribute to the broader definition.
5. Is the diction in this essay concrete or abstract? Specific or general? Identify several passages to support your answer.
6. Consider the essay as an argument. What is the claim? What is the supporting evidence? What warrants underpin the argument? How effective is the argument, and why?

WRITING

1. Working in a group, create a list of all the features of traditional Pueblo culture that Silko discusses. Choose two or three and write brief summaries of each.
2. Using Silko's essay as a frame of reference, write a comparative essay in which you discuss contemporary American cultural values in relationship to "old-time" Pueblo values and traditions.
3. **Writing an Argument:** Argue for or against the proposition that traditional Pueblo culture is superior to contemporary American culture. Use at least three topics drawn from Silko's essay—for example, approach to diversity and difference, treatment of women, or respect for the environment—to develop your argumentative essay.

NETWORKING
Applying 21st-Century Literacies

Vetting Online Sources (a Public Domain e-Book): From the Chapter 7 Networking page (at *www.mhhe.com/mhreader11e*), link to this compilation of Pueblo stories, written in 1910 by Charles Lummis. Click on the link to the book's introduction, titled "The Brown Story-Tellers," and consider how Lummis's purpose for sharing these stories differs from Silko's. Would you use Lummis's retellings as sources in a paper? Why, why not, and if so, in what context?

A World Not Neatly Divided

Amartya Sen

Amartya Sen (b. 1933), born in Santiniketan, India, was awarded the Nobel Prize in Economics in 1988 for his groundbreaking work on welfare economics. Educated at Presidency College in Calcutta and Cambridge University (PhD, 1959), Sen has taught at Harvard University, the London School of Economics, and Oxford University; currently, he is a professor at Trinity College, Cambridge University. His major works, all of which investigate the role of poverty and inequality in the world, include Collective Choice and Social Welfare *(1970),* On Economic Inequality *(1973),* Poverty and Famines: An Essay on Entitlement and Deprivation *(1981),* Commodities and Capabilities *(1985),* Development as Freedom *(1999), and* Identity and Violence: The Illusion of Destiny *(2006). In the following essay, which appeared in the* New York Times *in 2001, Sen suggests that generalizations about "civilization" tend to blur the realities of complex cultures.*

When people talk about clashing civilizations, as so many politicians and academics do now, they can sometimes miss the central issue. The inadequacy of this thesis begins well before we get to the question of whether civilizations must clash. The basic weakness of the theory lies in its program of categorizing people of the world according to a unique, allegedly commanding system of classification. This is problematic because civilizational categories are crude and inconsistent and also because there are other ways of seeing people (linked to politics, language, literature, class, occupation, or other affiliations).

The befuddling influence of a singular classification also traps those who dispute the thesis of a clash: To talk about "the Islamic world" or "the Western world" is already to adopt an impoverished vision of humanity as unalterably divided. In fact, civilizations are hard to partition in this way, given the diversities within each society as well as the linkages among different countries and cultures. For example, describing India as a "Hindu civilization" misses the fact that India has more Muslims than any other country except Indonesia and possibly Pakistan. It is futile to try to understand Indian art, literature, music, food, or politics without seeing the extensive interactions across barriers of religious communities. These include Hindus and Muslims, Buddhists, Jains, Sikhs, Parsees, Christians (who have been in India since at least the fourth century, well before England's conversion to Christianity), Jews (present since the fall of Jerusalem), and even atheists and agnostics. Sanskrit has a larger atheistic literature than exists in any other classical language. Speaking of India as a Hindu civilization may be comforting to the Hindu fundamentalist, but it is an odd reading of India.

3   A similar coarseness can be seen in the other categories invoked, like "the Islamic world." Consider Akbar and Aurangzeb, two Muslim emperors of the Mogul dynasty in India. Aurangzeb tried hard to convert Hindus into Muslims and instituted various policies in that direction, of which taxing the non-Muslims was only one example. In contrast, Akbar reveled in his multiethnic court and pluralist laws, and issued official proclamations insisting that no one "should be interfered with on account of religion" and that "anyone is to be allowed to go over to a religion that pleases him."

4   If a homogeneous view of Islam were to be taken, then only one of these emperors could count as a true Muslim. The Islamic fundamentalist would have no time for Akbar; Prime Minister Tony Blair, given his insistence that tolerance is a defining characteristic of Islam, would have to consider excommunicating Aurangzeb. I expect both Akbar and Aurangzeb would protest, and so would I. A similar crudity is present in the characterization of what is called "Western civilization." Tolerance and individual freedom have certainly been present in European history. But there is no dearth of diversity here, either. When Akbar was making his pronouncements on religious tolerance in Agra, in the 1590s, the Inquisitions were still going on; in 1600, Giordano Bruno was burned at the stake, for heresy, in Campo dei Fiori in Rome.

5   Dividing the world into discrete civilizations is not just crude. It propels us into the absurd belief that this partitioning is natural and necessary and must overwhelm all other ways of identifying people. That imperious view goes not only against the sentiment that "we human beings are all much the same," but also against the more plausible understanding that we are diversely different. For example, Bangladesh's split from Pakistan was not connected with religion, but with language and politics.

6   Each of us has many features in our self-conception. Our religion, important as it may be, cannot be an all-engulfing identity. Even a shared poverty can be a source of solidarity across the borders. The kind of division highlighted by, say, the so-called "antiglobalization" protesters—whose movement is, incidentally, one of the most globalized in the world—tries to unite the underdogs of the world economy and goes firmly against religious, national, or "civilizational" lines of division.

The main hope of harmony lies not in any imagined uniformity, but in the 7 plurality of our identities, which cut across each other and work against sharp divisions into impenetrable civilizational camps. Political leaders who think and act in terms of sectioning off humanity into various "worlds" stand to make the world more flammable—even when their intentions are very different. They also end up, in the case of civilizations defined by religion, lending authority to religious leaders seen as spokesmen for their "worlds." In the process, other voices are muffled and other concerns silenced. The robbing of our plural identities not only reduces us; it impoverishes the world.

COMPREHENSION

1. According to Sen, what is the "basic weakness" underlying the idea that the world is composed of "clashing civilizations" (paragraph 1)?
2. What does the writer mean by "singular classification" (paragraph 2)? Why is classifying people in terms of their civilization "crude and inconsistent"? Why is applying singular classification to religions and other features of society wrong?
3. What, according to Sen, is "the main hope of harmony" (paragraph 7) in the world?

RHETORIC

1. What argumentative strategy does Sen employ in the introductory paragraph? What point of view is he arguing against?
2. While arguing against a certain type of classification, Sen actually uses classification as a rhetorical strategy. How, precisely, does he employ classification to organize his argument?
3. What examples does Sen use to support his argument? Why does he use them? Why does he decide not to provide illustrations near the end of the selection?
4. What transitional devices serve to unify the essay?
5. How effective is Sen's concluding paragraph? Does it serve to confirm his claim? Why or why not?

WRITING

1. Write an essay about the problems you see in your community or on campus. Explain how singular classification might explain some of these problems.
2. In an analytical essay, explain how singular classification might help explain the events of September 11, 2001.
3. **Writing an Argument:** Write an essay in which you demonstrate that singular classification actually can be helpful in framing public discourse about groups, nations, or civilizations.

NETWORKING
Applying 21st-Century Literacies

Scripting a Presentation: Use PowerPoint or a similar storyboarding program to create an oral presentation responding to question 1 under Writing. Use animation, images, and text together to effectively illustrate your point about singular classification's role in a specific problem or problems on your campus.

The Arab World

Edward T. Hall

Edward T. Hall (b. 1914) was born in Missouri and earned a master's degree at the University of Arkansas and a PhD in anthropology at Columbia University. He was a professor of anthropology at the Illinois Institute of Technology and at Northwestern University. Hall is also the author of many books on anthropology and culture, among the most famous of which are The Silent Language *(1959),* The Hidden Dimension *(1966),* The Dance of Life *(1983),* Hidden Differences: Doing Business with the Japanese *(1987), and* Understanding Cultural Differences: Germans, French and Americans *(1990). In this selection from* The Hidden Dimension, *Hall demonstrates how such basic concepts as public and private space are perceived far differently depending on one's culture of origin.*

1 In spite of over two thousand years of contact, Westerners and Arabs still do not understand each other. Proxemic research reveals some insights into this difficulty. Americans in the Middle East are immediately struck by two conflicting sensations. In public they are compressed and overwhelmed by smells, crowding, and high noise levels; in Arab homes Americans are apt to rattle around, feeling exposed and often somewhat inadequate because of too much space! (The Arab houses and apartments of the middle and upper classes which Americans stationed abroad commonly occupy are much larger than the dwellings such Americans usually inhabit.) Both the high sensory stimulation which is experienced in public places and the basic insecurity which comes from being in a dwelling that is too large provide Americans with an introduction to the sensory world of the Arab.

Behavior in Public

2 Pushing and shoving in public places is characteristic of Middle Eastern culture. Yet it is not entirely what Americans think it is (being pushy and rude) but stems from a different set of assumptions concerning not only the relations between

people but how one experiences the body as well. Paradoxically, Arabs consider northern Europeans and Americans pushy, too. This was very puzzling to me when I started investigating these two views. How could Americans who stand aside and avoid touching be considered pushy? I used to ask Arabs to explain this paradox. None of my subjects was able to tell me specifically what particulars of American behavior were responsible, yet they all agreed that the impression was widespread among Arabs. After repeated unsuccessful attempts to gain insight into the cognitive world of the Arab on this particular point, I filed it away as a question that only time would answer. When the answer came, it was because of a seemingly inconsequential annoyance.

While waiting for a friend in a Washington, D.C., hotel lobby and wanting ₃ to be both visible and alone, I had seated myself in a solitary chair outside the normal stream of traffic. In such a setting most Americans follow a rule, which is all the more binding because we seldom think about it, that can be stated as follows: As soon as a person stops or is seated in a public place, there balloons around him a small sphere of privacy which is considered inviolate. The size of the sphere varies with the degree of crowding, the age, sex, and the importance of the person, as well as the general surroundings. Anyone who enters this zone and stays there is intruding. In fact, a stranger who intrudes, even for a specific purpose, acknowledges the fact that he has intruded by beginning his request with "Pardon me, but can you tell me . . . ?"

To continue, as I waited in the deserted lobby, a stranger walked up to ₄ where I was sitting and stood close enough so that not only could I easily touch him but I could even hear him breathing. In addition, the dark mass of his body filled the peripheral field of vision on my left side. If the lobby had been crowded with people, I would have understood his behavior, but in an empty lobby his presence made me exceedingly uncomfortable. Feeling annoyed by this intrusion, I moved my body in such a way as to communicate annoyance. Strangely enough, instead of moving away, my actions seemed only to encourage him, because he moved even closer. In spite of the temptation to escape the annoyance, I put aside thoughts of abandoning my post, thinking, "To hell with it. Why should I move? I was here first and I'm not going to let this fellow drive me out even if he is a boor." Fortunately, a group of people soon arrived whom my tormentor immediately joined. Their mannerisms explained his behavior, for I knew from both speech and gestures that they were Arabs. I had not been able to make this crucial identification by looking at my subject when he was alone because he wasn't talking and he was wearing American clothes.

In describing the scene later to an Arab colleague, two contrasting patterns ₅ emerged. My concept and my feelings about my own circle of privacy in a "public" place immediately struck my Arab friend as strange and puzzling. He said, "After all, it's a public place, isn't it?" Pursuing this line of inquiry, I found that in Arab thought I had no rights whatsoever by virtue of occupying a given spot; neither my place nor my body was inviolate! For the Arab, there is no such thing as an intrusion in public. Public means public. With this insight, a great range of Arab behavior that had been puzzling, annoying, and sometimes even frightening began to make sense. I learned, for example, that if *A* is standing on a street corner and *B* wants his spot, *B* is within his rights if he does what he can to make *A* uncomfortable enough to move. In Beirut only the hardy sit in the last row in a movie theater, because there are usually standees who want seats and who push and shove and make such a nuisance that most people give up and leave. Seen in this light, the Arab who "intruded" on my space in the hotel lobby had apparently selected it for the very reason I had: It was a good place to watch two doors and the elevator. My show of annoyance, instead of driving him away, had only encouraged him. He thought he was about to get me to move.

6   Another silent source of friction between Americans and Arabs is in an area that Americans treat very informally—the manners and rights of the road. In general, in the United States we tend to defer to the vehicle that is bigger, more powerful, faster, and heavily laden. While a pedestrian walking along a road may feel annoyed he will not think it unusual to step aside for a fast-moving automobile. He knows that because he is moving he does not have the right to the space around him that he has when he is standing still (as I was in the hotel lobby). It appears that the reverse is true with the Arabs who apparently *take on rights to space as they move.* For someone else to move into a space an Arab is also moving into is a violation of his rights. It is infuriating to an Arab to have someone else cut in front of him on the highway. It is the American's cavalier treatment of moving space that makes the Arab call him aggressive and pushy.

Concepts of Privacy

7 The experience described above and many others suggested to me that Arabs might actually have a wholly contrasting set of assumptions concerning the body and the rights associated with it. Certainly the Arab tendency to shove and push each other in public and to feel and pinch women in public conveyances would not be tolerated by Westerners. It appeared to me that they must not have any concept of a private zone outside the body. This proved to be precisely the case.

8   In the Western world, the person is synonymous with an individual inside a skin. And in northern Europe generally, the skin and even the clothes may be inviolate. You need permission to touch either if you are a stranger. This rule applies in some parts of France, where the mere touching of another person during an argument used to be legally defined as assault. For the Arab the location of the person in relation to the body is quite different. The person exists somewhere down inside the body. The ego is not completely hidden, however, because it can be reached very easily with an insult. It is protected from touch but not from words. The dissociation of the body and the ego may explain why the public amputation of a thief's hand is tolerated as standard punishment in Saudi Arabia. It also sheds light on why an Arab employer living in a modern apartment can provide his servant with a room that is a boxlike cubicle approximately 5 by 10 by 4 feet in size that is not only hung from the ceiling to conserve floor space but has an opening so that the servant can be spied on.

As one might suspect, deep orientations toward the self such as the one just 9
described are also reflected in the language. This was brought to my attention
one afternoon when an Arab colleague who is the author of an Arab-English
dictionary arrived in my office and threw himself into a chair in a state of obvious exhaustion. When I asked him what had been going on, he said: "I have
spent the entire afternoon trying to find the Arab equivalent of the English
word 'rape.' There is no such word in Arabic. All my sources, both written and
spoken, can come up with no more than an approximation, such as 'He took her
against her will.' There is nothing in Arabic approaching your meaning as it is
expressed in that one word."

Differing concepts of the placement of the ego in relation to the body are 10
not easily grasped. Once an idea like this is accepted, however, it is possible to
understand many other facets of Arab life that would otherwise be difficult to
explain. One of these is the high population density of Arab cities like Cairo,
Beirut, and Damascus. According to the animal studies described in the earlier
chapters [of *The Hidden Dimension*], the Arabs should be living in a perpetual
behavioral sink. While it is probable that Arabs are suffering from population
pressures, it is also just as possible that continued pressure from the desert has
resulted in a cultural adaptation to high density which takes the form described
above. Tucking the ego down inside the body shell not only would permit
higher population densities but would explain why it is that Arab communications are stepped up as much as they are when compared to northern European
communication patterns. Not only is the sheer noise level much higher, but the
piercing look of the eyes, the touch of the hands, and the mutual bathing in the
warm moist breath during conversation represent stepped up sensory inputs to
a level which many Europeans find unbearably intense.

The Arab dream is for lots of space in the home, which unfortunately many 11
Arabs cannot afford. Yet when he has space, it is very different from what one
finds in most American homes. Arab spaces inside their upper middle-class
homes are tremendous by our standards. They avoid partitions because Arabs
do not like to be alone. The form of the home is such as to hold the family together
inside a single protective shell, because Arabs are deeply involved with each
other. Their personalities are intermingled and take nourishment from each
other like the roots and soil. If one is not with people and actively involved in
some way, one is deprived of life. An old Arab saying reflects this value: "Paradise without people should not be entered because it is Hell." Therefore, Arabs
in the United States often feel socially and sensorially deprived and long to be
back where there is human warmth and contact.

Since there is no physical privacy as we know it in the Arab family, not even 12
a word for privacy, one could expect that the Arabs might use some other
means to be alone. Their way to be alone is to stop talking. Like the English, an
Arab who shuts himself off in this way is not indicating that anything is wrong
or that he is withdrawing, only that he wants to be alone with his own thoughts
or does not want to be intruded upon. One subject said that her father would
come and go for days at a time without saying a word, and no one in the family

thought anything of it. Yet for this very reason, an Arab exchange student visiting a Kansas farm failed to pick up the cue that his American hosts were mad at him when they gave him the "silent treatment." He only discovered something was wrong when they took him to town and tried forcibly to put him on a bus to Washington, D.C., the headquarters of the exchange program responsible for his presence in the U.S.

Arab Personal Distances

13 Like everyone else in the world, Arabs are unable to formulate specific rules for their informal behavior patterns. In fact, they often deny that there are any rules, and they are made anxious by suggestions that such is the case. Therefore, in order to determine how the Arab sets distances, I investigated the use of each sense separately. Gradually, definite and distinctive behavioral patterns began to emerge.

14   Olfaction occupies a prominent place in the Arab life. Not only is it one of the distance-setting mechanisms, but it is a vital part of a complex system of behavior. Arabs consistently breathe on people when they talk. However, this habit is more than a matter of different manners. To the Arab good smells are pleasing and a way of being involved with each other. To smell one's friend is not only nice but desirable, for to deny him your breath is to act ashamed. Americans, on the other hand, trained as they are not to breathe in people's faces, automatically communicate shame in trying to be polite. Who would expect that when our highest diplomats are putting on their best manners they are also communicating shame? Yet this is what occurs constantly, because diplomacy is not only "eyeball to eyeball" but breath to breath.

15   By stressing olfaction, Arabs do not try to eliminate all the body's odors, only to enhance them and use them in building human relationships. Nor are they self-conscious about telling others when they don't like the way they smell. A man leaving his house in the morning may be told by his uncle, "Habib, your stomach is sour and your breath doesn't smell too good. Better not talk too close to people today." Smell is even considered in the choice of a mate. When couples are being matched for marriage, the man's go-between will sometimes ask to smell the girl, who may be turned down if she doesn't "smell nice." Arabs recognize that smell and disposition may be linked.

16   In a word, the olfactory boundary performs two roles in Arab life. It enfolds those who want to relate and separates those who don't. The Arab finds it essential to stay inside the olfactory zone as a means of keeping tab on changes in emotion. What is more, he may feel crowded as soon as he smells something unpleasant. While not much is known about "olfactory crowding," this may prove to be as significant as any other variable in the crowding complex because it is tied directly to the body chemistry and hence to the state of health and emotions. . . . It is not surprising, therefore, that the olfactory boundary constitutes for the Arabs an informal distance-setting mechanism in contrast to the visual mechanisms of the Westerner.

Facing and Not Facing

One of my earliest discoveries in the field of intercultural communication was 17
that the position of the bodies of people in conversation varies with the culture.
Even so, it used to puzzle me that a special Arab friend seemed unable to walk
and talk at the same time. After years in the United States, he could not bring
himself to stroll along, facing forward while talking. Our progress would be arrested while he edged ahead, cutting slightly in front of me and turning side-
ways so we could see each other. Once in this position, he would stop. His
behavior was explained when I learned that for the Arabs to view the other
person peripherally is regarded as impolite, and to sit or stand back-to-back is
considered very rude. You must be involved when interacting with Arabs who
are friends.

One mistaken American notion is that Arabs conduct all conversations at 18
close distances. This is not the case at all. On social occasions, they may sit on
opposite sides of the room and talk across the room to each other. They are,
however, apt to take offense when Americans use what are to them ambiguous
distances, such as the four- to seven-foot social-consultative distance. They frequently complain that Americans are cold or aloof or "don't care." This was
what an elderly Arab diplomat in an American hospital thought when the
American nurses used "professional" distance. He had the feeling that he was
being ignored, that they might not take good care of him. Another Arab subject
remarked, referring to American behavior, "What's the matter? Do I smell bad?
Or are they afraid of me?"

Arabs who interact with Americans report experiencing a certain flatness 19
traceable in part to a very different use of the eyes in private and in public as
well as between friends and strangers. Even though it is rude for a guest to
walk around the Arab home eyeing things, Arabs look at each other in ways
which seem hostile or challenging to the American. One Arab informant said
that he was in constant hot water with Americans because of the way he looked
at them without the slightest intention of offending. In fact, he had on several
occasions barely avoided fights with American men who apparently thought
their masculinity was being challenged because of the way he was looking at
them. As noted earlier, Arabs look each other in the eye when talking with an
intensity that makes most Americans highly uncomfortable.

Involvement

As the reader must gather by now, Arabs are involved with each other on many 20
different levels simultaneously. Privacy in a public place is foreign to them.
Business transactions in the bazaar, for example, are not just between buyer and
seller, but are participated in by everyone. Anyone who is standing around may
join in. If a grownup sees a boy breaking a window, he must stop him even if he
doesn't know him. Involvement and participation are expressed in other ways
as well. If two men are fighting, the crowd must intervene. On the political

level, *to fail to intervene* when trouble is brewing is to take sides, which is what our State Department always seems to be doing. Given the fact that few people in the world today are even remotely aware of the cultural mold that forms their thoughts, it is normal for Arabs to view *our* behavior as though it stemmed from *their* own hidden set of assumptions.

Feelings about Enclosed Spaces

21 In the course of my interviews with Arabs the term "tomb" kept cropping up in conjunction with enclosed space. In a word, Arabs don't mind being crowded by people but hate to be hemmed in by walls. They show a much greater overt sensitivity to architectural crowding than we do. Enclosed space must meet at least three requirements that I know of if it is to satisfy the Arabs: There must be plenty of unobstructed space in which to move around (possibly as much as a thousand square feet); very high ceilings—so high in fact that they do not normally impinge on the visual field; and, in addition, there must be an unobstructed view. It was spaces such as these in which the Americans referred to earlier felt so uncomfortable. One sees the Arab's need for a view expressed in many ways, even negatively, for to cut off a neighbor's view is one of the most effective ways of spiting him. In Beirut one can see what is known locally as the "spite house." It is nothing more than a thick, four-story wall, built at the end of a long fight between neighbors, on a narrow strip of land for the express purpose of denying a view of the Mediterranean to any house built on the land behind. According to one of my informants, there is also a house on a small plot of land between Beirut and Damascus which is completely sur-rounded by a neighbor's wall built high enough to cut off the view from all windows!

Boundaries

22 Proxemic patterns tell us other things about Arab culture. For example, the whole concept of the boundary as an abstraction is almost impossible to pin down. In one sense, there are no boundaries. "Edges" of towns, yes, but perma-nent boundaries out in the country (hidden lines), no. In the course of my work with Arab subjects I had a difficult time translating our concept of a boundary into terms which could be equated with theirs. In order to clarify the distinc-tions between the two very different definitions, I thought it might be helpful to pinpoint acts which constituted trespass. To date, I have been unable to dis-cover anything even remotely resembling our own legal concept of trespass.

23 Arab behavior in regard to their own real estate is apparently an extension of, and therefore consistent with, their approach to the body. My subjects sim-ply failed to respond whenever trespass was mentioned. They didn't seem to understand what I meant by this term. This may be explained by the fact that

they organize relationships with each other according to closed social systems rather than spatially. For thousands of years Moslems, Marinites, Druses, and Jews have lived in their own villages, each with strong kin affiliations. Their hierarchy of loyalties is: first to one's self, then to kinsman, townsman, or tribesman, co-religionist and/or countryman. Anyone not in these categories is a stranger. Strangers and enemies are very closely linked, if not synonymous, in Arab thought. Trespass in this context is a matter of who you are, rather than a piece of land or a space with a boundary that can be denied to anyone and everyone, friend and foe alike.

In summary, proxemic patterns differ. By examining them it is possible to 24 reveal hidden cultural frames that determine the structure of a given people's perceptual world. Perceiving the world differently leads to differential definitions of what constitutes crowded living, different interpersonal relations, and a different approach to both local and international politics.

COMPREHENSION

1. This excerpt is from Hall's book *The Hidden Dimension*. What is the hidden dimension, according to the author?
2. In paragraph 10, Hall explains that "differing concepts of the placement of the ego in relation to the body are not easily grasped." What does he mean by this statement? How is it relevant to the theme of his essay?
3. The title of this essay is "The Arab World." What does the term *world* mean within the context of the essay?
4. Define the following words: *proxemic* (paragraph 1), *paradox* (paragraph 2), *inviolate* (paragraph 3), *defer* (paragraph 6), *olfaction* (paragraph 14), and *peripherally* (paragraph 17).

RHETORIC

1. Anthropology is often thought of as an intellectual pursuit. How would you characterize Hall's voice, considering his style of language and method of analysis?
2. How does Hall develop his comparison and contrast of the American versus the Arab perception of manners and driving?
3. People often favor their own perspective of life over a foreign perspective. Is Hall's comparison value-free, or does he seem to prefer one cultural system to another? Explain by making reference to his tone.
4. Who is the implied audience for this essay? Explain your view.
5. Hall makes use of personal anecdote in explaining his theme. What other forms of support does he offer? Cite at least two others and provide an example of each.
6. Writers often have various purposes in writing—for example, to entertain, to inform, to effect change, to advise, or to persuade. What is Hall's purpose or purposes in writing this essay? Explain your view.

WRITING

1. Write an expository essay in which you explain the use and interpretation of personal space by observing students in social situations at your college or university.
2. Write a personal anecdote about a time in your life when cultural perception caused a conflict between yourself and another person.
3. **Writing an Argument:** In a persuasive essay, argue for or against the proposition that some cultures are better than others.

NETWORKING
Applying 21st-Century Literacies

Creating a Poster Series: Design a series of posters that explore the use and interpretation of personal space on your campus—and that, collectively, make a point about it. As in question 1 under Writing, observe students in social contexts on campus: Then either take photographs, create illustrations or creative figures (such as graphs), or use images from other sources to depict what you observed. Use these images as a prominent component of your posters, and use minimal, effective text (a tagline, a series of parallel words or phrases) to clarify or cleverly suggest your purpose or point. (*Note:* If you take your own photos, whether they are staged shots or cameos, be sure to ask your subjects for permission to feature them in your poster series.)

Synthesis: Connections for Critical Thinking

1. Cofer writes about Latino culture and Silko about Native American culture in their respective essays. What connections do they make between their subjects and cultural affiliation and alienation? How do they present their ideas? How are their tones similar? How are they different?
2. Write an essay exploring the topic of culture and civilization in the essays by Ecenbarger, Sen, and Silko.
3. Consider the current position of women in our culture. Refer to any three essays in this chapter to support your main observations.
4. How does one's experience of being an outsider or stranger to a culture affect one's understanding of that culture? Use essays from this chapter to support your key points.
5. Write an essay exploring the shape of contemporary civilization as it is reflected in the essays in this chapter. Cite specific support from at least three of the selections you have read.
6. How does a nation maintain a strong sense of self and still remain open to outside influences? Is a national identity crucial to a nation's survival? Use the opinions of representative authors in this chapter to address the question.
7. Is there such a thing as ethnic character, something that distinguishes Native Americans from African Americans, or Latinos from Asian Americans? What factors

contribute to identification with culture and with nation? Cite at least three essays in this chapter.

8. Argue for or against the proposition that Americans are ignorant of both the contributions and the values of non-Western cultures in our country. Refer specifically to Reed, Hall, Silko, and Hoagland.

NETWORKING
Applying 21st-Century Literacies

1. Set up a chat room or blog with five class members, and discuss the differences in cultural perspectives among the writers in this chapter. Use hyperlinks to drive the discussion to additional sources.
2. Conduct an online search for reliable information on Judith Ortiz Cofer and Ishmael Reed. Keeping track of your sources, and using sources from at least three different media, write a brief research paper on these writers' perceptions of ethnicity and the American experience.

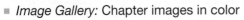

CH 7   **www.mhhe.com/mhreader11e**

- *Image Gallery:* Chapter images in color
- *History, Culture, and Civilization:* Information on the authors in this chapter
- *Ch. 7 Networking*

chapter *8*

Government, Politics, and Social Justice
How Do We Decide What Is Fair?

Recent studies indicate that American students have an extremely limited understanding of government and politics. In fact, one-third of all high school juniors cannot identify the main purpose of the Declaration of Independence or say in which century it was signed. This document is one of the selections in this chapter. If we are ignorant of such a basic instrument in the making of our history and society, what might that say about our concepts of citizenship? Do we now see ourselves purely as economic units—that is, in terms of our ability or potential to make money—or as consumers—that is, in terms of the roles we play in spending it? Other notable essays on government, politics, and social justice in this chapter will help us understand our cultural legacies and what has traditionally been thought of as the impetus in developing America as a country.

Skilled writers can bring politics and issues of social justice to life, enabling us to develop a sense of the various processes that have influenced the development of cultures over time. By studying the course of history and politics, we develop causal notions of how events are interrelated and how traditions have evolved. The study of history and politics can be an antidote to the continuous "present tense" of the media, which often have the power to make us believe we live from moment to moment, discouraging reflection on serious issues such as why we live the way we do and how we came to be the people we are. Essays, speeches, documents, biographies, narratives, and many other literary forms capture events and illuminate the past while holding up a mirror to the present. On the one hand, our political story can be brought to life out of the plain but painfully eloquent artifacts of oral culture. On the other, Thomas Jefferson employs classical rhetorical structures—notably argumentation—in outlining democratic vistas in the Declaration of Independence.

Even the briefest reflection will remind us of how important political processes and institutions are. Put simply, a knowledge of government and politics, and of our quest for social justice, validates our memory, a remembrance of how important the past is to our current existence. When, for example, Martin Luther King Jr. approaches the subject of oppression from a theological perspective, we are reminded of how important the concept of freedom is to our heritage and the various ways it can be addressed. Indeed, had we been more familiar with chapters in human history, we might have avoided some of the commensurate responses to the crises in our own era. The essays in this chapter help remind us—as the philosopher Santayana warned—that "those who forget the lessons of history are doomed to repeat them."

Only with a knowledge of government and politics can we make informed choices. Through a study of government and politics, we learn about challenges and opportunities, conflicts and their resolutions, and the use and abuse of power across time in numerous cultures and civilizations. It is through the study of historical processes and political institutions that we seek to define ourselves and to learn how we have evolved.

PREVIEWING THE CHAPTER

As you read the selections in this chapter and respond to them in discussion and writing, consider the following questions:

- On what specific events does the author concentrate? What is the time frame?
- What larger historical and political issues concern the author?
- From what perspective does the author treat the subject—from that of participant, observer, commentator, or some other role?
- What is the author's purpose in treating events and personalities—to explain, to instruct, to amuse, to criticize, or to celebrate?
- What does the author learn about history and politics from his or her inquiry into events?
- What sorts of conflicts—historical, political, economic, social, religious—emerge in the essay?
- Are there any correspondences among the essays? What analogies do the authors themselves draw?
- What is the relationship of people and personalities to the events under consideration?
- Which biases and ideological positions do you detect in the authors' works?
- How has your understanding of history and politics been challenged by the essays in this chapter?

Classic and Contemporary Images

HAVE WE MADE ADVANCES IN CIVIL RIGHTS?

Using a Critical Perspective   Are you optimistic or skeptical about the lofty words in the Declaration of Independence announcing that everyone is created equal? How do these two visual texts, one advertising a slave auction and the other presenting a campaign poster for President Barack Obama, affect your response? What aspects of these visual texts stand out? What is your emotional and ethical response to the images? What do the two illustrations tell us about the evolution of equal rights and justice in the United States?

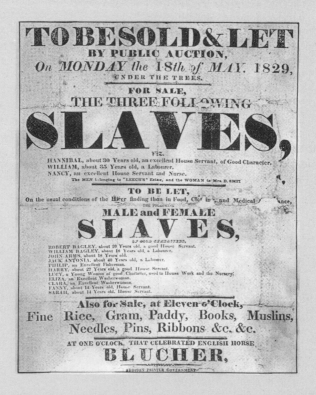

Advertisement of slaves for sale by the company Hewlett & Bright,
May 13, 1835.

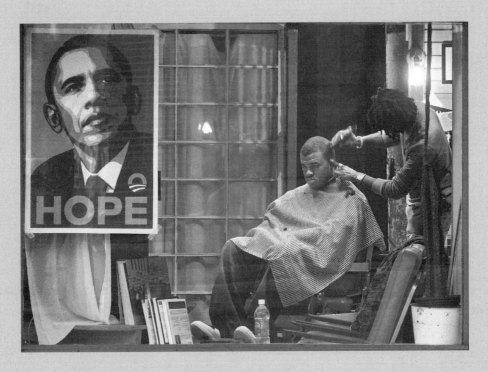

Hope, by Shepard Fairey. Street artist and illustrator Shepard Fairey created this iconic poster, based on an Associated Press photograph, for the 2008 Obama presidential campaign.

Classic and Contemporary Essays
WHAT IS THE AMERICAN DREAM?

Both Thomas Jefferson and Martin Luther King Jr. are now safely ensconced within the pantheon of American historical figures. The following two writing samples help indicate why. Both are concerned with perhaps the most significant issue that concerns contemporary humankind: freedom. Jefferson creates a doctrine that is powerful owing to his use of concise and powerful language, which he employs both to enumerate British offenses and to call on his fellow Americans to revolt if need be. While his list of grievances may seem unquestionably correct to the contemporary mind, one must consider that Jefferson was a product of the Enlightenment, when philosophers had finally turned their attention to the primacy of individual rights after millennia of living under monarchic rule. King also provides us with the powerful theme of freedom in his famous speech; while his reflections address the peculiarly American racial divide, his style contains many biblical references, and his rhetoric is that of the sermon. You should consider why these two documents, regardless of their historical context, seem to be milestones in our nation's history.

The Declaration of Independence
In Congress, July 4, 1776

Thomas Jefferson

Thomas Jefferson (1743–1826) was governor of Virginia during the American Revolution, America's first secretary of state, and the third president of the United States. He had a varied and monumental career as politician, public servant, scientist, architect, educator (he founded the University of Virginia), and man of letters. Jefferson attended the Continental Congress in 1775, where he wrote the rough draft of the Declaration of Independence. Other hands made contributions to the document that was signed on July 4, 1776, but the wording, style, structure, and spirit of the final version are distinctly Jefferson's. Like Thomas Paine, Benjamin Franklin, James Madison, and other major figures of the Revolutionary era, Jefferson was notable for his use of prose as an instrument for social and political change. In the Declaration of Independence, we see the direct, precise, logical, and persuasive statement of revolutionary principles that makes the document one of the best-known and best-written texts in world history. Jefferson died in his home at Monticello on July 4, 50 years to the day from the signing of the Declaration of Independence.

When in the Course of human events it becomes necessary for one people to 1
dissolve the political bands which have connected them with another, and to
assume among the powers of the earth, the separate and equal station to which
the Laws of Nature and of Nature's God entitle them, a decent respect to the
opinions of mankind requires that they should declare the causes which impel
them to the separation.

We hold these truths to be self-evident, that all men are created equal, that 2
they are endowed by their Creator with certain unalienable Rights, that among
these are Life, Liberty and the pursuit of Happiness.—That to secure these
rights, Governments are instituted among Men, deriving their just powers from
the consent of the governed.—That whenever any Form of Government becomes destructive of these ends, it is the Right of the People to alter or to abolish it, and to institute new Government, laying its foundation on such principles
and organizing its powers in such form, as to them shall seem most likely to
effect their Safety and Happiness. Prudence, indeed, will dictate that Governments long established should not be changed for light and transient causes;
and accordingly all experience hath shewn that mankind are more disposed to
suffer, while evils are sufferable, than to right themselves by abolishing the
forms to which they are accustomed. But when a long train of abuses and usurpations, pursuing invariably the same Object evinces a design to reduce them
under absolute Despotism, it is their right, it is their duty, to throw off such
Government, and to provide new Guards for their future security.—Such has
been the patient sufferance of these Colonies; and such is now the necessity
which constrains them to alter their former Systems of Government. The history of the present King of Great Britain is a history of repeated injuries and
usurpations, all having in direct object the establishment of an absolute Tyranny over these States. To prove this, let Facts be submitted to a candid world.

He has refused his Assent to Laws, the most wholesome and necessary for 3
the public good.

He has forbidden his Governors to pass Laws of immediate and pressing 4
importance, unless suspended in their operation till his Assent should be obtained; and when so suspended, he has utterly neglected to attend to them.

He has refused to pass other Laws for the accommodation of large districts 5
of people, unless those people would relinquish the right of Representation in
the Legislature, a right inestimable to them and formidable to tyrants only.

He has called together legislative bodies at places unusual, uncomfortable, 6
and distant from the depository of their public Records, for the sole purpose of
fatiguing them into compliance with his measures.

He has dissolved Representative Houses repeatedly, for opposing with 7
manly firmness his invasions on the rights of the people.

He has refused for a long time, after such dissolutions, to cause others to be 8
elected; whereby the Legislative powers, incapable of Annihilation, have returned

to the People at large for their exercise; the State remaining in the mean time exposed to all the dangers of invasion from without, and convulsions within.

9   He has endeavored to prevent the population of these States; for that purpose obstructing the Laws for Naturalization of Foreigners; refusing to pass others to encourage their migrations hither, and raising the conditions of new Appropriations of Lands.

10   He has obstructed the Administration of Justice, by refusing his Assent to Laws for establishing Judiciary powers.

11   He has made Judges dependent on his Will alone, for the tenure of their offices, and the amount and payment of their salaries.

12   He has erected a multitude of New Offices, and sent hither swarms of Officers to harass our people, and eat out their substance.

13   He has kept among us, in times of peace, Standing Armies without the Consent of our legislatures.

14   He has affected to render the Military independent of and superior to the Civil power.

15   He has combined with others to subject us to a jurisdiction foreign to our constitution, and unacknowledged by our laws; giving his Assent to their Acts of pretended Legislation:

> For quartering large bodies of armed troops among us:

> For protecting them, by a mock Trial, from punishment for any Murders which they should commit on the Inhabitants of these States:

> For cutting off our Trade with all parts of the world:

> For imposing Taxes on us without our Consent:

> For depriving us in many cases, of the benefits of Trial by jury:

> For transporting us beyond Seas to be tried for pretended offences:

> For abolishing the free System of English Laws in a neighboring Province, establishing therein an Arbitrary government, and enlarging its Boundaries so as to render it at once an example and fit instrument for introducing the same absolute rule into these Colonies:

> For taking away our Charters, abolishing our most valuable Laws and altering fundamentally the Forms of our Governments:

> For suspending our own Legislatures, and declaring themselves invested with power to legislate for us in all cases whatsoever.

16   He has abdicated Government here, by declaring us out of his Protection and waging War against us.

17   He has plundered our seas, ravaged our Coasts, burnt our towns, and destroyed the lives of our people.

18   He is at this time transporting large Armies of foreign Mercenaries to complete the works of death, desolation and tyranny, already begun with

circumstances of Cruelty & Perfidy scarcely paralleled in the most barbarous ages, and totally unworthy the Head of a civilized nation.

He has constrained our fellow Citizens taken Captive on the high Seas to 19 bear Arms against their Country, to become the executioners of their friends and Brethren, or to fall themselves by their Hands.

He has excited domestic insurrections amongst us, and has endeavored to 20 bring on the inhabitants of our frontiers, the merciless Indian Savages, whose known rule of warfare, is an undistinguished destruction of all ages, sexes and conditions.

In every stage of these Oppressions We have Petitioned for Redress in the 21 most humble terms: Our repeated Petitions have been answered only by repeated injury. A Prince, whose character is thus marked by every act which may define a Tyrant, is unfit to be the ruler of a free people.

Nor have We been wanting in attentions to our British brethren. We have 22 warned them from time to time of attempts by their legislature to extend an unwarrantable jurisdiction over us. We have reminded them of the circumstances of our emigration and settlement here. We have appealed to their native justice and magnanimity, and we have conjured them by the ties of our common kindred to disavow these usurpations, which would inevitably interrupt our connections and correspondence. They too have been deaf to the voice of justice and of consanguinity. We must, therefore, acquiesce in the necessity, which denounces our Separation, and hold them, as we hold the rest of mankind, Enemies in War, in Peace Friends.

We, therefore, the Representatives of the United States of America, in 23 General Congress, Assembled, appealing to the Supreme Judge of the world for the rectitude of our intentions, do, in the Name, and by Authority of the good People of these Colonies, solemnly publish and declare, That these United Colonies are, and of Right ought to be Free and Independent States; that they are Absolved from all Allegiance to the British Crown, and that all political connection between them and the State of Great Britain, is and ought to be totally dissolved; and that as Free and Independent States, they have full Power to levy War, conclude Peace, contract Alliances, establish Commerce, and to do all other Acts and Things which Independent States may of right do. And for the support of this Declaration, with a firm reliance on the protection of divine Providence, we mutually pledge to each other our Lives, our Fortunes and our sacred Honor.

COMPREHENSION

1. Explain Jefferson's main and subordinate purposes in this document.
2. What is Jefferson's key assertion or argument? Mention several reasons that he gives to support his argument.
3. Summarize Jefferson's definition of human nature and government.

RHETORIC

1. There are many striking words and phrases in the Declaration of Independence, notably in the beginning. Locate three such examples, and explain their connotative power and effectiveness.
2. Jefferson and his colleagues had to draft a document designed for several audiences. What audiences did they have in mind? How do their language and style reflect their awareness of multiple audiences?
3. The Declaration of Independence is a classic model of syllogistic reasoning and deductive argument (see the Glossary). What is its major premise, and where is this premise stated? The minor premise? The conclusion?
4. What sort of inductive evidence does Jefferson offer?
5. Why is the middle portion, or body, of the Declaration of Independence considerably longer than the introduction or conclusion? What holds the body together?
6. Explain the function and effect of parallel structure in this document.

WRITING

1. Discuss the relevance of the Declaration of Independence to politics today.
2. Explain in an essay why the Declaration of Independence is a model of effective prose.
3. Write your own declaration of independence—from family, employer, required courses, or the like. Develop this declaration as an op-ed piece for a newspaper.
4. **Writing an Argument:** Do you believe that "all men are created equal"? Justify your answer in an argumentative essay.

NETWORKING
Applying 21st-Century Literacies

Reading and Responding to a Web Site: At the Chapter 8 Networking page (*www.mhhe.com/mhreader11e*), link to *ushistory.org*'s Web site about the Declaration of Independence. In the menu on the left side of the page, choose several sections to explore: under "Document," you can see images of actual drafts of the text and read transcripts of it in several incarnations, including its final form. The "Related Information" page links to information about people, events, and other laws that influenced the document. Among other resources are two timelines (one chronicling the events of the Revolutionary War) and Jefferson's personal account of writing the Declaration of Independence. After spending some time with the site and the texts and links on it, write a reader response essay arguing that this site's contextual information either enhances or distracts from the content of the document itself. Explain how and why this was your reading experience; support your position with specific examples.

I Have a Dream

Martin Luther King Jr.

Martin Luther King Jr. (1929–1968) was born in Atlanta, Georgia, and received degrees from Morehouse College, Crozer Theological Seminary, Boston University, and Chicago Theological Seminary. As Baptist clergyman, civil rights leader, founder and president of the Southern Christian Leadership Conference, and 1964 Nobel Peace Prize winner, King was a celebrated advocate of nonviolent resistance to achieve equality and racial integration in the world. King was a gifted orator and a highly persuasive writer. His books include Stride toward Freedom *(1958),* Letter from Birmingham City Jail *(1963),* Strength to Love *(1963),* Why We Can't Wait *(1964), and* Where Do We Go from Here: Chaos or Community? *(1967), a book published shortly before he was assassinated on April 4, 1968, in Memphis, Tennessee. This selection, a milestone of American oratory, was the keynote address at the March on Washington, August 28, 1963.*

I am happy to join with you today in what will go down in history as the great- 1
est demonstration for freedom in the history of our nation.

Fivescore years ago, a great American, in whose symbolic shadow we stand 2
today, signed the Emancipation Proclamation. This momentous decree came as
a great beacon light of hope to millions of Negro slaves who had been seared in
the flames of withering injustice. It came as a joyous daybreak to end the long
night of their captivity.

But one hundred years later, the Negro still is not free; one hundred years 3
later, the life of the Negro is still sadly crippled by the manacles of segregation
and the chains of discrimination; one hundred years later, the Negro lives on a
lonely island of poverty in the midst of a vast ocean of material prosperity; one
hundred years later, the Negro is still languishing in the corners of American
society and finds himself in exile in his own land.

So we've come here today to dramatize a shameful condition. In a sense 4
we've come to our nation's capital to cash a check. When the architects of our
republic wrote the magnificent words of the Constitution and the Declaration
of Independence, they were signing a promissory note to which every American was to fall heir. This note was the promise that all men, yes, black men
as well as white men, would be guaranteed the unalienable rights of life, liberty,
and the pursuit of happiness.

It is obvious today that America has defaulted on this promissory note in so 5
far as her citizens of color are concerned. Instead of honoring this sacred obligation, America has given the Negro people a bad check; a check which has come
back marked "insufficient funds." We refuse to believe that there are insufficient funds in the great vaults of opportunity of this nation. And so we've come

to cash this check, a check that will give us upon demand the riches of freedom and the security of justice.

6   We have also come to this hallowed spot to remind America of the fierce urgency of now. This is no time to engage in the luxury of cooling off or to take the tranquilizing drug of gradualism. Now is the time to make real the promises of democracy; now is the time to rise from the dark and desolate valley of segregation to the sunlit path of racial justice; now is the time to lift our nation from the quicksands of racial injustice to the solid rock of brotherhood; now is the time to make justice a reality for all God's children. It would be fatal for the nation to overlook the urgency of the moment. This sweltering summer of the Negro's legitimate discontent will not pass until there is an invigorating autumn of freedom and equality.

7   Nineteen sixty-three is not an end, but a beginning. And those who hope that the Negro needed to blow off steam and will now be content, will have a rude awakening if the nation returns to business as usual.

8   There will be neither rest nor tranquility in America until the Negro is granted his citizenship rights. The whirlwinds of revolt will continue to shake the foundations of our nation until the bright day of justice emerges.

9   But there is something that I must say to my people who stand on the warm threshold which leads into the palace of justice. In the process of gaining our rightful place we must not be guilty of wrongful deeds.

10   Let us not seek to satisfy our thirst for freedom by drinking from the cup of bitterness and hatred. We must forever conduct our struggle on the high plane of dignity and discipline. We must not allow our creative protest to degenerate into physical violence. Again and again we must rise to the majestic heights of meeting physical force with soul force.

11   The marvelous new militancy which has engulfed the Negro community must not lead us to a distrust of all white people, for many of our white brothers, as evidenced by their presence here today, have come to realize that their destiny is tied up with our destiny and they have come to realize that their freedom is inextricably bound to our freedom. This offense we share mounted to storm the battlements of injustice must be carried forth by a biracial army. We cannot walk alone.

12   And as we walk, we must make the pledge that we shall always march ahead. We cannot turn back. There are those who are asking the devotees of civil rights, "When will you be satisfied?" We can never be satisfied as long as the Negro is the victim of the unspeakable horrors of police brutality.

13   We can never be satisfied as long as our bodies, heavy with fatigue of travel, cannot gain lodging in the motels of the highways and the hotels of the cities. We cannot be satisfied as long as the Negro's basic mobility is from a smaller ghetto to a larger one.

14   We can never be satisfied as long as our children are stripped of their selfhood and robbed of their dignity by signs stating "for whites only." We cannot be satisfied as long as a Negro in Mississippi cannot vote and a Negro in New York believes he has nothing for which to vote. No, we are not satisfied, and we

will not be satisfied until justice rolls down like waters and righteousness like a mighty stream.

I am not unmindful that some of you have come here out of excessive trials 15 and tribulation. Some of you have come fresh from narrow jail cells. Some of you have come from areas where your quest for freedom left you battered by the storms of persecution and staggered by the winds of police brutality. You have been the veterans of creative suffering. Continue to work with the faith that unearned suffering is redemptive.

Go back to Mississippi; go back to Alabama; go back to South Carolina; go 16 back to Georgia; go back to Louisiana; go back to the slums and ghettos of the northern cities, knowing that somehow this situation can, and will be changed. Let us not wallow in the valley of despair.

So I say to you, my friends, that even though we must face the difficulties of 17 today and tomorrow, I still have a dream. It is a dream deeply rooted in the American dream that one day this nation will rise up and live out the true meaning of its creed—we hold these truths to be self-evident, that all men are created equal.

I have a dream that one day on the red hills of Georgia, sons of former 18 slaves and sons of former slave-owners will be able to sit down together at the table of brotherhood.

I have a dream that one day, even the state of Mississippi, a state sweltering 19 with the heat of injustice, sweltering with the heat of oppression, will be transformed into an oasis of freedom and justice.

I have a dream my four little children will one day live in a nation where 20 they will not be judged by the color of their skin but by the content of their character. I have a dream today!

I have a dream that one day, down in Alabama, with its vicious racists, with 21 its governor having his lips dripping with the words of interposition and nullification, that one day, right there in Alabama, little black boys and black girls will be able to join hands with little white boys and white girls as sisters and brothers. I have a dream today!

I have a dream that one day every valley shall be exalted, every hill and 22 mountain shall be made low, the rough places shall be made plain, and the crooked places shall be made straight and the glory of the Lord will be revealed and all flesh shall see it together.

This is our hope. This is the faith that I go back to the South with. 23

With this faith we will be able to hear out of the mountain of despair a stone 24 of hope. With this faith we will be able to transform the jangling discords of our nation into a beautiful symphony of brotherhood.

With this faith we will be able to work together, to pray together, to struggle 25 together, to go to jail together, to stand up for freedom together, knowing that we will be free one day. This will be the day when all of God's children will be able to sing with new meaning—"my country 'tis of thee; sweet land of liberty; of thee I sing; land where my fathers died, land of the pilgrims' pride; from every mountain side, let freedom ring"—and if America is to be a great nation, this must become true.

26   So let freedom ring from the prodigious hilltops of New Hampshire.

27   Let freedom ring from the mighty mountains of New York.

28   Let freedom ring from the heightening Alleghenies of Pennsylvania.

29   Let freedom ring from the snow-capped Rockies of Colorado.

30   Let freedom ring from the curvaceous slopes of California.

31   But not only that.

32   Let freedom ring from Stone Mountain of Georgia.

33   Let freedom ring from Lookout Mountain of Tennessee.

34   Let freedom ring from every hill and molehill of Mississippi, from every mountainside, let freedom ring.

35   And when we allow freedom to ring, when we let it ring from every village and hamlet, from every state and city, we will be able to speed up that day when all of God's children—black men and white men, Jews and Gentiles, Catholics and Protestants—will be able to join hands and to sing in the words of the old Negro spiritual, "Free at last, free at last; thank God Almighty, we are free at last."

COMPREHENSION

1. What is the main purpose of this speech? Where does King state this purpose most clearly?
2. Why does King make use of "fivescore years ago" (paragraph 2)? How is this more appropriate than simply saying "a hundred years ago"?
3. Who is King's audience? Where does he acknowledge the special historical circumstances influencing his speech?

RHETORIC

1. From what sources does King adapt phrases to give his work allusive richness?
2. What do the terms *interposition* and *nullification* (paragraph 21) mean? What is their historical significance?
3. Why does King make use of repetition? Does this technique work well in print? Explain.
4. What is the purpose of the extended metaphor in paragraphs 4 and 5? Which point in paragraph 3 does it refer to?
5. In which paragraphs does King address the problems of African Americans?
6. Why is this selection titled "I Have a Dream"? How do dreams serve as a motif for this speech?

WRITING

1. "I Have a Dream" is considered by many people to be among the greatest speeches delivered by an American. Do you think it deserves to be? Explain in an essay.
2. Write a comparative essay analyzing King's assessment of black Americans' condition in 1963 and their condition today. What do you think King would say if he knew of contemporary conditions?

3. Write your own "I Have a Dream" essay, basing it on your vision of America or of a special people.
4. **Writing an Argument:** Prepare a newspaper editorial advocating a solution to one aspect of racial, ethnic, or sexual injustice.

NETWORKING
Applying 21st-Century Literacies

Seeing vs. Reading the Text of a Speech: At the Chapter 8 Networking page (*www.mhhe.com/mhreader11e*), link to the video of Martin Luther King giving his famous "I Have a Dream" speech. How is the experience of watching and listening to this speech different from reading it? Compare and contrast these two types of experiencing a text, using "I Have a Dream" as an example. Consider what, beyond the words themselves, is *happening* in this video.

Synthesis: Classic and Contemporary Questions for Comparison

1. Compare the Declaration of Independence with King's speech in terms of language, style, and content. Are they equally powerful and resonant? Cite specific passages from the essays to illustrate your response.
2. Rewrite the Declaration of Independence in modern English as you believe Dr. King might have written it, reflecting his concerns about the African American and other minorities in this country. Include a list of grievances similar to the ones concerning British rule.
3. Write a research paper about the lives and times of King and Jefferson. Compare and contrast any significant events or pertinent biographical data in their backgrounds.

We're All Torturers Now

Dahlia Lithwick

Dahlia Lithwick (b. 1972) *was born in Canada and is a Canadian citizen. She received her education in the United States, however, first attending Yale University (BA, 1990) and then taking a law degree at Stanford University (JD, 1996). Lithwick practiced law for a brief period before embarking on a writing and editorial career. She has written for the* New Republic, Elle, *the* Washington Post, *and CNN.com, and she is a contributing editor at* Newsweek *and senior editor and legal correspondent at* Slate. *Lithwick is co-author with Larry Berger of* I Will Sing Life: Voices from the Hole in the Wall Gang Camp *(1992) and with Brandt Goldstein of* ME v. Everybody: Absurd Contracts for an Absurd World *(2003). In this essay, which appeared in* Slate *in 2009, Lithwick speculates on why we are no longer scandalized by the idea of torture.*

1   In April of 2004, the world first learned that American soldiers in Iraq had abused detainees at the Abu Ghraib prison. Images first revealed on CBS and in the *New Yorker* showed prisoners standing hooded on a box with wires attached to their hands and genitals; piles of naked prisoners stacked into a pyramid; and detainees forced to simulate sexual acts upon one another, often with grinning GIs on hand to point and offer a jaunty thumbs up.

2   The reaction to the Abu Ghraib scandal was swift and bipartisan. Within days, President George W. Bush had offered a public apology for "the terrible and horrible acts," and his secretary of defense, Donald Rumsfeld, took "full responsibility" for the scandal, promising that the offenders would be brought to justice, because the victims "are human beings. They were in U.S. custody. Our country had an obligation to treat them right. We didn't do that." With the exception of a handful of outliers—Rush Limbaugh said the abuse was "no different than what happens at the Skull and Bones initiation," and Sen. James Inhofe, R-Okla., claimed to be "more outraged by the outrage than . . . by the treatment"— Americans reacted with almost universal surprise and revulsion.

3   In April of 2009, President Barack Obama released four government memos, written in 2002 and 2005, laying out legal justifications for prisoner abuse far more shocking than anything we had seen in the images from Abu Ghraib. Among other things, U.S. prisoners could be thrown into walls, water-boarded, shackled to the ceiling for hours, deprived of sleep for up to 11 days, and locked in coffinlike boxes. But the reaction could not have been more different. Former CIA Director Michael Hayden and former Attorney General Michael Mukasey quickly penned an editorial in the *Wall Street Journal* condemning the release of the memos and defending the interrogation techniques. Former Vice President Dick Cheney insisted that the Obama administration now needs to "put out the memos that showed the success of the effort." Conservative pundits casually likened water-boarding to prep school initiation and claimed that anyone who opposes prisoner abuse must simply hate America. The many ordinary Americans who want to see torture allegations investigated—evidently a majority of them, in fact—have been dismissed by these same pundits as members of a bloodthirsty "hard left." The president himself asks us all to move on. And if we're moving on, it can't have been all that bad.

4   In some ways, it's easy to account for the differences between the response to Abu Ghraib in 2004 and the reaction to the torture memos this month: The torture at Abu Ghraib was documented in pictures, rather than mere words,

making it harder to play down or parse out. The OLC's torture memos—written in dispassionate legalese with much legal citation—are easier to defend than the brutal images of what they permitted (and that's why the CIA saw fit to destroy its interrogation tapes). The abuses at Abu Ghraib were of low-level prisoners, whereas the torture memos purport to target "ticking time bombs": high-level terrorists with critical information about imminent strikes that continue to exist mainly in thought experiments and the mind of Dick Cheney.

But there's one other fact that accounts for the horror differential between 5 the torture memos and Abu Ghraib, and that's the fact of Abu Ghraib. Because, as I have suggested before, after Abu Ghraib, America seems to have lost its capacity to be truly shocked by anything America might do. As chilling and brutal as the images were at the time, they have, in the years between, lost much of their power to repel us. They have become—abetted by endless viewings of Jack Bauer on 24 and an interminable national debate about torture—emblems of what America is at least willing to consider doing. They are no longer postcards from the unthinkable. They are what we have become.

When we first saw those now-iconic photos from Abu Ghraib, most of us 6 still had no notion that our government would degrade and terrorize prisoners. We had no inkling at that time that—in violation of domestic and international law—the U.S. government had already water-boarded Khalid Sheikh Mohammed 183 times in one month in 2003. Discovery of the sexual humiliation and stress positions used at Abu Ghraib represented a brief and terrible loss of innocence for Americans. But maybe you can lose your innocence only once.

After Abu Ghraib, the idea that prisoners could be stripped naked and hu- 7 miliated, or terrorized by dogs, or piled up like Tinkertoys, was not just in the backs of our minds but also back on the table. Less than two years after we learned of the goings-on at Abu Ghraib, Congress had passed legislation legalizing many of the "alternative interrogation tactics"—the stress positions and sexual humiliations—that had so offended us months before. Prisoner abuse that flattened us in 2004 was normalized to the point that it was open to political debate only a year later. And once you have been desensitized to hoodings and nudity, is a little simulated drowning or being bounced off a wall really all that much worse?

The MPs caught abusing prisoners at Abu Ghraib later claimed that they did 8 so because they were merely following orders from superiors, orders to "soften up" the detainees who would then be more amenable to interrogation. I keep wondering whether they inadvertently softened up the rest of us as well. We have become so casual about torture that we now openly debate its efficacy—something nobody would have dared do in the first days after Abu Ghraib. The fight playing out between the left and the right now isn't "Did we waterboard?" We already knew we did. It is barely even "Was it legal?" Virtually nobody seriously argues that it was. The fight we are having in America now is "Did it work?" And if we manage to persuade ourselves that torture does work, whether it's legal or even moral will no longer matter. And such tactics will never be able to horrify us again.

COMPREHENSION

1. What is Lithwick's moral position regarding torture?
2. What happened at Abu Ghraib? How much information does Lithwick provide about this event?
3. How does Lithwick treat conservatives and liberals in this essay? Do you think she is balanced or biased? Justify your response.

RHETORIC

1. Lithwick wrote this article for *Slate*. (A slightly different version appeared subsequently in *Newsweek*.) What assumptions does she make about the values of her readers? Why might she have special authority in dealing with cases of torture?
2. Do you find Lithwick's title to be effective? Why or why not?
3. Why does Lithwick begin and end her essay with reference to Abu Ghraib?
4. What is Lithwick's premise, and how does she develop it? Do you find her argument to be convincing, or would you like to see more supporting reasons and evidence? Explain.
5. What comparisons does Lithwick draw in this essay? What is her purpose in using the comparative method?

WRITING

1. Write an analysis of the strategies that Lithwick uses to make a legal case about our complicity in torture.
2. **Writing an Argument:** Either support or rebut Lithwick's claim that "we are all torturers now."

NETWORKING
Applying 21st-Century Literacies

Conducting Online Research: Do research on Abu Ghraib, making sure to use only trustworthy sources. Then write a brief investigative report on your findings including hyperlinks to, as well as traditional citations of, your sources.

Is Texas America?

Molly Ivins

Molly Ivins (1944–2007), a humorous and typically irreverent newspaper commentator whose syndicated column appeared in about 350 newspapers, was born in California but grew up in Texas. The Lone Star State—and especially the Bush family—animated

Ivins's writing and prompted her satirical assessment of Texas; its people, politics, and culture. She called Texas the Great State, "reactionary, cantankerous, and hilarious." Growing up in an affluent family, she learned to confront her conservative Republican father, arguing with him over civil rights and the Vietnam War. Ivins attended Smith College and the Institute for Political Science in Paris before earning a master's degree at the Columbia Graduate School of Journalism. She worked for several newspapers, including the New York Times *and the monthly* Texas Observer, *and published six books, among them* Molly Ivins Can't Say That, Can She? *(1991) and two books on George Bush,* Shrub: The Short but Happy Life of George Bush *(2000) and* Bushwacked *(2003). "There are two kinds of humor," Ivins once observed; one "makes us chuckle about our foibles and shared humanity. The other kind holds people up to public contempt and ridicule. That's what I do." In fact, the following essay, published in the* Nation *in 2003, indicates that Ivins is adept at both kinds of humor.*

Well, sheesh. I don't know whether to warn you that because George Dubya 1 Bush is President the whole damn country is about to be turned into Texas (a singularly horrible fate: as the country song has it: "Lubbock on Everythang") or if I should try to stand up for us and convince the rest of the country we're not all that insane.

Truth is, I've spent much of my life trying, unsuccessfully, to explode the 2 myths about Texas. One attempts to explain—with all good will, historical evidence, nasty statistics and just a bow of recognition to our racism—that Texas is not *The Alamo* starring John Wayne. We're not *Giant,* we ain't a John Ford western. The first real Texan I ever saw on TV was *King of the Hill*'s Boomhauer, the guy who's always drinking beer and you can't understand a word he says.

So, how come trying to explode myths about Texas always winds up rein- 3 forcing them? After all these years, I do not think it is my fault. The fact is, it's a damned peculiar place. Given all the horseshit, there's bound to be a pony in here somewhere. Just by trying to be honest about it, one accidentally underlines its sheer strangeness.

Here's the deal on Texas. It's big. So big there's about five distinct and dif- 4 ferent places here, separated from one another geologically, topographically, botanically, ethnically, culturally and climatically. Hence our boring habit of specifying East, West and South Texas, plus the Panhandle and the Hill Country. The majority of the state's blacks live in East Texas, making it more like the Old South than the Old South is anymore. West Texas is, more or less, like *Giant,* except, like every place else in the state, it has an incurable tendency toward the tacky and all the cowboys are brown. South Texas is 80 percent Hispanic and a weird amalgam of cultures. You get names now like Shannon Rodriguez, Hannah Gonzalez and Tiffany Ruiz. Even the Anglos speak English with a Spanish accent. The Panhandle, which sticks up to damn near Kansas, is High Plains, like one of those square states, Nebraska or the Dakotas, except more brown folks. The Hill Country, smack dab in the middle, resembles nothing else in the state.

Plus, plopped on top of all this, we have three huge cities, all among the ten 5 largest in the country. Houston is Los Angeles with the climate of Calcutta, Dallas is Dutch (clean, orderly and conformist), while San Antonio is Monterrey North.

Copyright © 2002 by Karen Caldicott.

Many years ago I wrote of this state: "The reason the sky is bigger here is because there aren't any trees. The reason folks here eat grits is because they ain't
got no taste. Cowboys mostly stink and it's hot, oh God, is it hot. . . . Texas is a
mosaic of cultures, which overlap in several parts of the state, with the darker
layers on the bottom. The cultures are black, Chicano, Southern, freak, suburban and shitkicker. (Shitkicker is dominant.) They are all rotten for women." All
that's changed in thirty years is that suburban is now dominant, shitkicker isn't
so ugly as it once was and the freaks are now Goths or something. So it could be
argued we're becoming more civilized.

6   In fact, it was always easy to argue that: Texas has symphony orchestras
and great universities and perfect jewels of art museums (mostly in Fort Worth,
of all places). It has lots of people who birdwatch, write PhD theses on esoteric
subjects and speak French, for chrissake. But what still makes Texas Texas is
that it's ignorant, cantankerous and ridiculously friendly. Texas is still resistant
to Howard Johnsons, Interstate highways and some forms of phoniness. It is
the place least likely to become a replica of everyplace else. It's authentically
awful, comic and weirdly charming, all at the same time.

7   Culturally, Texans rather resemble both Alaskans (hunt, fish, hate government) and Australians (drink beer, hate snobs). The food is quite good—
Mexican, barbecue, chili, shrimp and chicken-fried steak, an acquired taste. The
music is country, blues, folk, mariachi, rockabilly and everything else you can
think of. Mexican music—norteño, ranchero—is poised to cross over, as black
music did in the 1950s.

8   If you want to understand George W. Bush—unlike his daddy, an unfortunate example of a truly Texas-identified citizen—you have to stretch your imagination around a weird Texas amalgam: religion, anti-intellectualism and
machismo. All big, deep strains here, but still an odd combination. Then add that
Bush is just another li'l upper-class white boy out trying to prove he's tough.

The politics are probably the weirdest thing about Texas. The state has gone 9
from one-party Democrat to one-party Republican in thirty years. Lyndon said
when he signed the Civil Rights Act in 1964 that it would take two generations
and cost the Democrats the South. Right on both counts. We like to think we're
"past race" in Texas, but of course East Texas remains an ugly, glaring exception. After James Byrd Jr. was dragged to death near Jasper, only one prominent
white politician attended his funeral—US Senator Kay Bailey Hutchison.
Dubya, then governor, put the kibosh on the anti–hate crimes bill named in
Byrd's memory. (The deal-breaker for Bush was including gays and lesbians. At
a meeting last year of the Texas Civil Liberties Union board, vicious hate crimes
against gays in both Dallas and Houston were discussed. I asked the board
member from Midland if they'd been having any trouble with gay-bashing out
there. "Hell, honey," she said, with that disastrous frankness one can grow so
fond of, "there's not a gay in Midland would come out of the closet for fear
people would think they're a Democrat.")

Among the various strains of Texas right-wingism (it is factually incorrect to 10
call it conservatism) is some leftover loony John Birchism, now morphed into mi-
litias; country-club economic conservatism, à la George Bush *père;* and the usual
batty antigovernment strain. Of course Texas grew on the tender mercies of the
federal government—rural electrification, dams, generations of master pork-
barrel politicians and vast subsidies to the oil and gas industry. But that has never
interfered with Texans' touching but entirely erroneous belief that this is the Frontier, and that in the Old West every man pulled his own weight and depended on
no one else. The myth of rugged individualism continues to afflict a generation
raised entirely in suburbs with names like "Flowering Forest Hills of Lubbock."

The Populist movement was born in the Texas Hill Country, as genuinely 11
democratic an uprising as this country has ever known. It produced legendary
politicians for generations, including Ralph Yarborough, Sam Rayburn, Lyndon
and even into the 1990s, with Agriculture Commissioner Jim Hightower. I think
it is not gone, but only sleeping.

Texans retain an exaggerated sense of state identification, routinely identifying 12
themselves when abroad as Texans, rather than Americans or from the United
States. That aggravated provincialism has three sources. First, the state is so big
(though not so big as Alaska, as they are sure to remind us) that it can take a
couple of days hard travel just to get out of it. Second, we reinforce the sense of
difference by requiring kids to study Texas history, including roughly ten years
as an independent country. In state colleges, the course in Texas government is
mandatory. Third, even national advertising campaigns pitch brands with a
Texas accent here and certain products, like the pickup truck, are almost invariably sold with a Texas pitch. (Makes sense: Texas leads the nation with more
than four million registered pickups.)

The founding myth is the Alamo. I was raised on the Revised Standard Ver- 13
sion, which holds that while it was stupid of Travis and the gang to be there at
all (Sam Houston told them to get the hell out), it was still an amazing last

stand. Stephen Harrigan in *The Gates of the Alamo* is closer to reality, but even he admits in the end there was something romantic and even noble about the episode, like having served in the Abraham Lincoln Brigade during the Spanish Civil War.

14 According to the demographers at Texas A&M (itself a source of much Texas lore), Texas will become "majority minority" in 2008. Unfortunately, we won't see it in the voting patterns for at least a generation, and by then the Republicans will have the state so tied up by redistricting (recently the subject of a massive standoff, now over, in the legislature), it's unlikely to shift for another generation beyond that. The Christian right is heavily dominant in the Texas Republican Party. It was the genius of Karl Rove/George W. Bush to straddle the divide between the Christian right and the country club conservatives, which is actually a significant class split. The politics of resentment plays a large role on the Christian right: Fundamentalists are perfectly aware that they are held in contempt by "the intellectuals." (William Brann of Waco once observed, "The trouble with our Texas Baptists is that we do not hold them under water long enough." He was shot to death by an irate Baptist.) In Texas, "intellectual" is often used as a synonym for "snob." George W. Bush perfectly exemplifies that attitude.

15 Here in the National Laboratory for Bad Government, we have an antiquated and regressive tax structure—high property, high sales, no income tax. We consistently rank near the bottom by every measure of social service, education and quality of life (leading to one of our state mottoes, "Thank God for Mississippi"). Yet the state is incredibly rich in more than natural resources. The economy is now fully diversified, so plunges in the oil market can no longer throw the state into the bust cycle.

16 It is widely believed in Texas that the highest purpose of government is to create "a healthy bidness climate." The legislature is so dominated by special interests that the gallery where the lobbyists sit is called "the owners' box." The consequences of unregulated capitalism, of special interests being able to buy government through campaign contributions, are more evident here because Texas is "first and worst" in this area. That Enron was a Texas company is no accident: Texas was also Ground Zero in the savings-and-loan scandals, is continually the site of major ripoffs by the insurance industry and has a rich history of gigantic chicanery going way back. Leland Beatty, an agricultural consultant, calls Enron "Billie Sol Estes Goes to College." Economists call it "control fraud" when a corporation is rotten from the head down. I sometimes think Texas government is a case of control fraud too.

17 We are currently saddled with a right-wing ideologue sugar daddy, James Leininger out of San Antonio, who gives immense campaign contributions and wants school vouchers, abstinence education and the like in return. The result is a crew of breathtakingly right-wing legislators. This session, Representative Debbie Riddle of Houston said during a hearing, "Where did this idea come from that everybody deserves free education, free medical care, free whatever? It comes from Moscow, from Russia. It comes straight out of the pit of hell."

Texans for Lawsuit Reform, *aka* the bidness lobby, is a major player and has ef- 18
fectively eviscerated the judiciary with a two-pronged attack. While round after
round of "tort reform" was shoved through the legislature, closing off access to
the courts and protecting corporations from liability for their misdeeds, Karl
Rove was busy electing all nine state Supreme Court justices. So even if you
should somehow manage to get into court, you are faced with a bench noted for
its canine fidelity to corporate special interests.

Here's how we make progress in Texas. Two summers ago, Governor 19
Goodhair Perry (the man has a head of hair every Texan can be proud of, regardless of party) appointed an Enron executive to the Public Utilities Commission. The next day, Governor Goodhair got a $25,000 check from Ken Lay. Some
thought there might be a connection. The guv was forced to hold a press conference, at which he explained that the whole thing was "totally coincidental." So
that was a big relief.

We don't have a sunshine law in Texas; it's more like a partly cloudy law. 20
But even here a major state appointee has to fill out a bunch of forms that are
then public record. When the governor's office put out the forms on the Enron
guy, members of the press, that alert guardian watchdog of democracy, noticed
that the question about any unfortunate involvement with law enforcement
looked funny. The governor's office had whited out the answers. A sophisticated cover-up. The alert guardian watchdogs were on the trail. We soon un-
covered a couple of minor traffic violations and the following item: While out
hunting a few years earlier, the Enron guy accidentally shot a whooping crane.
As a result he had to pay a $15,000 fine under what is known in Texas as the In
Danger Species Act. We print this. A state full of sympathetic hunters reacted
with, "Hell, anybody could accidentally shoot a whooper." But the press stayed
on the story and was able to report that the guy shot the whooper while on a
goose hunt. Now the whooper is a large bird—runs up to five feet tall. The
goose—short. Now we have a state full of hunters saying, "Hell, if this boy is
too dumb to tell a whooper from a goose, maybe he shouldn't be regulatin'
public utilities." He was forced to resign.

As Willie Nelson sings, if we couldn't laugh, we would all go insane. This 21
is our redeeming social value and perhaps our one gift to progressives outside
our borders. We do laugh. We have no choice. We have to have fun while trying
to stave off the forces of darkness because we hardly ever win, so it's the only
fun we get to have. We find beer and imagination helpful. The Billion Bubba
March, the Spam-o-rama, the time we mooned the Klan, being embedded with
the troops at the Holiday Inn in Ardmore, Oklahoma, singing "I'm Just an Ass-
hole from El Paso" with Kinky Friedman and the Texas Jewboys, and "Up
Against the Wall, Redneck Mother" with Ray Wylie Hubbard laughing at the
loonies in the lege—does it get better than this? The late Bill Kugle of Athens is
buried in the Texas State Cemetery. On the front of his stone are listed his service in the Marines in World War II, his years in the legislature, other titles and
honors. On the back of the stone is, "He never voted for a Republican and never
had much to do with them either."

22   We have lost some great freedom fighters in Texas during the past year. Billie Carr, the great Houston political organizer (you'd've loved her: She got invited to the White House during the middle of the Monica mess, sashayed through the receiving line, looked Bill Clinton in the eye and said, "You dumb son of a bitch"), always said she wanted her funeral to be like her whole life in politics: It should start half an hour late, she wanted a balanced delegation of pallbearers— one black, one brown, two women—and she wanted an open casket and a name tag stuck over her left tit that said, "Hi there! My name is Billie Carr." We did it all for her.

23   At the funeral of Malcolm McGregor, the beloved legislator and bibliophile from El Paso, we heard "The Eyes of Texas" and the Aggie War Hymn played on the bagpipes. At the service for Maury Maverick Jr. of San Antonio, and at his request, J. Frank Dobie's poem "The Mustangs" was read by the poet Naomi Shihab Nye. The last stanza is:

> So sometimes yet, in the realities of silence and solitude,
> For a few people unhampered a while by things,
> The mustangs walk out with dawn, stand high, then
> Sweep away, wild with sheer life, and free, free, free—
> Free of all confines of time and flesh.

COMPREHENSION

1. How does Ivins answer the question posed by her title? In other words, what does Texas have that the United States in general possesses? What, according to Ivins, is unique about Texas?
2. In paragraph 9, Ivins writes, "The politics are probably the weirdest thing about Texas." What examples does she give to support her statement?
3. Ivins seems to warn us about the excesses of Texas life and politics, but clearly she is also fascinated by her home state. Does she reconcile these conflicting perspectives? Why or why not?

RHETORIC

1. What is Ivins's claim or main proposition? What are her minor propositions? Do you think that her argument is sound or valid? Justify your response.
2. How does Ivins establish herself as an authority on Texas? Would you accuse her of bias? Why or why not? Why might her opinions be congenial to an audience reading the *Nation*?
3. Ivins uses phrases like "Well, sheesh" (paragraph 1), "plopped on top"(paragraph 5), and "for crissake" (paragraph 6) in the essay. What is the effect of this colloquial style and tone? What is her purpose?
4. Locate varieties of humor in the essay. Do you think that Ivins employs humor effectively to advance her argument? Explain your response.
5. The essay contains four main sections. What is the core topic of each section? How do these topics overlap? What transitions serve to link the parts?

6. Throughout the essay, Ivins alludes to many aspects of Texas life, culture, people, and politics that we might not be familiar with. Do these allusions detract from the essay or make it too topical? Why, for instance, would Ivins want to end her essay with reference to the deaths of two Texans and an allusion to a poem by J. Frank Dobie?

WRITING

1. Write a humorous essay on the state in which you grew up. Decide in advance what varieties of humor and what tone you want to use.
2. Go online or to a library and find out more about a Texan (for instance, George W. Bush), a Texas trait (like *machismo*), or a Texas institution (for example, the state legislature), and then write an essay that seeks to either confirm or refute Ivins's presentation of the subject.
3. **Writing an Argument:** In an essay, argue for or against the proposition that Ivins is too biased and cruel in her exposé of Texas. Defend or refute her argument on a point-by-point basis.

NETWORKING
Applying 21st-Century Literacies

Reading a Visual in Context: In a two- or three-page response, summarize, analyze, and interpret the illustration that accompanies this essay (see p. 414). In your response, consider how it works with this piece and what each text lends to the other.

Cyberspace: If You Don't Love It, Leave It

Esther Dyson

Esther Dyson (b. 1951) was born in Zurich, Switzerland; grew up in Princeton, New Jersey; and received a BA in economics from Harvard University. She is the daughter of Freeman Dyson, a physicist prominent in arms control. She is the editor and publisher of the widely respected computer newsletter Release 1.0, *which is circulated to many computer industry leaders. She is also chairperson of the Electronic Frontier Foundation and on the boards of the Santa Fe Institute, the Global Business Network, and the Institute for East/West Studies. She served as a reporter for* Forbes *magazine for four years. The following essay appeared in the* New York Times Magazine *in July 1995. In it, Dyson defends the free-market approach to cyberspace content, arguing that regulation of the Internet is simply impossible and counterproductive.*

1   Something in the American psyche loves new frontiers. We hanker after wide-open spaces; we like to explore; we like to make rules instead of follow them. But in this age of political correctness and other intrusions on our national cult of independence, it's hard to find a place where you can go and be yourself without worrying about the neighbors.

2   There is such a place: cyberspace. Lost in the furor over porn on the Net is the exhilarating sense of freedom that this new frontier once promised—and still does in some quarters. Formerly a playground for computer nerds and techies, cyberspace now embraces every conceivable constituency: schoolchildren, flirtatious singles, Hungarian-Americans, accountants—along with pederasts and porn fans. Can they all get along? Or will our fear of kids surfing for cyberporn behind their bedroom doors provoke a crackdown?

3   The first order of business is to grasp what cyberspace *is*. It might help to leave behind metaphors of highways and frontiers and to think instead of real estate. Real estate, remember, is an intellectual, legal, artificial environment constructed *on top of* land. Real estate recognizes the difference between parkland and shopping mall, between red-light zone and school district, between church, state and drugstore.

4   In the same way, you could think of cyberspace as a giant and unbounded world of virtual real estate. Some property is privately owned and rented out; other property is common land; some places are suitable for children, and others are best avoided by all but the kinkiest citizens. Unfortunately, it's those places that are now capturing the popular imagination: places that offer bomb-making instructions, pornography, advice on how to procure stolen credit cards. They make cyberspace sound like a nasty place. Good citizens jump to a conclusion: Better regulate it.

5   The most recent manifestation of this impulse is the Exon-Coats Amendment, a well-meaning but misguided bill drafted by Senators Jim Exon, Democrat of Nebraska, and Daniel R. Coats, Republican of Indiana, to make cyberspace "safer" for children. Part of the telecommunications reform bill passed by the Senate and awaiting consideration by the House, the amendment would outlaw making "indecent communication" available to anyone under 18.[1] Then there's the Amateur Action bulletin board case, in which the owners of a porn service in Milpitas, Calif., were convicted in a Tennessee court of violating "community standards" after a local postal inspector requested that the material be transmitted to him.

6   Regardless of how many laws or lawsuits are launched, regulation won't work.

7   Aside from being unconstitutional, using censorship to counter indecency and other troubling "speech" fundamentally misinterprets the nature of cyberspace. Cyberspace isn't a frontier where wicked people can grab unsuspecting children, nor is it a giant television system that can beam offensive messages at unwilling viewers. In this kind of real estate, users have to *choose* where they

---

[1]The Communication Decency Act (CDA) was passed by Congress, but the Supreme Court ruled that it was unconstitutional in 1996.

visit, what they see, what they do. It's optional, and it's much easier to bypass a place on the Net than it is to avoid walking past an unsavory block of stores on the way to your local 7-Eleven.

Put plainly, cyberspace is a voluntary destination—in reality, many destina- 8 tions. You don't just get "onto the net"; you have to go someplace in particular. That means that people can choose where to go and what to see. Yes, commu- nity standards should be enforced, but those standards should be set by cyber- space communities themselves, not by the courts or by politicians in Washington. What we need isn't Government control over all these electronic communities: We need self-rule.

What makes cyberspace so alluring is precisely the way in which it's *different* 9 from shopping malls, television, highways and other terrestrial jurisdictions. But let's define the territory:

First, there are private e-mail conversations, akin to the conversations you 10 have over the telephone or voice mail. These are private and consensual and require no regulation at all.

Second, there are information and entertainment services, where people 11 can download anything from legal texts and lists of "great new restaurants" to game software or dirty pictures. These places are like bookstores, malls and movie houses—places where you go to buy something. The customer needs to request an item or sign up for a subscription; stuff (especially pornography) is not sent out to people who don't ask for it. Some of these services are free or included as part of a broader service like Compuserve or America Online; oth- ers charge and may bill their customers directly.

Third, there are "real" communities—groups of people who communicate 12 among themselves. In real-estate terms, they're like bars or restaurants or bath- houses. Each active participant contributes to a general conversation, generally through posted messages. Other participants may simply listen or watch. Some are supervised by a moderator; others are more like bulletin boards—anyone is free to post anything. Many of these services started out unmoderated but are now imposing rules to keep out unwanted advertising, extraneous discussions or increasingly rude participants. Without a moderator, the decibel level often gets too high.

Ultimately, it's the rules that determine the success of such places. Some of 13 the rules are determined by the supplier of content; some of the rules concern prices and membership fees. The rules may be simple: "Only high-quality con- tent about oil-industry liability and pollution legislation: $120 an hour." Or: "This forum is unmoderated, and restricted to information about copyright is- sues. People who insist on posting advertising or unrelated material will be asked to desist (and may eventually be barred)." Or: "Only children 8 to 12, on school-related topics and only clean words. The moderator will decide what's acceptable."

Cyberspace communities evolve just the way terrestrial communities do: 14 People with like-minded interests band together. Every cyberspace community has its own character. Overall, the communities on Compuserve tend to be more techy or professional; those on America Online, affluent young singles; Prodigy, family oriented. Then there are independents like Echo, a hip, downtown New York service, or Women's Wire, targeted to women who want to avoid the male culture prevalent elsewhere on the Net. There's SurfWatch, a new program allowing access only to locations deemed suitable for children. On the Internet itself, there are lots of passionate noncommercial discussion groups on topics ranging from Hungarian politics (Hungary-Online) to copyright law.

15   And yes, there are also porn-oriented services, where people share dirty pictures and communicate with one another about all kinds of practices, often anonymously. Whether these services encourage the fantasies they depict is subject to debate—the same debate that has raged about pornography in other media. But the point is that no one is forcing this stuff on anybody.

16   What's unique about cyberspace is that it liberates us from the tyranny of government, where everyone lives by the rule of the majority. In a democracy, minority groups and minority preferences tend to get squeezed out, whether they are minorities of race and culture or minorities of individual taste. Cyberspace allows communities of any size and kind to flourish; in cyberspace, communities are chosen by the users, not forced on them by accidents of geography. This freedom gives the rules that preside in cyberspace a moral authority that rules in terrestrial environments don't have. Most people are stuck in the country of their birth, but if you don't like the rules of a cyberspace community, you can just sign off. Love it or leave it. Likewise, if parents don't like the rules of a given cyberspace community, they can restrict their children's access to it.

17   What's likely to happen in cyberspace is the formation of new communities, free of the constraints that cause conflict on earth. Instead of a global village, which is a nice dream but impossible to manage, we'll have invented another world of self-contained communities that cater to their own members' inclinations without interfering with anyone else's. The possibility of a real market-style evolution of governance is at hand. In cyberspace, we'll be able to test and evolve rules governing what needs to be governed—intellectual property, content and access control, rules about privacy and free speech. Some communities will allow anyone in; others will restrict access to members who qualify on one basis or another. Those communities that prove self-sustaining will prosper (and perhaps grow and split into subsets with ever-more-particular interests and identities). Those that can't survive—either because people lose interest or get scared off—will simply wither away.

18   In the near future, explorers in cyberspace will need to get better at defining and identifying their communities. They will need to put in place—and accept—their own local governments, just as the owners of expensive real estate often prefer to have their own security guards rather than call in the police. But they will rarely need help from any terrestrial government.

19   Of course, terrestrial governments may not agree. What to do, for instance, about pornography? The answer is labeling—not banning—questionable

material. In order to avoid censorship and lower the political temperature, it makes sense for cyberspace participants themselves to agree on a scheme for questionable items, so that people or automatic filters can avoid them. In other words, posting pornography in "alt.sex.bestiality" would be OK; it's easy enough for software manufacturers to build an automatic filter that would prevent you—or your child—from ever seeing that item on a menu. (It's as if all the items were wrapped with labels on the wrapper.) Someone who posted the same material under the title "Kid-Fun" could be sued for mislabeling.

Without a lot of fanfare, private enterprises and local groups are already 20 producing a variety of labeling and ranking services, along with kid-oriented sites like Kidlink, EdWeb and Kids' Space. People differ in their tastes and values and can find services or reviewers on the Net that suit them in the same way they select books and magazines. Or they can wander freely if they prefer, making up their own itinerary.

In the end, our society needs to grow up. Growing up means understand- 21 ing that there are no perfect answers, no all-purpose solutions, no government-sanctioned safe havens. We haven't created a perfect society on earth and we won't have one in cyberspace either. But at least we can have individual choice—and individual responsibility.

COMPREHENSION

1. The title of the essay is a variation of a phrase popularized in the 1960s. What is the original expression, and what was its significance? What is its relevance to this essay?
2. What is Dyson's thesis? Is it stated explicitly? If so, where in the essay does it occur? If it is merely suggested, how is it suggested, and where?
3. There are many forms of new media that are not considered communities. Why does Dyson refer to cyberspace as a community?
4. According to Dyson, what distinguishes cyberspace from physical space?
5. What does Dyson mean when she states that cyberspace needs "self-rule" (paragraph 8)?

RHETORIC

1. How does Dyson use her introduction to foreshadow her main concerns about censorship in cyberspace?
2. How does Dyson use metaphor in paragraphs 10–12 to help us understand the structure of cyberspace? Why is metaphor a particularly useful literary device when explaining a new concept?
3. Key to Dyson's views on cyberspace is that it is a "voluntary destination" (paragraph 8). What evidence does Dyson present that it is voluntary? What argument can be made that it is not always "voluntary"?
4. Who is the implied audience for this essay? What level of education does one need to have and how sophisticated about the world of cyberspace does one need to be in order to comprehend and process the author's views? Explain your answer.

5. Dyson refers to laws, rules, and regulations as strategies that various interest groups may use to determine access to content in cyberspace. How does Dyson distinguish these three related tactics? What significance does differentiating these methods have in her presentation of her argument?
6. Dyson concludes her essay with an analogy between human society and cyberspace culture. Why does she save this final support for last? How does it extend her argument rather than merely restate it?

WRITING

1. In paragraph 17, Dyson refers to the "global village," a term coined by the media critic Marshall McLuhan. For a research project, study McLuhan's views on the nature of the global village, and compare and contrast them to Dyson's views of the nature of cyberspace.
2. **Writing an Argument:** Dyson argues that technology can create filters, labeling and ranking services to prevent children from viewing inappropriate material. In an essay, argue for or against the proposition that there can be a nontechnological solution to this issue—for example, instilling values in children or developing a society that does not create a mystique about taboo subject matter.

NETWORKING
Applying 21st-Century Literacies

Exploring Virtual Communities: In a comparison-and-contrast essay, select three cyberspace communities and describe each one's character (refer to Dyson's reference to cyberspace characters in paragraph 14).

Obama vs. Marx

Alan Wolfe

Alan Wolfe (b. 1942) is an American educator and journalist. He was born in Philadelphia, attending Temple University (BS, 1963) and the University of Pennsylvania (PhD, 1967), where he majored in sociology and political science. Currently a professor at Queens College, City University of New York, Wolfe straddles the academic and journalistic worlds. He writes, "I am trying to keep alive a tradition of informed commentary on public affairs in the face of sterile academic research and a journalistic tradition that refuses to go into historical and political background." Among Wolfe's many books are The Seamy Side of Democracy *(1973, 1978),* One Nation, After All *(1998),* Moral Freedom *(2001),* Return to Greatness *(2005), and* The Future of

Liberalism *(2009). In this essay, published in the* New Republic *in 2009, Wolfe offers insights into liberalism, conservatism, and socialism—and where Barack Obama fits within these political traditions.*

The word "liberal" was first used in its modern political sense in 1812, when   1
Spaniards wrote a new constitution liberating themselves from monarchical
rule. As it happens, the word "socialism" originated in roughly the same period; it came into existence to describe the utopian ideas of the British reformer
Robert Owen. Such timing suggests two possibilities: Either the fates of liberalism and socialism are so interlinked that one is all but synonymous with the
other—or the two are actually competitors developed to meet similar conditions, in which case victory for one marks the defeat of the other.

These days, one could be forgiven for believing that the former conclusion   2
is correct. It was not so long ago that conservatives were equating liberalism
with fascism; today, they have executed a 180-degree swing in order to argue
that liberalism is actually synonymous with socialism. "Americans," proclaimed Republican Senator Jim DeMint at the recent meeting of the Conservative Political Action Conference, "have gotten a glimpse of the big-government
plans of Obama and the Democrats and are ready to stand up, speak out, and,
yes, even to take to the streets to stop America's slide into socialism." But it isn't
just the right that has worked itself into a frenzy; on the question of whether we
are approaching a new age of socialism, there seems to be remarkable political
consensus. In recent weeks, the covers of *National Review* ("Our Socialist Future"), the *Nation* ("Reinventing Capitalism, Reimagining Socialism"), and
Newsweek ("We Are All Socialists Now") have—respectively—lamented, heralded, and observed the coming rise of socialism.

But all these commentators—right, left, and middle—may want to take a   3
deep breath. We aren't headed for an era of socialism at all, since socialism is
not a natural outgrowth of liberalism. Liberalism is a political philosophy that
seeks to extend personal autonomy to as many people as possible, if necessary
through positive government action; socialism, by contrast, seeks as much
equality as possible, even if doing so curtails individual liberty. These are differences of kind, not degree—differences that have historically placed the two philosophies in direct competition. Today, socialism is on the decline, in large part
because liberalism has lately been on the rise. And, if Barack Obama's version
of liberalism succeeds, socialism will be even less popular than it already is.

Socialism was born in political conditions that no longer exist. In its most radi-   4
cal form, the one associated with Marx and Engels, it had far more in common
with European romanticism than with the moderate reformism of a John Stuart
Mill or a Thomas Hill Green, two of Great Britain's most important liberal
thinkers. Socialism seemed possible when anything seemed possible. It was an
ideology of progress when progress was an unquestioned good. Even its less
revolutionary adherents, those more likely to call themselves social democrats
rather than socialists, believed in economic planning and social transformation

in ways that seem embarrassing now. Once it appeared possible for government to control the major means of production. Now it seems impossible to build a high-speed rail between Boston and Washington.

5   The story of socialism's decline is essentially a European story. Socialism has never had much appeal in the United States, but that was not always the case on the other side of the Atlantic. The temptation toward socialism was not just on display in Eastern Europe; in the western half of the continent, too, left-wing governments and parties quite openly embraced socialist programs for much of the twentieth century. Those days, however, are largely over. In Britain, the Labour Party no longer pays much homage to its socialist roots. Tony Blair revived the party only after leading a campaign to alter its notorious Clause IV, which had explicitly endorsed the "common ownership of the means of production." The revised version proclaimed Labour a "democratic socialist" party, but the wording was so vague, and Blair so consistently ignored it, that its purposes were symbolic only. On this crucial point, Gordon Brown has not backtracked in the least.

6   Elsewhere in Europe, the same movement against socialism dominates the political landscape. Socialism in the form of social democracy was long the governing ideology of Scandinavia, but Swedes never much liked the idea of nationalizing industries, and the Danes have for some time been governed by conservatives—called, in European parlance, liberals. Angela Merkel is anything but a socialist; the same is true for Nicolas Sarkozy. "Americanization" was once a dirty word in France. Now it fairly well describes Sarkozy's domestic program. There is talk of reforming the country's Napoleonic legal system with

something more resembling our insistence upon rights. Public bureaucracies, including France's complex system of higher education, are to be reformed along more "modern"—read American—lines. Spain, meanwhile, does have a socialist government; but its leftism is a reaction to the extreme conservatism that governed the country for much of the twentieth century. For their part, the Eastern European countries now outdo each other in their love for the free market.

It is true that European societies are committed to an active role for govern- 7 ment and that a number of their public policies, such as national health insurance, owe something to the socialist tradition. But the roots of the European welfare state are much more complex than is commonly acknowledged. European ideas about government have Christian as well as socialist origins. Two great papal encyclicals—*Rerum Novarum* (1891) and *Quadragesimo Anno* (1931)— spurred Catholic countries to adopt the idea that government should protect the rights of workers and that society has an obligation to help all. One of Great Britain's most eloquent defenders of equality, the Fabian socialist R. H. Tawney, was a devout Protestant. After World War II, Christian parties siphoned off votes that might have gone to more radical politicians by emphasizing traditions of solidarity and community. If Obama is really leading us down the road to Europeanization, an equally accurate *Newsweek* headline might be, "We Are All Christian Democrats Now."

And the origins of big government in Europe run deeper than either Marx 8 or Christian politics. It is not exactly socialism that has stifled so much of French economic life with cumbersome regulations but a blunderbuss government that dates back to the *ancien régime*. Socialist politicians in France did not invent the idea of big government. They instead relied on traditions of *étatism* that had long preceded them. Given all this, it's no wonder that liberalism is experiencing a comeback in Europe. The revival of liberal sentiment is as much a reaction against both Christianity and feudalism as anything else.

As for Obama, it is absurd to view his program as a step toward socialism. First 9 of all, while he is planning to raise taxes, they will still be lower than what is common in other Western countries. And, according to Brian Reidl of the Heritage Foundation, Obama's budget would increase government spending from 20 percent of GDP to 22 percent. Is it really possible that a society is capitalist when government spending represents 20 percent of GDP—but socialist at 22 percent?

Next, consider Obama's stances on the defining issues of our time. At most, 10 his administration might nationalize banks temporarily; a socialist would nationalize them for good. He proposes to fix free trade, not abolish it. He does not favor a single-payer health care system, and any proposal he eventually puts forward is going to involve competition in some form. (It is worth noting that arguably the biggest beneficiaries of health care reform will be businesses, many of which struggle to pay their employees' health care costs.) To address global warming, Obama favors cap and trade, a market-oriented solution to our gravest environmental problem. That's right: This alleged socialist has so much faith in capitalism, he is willing to put the future of our planet more or less in the hands of a market.

11   What these ideas have in common is, first, an attachment to economic freedom that no self-respecting socialist would countenance. In fact, most of Obama's measures are designed to save, not destroy, the instruments of capitalism—businesses and the markets in which they compete. Should Obama get everything he wants, liberals will have once again—as has happened so often in the United States—gone a long way toward rescuing capitalism from its worst excesses.

12   Moreover, it has for some time now been established that the moderate use of government to improve the lives of large numbers of citizens, while producing minor advances in equality, is primarily about giving citizens more liberty. People who, with the help of government, need not postpone medical care or can avoid going into lifetime debt to pay for it are freer people. Progressive taxation, especially the way Obama talks about it, is not about confiscating the wealth of the rich but about giving those at the bottom of the ladder more opportunity. Modest enhancements of what has been called "positive liberty" do not come anywhere close to socialism; they instead make liberalism's benefits more widespread.

13   Conservatives seem to think that any increase in the size of government means a step toward socialism. But, if this is the case, then George W. Bush ought to come out of the closet as a socialist. It is not just that Bush spent uncountable sums on his Iraqi adventure. Nor is it that he put Keynes to shame by spending money he did not have. Bush, at least at the start of his presidency, wanted to be known for his compassion and sponsored reforms of both Medicare and education that, had a Democrat proposed them, would have been widely denounced by conservatives as socialism run rampant. Socialism, in the Republican imagination, is only something Democrats do, never something they themselves do.

14   In the United States, liberalism is the alternative to which we turn when conservatism fails, just as in Europe it is what people look to when socialism sputters, Christianity no longer appeals, and the old feudal statism appears moribund. Liberalism has always been more comfortable finding its place between the extremes than mimicking either one of them. Americans tend to be most familiar with the ways in which liberalism distinguishes itself from conservatism. But liberalism has gone to great lengths to distinguish itself from the left as well—from the gulag, the Soviet occupation of Eastern European countries against the will of their people, and all the various forms of socialism from Baathism to Castroism associated with Third World tyrants. These distinctions have reaffirmed the liberal dedication to human rights—and this at a time when conservatives like Bush and Cheney were prepared to dispense with them. Conservatives may denounce Obama for his socialism, but it is he, and not they, who is returning the United States to such liberal commitments as the separation of powers, habeas corpus, and transparency in government.

If Barack Obama is a socialist, he sure is good at fooling people. Americans 15 seem to like his quiet demeanor, his sense of caution, his efforts at inclusion. With its emphasis on intellectual modesty and pragmatism, liberalism is a temperament as well as a set of ideas; and Obama's disposition is quintessentially liberal.

We cannot at this point know what his legacy will be. But we do know what 16 it will not be. Eight years of Obama, and the United States has its best chance in decades to return to the liberalism that has long defined its heritage. There would be no greater blow to socialism—in America, in Europe, or anywhere else—than for this venture to succeed.

COMPREHENSION

1. How does Wolfe define liberalism and socialism?
2. According to Wolfe, is Barack Obama a liberal, socialist, or conservative? Justify your response by referring to the text.
3. What explanation does Wolfe give for the decline of socialism in Europe? What role has the Christian Church played in this process?

RHETORIC

1. Wolfe's essay appeared in the *New Republic*, a magazine devoted to politics. What aspects of diction, tone, syntax, and paragraph development suggest that he is writing for a highly educated audience—and a readership interested in political discourse?
2. Where does Wolfe state most concisely the thesis or claim that governs his essay?
3. Wolfe divides his essay into three parts. What topic dominates each part? How are the parts interrelated? Comment on whether or not you think the essay is unified.
4. How does Wolfe use comparison and contrast, extended definition, and causal analysis to develop his essay? Identify specific passages that illustrate these rhetorical strategies.
5. Based on your analysis of Wolfe's argument, in what ways would you agree or disagree with the writer's understanding of Barack Obama's politics? Refer to the text to explain your answer. Be as specific as possible.

WRITING

1. Explain your political beliefs in a brief essay.
2. Write an extended definition of liberalism, conservatism, or socialism. Use the comparative method to distinguish your choice from the other two ideologies.
3. **Writing an Argument:** Given your understanding of President Barack Obama's policies, argue for or against the proposition that he is a socialist.

NETWORKING
Applying 21st-Century Literacies

Comparing and Contrasting Visuals: What purpose and point does the photograph (p. 425) that accompanies this essay serve? Write an essay comparing and contrasting its relationship with this article, to the relationship of the illustration (p. 414) in Molly Ivins's "Is Texas America?" with that essay.

Grant and Lee: A Study in Contrasts

Bruce Catton

Bruce Catton (1899–1978) was born in Petosky, Michigan. After serving in the Navy during World War I, he attended Oberlin College but left in his junior year to pursue a career in journalism. From 1942 to 1952, Catton served in the government, first on the War Production Board and later in the departments of Commerce and the Interior. He left government to devote himself to literary work as a columnist for the Nation *and a historian of the Civil War. His many works include* A Stillness at Appomattox *(1953), which won the 1954 Pulitzer Prize;* Mr. Lincoln's Army *(1951);* The Centennial History of the Civil War *(1961–1965); and* Prefaces to History *(1970). In the following selection, Catton presents vivid portraits of two well-known but little understood figures from American history.*

1   When Ulysses S. Grant and Robert E. Lee met in the parlor of a modest house at Appomattox Court House, Virginia, on April 9, 1865, to work out the terms for the surrender of Lee's Army of Northern Virginia, a great chapter in American life came to a close, and a great new chapter began.

2   These men were bringing the Civil War to its virtual finish. To be sure, other armies had yet to surrender, and for a few days the fugitive Confederate government would struggle desperately and vainly, trying to find some way to go on living now that its chief support was gone. But in effect it was all over when Grant and Lee signed the papers. And the little room where they wrote out the terms was the scene of one of the poignant, dramatic contrasts in American history.

3   They were two strong men, these oddly different generals, and they represented the strengths of two conflicting currents that, through them, had come into final collision.

4   Back of Robert E. Lee was the notion that the old aristocratic concept might somehow survive and be dominant in American life.

Lee was tidewater Virginia, and in his background were family, culture, 5 and tradition . . . the age of chivalry transplanted to a New World which was making its own legends and its own myths. He embodied a way of life that had come down through the age of knighthood and the English country squire. America was a land that was beginning all over again, dedicated to nothing much more complicated than the rather hazy belief that all men had equal rights and should have an equal chance in the world. In such a land Lee stood for the feeling that it was somehow of advantage to human society to have a pronounced inequality in the social structure. There should be a leisure class, backed by ownership of land; in turn, society itself should be keyed to the land as the chief source of wealth and influence. It would bring forth (according to this ideal) a class of men with a strong sense of obligation to the community; men who lived not to gain advantage for themselves, but to meet the solemn obligations which had been laid on them by the very fact that they were privileged. From them the country would get its leadership; to them it could look for the higher values—of thought, of conduct, of personal deportment—to give it strength and virtue.

Lee embodied the noblest elements of this aristocratic ideal. Through him, 6 the landed nobility justified itself. For four years, the Southern states had fought a desperate war to uphold the ideals for which Lee stood. In the end, it almost seemed as if the Confederacy fought for Lee; as if he himself was the Confederacy . . . the best thing that the way of life for which the Confederacy stood could ever have to offer. He had passed into legend before Appomattox. Thousands of tired, underfed, poorly clothed Confederate soldiers, long since past the simple enthusiasm of the early days of the struggle, somehow considered Lee the symbol of everything for which they had been willing to die. But they could not quite put this feeling into words. If the Lost Cause, sanctified by so much heroism and so many deaths, had a living justification, its justification was General Lee.

Grant, the son of a tanner on the Western frontier, was everything Lee was 7 not. He had come up the hard way and embodied nothing in particular except the eternal toughness and sinewy fiber of the men who grew up beyond the mountains. He was one of a body of men who owed reverence and obeisance to no one, who were self-reliant to a fault, who cared hardly anything for the past but who had a sharp eye for the future.

These frontier men were the precise opposites of the tidewater aristocrats. 8 Back of them, in the great surge that had taken people over the Alleghenies and into the opening Western country, there was a deep, implicit dissatisfaction with a past that had settled into grooves. They stood for democracy, not from any reasoned conclusion about the proper ordering of human society, but simply because they had grown up in the middle of democracy and knew how it worked. Their society might have privileges, but they would be privileges each man had won for himself. Forms and patterns meant nothing. No man was born to anything, except perhaps to a chance to show how far he could rise. Life was competition.

9   Yet along with this feeling had come a deep sense of belonging to a national community. The Westerner who developed a farm, opened a shop, or set up in business as a trader, could hope to prosper only as his own community prospered—and his community ran from the Atlantic to the Pacific and from Canada down to Mexico. If the land was settled, with towns and highways and accessible markets, he could better himself. He saw his fate in terms of the nation's own destiny. As its horizons expanded, so did his. He had, in other words, an acute dollars-and-cents stake in the continued growth and development of his country.

10   And that, perhaps, is where the contrast between Grant and Lee becomes most striking. The Virginia aristocrat, inevitably, saw himself in relation to his own region. He lived in a static society which could endure almost anything except change. Instinctively, his first loyalty would go to the locality in which that society existed. He would fight to the limit of endurance to defend it, because in defending it he was defending everything that gave his own life its deepest meaning.

11   The Westerner, on the other hand, would fight with an equal tenacity for the broader concept of society. He fought so because everything he lived by was tied to growth, expansion, and a constantly widening horizon. What he lived by would survive or fall with the nation itself. He could not possibly stand by unmoved in the face of an attempt to destroy the Union. He would combat it with everything he had, because he could only see it as an effort to cut the ground out from under his feet.

12   So Grant and Lee were in complete contrast, representing two diametrically opposed elements in American life. Grant was the modern man emerging; beyond him, ready to come on the stage, was the great age of steel and machinery, of crowded cities and a restless burgeoning vitality. Lee might have ridden down from the old age of chivalry, lance in hand, silken banner fluttering over his head. Each man was the perfect champion of his cause, drawing both his strengths and his weaknesses from the people he led.

13   Yet it was not all contrast, after all. Different as they were—in background, in personality, in underlying aspiration—these two great soldiers had much in common. Under everything else, they were marvelous fighters. Furthermore, their fighting qualities were really very much alike.

14   Each man had, to begin with, the great virtue of utter tenacity and fidelity. Grant fought his way down the Mississippi Valley in spite of acute personal discouragement and profound military handicaps. Lee hung on in the trenches at Petersburg after hope itself had died. In each man there was an indomitable quality . . . the born fighter's refusal to give up as long as he can still remain on his feet and lift his two fists.

15   Daring and resourcefulness they had, too; the ability to think faster and move faster than the enemy. These were the qualities which gave Lee the dazzling campaigns of Second Manassas and Chancellorsville and won Vicksburg for Grant.

16   Lastly, and perhaps greatest of all, there was the ability, at the end, to turn quickly from war to peace once the fighting was over. Out of the way these two

men behaved at Appomattox came the possibility of a peace of reconciliation. It was a possibility not wholly realized, in the years to come, but which did, in the end, help the two sections to become one nation again . . . after a war whose bitterness might have seemed to make such a reunion wholly impossible. No part of either man's life became him more than the part he played in their brief meeting in the McLean house at Appomattox. Their behavior there put all succeeding generations of Americans in their debt. Two great Americans, Grant and Lee—very different, yet under everything very much alike. Their encounter at Appomattox was one of the great moments of American history.

COMPREHENSION

1. What is the central purpose of Catton's study? Cite evidence to support your view. Who is his audience?
2. What is the primary appeal to readers of describing history through the study of individuals rather than through the recording of events? How does Catton's essay reflect this appeal?
3. According to Catton, what special qualities did Grant and Lee share, and what qualities set them apart?

RHETORIC

1. What role does the opening paragraph play in setting the tone for the essay? Is the tone typical of what you would expect of an essay describing military generals? Explain your view. How does the conclusion echo the introductory paragraph?
2. Note that the sentence "Two great Americans, Grant and Lee—very different, yet under everything very much alike" (paragraph 16) has no verb. What does this indicate about Catton's style? What other sentences contain atypical syntax? What is their contribution to the unique quality of the writing?
3. Although this essay is about a historical era, there is a notable lack of specific facts—dates, statistics, and events. What has Catton focused on instead?
4. What is the function of the one-sentence paragraph 3?
5. Paragraphs 9, 10, 12, and 13 begin with coordinating conjunctions. How do these transitional words give the paragraphs their special coherence? How would more typical introductory expressions, such as *in addition, furthermore,* or *moreover,* have altered this coherence?
6. What strategy does Catton use in comparing and contrasting the two generals? Study paragraphs 5–16. Which are devoted to describing each man separately, and which include aspects of both men? What is the overall effectiveness of the comparisons?

WRITING

1. Does Lee's vision of society exist in the United States today? If not, why not? If so, where do you find this vision? Write a brief essay on this topic.

2. Select two well-known individuals in the same profession—for example, politics, entertainment, or sports. Make a list for each, enumerating the different aspects of their character, behavior, beliefs, and background. Using this as an outline, devise an essay comparing and contrasting the two.

3. **Writing an Argument:** Apply, in an argumentative essay, Catton's observation about "two diametrically opposed elements in American life" (paragraph 12) to the current national scene.

NETWORKING
Applying 21st-Century Literacies

Creating a Hyperlinked Essay: Approach question 2 under Writing as an electronic essay that links readers to relevant Web sites to enhance their reading experience. Link to at least six locations.

American Dreamer

Bharati Mukherjee

Bharati Mukherjee (b. 1940) was born in Calcutta, India, and learned to read and write by age three. In 1947, she moved to Britain with her family. After receiving her BA from the University of Calcutta and her MA in English and ancient Indian culture from the University of Boroda, she came to the United States, where she received an MFA in creative writing and a PhD in English and comparative literature at the University of Iowa. Mukherjee is the author of Jasmine *(1989) and* The Middleman and Other Stories, *which won the 1988 National Book Critic's Circle Award for Fiction. Her more recent work includes the novels* Desirable Daughters *(2002) and* The Tree Bride *(2004). She is currently a professor at the University of California, Berkeley. Mukherjee is often interested in and writing about issues of cultural identity. In the following essay, which first appeared in the magazine* Mother Jones *in 1997, she examines why "hyphenated Americans" always seem to be members of nonwhite groups.*

1   The United States exists as a sovereign nation. "America," in contrast, exists as a myth of democracy and equal opportunity to live by, or as an ideal goal to reach.

2   I am a naturalized U.S. citizen, which means that, unlike native-born citizens, I had to prove to the U.S. government that I merited citizenship. What I didn't have to disclose was that I desired "America," which to me is the stage for the drama of self-transformation.

3   I was born in Calcutta and first came to the United States—to Iowa City, to be precise—on a summer evening in 1961. I flew into a small airport surrounded by cornfields and pastures, ready to carry out the two commands my father had

written out for me the night before I left Calcutta: Spend two years studying creative writing at the Iowa Writers' Workshop, then come back home and marry the bridegroom he selected for me from our caste and class.

In traditional Hindu families like ours, men provided and women were pro- 4 vided for. My father was a patriarch and I a pliant daughter. The neighborhood I'd grown up in was homogeneously Hindu, Bengali-speaking, and middle-class. I didn't expect myself to ever disobey or disappoint my father by setting my own goals and taking charge of my future.

When I landed in Iowa 35 years ago, I found myself in a society in which 5 almost everyone was Christian, white, and moderately well-off. In the women's dormitory I lived in my first year, apart from six international graduate students (all of us were from Asia and considered "exotic"), the only non-Christian was Jewish, and the only nonwhite an African-American from Georgia. I didn't anticipate then, that over the next 35 years, the Iowa population would become so diverse that it would have 6,931 children from non-English-speaking homes registered as students in its schools, nor that Iowans would be in the grip of a cultural crisis in which resentment against immigrants, particularly refugees from Vietnam, Sudan, and Bosnia, as well as unskilled Spanish-speaking workers, would become politicized enough to cause the Immigration and Naturalization Service to open an "enforcement" office in Cedar Rapids in October for the tracking and deporting of undocumented aliens.

In Calcutta in the '50s, I heard no talk of "identity crisis"—communal or 6 individual. The concept itself—a person not knowing who he or she is—was unimaginable in our hierarchical, classification-obsessed society. One's identity was fixed, derived from religion, caste, patrimony, and mother tongue. A Hindu Indian's last name announced his or her forefathers' caste and place of origin. A Mukherjee could only be a Brahmin from Bengal. Hindu tradition forbade intercaste, interlanguage, interethnic marriages. Bengali tradition even discouraged emigration: To remove oneself from Bengal was to dilute true culture.

Until the age of 8, I lived in a house crowded with 40 or 50 relatives. My 7 identity was viscerally connected with ancestral soil and genealogy. I was who I was because I was Dr. Sudhir Lal Mukherjee's daughter, because I was a Hindu Brahmin, because I was Bengali-speaking, and because my *desh*—the Bengali word for homeland—was an East Bengal village called Faridpur.

The University of Iowa classroom was my first experience of coeducation. And 8 after not too long, I fell in love with a fellow student named Clark Blaise, an American of Canadian origin, and impulsively married him during a lunch break in a lawyer's office above a coffee shop.

That act cut me off forever from the rules and ways of upper-middle-class 9 life in Bengal, and hurled me into a New World life of scary improvisations and heady explorations. Until my lunch-break wedding, I had seen myself as an Indian foreign student who intended to return to India to live. The five-minute ceremony in the lawyer's office suddenly changed me into a transient with conflicting loyalties to two very different cultures.

10   The first 10 years into marriage, years spent mostly in my husband's native Canada, I thought of myself as an expatriate Bengali permanently stranded in North America because of destiny or desire. My first novel, *The Tiger's Daughter*, embodies the loneliness I felt but could not acknowledge, even to myself, as I negotiated the no man's land between the country of my past and the continent of my present. Shaped by memory, textured with nostalgia for a class and culture I had abandoned, this novel quite naturally became an expression of the expatriate consciousness.

11   It took me a decade of painful introspection to put nostalgia in perspective and to make the transition from expatriate to immigrant. After a 14-year stay in Canada, I forced my husband and our two sons to relocate to the United States. But the transition from foreign student to U.S. citizen, from detached onlooker to committed immigrant, has not been easy.

12   The years in Canada were particularly harsh. Canada is a country that officially, and proudly, resists cultural fusion. For all its rhetoric about a cultural "mosaic," Canada refuses to renovate its national self-image to include its changing complexion. It is a New World country with Old World concepts of a fixed, exclusivist national identity. Canadian official rhetoric designated me as one of the "visible minority" who, even though I spoke the Canadian languages of English and French, was straining "the absorptive capacity" of Canada. Canadians of color were routinely treated as "not real" Canadians. One example: In 1985 a terrorist bomb, planted in an Air-India jet on Canadian soil, blew up after leaving Montreal, killing 329 passengers, most of whom were Canadians of Indian origin. The prime minister of Canada at the time, Brian Mulroney, phoned the prime minister of India to offer Canada's condolences for India's loss.

13   Those years of race-related harassments in Canada politicized me and deepened my love of the ideals embedded in the American Bill of Rights. I don't forget that the architects of the Constitution and the Bill of Rights were white males and slaveholders. But through their declaration, they provided us with the enthusiasm for human rights, and the initial framework from which other empowerments could be conceived and enfranchised communities expanded.

14   I am a naturalized U.S. citizen and I take my American citizenship very seriously. I am not an economic refugee, nor am I a seeker of political asylum. I am a voluntary immigrant. I became a citizen by choice, not by simple accident of birth.

15   Yet these days, questions such as who is an American and what is American culture are being posed with belligerence, and being answered with violence. Scapegoating of immigrants has once again become the politicians' easy remedy for all that ails the nation. Hate speeches fill auditoriums for demagogues willing to profit from stirring up racial animosity. An April [1996] Gallup poll indicated that half of Americans would like to bar almost all legal immigration for the next five years.

16   The United States, like every sovereign nation, has a right to formulate its immigration policies. But in this decade of continual, large-scale diasporas, it is

imperative that we come to some agreement about who "we" are, and what our goals are for the nation, now that our community includes people of many races, ethnicities, languages, and religions.

The debate about American culture and American identity has to date been 17 monopolized largely by Eurocentrists and ethnocentrists whose rhetoric has been flamboyantly divisive, pitting a phantom "us" against a demonized "them."

All countries view themselves by their ideals. Indians idealize the cultural con- 18 tinuum, the inherent value system of India, and are properly incensed when foreigners see nothing but poverty, intolerance, strife, and injustice. Americans see themselves as the embodiments of liberty, openness, and individualism, even as the world judges them for drugs, crime, violence, bigotry, militarism, and homelessness. I was in Singapore in 1994 when the American teenager Michael Fay was sentenced to caning for having spraypainted some cars. While I saw Fay's actions as those of an individual, and his sentence as too harsh, the overwhelming local sentiment was that vandalism was an "American" crime, and that flogging Fay would deter Singapore youths from becoming "Americanized."

Conversely, in 1994, in Tavares, Florida, the Lake County School Board 19 announced its policy (since overturned) requiring middle school teachers to instruct their students that American culture, by which the board meant European-American culture, is inherently "superior to other foreign or historic cultures." The policy's misguided implication was that culture in the United States has not been affected by the American Indian, African-American, Latin-American, and Asian-American segments of the population. The sinister implication was that our national identity is so fragile that it can absorb diverse and immigrant cultures only by recontextualizing them as deficient.

Our nation is unique in human history in that the founding idea of "America" 20 was in opposition to the tenet that a nation is a collection of like-looking, like-speaking, like-worshipping people. The primary criterion for nationhood in Europe is homogeneity of culture, race, and religion—which has contributed to blood-soaked balkanization in the former Yugoslavia and the former Soviet Union.

America's pioneering European ancestors gave up the easy homogeneity of 21 their native countries for a new version of Utopia. Now, in the 1990s, we have the exciting chance to follow that tradition and assist in the making of a new American culture that differs from both the enforced assimilation of a "melting pot" and the Canadian model of a multicultural "mosaic."

The multicultural mosaic implies a contiguity of fixed, self-sufficient, ut- 22 terly distinct cultures. Multiculturalism, as it has been practiced in the United States in the past 10 years, implies the existence of a central culture, ringed by peripheral cultures. The fallout of official multiculturalism is the establishment of one culture as the norm and the rest as aberrations. At the same time, the multiculturalist emphasis on race- and ethnicity-based group identity leads to a lack of respect for individual differences within each group, and to vilification of those individuals who place the good of the nation above the interests of their particular racial or ethnic communities.

23   We must be alert to the dangers of an "us" vs. "them" mentality. In California, this mentality is manifesting itself as increased violence between minority, ethnic communities. The attack on Korean-American merchants in South Central Los Angeles in the wake of the Rodney King beating trial is only one recent example of the tragic side effects of this mentality. On the national level, the politicization of ethnic identities has encouraged the scapegoating of legal immigrants, who are blamed for economic and social problems brought about by flawed domestic and foreign policies.

24   We need to discourage the retention of cultural memory if the aim of that retention is cultural balkanization. We must think of American culture and nationhood as a constantly reforming, transmogrifying "we."

25   In this age of diasporas, one's biological identity may not be one's only identity. Erosions and accretions come with the act of emigration. The experience of cutting myself off from a biological homeland and settling in an adopted homeland that is not always welcoming to its dark-complexioned citizens has tested me as a person, and made me the writer I am today.

26   I choose to describe myself on my own terms, as an American, rather than as an Asian-American. Why is it that hyphenation is imposed only on nonwhite Americans? Rejecting hyphenation is my refusal to categorize the cultural landscape into a center and its peripheries; it is to demand that the American nation deliver the promises of its dream and its Constitution to all its citizens equally.

27   My rejection of hyphenation has been misrepresented as race treachery by some India-born academics on U.S. campuses who have appointed themselves guardians of the "purity" of ethnic cultures. Many of them, though they reside permanently in the United States and participate in its economy, consistently denounce American ideals and institutions. They direct their rage at me because, by becoming a U.S. citizen and exercising my voting rights, I have invested in the present and not the past; because I have committed myself to help shape the future of my adopted homeland; and because I celebrate racial and cultural mongrelization.

28   What excites me is that as a nation we have not only the chance to retain those values we treasure from our original cultures but also the chance to acknowledge that the outer forms of those values are likely to change. Among Indian immigrants, I see a great deal of guilt about the inability to hang on to what they commonly term "pure culture." Parents express rage or despair at their U.S.-born children's forgetting of, or indifference to, some aspects of Indian culture. Of those parents I would ask: What is it we have lost if our children are acculturating into the culture in which we are living? Is it so terrible that our children are discovering or are inventing homelands for themselves?

29   Some first-generation Indo-Americans, embittered by racism and by unofficial "glass ceilings," construct a phantom identity, more-Indian-than-Indians-in-India, as a defense against marginalization. I ask: Why don't you get actively involved in fighting discrimination? Make your voice heard. Choose the forum

most appropriate for you. If you are a citizen, let your vote count. Reinvest your energy and resources into revitalizing your city's disadvantaged residents and neighborhoods. Know your constitutional rights, and when they are violated, use the agencies of redress the Constitution makes available to you. Expect change, and when it comes, deal with it!

As a writer, my literary agenda begins by acknowledging that America has 30 transformed me. It does not end until I show that I (along with the hundreds of thousands of immigrants like me) am minute by minute transforming America. The transformation is a two-way process: It affects both the individual and the national-cultural identity.

Others who write stories of migration often talk of arrival at a new place as 31 a loss, the loss of communal memory and the erosion of an original culture. I want to talk of arrival as a gain.

COMPREHENSION

1. What is the significance of the title? In what way is Mukherjee a "dreamer"? In what way does the United States inspire "dreaming"?
2. In paragraph 6, Mukherjee states that in India she had a strong sense of identity. Why was it difficult for her to feel at ease with her American identity?
3. A country is a geographical area with national boundaries as well as an underlying concept and ideal. Does Mukherjee focus on these aspects of the United States and Canada equally, or does she emphasize one more than the other? Explain.

RHETORIC

1. The essay is divided into four parts. Why did the author adopt this structure? What is the focus of each? How does each section function rhetorically in relation to the other three?
2. Mukherjee introduces her essay with her own explanations of the terms "America" and "the United States." What is her purpose, considering that this is an autobiographical essay?
3. Mukherjee explores her transition from "expatriate" to "immigrant" to "U.S. citizen" in paragraphs 10 and 11. Explain the significance of each term in general and each term's particular role in the author's cultural metamorphosis.
4. Mukherjee rejects and condemns the belligerence toward and scapegoating of immigrants. How would you characterize the effect of these attacks on Mukherjee, an immigrant herself? Note, in particular, her statements in paragraphs 13 and 26.
5. How does Mukherjee employ irony in paragraph 12 to demonstrate the double standard imposed on individuals who do not fit the stereotypical mold of what it means to be a "citizen"?
6. In paragraph 14, the author states, "I take my American citizenship very seriously." Is the tone of the essay serious? Explain your view.
7. As you define the following words, identify the intended audience for this essay: *exclusivist* (paragraph 12), *demagogues* (paragraph 15), *diasporas* (paragraph 16), *ethnocentrists* and *demonized* (paragraph 17), and *balkanization* (paragraph 24).

WRITING

1. In a personal essay, write about a time in your life when your allegiance, honesty, or integrity was unfairly questioned. Be sure to use specifics such as the circumstances of who, what, where, when, and why. Also describe your feelings at the time and the emotional outcome.
2. Write an essay based on personal experience or observation, explaining whether Mukherjee is correct in stating that "hyphenation is imposed only on nonwhite Americans" (paragraph 26). A variation on this theme might be an exploration why "hyphenated" terms used to describe certain white American groups have a different tone and purpose than terms used for nonwhites.
3. **Writing an Argument:** In her conclusion, Mukherjee criticizes "guardians of the 'purity' of ethnic cultures." Is there such a thing as a "pure" ethnic culture? Write an essay arguing your viewpoint.

NETWORKING
Applying 21st-Century Literacies

Making an Oral Argument: Write a speech, arguing for or against the proposition that a course on cultural diversity should be taught at your college or university. Consider whether other ways of approaching the subject would be more profitable, or whether the subject needs to be addressed at all. Use logical, ethical, and emotional appeals.

Stranger in the Village

James Baldwin

James Baldwin (1924–1988), a major American essayist, novelist, short-story writer, and playwright, was born and grew up in Harlem. He won a Eugene Saxon Fellowship and lived in Europe from 1948 to 1956. Always an activist in civil rights causes, Baldwin focused in his essays and fiction on the black search for identity in modern America and on the myth of white superiority. Among his principal works are Go Tell It on the Mountain *(1953),* Notes of a Native Son *(1955),* Giovanni's Room *(1956),* Nobody Knows My Name *(1961),* Another Country *(1962), and* If Beale Street Could Talk *(1974). One of the finest contemporary essayists, Baldwin had a rare talent for portraying the deepest concerns about civilization in an intensely personal style, as the following essay indicates.*

1 From all available evidence no black man had ever set foot in this tiny Swiss village before I came. I was told before arriving that I would probably be a

"sight" for the village; I took this to mean that people of my complexion were rarely seen in Switzerland, and also that city people are always something of a "sight" outside of the city. It did not occur to me—possibly because I am an American—that there could be people anywhere who had never seen a Negro.

It is a fact that cannot be explained on the basis of the inaccessibility of the village. The village is very high, but it is only four hours from Milan and three hours from Lausanne. It is true that it is virtually unknown. Few people making plans for a holiday would elect to come here. On the other hand, the villagers are able, presumably, to come and go as they please—which they do: to another town at the foot of the mountain, with a population of approximately five thousand, the nearest place to see a movie or go to the bank. In the village there is no movie house, no bank, no library, no theater; very few radios, one jeep, one station wagon; and, at the moment, one typewriter, mine, an invention which the woman next door to me here had never seen. There are about six hundred people living here, all Catholic—I conclude this from the fact that the Catholic church is open all year round, whereas the Protestant chapel, set off on a hill a little removed from the village, is open only in the summertime when the tourists arrive. There are four or five hotels, all closed now, and four or five *bistros,* of which, however, only two do any business during the winter. These two do not do a great deal, for life in the village seems to end around nine or ten o'clock. There are a few stores, butcher, baker, *épicerie,* a hardware store, and a money-changer—who cannot change travelers' checks, but must send them down to the bank, an operation which takes two or three days. There is something called the *Ballet Haus,* closed in the winter and used for God knows what, certainly not ballet, during the summer. There seems to be only one schoolhouse in the village, and this for the quite young children; I suppose this to mean that their older brothers and sisters at some point descend from these mountains in order to complete their education—possibly, again, to the town just below. The landscape is absolutely forbidding, mountains towering on all four sides, ice and snow as far as the eye can reach. In this white wilderness, men and women and children move all day, carrying washing, wood, buckets of milk or water, sometimes skiing on Sunday afternoons. All week long boys and young men are to be seen shoveling snow off the rooftops, or dragging wood down from the forest in sleds.

The village's only real attraction, which explains the tourist season, is the hot spring water. A disquietingly high proportion of these tourists are cripples, or semi-cripples, who come year after year—from other parts of Switzerland, usually—to take the waters. This lends the village, at the height of the season, a rather terrifying air of sanctity, as though it were a lesser Lourdes. There is often something beautiful, there is always something awful, in the spectacle of a person who has lost one of his faculties, a faculty he never questioned until it was gone, and who struggles to recover it. Yet people remain people, on crutches or indeed on deathbeds; and wherever I passed, the first summer I was here, among the native villagers or among the lame, a wind passed with me—of astonishment, curiosity, amusement, and outrage. The first summer I stayed two weeks and never intended to return. But I did return in the winter, to work; the village offers, obviously, no distractions whatever and has the further advantage of being extremely cheap. Now it is winter again, a year later, and I am here again. Everyone in the village knows my name, though they scarcely ever use it, knows that I come from America—though this, apparently, they will never really believe: black men come from Africa—and everyone knows that I am the friend of the son of a woman who was born here, and that I am staying in their chalet. But I remain as much a stranger today as I was the first day I arrived, and the children shout *Neger! Neger!* as I walk along the streets.

4   It must be admitted that in the beginning I was far too shocked to have any real reaction. In so far as I reacted at all, I reacted by trying to be pleasant—it being a great part of the American Negro's education (long before he goes to school) that he must make people "like" him. This smile-and-the-world-smiles-with-you routine worked about as well in this situation as it had in the situation for which it was designed, which is to say that it did not work at all. No one, after all, can be liked whose human weight and complexity cannot be, or has not been, admitted. My smile was simply another unheard-of phenomenon which allowed them to see my teeth—they did not, really, see my smile and I began to think that, should I take to snarling, no one would notice any difference. All of the physical characteristics of the Negro which had caused me, in America, a very different and almost forgotten pain were nothing less than miraculous—or infernal—in the eyes of the village people. Some thought my hair was the color of tar, that it had the texture of wire, or the texture of cotton. It was jocularly suggested that I might let it all grow long and make myself a winter coat. If I sat in the sun for more than five minutes some daring creature was certain to come along and gingerly put his fingers on my hair, as though he were afraid of an electric shock, or put his hand on my hand, astonished that the color did not rub off. In all of this, in which it must be conceded there was the charm of genuine wonder and in which there was certainly no element of intentional unkindness, there was yet no suggestion that I was human: I was simply a living wonder.

5   I knew that they did not mean to be unkind, and I know it now; it is necessary, nevertheless, for me to repeat this to myself each time I walk out of the chalet. The children who shout *Neger!* have no way of knowing the echoes this sound raises in me. They are brimming with good humor and the more daring swell with pride when I stop to speak with them. Just the same, there are days when I cannot pause and smile, when I have no heart to play with them; when, indeed, I mutter sourly to myself, exactly as I muttered on the streets of a city these children have never seen, when I was no bigger than these children are now: *Your* mother *was a nigger.* Joyce is right about history being a nightmare—but it may be the nightmare from which no one can awaken. People are trapped in history and history is trapped in them.

6   There is a custom in the village—I am told it is repeated in many villages—of "buying" African natives for the purpose of converting them to Christianity. There stands in the church all year round a small box with a slot for money,

decorated with a black figurine, and into this box the villagers drop their francs. During the *carnaval* which precedes Lent, two village children have their faces blackened—out of which bloodless darkness their blue eyes shine like ice—and fantastic horsehair wigs are placed on their blond heads; thus disguised, they solicit among the villagers for money for the missionaries in Africa. Between the box in the church and the blackened children, the village "bought" last year six or eight African natives. This was reported to me with pride by the wife of one of the *bistro* owners and I was careful to express astonishment and pleasure at the solicitude shown by the village for the souls of black folk. The *bistro* owner's wife beamed with a pleasure far more genuine than my own and seemed to feel that I might now breathe more easily concerning the souls of at least six of my kinsmen.

I tried not to think of these so lately baptized kinsmen, of the price paid for 7 them, or the peculiar price they themselves would pay, and said nothing about my father, who having taken his own conversion too literally never, at bottom, forgave the white world (which he described as heathen) for having saddled him with a Christ in whom, to judge at least from their treatment of him, they themselves no longer believed. I thought of white men arriving for the first time in an African village, strangers there, as I am a stranger here, and tried to imagine the astounded populace touching their hair and marveling at the color of their skin. But there is a great difference between being the first white man to be seen by Africans and being the first black man to be seen by whites. The white man takes the astonishment as tribute, for he arrives to conquer and to convert the natives, whose inferiority in relation to himself is not even to be questioned; whereas I, without a thought of conquest, find myself among a people whose culture controls me, has even, in a sense, created me, people who have cost me more in anguish and rage than they will ever know, who yet do not even know of my existence. The astonishment with which I might have greeted them, should they have stumbled into my African village a few hundred years ago, might have rejoiced their hearts. But the astonishment with which they greet me today can only poison mine.

And this is so despite everything I may do to feel differently, despite my 8 friendly conversations with the *bistro* owner's wife, despite their three-year-old son who has at last become my friend, despite the *saluts* and *bonsoirs* which I exchange with people as I walk, despite the fact that I know that no individual can be taken to task for what history is doing, or has done. I say that the culture of these people controls me—but they can scarcely be held responsible for European culture. America comes out of Europe, but these people have never seen America nor have most of them seen more of Europe than the hamlet at the foot of their mountain. Yet they move with an authority which I shall never have; and they regard me, quite rightly, not only as a stranger in their village but as a suspect latecomer, bearing no credentials, to everything they have—however unconsciously—inherited.

For this village, even were it incomparably more remote and incredibly 9 more primitive, is the West, the West onto which I have been so strangely grafted. These people cannot be, from the point of view of power, strangers anywhere in the world; they have made the modern world, in effect, even if they do not know it. The most illiterate among them is related, in a way that I am not, to Dante, Shakespeare, Michelangelo, Aeschylus, da Vinci, Rembrandt, and Racine; the cathedral at Chartres says something to them which it cannot say to me, as indeed would New York's Empire State Building, should anyone here ever see it. Out of their hymns and dances come Beethoven and Bach. Go back a few centuries and they are in their full glory—but I am in Africa, watching the conquerors arrive.

10   The rage of the disesteemed is personally fruitless, but it is also absolutely inevitable; this rage, so generally discounted, so little understood even among the people whose daily bread it is, is one of the things that makes history. Rage can only with difficulty, and never entirely, be brought under the domination of the intelligence and is therefore not susceptible to any arguments whatever. This is a fact which ordinary representatives of the *Herrenvolk,* having never felt this rage and being unable to imagine it, quite fail to understand. Also, rage cannot be hidden, it can only be dissembled. This dissembling deludes the thoughtless, and strengthens rage and adds, to rage, contempt. There are, no doubt, as many ways of coping with the resulting complex of tensions as there are black men in the world, but no black man can hope ever to be entirely liberated from this internal warfare—rage, dissembling, and contempt having inevitably accompanied his first realization of the power of white men. What is crucial here is that, since white men represent in the black man's world so heavy a weight, white men have for black men a reality which is far from being reciprocal; and hence all black men have toward all white men an attitude which is designed, really, either to rob the white man of the jewel of his naïveté, or else to make it cost him dear.

11   The black man insists, by whatever means he finds at his disposal, that the white man cease to regard him as an exotic rarity and recognize him as a human being. This is a very charged and difficult moment, for there is a great deal of will power involved in the white man's naïveté. Most people are not naturally reflective any more than they are naturally malicious, and the white man prefers to keep the black man at a certain human remove because it is easier for him thus to preserve his simplicity and avoid being called to account for crimes committed by his forefathers, or his neighbors. He is inescapably aware, nevertheless, that he is in a better position in the world than black men are, nor can he quite put to death the suspicion that he is hated by black men therefore. He does not wish to be hated, neither does he wish to change places, and at this point in his uneasiness he can scarcely avoid having recourse to those legends which white men have created about black men, the most usual effect of which is that the white man finds himself enmeshed, so to speak, in his own language which describes hell, as well as the attributes which lead one to hell, as being as black as night.

12   Every legend, moreover, contains its residuum of truth, and the root function of language is to control the universe by describing it. It is of quite considerable

significance that black men remain, in the imagination, and in overwhelming numbers in fact, beyond the disciplines of salvation; and this despite the fact the West has been "buying" African natives for centuries. There is, I should hazard, an instantaneous necessity to be divorced from this so visibly unsaved stranger, in whose heart, moreover, one cannot guess what dreams of vengeance are being nourished; and, at the same time, there are few things on earth more attractive than the idea of the unspeakable liberty which is allowed the unredeemed. When, beneath the black mask, a human being begins to make himself felt one cannot escape a certain awful wonder as to what kind of human being it is. What one's imagination makes of other people is dictated, of course, by the laws of one's own personality and it is one of the ironies of black-white relations that, by means of what the white man imagines the black man to be, the black man is enabled to know who the white man is.

I have said, for example, that I am as much a stranger in this village today 13 as I was the first summer I arrived, but this is not quite true. The villagers wonder less about the texture of my hair than they did then, and wonder rather more about me. And the fact that their wonder now exists on another level is reflected in their attitudes and in their eyes. There are the children who make those delightful, hilarious, sometimes astonishingly grave overtures of friendship in the unpredictable fashion of children; other children, having been taught that the devil is a black man, scream in genuine anguish as I approach. Some of the older women never pass without a friendly greeting, never pass, indeed, if it seems that they will be able to engage me in conversation; other women look down or look away or rather contemptuously smirk. Some of the men drink with me and suggest that I learn how to ski—partly, I gather, because they cannot imagine what I would look like on skis—and want to know if I am married, and ask questions about my *métier*. But some of the men have accused *le sale négre*—behind my back—of stealing wood and there is already in the eyes of some of them that peculiar, intent, paranoiac malevolence which one sometimes surprises in the eyes of American white men when, out walking with their Sunday girl, they see a Negro male approach.

There is a dreadful abyss between the streets of this village and the streets of 14 the city in which I was born, between the children who shout *Neger!* today and those who shouted *Nigger!* yesterday—the abyss is experience, the American experience. The syllable hurled behind me today expresses, above all, wonder: I am a stranger here. But I am not a stranger in America and the same syllable riding on the American air expresses the war my presence has occasioned in the American soul.

For this village brings home to me this fact: that there was a day, and not 15 really a very distant day, when Americans were scarcely Americans at all but discontented Europeans, facing a great unconquered continent and strolling, say, into a marketplace and seeing black men for the first time. The shock this spectacle afforded is suggested, surely, by the promptness with which they decided that these black men were not really men but cattle. It is true that the necessity on the part of the settlers of the New World of reconciling their moral assumptions with the fact—and the necessity—of slavery enhanced immensely the charm of this idea, and it is also true that this idea expresses, with a truly American bluntness, the attitude which to varying extents all masters have had toward all slaves.

16   But between all former slaves and slave owners and the drama which begins for Americans over three hundred years ago at Jamestown, there are at least two differences to be observed. The American Negro slave could not suppose, for one thing, as slaves in past epochs had supposed and often done, that he would ever be able to wrest the power from his master's hands. This was a supposition which the modern era, which was to bring about such vast changes in the aims and dimensions of power, put to death; it only begins, in unprecedented fashion, and with dreadful implications, to be resurrected today. But even had this supposition persisted with undiminished force, the American Negro slave could not have used it to lend his condition dignity, for the reason that this supposition rests on another: that the slave in exile yet remains related to his past, has some means—if only in memory—of revering and sustaining the forms of his former life, is able, in short, to maintain his identity.

17   This was not the case with the American Negro slave. He is unique among the black men of the world in that his past was taken from him, almost literally, at one blow. One wonders what on earth the first slave found to say to the first dark child he bore. I am told that there are Haitians able to trace their ancestry back to African kings, but any American Negro wishing to go back so far will find his journey through time abruptly arrested by the signature on the bill of sale which served as the entrance paper for his ancestor. At the time—to say nothing of the circumstances—of the enslavement of the captive black man who was to become the American Negro, there was not the remotest possibility that he would ever take power from his master's hands. There was no reason to suppose that his situation would ever change, nor was there, shortly, anything to indicate that his situation had ever been different. It was his necessity, in the words of E. Franklin Frazier, to find a "motive for living under American culture or die." The identity of the American Negro comes out of this extreme situation, and the evolution of this identity was a source of the most intolerable anxiety in the minds and the lives of his masters.

18   For the history of the American Negro is unique also in this: that the question of his humanity, and of his rights therefore as a human being, became a burning one for several generations of Americans, so burning a question that it ultimately became one of those used to divide the nation. It is out of this argument that the venom of the epithet *Nigger!* is derived. It is an argument which Europe has never had, and hence Europe quite sincerely fails to understand how or why the argument arose in the first place, why its effects are so frequently disastrous and always so unpredictable, why it refuses until today to be entirely settled. Europe's black possessions remained—and do remain—in Europe's colonies, at which remove they represented no threat whatever to European identity. If they posed any problem at all for the European conscience, it was a problem which remained comfortingly abstract: in effect, the black man,

as a man, did not exist for Europe. But in America, even as a slave, he was an inescapable part of the general social fabric and no American could escape having an attitude toward him. Americans attempt until today to make an abstraction of the Negro, but the very nature of these abstractions reveals the tremendous effects the presence of the Negro has had on the American character.

When one considers the history of the Negro in America it is of the greatest ₁₉ importance to recognize that the moral beliefs of a person, or a people, are never really as tenuous as life—which is not moral—very often causes them to appear; these create for them a frame of reference and a necessary hope, the hope being that when life has done its worst they will be enabled to rise above themselves and to triumph over life. Life would scarcely be bearable if this hope did not exist. Again, even when the worst has been said, to betray a belief is not by any means to have put oneself beyond its power; the betrayal of a belief is not the same thing as ceasing to believe. If this were not so there would be no moral standards in the world at all. Yet one must also recognize that morality is based on ideas and that all ideas are dangerous—dangerous because ideas can only lead to action and where the action leads no man can say. And dangerous in this respect: that confronted with the impossibility of becoming free of them, one can be driven to the most inhuman excesses. The ideas on which American beliefs are based are not, though Americans often seem to think so, ideas which originated in America. They came out of Europe. And the establishment of democracy on the American continent was scarcely as radical a break with the past as was the necessity, which Americans faced, of broadening this concept to include black men.

This was, literally, a hard necessity. It was impossible, for one thing, for ₂₀ Americans to abandon their beliefs, not only because these beliefs alone seemed able to justify the sacrifices they had endured and the blood that they had spilled, but also because these beliefs afforded them their only bulwark against a moral chaos as absolute as the physical chaos of the continent it was their destiny to conquer. But in the situation in which Americans found themselves, these beliefs threatened an idea which, whether or not one likes to think so, is the very warp and woof of the heritage of the West, the idea of white supremacy.

Americans have made themselves notorious by the shrillness and the bru- ₂₁ tality with which they have insisted on this idea, but they did not invent it; and it has escaped the world's notice that those very excesses of which Americans have been guilty imply a certain, unprecedented uneasiness over the idea's life and power, if not, indeed, the idea's validity. The idea of white supremacy rests simply on the fact that white men are the creators of civilization (the present civilization, which is the only one that matters; all previous civilizations are simply "contributions" to our own) and are therefore civilization's guardians and defenders. Thus it was impossible for Americans to accept the black man as one of themselves, for to do so was to jeopardize their status as white men. But not so to accept him was to deny his human reality, his human weight and complexity, and the strain of denying the overwhelmingly undeniable forced Americans into rationalizations so fantastic that they approached the pathological.

22   At the root of the American Negro problem is the necessity of the American white man to find a way of living with the Negro in order to be able to live with himself. And the history of this problem can be reduced to the means used by Americans—lynch law and law, segregation and legal acceptance, terrorization and concession—either to come to terms with this necessity, or to find a way around it, or (most usually) to find a way of doing both these things at once. The resulting spectacle, at once foolish and dreadful, led someone to make the quite accurate observation that "the Negro-in-America is a form of insanity which overtakes white men."

23   In this long battle, a battle by no means finished, the unforeseeable effects of which will be felt by many future generations, the white man's motive was the protection of his identity; the black man was motivated by the need to establish an identity. And despite the terrorization which the Negro in America endured and endures sporadically until today, despite the cruel and totally inescapable ambivalence of his status in his country, the battle for his identity has long ago been won. He is not a visitor to the West, but a citizen there, an American; as American as the Americans who despise him, the Americans who fear him, the Americans who love him—the Americans who became less than themselves, or rose to be greater than themselves by virtue of the fact that the challenge he represented was inescapable. He is perhaps the only black man in the world whose relationship to white men is more terrible, more subtle, and more meaningful than the relationship of bitter possessed to uncertain possessor. His survival depended, and his development depends, on his ability to turn his peculiar status in the Western world to his own advantage and, it may be, to the very great advantage of that world. It remains for him to fashion out of his experience that which will give him sustenance, and a voice.

24   The cathedral at Chartres, I have said, says something to the people of this village which it cannot say to me; but it is important to understand that this cathedral says something to me which it cannot say to them. Perhaps they are struck by the power of the spires, the glory of the windows; but they have known God, after all, longer than I have known him, and in a different way, and I am terrified by the slippery bottomless well to be found in the crypt, down which heretics were hurled to death, and by the obscene, inescapable gargoyles jutting out of the stone and seeming to say that God and the devil can never be divorced. I doubt that the villagers think of the devil when they face a cathedral because they have never been identified with the devil. But I must accept the status which myth, if nothing else, gives me in the West before I can hope to change the myth.

25   Yet, if the American Negro has arrived at his identity by virtue of the absoluteness of his estrangement from his past, American white men still nourish the illusion that there is some means of recovering the European innocence, of returning to a state in which black men do not exist. This is one of the greatest errors Americans can make. The identity they fought so hard to protect has, by virtue of that battle, undergone a change: Americans are as unlike any other white people in the world as it is possible to be. I do not think, for example, that

it is too much to suggest that the American vision of the world—which allows so little reality, generally speaking, for any of the darker forces in human life, which tends until today to paint moral issues in glaring black and white—owes a great deal to the battle waged by Americans to maintain between themselves and black men a human separation which could not be bridged. It is only now beginning to be borne in on us—very faintly, it must be admitted, very slowly, and very much against our will—that this vision of the world is dangerously inaccurate, and perfectly useless. For it protects our moral high-mindedness at the terrible expense of weakening our grasp of reality. People who shut their eyes to reality simply invite their own destruction, and anyone who insists on remaining in a state of innocence long after that innocence is dead turns himself into a monster.

The time has come to realize that the interracial drama acted out on the American continent has not only created a new black man, it has created a new white man, too. No road whatever will lead Americans back to the simplicity of this European village where white men still have the luxury of looking on me as a stranger. I am not, really, a stranger any longer for any American alive. One of the things that distinguishes Americans from other people is that no other people has ever been so deeply involved in the lives of black men, and vice versa. This fact faced, with all its implications, it can be seen that the history of the American Negro problem is not merely shameful, it is also something of an achievement. For even when the worst has been said, it must also be added that the perpetual challenge posed by this problem was always, somehow, perpetually met. It is precisely this black-white experience which may prove of indispensable value to us in the world we face today. This world is white no longer, and it will never be white again. 26

COMPREHENSION

1. According to Baldwin, what distinguishes Americans from other people? What is his purpose in highlighting these differences?
2. What connections between Europe, Africa, and America emerge from this essay? What is the relevance of the Swiss village to this frame of reference?
3. In the context of the essay, explain what Baldwin means by his statement "People are trapped in history and history is trapped in them" (paragraph 5).

RHETORIC

1. Analyze the effect of Baldwin's repetition of "there is" and "there are" constructions in paragraph 2. What does the parallelism at the start of paragraph 8 accomplish? Locate other examples of parallelism in the essay.
2. Analyze the image of winter in paragraph 2 and its relation to the rest of the essay.
3. Where in the essay is Baldwin's complex thesis condensed for the reader? What does this placement of thesis reveal about the logical method of development in the essay?

4. How does Baldwin create his introduction? What is the focus? What key motifs does he present that will inform the rest of the essay? What is the relationship of paragraph 5 to paragraph 6?
5. What paragraphs constitute the second section of the essay? What example serves to unify this section? What major shift in emphasis occurs in the third part of the essay? Explain the cathedral of Chartres as a controlling motif between these two sections.
6. What comparisons and contrasts help structure and unify the essay?

WRITING

1. Examine the paradox implicit in Baldwin's statement in the final paragraph that the history of the American Negro problem is "something of an achievement."
2. Describe a time when you felt yourself a "stranger" in a certain culture.
3. **Writing an Argument:** Write an argumentative essay on civilization based on the last sentence in Baldwin's essay: "This world is white no longer, and it will never be white again."

NETWORKING
Applying 21st-Century Literacies

Analyzing a Debate: On the Chapter 8 Networking page (at *www.mhhe.com/ mhreader11e*), follow the link to a video of a Cambridge University debate between James Baldwin and William F. Buckley Jr. What is the central disagreement between these two men? How are the issues raised in "Stranger in the Village" also addressed in this argument? Who do you see as "winning" this debate, and why?

Synthesis: Connections for Critical Thinking

1. Discuss the views that Mukherjee and Baldwin have in common regarding the refusal of American culture to accept the "otherness" of those it perceives as not behaving like or looking like the conventional "American." Expand your discussion to present your own views about the similarities and differences in the ways "white" America views immigrants and "black" Americans.
2. Compare and contrast the diction, level of discourse, style, and vocabulary of Ivins and Lithwick.
3. Both Thomas Jefferson and Martin Luther King Jr. made powerful appeals to the government in power on behalf of their people. Write a comparison-and-contrast essay that examines the language, style, and content of both essays.
4. Select the three essays you find the most and the least appealing or compelling in this chapter. Discuss why you selected them, and explore the way you developed your viewpoint.
5. Analyze the comparative methods of Catton and Wolfe.

6. Compare and contrast the difficulties Baldwin had in attempting to "fit in" to an alien European culture with the experiences Mukherjee describes of a nonwhite American trying to assimilate into the dominant culture.
7. Interview five parents who have children under age 10, and ask them if and how they control the online content their children view. Report your findings to your class.

NETWORKING
Applying 21st-Century Literacies

1. On Facebook or in a chat room, discuss with classmates Dyson's views on cyberspace regulation. Write a summary of your discussion.
2. Conduct online research on Ivins, Mukherjee, and Baldwin. Write an analysis of how their senses of place influence their ideas.

CH 8   **www.mhhe.com/mhreader11e**

- *Image Gallery:* Chapter images in color
- *Government, Politics, and Social Justice:* Information on the authors in this chapter
- *Ch. 8 Networking*

chapter *9*

Business and Economics
How Do We Earn Our Keep?

Work is central to the human experience; in fact, it is work and its economic and social outcomes that provide us with the keys to an understanding of culture and civilization. Work tells us much about scarcity and abundance, poverty and affluence, the haves and have-nots in any society, as well as a nation's economic imperatives. Whether it is the rise and fall of cities, the conduct of business and corporations, or the economic policies of government, we see in the culture of work an attempt to impose order on nature. Work is our handprint on the world.

The work we perform and the careers we pursue also define us in very personal ways. "I'm a professor at Harvard" or "I work for Google" serve as identity badges. (Robert Reich, a contributor to this chapter, once worked at Harvard.) For what we do explains, at least in part, what and who we are. The very act of looking for work illuminates one's status in society, one's background, one's aspirations. Jonathan Swift, in his classic essay "A Modest Proposal," written in 1729, demonstrates how labor reveals economic and political configurations of power. Over 250 years later, Reich tells us the same thing in his analysis of the changing nature of work and the way these changes create an even broader gap between rich and poor.

Work is not merely an important human activity but an essential one for social and psychological health. You might like your work, or you might loathe it; be employed or unemployed; enjoy the reputation of a workaholic or a person who lives for leisure time; view work as a curse or as a duty. Regardless, it is work that occupies a central position in your relationship to society. In fact, Sigmund Freud spoke of work as the basis of one's social reality.

Regardless of your perspective on the issue, it is important to understand the multiple dimensions of work. In both traditional and modern societies, work prepares us for economic and social roles. It affects families, school curricula, and public policy. Ultimately, as many authors here suggest, it determines our self-esteem. Through work we come to terms with ourselves and our environment. The nature and purpose of the work we do provide us with a powerful measure of our worth.

PREVIEWING THE CHAPTER

As you read the essays in this chapter and respond to them in discussion and writing, consider the following questions:

- What are the significant forms of support the author uses in viewing the world of work: observation, statistics, personal experience, history, and so on?
- What assumptions does the author make about the value of work?
- Does the author discuss work in general or focus on one particular aspect of work?
- How does the writer define *work*? In what ways, if any, does she or he expand on the simple definition of work as "paid employment"?
- What issues of race, class, and gender does the author raise?
- What is the relationship of work to the changing social, political, and economic systems depicted in the author's essay?
- What tone does the writer take in his or her presentation of the work experience?
- What psychological insights does the author offer into the culture of work?
- What does the writer's style reveal about her or his attitude toward work?

Classic and Contemporary Images
WILL WORKERS BE DISPLACED BY MACHINES?

Using a Critical Perspective   Diego Rivera's mural and the photograph of an automobile assembly line present industrial scenes that reveal the impact of technology on workers. What details are emphasized in each illustration? How are these two images similar and dissimilar? What, for example, is the relation of human beings to the machines that are the centerpiece of each photograph? Are the artist and photographer objective or subjective in the presentation of each scene? Explain.

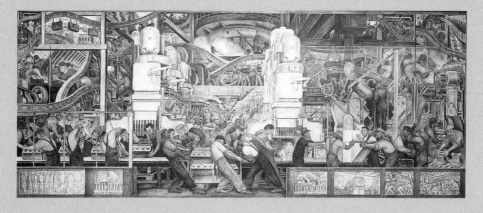

In the era known as the "Machine Age," 1918–1941, many artists, industrial designers, and architects in the United States and Europe evoked the mechanisms and images of industry in their works. During this time, the Mexican painter Diego Rivera (1886–1957) created a mural for the Detroit Institute of Arts (1932–33), a portion of which is reprinted here.

Today, computers are used to help
control assembly lines, as shown in
this photo of an automobile assembly line.

Classic and Contemporary Essays
Does Equal Opportunity Exist?

Virginia Woolf's "Professions for Women" is ironic from the start as she readily admits she can speak expertly of only one profession, her own, which is writing. But her message is clear regarding the effect of living in a male-dominated society. Simply put, it is very difficult to break the shackles of conditioning that one acquires from being told over and over again by one's culture that gender is destiny, regardless of what one aspires to. The author—through personal experience—demonstrates how this discrimination has a profound effect on the ability to see with one's own eyes and to think with one's own mind. Henry Louis Gates Jr. presents an interesting variation on this theme. Although the outcome is the same, the premise is reversed. He demonstrates how correlating supposedly positive attributes to a group—that is, superior athletic performance and race—results in the same deadening of the sense of personal ambition and a limiting of the scope of what one can aspire to. The thoughtful reader should be able to learn valuable lessons from comparing and contrasting these essays—one of which is that misguided perception all too often can be a self-fulfilling prophecy.

Professions for Women

Virginia Woolf

Virginia Woolf (1882–1941), novelist and essayist, was the daughter of Sir Leslie Stephen, a famous critic and writer on economics. An experimental novelist, Woolf attempted to portray consciousness through a poetic, symbolic, and concrete style. Her novels include Jacob's Room *(1922),* Mrs. Dalloway *(1925),* To the Lighthouse *(1927), and* The Waves *(1931). She was also a perceptive reader and critic; her criticism appears in* The Common Reader *(1925) and* The Second Common Reader *(1933). In the following essay, which was delivered originally as a speech to the Women's Service League in 1931, Woolf argues that women must overcome several "angels," or phantoms, in order to succeed in professional careers.*

1 When your secretary invited me to come here, she told me that your Society is concerned with the employment of women and she suggested that I might tell you something about my own professional experiences. It is true I am a woman; it is true I am employed; but what professional experiences have I had? It is difficult to say. My profession is literature; and in that profession there are fewer

experiences for women than in any other, with the exception of the stage—fewer, I mean, that are peculiar to women. For the road was cut many years ago—by Fanny Burney, by Aphra Behn, by Harriet Martineau, by Jane Austen, by George Eliot—many famous women, and many more unknown and forgotten, have been before me, making the path smooth, and regulating my steps. Thus, when I came to write, there were very few material obstacles in my way. Writing was a reputable and harmless occupation. The family peace was not broken by the scratching of a pen. No demand was made upon the family purse. For ten and sixpence one can buy paper enough to write all the plays of Shakespeare—if one has a mind that way. Pianos and models, Paris, Vienna and Berlin, masters and mistresses, are not needed by a writer. The cheapness of writing paper is, of course, the reason why women have succeeded as writers before they have succeeded in the other professions.

But to tell you my story—it is a simple one. You have only got to figure to 2 yourselves a girl in a bedroom with a pen in her hand. She had only to move that pen from left to right—from ten o'clock to one. Then it occurred to her to do what is simple and cheap enough after all—to slip a few of those pages into an envelope, fix a penny stamp in the corner, and drop the envelope into the red box at the corner. It was thus that I became a journalist; and my effort was rewarded on the first day of the following month—a very glorious day it was for me—by a letter from an editor containing a check for one pound ten shillings and sixpence. But to show you how little I deserve to be called a professional woman, how little I know of the struggles and difficulties of such lives, I have to admit that instead of spending that sum upon bread and butter, rent, shoes and stockings, or butcher's bills, I went out and bought a cat—a beautiful cat, a Persian cat, which very soon involved me in bitter disputes with my neighbors.

What could be easier than to write articles and to buy Persian cats with the 3 profits? But wait a moment. Articles have to be about something. Mine, I seem to remember, was about a novel by a famous man. And while I was writing this review, I discovered that if I were going to review books I should need to do battle with a certain phantom. And the phantom was a woman, and when I came to know her better I called her after the heroine of a famous poem, "The Angel in the House." It was she who used to come between me and my paper when I was writing reviews. It was she who bothered me and wasted my time and so tormented me that at last I killed her. You who come of a younger and happier generation may not have heard of her—you may not know what I mean by the Angel in the House. I will describe her as shortly as I can. She was intensely sympathetic. She was immensely charming. She was utterly unselfish. She excelled in the difficult arts of family life. She sacrificed herself daily. If there was a chicken, she took the leg; if there was a draught she sat in it—in short she was so constituted that she never had a mind or a wish of her own, but preferred to sympathize always with the minds and wishes of others. Above all—I need not say it—she was pure. Her purity was supposed to be her chief beauty—her blushes, her great grace. In those days—the last of Queen

Victoria—every house had its Angel. And when I came to write I encountered her with the very first words. The shadow of her wings fell on my page; I heard the rustling of her skirts in the room. Directly, that is to say, I took my pen in hand to review that novel by a famous man, she slipped behind me and whispered: "My dear, you are a young woman. You are writing about a book that has been written by a man. Be sympathetic; be tender; flatter; deceive; use all the arts and wiles of our sex. Never let anybody guess that you have a mind of your own. Above all, be pure." And she made as if to guide my pen. I now record the one act for which I take some credit to myself, though the credit rightly belongs to some excellent ancestors of mine who left me a certain sum of money—shall we say five hundred pounds a year—so that it was not necessary for me to depend solely on charm for my living. I turned upon her and caught her by the throat. I did my best to kill her. My excuse, if I were to be had up in a court of law, would be that I acted in self-defense. Had I not killed her she would have killed me. She would have plucked the heart out of my writing. For, as I found, directly I put pen to paper, you cannot review even a novel without having a mind of your own, without expressing what you think to be the truth about human relations, morality, sex. And all these questions, according to the Angel in the House, cannot be dealt with freely and openly by women; they must charm, they must conciliate, they must—to put it bluntly—tell lies if they are to succeed. Thus, whenever I felt the shadow of her wing or the radiance of her halo upon my page, I took up the inkpot and flung it at her. She died hard. Her fictitious nature was of great assistance to her. It is far harder to kill a phantom than a reality. She was always creeping back when I thought I had dispatched her. Though I flatter myself that I killed her in the end, the struggle was severe; it took much time that had better have been spent upon learning Greek grammar; or in roaming the world in search of adventures. But it was a real experience; it was an experience that was bound to befall all women writers at that time. Killing the Angel in the House was part of the occupation of a woman writer.

4   But to continue my story. The Angel was dead; what then remained? You may say that what remained was a simple and common object—a young woman in a bedroom with an inkpot. In other words, now that she had rid herself of falsehood, that young woman had only to be herself. Ah, but what is "herself"? I mean, what is a woman? I assure you, I do not know. I do not believe that you know. I do not believe that anybody can know until she has expressed herself in all the arts and professions open to human skill. That indeed is one of the reasons why I have come here—out of respect for you, who are in process of showing us by your experiments what a woman is, who are in process of providing us, by your failures and successes, with that extremely important piece of information.

5   But to continue the story of my professional experiences. I made one pound ten and six by my first review; and I bought a Persian cat with the proceeds. Then I grew ambitious. A Persian cat is all very well, I said; but a Persian cat is not enough. I must have a motor car. And it was thus that I became a novelist—for it is a very strange thing that people will give you a motor car if you will tell

them a story. It is a still stranger thing that there is nothing so delightful in the world as telling stories. It is far pleasanter than writing reviews of famous novels. And yet, if I am to obey your secretary and tell you my professional experiences as a novelist, I must tell you about a very strange experience that befell me as a novelist. And to understand it you must try first to imagine a novelist's state of mind. I hope I am not giving away professional secrets if I say that a novelist's chief desire is to be as unconscious as possible. He has to induce in himself a state of perpetual lethargy. He wants life to proceed with the utmost quiet and regularity. He wants to see the same faces, to read the same books, to do the same things day after day, month after month, while he is writing, so that nothing may break the illusion in which he is living—so that nothing may disturb or disquiet the mysterious nosings about, feelings round, darts, dashes and sudden discoveries of that very shy and illusive spirit, the imagination. I suspect that this state is the same both for men and women. Be that as it may, I want you to imagine me writing a novel in a state of trance. I want you to figure to yourselves a girl sitting with a pen in her hand, which for minutes, and indeed for hours, she never dips into the inkpot. The image that comes to my mind when I think of this girl is the image of a fisherman lying sunk in dreams on the verge of a deep lake with a rod held out over the water. She was letting her imagination sweep unchecked round every rock and cranny of the world that lies submerged in the depths of our unconscious being. Now came the experience, the experience that I believe to be far commoner with women writers than with men. The line raced through the girl's fingers. Her imagination had rushed away. It had sought the pools, the depths, the dark places where the largest fish slumber. And then there was a smash. There was an explosion. There was foam and confusion. The imagination had dashed itself against something hard. The girl was roused from her dream. She was indeed in a state of the most acute and difficult distress. To speak without figure she had thought of something, something about the body, about the passions which it was unfitting for her as a woman to say. Men, her reason told her, would be shocked. The consciousness of what men will say of a woman who speaks the truth about her passions had roused her from her artist's state of unconsciousness. She could write no more. The trance was over. Her imagination could work no longer. This I believe to be a very common experience with women writers—they are impeded by the extreme conventionality of the other sex. For though men sensibly allow themselves great freedom in these respects, I doubt that they realize or can control the extreme severity with which they condemn such freedom in women.

These then were two very genuine experiences of my own. These were two 6 of the adventures of my professional life. The first—killing the Angel in the House—I think I solved. She died. But the second, telling the truth about my own experiences as a body, I do not think I solved. I doubt that any woman has solved it yet. The obstacles against her are still immensely powerful—and yet they are very difficult to define. Outwardly, what is simpler than to write books? Outwardly, what obstacles are there for a woman rather than for a man? Inwardly, I think, the case is very different; she has still many ghosts to fight, many prejudices to overcome. Indeed it will be a long time still, I think, before a woman can sit down to write a book without finding a phantom to be slain, a rock to be dashed against. And if this is so in literature, the freest of all professions for women, how is it in the new professions which you are now for the first time entering?

7   Those are the questions that I should like, had I time, to ask you. And indeed, if I have laid stress upon these professional experiences of mine, it is because I believe that they are, though in different forms, yours also. Even when the path is nominally open—when there is nothing to prevent a woman from being a doctor, a lawyer, a civil servant—there are many phantoms and obstacles, as I believe, looming in her way. To discuss and define them is I think of great value and importance; for thus only can the labor be shared, the difficulties be solved. But besides this, it is necessary also to discuss the ends and the aims for which we are fighting, for which we are doing battle with these formidable obstacles. Those aims cannot be taken for granted; they must be perpetually questioned and examined. The whole position, as I see it—here in this hall surrounded by women practicing for the first time in history I know not how many different professions—is one of extraordinary interest and importance. You have won rooms of your own in the house hitherto exclusively owned by men. You are able, though not without great labor and effort, to pay the rent. You are earning your five hundred pounds a year. But this freedom is only a beginning; the room is your own, but it is still bare. It has to be furnished; it has to be decorated; it has to be shared. How are you going to furnish it, how are you going to decorate it? With whom are you going to share it, and upon what terms? These, I think, are questions of the utmost importance and interest. For the first time in history you are able to ask them; for the first time you are able to decide for yourselves what the answers should be. Willingly would I stay and discuss those questions and answers—but not tonight. My time is up; and I must cease.

COMPREHENSION

1. This essay was presented originally as a speech. What internal evidence indicates that it was intended as a talk? How do you respond to it today as a reader?
2. Who or what is the "angel" that Woolf describes in this essay? Why must she kill it? What other obstacles does a professional woman encounter?
3. Paraphrase the last two paragraphs of this essay. What is the essence of Woolf's argument?

RHETORIC

1. There is a significant amount of figurative language in the essay. Locate and explain examples. What does the figurative language contribute to the tone of the essay?
2. How do we know that Woolf is addressing an audience of women? Why does she pose so many questions, and what does this strategy contribute to the rapport she wants to establish? Explain the effect of the last two sentences.

3. How does Woolf use analogy to structure part of her argument?
4. Why does Woolf rely on personal narration? How does it affect the logic of her argument?
5. Evaluate Woolf's use of contrast to advance her argument.
6. Where does Woolf place her main proposition? How emphatic is it, and why?

WRITING

1. How effectively does Woolf use her own example as a professional writer to advance a broader proposition concerning all women entering professional life? Answer this question in a brief essay.
2. Discuss the problems and obstacles that you anticipate when you enter your chosen career.
3. **Writing an Argument:** Argue for or against the proposition that Woolf's essay has little relevance for women planning careers today.

NETWORKING
Applying 21st-Century Literacies

Repurposing Text for a New Genre: Condense and rewrite Woolf's speech/essay as a blog entry. Preserve and do not distort her central message, but do not use more than 500 words. What else, besides length, will you modify to fit this new form?

Delusions of Grandeur

Henry Louis Gates Jr.

Henry Louis Gates Jr. (b. 1950) is an educator, writer, and editor. He was born in West Virginia and educated at Yale and at Clare College in Cambridge. Gates has had a varied career, working as a general anesthetist in Tanzania and as a staff correspondent for Time *magazine in London. His essays have appeared in such diverse publications as* Black American Literature Forum, Yale Review, New York Times Book Review, *and* Sports Illustrated. *He is also the author of* Figures in Black: Words, Signs and the Racial Self *(1987) and* The Signifying Monkey: A Theory of Afro-American Literary Criticism *(1988) and is the editor, with Nellie Y. McKey, of* The Norton Anthology of African American Literature *(1996), and, with Hollis Robbins,* The Annotated Uncle Tom's Cabin *(2007). In this article from* Sports Illustrated, *Gates turns his attention to the limited career choices presented as viable to African American youth and to public misconceptions about blacks in sports.*

1   Standing at the bar of an all-black VFW post in my hometown of Piedmont, W.Va., I offered five dollars to anyone who could tell me how many African-American professional athletes were at work today. There are 35 million African-Americans, I said.

2   "Ten million!" yelled one intrepid soul, too far into his cups.

3   "No way . . . more like 500,000," said another.

4   "You mean *all* professional sports," someone interjected, "including golf and tennis, but not counting the brothers from Puerto Rico?" Everyone laughed.

5   "Fifty thousand, minimum," was another guess.

6   Here are the facts:

There are 1,200 black professional athletes in the U.S.

There are 12 times more black lawyers than black athletes.

There are 2½ times more black dentists than black athletes.

There are 15 times more black doctors than black athletes.

7   Nobody in my local VFW believed these statistics; in fact, few people would believe them if they weren't reading them in the pages of *Sports Illustrated.* In spite of these statistics, too many African-American youngsters still believe that they have a much better chance of becoming another Magic Johnson or Michael Jordan than they do of matching the achievements of Baltimore Mayor Kurt Schmoke or neurosurgeon Dr. Benjamin Carson, both of whom, like Johnson and Jordan, are black.

8   In reality, an African-American youngster has about as much chance of becoming a professional athlete as he or she does of winning the lottery. The tragedy for our people, however, is that few of us accept that truth.

9   Let me confess that I love sports. Like most black people of my generation—I'm 40—I was raised to revere the great black athletic heroes, and I never tired of listening to the stories of triumph and defeat that, for blacks, amount to a collective epic much like those of the ancient Greeks: Joe Louis's demolition of Max Schmeling; Satchel Paige's dazzling repertoire of pitches; Jesse Owens's in-your-face performance in Hitler's 1936 Olympics; Willie Mays's over-the-shoulder basket catch; Jackie Robinson's quiet strength when assaulted by racist taunts; and a thousand other grand tales.

10 Nevertheless, the blind pursuit of attainment in sports is having a devastating effect on our people. Imbued with a belief that our principal avenue to fame and profit is through sport, and seduced by a win-at-any-cost system that corrupts even elementary school students, far too many black kids treat basketball courts and football fields as if they were classrooms in an alternative school system. "O.K., I flunked English," a young athlete will say. "But I got an A plus in slamdunking."

11 The failure of our public schools to educate athletes is part and parcel of the schools' failure to educate almost everyone. A recent survey of the Philadelphia school system, for example, stated that "more than half of all students

in the third, fifth and eighth grades cannot perform minimum math and language tasks." One in four middle school students in that city fails to pass to the next grade each year. It is a sad truth that such statistics are repeated in cities throughout the nation. Young athletes—particularly young black athletes—are especially ill-served. Many of them are functionally illiterate, yet they are passed along from year to year for the greater glory of good old Hometown High. We should not be surprised to learn, then, that only 26.6 percent of black athletes at the collegiate level earn their degrees. For every successful educated black professional athlete, there are thousands of dead and wounded. Yet young blacks continue to aspire to careers as athletes, and it's no wonder why; when the University of North Carolina recently commissioned a sculptor to create archetypes of its student body, guess which ethnic group was selected to represent athletes?

Those relatively few black athletes who do make it in the professional ranks 12 must be prevailed upon to play a significant role in the education of all of our young people, athlete and nonathlete alike. While some have done so, many others have shirked their social obligations: to earmark small percentages of their incomes for the United Negro College Fund; to appear on television for educational purposes rather than merely to sell sneakers; to let children know the message that becoming a lawyer, a teacher or a doctor does more good for our people than winning the Super Bowl; and to form productive liaisons with educators to help forge solutions to the many ills that beset the black community. These are merely a few modest proposals.

A similar burden falls upon successful blacks in all walks of life. Each of us 13 must strive to make our young people understand the realities. Tell them to cheer Bo Jackson but to emulate novelist Toni Morrison or businessman Reginald Lewis or historian John Hope Franklin or Spelman College president Johnetta Cole—the list is long.

Of course, society as a whole bears responsibility as well. Until colleges 14 stop using young blacks as cannon fodder in the big-business wars of so-called nonprofessional sports, until training a young black's mind becomes as important as training his or her body, we will continue to perpetuate a system akin to that of the Roman gladiators, sacrificing a class of people for the entertainment of the mob.

COMPREHENSION

1. What does Gates suggest is the general assumption made about blacks in sports?
2. Why do American schools continue to perpetuate the myth that Gates is writing about?
3. According to Gates, what should successful black athletes do to help guide the career choices of young black?

RHETORIC

1. What is Gates's thesis? Where does it appear?
2. How does the introductory paragraph work to set up the writer's focus?
3. State Gates's purpose in using statistics in his essay.
4. What is the tone of Gates's essay? Cite specific sections where this tone seems strongest.
5. Examine the accumulation of facts in paragraph 11. How does this technique underscore Gates's point?
6. Explain Gates's allusion to Roman gladiators in his conclusion. How does it aid in emphasizing his main point?

WRITING

1. Write a brief essay in which you analyze your personal reaction to Gates's statistics. Were you surprised by them? What assumptions did you have about the number of black professional athletes? Why do you think most Americans share these assumptions?
2. Write a biographical research paper on the life and career of a black athlete.
3. **Writing an Argument:** Pretend you are addressing a group of young African Americans at an elementary school. Argue that sports and entertainment should (or should not) be their career choices.

NETWORKING
Applying 21st-Century Literacies

Creating a Graphic from Data: Use select statistics from this essay to create an effective graph, table, or chart.

Synthesis: Classic and Contemporary Questions for Comparison

1. Examine the argumentative styles of Woolf and Gates. What are their main propositions? Their minor propositions? What evidence do they provide?
2. Woolf first presented her paper as a speech before an audience of women. Gates wrote his essay as an opinion piece for *Sports Illustrated*. Write a comparative audience analysis of the two selections. Analyze the purpose, tone, style, and any other relevant aspects of these essays.
3. Argue for or against the proposition that white women and black men face the same barriers to employment in today's professions. Refer to the essays by Woolf and Gates to support your position.

The Death of Horatio Alger

Paul Krugman

Paul Krugman (b. 1953), who teaches at Princeton University, received the Nobel Prize for Economics in 2008 for his analysis of trade patterns and economic activity. Raised in the suburbs of New York City, Krugman attended Yale University for two years before transferring to Massachusetts Institute of Technology, where he received his PhD in economics in 1977. Krugman has published many highly specialized texts in economic theory, but also more popular works like Peddling Prosperity *(1994),* The Accidental Theorist: And Other Dispatches from the Dismal Science *(1998), and* The Return of Depression Economics and the Crisis of 2008 *(2008). A frequent contributor to such newspapers and magazines as the* New Republic, Financial Times, *and* Mother Jones, *Krugman currently is an op-ed columnist for the* New York Times. *Known for his trenchant style and oppositional viewpoints, Krugman attempts to make complex economic trends comprehensible to a broad audience. In this essay from the* Nation, *published in 2004, Krugman looks into the causes of economic inequality.*

The other day I found myself reading a leftist rag that made outrageous claims 1 about America. It said that we are becoming a society in which the poor tend to stay poor, no matter how hard they work; in which sons are much more likely to inherit the socioeconomic status of their father than they were a generation ago.

The name of the leftist rag? *BusinessWeek,* which published an article titled 2 "Waking Up from the American Dream." The article summarizes recent research showing that social mobility in the United States (which was never as high as legend had it) has declined considerably over the past few decades. If you put that research together with other research that shows a drastic increase in income and wealth inequality, you reach an uncomfortable conclusion: America looks more and more like a class-ridden society.

And guess what? Our political leaders are doing everything they can to 3 fortify class inequality, while denouncing anyone who complains—or even points out what is happening—as a practitioner of "class warfare."

Let's talk first about the facts on income distribution. Thirty years ago we 4 were a relatively middle-class nation. It had not always been thus: Gilded Age America was a highly unequal society, and it stayed that way through the 1920s. During the 1930s and '40s, however, America experienced what the economic historians Claudia Goldin and Robert Margo have dubbed the Great Compression: a drastic narrowing of income gaps, probably as a result of New Deal policies. And the new economic order persisted for more than a generation: Strong unions; taxes on inherited wealth, corporate profits and high incomes;

close public scrutiny of corporate management—all helped to keep income gaps relatively small. The economy was hardly egalitarian, but a generation ago the gross inequalities of the 1920s seemed very distant.

5   Now they're back. According to estimates by the economists Thomas Piketty and Emmanuel Saez—confirmed by data from the Congressional Budget Office—between 1973 and 2000 the average real income of the bottom 90 percent of American taxpayers actually fell by 7 percent. Meanwhile, the income of the top 1 percent rose by 148 percent, the income of the top 0.1 percent rose by 343 percent and the income of the top 0.01 percent rose 599 percent. (Those numbers exclude capital gains, so they're not an artifact of the stock-market bubble.) The distribution of income in the United States has gone right back to Gilded Age levels of inequality.

6   Never mind, say the apologists, who churn out papers with titles like that of a 2001 Heritage Foundation piece, "Income Mobility and the Fallacy of Class-Warfare Arguments." America, they say, isn't a caste society—people with high incomes this year may have low incomes next year and vice versa, and the route to wealth is open to all. That's where those commies at *BusinessWeek* come in: As they point out (and as economists and sociologists have been pointing out for some time), America actually is more of a caste society than we like to think. And the caste lines have lately become a lot more rigid.

7   The myth of income mobility has always exceeded the reality: As a general rule, once they've reached their 30s, people don't move up and down the income ladder very much. Conservatives often cite studies like a 1992 report by Glenn Hubbard, a Treasury official under the elder Bush who later became chief economic adviser to the younger Bush, that purport to show large numbers of Americans moving from low-wage to high-wage jobs during their working lives. But what these studies measure, as the economist Kevin Murphy put it, is mainly "the guy who works in the college bookstore and has a real job by his early 30s." Serious studies that exclude this sort of pseudo-mobility show that inequality in average incomes over long periods isn't much smaller than inequality in annual incomes.

8   It is true, however, that America was once a place of substantial intergenerational mobility: Sons often did much better than their fathers. A classic 1978 survey found that among adult men whose fathers were in the bottom 25 percent of the population as ranked by social and economic status, 23 percent had made it into the top 25 percent. In other words, during the first thirty years or so after World War II, the American dream of upward mobility was a real experience for many people.

9   Now for the shocker: The *BusinessWeek* piece cites a new survey of today's adult men, which finds that this number has dropped to only 10 percent. That is, over the past generation upward mobility has fallen drastically. Very few children of the lower class are making their way to even moderate affluence. This goes along with other studies indicating that rags-to-riches stories have become vanishingly rare, and that the correlation between fathers' and sons' incomes has risen in recent decades. In modern America, it

seems, you're quite likely to stay in the social and economic class into which you were born.

BusinessWeek attributes this to the "Wal-Martization" of the economy, the 10 proliferation of dead-end, low-wage jobs and the disappearance of jobs that provide entry to the middle class. That's surely part of the explanation. But public policy plays a role—and will, if present trends continue, play an even bigger role in the future.

Put it this way: Suppose that you actually liked a caste society, and you 11 were seeking ways to use your control of the government to further entrench the advantages of the haves against the have-nots. What would you do?

One thing you would definitely do is get rid of the estate tax, so that large 12 fortunes can be passed on to the next generation. More broadly, you would seek to reduce tax rates both on corporate profits and on unearned income such as dividends and capital gains, so that those with large accumulated or inherited wealth could more easily accumulate even more. You'd also try to create tax shelters mainly useful for the rich. And more broadly still, you'd try to reduce tax rates on people with high incomes, shifting the burden to the payroll tax and other revenue sources that bear most heavily on people with lower incomes.

Meanwhile, on the spending side, you'd cut back on healthcare for the 13 poor, on the quality of public education and on state aid for higher education. This would make it more difficult for people with low incomes to climb out of their difficulties and acquire the education essential to upward mobility in the modern economy.

And just to close off as many routes to upward mobility as possible, you'd 14 do everything possible to break the power of unions, and you'd privatize government functions so that well-paid civil servants could be replaced with poorly paid private employees.

It all sounds sort of familiar, doesn't it?   15

Where is this taking us? Thomas Piketty, whose work with Saez has trans- 16 formed our understanding of income distribution, warns that current policies will eventually create "a class of rentiers in the U.S., whereby a small group of wealthy but untalented children controls vast segments of the US economy and penniless, talented children simply can't compete." If he's right—and I fear that he is—we will end up suffering not only from injustice, but from a vast waste of human potential.

Goodbye, Horatio Alger. And goodbye, American Dream.   17

COMPREHENSION

1. What reasons does Krugman give for the creation of a caste society in the United States?
2. Who is Horatio Alger? Why doesn't Krugman explain who he is in his essay?
3. Krugman alludes to the "leftist rag" *BusinessWeek*. What can you infer about the contents and political opinions of this publication?

RHETORIC

1. What is Krugman's claim, and where does he state it most clearly?
2. Comment on the types of evidence that Krugman uses to support his argument. Do you find this evidence to be sufficient and convincing? Why or why not?
3. Krugman's style is quite impersonal. Locate examples of this style, and explain the overall effect.
4. Much of this essay involves comparative analysis. What subjects and ideas does Krugman compare and contrast?
5. Krugman's conclusion is very brief. Do you find it effective? Explain.

WRITING

1. Do you think that your life will be better economically than that of your parents? Write a personal essay in response to this question.
2. Write your own analysis of class inequality in the United States or in another nation that you are familiar with.
3. **Writing an Argument:** Write a rebuttal to Krugman, arguing that the American Dream is still alive and well.

NETWORKING
Applying 21st-Century Literacies

Making a Brochure: Create a brochure titled either "The American Dream Is Alive and Well" or "The Myth of Upward Mobility." Avoiding propaganda or other fallacious forms of argument, make a solid, convincing case. Consider creating or finding visuals to use in this project.

Tails of Manhattan

Woody Allen

Woody Allen (b. 1935), born Allen Stewart Konigsberg in Brooklyn, New York, is one of the most renowned auteurs in American film. He also is an actor, comedian, writer, occasional musician, and celebrity. Allen's notable early screenplays include What's New, Pussycat? *(1965),* Bananas *(1970),* Play It Again, Sam *(1972),* Sleeper *(1973), and* Annie Hall *(1977), a film that won the Academy Award, with Allen also receiving honors for best director and best original screenplay. Later films include* Stardust Memories *(1980), the Academy Award–winning* Hannah and Her Sisters *(1986), and* Vicky Cristina Barcelona *(2008). Allen also has written for* Playboy, New Yorker, Esquire, *and other publications. His books, filled with the same comic genius as his best films, include*

*Getting Even (1971), Without Feathers (1975), and Side Effects (1980). This essay,
published in the* New Yorker *in 2009, offers a slapstick "tail" about Bernard Madoff, the
financial manipulator who devised the greatest Ponzi scheme in modern history.*

Two weeks ago, Abe Moscowitz dropped dead of a heart attack and was reincar- 1
nated as a lobster. Trapped off the coast of Maine, he was shipped to Manhattan
and dumped into a tank at a posh Upper East Side seafood restaurant. In the
tank there were several other lobsters, one of whom recognized him. "Abe, is
that you?" the creature asked, his antennae perking up.

"Who's that? Who's talking to me?" Moscowitz said, still dazed by the 2
mystical slam-bang postmortem that had transmogrified him into a crustacean.

"It's me, Moe Silverman," the other lobster said.   3

"O.M.G.!" Moscowitz piped, recognizing the voice of an old gin-rummy 4
colleague. "What's going on?"

"We're reborn," Moe explained. "As a couple of two-pounders."   5

"Lobsters? This is how I wind up after leading a just life? In a tank on Third 6
Avenue?"

"The Lord works in strange ways," Moe Silverman explained. "Take Phil 7
Pinchuck. The man keeled over with an aneurysm, he's now a hamster. All day,
running at the stupid wheel. For years he was a Yale professor. My point is he's
gotten to like the wheel. He pedals and pedals, running nowhere, but he smiles."

Moscowitz did not like *his* new condition at all. Why should a decent citizen 8
like himself, a dentist, a mensch who deserved to relive life as a soaring eagle or
ensconced in the lap of some sexy socialite getting his fur stroked, come back
ignominiously as an entrée on a menu? It was his cruel fate to be delicious, to
turn up as Today's Special, along with a baked potato and dessert. This led to a
discussion by the two lobsters of the mysteries of existence, of religion, and how
capricious the universe was, when someone like Sol Drazin, a schlemiel they
knew from the catering business, came back after a fatal stroke as a stud horse
impregnating cute little thoroughbred fillies for high fees. Feeling sorry for himself and angry, Moscowitz swam about, unable to buy into Silverman's Buddha-
like resignation over the prospect of being served thermidor.

At that moment, who walked into the restaurant and sits down at a nearby 9
table but Bernie Madoff. If Moscowitz had been bitter and agitated before, now
he gasped as his tail started churning the water like an Evinrude.

"I don't believe this," he said, pressing his little black peepers to the glass 10
walls. "That goniff who should be doing time, chopping rocks, making license
plates, somehow slipped out of his apartment confinement and he's treating
himself to a shore dinner."

"Clock the ice on his immortal beloved," Moe observed, scanning Mrs. M.'s 11
rings and bracelets.

Moscowitz fought back his acid reflux, a condition that had followed him 12
from his former life. "He's the reason I'm here," he said, riled to a fever pitch.

13   "Tell me about it," Moe Silverman said. "I played golf with the man in Florida, which incidentally he'll move the ball with his foot if you're not watching."

14   "Each month I got a statement from him," Moscowitz ranted. "I knew such numbers looked too good to be kosher, and when I joked to him how it sounded like a Ponzi scheme he choked on his kugel. I had to do the Heimlich maneuver. Finally, after all that high living, it comes out he was a fraud and my net worth was bupkes. P.S., I had a myocardial infarction that registered at the oceanography lab in Tokyo."

15   "With me he played it coy," Silverman said, instinctively frisking his carapace for a Xanax. "He told me at first he had no room for another investor. The more he put me off, the more I wanted in. I had him to dinner, and because he liked Rosalee's blintzes he promised me the next opening would be mine. The day I found out he could handle my account I was so thrilled I cut my wife's head out of our wedding photo and put his in. When I learned I was broke, I committed suicide by jumping off the roof of our golf club in Palm Beach. I had to wait half an hour to jump, I was twelfth in line."

16   At this moment, the captain escorted Madoff to the lobster tank, where the unctuous sharpie analyzed the assorted saltwater candidates for potential succulence and pointed to Moscowitz and Silverman. An obliging smile played on the captain's face as he summoned a waiter to extract the pair from the tank.

17   "This is the last straw!" Moscowitz cried, bracing himself for the consummate outrage. "To swindle me out of my life's savings and then to nosh me in butter sauce! What kind of universe is this?"

18   Moscowitz and Silverman, their ire reaching cosmic dimensions, rocked the tank to and fro until it toppled off its table, smashing its glass walls and flooding the hexagonal-tile floor. Heads turned as the alarmed captain looked on in stunned disbelief. Bent on vengeance, the two lobsters scuttled swiftly after Madoff. They reached his table in an instant, and Silverman went for his ankle. Moscowitz, summoning the strength of a madman, leaped from the floor and with one giant pincer took firm hold of Madoff's nose. Screaming with pain, the gray-haired con artist hopped from the chair as Silverman strangled his instep with both claws. Patrons could not believe their eyes as they recognized Madoff, and began to cheer the lobsters.

19   "This is for the widows and charities!" yelled Moscowitz. "Thanks to you, Hatikvah Hospital is now a skating rink!"

20   Madoff, unable to free himself from the two Atlantic denizens, bolted from the restaurant and fled yelping into traffic. When Moscowitz tightened his vise-like grip on his septum and Silverman tore through his shoe, they persuaded the oily scammer to plead guilty and apologize for his monumental hustle.

21   By the end of the day, Madoff was in Lenox Hill Hospital, awash in welts and abrasions. The two renegade main courses, their rage slaked, had just enough strength left to flop away into the cold, deep waters of Sheepshead Bay, where, if I'm not mistaken, Moscowitz lives to this day with Yetta Belkin, whom he recognized from shopping at Fairway. In life she had always resembled a flounder, and after her fatal plane crash she came back as one.

COMPREHENSION

1. Why does Allen call his essay "tails" of Manhattan and not "tales"? What is his purpose here?
2. Who are Abe Moscowitz and Moe Silverman? Why do they hate Bernie Madoff?
3. Why is New York City an appropriate backdrop for this story? What aspects of New York culture does Allen exploit?

RHETORIC

1. How would you characterize the tone of this selection? What elements contribute to this tone?
2. Evaluate Allen's ability to create a setting, describe characters, and concisely plot the action. Would you say that his technique is cinematic? Why or why not?
3. Does Allen have a thesis or claim? Does the story have a moral? Explain.
4. Allen's dialogue reflects Jewish American diction and locutions. Cite examples of this strategy. Do you find it effective? Might some call it stereotyping? Justify your response.
5. Comedy can sometimes be short-lived; at other times, it can be timeless. How would you characterize the shelf life of this piece? Will the humor fade as the Bernard Madoff affair recedes into history? Explain.

WRITING

1. Write your own brief comic tale about Bernard Madoff. If necessary go online to find out more about him.
2. Write an extended definition of the Ponzi scheme. Conduct research if necessary.
3. **Writing an Argument:** Argue for or against the proposition that people who invest in financial schemes that are too good to be true (Madoff's clients received 12–20 percent profits every year until the scheme unraveled) deserve to lose their investments.

NETWORKING
Applying 21st-Century Literacies

Navigating Blogosphere Reactions: From the Chapter 9 Networking page (at *www.mhhe.com/mhreader11e*), click to find a launch page of links to various bloggers' responses to Woody Allen's essay. Scroll through the results and choose a few to click on and analyze. For each source, note whether the blogger or other type of poster seems reliable, why he or she discusses and/or links to the essay, what his or her response to it is, and how valuable you consider this contribution to the blogosphere to be. Synthesize your findings in a short essay.

Globalization: The Super-Story

Thomas L. Friedman

Thomas L. Friedman (b. 1953) was born in Minneapolis, Minnesota. He majored in Mediterranean studies at Brandeis University (BA 1975) and received an MA in modern Middle Eastern studies from Oxford University in 1978. As journalist, author, television commentator, and op-ed contributor to the New York Times, *Friedman tries to provide unbiased viewpoints on cultural, political, and economic issues. From 1979 to 1984 he was the* Times *correspondent in Beirut, Lebanon, and subsequently until 1988 served as bureau chief in Jerusalem. His book recounting his 10 years in the Middle East,* From Beirut to Jerusalem *(1983), received the National Book Award for nonfiction. Friedman also has published* The Lexus and the Olive Tree: Understanding Globalization *(2000),* The World Is Flat: A Brief History of the Twenty-First Century *(2005),* Hot, Flat, and Crowded: Why we Need a Green Revolution—And How It Can Renew America *(2008), and a collection of essays,* Longitudes and Attitudes: Explaining the World after September 11 *(2002), which contains the following selection.*

1 I am a big believer in the idea of the super-story, the notion that we all carry around with us a big lens, a big framework, through which we look at the world, order events, and decide what is important and what is not. The events of 9/11 did not happen in a vacuum. They happened in the context of a new international system—a system that cannot explain everything but *can* explain and connect more things in more places on more days than anything else. That new international system is called globalization. It came together in the late 1980s and replaced the previous international system, the cold war system, which had reigned since the end of World War II. This new system is the lens, the super-story, through which I viewed the events of 9/11.

2 I define globalization as the inexorable integration of markets, transportation systems, and communication systems to a degree never witnessed before—in a way that is enabling corporations, countries, and individuals to reach around the world farther, faster, deeper, and cheaper than ever before, and in a way that is enabling the world to reach into corporations, countries, and individuals farther, faster, deeper, and cheaper than ever before.

3 Several important features of this globalization system differ from those of the cold war system in ways that are quite relevant for understanding the events of 9/11. I examined them in detail in my previous book, *The Lexus and the Olive Tree,* and want to simply highlight them here.

4 The cold war system was characterized by one overarching feature—and that was *division.* That world was a divided-up, chopped-up place, and whether you were a country or a company, your threats and opportunities in the cold war

system tended to grow out of who you were divided from. Appropriately, this cold war system was symbolized by a single word—*wall*, the Berlin Wall.

The globalization system is different. It also has one overarching feature— 5 and that is *integration*. The world has become an increasingly interwoven place, and today, whether you are a company or a country, your threats and opportunities increasingly derive from who you are connected to. This globalization system is also characterized by a single word—*web*, the World Wide Web. So in the broadest sense we have gone from an international system built around division and walls to a system increasingly built around integration and webs. In the cold war we reached for the hotline, which was a symbol that we were divided but at least two people were in charge—the leaders of the United States and the Soviet Union. In the globalization system we reach for the Internet, which is a symbol that we are all connected and nobody is quite in charge.

Everyone in the world is directly or indirectly affected by this new system, 6 but not everyone benefits from it, not by a long shot, which is why the more it becomes diffused, the more it also produces a backlash by people who feel overwhelmed by it, homogenized by it, or unable to keep pace with its demands.

The other key difference between the cold war system and the globalization 7 system is how power is structured within them. The cold war system was built primarily around nation-states. You acted on the world in that system through your state. The cold war was a drama of states confronting states, balancing states, and aligning with states. And, as a system, the cold war was balanced at the center by two superstates, two superpowers: the United States and the Soviet Union.

The globalization system, by contrast, is built around three balances, which 8 overlap and affect one another. The first is the traditional balance of power between nation-states. In the globalization system, the United States is now the sole and dominant superpower and all other nations are subordinate to it to one degree or another. The shifting balance of power between the United States and other states, or simply between other states, still very much matters for the stability of this system. And it can still explain a lot of the news you read on the front page of the paper, whether it is the news of China balancing Russia, Iran balancing Iraq, or India confronting Pakistan.

The second important power balance in the globalization system is between 9 nation-states and global markets. These global markets are made up of millions of investors moving money around the world with the click of a mouse. I call them the Electronic Herd, and this herd gathers in key global financial centers—such as Wall Street, Hong Kong, London, and Frankfurt—which I call the Supermarkets. The attitudes and actions of the Electronic Herd and the Supermarkets can have a huge impact on nation-states today, even to the point of triggering the downfall of governments. Who ousted Suharto in Indonesia in 1998? It wasn't another state, it was the Supermarkets, by withdrawing their support for, and confidence in, the Indonesian economy. You also will not understand the front page of the newspaper today unless you bring the Supermarkets into your analysis. Because the United States can destroy you by dropping bombs, but the Supermarkets can destroy you by downgrading your bonds. In other words, the United States is the dominant player in maintaining the glo-balization game board, but it is hardly alone in influencing the moves on that game board.

10   The third balance that you have to pay attention to—the one that is really the newest of all and the most relevant to the events of 9/11—is the balance between individuals and nation-states. Because globalization has brought down many of the walls that limited the movement and reach of people, and because it has simultaneously wired the world into networks, it gives more power to *individuals* to influence both markets and nation-states than at any other time in history. Whether by enabling people to use the Internet to com-municate instantly at almost no cost over vast distances, or by enabling them to use the Web to transfer money or obtain weapons designs that normally would have been controlled by states, or by enabling them to go into a hardware store now and buy a five-hundred-dollar global positioning device, connected to a satellite, that can direct a hijacked airplane—globalization can be an incredible force-multiplier for individuals. Individuals can increasingly act on the world stage directly, unmediated by a state.

11   So you have today not only a superpower, not only Supermarkets, but also what I call "super-empowered individuals." Some of these super-empowered in-dividuals are quite angry, some of them quite wonderful—but all of them are now able to act much more directly and much more powerfully on the world stage.

12   Osama bin Laden declared war on the United States in the late 1990s. After he organized the bombing of two American embassies in Africa, the U.S. Air Force retaliated with a cruise missile attack on his bases in Afghanistan as though he were another nation-state. Think about that: on one day in 1998, the United States fired 75 cruise missiles at bin Laden. The United States fired 75 cruise missiles, at $1 million apiece, at a person! That was the first battle in his-tory between a superpower and a super-empowered angry man. September 11 was just the second such battle.

13   Jody Williams won the Nobel Peace Prize in 1997 for helping to build an international coalition to bring about a treaty outlawing land mines. Although nearly 120 governments endorsed the treaty, it was opposed by Russia, China, and the United States. When Jody Williams was asked, "How did you do that? How did you organize one thousand different citizens' groups and nongovern-mental organizations on five continents to forge a treaty that was opposed by the major powers?" she had a very brief answer: "E-mail." Jody Williams used e-mail and the networked world to super-empower herself.

14   Nation-states, and the American superpower in particular, are still hugely important today, but so too now are Supermarkets and super-empowered indi-viduals. You will never understand the globalization system, or the front page of the morning paper—or 9/11—unless you see each as a complex interaction between all three of these actors: states bumping up against states, states bumping up against Supermarkets, and Supermarkets and states bumping up against super-empowered individuals—many of whom, unfortunately, are super-empowered angry men.

COMPREHENSION

1. What is Friedman's "super-story"? How does he define it?
2. What are the main features of globalization? How does globalization differ from the system characterized by the cold war? Explain the "three balances" (paragraphs 8–10) that Friedman writes about.
3. What does Friedman mean by "super-empowered" individuals (paragraph 11)?

RHETORIC

1. What is Friedman's thesis or claim in this essay? Where does it appear?
2. How and why does Friedman create a personal voice as well as a colloquial style in this selection? What is the effect?
3. What definitions does Friedman establish? Are the definitions too abstract, or does he provide sufficient explanations and evidence? Explain.
4. Locate instances of classification and of comparison and contrast. Why does Friedman use these rhetorical strategies? How do the two methods complement each other?
5. Friedman uses several metaphors in this essay. What are they, and how do they function to enhance meaning?
6. Why does the writer discuss 9/11 in the final three paragraphs? What is the effect on the overall message and purpose of the essay?

WRITING

1. In groups of three or four, use Friedman's essay to brainstorm about globalization. Construct a list of ideas and attributes. Using this list, write a definition essay exploring the subject of globalization. Include comparison and contrast or classification, or both, to help organize the essay.
2. Write a personal essay on how you think globalization is affecting your life.
3. **Writing an Argument:** Write a letter to Friedman, either agreeing or disagreeing with his opinions concerning globalization, supporting or refuting his ideas, or offering alternative views.

NETWORKING
Applying 21st-Century Literacies

Crafting a Comment: Like letters to the editors of newspapers, comments on online articles and blog posts offer readers a chance to question or otherwise engage with published texts. Approach question 3 under Writing from a more concise angle: Imagine as you craft your response that it will be a comment posted after the article, a comment visible, potentially, to anyone from around the world. Include one or two link(s) to credible articles, data, or Web sites that support your response.

Nickel and Dimed

Barbara Ehrenreich

Barbara Ehrenreich (b. 1941) was born in Butte, Montana. The daughter of working-class parents, she attended Reed College (BA 1963) and Rockefeller University, where she received a PhD in biology in 1968. After deciding not to pursue a career in science, Ehrenreich turned to political causes, using her scientific training to investigate a broad range of social issues. A prolific writer, Ehrenreich has contributed to Time, *the* New Republic, *the* Progressive, *and other magazines. She also has written several books, including* The American Health Empire *(1970),* Complaints and Disorders: The Sexual Politics of Sickness *(1978),* Nickel and Dimed: On (Not) Getting By in America *(2001),* Dancing in the Streets *(2007), and a collection of essays,* This Land Is Their Land: Reports from a Divided Nation *(2008). In the following excerpt from* Nickel and Dimed, *Ehrenreich recounts her experience working for a large cleaning agency.*

1   I am rested and ready for anything when I arrive at The Maids' office suite Monday at 7:30 A.M. I know nothing about cleaning services like this one, which, according to the brochure I am given, has over three hundred franchises nationwide, and most of what I know about domestics in general comes from nineteenth-century British novels and *Upstairs, Downstairs.* Prophetically enough, I caught a rerun of that very show on PBS over the weekend and was struck by how terribly correct the servants looked in their black-and-white uniforms and how much wiser they were than their callow, egotistical masters. We too have uniforms, though they are more oafish than dignified—ill-fitting and in an overloud combination of kelly-green pants and a blinding sunflower-yellow polo shirt. And, as is explained in writing and over the next day and a half of training, we too have a special code of decorum. No smoking anywhere, or at least not within fifteen minutes of arrival at a house. No drinking, eating, or gum chewing in a house. No cursing in a house, even if the owner is not present, and—perhaps to keep us in practice—no obscenities even in the office. So this is Downstairs, is my chirpy first thought. But I have no idea, of course, just how far down these stairs will take me.

2   Forty minutes go by before anyone acknowledges my presence with more than a harried nod. During this time the other employees arrive, about twenty of them, already glowing in their uniforms, and breakfast on the free coffee, bagels, and doughnuts The Maids kindly provides for us. All but one of the others are female, with an average age I would guess in the late twenties, though the range seems to go from prom-fresh to well into the Medicare years. There is a pleasant sort of bustle as people get their breakfasts and fill plastic buckets with rags and bottles of cleaning fluids, but surprisingly little conversation

outside of a few references to what people ate (pizza) and drank (Jell-O shots are mentioned) over the weekend. Since the room in which we gather contains only two folding chairs, both of them occupied, the other new girl and I sit cross-legged on the floor, silent and alert, while the regulars get sorted into teams of three or four and dispatched to the day's list of houses. One of the women explains to me that teams do not necessarily return to the same houses week after week, nor do you have any guarantee of being on the same team from one day to the next. This, I suppose, is one of the advantages of a corporate cleaning service to its customers: There are no sticky and possibly guilt-ridden relationships involved, because the customers communicate almost entirely with Tammy, the office manager, or with Ted, the franchise owner and our boss. The advantage to the cleaning person is harder to determine, since the pay compares so poorly to what an independent cleaner is likely to earn—up to $15 an hour, I've heard. While I wait in the inner room, where the phone is and Tammy has her desk, to be issued a uniform, I hear her tell a potential customer on the phone that The Maids charges $25 per person-hour. The company gets $25 and we get $6.65 for each hour we work? I think I must have misheard, but a few minutes later I hear her say the same thing to another inquirer. So the only advantage of working here as opposed to freelancing is that you don't need a clientele or even a car. You can arrive straight from welfare or, in my case, the bus station—fresh off the boat.

At last, after all the other employees have sped off in the company's eye- 3 catching green-and-yellow cars, I am led into a tiny closet-sized room off the inner office to learn my trade via videotape. The manager at another maid service where I'd applied had told me she didn't like to hire people who had done cleaning before because they were resistant to learning the company's system, so I prepare to empty my mind of all prior house-cleaning experience. There are four tapes—dusting, bathrooms, kitchen, and vacuuming—each starring an attractive, possibly Hispanic young woman who moves about serenely in obedience to the male voiceover: For vacuuming, begin in the master bedroom; when dusting, begin with the room directly off the kitchen. When you enter a room, mentally divide it into sections no wider than your reach. Begin in the section to your left and, within each section, move from left to right and top to bottom. This way nothing is ever overlooked.

I like *Dusting* best, for its undeniable logic and a certain kind of austere 4 beauty. When you enter a house, you spray a white rag with Windex and place it in the left pocket of your green apron. Another rag, sprayed with disinfectant, goes in the middle pocket, and a yellow rag bearing wood polish in the right-hand pocket. A dry rag, for buffing surfaces, occupies the right-hand pocket of your slacks. Shiny surfaces get Windexed, wood gets wood polish, and everything else is wiped dust-free with disinfectant. Every now and then Ted pops in to watch with me, pausing the video to underscore a particularly dramatic moment: "See how she's working around the vase? That's an accident waiting to happen." If Ted himself were in a video, it would have to be a cartoon, because the only features sketched onto his pudgy face are brown buttonlike eyes and a tiny pug nose; his belly, encased in a polo shirt, overhangs the waistline of his shorts. "You know, all this was figured out with a stopwatch," he tells me with something like pride. When the video warns against oversoaking our rags with cleaning fluids, he pauses it to tell me there's a danger in undersoaking too, especially if it's going to slow me down. "Cleaning fluids are less expensive than your time." It's good to know that *something* is cheaper than my time, or that in the hierarchy of the company's values I rank above Windex.

5   *Vacuuming* is the most disturbing video, actually a double feature beginning with an introduction to the special backpack vacuum we are to use. Yes, the vacuum cleaner actually straps onto your back, a chubby fellow who introduces himself as its inventor explains. He suits up, pulling the straps tight across and under his chest and then says proudly into the camera: "See, I *am* the vacuum cleaner." It weighs only ten pounds, he claims, although, as I soon find out, with the attachments dangling from the strap around your waist, the total is probably more like fourteen. What about my petulant and much-pampered lower back? The inventor returns to the theme of human/machine merger: When properly strapped in, we too will be vacuum cleaners, constrained only by the cord that attaches us to an electrical outlet, and vacuum cleaners don't have backaches. Somehow all this information exhausts me, and I watch the second video, which explains the actual procedures for vacuuming, with the detached interest of a cineast. Could the model maid be an actual maid and the model home someone's actual dwelling? And who are these people whose idea of decorating is matched pictures of mallard ducks in flight and whose house is perfectly characterless and pristine even before the model maid sets to work?

6   At first I find the videos on kitchens and bathrooms baffling, and it takes me several minutes to realize why: There is no *water,* or almost no water, involved. I was taught to clean by my mother, a compulsive housekeeper who employed water so hot you needed rubber gloves to get into it and in such Niagara-like quantities that most microbes were probably crushed by the force of it before the soap suds had a chance to rupture their cell walls. But germs are never mentioned in the videos provided by The Maids. Our antagonists exist entirely in the visible world—soap scum, dust, counter crud, dog hair, stains, and smears— and are to be attacked by damp rag or, in hard-core cases, by Dobie (the brand of plastic scouring pad we use). We scrub only to remove impurities that might be detectable to a customer by hand or by eye; otherwise our only job is to wipe. Nothing is said about the possibility of transporting bacteria, by rag or by hand, from bathroom to kitchen or even from one house to the next. It is the "cosmetic touches" that the videos emphasize and that Ted, when he wanders back into the room, continually directs my eye to. Fluff up all throw pillows and arrange them symmetrically. Brighten up stainless steel sinks with baby oil. Leave all spice jars, shampoos, etc., with their labels facing outward. Comb out the fringes of Persian carpets with a pick. Use the vacuum cleaner to create a special, fernlike pattern in the carpets. The loose ends of toilet paper and paper towel rolls have to be given a special fold (the same one you'll find in hotel

bathrooms). "Messes" of loose paper, clothing, or toys are to be stacked into "neat messes." Finally, the house is to be sprayed with the cleaning service's signature floral-scented air freshener, which will signal to the owners, the moment they return home, that, yes, their house has been "cleaned."

After a day's training, I am judged fit to go out with a team, where I soon 7 discover that life is nothing like the movies, at least not if the movie is *Dusting*. For one thing, compared with our actual pace, the training videos were all in slow motion. We do not walk to the cars with our buckets full of cleaning fluids and utensils in the morning, we run, and when we pull up to a house, we run with our buckets to the door. Liza, a good-natured woman in her thirties who is my first team leader, explains that we are given only so many minutes per house, ranging from under sixty for a 1½-bathroom apartment to two hundred or more for a multibathroom "first timer." I'd like to know why anybody worries about Ted's time limits if we're being paid by the hour but hesitate to display anything that might be interpreted as attitude. As we get to each house, Liza assigns our tasks, and I cross my fingers to ward off bathrooms and vacuuming. Even dusting, though, gets aerobic under pressure, and after about an hour of it—reaching to get door tops, crawling along floors to wipe baseboards, standing on my bucket to attack the higher shelves—I wouldn't mind sitting down with a tall glass of water. But as soon as you complete your assigned task, you report to the team leader to be assigned to help someone else. Once or twice, when the normal process of evaporation is deemed too slow, I am assigned to dry a scrubbed floor by putting rags under my feet and skating around on it. Usually, by the time I get out to the car and am dumping the dirty water used on floors and wringing out rags, the rest of the team is already in the car with the motor running. Liza assures me that they've never left anyone behind at a house, not even, presumably, a very new person whom nobody knows.

In my interview, I had been promised a thirty-minute lunch break, but this 8 turns out to be a five-minute pit stop at a convenience store, if that. I bring my own sandwich—the same turkey breast and cheese every day—as do a couple of the others; the rest eat convenience store fare, a bagel or doughnut salvaged from our free breakfast, or nothing at all. The two older married women I'm teamed up with eat best—sandwiches and fruit. Among the younger women, lunch consists of a slice of pizza, a "pizza pocket" (a roll of dough surrounding some pizza sauce), or a small bag of chips. Bear in mind we are not office workers, sitting around idling at the basal metabolic rate. A poster on the wall in the office cheerily displays the number of calories burned per minute at our various tasks, ranging from about 3.5 for dusting to 7 for vacuuming. If you assume an average of 5 calories per minute in a seven-hour day (eight hours minus time for travel between houses), you need to be taking in 2,100 calories in addition to the resting minimum of, say, 900 or so. I get pushy with Rosalie, who is new like me and fresh from high school in a rural northern part of the state, about the meagerness of her lunches, which consist solely of Doritos—a half-bag from the day before or a freshly purchased small-sized bag. She just didn't have anything in the house, she says (though she lives with her boyfriend and his mother), and she certainly doesn't have any money to buy lunch, as I find out when I offer to fetch her a soda from a Quik Mart and she has to admit she doesn't have eighty-nine cents. I treat her to the soda, wishing I could force her, mommylike, to take milk instead. So how does she hold up for an eight- or even nine-hour day? "Well," she concedes, "I get dizzy sometimes."

9   How poor are they, my coworkers? The fact that anyone is working this job at all can be taken as prima facie evidence of some kind of desperation or at least a history of mistakes and disappointments, but it's not for me to ask. In the prison movies that provide me with a mental guide to comportment, the new guy doesn't go around shaking hands and asking, "Hi there, what are you in for?" So I listen, in the cars and when we're assembled in the office, and learn, first, that no one seems to be homeless. Almost everyone is embedded in extended families or families artificially extended with housemates. People talk about visiting grandparents in the hospital or sending birthday cards to a niece's husband; single mothers live with their own mothers or share apartments with a coworker or boyfriend. Pauline, the oldest of us, owns her own home, but she sleeps on the living room sofa, while her four grown children and three grandchildren fill up the bedrooms.

10   But although no one, apparently, is sleeping in a car, there are signs, even at the beginning, of real difficulty if not actual misery. Half-smoked cigarettes are returned to the pack. There are discussions about who will come up with fifty cents for a toll and whether Ted can be counted on for prompt reimbursement. One of my teammates gets frantic about a painfully impacted wisdom tooth and keeps making calls from our houses to try to locate a source of free dental care. When my—or, I should say, Liza's—team discovers there is not a single Dobie in our buckets, I suggest that we stop at a convenience store and buy one rather than drive all the way back to the office. But it turns out I haven't brought any money with me and we cannot put together $2 between the four of us.

11   The Friday of my first week at The Maids is unnaturally hot for Maine in early September—95 degrees, according to the digital time-and-temperature displays offered by banks that we pass. I'm teamed up with the sad-faced Rosalie and our leader, Maddy, whose sullenness, under the circumstances, is almost a relief after Liza's relentless good cheer. Liza, I've learned, is the highest-ranking cleaner, a sort of supervisor really, and said to be something of a snitch, but Maddy, a single mom of maybe twenty-seven or so, has worked for only three months and broods about her child care problems. Her boyfriend's sister, she tells me on the drive to our first house, watches her eighteen-month-old for $50 a week, which is a stretch on The Maids' pay, plus she doesn't entirely trust the sister, but a real day care center could be as much as $90 a week. After polishing off the first house, no problem, we grab "lunch"—Doritos for Rosalie and a bag of Pepperidge Farm Goldfish for Maddy—and head out into the exurbs for what our instruction sheet warns is a five-bathroom spread and a first-timer to boot. Still, the size of the place makes us pause for a moment, buckets in hand, before searching out an appropriately humble entrance. It sits there like a beached

ocean liner, the prow cutting through swells of green turf, windows without number. "Well, well," Maddy says, reading the owner's name from our instruction sheet. "Mrs. W. and her big-ass house. I hope she's going to give us lunch."

Mrs. W. is not in fact happy to see us, grimacing with exasperation when 12 the black nanny ushers us into the family room or sunroom or den or whatever kind of specialized space she is sitting in. After all, she already has the nanny, a cooklike person, and a crew of men doing some sort of finishing touches on the construction to supervise. No, she doesn't want to take us around the house, because she already explained everything to the office on the phone, but Maddy stands there, with Rosalie and me behind her, until she relents. We are to move everything on all surfaces, she instructs during the tour, and get underneath and be sure to do every bit of the several miles, I calculate, of baseboards. And be mindful of the baby, who's napping and can't have cleaning fluids of any kind near her.

Then I am let loose to dust. In a situation like this, where I don't even know 13 how to name the various kinds of rooms, The Maids' special system turns out to be a lifesaver. All I have to do is keep moving from left to right, within rooms and between rooms, trying to identify landmarks so I don't accidentally do a room or a hallway twice. Dusters get the most complete biographical overview, due to the necessity of lifting each object and tchotchke individually, and I learn that Mrs. W. is an alumna of an important women's college, now occupying herself by monitoring her investments and the baby's bowel movements. I find special charts for this latter purpose, with spaces for time of day, most recent fluid intake, consistency, and color. In the master bedroom, I dust a whole shelf of books on pregnancy, breastfeeding, the first six months, the first year, the first two years—and I wonder what the child care–deprived Maddy makes of all this. Maybe there's been some secret division of the world's women into breeders and drones, and those at the maid level are no longer supposed to be reproducing at all. Maybe this is why our office manager, Tammy, who was once a maid herself, wears inch-long fake nails and tarty little outfits—to show she's advanced to the breeder caste and can't be sent out to clean anymore.

It is hotter inside than out, un-air-conditioned for the benefit of the baby, I 14 suppose, but I do all right until I encounter the banks of glass doors that line the side and back of the ground floor. Each one has to be Windexed, wiped, and buffed—inside and out, top to bottom, left to right, until it's as streakless and invisible as a material substance can be. Outside, I can see the construction guys knocking back Gatorade, but the rule is that no fluid or food item can touch a maid's lips when she's inside a house. Now, sweat, even in unseemly quantities, is nothing new to me. I live in a subtropical area where even the inactive can expect to be moist nine months out of the year. I work out, too, in my normal life and take a certain macho pride in the Vs of sweat that form on my T-shirt after ten minutes or more on the StairMaster. But in normal life fluids lost are immediately replaced. Everyone in yuppie-land—airports, for example—looks like a nursing baby these days, inseparable from their plastic bottles of water. Here, however, I sweat without replacement or pause, not in individual drops but in continuous sheets of fluid soaking through my polo shirt, pouring down the backs of my legs. The eyeliner I put on in the morning—vain twit that I am—has long since streaked down onto my cheeks, and I could wring my braid out if I wanted to. Working my way through the living room(s), I wonder if Mrs. W. will ever have occasion to realize that every single doodad and *objet* through which she expresses her unique, individual self is, from another vantage point, only an obstacle between some thirsty person and a glass of water.

15　　When I can find no more surfaces to wipe and have finally exhausted the supply of rooms, Maddy assigns me to do the kitchen floor. OK, except that Mrs. W. is *in* the kitchen, so I have to go down on my hands and knees practically at her feet. No, we don't have sponge mops like the one I use in my own house; the hands-and-knees approach is a definite selling point for corporate cleaning services like The Maids. "We clean floors the old-fashioned way—*on our hands and knees*" (emphasis added), the brochure for a competing firm boasts. In fact, whatever advantages there may be to the hands-and-knees approach—you're closer to your work, of course, and less likely to miss a grimy patch—are undermined by the artificial drought imposed by The Maids' cleaning system. We are instructed to use less than half a small bucket of lukewarm water for a kitchen and all adjacent scrubbable floors (breakfast nooks and other dining areas), meaning that within a few minutes we are doing nothing more than redistributing the dirt evenly around the floor. There are occasional customer complaints about the cleanliness of our floors—for example, from a man who wiped up a spill on his freshly "cleaned" floor only to find the paper towel he employed for this purpose had turned gray. A mop and a full bucket of hot soapy water would not only get a floor cleaner but would be a lot more dignified for the person who does the cleaning. But it is this primal posture of submission—and of what is ultimately anal accessibility—that seems to gratify the consumers of maid services.

16　　I don't know, but Mrs. W.'s floor is hard—stone, I think, or at least a stonelike substance—and we have no knee pads with us today. I had thought in my middle-class innocence that knee pads were one of Monica Lewinsky's prurient fantasies, but no, they actually exist, and they're usually a standard part of our equipment. So here I am on my knees, working my way around the room like some fanatical penitent crawling through the stations of the cross, when I realize that Mrs. W. is staring at me fixedly—so fixedly that I am gripped for a moment by the wild possibility that I may have once given a lecture at her alma mater and she's trying to figure out where she's seen me before. If I were recognized, would I be fired? Would she at least be inspired to offer me a drink of water? Because I have decided that if water is actually offered, I'm taking it, rules or no rules, and if word of this infraction gets back to Ted, I'll just say I thought it would be rude to refuse. Not to worry, though. She's just watching that I don't leave out some stray square inch, and when I rise painfully to my feet again, blinking through the sweat, she says, "Could you just scrub the floor in the entryway while you're at it?"

17　　I rush home to the Blue Haven at the end of the day, pull down the blinds for privacy, strip off my uniform in the kitchen—the bathroom being too small for both a person and her discarded clothes—and stand in the shower for a good ten minutes, thinking all this water is *mine*. I have paid for it, in fact, I have earned it. I have gotten through a week at The Maids without mishap, injury, or insurrection. My back feels fine, meaning I'm not feeling it at all; even my wrists, damaged by carpal tunnel syndrome years ago, are issuing no complaints. Coworkers warned me that the first time they donned the backpack vacuum they felt faint, but not me. I am strong and I am, more than that, good. Did I toss my bucket of filthy water onto Mrs. W.'s casual white summer outfit? No. Did I take the wand of my vacuum cleaner and smash someone's Chinese porcelain statues or Hummel figurines? Not once. I was at all times cheerful, energetic, helpful, and as competent as a new hire can be expected to be. If I can do one week, I can do another, and might as well, since there's never been a moment for job-hunting. The 3:30 quitting time turns out to be a myth; often we don't return to the office until 4:30 or 5:00. And what did I think? That I was going to go out to interviews in my soaked and stinky postwork condition? I decide to reward myself with a sunset walk on Old Orchard Beach.

On account of the heat, there are still a few actual bathers on the beach, but 18 I am content to sit in shorts and T-shirt and watch the ocean pummel the sand. When the sun goes down I walk back into the town to find my car and am amazed to hear a sound I associate with cities like New York and Berlin. There's a couple of Peruvian musicians playing in the little grassy island in the street near the pier, and maybe fifty people—locals and vacationers—have gathered around, offering their bland end-of-summer faces to the sound. I edge my way through the crowd and find a seat where I can see the musicians up close—the beautiful young guitarist and the taller man playing the flute. What are they doing in this rinky-dink blue-collar resort, and what does the audience make of this surprise visit from the dark-skinned South? The melody the flute lays out over the percussion is both utterly strange and completely familiar, as if it had been imprinted in the minds of my own peasant ancestors centuries ago and forgotten until this very moment. Everyone else seems to be as transfixed as I am. The musicians wink and smile at each other as they play, and I see then that they are the secret emissaries of a worldwide lower-class conspiracy to snatch joy out of degradation and filth. When the song ends, I give them a dollar, the equivalent of about ten minutes of sweat.

COMPREHENSION

1. Why do women work for The Maids when they could earn more money as independent cleaners? How does Ehrenreich distinguish her cleaning practices from her coworkers'? Why do the maids emphasize "cosmetic touches" (paragraph 6)?
2. Describe the plight of Ehrenreich's coworkers. What "signs . . . of real difficulty if not actual misery" (paragraph 10) does she detect? What, if anything, does she do to help them?
3. Who is Mrs. W? What is her lifestyle like, and what does she expect of the maids? How does she treat Ehrenreich?

RHETORIC

1. How does Ehrenreich structure her narrative? How much time elapses? What elements of conflict develop? What transitional devices does she employ to unify the action?
2. Where does the writer employ description, and for what purpose? What descriptive details seem most striking to you? How, for example, does Ehrenreich bring her coworkers and Mrs. W. to life?
3. Identify those instances where the writer uses process analysis and comparison and contrast to organize her essay. Why does she select these strategies?
4. Explain the tone of this selection. What elements of irony and sarcasm do you detect?
5. Do you think this essay provides a straightforward account of Ehrenreich's experience working for The Maids, or does she have an argumentative point? Justify your response.
6. How does the writer conclude this selection? What elements in the last paragraph capture the main purpose behind her account?

WRITING

1. Write a narrative and descriptive essay of a job you have held that involved menial labor. Establish a time frame. Describe any colleagues who worked with you. Have a thesis or an argument that you either state explicitly or permit to emerge from the account.
2. Compare and contrast a bad job that you have held and a job that provided you with a degree of satisfaction.
3. **Writing an Argument:** In *Nickel and Dimed*, Ehrenreich set out to find minimum-wage jobs in several parts of the United States, including a Wal-Mart in Minnesota and a restaurant in Florida. However, she knew at the outset that these jobs were temporary and that she had the luxury of going back to her comfortable life and her career as a writer and activist. Argue for or against the proposition that Ehrenreich was being unethical and exploitative in her behavior. Refer to this selection to support your position.

NETWORKING
Applying 21st-Century Literacies

Examining Comments on a Blog: From the Chapter 9 Networking page (at *www.mhhe.com/mhreader11e*), link to the 2009 entry "Rich Get Poorer, Poor Disappear" on Barbara Ehrenreich's blog. After reading the entry itself at least twice, go through the comments. How many, and which commenters, make valuable contributions to the conversation? How many, and which do not? Based on your findings, what makes a good blog comment? Do you think blog comments should be moderated by the blog's author? Why or why not?

Why the Rich Are Getting Richer and the Poor, Poorer

Robert Reich

Robert Reich (b. 1946) is a professor of Public Policy at the University of California at Berkeley. He served as secretary of labor in the first Clinton administration and, before that, as a professor of economics at Harvard University. He has written numerous books on economics and has been a prominent lecturer for a dozen years. His books include The Next American Frontier *(1983) and* The Work of Nations *(1991), which takes its title from Adam Smith's classic work on economics* The Wealth of Nations, *written in 1776. Reich is known for his ability to "think outside the box," in other words, to see things from a unique and original perspective. Here he warns of what exists—perhaps in front of our very noses—but that we are too caught up in the moment to consider.*

> *The division of labor is limited by the extent of the market.*
> —*Adam Smith,* An Inquiry into the Nature and Causes
> of the Wealth of Nations *(1776)*

Regardless of how your job is officially classified (manufacturing, service, man- 1
agerial, technical, secretarial, and so on), or the industry in which you work
(automotive, steel, computer, advertising, finance, food processing), your real
competitive position in the world economy is coming to depend on the function
you perform in it. Herein lies the basic reason why incomes are diverging. The
fortunes of routine producers are declining. In-person servers are also becoming poorer, although their fates are less clear-cut. But symbolic analysts—who
solve, identify, and broker new problems—are, by and large, succeeding in the
world economy.

All Americans used to be in roughly the same economic boat. Most rose or 2
fell together as the corporations in which they were employed, the industries
comprising such corporations, and the national economy as a whole became
more productive—or languished. But national borders no longer define our
economic fates. We are now in different boats, one sinking rapidly, one sinking
more slowly, and the third rising steadily.

The boat containing routine producers is sinking rapidly. Recall that by mid- 3
century routine production workers in the United States were paid relatively
well. The giant pyramidlike organizations at the core of each major industry
coordinated their prices and investments—avoiding the harsh winds of competition and thus maintaining healthy earnings. Some of these earnings, in turn,

were reinvested in new plants and equipment (yielding ever-larger-scale economies); another portion went to top managers and investors. But a large and increasing portion went to middle managers and production workers. Work
stoppages posed such a threat to high-volume production that organized labor
was able to exact an ever-larger premium for its cooperation. And the pattern of
wages established within the core corporations influenced the pattern throughout the national economy. Thus the growth of a relatively affluent middle class,
able to purchase all the wondrous things produced in high volume by the core
corporations.

4   But, as has been observed, the core is rapidly breaking down into global
webs which earn their largest profits from clever problem-solving, -identifying,
and brokering. As the costs of transporting standard things and of communicating information about them continue to drop, profit margins on high-volume,
standardized production are thinning, because there are few barriers to entry.
Modern factories and state-of-the-art machinery can be installed almost anywhere on the globe. Routine producers in the United States, then, are in direct
competition with millions of routine producers in other nations. Twelve thousand people are added to the world's population every hour, most of whom,
eventually, will happily work for a small fraction of the wages of routine producers in America.[1]

5   The consequence is clearest in older, heavy industries, where high-volume,
standardized production continues its ineluctable move to where labor is
cheapest and most accessible around the world. Thus, for example, the Maqui-
ladora factories cluttered along the Mexican side of the U.S. border in the
sprawling shanty towns of Tijuana, Mexicali, Nogales, Agua Prieta, and Ciudad
Juárez—factories owned mostly by Americans, but increasingly by Japanese—
in which more than a half million routine producers assemble parts into finished goods to be shipped into the United States.

6   The same story is unfolding worldwide. Until the late 1970s, AT&T had
depended on routine producers in Shreveport, Louisiana, to assemble standard
telephones. It then discovered that routine producers in Singapore would perform the same tasks at a far lower cost. Facing intense competition from other
global webs, AT&T's strategic brokers felt compelled to switch. So in the early
1980s they stopped hiring routine producers in Shreveport and began hiring
cheaper routine producers in Singapore. But under this kind of pressure for
ever lower high-volume production costs, today's Singaporean can easily end
up as yesterday's Louisianan. By the late 1980s, AT&T's strategic brokers found
that routine producers in Thailand were eager to assemble telephones for a
small fraction of the wages of routine producers in Singapore. Thus, in 1989,

---

[1]The reader should note, of course, that lower wages in other areas of the world are of no particular attraction to global capital unless workers there are sufficiently productive to make the labor
cost of producing *each unit* lower there than in higher-wage regions. Productivity in many low-
wage areas of the world has improved due to the ease with which state-of-the-art factories and
equipment can be installed there.

AT&T stopped hiring Singaporeans to make telephones and began hiring even cheaper routine producers in Thailand.

The search for ever lower wages has not been confined to heavy industry. 7 Routine data processing is equally footloose. Keypunch operators located anywhere around the world can enter data into computers, linked by satellite or transoceanic fiber-optic cable, and take it out again. As the rates charged by satellite networks continue to drop, and as more satellites and fiber-optic cables become available (reducing communication costs still further), routine data processors in the United States find themselves in ever more direct competition with their counterparts abroad, who are often eager to work for far less.

By 1990, keypunch operators in the United States were earning, at most, 8 $6.50 per hour. But keypunch operators throughout the rest of the world were willing to work for a fraction of this. Thus, many potential American data-processing jobs were disappearing, and the wages and benefits of the remaining ones were in decline. Typical was Saztec International, a $20-million-a-year data-processing firm headquartered in Kansas City, whose American strategic brokers contracted with routine data processors in Manila and with American-owned firms that needed such data-processing services. Compared with the average Philippine income of $1,700 per year, data-entry operators working for Saztec earn the princely sum of $2,650. The remainder of Saztec's employees were American problem-solvers and -identifiers, searching for ways to improve the worldwide system and find new uses to which it could be put.[2]

By 1990, American Airlines was employing over 1,000 data processors in 9 Barbados and the Dominican Republic to enter names and flight numbers from used airline tickets (flown daily to Barbados from airports around the United States) into a giant computer bank located in Dallas. Chicago publisher R. R. Donnelley was sending entire manuscripts to Barbados for entry into computers in preparation for printing. The New York Life Insurance Company was dispatching insurance claims to Castleisland, Ireland, where routine producers, guided by simple directions, entered the claims and determined the amounts due, then instantly transmitted the computations back to the United States. (When the firm advertised in Ireland for twenty-five data-processing jobs, it received six hundred applications.) And McGraw-Hill was processing subscription renewal and marketing information for its magazines in nearby Galway. Indeed, literally millions of routine workers around the world were receiving information, converting it into computer-readable form, and then sending it back—at the speed of electronic impulses—whence it came.

The simple coding of computer software has also entered into world com- 10 merce. India, with a large English-speaking population of technicians happy to do routine programming cheaply, is proving to be particularly attractive to global webs in need of this service. By 1990, Texas Instruments maintained a software development facility in Bangalore, linking fifty Indian programmers

[2]John Maxwell Hamilton, "A Bit Player Buys into the Computer Age," *New York Times Business World*, December 3, 1989, p. 14.

by satellite to TI's Dallas headquarters. Spurred by this and similar ventures, the Indian government was building a teleport in Poona, intended to make it easier and less expensive for many other firms to send their routine software design specifications for coding.[3]

11   This shift of routine production jobs from advanced to developing nations is a great boon to many workers in such nations who otherwise would be jobless or working for much lower wages. These workers, in turn, now have more money with which to purchase symbolic-analytic services from advanced nations (often embedded within all sorts of complex products). The trend is also beneficial to everyone around the world who can now obtain high-volume, standardized products (including information and software) more cheaply than before.

12   But these benefits do not come without certain costs. In particular the burden is borne by those who no longer have good-paying routine production jobs within advanced economies like the United States. Many of these people used to belong to unions or at least benefited from prevailing wage rates established in collective bargaining agreements. But as the old corporate bureaucracies have flattened into global webs, bargaining leverage has been lost. Indeed, the tacit national bargain is no more.

13   Despite the growth in the number of new jobs in the United States, union membership has withered. In 1960, 35 percent of all nonagricultural workers in America belonged to a union. But by 1980 that portion had fallen to just under a quarter, and by 1989 to about 17 percent. Excluding government employees, union membership was down to 13.4 percent.[4] This was a smaller proportion even than in the early 1930s, before the National Labor Relations Act created a legally protected right to labor representation. The drop in membership has been accompanied by a growing number of collective bargaining agreements to freeze wages at current levels, reduce wage levels of entering workers, or reduce wages overall. This is an important reason why the long economic recovery that began in 1982 produced a smaller rise in unit labor costs than any of the eight recoveries since World War II—the low rate of unemployment during its course notwithstanding.

14   Routine production jobs have vanished fastest in traditional unionized industries (autos, steel, and rubber, for example), where average wages have kept up with inflation. This is because the jobs of older workers in such industries are protected by seniority; the youngest workers are the first to be laid off. Faced with a choice of cutting wages or cutting the number of jobs, a majority of union members (secure in the knowledge that there are many who are junior to them who will be laid off first) often have voted for the latter.

---

[3]Udayan Gupta, "U.S.-Indian Satellite Link Stands to Cut Software Costs," *Wall Street Journal,* March 6, 1989, p. B2.
[4]*Statistical Abstract of the United States* (Washington, D.C.: U.S. Government Printing Office, 1989), p. 416, table 684.

Thus the decline in union membership has been most striking among 15
young men entering the work force without a college education. In the early
1950s, more than 40 percent of this group joined unions; by the late 1980s, less
than 20 percent (if public employees are excluded, less than 10 percent).[5] In
steelmaking, for example, although many older workers remained employed,
almost half of all routine steelmaking jobs in America vanished between 1974
and 1988 (from 480,000 to 260,000). Similarly with automobiles: During the
1980s, the United Auto Workers lost 500,000 members—one-third of their total
at the start of the decade. General Motors alone cut 150,000 American production jobs during the 1980s (even as it added employment abroad). Another consequence of the same phenomenon: The gap between the average wages of
unionized and nonunionized workers widened dramatically—from 14.6 percent in 1973 to 20.4 percent by the end of the 1980s.[6] The lesson is clear. If you
drop out of high school or have no more than a high school diploma, do not
expect a good routine production job to be awaiting you.

Also vanishing are lower- and middle-level management jobs involving 16
routine production. Between 1981 and 1986, more than 780,000 foremen, super-
visors, and section chiefs lost their jobs through plant closings and layoffs.[7]
Large numbers of assistant division heads, assistant directors, assistant managers, and vice presidents also found themselves jobless. GM shed more than
40,000 white-collar employees and planned to eliminate another 25,000 by the
mid-1990s.[8] As America's core pyramids metamorphosed into global webs,
many middle-level routine producers were as obsolete as routine workers on
the line.

As has been noted, foreign-owned webs are hiring some Americans to do 17
routine production in the United States. Philips, Sony, and Toyota factories are
popping up all over—to the self-congratulatory applause of the nation's governors and mayors, who have lured them with promises of tax abatements and
new sewers, among other amenities. But as these ebullient politicians will soon
discover, the foreign-owned factories are highly automated and will become far
more so in years to come. Routine production jobs account for a small fraction of
the cost of producing most items in the United States and other advanced nations, and this fraction will continue to decline sharply as computer-integrated
robots take over. In 1977, it took routine producers thirty-five hours to assemble an automobile in the United States; it is estimated that by the mid-1990s,
Japanese-owned factories in America will be producing finished automobiles
using only eight hours of a routine producer's time.[9]

[5]Calculations from Current Population Surveys by L. Katz and A. Revenga, "Changes in the
Structure of Wages: U.S. and Japan," National Bureau of Economic Research, September 1989.
[6]U.S. Department of Commerce, Bureau of Labor Statistics, "Wages of Unionized and
Nonunionized Workers," various issues.
[7]U.S. Department of Labor, Bureau of Labor Statistics, "Reemployment Increases among Displaced
Workers," *BLS News*, USDL 86-414, October 14, 1986, table 6.
[8]*Wall Street Journal*, February 16, 1990, p. A5.
[9]Figures from the International Motor Vehicles Program, Massachusetts Institute of Technology, 1989.

18   The productivity and resulting wages of American workers who run such robotic machinery may be relatively high, but there may not be many such jobs to go around. A case in point: In the late 1980s, Nippon Steel joined with America's ailing Inland Steel to build a new $400 million cold-rolling mill fifty miles west of Gary, Indiana. The mill was celebrated for its state-of-the-art technology, which cut the time to produce a coil of steel from twelve days to about one hour. In fact, the entire plant could be run by a small team of technicians, which became clear when Inland subsequently closed two of its old cold-rolling mills, laying off hundreds of routine workers. Governors and mayors take note: Your much-ballyhooed foreign factories may end up employing distressingly few of your constituents.

19   Overall, the decline in routine jobs has hurt men more than women. This is because the routine production jobs held by men in high-volume metal bending manufacturing industries had paid higher wages than the routine production jobs held by women in textiles and data processing. As both sets of jobs have been lost, American women in routine production have gained more equal footing with American men—equally poor footing, that is. This is a major reason why the gender gap between male and female wages began to close during the 1980s.

20 The second of the three boats, carrying in-person servers, is sinking as well, but somewhat more slowly and unevenly. Most in-person servers are paid at or just slightly above the minimum wage and many work only part-time, with the result that their take-home pay is modest, to say the least. Nor do they typically receive all the benefits (health care, life insurance, disability, and so forth) garnered by routine producers in large manufacturing corporations or by symbolic analysts affiliated with the more affluent threads of global webs.[10] In-person servers are sheltered from the direct effects of global competition and, like everyone else, benefit from access to lower-cost products from around the world. But they are not immune to its indirect effects.

21   For one thing, in-person servers increasingly compete with former routine production workers, who, no longer able to find well-paying routine production jobs, have few alternatives but to seek in-person service jobs. The Bureau of Labor Statistics estimates that of the 2.8 million manufacturing workers who lost their jobs during the early 1980s, fully one-third were rehired in service jobs paying at least 20 percent less.[11] In-person servers must also compete with high school graduates and dropouts who years before had moved easily into routine production jobs but no longer can. And if demographic predictions about the American work force in the first decades of the twenty-first century are correct (and they are likely to be, since most of the people who will comprise the work

---

[10]The growing portion of the American labor force engaged in in-person services, relative to routine production, thus helps explain why the number of Americans lacking health insurance increased by at least 6 million during the 1980s.

[11]U.S. Department of Labor, Bureau of Labor Statistics, "Reemployment Increases among Disabled Workers," October 14, 1986.

force are already identifiable), most new entrants into the job market will be black or Hispanic men, or women—groups that in years past have possessed relatively weak technical skills. This will result in an even larger number of people crowding into in-person services. Finally, in-person servers will be competing with growing numbers of immigrants, both legal and illegal, for whom in-person services will comprise the most accessible jobs. (It is estimated that between the mid-1980s and the end of the century, about a quarter of all workers entering the American labor force will be immigrants.[12])

Perhaps the fiercest competition that in-person servers face comes from 22 labor-saving machinery (much of it invented, designed, fabricated, or assembled in other nations, of course). Automated tellers, computerized cashiers, automatic car washes, robotized vending machines, self-service gasoline pumps, and all similar gadgets substitute for the human beings that customers once encountered. Even telephone operators are fast disappearing, as electronic sensors and voice simulators become capable of carrying on conversations that are reasonably intelligent and always polite. Retail sales workers—among the largest groups of in-person servers—are similarly imperiled. Through personal computers linked to television screens, tomorrow's consumers will be able to buy furniture, appliances, and all sorts of electronic toys from their living rooms— examining the merchandise from all angles, selecting whatever color, size, special features, and price seem most appealing, and then transmitting the order instantly to warehouses from which the selections will be shipped directly to their homes. So, too, with financial transactions, airline and hotel reservations, rental car agreements, and similar contracts, which will be executed between consumers in their homes and computer banks somewhere else on the globe.[13]

Advanced economies like the United States will continue to generate siz- 23 able numbers of new in-person service jobs, of course, the automation of older ones notwithstanding. For every bank teller who loses her job to an automated teller, three new jobs open for aerobics instructors. Human beings, it seems, have an almost insatiable desire for personal attention. But the intense competition nevertheless ensures that the wages of in-person servers will remain relatively low. In-person servers—working on their own, or else dispersed widely amid many small establishments, filling all sorts of personal-care niches—cannot readily organize themselves into labor unions or create powerful lobbies to limit the impact of such competition.

In two respects, demographics will work in favor of in-person servers, 24 buoying their collective boat slightly. First, as has been noted, the rate of growth of the American work force is slowing. In particular, the number of young workers is shrinking. Between 1985 and 1995, the number of the eighteen- to twenty-four-year-olds will have declined by 17.5 percent. Thus, employers will

---

[12]Federal Immigration and Naturalization Service, *Statistical Yearbook* (Washington, D.C.: U.S. Government Printing Office, 1986, 1987).
[13]See Claudia H. Deutsch, "The Powerful Push for Self-Service," *New York Times*, April 9, 1989, section 3, p. 1.

have more incentive to hire and train in-person servers whom they might previously have avoided. But this demographic relief from the competitive pressures will be only temporary. The cumulative procreative energies of the postwar baby-boomers (born between 1946 and 1964) will result in a new surge of workers by 2010 or thereabouts.[14] And immigration—both legal and illegal—shows every sign of increasing in years to come.

25   Next, by the second decade of the twenty-first century, the number of Americans aged sixty-five and over will be rising precipitously, as the baby-boomers reach retirement age and live longer. Their life expectancies will lengthen not just because fewer of them will have smoked their way to their graves and more will have eaten better than their parents, but also because they will receive all sorts of expensive drugs and therapies designed to keep them alive—barely. By 2035, twice as many Americans will be elderly as in 1988, and the number of octogenarians is expected to triple. As these decaying baby-boomers ingest all the chemicals and receive all the treatments, they will need a great deal of personal attention. Millions of deteriorating bodies will require nurses, nursing-home operators, hospital administrators, orderlies, home-care providers, hospice aides, and technicians to operate and maintain all the expensive machinery that will monitor and temporarily stave off final disintegration. There might even be a booming market for euthanasia specialists. In-person servers catering to the old and ailing will be in strong demand.[15]

26   One small problem: the decaying baby-boomers will not have enough money to pay for these services. They will have used up their personal savings years before. Their Social Security payments will, of course, have been used by the government to pay for the previous generation's retirement and to finance much of the budget deficits of the 1980s. Moreover, with relatively fewer young Americans in the population, the supply of housing will likely exceed the demand, with the result that the boomers' major investments—their homes—will be worth less (in inflation-adjusted dollars) when they retire than they planned for. In consequence, the huge cost of caring for the graying boomers will fall on many of the same people who will be paid to care for them. It will be like a great sump pump: In-person servers of the twenty-first century will have an abundance of health-care jobs, but a large portion of their earnings will be devoted to Social Security payments and income taxes, which will in turn be used to pay their salaries. The net result: No real improvement in their standard of living.

27   The standard of living of in-person servers also depends, indirectly, on the standard of living of the Americans they serve who are engaged in world commerce. To the extent that *these* Americans are richly rewarded by the rest of the world for what they contribute, they will have more money to lavish upon

---

[14]U.S. Bureau of the Census, Current Population Reports, Series P-23, no. 138, tables 2-1, 4-6. See W. Johnson, A. Packer, et al., *Workforce 2000: Work and Workers for the 21st Century* (Indianapolis: Hudson Institute, 1987).

[15]The Census Bureau estimates that by the year 2000, at least 12 million Americans will work in health services—well over 6 percent of the total work force.

in-person services. Here we find the only form of "trickle-down" economics that has a basis in reality. A waitress in a town whose major factory has just been closed is unlikely to earn a high wage or enjoy much job security; in a swank resort populated by film producers and banking moguls, she is apt to do reasonably well. So, too, with nations. In-person servers in Bangladesh may spend their days performing roughly the same tasks as in-person servers in the United States, but have a far lower standard of living for their efforts. The difference comes in the value that their customers add to the world economy.

Unlike the boats of routine producers and in-person servers, however, the   28 vessel containing America's symbolic analysts is rising. Worldwide demand for their insights is growing as the ease and speed of communicating them steadily increases. Not every symbolic analyst is rising as quickly or as dramatically as every other, of course; symbolic analysts at the low end are barely holding their own in the world economy. But symbolic analysts at the top are in such great demand worldwide that they have difficulty keeping track of all their earnings. Never before in history has opulence on such a scale been gained by people who have earned it, and done so legally.

Among symbolic analysts in the middle range are American scientists and   29 researchers who are busily selling their discoveries to global enterprise webs. They are not limited to American customers. If the strategic brokers in General Motors' headquarters refuse to pay a high price for a new means of making high-strength ceramic engines dreamed up by a team of engineers affiliated with Carnegie Mellon University in Pittsburgh, the strategic brokers of Honda or Mercedes-Benz are likely to be more than willing.

So, too, with the insights of America's ubiquitous management consultants,   30 which are being sold for large sums to eager entrepreneurs in Europe and Latin America. Also, the insights of America's energy consultants, sold for even larger sums to Arab sheikhs. American design engineers are providing insights to Olivetti, Mazda, Siemens, and other global webs; American marketers, techniques for learning what worldwide consumers will buy; American advertisers, ploys for ensuring that they actually do. American architects are issuing designs and blueprints for opera houses, art galleries, museums, luxury hotels, and residential complexes in the world's major cities; American commercial property developers, marketing these properties to worldwide investors and purchasers.

Americans who specialize in the gentle art of public relations are in de-   31 mand by corporations, governments, and politicians in virtually every nation. So, too, are American political consultants, some of whom, at this writing, are advising the Hungarian Socialist Party, the remnant of Hungary's ruling Communists, on how to salvage a few parliamentary seats in the nation's first free election in more than forty years. Also at this writing, a team of American agricultural consultants is advising the managers of a Soviet farm collective employing 1,700 Russians eighty miles outside Moscow. As noted, American investment bankers and lawyers specializing in financial circumnavigations are selling their insights to Asians and Europeans who are eager to discover how to make large amounts of money by moving large amounts of money.

32   Developing nations, meanwhile, are hiring American civil engineers to advise on building roads and dams. The present thaw in the Cold War will no doubt expand these opportunities. American engineers from Bechtel (a global firm notable for having employed both Caspar Weinberger and George Shultz for much larger sums than either earned in the Reagan administration) have begun helping the Soviets design and install a new generation of nuclear reactors. Nations also are hiring American bankers and lawyers to help them renegotiate the terms of their loans with global banks, and Washington lobbyists to help them with Congress, the Treasury, the World Bank, the IMF, and other politically sensitive institutions. In fits of obvious desperation, several nations emerging from communism have even hired American economists to teach them about capitalism.

33   Almost everyone around the world is buying the skills and insights of Americans who manipulate oral and visual symbols—musicians, sound engineers, film producers, makeup artists, directors, cinematographers, actors and actresses, boxers, scriptwriters, songwriters, and set designers. Among the wealthiest of symbolic analysts are Steven Spielberg, Bill Cosby, Charles Schulz, Eddie Murphy, Sylvester Stallone, Madonna, and other star directors and performers—who are almost as well known on the streets of Dresden and Tokyo as in the Back Bay of Boston. Less well rewarded but no less renowned are the unctuous anchors on Turner Broadcasting's Cable News, who appear daily, via satellite, in places ranging from Vietnam to Nigeria. Vanna White is the world's most-watched game-show hostess. Behind each of these familiar faces is a collection of American problem-solvers, -identifiers, and brokers who train, coach, advise, promote, amplify, direct, groom, represent, and otherwise add value to their talents.[16]

34   There are also the insights of senior American executives who occupy the world headquarters of global "American" corporations and the national or regional headquarters of global "foreign" corporations. Their insights are duly exported to the rest of the world through the webs of global enterprise. IBM does not export many machines from the United States, for example. Big Blue makes machines all over the globe and services them on the spot. Its prime American exports are symbolic and analytic. From IBM's world headquarters in Armonk, New York, emanate strategic brokerage and related management services bound for the rest of the world. In return, IBM's top executives are generously rewarded.

35 The most important reason for this expanding world market and increasing global demand for the symbolic and analytic insights of Americans has been the dramatic improvement in worldwide communication and transportation technologies. Designs, instructions, advice, and visual and audio symbols can be communicated more and more rapidly around the globe, with ever greater precision and at ever-lower cost. Madonna's voice can be transported to billions of listeners, with perfect clarity, on digital compact discs. A new invention

---

[16]In 1989, the entertainment business summoned to the United States $5.5 billion in foreign earnings—making it among the nation's largest export industries, just behind aerospace. U.S. Department of Commerce, International Trade Commission, "Composition of U.S. Exports," various issues.

emanating from engineers in Battelle's laboratory in Columbus, Ohio, can be sent almost anywhere via modem, in a form that will allow others to examine it in three dimensions through enhanced computer graphics. When face-to-face meetings are still required—and videoconferencing will not suffice—it is relatively easy for designers, consultants, advisers, artists, and executives to board supersonic jets and, in a matter of hours, meet directly with their worldwide clients, customers, audiences, and employees.

With rising demand comes rising compensation. Whether in the form of li- 36 censing fees, fees for service, salaries, or shares in final profits, the economic result is much the same. There are also nonpecuniary rewards. One of the best-kept secrets among symbolic analysts is that so many of them enjoy their work. In fact, much of it does not count as work at all, in the traditional sense. The work of routine producers and in-person servers is typically monotonous; it causes muscles to tire or weaken and involves little independence or discretion. The "work" of symbolic analysts, by contrast, often involves puzzles, experiments, games, a significant amount of chatter, and substantial discretion over what to do next. Few routine producers or in-person servers would "work" if they did not need to earn the money. Many symbolic analysts would "work" even if money were no object.

At mid-century, when America was a national market dominated by core 37 pyramid-shaped corporations, there were constraints on the earnings of people at the highest rungs. First and most obviously, the market for their services was largely limited to the borders of the nation. In addition, whatever conceptual value they might contribute was small relative to the value gleaned from large scale—and it was dependent on large scale for whatever income it was to summon. Most of the problems to be identified and solved had to do with enhancing the efficiency of production and improving the flow of materials, parts, assembly, and distribution. Inventors searched for the rare breakthrough revealing an entirely new product to be made in high volume; management consultants, executives, and engineers thereafter tried to speed and synchronize its manufacture, to better achieve scale efficiencies; advertisers and marketers sought then to whet the public's appetite for the standard item that emerged. Since white-collar earnings increased with larger scale, there was considerable incentive to expand the firm; indeed, many of America's core corporations grew far larger than scale economies would appear to have justified.

By the 1990s, in contrast, the earnings of symbolic analysts were limited 38 neither by the size of the national market nor by the volume of production of the firms with which they were affiliated. The marketplace was worldwide, and conceptual value was high relative to value added from scale efficiencies.

There had been another constraint on high earnings, which also gave way by 39 the 1990s. At mid-century, the compensation awarded to top executives and advisers of the largest of America's core corporations could not be grossly out of proportion to that of low-level production workers. It would be unseemly for executives who engaged in highly visible rounds of bargaining with labor unions, and who routinely responded to government requests to moderate prices, to take home wages and benefits wildly in excess of what other Americans earned.

Unless white-collar executives restrained themselves, moreover, blue-collar production workers could not be expected to restrain their own demands for higher
wages. Unless both groups exercised restraint, the government could not be expected to forbear from imposing direct controls and regulations.

40   At the same time, the wages of production workers could not be allowed to
sink too low, lest there be insufficient purchasing power in the economy. After
all, who would buy all the goods flowing out of American factories if not American workers? This, too, was part of the tacit bargain struck between American
managers and their workers.

41   Recall the oft-repeated corporate platitude of the era about the chief executive's responsibility to carefully weigh and balance the interests of the corporation's disparate stakeholders. Under the stewardship of the corporate statesman,
no set of stakeholders—least of all white-collar executives—was to gain a disproportionately large share of the benefits of corporate activity; nor was any
stakeholder—especially the average worker—to be left with a share that was
disproportionately small. Banal though it was, this idea helped to maintain the
legitimacy of the core American corporation in the eyes of most Americans, and
to ensure continued economic growth.

42   But by the 1990s, these informal norms were evaporating, just as (and
largely because) the core American corporation was vanishing. The links between top executives and the American production worker were fading: An
ever-increasing number of subordinates and contractees were foreign, and a
steadily growing number of American routine producers were working for
foreign-owned firms. An entire cohort of middle-level managers, who had once
been deemed "white collar," had disappeared; and, increasingly, American executives were exporting their insights to global enterprise webs.

43   As the American corporation itself became a global web almost indistin-
guishable from any other, its stakeholders were turning into a large and diffuse
group, spread over the world. Such global stakeholders were less visible, and
far less noisy, than national stakeholders. And as the American corporation sold
its goods and services all over the world, the purchasing power of American
workers became far less relevant to its economic survival.

44   Thus have the inhibitions been removed. The salaries and benefits of America's top executives, and many of their advisers and consultants, have soared to
what years before would have been unimaginable heights, even as those of
other Americans have declined.

COMPREHENSION

1. To what does the title allude? Why is this allusion significant to the meaning of the
   title?
2. To whom does Reich refer when he mentions "symbolic analysts"? Regardless of
   their occupation, what do all symbolic analysts have in common regarding the nature of their work?

3. What has traditionally been the image of and the nature of work among the white-collar workers to whom Reich alludes? Why are they now one of the groups in danger of losing employment opportunities?

RHETORIC

1. Reich uses the central metaphor of the "boat" in describing the state of economics and employment. Why? What connotations are associated with this image in regard to financial security?
2. How does Reich's introduction prepare you for the major themes he addresses in the body of his essay?
3. Examine the section breaks at the start of paragraphs 3, 11, 20, 35, and 37. How does each section relate to the theme of the essay as a whole? What transitional devices does Reich use to bridge one section to the next?
4. Paragraphs 5, 6, 9, and 16 cite specific and detailed examples of the effects of the changing global economy. How does this contribute to conveying Reich's authority regarding the subject he is discussing?
5. Reich describes a dire situation for the American worker. How would you characterize the tone of this description? Is it angry, resigned, impartial, or accusatory? You may use these or any other adjectives as long as you explain your view.
6. Why does Reich open his essay with an epigraph from Adam Smith? What is the relationship of the quotation to the overall theme of the essay? How does the tone of the epigraph contrast with the tone of the title?
7. What is the author's purpose? Is it to inform, to explain, to warn, to enlighten, to offer solutions, or a combination of any of these? Explain your view.

WRITING

1. In a classification essay, describe three areas of academic concentration at your college or university that can help prepare one for a job as a symbolic analyst.
2. In an expository essay, explain whether you believe the discrepancy between high-wage and low-wage workers will increase, decrease, or remain the same.
3. **Writing an Argument:** In an essay, argue for or against the proposition that as long as one knows which careers command the highest salaries, it is up to the individual to decide whether he or she should pursue a job in those fields.

NETWORKING
Applying 21st-Century Literacies

Participating in a Newsgroup: Join a newsgroup with a special interest in the global economy. Post a general question to its members, asking whether they agree with Reich's analysis of the changing job market. Collect and synthesize the responses.

A Modest Proposal
Preventing the Children of Poor People
in Ireland from Being a Burden to Their
Parents or Country, and for Making
Them Beneficial to the Public

Jonathan Swift

Jonathan Swift (1667–1745) is best known as the author of three satires: A Tale of a
Tub *(1704),* Gulliver's Travels *(1726), and* A Modest Proposal *(1729). In these
satires, Swift pricks the balloon of many of his contemporaries' and our own most cherished prejudices, pomposities, and delusions. He was also a famous churchman, an eloquent spokesman for Irish rights, and a political journalist. The following selection,
perhaps the most famous satiric essay in the English language, offers modest advice to
a nation suffering from poverty, overpopulation, and political injustice.*

1   It is a melancholy object to those who walk through this great town or travel in
the country, when they see the streets, the roads, and cabin doors, crowded
with beggars of the female-sex, followed by three, four, or six children, all in
rags and importuning every passenger for an alms. These mothers, instead of
being able to work for their honest livelihood, are forced to employ all their
time in strolling to beg sustenance for their helpless infants, who, as they grow
up, either turn thieves for want of work, or leave their dear native country to
fight for the Pretender in Spain, or sell themselves to the Barbadoes.

2   I think it is agreed by all parties that this prodigious number of children in
the arms, or on the backs, or at the heels of their mothers, and frequently of
their fathers, is in the present deplorable state of the kingdom a very great additional grievance; and therefore whoever could find out a fair, cheap, and easy
method of making these children sound, useful members of the commonwealth
would deserve so well of the public as to have his statue set up for a preserver
of the nation.

3   But my intention is very far from being confined to provide only for the
children of professed beggars; it is of a much greater extent, and shall take in
the whole number of infants at a certain age who are born of parents in effect as
little able to support them as those who demand our charity in the streets.

4   As to my own part, having turned my thoughts for many years upon this
important subject, and maturely weighted the several schemes of other projec-
tors, I have always found them grossly mistaken in their computation. It is
true, a child just dropped from its dam may be supported by her milk for a

solar year, with little other nourishment; at most not above the value of two shillings, which the mother may certainly get, or the value in scraps, by her lawful occupation of begging; and it is exactly at one year old that I propose to provide for them in such a manner as instead of being a charge upon their parents or the parish, or wanting food and raiment for the rest of their lives, they shall on the contrary contribute to the feeding, and partly to the clothing, of many thousands.

There is likewise another great advantage in my scheme, that it will prevent ₅ those voluntary abortions, and that horrid practice of women murdering their bastard children, alas, too frequent among us, sacrificing the poor innocent babes, I doubt, more to avoid the expense than the shame, which would move tears and pity in the most savage and inhuman breast.

The number of souls in this kingdom being usually reckoned one million ₆ and a half, of these I calculate there may be about two hundred thousand couples whose wives are breeders; from which number I subtract thirty thousand couples who are able to maintain their own children, although I apprehend there cannot be so many under the present distresses of the kingdom; but this being granted, there will remain an hundred and seventy thousand breeders. I again subtract fifty thousand for those women who miscarry, or whose children die by accident or disease within the year. There only remain an hundred and twenty thousand children of poor parents annually born. The question therefore is, how this number shall be reared and provided for, which, as I have already said, under the present situation of affairs, is utterly impossible by all the methods hitherto proposed. For we can neither employ them in handicraft or agriculture; we neither build houses (I mean in the country) nor cultivate land. They can very seldom pick up a livelihood by stealing till they arrive at six years old, except where they are of towardly parts; although I confess they learn the rudiments much earlier, during which time they can however be looked upon only as probationers, as I have been informed by a principal gentleman in the county of Cavan, who protested to me that he never knew above one or two instances under the age of six, even in a part of the kingdom so renowned for the quickest proficiency in that art.

I am assured by our merchants that a boy or girl before twelve years old is ₇ no salable commodity; and even when they come to this age they will not yield above three pounds, or three pounds and half a crown at most on the Exchange; which cannot turn to account either to the parents or the kingdom, the charge of nutriment and rags having been at least four times that value.

I shall now therefore humbly propose my own thoughts, which I hope will ₈ not be liable to the least objection.

I have been assured by a very knowing American of my acquaintance in ₉ London, that a young healthy child well nursed is at a year old a most delicious, nourishing, and wholesome food, whether stewed, roasted, baked or boiled; and I make no doubt that it will equally serve in a fricassee or a ragout.

I do therefore humbly offer it to public consideration that of the hundred ₁₀ and twenty thousand children, already computed, twenty thousand may be reserved for breed, whereof only one fourth part to be males, which is more than we allow to sheep, black cattle, or swine; and my reason is that these children are seldom the fruits of marriage, a circumstance not much regarded by our savages, therefore one male will be sufficient to serve four females. That the remaining hundred thousand may at a year old be offered in sale to the persons of quality and fortune through the kingdom, always advising the mother to let them suck plentifully in the last month, so as to render them plump and fat for a good table. A child will make two dishes at an entertainment for friends; and when the family dines alone, the fore or hind quarter will make a reasonable dish, and seasoned with a little pepper or salt will be very good boiled on the fourth day, especially in winter.

11   I have reckoned upon a medium that a child just born will weigh twelve pounds, and in a solar year if tolerably nursed increaseth to twenty-eight pounds.

12   I grant this food will be somewhat dear, and therefore very proper for landlords, who, as they have already devoured most of the parents, seem to have the best title to the children.

13   Infant's flesh will be in season throughout the year, but more plentiful in March, and a little before and after. For we are told by a grave author, an eminent French physician, that fish being a prolific diet, there are more children born in Roman Catholic countries about nine months after Lent than at any other season: therefore, reckoning a year after Lent, the markets will be more glutted than usual, because the number of popish infants is at least three to one in this kingdom; and therefore it will have one other collateral advantage, by lessening the number of Papists among us.

14   I have already computed the charge of nursing a beggar's child (in which list I reckon all cottagers, laborers, and four fifths of the farmers) to be about two shillings per annum, rags included: and I believe no gentleman would repine to give ten shillings for the carcass of a good fat child, which, as I have said, will make four dishes of excellent nutritive meat, when he hath only some particular friend or his own family to dine with him. Thus the squire will learn to be a good landlord, and grow popular among the tenants; the mother will have eight shillings net profit, and be fit for work till she produces another child.

15   Those who are more thrifty (as I must confess the times require) may flay the carcass; the skin of which artificially dressed will make admirable gloves for ladies, and summer boots for fine gentlemen.

16   As to our city of Dublin, shambles may be appointed for this purpose in the most convenient parts of it, and butchers we may be assured will not be wanting; although I rather recommend buying the children alive, and dressing them hot from the knife as we do roasting pigs.

17   A very worthy person, a true lover of his country, and whose virtues I highly esteem, was lately pleased in discoursing on this matter to offer a refinement upon my scheme. He said that many gentlemen of this kingdom, having of late destroyed their deer, he conceived that the want of venison might be

well supplied by the bodies of young lads and maidens, not exceeding fourteen years of age nor under twelve, so great a number of both sexes in every county being now ready to starve for want of work and service; and these to be disposed of by their parents, if alive, or otherwise by their nearest relations. But with due deference to so excellent a friend and so deserving a patriot, I cannot be altogether in his sentiments; for as to the males, my American acquaintance assured me from frequent experience that their flesh was generally tough and lean, like that of our schoolboys, by continual exercise, and their taste disagreeable; and to fatten them would not answer the charge. Then as to the females, it would, I think with humble submission, be a loss to the public, because they soon would become breeders themselves: and besides, it is not improbable that some scrupulous people might be apt to censure such a practice (although indeed very unjustly) as a little bordering upon cruelty; which, I confess, hath always been with me the strongest objection against any project, how well so ever intended.

But in order to justify my friend, he confessed that this expedient was put 18 into his head by the famous Psalmanazar, a native of the island Formosa, who came from thence to London above twenty years ago, and in conversation told my friend that in his country when any young person happened to be put to death, the executioner sold the carcass to persons of quality as a prime dainty; and that in his time the body of a plump girl of fifteen, who was crucified for an attempt to poison the emperor, was sold to his Imperial Majesty's prime minister of state, and other great mandarins of the court, in joints from the gibbet, at four hundred crowns. Neither indeed can I deny that if the same use were made of several plump young girls in this town, who without one single groat to their fortunes cannot stir abroad without a chair, and appear at the playhouse and assemblies in foreign fineries which they never will pay for, the kingdom would not be the worse.

Some persons of a desponding spirit are in great concern about that vast 19 number of poor people who are aged, diseased, or maimed, and I have been desired to employ my thoughts what course may be taken to ease the nation of so grievous an encumbrance. But I am not in the least pain upon that matter, because it is very well known that they are every day dying and rotting by cold and famine, and filth and vermin, as fast as can be reasonably expected. And as to the younger laborers, they are now in almost as hopeful a condition. They cannot get work, and consequently pine away for want of nourishment to a degree that if at any time they are accidentally hired to common labor, they have not strength to perform it; and thus the country and themselves are happily delivered from the evils to come.

I have too long digressed, and therefore shall return to my subject. I think 20 the advantages by the proposal which I have made are obvious and many, as well as of the highest importance.

For first, as I have already observed, it would greatly lessen the number 21 of Papists, with whom we are yearly overrun, being the principal breeders of the nation as well as our most dangerous enemies; and who stay at home on purpose to deliver the kingdom to the Pretender, hoping to take their advantage by the absence of so many good Protestants, who have chosen rather to leave their country than to stay at home and pay tithes against their conscience to an Episcopal curate.

22 Secondly, the poorer tenants will have something valuable of their own, which by law may be made liable to distress, and help to pay their landlord's rent, their corn and cattle being already seized and money a thing unknown.

23 Thirdly, whereas the maintenance of an hundred thousand children, from two years old and upwards, cannot be computed at less than ten shillings a piece per annum, the nation's stock will be thereby increased fifty thousand pounds per annum, besides the profit of a new dish introduced to the tables of all gentlemen of fortune in the kingdom who have any refinement in taste. And the money will circulate among ourselves, the goods being entirely of our own growth and manufacture.

24 Fourthly, the constant breeders, besides the gain of eight shillings sterling per annum by the sale of their children, will be rid of the charge of maintaining them after the first year.

25 Fifthly, this food would likewise bring great custom to taverns, where the vintners will certainly be so prudent as to procure the best receipts for dressing it to perfection, and consequently have their houses frequented by all the fine gentlemen, who justly value themselves upon their knowledge in good eating; and a skillful cook, who understands how to oblige his guests, will contrive to make it as expensive as they please.

26 Sixthly, this would be a great inducement to marriage, which all wise nations have either encouraged by rewards or enforced by laws and penalties. It would increase the care and tenderness of mothers toward their children, when they were sure of a settlement for life to the poor babes, provided in some sort by the public, to their annual profit instead of expense. We should see an honest emulation among the married women, which of them could bring the fattest child to the market. Men would become as fond of their wives during the time of their pregnancy as they are now of their mares in foal, their cows in calf, or sows when they are ready to farrow; nor offer to beat or kick them (as is too frequent a practice) for fear of a miscarriage.

27 Many other advantages might be enumerated. For instance, the addition of some thousand carcasses in our exportation of barreled beef, the propagation of swine's flesh, and improvement in the art of making good bacon, so much wanted among us by the great destruction of pigs, too frequent at our tables, which are no way comparable in taste or magnificence to a well-grown, fat yearling child, which roasted whole will make a considerable figure at a lord mayor's feast or any other public entertainment. But this and many others I omit, being studious of brevity.

28 Supposing that one thousand families in this city would be constant customers for infants' flesh, besides others who might have it at merry meetings, particularly weddings and christenings, I compute that Dublin would take off annually about twenty thousand carcasses, and the rest of the kingdom

(where probably they will be sold somewhat cheaper) the remaining eighty thousand.

I can think of no one objection that will possibly be raised against this pro- 29 posal, unless it should be urged that the number of people will be thereby much lessened in the kingdom. This I freely own, and it was indeed one principal design in offering it to the world. I desire the reader will observe, that I calculate my remedy for this one individual kingdom of Ireland and for no other that ever was, is, or I think ever can be upon earth. Therefore let no man talk to me of other expedients: of taxing our absentees at five shillings a pound: of using neither clothes nor household furniture except what is of our own growth and manufacture: of utterly rejecting the materials and instruments that promote foreign luxury: of curing the expensiveness of pride, vanity, idleness, and gaming in our women: of introducing a vein of parsimony, prudence, and temperance: of learning to love our country, in the want of which we differ even from Laplanders and the inhabitants of Topinamboo: of quitting our animosities and factions, nor acting any longer like the Jews, who were murdering one another at the very moment their city was taken: of being a little cautious not to sell our country and conscience for nothing: of teaching landlords to have at least one degree of mercy toward their tenants: lastly, of putting a spirit of honesty, industry, and skill into our shopkeepers; who, if a resolution could be now taken to buy only our native goods, would immediately unite to cheat and exact upon us in the price, the measure and the goodness, nor could ever yet be brought to make one fair proposal of just dealing, though often and earnestly invited to it.

Therefore I repeat, let no man talk to me of these and the like expedients, till 30 he hath at least some glimpse of hope that there will ever be some hearty and sincere attempt to put them in practice.

But as to myself, having been wearied out for many years with offering 31 vain, idle, visionary thoughts, and at length utterly despairing of success, I fortunately fell upon this proposal, which, as it is wholly new, so it hath something solid and real, of no expense and little trouble, full in our own power, and whereby we can incur no danger in disobliging England. For this kind of commodity will not bear exportation, the flesh being of too tender a consistence to admit a long continuance in salt, although perhaps I could name a country which would be glad to eat up our whole nation without it.

After all, I am not so violently bent upon my own opinion as to reject any 32 offer proposed by wise men, which shall be found equally innocent, cheap, easy, and effectual. But before something of that kind shall be advanced in contradiction to my scheme, and offering a better, I desire the author or authors will be pleased maturely to consider two points. First, as things now stand, how they will be able to find food and raiment for an hundred thousand useless mouths and backs. And secondly, there being a round million of creatures in human figure throughout this kingdom, whose sole subsistence put into a common stock would leave them in debt two millions of pounds sterling, adding those who are beggars by profession to the bulk of farmers, cottagers, and laborers, with their wives and children who are beggars in effect; I desire those politicians who dislike my overture, and may perhaps be so bold to attempt an answer, that they will first ask the parents of these mortals whether they would not at this day think it a great happiness to have been sold for food at a year old in the manner I prescribe, and thereby have avoided such a perpetual scene of misfortunes as they have since gone through by the oppression of landlords, the impossibility of paying rent without money or trade, the want of common sustenance, with neither house nor clothes to cover them from the inclemencies of the weather, and the most inevitable prospect of entailing the like or greater miseries upon their breed forever.

33   I profess, in the sincerity of my heart, that I have not the least personal interest in endeavoring to promote this necessary work, having no other motive than the public good of my country, by advancing our trade, providing for infants, relieving the poor, and giving some pleasure to the rich. I have no children by which I can propose to get a single penny; the youngest being nine years old, and my wife past childbearing.

COMPREHENSION

1. Who is Swift's audience for this essay? Defend your answer.
2. Describe the persona in this essay. How is the unusual narrative personality (as distinguished from Swift's personality) revealed by the author in degrees? How can we tell that the speaker's opinions are not shared by Swift?
3. What are the major propositions behind Swift's modest proposal? What are the minor propositions?

RHETORIC

1. Explain the importance of the word *modest* in the title. What stylistic devices does this "modesty" contrast with?
2. What is the effect of Swift's persistent reference to people as "breeders," "dams," "carcass," and the like? Why does he define *children* in economic terms? Find other words that contribute to this motif.
3. Analyze the purpose of the relatively long introduction, consisting of paragraphs 1–7. How does Swift establish his ironic-satiric tone in this initial section?
4. What contrasts and discrepancies are at the heart of Swift's ironic statement in paragraphs 9 and 10? Explain both the subtlety and savagery of the satire in paragraph 12.
5. Paragraphs 13–20 develop six advantages of Swift's proposal, while paragraphs 21–26 list them in enumerative manner. Analyze the progression of these propositions. What is the effect of the listing? Why is Swift parodying argumentative techniques?
6. How does the author both sustain and suspend the irony in paragraph 29? How is the strategy repeated in paragraph 32? How does the concluding paragraph cap his satiric commentary on human nature?

WRITING

1. Discuss Swift's social, political, religious, and economic views as they are revealed in the essay.
2. Write a comprehensive critique of America's failure to address the needs of its poor.
3. **Writing an Argument:** Write a modest proposal—on, for example, how to end the drug problem—advancing an absurd proposition through various argumentative techniques.

NETWORKING
Applying 21st-Century Literacies

Navigating Online Criticism: Go online to locate various critical responses to Swift's famous essay. Review at least five entries from online journals, magazines, or blogs that you would determine *credible sources*, analyzing the basic thesis or claim by each writer. Synthesize your findings in a brief essay.

Synthesis: Connections for Critical Thinking

1. Using the essays of Ehrenreich and Reich, compare the effects of work on human relationships.
2. Write a definition essay titled "What Is Work?" Refer to any of the selections in this chapter to substantiate your opinions.
3. Describe the potential effect of the global marketplace as described by Reich and Friedman.
4. Compare the writings of Swift, Ehrenreich, Krugman, and Reich in terms of the options of those on the lowest rungs of the economic system in Western society.
5. Woolf and Swift are considered to be "classic" writers. What makes their essays "classics"?
6. Monitor and record three business news television shows that focus on analysis and commentary. Analyze the discourse of the moderators, hosts, and guests. As an alternative method, review selected business news Web sites, and subject them to the same analysis.
7. To what extent is American society guided by a business ethic? For example, have Americans historically been so preoccupied with wealth that the quest for money has actually become a distinguishing mark of the national character? Or does the merging of business and religion (what social scientists term the Protestant work ethic) reflect a uniquely American trait? Discuss these issues in an analytical and argumentative essay.
8. Compare and contrast the use of irony and satire in the essays by Allen and Swift.

NETWORKING
Applying 21st-Century Literacies

1. Locate the online editions of three major newspapers in three different large cities in America. Review their classified sections, and compare and contrast the types of jobs advertised in the three cities. Do a similar search and comparison for federal and state government jobs.
2. Examine your own college's or university's Web site, and review its philosophy regarding the relationship of college studies to the world of work.
3. Locate several Web sites for job seekers—for example, Monster.com, Idealist.org, and Craigslist. Enter the job classification you are interested in, and compare and contrast the number and types of jobs advertised for three cities. Do a similar search and comparison for federal and state government jobs advertised online.

CH 9   **www.mhhe.com/mhreader11e**

- *Image Gallery:* Chapter images in color
- *Business and Economics:* Information on the authors in this chapter
- *Ch. 9 Networking*

chapter *10*

Media and Popular Culture
What Is the Message?

We are surrounded today as never before by images, sounds, and texts—by what Todd Gitlin, who has an essay in this chapter, terms a "media torrent." Radio and television programs, newspapers and Internet sites, MTV and video games, iPods and cell phone gadgetry increasingly mold our place in culture and society. Indeed, the power of media in our waking and subliminal lives might very well condition our understanding (or misunderstanding) of reality. Today, we can download "reality."

Today's media universe, fueled by new technology, is transforming our sense of the world. Consider the ways in which computers permit us to enter the media stream, making us willing, even compulsive, participants in and consumers of popular culture. Video games, streaming advertisements, wraparound music, newsgroups, chat rooms, and more—all provide data and sensation at warp computer speed. Some slow down the torrent: Bloggers (a word that didn't exist until recently) interrogate their lives and the "facts," even holding newspapers and television news channels accountable for information. But if, as Marshall McLuhan declared, the medium is the message, then any medium, whether old or new, has the power to reflect or construct versions of reality.

Perhaps Americans have moved from a print-based culture to an aural/visual one, preferring electronic media for information, distraction, and entertainment. For centuries books were the molders of popular taste and culture. Tocqueville in *Democracy in America* was amazed by the fact that in the rudest pioneer's hut there was a copy of Shakespeare—and probably, we might add, a copy of the best seller of all time, the Bible. Today's typical household might have more media for DVD players, MP3 players, and gaming consoles than books in a library. Of course, print media—say, a book on the ways in which major political parties manipulate the media—offer us the opportunity to scrutinize facts and sources in ways that shock jocks on radio, or talk show hosts on television, or participants in chat rooms cannot. The *medium* or *source* from which we receive sounds, images, and text—the place from which we enter the media torrent—determines the version of reality we carry with us. We can even drown in this torrent, as people who have been captured in virtual reality can attest.

The writers in this chapter invite us to enter the media torrent from a variety of places. They ask broad cultural questions about how we conduct our everyday lives and what choices we make. These questions have both local and worldwide implications, because media and their technological helpmates have created a global village permitting the instant transmission of ideas and images, as well as a subtle transfer of culture—typically American—to the remotest parts of the planet. Whether we navigate the torrent intelligently or succumb passively to the images and sounds washing over us, it is clear that the media in this century will have an increasingly significant impact on human experience.

PREVIEWING THE CHAPTER

As you read the essays in this chapter and respond to them in discussion and writing, consider the following questions:

- What is the main media form and issue on which the author focuses?
- What tone or attitude does the author take toward the subject?
- How does the author fit his or her analysis into the context of popular culture? What social, economic, psychological, or political problems or controversies are treated?
- Which areas of expertise does the author bring to bear on the subject?
- What form of rhetoric—narration and description, exposition, argument—does the writer use? If argument, what is the author's claim? What evidence does she or he provide to support this claim?
- Which essays are similar in subject, thesis, style, purpose, or method, and why?
- What have you learned about the media and popular culture from reading these essays?
- Which essays did you find the most compelling or persuasive? The least? Why?

Classic and Contemporary Images
WHAT DO GANGSTER FILMS REVEAL ABOUT US?

Using a Critical Perspective The best gangster films—like *Little Caesar*, *The God-father*, and the *Sopranos* series—challenge viewers to form ethical opinions about and interpretations of the tale of crime that unfolds. Even if you haven't seen either the film or TV show depicted here, what do you think is happening in each frame? What details do you focus on? Do the two characters capture the essence of the gangster life, and why? What aspects of film art—framing, the use of close-up or distance shots, the handling of light, shadow, and color—convey an ethical statement? More broadly, in what ways can film art serve as a commentary on American life?

During the 1930s, the first decade of sound films, actors such as
Edward G. Robinson, James Cagney, and Paul Muni created the
classic portrait of the gangster as a tough-talking, violent outlaw
in films such as *Little Caesar* (1930), *The Public Enemy* (1931),
and *Scarface* (1932).

HBO's award-winning series *The Sopranos* provided a more nuanced portrait of the gangster as a member of a corrupt, and corrupting, organization with shifting loyalties. For example, Tony Soprano, the character played by James Gandolfini, is a family man beset by so many problems that he must seek psychiatric help.

Classic and Contemporary Essays
WHY ARE WE FASCINATED BY BAD MEN
IN POPULAR CULTURE?

Both Robert Warshow and Lauren Goodlad examine the portrayal of "bad" men in popular culture, and specifically our fascination with this type in television and film. Warshow in his highly allusive essay argues that the gangster in American film is a type of urban tragic hero. On the other hand, Goodlad, whose essay is also filled with references to other works, argues from a feminist perspective that Don Draper, the protagonist in the wildly popular AMC series *Mad Men*, is an "icon of masculinity-in-crisis." Essentially, both writers suggest that bad, mad men—gangsters, rogues, outlaws, even some businessmen—exert a powerful hold on our imagination because they represent a flawed mythology of American success. These bad men are ill-fated from the start because they are compelled to operate in an unforgiving cultural and economic universe. They are doomed to anxiety and failure because their key point of cultural reference— the American Dream—is intrinsically corrupt. Ultimately both writers urge us to go beyond our fascination with media types of tragic men to examine the ethical dimensions of the world they inhabit.

The Gangster as Tragic Hero

Robert Warshow

Robert Warshow (1917–1955) attended the University of Michigan and worked for the U.S. Army Security Agency from 1942 to 1946. After the war, he served as an editor of Commentary, *writing film criticism for this magazine and also for* Partisan Review. *Before his untimely death from a heart attack, Warshow had written several brilliant essays on film and on popular culture. Writing of Warshow, Lionel Trilling observed, "I believe that certain of his pieces establish themselves in the line of Hazlitt, a tradition in which I would place only one other writer of our time, George Orwell." One of these brilliant essays, focusing on the interrelation of film and society, is "The Gangster as Tragic Hero," which appeared in* The Immediate Experience: Movies, Games, Theatre and Other Aspects of Popular Culture *(1962).*

1   America, as a social and political organization, is committed to a cheerful view of life. It could not be otherwise. The sense of tragedy is a luxury of aristocratic societies, where the fate of the individual is not conceived of as having a direct

and legitimate political importance, being determined by a fixed and supra-
political—that is, non-controversial—moral order or fate. Modern equalitarian
societies, however, whether democratic or authoritarian in their political forms,
always base themselves on the claim that they are making life happier; the
avowed function of the modern state, at least in its ultimate terms, is not only to
regulate social relations, but also to determine the quality and possibilities of
human life in general. Happiness thus becomes the chief political issue—in a
sense, the only political issue—and for that reason it can never be treated as an
issue at all. If an American or a Russian is unhappy, it implies a certain reproba-
tion of his society, and therefore, by a logic of which we can all recognize the
necessity, it becomes an obligation of citizenship to be cheerful; if the authorities find it necessary, the citizen may even be compelled to make a public display of his cheerfulness on important occasions, just as he may be conscripted
into the army in time of war.

Naturally, this civic responsibility rests most strongly upon the organs of 2
mass culture. The individual citizen may still be permitted his private unhappi-
ness so long as it does not take on political significance, the extent of this tolerance being determined by how large an area of private life the society can
accommodate. But every production of mass culture is a public act and must
conform with accepted notions of the public good. Nobody seriously questions
the principle that it is the function of mass culture to maintain public morale,
and certainly nobody in the mass audience objects to having his morale maintained.[1] At a time when the normal condition of the citizen is a state of anxiety,
euphoria spreads over our culture like the broad smile of an idiot. In terms of
attitudes towards life, there is very little difference between a "happy" movie
like *Good News,* which ignores death and suffering, and a "sad" movie like *A
Tree Grows in Brooklyn,* which uses death and suffering as incidents in the service of a higher optimism.

But, whatever its effectiveness as a source of consolation and a means of 3
pressure for maintaining "positive" social attitudes, this optimism is fundamentally satisfying to no one, not even to those who would be most disoriented
without its support. Even within the area of mass culture, there always exists a
current of opposition, seeking to express by whatever means are available to it
that sense of desperation and inevitable failure which optimism itself helps to
create. Most often, this opposition is confined to rudimentary or semi-literate
forms: in mob politics and journalism, for example, or in certain kinds of religious enthusiasm. When it does enter the field of art, it is likely to be disguised
or attenuated: in an unspecific form of expression like jazz, in the basically
harmless nihilism of the Marx Brothers, in the continually reasserted strain of
hopelessness that often seems to be the real meaning of the soap opera. The

---

[1]In her testimony before the House Committee on Un-American Activities, Mrs. Leila Rogers said
that the movie *None But the Lonely Heart* was un-American because it was gloomy. Like so much
else that was said during the unhappy investigation of Hollywood, this statement was at once stupid and illuminating. One knew immediately what Mrs. Rogers was talking about; she had simply
been insensitive enough to carry her philistinism to its conclusion.

gangster film is remarkable in that it fills the need for disguise (though not sufficiently to avoid arousing uneasiness) without requiring any serious distortion. From its beginnings, it has been a consistent and astonishingly complete presentation of the modern sense of tragedy.[2]

4   In its initial character, the gangster film is simply one example of the movies' constant tendency to create fixed dramatic patterns that can be repeated indefinitely with a reasonable expectation of profit. One gangster film follows another as one musical or one Western follows another. But this rigidity is not necessarily opposed to the requirements of art. There have been very successful types of art in the past which developed such specific and detailed conventions as almost to make individual examples of the type interchangeable. This is true, for example, of Elizabethan revenge tragedy and Restoration comedy.

5   For such a type to be successful means that its conventions have imposed themselves upon the general consciousness and become the accepted vehicles of a particular set of attitudes and a particular aesthetic effect. One goes to any individual example of the type with very definite expectations, and originality is to be welcomed only in the degree that it intensifies the expected experience without fundamentally altering it. Moreover, the relationship between the conventions which go to make up such a type and the real experience of its audience or the real facts of whatever situation it pretends to describe is of only secondary importance and does not determine its aesthetic force. It is only in an ultimate sense that the type appeals to its audience's experience of reality; much more immediately, it appeals to previous experience of the type itself: It creates its own field of reference.

6   Thus the importance of the gangster film, and the nature and intensity of its emotional and aesthetic impact, cannot be measured in terms of the place of the gangster himself or the importance of the problem of crime in American life. Those European moviegoers who think there is a gangster on every corner in New York are certainly deceived, but defenders of the "positive" side of American culture are equally deceived if they think it relevant to point out that most Americans have never seen a gangster. What matters is that the experience of the gangster *as an experience of art* is universal to Americans. There is almost nothing we understand better or react to more readily or with quicker intelligence. The Western film, though it seems never to diminish in popularity, is for most of us no more than the folklore of the past, familiar and understandable only because it has been repeated so often. The gangster film comes much closer. In ways that we do not easily or willingly define, the gangster speaks for us, expressing that part of the American psyche which rejects the qualities and the demands of modern life, which rejects "Americanism" itself.

7   The gangster is the man of the city, with the city's language and knowledge, with its queer and dishonest skills and its terrible daring, carrying his life in his

---

[2]Efforts have been made from time to time to bring the gangster film into line with the prevailing optimism and social constructiveness of our culture; *Kiss of Death* is a recent example. These efforts are usually unsuccessful; the reasons for their lack of success are interesting in themselves, but I shall not be able to discuss them here.

hands like a placard, like a club. For everyone else, there is at least the theoretical possibility of another world—in that happier American culture which the gangster denies, the city does not really exist; it is only a more crowded and more brightly lit country—but for the gangster there is only the city; he must inhabit it in order to personify it: not the real city, but that dangerous and sad city of the imagination which is so much more important, which is the modern world. And the gangster—though there are real gangsters—is also, and primarily, a creature of the imagination. The real city, one might say, produces only criminals; the imaginary city produces the gangster: He is what we want to be and what we are afraid we may become.

Thrown into the crowd without background or advantages, with only those ambiguous skills which the rest of us—the real people of the real city—can only pretend to have, the gangster is required to make his way, to make his life and impose it on others. Usually, when we come upon him, he has already made his choice or the choice has already been made for him, it doesn't matter which: We are not permitted to ask whether at some point he could have chosen to be something else than what he is. 8

The gangster's activity is actually a form of rational enterprise, involving fairly definite goals and various techniques for achieving them. But thus rationality is usually no more than a vague background; we know, perhaps, that the gangster sells liquor or that he operates a numbers racket; often we are not given even that much information. So his activity becomes a kind of pure criminality: He hurts people. Certainly our response to the gangster film is most consistently and most universally a response to sadism; we gain the double satisfaction of participating vicariously in the gangster's sadism and then seeing it turned against the gangster himself. 9

But on another level the quality of irrational brutality and the quality of rational enterprise become one. Since we do not see the rational and routine aspects of the gangster's behavior, the practice of brutality—the quality of unmixed criminality—becomes the totality of his career. At the same time, we are always conscious that the whole meaning of this career is a drive for success: the typical gangster film presents a steady upward progress followed by a very precipitate fall. Thus brutality itself becomes at once the means to success and the content of success—a success that is defined in its most general terms, not as accomplishment or specific gain, but simply as the unlimited possibility of aggression. (In the same way, film presentations of businessmen tend to make it appear that they achieve their success by talking on the telephone and holding conferences and that success *is* talking on the telephone and holding conferences.) 10

From this point of view, the initial contact between the film and its audience is an agreed conception of human life: that man is a being with the possibilities of success or failure. This principle, too, belongs to the city; one must emerge from the crowd or else one is nothing. On that basis the necessity of the action is established, and it progresses, by inalterable paths to the point where the gangster lies dead and the principle has been modified: There is really only one possibility—failure. The final meaning of the city is anonymity and death. 11

12   In the opening scene of *Scarface,* we are shown a successful man; we know he is successful because he has just given a party of opulent proportions and because he is called Big Louie. Through some monstrous lack of caution, he permits himself to be alone for a few moments. We understand from this immediately that he is about to be killed. No convention of the gangster film is more strongly established than this: It is dangerous to be alone. And yet the very conditions of success make it impossible not to be alone, for success is always the establishment of an *individual* pre-eminence that must be imposed on others, in whom it automatically arouses hatred; the successful man is an outlaw. The gangster's whole life is an effort to assert himself as an individual, to draw himself out of the crowd, and he always dies *because* he is an individual; the final bullet thrusts him back, makes him, after all, a failure. "Mother of God," says the dying Little Caesar, "is this the end of Rico?"—speaking of himself thus in the third person because what has been brought low is not the undifferentiated *man,* but the individual with a name, the gangster, the success; even to himself he is a creature of the imagination. (T. S. Eliot has pointed out that a number of Shakespeare's tragic heroes have this trick of looking at themselves dramatically; their true identity, the thing that is destroyed when they die, is something outside themselves—not a man, but a style of life, a kind of meaning.)

13   At bottom, the gangster is doomed because he is under the obligation to succeed, not because the means he employs are unlawful. In the deeper layers of the modern consciousness, *all* means are unlawful, every attempt to succeed is an act of aggression, leaving one alone and guilty and defenseless among enemies: One is *punished* for success. This is our intolerable dilemma: that failure is a kind of death and success is evil and dangerous, is—ultimately—impossible. The effect of the gangster film is to embody this dilemma in the person of the gangster and resolve it by his death. The dilemma is resolved because it is *his* death, not ours. We are safe; for the moment, we can acquiesce in our failure, we can choose to fail.

COMPREHENSION

1. What are the "organs of mass culture" (paragraph 2)? What properties do they all have in common?
2. Define the term *tragic hero* as Warshow uses it in his title.
3. Compare and contrast Warshow's concepts of the "real city" with those of the "imaginary city" as they relate to modern life and mass culture.

RHETORIC

1. Although the ultimate focus of the essay is on the "gangster," the subject is not referred to until paragraph 4. Why does Warshow need so much exposition before focusing on his main topic?

2. What do terms such as *supra-political* (paragraph 1), *harmless nihilism* (paragraph 3), and *general consciousness* (paragraph 5) suggest about the tone of the essay? What do they imply concerning the target audience for the essay?
3. Study the topic sentence of each paragraph. Are the topic sentences successful in setting up the material that follows? How does this strategy enhance or detract from the coherence of the author's argument?
4. Essayists usually provide their thesis at the beginning of their essays. Where does Warshow provide the thesis in his essay? What is the purpose and effect of placing it where he does?
5. The author explains the nature of the gangster film genre—its function, characters, themes, plots, meanings, and so on—*before* he cites specific films. Is this a rhetorical weakness in the essay, or does it give the essay particular potency? Explain.
6. Does the conclusion summarize the main points of the essay, bolster them, or provide new insights into them? Or does it do a combination of these things? Explain.
7. Study the introductory paragraph and the conclusion. What themes are reiterated or complemented? How do these two paragraphs serve to provide both thematic and structural coherence?

WRITING

1. Select a genre of television show or movie. Analyze its conventions and the degree to which these conventions transgress the implicit values of our society.
2. **Writing an Argument:** Argue for or against the proposition that genre movies are a form of escapism that distorts the individual's concept of the actual society he or she lives in and its citizens.

NETWORKING
Applying 21st-Century Literacies

Analyzing a Film: Select a contemporary gangster movie. Using Warshow's criteria, demonstrate—via reference to its characters, plot, and theme—how your selection reinforces the author's thesis.

Why We Love "Mad Men"

Lauren M. E. Goodlad

Lauren M. E. Goodlad has degrees from Cornell University (BS), New York University (MA), and Columbia University (PhD). She is an associate professor of English at the University of Illinois at Urbana-Champaign, where she teaches Victorian literature and directs the Unit for Criticism and Interpretative Theory. Goodlad has published

Victorian Literature and the Victorian State (2003) and most recently is a co-editor of Goth: Undead Subculture *(2007). She worked in the 1980s as a cosmetics and fragrance copywriter in New York City. In the following essay, which was published in the* Chronicle of Higher Education *in 2009, Goodlad combines her personal response to* Mad Men *with unique feminist critical inquiry.*

1   Like most women who call themselves feminists, I've spent my life avoiding men like Don Draper, the incorrigible ladies' man at the center of *Mad Men*, a show about a Madison Avenue advertising agency in the early 1960s. I took a pass on the show during its first season, catching up with it on DVD when the mounting enthusiasm of friends and co-workers piqued my curiosity.

2   By the time the season-three premier was promoted this month, my friends (men and women in their 30s and 40s) had taken to posting Madmenized avatars of themselves on their Facebook pages. And I was one of them, styling myself on madmenyourself.com in a chic red dress, gloves, and cat's-eye glasses. What had happened to make these politically progressive adults in the last days of their youth identify with characters from their parents' generation?

3   I have been intrigued by the mysteries of culture before. In the 1990s, I was writing on gothic subculture and the phenomenon of "men who feel and cry"—men like Anne Rice's vampires, Tim Burton's Edward Scissorhands, and Nine Inch Nails' Trent Reznor, all of whom beckoned young men to dramatize emotion in ways that previous generations had scorned as unmasculine. Alongside those men in black were harsher specimens of masculinity in crisis: men like Tyler Durden, the split personality who launches an underground subculture called Fight Club.

4   While superficially different, both kinds of men were desperate to feel, through catharsis or brutal violence. Yet most of these tales focused on men's relationships with one another, like Tyler's two halves, or Lestat and Louis in Rice's *Interview with the Vampire*. They were men searching for their feelings in the company of other men.

5   And now comes Don Draper, icon of masculinity-in-crisis for the 21st century. Don is in pain, yes, and hurting himself, too (for all his spectacular emotional reserve). But he is also different. No tears or blood on that impeccably pressed suit. No close ties to other men. What is it that makes this odd blend of Jay Gatsby, American Gigolo, and the Man in the Gray Flannel Suit so captivating a figure for today?

6   When I asked a sample of folks close to hand what they thought of the show, strangely enough, the first three said virtually the same thing—all references to Don: *"The guy is hot."* (OK, my mother, a veteran of the *Mad Men* era, said "very handsome," not "hot".) To be sure, the show need not be experienced as the story of a "hot" guy in crisis. A close female colleague, indifferent to Don's eros, tunes in mostly for the Peggy Olson narrative. And there is my husband, who enjoys the show for its complexity and period detail, but hates Don Draper for his selfishness and lies. Like Don, my husband is a

Jon Hamm as Don Draper in the AMC series *Mad Men*.

hard-working professional father of two in his late 30s. Unlike Don . . . well, you could call him the anti-Don.

Although Don Draper is the show's center of gravity, a constellation of in- 7 triguing personalities surrounds him. Several of those characters suggest series that might have been: *Mad Women,* in which Joan Holloway and Peggy Olson take different paths in the struggle for integrity in a man's world; *Mad Closet,* the story of Salvatore Romano's slow-motion sexual awakening; *Bad Men,* a close study of Pete Campbell's toxic cocktail of ambition and insecurity; *Race Men,* in which Paul Kinsey strives to be a hero in the civil-rights movement without exposing himself as an insufferable honkie; *Sad Men,* a nighttime soap in which Roger Sterling deludes himself about his impending mortality; and of course *Mod Men,* a show about style.

And then there is Don's beautiful wife, Betty, who, though clearly his better 8 half, is not his patsy. A kind of Donna Reed on steroids, she is much, much more than the first woman on television to have a passionate affair with a household appliance. Her vigorous horsemanship, her facility with a shotgun: These are the signs that though raised to follow the grooves, Betty cannot be underestimated.

Witness the end of the first season when, opening the phone bill, she learns that Don has been checking up on her with her psychoanalyst. We think she is in the dark about Don's infidelity; but then, as she lies on the couch, we learn that she has known all along. Betty's decision to tell the good doctor wasn't Freud's talking cure but a savvy move on the chess board that is the Draper marriage. She knows that the shrink will tell Don, so that Don will learn, with a minimum of confrontation, that his fooling around isn't fooling anyone.

9   Conventional wisdom says that women are irresistibly attracted to power. And yet, professionally speaking, Don's position is precarious. Less Gordon Gekko in *Wall Street* than Montgomery Clift's character in *A Place in the Sun*, he is vulnerable to corporate management, professional rivals, and the whims of clients. With no family connections to buttress him, Don has nothing to sell but himself. If he is powerful, it's because the particular commodity he has to offer is selling itself: the trick of making selling seem magical in a consumer society. That is why Don's "hotness" is not the garden-variety sort—not the televised equivalent of an Abercrombie & Fitch ad—but the aspect of his character that connects his existential crisis to ours.

10   Don's sexual tensions bespeak his brilliance as an ad man. His genius for spinning fantasies works in boardroom and bedroom alike. Though superficially a "man's man," he does not long for intimacy with other men. Women are his métier; their desire is the complement to the seductive powers his clients pay him to wield. This is not to say that "sex sells"—a crude logic that Don despises. It is to say that in a consumer society, the fine art of selling is a lot like sex.

11   While his milieu is fundamentally misogynistic, Don himself is far less so. At home he is a possessive, philandering husband, but at work he is the least sexist of the lot, respecting the feelings of middle-age women and promoting his talented secretary.

12   If Betty is stuck playing Don's Madonna—the angelic mother he never had— the other women in his life are more like female variations on Don. There is Midge, the independent bohemian who doesn't make breakfast; Bobbie Barrett, the shrewd businesswoman whose frank sexual hunger ignites Don's kinky side; and Rachel, also a businesswoman, but memorable as the one who got away. Her Jewishness stands for a kind of depth that might cut through Don's mad world if only his desire to connect could trump his need to seduce. In one of many grace notes, Don, in need of a pseudonym, calls himself Tilden Katz— the man Rachel marries after she ends their affair. It is Don imagining himself as an anti-Don.

13   In the title poem of *Meditations in an Emergency*, a collection by Frank O'Hara that Don reads, the speaker writes, "no one trusts me" because "I am always looking away." As we eventually learn, Don sends this book to the widow of the man whose identity he stole. But Don's past is really window dressing for a more systemic crisis. There are lots of men with Don's issues who aren't orphans and didn't change their names. If there is anyone who trusts Don it is Peggy, a woman whose loyalty he values too much to throw away—perhaps because he knows that she is like him: Her talent for selling will take her places.

For some viewers, the secret of *Mad Men*'s success is the pleasure of watch- 14
ing characters who don't know, as we do, that "change is gonna come." If that's
true, we have more reason to be anxious voyeurs than smug ones. We may know
more than Don, Roger, and Betty about the dangers of booze and cigarettes—but
we still die as they do (and die increasingly of cancer). And while we have
made real gains in sexual and racial equality, the price we have paid is the reactionary anger that haunts every aspect of our social being.

The open secret of our time is that we are less secure than were our pre- 15
cursors in the *Mad Men* era. If we know them to be in the grips of a cold war
that finally came to an end, we know ourselves to be losing wars of our own
making—a boundless "war on terror" and the destruction of our own environment. We do not watch *Mad Men* because we imagine ourselves as free of vice
and illusions; we watch it because we know that our lives, too, are one long
meditation in an emergency.

In the dwindling prosperity that is capitalism in the 21st century, every one 16
of us knows that we must sell ourselves, make our pitch, compete for our place
in the sun. Though Don has a nice house and car, like most of us, he will never
join the big leagues. Among us today, he would not be a Wall Street banker or
CEO, for he is not cut from that cloth. His golden parachute is the dream of
another life in a California that, if it ever existed, exists no more.

"The guy is hot." If we feast our eyes on Don, wanting him and wanting to 17
be like him, it is perhaps because we, too, want to make it look that good. As
Frank O'Hara wrote, "It is easy to be beautiful; it is difficult to appear so." Don
gratifies the illusion that a life lived as a commodity can somehow be meaningful; that if we close our eyes, the art of selling will be like the best sex we
ever had.

COMPREHENSION

1. Why does Goodlad identify herself as a feminist and why would a self-styled
   feminist defend a character like Don Draper? How does this defense of Don work
   in Goodlad's feminist interpretation of *Mad Men*? Provide examples from the essay
   to support your response.
2. According to Goodlad, the main character in *Mad Men*, Don Draper, is an "icon of
   masculinity-in-crisis" (paragraph 5). What does she mean by this phrase? Where in
   the essay does she explore this idea?
3. What observations does Goodlad make about American culture in this essay?

RHETORIC

1. Goodlad summarizes various plotlines and introduces primary characters in *Mad
   Men*. Why does she devote so much space to this overview? What assumptions is
   she making about her primary audience, who typically would be college teachers
   and administrators? (Recall that this essay appeared in the *Chronicle of Higher*

Education.) What information does she convey that the average viewer might not know or find interesting?

2. What is Goodlad's thesis? Does she state or imply her main idea? Explain.

3. Identify the allusions that Goodlad uses in this essay. What is her purpose in referring to other characters and works, ranging from Anne Rice's vampires to Frank O'Hara? (Who *was* Frank O'Hara?)

4. Goodlad makes a number of assertions regarding the cultural significance of *Mad Men*. What are they, and do they effectively support her thesis? Are these assertions facts or opinions? Explain your viewpoint.

5. Which paragraphs constitute what we might consider to be Goodlad's conclusion? Is this conclusion effective? Why or why not?

WRITING

1. Watch one episode of *Mad Men*, and then write your own critical response to it.

2. **Writing an Argument:** It could be argued that television series like *Mad Men, The Sopranos,* and *Breaking Bad* engage in negative stereotyping. Which side of the debate do you take? Write an argumentative essay on this topic. State your claim, offer evidence, and structure the argument carefully in a series of key reasons in support of your claim.

NETWORKING
Applying 21st-Century Literacies

Critically Interpreting a Television Series: Write a feminist interpretation of a television series that you watch regularly or are familiar with.

Synthesis: Classic and Contemporary Questions for Comparison

1. Warshow critiques the function and role of the gangster in popular media, whereas Goodlad focuses on an analysis of one television series in which the life of an ad man is articulated. How do these different focuses determine the thesis of each essay? What are the positive and negative consequences of addressing a broad issue in "The Gangster as Tragic Hero" without using one extended example, as opposed to the detailed analysis of one TV series in "Why We Love 'Mad Men'"?

2. Goodlad writes an admittedly feminist critique of *Mad Men*. How would you categorize Warshow's critical approach? Is he interested in theory? Why or why not?

3. Compare and contrast Warshow's and Goodlad's observations about American culture in their respective essays. In which of these essays do you find these cultural insights to be most convincing, and why?

2 Live Crew, Decoded

Henry Louis Gates Jr.

*Henry Louis Gates Jr. (b. 1950) was born in Keyser, West Virginia, and was edu-
cated at Yale University and Clare College, Cambridge, where he received his PhD in
1979. He now teaches at Harvard University. Gates has edited numerous books addressing the issues of race, identity, and African American history and has contributed
to over a dozen periodicals and journals, including* Critical Inquiry, Black World, *the*
Yale Review, *and the* Antioch Review. *His work attempts to apply contemporary
literary theories, such as structuralism and poststructuralism, to African and African
American literature so that readers can develop a deep understanding of the structure,
significance, methods, and meanings of this body of work. Many of his theoretical insights are summed up in his book* The Signifying Monkey: Towards a Theory of
Afro-American Literary Criticism *(1988). Among his awards and honors have been
a Carnegie Foundation fellowship, a MacArthur Prize fellowship, and a Mellon fellowship from Yale University. In the following essay, published in the* New York Times
in 1990, Gates offers a keen analysis of the rap music phenomenon.

The rap group 2 Live Crew and their controversial hit recording, "As Nasty as 1
They Wanna Be," may well earn a signal place in the history of First Amendment rights. But just as important is how these lyrics will be interpreted and by
whom.

For centuries, African Americans have been forced to develop coded ways 2
of communicating to protect them from danger. Allegories and double meanings, words redefined to mean their opposites ("bad" meaning "good," for instance), even neologisms ("bodacious") have enabled blacks to share messages
only the initiated understand.

Many blacks were amused by the transcripts of Marion Barry's sting opera- 3
tion, which reveals that he used the traditional black expression about one's
"nose being opened." This referred to a love affair and not, as Mr. Barry's prosecutors have suggested, to the inhalation of drugs. Understanding this phrase
could very well spell the difference (for the Mayor) between prison and freedom.

2 Live Crew is engaged in heavy-handed parody, turning the stereotypes of 4
black and white American culture on their heads. These young artists are acting
out, to lively dance music, a parodic exaggeration of the age-old stereotypes of
the oversexed black female and male. Their exuberant use of hyperbole (phan-
tasmagoric sexual organs, for example) undermines—for anyone fluent in black
cultural codes—a too literal-minded hearing of the lyrics.

This is the street tradition called "signifying" or "playing the dozens," 5
which has generally been risqué, and where the best signifier or "rapper" is the

one who invents the most extravagant images, the biggest "lies," as the culture says. (H. "Rap" Brown earned his nickname in just this way.) In the face of racist stereotypes about black sexuality, you can do one of two things: You can disavow them or explode them with exaggeration.

6   2 Live Crew, like many "hip-hop" groups, is engaged in sexual carnivalesque. Parody reigns supreme; from a take-off of standard blues to a spoof of the black power movement, their off-color nursery rhymes are part of a venerable Western tradition. The group even satirizes the culture of commerce when it appropriates popular advertising slogans ("Tastes great!" "Less filling!") and puts them in a bawdy context.

7   2 Live Crew must be interpreted within the context of black culture generally and of signifying specifically. Their novelty, and that of other adventuresome rap groups, is that their defiant rejection of euphemism now voices for the mainstream what before existed largely in the "race record" market—where the records of Redd Foxx and Rudy Ray Moore once were forced to reside.

8   Rock songs have always been about sex but have used elaborate subterfuges to convey that fact. 2 Live Crew uses Anglo-Saxon words and is self-conscious about it: A parody of a white voice in one song refers to "private personal parts," as a coy counterpart to the group's bluntness.

9   Much more troubling than its so-called obscenity is the group's overt sexism. Their sexism is so flagrant, however, that it almost cancels itself out in a hyperbolic war between the sexes. In this, it recalls the inter-sexual jousting in Zora Neale Hurston's novels. Still, many of us look toward the emergence of more female rappers to redress sexual stereotypes. And we must not allow ourselves to sentimentalize street culture: The appreciation of verbal virtuosity does not lessen one's obligation to critique bigotry in all of its pernicious forms.

10   Is 2 Live Crew more "obscene" than, say, the comic Andrew Dice Clay? Clearly, this rap group is seen as more threatening than others that are just as sexually explicit. Can this be completely unrelated to the specter of the young black male as a figure of sexual and social disruption, the very stereotypes 2 Live Crew seem determined to undermine?

11   This question—and the very large question of obscenity and the First Amendment—cannot even be addressed until those who would answer them become literate in the vernacular traditions of African Americans. To do less is to censor through the equivalent of intellectual prior restraint—and censorship is to art what lynching is to justice.

COMPREHENSION

1. What is the author's thesis?
2. According to Gates, what must one know before engaging in a critique of 2 Live Crew?
3. Does Gates consider 2 Live Crew's music obscene? Why or why not?

RHETORIC

1. The paragraphs in this essay are fairly short. How does this affect Gates's argument?
2. How does the author use definition to decode certain aspects of African American culture? Why is definition an important strategy in his argument?
3. Gates uses the word *hyperbole* in paragraph 4 and the word *hyperbolic* in paragraph 9. Why is it necessary for him to emphasize this concept to develop his argument?
4. Does the author appear to use a particular tone toward his subject matter? Does he appear to support the art of his subject, condemn it, explain it, or provide a mixture of all three approaches?
5. For whom is this essay written? What is its intended purpose? Explain your view.
6. Examine the final sentence of the essay. Does it provide an effective closure? Why is it particularly pertinent considering 2 Live Crew is an African American music group? Explain your view.

WRITING

1. In an essay, explain your position on rap music as (in Gates's words) "sexual carnivalesque."
2. For a research project, write a paper on one of your favorite singers or music groups, and how this artist or group mirrors contemporary patterns of culture.
3. **Writing an Argument:** Argue for or against the proposition that the music of 2 Live Crew or any more contemporary rap artist or group is obscene, basing your argument on the points raised in the article by Gates.

NETWORKING
Applying 21st-Century Literacies

Incorporating Audio as Support: Just as you can use visuals in a conventional paper, you can also link or refer readers to audio files or clips in an electronic essay. In your response to question 2 under Writing, refer readers to free, legal samples of the artist's work on the band's MySpace page, home page, or similar source, and discuss these specific songs in your essay, referring to or extending from something the reader will be able to listen to.

My Creature from the Black Lagoon

Stephen King

Stephen King (b. 1947) was born in Portland, Maine. Raised by his mother, he spent parts of his childhood in Indiana, Connecticut, Massachusetts, and Maine. He graduated from the University of Maine at Orono in 1970 with a degree in English. During his early writing career, he sold several stories to mass market men's magazines and taught English in Hampden, Maine. In 1973, his novel Carrie *sold enough copies that he could devote his energies to writing full-time. He is the author of about 100 books, most focusing on horror and the occult. A number have been adapted for film and television, including* Carrie, The Dead Zone, The Shining, Christine, Pet Sematary, Stand by Me, *and* The Green Mile. *Besides writing, he belongs to an all-writers rock-and-roll band (with Dave Barry and Amy Tan) and is a major contributor to local and national charities. In the following selection, taken from* Danse Macabre (1981), *King compares and contrasts the responses of adults and children to horror movies.*

1   The first movie I can remember seeing as a kid was *Creature from the Black Lagoon.* It was at the drive-in, and unless it was a second-run job I must have been about seven, because the film, which starred Richard Carlson and Richard Denning, was released in 1954. It was also originally released in 3-D, but I cannot remember wearing the glasses, so perhaps I did see a rerelease.

2   I remember only one scene clearly from the movie, but it left a lasting impression. The hero (Carlson) and the heroine (Julia Adams, who looked absolutely spectacular in a one-piece white bathing suit) are on an expedition somewhere in the Amazon basin. They make their way up a swampy, narrow waterway and into a wide pond that seems an idyllic South American version of the Garden of Eden.

3   But the Creature is lurking—naturally. It's a scaly, batrachian monster that is remarkably like Lovecraft's half-breed, degenerate aberrations—the crazed and blasphemous results of liaisons between gods and human women (it's difficult to get away from Lovecraft). This monster is slowly and patiently barricading the mouth of the stream with sticks and branches, irrevocably sealing the party of anthropologists in.

4   I was barely old enough to read at that time, the discovery of my father's box of weird fiction still years away. I have a vague memory of boyfriends in my mom's life during that period—from 1952 until 1958 or so; enough of a memory to be sure she had a social life, not enough to even guess if she had a sex life. There was Norville, who smoked Luckies and kept three fans going in his two-room apartment during the summer; and there was Milt, who drove a Buick and wore gigantic blue shorts in the summertime; and another fellow, very small, who was, I believe, a cook in a French restaurant. So far as I know, my mother came close to marrying none of them. She'd gone that route once. Also, that was a time when a woman, once married, became a shadow figure in the process of decision-making and bread-winning. I think my mom, who could be stubborn, intractable, grimly persevering and nearly impossible to discourage, had gotten a taste for captaining her own life. And so she went out with guys, but none of them became permanent fixtures.

5   It was Milt we were out with that night, he of the Buick and the large blue shorts. He seemed to genuinely like my brother and me, and to genuinely not mind having us along in the back seat from time to time (it may be that when you have reached the calmer waters of your early forties, the idea of necking at the drive-in no longer appeals so strongly . . . even if you have a Buick as large

as a cabin cruiser to do it in). By the time the Creature made his appearance, my brother had slithered down onto the floor of the back and had fallen asleep. My mother and Milt were talking, perhaps passing a Kool back and forth. They don't matter, at least not in this context; nothing matters except the big black-and-white images up on the screen, where the unspeakable Thing is walling the handsome hero and the sexy heroine into . . . into . . . the Black Lagoon!

I knew, watching, that the Creature had become *my* Creature; I had bought 6 it. Even to a seven-year-old, it was not a terribly convincing Creature. I did not know then it was good old Ricou Browning, the famed underwater stuntman, in a molded latex suit, but I surely knew it was some guy in some kind of a monster suit . . . just as I knew that, later on that night, he would visit me in the black lagoon of my dreams, looking much more realistic. He might be waiting in the closet when we got back; he might be standing slumped in the blackness of the bathroom at the end of the hall, stinking of algae and swamp rot, all ready for a post-midnight snack of small boy. Seven isn't old, but it is old enough to know that you get what you pay for. You own it, you bought it, it's yours. It is old enough to feel the dowser suddenly come alive, grow heavy, and roll over in your hands, pointing at hidden water.

My reaction to the Creature on that night was perhaps the perfect reaction, 7 the one every writer of horror fiction or director who has worked in the field hopes for when he or she uncaps a pen or a lens: total emotional involvement, pretty much undiluted by any real thinking process—and you understand, don't you, that when it comes to horror movies, the only thought process really necessary to break the mood is for a friend to lean over and whisper, "See the zipper running down his back?"

I think that only people who have worked in the field for some time truly 8 understand how fragile this stuff really is, and what an amazing commitment it imposes on the reader or viewer of intellect and maturity. When Coleridge spoke of "the suspension of disbelief" in his essay on imaginative poetry, I be-lieve he knew that disbelief is not like a balloon, which may be suspended in air with a minimum of effort; it is like a lead weight, which has to be hoisted with a clean and a jerk and held up by main force. Disbelief isn't light; it's heavy. The difference in sales between Arthur Hailey and H. P. Lovecraft may exist because everyone believes in cars, and banks, but it takes a sophisticated and muscular intellectual act to believe, even for a little while, in Nyarlathotep, the Blind Faceless One, the Howler in the Night. And whenever I run into someone who expresses a feeling along the lines of, "I don't read fantasy or go to any of those movies; none of it's real," I feel a kind of sympathy. They simply can't lift the weight of fantasy. The muscles of the imagination have grown too weak.

In this sense, kids are the perfect audience for horror. The paradox is this: 9 Children, who are physically quite weak, lift the weight of unbelief with ease. They are the jugglers of the invisible world—a perfectly understandable phe-nomenon when you consider the perspective they must view things from. Children deftly manipulate the logistics of Santa Claus's entry on Christmas Eve (he can get down small chimneys by making himself small, and if there's no chimney there's the letter slot, and if there's no letter slot there's always the crack under the door), the Easter Bunny, God (big guy, sorta old, white beard, throne), Jesus ("How do you think he turned the water into wine?" I asked my son Joe when he—Joe, not Jesus—was five; Joe's idea was that he had something "kinda like magic Kool-Aid, you get what I mean?"), the devil (big guy, red skin, horse feet, tail with an arrow on the end of it, Snidely Whiplash moustache), Ronald McDonald, the Burger King, the Keebler Elves, Dorothy and Toto, the Lone Ranger and Tonto, a thousand more.

10   Most parents think they understand this openness better than, in many cases, they actually do, and try to keep their children away from anything that smacks too much of horror and terror—"Rated PG (or G in the case of *The Andromeda Strain*), but may be too intense for younger children," the ads for *Jaws* read—believing, I suppose, that to allow their kids to go to a real horror movie would be tantamount to rolling a live hand grenade into a nursery school.

11   But one of the odd Döppler effects that seems to occur during the selective forgetting that is so much a part of "growing up" is the fact that almost *everything* has a scare potential for the child under eight. Children are literally afraid of their own shadows at the right time and place. There is the story of the four-year-old who refused to go to bed at night without a light on in his closet. His parents at last discovered he was frightened of a creature he had heard his father speak of often; this creature, which had grown large and dreadful in the child's imagination, was the "twi-night double-header."

12   Seen in this light, even Disney movies are minefields of terror, and the animated cartoons, which will apparently be released and rereleased even unto the end of the world,[1] are usually the worst offenders. There are adults today, who, when questioned, will tell you that the most frightening thing they saw at the movies as children was Bambi's father shot by the hunter, or Bambi and his mother running before the forest fire. Other Disney memories which are right up there with the batrachian horror inhabiting the Black Lagoon include the marching brooms that have gone totally out of control in *Fantasia* (and for the small child, the real horror inherent in the situation is probably buried in the implied father-son relationship between Mickey Mouse and the old sorcerer; those brooms are making a terrible mess, and when the sorcerer/father gets home, there may be PUNISHMENT. . . . This sequence might well send the child of strict parents into an ecstasy of terror); the night on Bald Mountain from the same film; the witches in *Snow White* and *Sleeping Beauty*, one with her enticingly red poisoned apple (and what small child is not taught early to fear the

---

[1]In one of my favorite Arthur C. Clarke stories, this actually happens. In this vignette, aliens from space land on earth after the Big One has finally gone down. As the story closes, the best brains of this alien culture are trying to figure out the meaning of a film they have found and learned how to play back. The film ends with the words *A Walt Disney Production*. I have moments when I really believe that there would be no better epitaph for the human race, or for a world where the only sentient being absolutely guaranteed of immortality is not Hitler, Charlemagne, Albert Schweitzer, or even Jesus Christ—but is, instead, Richard M. Nixon, whose name is engraved on a plaque placed on the airless surface of the moon.

idea of POISON?), the other with her deadly spinning wheel; this holds all the way up to the relatively innocuous *One Hundred* and *One Dalmatians* which features the logical granddaughter of those Disney witches from the thirties and forties—the evil Cruella DeVille, with her scrawny, nasty face, her loud voice (grownups sometimes forget how terrified young children are of loud voices, which come from the giants of their world, the adults), and her plan to kill all the dalmatian puppies (read "children," if you're a little person) and turn them into dogskin coats.

Yet it is the parents, of course, who continue to underwrite the Disney procedure of release and rerelease, often discovering goosebumps on their own arms as they rediscover what terrified them as children . . . because what the good horror film (or horror sequence in what may be billed a "comedy" or an "animated cartoon") does above all else is to knock the adult props out from under us and tumble us back down the slide into childhood. And there our own shadow may once again become that of a mean dog, a gaping mouth, or a beckoning dark figure. 13

Perhaps the supreme realization of this return to childhood comes in David Cronenberg's marvelous horror film *The Brood*, where a disturbed woman is literally producing "children of rage" who go out and murder the members of her family, one by one. About halfway through the film, her father sits dispiritedly on the bed in an upstairs room, drinking and mourning his wife, who has been the first to feel the wrath of the brood. We cut to the bed itself . . . and clawed hands suddenly reach out from beneath it and dig into the carpeting near the doomed father's shoes. And so Cronenberg pushes us down the slide; we are four again, and all of our worst surmises about what might be lurking under the bed have turned out to be true. 14

The irony of all this is that children are better able to deal with fantasy and terror *on its own terms* than their elders are. You'll note I've italicized the phrase "on its own terms." An adult is able to deal with the cataclysmic terror of something like *The Texas Chainsaw Massacre* because he or she understands that it is all make-believe, and that when the take is done the dead people will simply get up and wash off the stage blood. The child is not so able to make this distinction, and *Chainsaw Massacre* is quite rightly rated R. Little kids do not need this scene, any more than they need the one at the end of *The Fury* where John Cassavetes quite literally blows apart. But the point is, if you put a little kid of six in the front row at a screening of *The Texas Chainsaw Massacre* along with an adult who was temporarily unable to distinguish between make-believe and "real things" (as Danny Torrance, the little boy in *The Shining* puts it)—if, for instance, you had given the adult a hit of Yellow Sunshine LSD about two hours before the movie started—my guess is that the kid would have maybe a week's worth of bad dreams. The adult might spend a year or so in a rubber room, writing home with Crayolas. 15

A certain amount of fantasy and horror in a child's life seems to me a perfectly okay, useful sort of thing. Because of the size of their imaginative capacity, children are able to handle it, and because of their unique position in life, 16 they are able to put such feelings to work. They understand their position very well, too. Even in such a relatively ordered society as our own, they understand that their survival is a matter almost totally out of their hands. Children are "dependents" up until the age of eight or so in every sense of the word; dependent on mother and father (or some reasonable facsimile thereof) not only for food, clothing, and shelter, but dependent on them not to crash the car into a bridge abutment, to meet the school bus on time, to walk them home from Cub Scouts or Brownies, to buy medicines with childproof caps, dependent on them to make sure they don't electrocute themselves while screwing around with the toaster or while trying to play with Barbie's Beauty Salon in the bathtub.

17   Running directly counter to this necessary dependence is the survival directive built into all of us. The child realizes his or her essential lack of control, and I suspect it is this very realization which makes the child uneasy. It is the same sort of free-floating anxiety that many air travelers feel. They are not afraid because they believe air travel to be unsafe; they are afraid because they have surrendered control, and if something goes wrong all they can do is sit there clutching airsick bags or the in-flight magazine. To surrender control runs counter to the survival directive. Conversely, while a thinking, informed person may understand intellectually that travel by car is much more dangerous than flying, he or she is still apt to feel much more comfortable behind the wheel, because she/he has control . . . or at least an illusion of it.

18   This hidden hostility and anxiety toward the airline pilots of their lives may be one explanation why, like the Disney pictures which are released during school vacations in perpetuity, the old fairy tales also seem to go on forever. A parent who would raise his or her hands in horror at the thought of taking his/her child to see *Dracula* or *The Changeling* (with its pervasive imagery of the drowning child) would be unlikely to object to the baby sitter reading "Hansel and Gretel" to the child before bedtime. But consider: The tale of Hansel and Gretel begins with deliberate abandonment (oh yes, the stepmother masterminds that one, but she is the symbolic mother all the same, and the father is a spaghetti-brained nurd who goes along with everything she suggests even though he knows it's wrong—thus we can see her as amoral, him as actively evil in the Biblical and Miltonian sense), it progresses to kidnapping (the witch in the candy house), enslavement, illegal detention, and finally justifiable homicide and cremation. Most mothers and fathers would never take their children to see *Survive*, that quickie Mexican exploitation flick about the rugby players who survived the aftermath of a plane crash in the Andes by eating their dead teammates, but these same parents find little to object to in "Hansel and Gretel," where the witch is fattening the children up so she can eat them. We give this stuff to the kids almost instinctively, understanding on a deeper level, perhaps, that such fairy stories are the perfect points of crystallization for those fears and hostilities.

19   Even anxiety-ridden air travelers have their own fairy tales—all those *Airport* movies, which, like "Hansel and Gretel" and all those Disney cartoons,

show every sign of going on forever . . . but which should only be viewed on Thanksgivings, since all of them feature a large cast of turkeys.

My gut reaction to *Creature from the Black Lagoon* on that long-ago night was 20 a kind of terrible, waking swoon. The nightmare was happening right in front of me; every hideous possibility that human flesh is heir to was being played out on that drive-in screen.

Approximately twenty-two years later, I had a chance to see *Creature from* 21 *the Black Lagoon* again—not on TV, with any kind of dramatic build and mood broken up by adverts for used cars, K-Tel disco anthologies, and Underalls pantyhose, thank God, but intact, uncut . . . and even in 3-D. Guys like me who wear glasses have a hell of a time with 3-D, you know; ask anyone who wears specs how they like those nifty little cardboard glasses they give you when you walk in the door. If 3-D ever comes back in a big way, I'm going to take myself down to the local Pearle Vision Center and invest seventy bucks in a special pair of prescription lenses: one red, one blue. Annoying glasses aside, I should add that I took my son Joe with me—he was then five, about the age I had been myself, that night at the drive-in (and imagine my surprise—my *rueful* surprise—to discover that the movie which had so terrified me on that long-ago night had been rated G by the MPAA . . . just like the Disney pictures).

As a result, I had a chance to experience that weird doubling back in time 22 that I believe most parents only experience at the Disney films with their children, or when reading them the Pooh books or perhaps taking them to the Shrine or the Barnum & Bailey circus. A popular record is apt to create a particular "set" in a listener's mind, precisely because of its brief life of six weeks to three months, and "golden oldies" continue to be played because they are the emotional equivalent of freeze-dried coffee. When the Beach Boys come on the radio singing "Help Me, Rhonda," there is always that wonderful second or two when I can re-experience the wonderful, guilty joy of copping my first feel (and if you do the mental subtraction from my present age of thirty-three, you'll see that I was a little backward in that respect). Movies and books do the same thing, although I would argue that the mental set, its depth and texture, tends to be a little richer, a little more complex, when re-experiencing films and a lot more complex when dealing with books.

With Joe that day I experienced *Creature from the Black Lagoon* from the other 23 end of the telescope, but this particular theory of set identification still applied; in fact, it prevailed. Time and age and experience have all left their marks on me, just as they have on you; time is not a river, as Einstein theorized—it's a big . . . buffalo herd that runs us down and eventually mashes us into the ground, dead and bleeding, with a hearing-aid plugged into one ear and a colostomy bag instead of a .44 clapped on one leg. Twenty-two years later I knew that the Creature was really good old Ricou Browning, the famed underwater stuntman, in a molded latex suit, and the suspension of disbelief, that mental clean-and-jerk, had become a lot harder to accomplish. But I did it, which may mean nothing, or which may mean (I hope!) that the buffalo haven't got me yet.

But when that weight of disbelief was finally up there, the old feelings came flooding in, as they flooded in some five years ago when I took Joe and my daughter Naomi to their first movie, a reissue of *Snow White and the Seven Dwarfs*. There is a scene in that film where, after Snow White has taken a bite from the poisoned apple, the dwarfs take her into the forest, weeping copiously. Half the audience of little kids was also in tears; the lower lips of the other half were trembling. The set identification in that case was strong enough so that I was also surprised into tears. I hated myself for being so blatantly manipulated, but manipulated I was, and there I sat, blubbering into my beard over a bunch of cartoon characters. But it wasn't Disney that manipulated me; I did it myself. It was the kid inside who wept, surprised out of dormancy and into schmaltzy tears . . . but at least awake for awhile.

24   During the final two reels of *Creature from the Black Lagoon*, the weight of disbelief is nicely balanced somewhere above my head, and once again director Jack Arnold places the symbols in front of me and produces the old equation of the fairy tales, each symbol as big and as easy to handle as a child's alphabet block. Watching, the child awakes again and knows that this is what dying is like. Dying is when the Creature from the Black Lagoon dams up the exit. Dying is when the monster gets you.

25   In the end, of course, the hero and heroine, very much alive, not only survive but triumph—as Hansel and Gretel do. As the drive-in floodlights over the screen came on and the projector flashed its GOOD NIGHT, DRIVE SAFELY slide on that big white space (along with the virtuous suggestion that you ATTEND THE CHURCH OF YOUR CHOICE), there was a brief feeling of relief, almost of resurrection. But the feeling that stuck longest was the swooning sensation that good old Richard Carlson and Julia Adams were surely going down for the third time, and the image that remains forever after is of the creature slowly and patiently walling its victims into the Black Lagoon; even now I can see it peering over that growing wall of mud and sticks.

26   Its eyes. Its ancient eyes.

COMPREHENSION

1. Why does King claim that it is harder for an author to successfully bring a horror tale to life than a standard "realistic" one? What special skills does the horror writer need?

2. Why are children the "perfect audience for horror" (paragraph 9)? What exists in the structure of most horror films that makes them suitable for children?

3. King titles his essay "My Creature from the Black Lagoon" rather than using the original title *The Creature from the Black Lagoon*. Why?

4. Why does King think it is ironic that many Disney movies are G-rated while "horror" movies often contain warnings about content for children?

5. In paragraph 23, King remarks that he is pleased that he is still able to get a thrill from watching a horror movie even though he is an adult and understands the artifice behind the monster. Why does he feel this is a positive response? Why does he believe it would be beneficial for most adults to react this way?

RHETORIC

1. In paragraph 9, King attempts to reproduce the sense of what it is like to think like a child. How does he achieve this effect? What is his purpose?
2. How does King structure paragraph 18 to compare and contrast horror movies with "fairy tales"? What is his rhetorical intent?
3. What vocabulary choices does King use in his introduction to set up his conversational style of writing? What relationship does King intend to create between the writer and reader by employing this type of discourse?
4. In paragraphs 4 and 5, King recounts a childhood anecdote. What is the purpose of describing the outing to the drive-in theater with his mother's boyfriend, Milt? How does King structure these two paragraphs so that they culminate rhetorically in a device similar to that employed in horror movies?
5. Although much of King's writing is informal, he does use references to popular culture, literature, and science in his writing. What is the significance and meaning of the following terms and phrases: *batrachian* (paragraph 3), *suspension of disbelief* (paragraph 8), *Döppler effects* (paragraph 11), *twi-night double-header* (paragraph 11), *possibility that human flesh is heir to* (paragraph 20), and *golden oldies* (paragraph 22)?
6. The conclusion is only five words: two sentence fragments. Why did King choose to end his essay this way?
7. King uses irony in his essay for comic effect; for example, in paragraph 25, what is the irony in the "sign-off" at the drive-in movie theater that reads: ATTEND THE CHURCH OF YOUR CHOICE?

WRITING

1. Compare and contrast the benefits or drawbacks, or both, of an adult reading a story to a child versus taking a child to the movies.
2. **Writing an Argument:** In an essay, argue for or against the proposition that horror movies are scarier when viewed at the movie theater than on home video.

NETWORKING
Applying 21st-Century Literacies

1. **Responding to Film:** Think of the first horror movie you recall vividly from your childhood. Write an expository essay about how the film scared you. Include both the dramatic elements on the screen and your own state of mind while you watched.
2. **Comparing Print and Film:** Select a horror or science fiction book you've read that has been adapted for the screen. Compare and contrast the effects of each version. Which was more captivating? More engaging? More horrifying? More believable? Explain your view.

Red, White, and Beer

Dave Barry

Dave Barry (b. 1947) was born in Armonk, New York. He graduated from Haverford College in 1969 and was a reporter and editor at the Daily Local News *from 1971 to 1975 and subsequently a columnist for the* Miami Herald. *Besides writing his columns, Barry has written numerous books, all with his unique, amusing point of view. His books include* Stay Fit and Healthy until You're Dead *(1985),* Dave Barry's Greatest Hits *(1988),* Dave Barry Turns 40 *(1990),* Dave Barry's Only Travel Guide You'll Ever Need *(1991), and* Dave Barry's History of the Millennium (So Far) *(2007). Barry won the 1988 Pulitzer Prize for commentary. In the following piece, he comments on the relation between television commercials and patriotism.*

1   Lately I've been feeling very patriotic, especially during commercials. Like, when I see those strongly pro-American Chrysler commercials, the ones where the winner of the Bruce Springsteen Sound-Alike Contest sings about how The Pride Is Back, the ones where Lee Iacocca himself comes striding out and practically challenges the president of Toyota to a knife fight, I get this warm, proud feeling inside, the same kind of feeling I get whenever we hold routine naval maneuvers off the coast of Libya.

2   But if you want to talk about *real* patriotism, of course, you have to talk about beer commercials. I would have to say that Miller is the most patriotic brand of beer. I grant you it tastes like rat saliva, but we are not talking about taste here. What we are talking about, according to the commercials, is that Miller is by God an *American* beer, "born and brewed in the U.S.A.," and the men who drink it are American men, the kind of men who aren't afraid to perspire freely and shake a man's hand. That's mainly what happens in Miller commercials: Burly American men go around, drenched in perspiration, shaking each other's hands in a violent and patriotic fashion.

3   You never find out exactly why these men spend so much time shaking hands. Maybe shaking hands is just their simple straightforward burly masculine American patriotic way of saying to each other: "Floyd, I am truly sorry I drank all that Miller beer last night and went to the bathroom in your glove compartment." Another possible explanation is that, since there are never any women in the part of America where beer commercials are made, the burly men have become lonesome and desperate for any form of physical contact. I have noticed that sometimes, in addition to shaking hands, they hug each other. Maybe very late at night, after the David Letterman show, there are Miller commercials in which the burly men engage in slow dancing. I don't know.

I do know that in one beer commercial, I think this is for Miller—although it ₄ could be for Budweiser, which is also a very patriotic beer—the burly men build a house. You see them all getting together and pushing up a brand-new wall. Me, I worry some about a house built by men drinking beer. In my experience, you run into trouble when you ask a group of beer-drinking men to perform any task more complex than remembering not to light the filter ends of cigarettes.

For example, in my younger days, whenever anybody in my circle of ₅ friends wanted to move, he'd get the rest of us to help, and, as an inducement, he'd buy a couple of cases of beer. This almost always produced unfortunate results, such as the time we were trying to move Dick "The Wretch" Curry from a horrible fourth-floor walk-up apartment in Manhattan's Lower East Side to another horrible fourth-floor walk-up apartment in Manhattan's Lower East Side, and we hit upon the labor-saving concept of, instead of carrying The Wretch's possessions manually down the stairs, simply dropping them out the window, down onto the street, where The Wretch was racing around, gathering up the broken pieces of his life and shrieking at us to stop helping him move, his emotions reaching a fever pitch when his bed, which had been swinging wildly from a rope, entered the apartment two floors below his through what had until seconds earlier been a window.

This is the kind of thinking you get, with beer. So I figure what happens, in ₆ the beer commercial where the burly men are building the house, is they push the wall up so it's vertical, and then, after the camera stops filming them, they just keep pushing, and the wall crashes down on the other side, possibly onto somebody's pickup truck. And then they all shake hands.

But other than that, I'm in favor of the upsurge in retail patriotism, which is ₇ lucky for me because the airwaves are saturated with pro-American commercials. Especially popular are commercials in which the newly restored Statue of Liberty—and by the way, I say Lee Iacocca should get some kind of medal for that, or at least be elected president—appears to be endorsing various products, as if she were Mary Lou Retton or somebody. I saw one commercial strongly suggesting that the Statue of Liberty uses Sure brand underarm deodorant.

I have yet to see a patriotic laxative commercial, but I imagine it's only a ₈ matter of time. They'll show some actors dressed up as hard-working country folk, maybe at a church picnic, smiling at each other and eating pieces of pie. At least one of them will be a black person. The Statue of Liberty will appear in the background. Then you'll hear a country-style singer singing:

Folks 'round here they love this land;
They stand by their beliefs;
An' when they git themselves stopped up;
They want some quick relief.

Well, what do you think? Pretty good commercial concept, huh? ₉

Nah, you're right. They'd never try to pull something like that. They'd put ₁₀ the statue in the *foreground.*

COMPREHENSION

1. What does Barry mean by "retail patriotism" (paragraph 7)? How does the essay's title illustrate this concept?
2. According to Barry, what makes beer commercials, especially those for Miller, patriotic?
3. In Barry's opinion, what do sexism, patriotism, and beer have in common?

RHETORIC

1. Barry doesn't explicitly state his thesis anywhere in the essay. In your own words, what is his implied thesis? Use evidence from the essay to support your view.
2. Barry uses irony and humor very effectively in this piece. Cite some examples of his humor, and analyze how he achieves the desired effect.
3. The writer uses specific brand names in his essay. How does this device help strengthen his argument? Would eliminating them make the essay less persuasive? Why or why not?
4. Barry seems to digress from his point in paragraphs 4–6. Why does he do this? How does this digression serve the purpose of the piece?
5. Does the anecdote Barry uses in paragraph 5 ring true? Why or why not? What purpose does it serve in the essay? Does its plausibility affect the strength of Barry's argument?
6. How does paragraph 10 function as a conclusion? Is it in keeping with the essay's tone and style? Is it an effective device? Justify your response.

WRITING

1. Write an essay titled "Patriotism," using both denotative and connotative definitions of the word.
2. **Writing an Argument:** In an essay, argue for or against the claim that television advertising has had a harmful impact on American and global consumers.

NETWORKING
Applying 21st-Century Literacies

Analyzing TV Commercials: Barry's essay examines how television sells patriotism. Write an essay analyzing how television sells other abstract ideas, such as success, love, freedom, or democracy. Pattern your essay after Barry's, using humor. Also, use specific television commercials you have seen as examples.

Wonder Woman

Gloria Steinem

Gloria Steinem (b. 1934) was born and raised in Toledo, Ohio; she attended Smith College, receiving a BA in government in 1956. A noted feminist and political activist, Steinem in 1968 helped to found New York *magazine; in 1971 she cofounded* Ms. *magazine and served as its editor. Whether campaigning for Robert Kennedy, defending raising money for the United Farm Workers, or championing women's reproductive rights, Steinem has been on the cutting edge of American politics and social activism for almost five decades. Her books include* The Thousand Indias *(1957),* Outrageous Acts and Everyday Rebellions *(1983),* Marilyn: Norma Jean *(1986),* Revolution from Within *(1992),* Moving beyond Words *(1994), and* Doing Sixty and Seventy *(2006). In the following essay, Steinem explains why the comic book heroine Wonder Woman (who was on the first cover of* Ms.*) was such a formative influence during her childhood.*

Wonder Woman is the only female super-hero to be published continuously since 1 comic books began—indeed, she is one of the few to have existed at all or to be anything other than part of a male super-hero group—but this may strike many readers as a difference without much distinction. After all, haven't comic books always been a little disreputable? Something that would never have been assigned in school? The answer to those questions is yes, which is exactly why they are important. Comic books have power—including over the child who still lives within each of us—because they are *not* part of the "serious" grown-up world.

I remember hundreds of nights reading comic books under the covers with 2 a flashlight; dozens of car trips while my parents told me I was ruining my eyes and perhaps my mind ("brain-deadeners" was what my mother called them); and countless hours spent hiding in a tree or some other inaccessible spot where I could pore over their pages in sweet freedom. Because my family's traveling meant I didn't go to school regularly until I was about twelve, comic books joined cereal boxes and ketchup labels as the primers that taught me how to read. They were even cheap enough to be the first things I bought on my own— a customer who couldn't see over the countertop but whose dignity was greatly enhanced by making a choice, counting out carefully hoarded coins, and completing a grown-up exchange.

I've always wondered if this seemingly innate drive toward independence in 3 children isn't more than just "a movement toward mastery," as psychologists say. After all, each of us is the result of millennia of environment and heredity, a unique combination that could never happen before—or again. Like a seed that contains a plant, a child is already a unique person; an ancient spirit born into a body too small to express itself, or even cope with the world. I remember feeling the greatest love for my parents whenever they allowed me to express my own will, whether that meant wearing an inappropriate hat for days on end, or eating dessert before I had finished dinner.

4   Perhaps it's our memories of past competence and dreams for the future that create the need for super-heroes in the first place. Leaping skyscrapers in a single bound, seeing through walls, and forcing people to tell the truth by encircling them in a magic lasso—all would be satisfying fantasies at any age, but they may be psychological necessities when we have trouble tying our shoes, escaping a worldview composed mainly of belts and knees, and getting grown-ups to *pay attention.*

5   The problem is that the super-heroes who perform magical feats—indeed, even mortal heroes who are merely competent—are almost always men. A female child is left to believe that, even when her body is as big as her spirit, she will still be helping with minor tasks, appreciating the accomplishments of others, and waiting to be rescued. Of course, pleasure is to be found in all these experiences of helping, appreciating, and being rescued; pleasure that should be open to boys, too. Even in comic books, heroes sometimes work in groups or are called upon to protect their own kind, not just helpless females. But the truth is that a male super-hero is more likely to be vulnerable, if only to create suspense, than a female character is to be powerful or independent. For little girls, the only alternative is suppressing a crucial part of ourselves by transplanting our consciousness into a male character—which usually means a white one, thus penalizing girls of color doubly, and boys of color, too. Otherwise, choices remain limited: in the case of girls, to an "ideal" life of sitting around like a Technicolor clotheshorse, getting into jams with villains, and saying things like, "Oh, Superman! I'll always be grateful to you"; in the case of boys of color, to identifying with villains who may be the only ethnic characters with any power; and in the case of girls of color, to making an impossible choice between parts of their identity. It hardly seems worth learning to tie our shoes.

6   I'm happy to say that I was rescued from this dependent fate at the age of seven or so; rescued (Great Hera!) by a woman. Not only did she have the wisdom of Athena and Aphrodite's power to inspire love, she was also faster than Mercury and stronger than Hercules. In her all-woman home on Paradise Island, a refuge of ancient Amazon culture protected from nosy travelers by magnetic thought-fields that created an area known to the world as the Bermuda Triangle, she had come to her many and amazing powers naturally. Together with her Amazon sisters, she had been trained in them from infancy and perfected them in Greek-style contests of dexterity, strength, and speed. The lesson was that each of us might have unknown powers within us, if we only believed and practiced them. (To me, it always seemed boring that Superman had bullet-proof skin, X-ray vision, and the ability to fly. Where was the contest?) Though definitely white, as were all her Amazon sisters, she was tall and strong, with dark hair and eyes—a relief from the weak, bosomy, blonde heroines of the 1940s.

Of course, this Amazon did need a few fantastic gadgets to help her once ⁷
she entered a modern world governed by Ares, God of War, not Aphrodite,
Goddess of Love: a magic golden lasso that compelled all within its coils to
obey her command, silver bracelets that repelled bullets, and an invisible plane
that carried her through time as well as space. But she still had to learn how to
throw the lasso with accuracy, be agile enough to deflect bullets from her silver-
encased wrists, and navigate an invisible plane.

Charles Moulton, whose name appeared on each episode as Wonder Wom- ⁸
an's writer and creator, had seen straight into my heart and understood the fears
of violence and humiliation hidden there. No longer did I have to pretend to like
the "POW!" and "SPLAT!" of boys' comic books, from Captain Marvel to the Green
Hornet. No longer did I have nightmares after looking at ghoulish images of
torture and murder, bloody scenes made all the more realistic by steel-booted
Nazis and fang-toothed Japanese who were caricatures of World War II enemies
then marching in every newsreel. (Eventually, the sadism of boys' comic books
was so extreme that it inspired Congressional hearings, and publishers were
asked to limit the number of severed heads and dripping entrails—a reminder
that television wasn't the first popular medium selling sadism to boys.) Best of
all, I could stop pretending to enjoy the ridicule, bossing-around, and constant
endangering of female characters. In these Amazon adventures, only the villains
bought the idea that "masculine" meant aggression and "feminine" meant submission. Only the occasional female accomplice said things like "Girls want
superior men to boss them around," and even they were usually converted to
the joys of self-respect by the story's end.

This was an Amazon super-hero who never killed her enemies. Instead, she ⁹
converted them to a belief in equality and peace, to self-reliance, and respect for
the rights of others. If villains destroyed themselves, it was through their own
actions or some unbloody accident. Otherwise, they might be conquered by
force, but it was a force tempered by love and justice.

In short, she was wise, beautiful, brave, and explicitly out to change "a ¹⁰
world torn by the hatreds and wars of men."

She was Wonder Woman. ¹¹

Only much later, when I was in my thirties and modern feminism had be- ¹²
gun to explain the political roots of women's status—instead of accepting some
"natural" inferiority decreed by biology, God, or Freud—did I realize how hard
Charles Moulton had tried to get an egalitarian worldview into comic book
form. From Wonder Woman's birth myth as Princess Diana of Paradise Island,
"that enlightened land," to her adventures in America disguised as Diana
Prince, a be-spectacled army nurse and intelligence officer (a clear steal from
Superman's Clark Kent), this female super-hero was devoted to democracy,
peace, justice, and "liberty and freedom for all womankind."

One typical story centers on Prudence, a young pioneer in the days of the ¹³
American Frontier, where Wonder Woman has been transported by the invisi-
ble plane that doubles as a time machine. After being rescued from a Perils of
Pauline life, Prudence finally realizes her own worth, and also the worth of all

women. "From now on," she says proudly to Wonder Woman, "I'll rely on myself, not on a man." Another story ends with Wonder Woman explaining her own long-running romance with Captain Steve Trevor, the American pilot whose crash-landing on Paradise Island was Aphrodite's signal that the strongest and wisest of all the Amazons must answer the call of a war-torn world. As Wonder Woman says of this colleague whom she so often rescues: "I can never love a dominant man."

14   The most consistent villain is Ares, God of War, a kind of metavillain who considers women "the natural spoils of war" and insists they stay home as the slaves of men. Otherwise, he fears women will spread their antiwar sentiments, create democracy in the world, and leave him dishonored and unemployed. That's why he keeps trying to trick Queen Hippolyte, Princess Diana's mother, into giving up her powers as Queen of the Amazons, thus allowing him to conquer Paradise Island and destroy the last refuge of ancient feminism. It is in memory of a past time when the Amazons did give in to the soldiers of Ares, and were enslaved by them, that Aphrodite requires each Amazon to wear a pair of cufflike bracelets. If captured and bound by them (as Wonder Woman sometimes is in particularly harrowing episodes), an Amazon loses all her power. Wearing them is a reminder of the fragility of female freedom.

15   In America, however, villains are marked not only by their violence, but by their prejudice and lust for money. Thomas Tighe, woman-hating industrialist, is typical. After being rescued by Wonder Woman from accidental imprisonment in his own bank vault, he refuses to give her the promised reward of a million dollars. Though the money is needed to support Holliday College, the home of the band of college girls who aid Wonder Woman, Tighe insists that its students must first complete impossible tests of strength and daring. Only after Wonder Woman's powers allow them to meet every challenge does Tighe finally admit: "You win, Wonder Woman! . . . I am no longer a woman hater." She replies: "Then you're the real winner, Mr. Tighe! Because when one ceases to hate, he becomes stronger!"

16   Other villains are not so easily converted. Chief among them is Dr. Psycho, perhaps a parody of Sigmund Freud. An "evil genius" who "abhors women," the mad doctor's intentions are summed up in this scene-setting preface to an episode called "Battle for Womanhood": "With weird cunning and dark, forbidden knowledge of the occult, Dr. Psycho prepares to change the independent status of modern American women back to the days of the sultans and slave markets, clanking chains and abject captivity. But sly and subtle Psycho reckons without Wonder Woman!"

17   When I looked into the origins of my proto-feminist super-hero, I discovered that her pseudonymous creator had been a very non-Freudian psychologist named William Moulton Marston. Also a lawyer, businessman, prison reformer, and inventor of the lie-detector test (no doubt the inspiration for Wonder Woman's magic lasso), he had invented Wonder Woman as a heroine for little girls, and also as a conscious alternative to the violence of comic books for boys. In fact, Wonder Woman did attract some boys as readers, but the

integrated world of comic book trading revealed her true status: at least three Wonder Woman comic books were necessary to trade for one of Superman. Among the many male super-heroes, only Superman and Batman were to be as long-lived as Wonder Woman, yet she was still a second-class citizen.

Of course, it's also true that Marston's message wasn't as feminist as it might have been. Instead of portraying the goal of full humanity for women and men, which is what feminism has in mind, he often got stuck in the sub-ject/object, winner/loser paradigm of "masculine" versus "feminine," and came up with female superiority instead. As he wrote: "Women represent love; men represent force. Man's use of force without love brings evil and unhappi-ness. Wonder Woman proves that women are superior to men because they have love in addition to force." No wonder I was inspired but confused by the isolationism of Paradise Island: Did women have to live separately in order to be happy and courageous? No wonder even boys who could accept equality might have felt less than good about themselves in some of these stories: Were there *any* men who could escape the cultural instruction to be violent? 18

Wonder Woman herself sometimes got trapped in this either/or choice. As she muses to herself: "Some girls love to have a man stronger than they are to make them do things. Do I like it? I don't know, it's sort of thrilling. But isn't it more fun to make a man obey?" Even female villains weren't capable of being evil on their own. Instead, they were hyperfeminine followers of men's commands. Consider Priscilla Rich, the upper-class antagonist who metamorphoses into the Cheetah, a dangerous she-animal. "Women have been submissive to men," wrote Marston, "and taken men's psychology [force without love] as their own." 19

In those wartime years, stories could verge on a jingoistic, even racist pa-triotism. Wonder Woman sometimes forgot her initial shock at America's unjust patriarchal system and confined herself to defeating a sinister foreign threat by proving that women could be just as loyal and brave as men in service of their country. Her costume was a version of the Stars and Stripes. Some of her adver-saries were suspiciously short, ugly, fat, or ethnic as a symbol of "un-American" status. In spite of her preaching against violence and for democracy, the good guys were often in uniform, and no country but the United States was seen as a bastion of freedom. 20

But Marston didn't succumb to stereotypes as often as most comic book writ-ers of the 1940s. Though Prudence, his frontier heroine, is threatened by monosyl-labic Indians, Prudence's father turns out to be the true villain, who has been cheating the Indians. And the irrepressible Etta Candy, one of Wonder Woman's band of college girls, is surely one of the few fat-girl heroines in comics. 21

There are other unusual rewards. Queen Hippolyte, for instance, is a rare example of a mother who is good, powerful, and a mentor to her daughter. She founds nations, fights to protect Paradise Island, and is a source of strength to Wonder Woman as she battles the forces of evil and inequality. Mother and daughter stay in touch through a sort of telepathic TV set, and the result is a team of equals who are separated only by experience. In the flashback episode in which Queen Hippolyte succumbs to Hercules, she is even seen as a sexual 22 being. How many girl children grew to adulthood with no such example of a strong, sensual mother—except for these slender stories? How many mothers preferred sons, or believed the patriarchal myth that competition is "natural" between mothers and daughters, or tamed their daughters instead of encouraging their wildness and strength? We are just beginning to realize the sense of anger and loss in girls whose mothers had no power to protect them, or forced them to conform out of fear for their safety, or left them to identify only with their fathers if they had any ambition at all.

23   Finally, there is Wonder Woman's ability to unleash the power of self-respect within the women around her; to help them work together and support each other. This may not seem revolutionary to male readers accustomed to stories that depict men working together, but for females who are usually seen as competing for the favors of men—especially little girls who may just be getting to the age when girlfriends betray each other for the approval of boys—this discovery of sisterhood can be exhilarating indeed. Women get a rare message of independence, of depending on themselves, not even on Wonder Woman. "You saved yourselves," as she says in one of her inevitable morals at story's end. "I only showed you that you could."

24   Whatever the shortcomings of William Marston, his virtues became clear after his death in 1947. Looking back at the post-Marston stories I had missed the first time around—for at twelve or thirteen, I thought I had outgrown Wonder Woman and had abandoned her—I could see how little her later writers understood her spirit. She became sexier-looking and more submissive, violent episodes increased, more of her adversaries were female, and Wonder Woman herself required more help from men in order to triumph. Like so many of her real-life sisters in the postwar era of conservatism and "togetherness" of the 1950s, she had fallen on very hard times.

25   By the 1960s, Wonder Woman had given up her magic lasso, her bullet-deflecting bracelets, her invisible plane, and all her Amazonian powers. Though she still had adventures and even practiced karate, any attractive man could disarm her. She had become a kind of female James Bond, though much more boring because she was denied his sexual freedom. She was Diana Prince, a mortal who walked about in boutique, car-hop clothes and took the advice of a male mastermind named "I Ching."

26   It was in this sad state that I first rediscovered my Amazon super-hero in 1972. *Ms.* magazine had just begun, and we were looking for a cover story for its first regular issue to appear in July. Since Joanne Edgar and other of its founding editors had also been rescued by Wonder Woman in their childhoods, we decided to rescue Wonder Woman in return. Though it wasn't easy to persuade her publishers to let us put her original image on the cover of a new and unknown feminist magazine, or to reprint her 1940s Golden Age episodes inside, we finally succeeded. Wonder Woman appeared on newsstands again in all her original glory, striding through city streets like a colossus, stopping planes and bombs with one hand and rescuing buildings with the other.

Clearly, there were many nostalgic grown-ups and heroine-starved readers 27
of all ages. The consensus of response seemed to be that if we had all read more
about Wonder Woman and less about Dick and Jane, we might have been a lot
better off. As for her publishers, they, too, were impressed. Under the direction
of Dorothy Woolfolk, the first woman editor of Wonder Woman in all her long
history, she was returned to her original Amazon status—golden lasso, bracelets, and all.

One day some months after her rebirth, I got a phone call from one of Won- 28
der Woman's tougher male writers. "Okay," he said, "she's got all her Amazon
powers back. She talks to the Amazons on Paradise Island. She even has a Black
Amazon sister named Nubia. Now will you leave me alone?"

I said we would.   29

In the 1970s, Wonder Woman became the star of a television series. As played 30
by Lynda Carter, she was a little blue of eye and large of breast, but she still retained her Amazon powers, her ability to convert instead of kill, and her appeal
for many young female viewers. There were some who refused to leave their
TV sets on Wonder Woman night. A few young boys even began to dress up as
Wonder Woman on Halloween—a true revolution.

In the 1980s, Wonder Woman's story line was revamped by DC Comics, which 31
reinvented its male super-heroes Superman and Batman at about the same time.
Steve Trevor became a veteran of Vietnam; he remained a friend, but was romanti-
cally involved with Etta Candy. Wonder Woman acquired a Katharine Hepburn–
Spencer Tracy relationship with a street-smart Boston detective named Ed
Indelicato, whose tough-guy attitude played off Wonder Woman's idealism. She
also gained a friend and surrogate mother in Julia Kapatelis, a leading archaeolo-
gist and professor of Greek culture at Harvard University who can understand the
ancient Greek that is Wonder Woman's native tongue, and be a model of a smart,
caring, single mother for girl readers. Julia's teenage daughter, Vanessa, is the age
of many readers and goes through all of their uncertainties, trials, and tribulations,
but has the joy of having a powerful older sister in Wonder Woman. There is even
Myndi Mayer, a slick Hollywood public relations agent who turns Wonder
Woman into America's hero, and is also in constant danger of betraying Diana's
idealistic spirit. In other words, there are many of the currents of society today,
from single mothers to the worries of teenage daughters and a commercial culture,
instead of the simpler plots of America's dangers in World War II.

You will see whether Wonder Woman carries her true Amazon spirit into 32
the present. If not, let her publishers know. She belongs to you.

Since Wonder Woman's beginnings more than a half century ago, however, a 33
strange thing has happened: The Amazon myth has been rethought as archaeological relics have come to light. Though Amazons had been considered figments
of the imagination, perhaps the mythological evidence of man's fear of woman,
there is a tentative but growing body of evidence to support the theory that
some Amazon-like societies did exist. In Europe, graves once thought to contain

male skeletons—because they were buried with weapons or were killed by battle wounds—have turned out to hold skeletons of females after all. In the jungles of Brazil, scientists have found caves of what appears to have been an all-female society. The caves are strikingly devoid of the usual phallic design and theme; they feature, instead, the triangular female symbol, and the only cave that does bear male designs is believed to have been the copulatorium, where Amazons mated with males from surrounding tribes, kept only the female children, and returned male infants to the tribe. Such archaeological finds have turned up not only along the Amazon River in Brazil, but at the foot of the Atlas Mountains in northwestern Africa, and on the European and Asiatic sides of the Black Sea.

34   There is still far more controversy than agreement, but a shared supposition of these myths is this: Imposing patriarchy on the gynocracy of pre-history took many centuries and great cruelty. Rather than give up freedom and worship only male gods, some bands of women resisted. They formed all-woman cultures that survived by capturing men from local tribes, mating with them, and raising their girl children to have great skills of body and mind. These bands became warriors and healers who were sometimes employed for their skills by patriarchal cultures around them. As a backlash culture, they were doomed, but they may also have lasted for centuries.

35   Perhaps that's the appeal of Wonder Woman, Paradise Island, and this comic book message. It's not only a child's need for a lost independence, but an adult's need for a lost balance between women and men, between humans and nature. As the new Wonder Woman says to Vanessa, "Remember your *power*, little sister."

36   However simplified, that is Wonder Woman's message: Remember Our Power.

COMPREHENSION

1. According to Steinem, why are children drawn to comic books and superheroes?
2. Why did Wonder Woman appeal especially to Steinem? What distinctions does she draw between the ways boys and girls view action heroes?
3. The writer traces the development of Wonder Woman from her inception during the 1940s to the 1980s. How did Wonder Woman change over the years? How did she remain true to her creator's (William Marston) conception of her? What does Steinem think about these changes?

RHETORIC

1. What is this essay's persuasive thesis?
2. At whom is this essay aimed—lovers of comic books, or women, or a general audience? On what do you base your conclusion?
3. In part, this is a personal essay. How does Steinem create her persona or self-image? Does the personal element enhance or detract from the analysis? Explain your response.
4. Sort out the complex cause-and-effect relationships in this essay. How does the comparative method reinforce the writer's analysis?

5. What types of evidence does the writer provide? Is it sufficient to convince readers? Where, if anywhere, would more detail be helpful?
6. Steinem divides the essay into five sections. What is her purpose? How successful is she in maintaining the essay's unity by employing this method?
7. What paragraphs form the writer's conclusion? How do they recapitulate and add to the substance of the overall essay?

WRITING

1. Compare and contrast the ways in which females and males approach action heroes. Refer to specific icons like Batman, Spiderman, Ellen Ripley, or Buffy the Vampire Slayer to support your assessment.
2. **Writing an Argument:** Think about the numerous action or superheroes that young children and adolescents encounter today in various media forms. Write an essay in which you contend that exposure to such superheroes either does or does not encourage violent behavior in young people.

NETWORKING
Applying 21st-Century Literacies

Reading Action Heroes in Different Media: Write a personal essay about your favorite action hero or heroine—drawn from comics, television shows, or computer games. Explain why this figure appeals to you and what this appeal reveals about the broader culture. In your exploration, include a discussion of how this particular medium/genre was ideal for this character.

Supersaturation, or, The Media Torrent and Disposable Feeling

Todd Gitlin

Todd Gitlin (b. 1943) was born and grew up in New York City. He received a PhD in sociology from the University of California at Berkeley and was president of Students for a Democratic Society (SDS) in the 1960s. Gitlin is professor of culture, journalism, and sociology at New York University and has held the chair in American civilization at the École des hautes études en sciences sociales *in Paris. Gitlin also lectures at home and abroad on contemporary culture and history. He is the North American editor of the Web site openDemocracy.net. Among his notable books are* Inside Prime Time *(1983),* The Twilight of Common Dreams: Why America Is Wracked by Culture Wars *(1995),* Media Unlimited: How the Torrent of Images and Sounds

Overwhelms Our Lives *(2001), and* The Bulldozer and the Big Tent: Blind Republicans *(2008). In the selection from* Media Unlimited *that follows, Gitlin offers
an overview of the ways in which the media influence our contemporary lives.*

1   On my bedroom wall hangs a print of Vermeer's *The Concert*, painted around
1660. A young woman is playing a spinet. A second woman, probably her maid,
holds a letter. A cavalier stands between them, his back to us. A landscape is
painted on the raised lid of the spinet, and on the wall hang two paintings, a
landscape and *The Procuress*, a work by Baburen, another Dutch artist, depicting
a man and two women in a brothel. As in many seventeenth-century Dutch
paintings, the domestic space is decorated by paintings. In wealthy Holland,
many homes, and not only bourgeois ones, featured such renderings of the
outer world. These pictures were pleasing, but more: They were proofs of taste
and prosperity, amusements and news at once.

2   Vermeer froze instants, but instants that spoke of the relative constancy
of the world in which his subjects lived. If he had painted the same room in
the same house an hour, a day, or a month later, the letter in the maid's hand
would have been different, and the woman might have been playing a different selection, but the paintings on the far wall would likely have been the
same. There might have been other paintings, etchings, and prints elsewhere
in the house, but they would not have changed much from month to month,
year to year.

3   In what was then the richest country in the world, "everyone strives to em-
bellish his house with precious pieces, especially the room toward the street,"
as one English visitor to Amsterdam wrote in 1640, noting that he had observed
paintings in bakeries, butcher's shops, and the workshops of blacksmiths and
cobblers.[1] Of course, the number of paintings, etchings, and prints in homes
varied considerably. One tailor owned five paintings, for example, while at the
high end, a 1665 inventory of a lavish patrician's house in Amsterdam held two
maps and thirteen paintings in one grand room, twelve paintings in his widow's bedroom, and seven in the maid's room. Still, compared with today's domestic imagery, the grandest Dutch inventories of that prosperous era were
tiny.[2] Even in the better-off households depicted by Vermeer, the visual field
inhabited by his figures was relatively scanty and fixed.[3]

---

[1] Peter Mundy, quoted by Geert Mak, *Amsterdam,* trans. Philipp Blom (Cambridge, Mass.: Harvard
University Press, 2000), p. 109.
[2] Simon Schama, *The Embarrassment of Riches: An Interpretation of Dutch Culture in the Golden Age*
(New York: Knopf, 1987), pp. 313–19. Schama notes that research in the relevant archives is "still
in its early days" (p. 315).
[3] Many bourgeois Dutch houses also featured a camera lucida, a mounted magnifying lens trained
on objects in the vicinity. Because the lens was movable, motion could be simulated—distant
objects being brought nearer and sent farther away. But because the apparatus was mounted
in a fixed location, the range of objects in motion was limited to those actually visible from the
window. (Svetlana Alpers, personal communication, October 8, 1999.)

Today, Vermeer's equivalent, if he were painting domestic scenes, or shoot- 4
ing a spread for *Vanity Fair,* or directing commercials or movies, would also
display his figures against a background of images; and if his work appeared
on-screen, there is a good chance that he would mix in a soundtrack as well.
Most of the images would be portraits of individuals who have never walked in
the door—not in the flesh—and yet are recognized and welcomed, though not
like actual persons. They would rapidly segue into others—either because they
had been edited into a video montage, or because they appear on pages meant
to be leafed through. Today's Vermeer would discover that the private space of
the home offers up vastly more impressions of the larger world than was possible in 1660. In seventeenth-century Delft, painters did not knock on the door
day and night offering fresh images for sale. Today, though living space has
been set apart from working space, as would have been the case only for the
wealthier burghers of Vermeer's time, the outside world has entered the home
with a vengeance—in the profusion of media.

The flow of images and sounds through the households of the rich world, 5
and the richer parts of the poor world, seems unremarkable today. Only a
visitor from an earlier century or an impoverished country could be startled
by the fact that life is now played out against a shimmering multitude of images and sounds, emanating from television, videotapes, videodiscs, video
games, VCRs, computer screens, digital displays of all sorts, always in flux,
chosen partly at will, partly by whim, supplemented by words, numbers,
symbols, phrases, fragments, all passing through screens that in a single minute can display more pictures than a prosperous seventeenth-century Dutch
household contained over several lifetimes, portraying in one day more individuals than the Dutch burgher would have beheld in the course of years,
and in one week more bits of what we have come to call "information" than
all the books in all the households in Vermeer's Delft. And this is not yet to
speak of our sonic surroundings: the music, voices, and sound effects from
radios, CD players, and turntables. Nor is it to speak of newspapers, magazines, newsletters, and books. Most of the faces we shall ever behold, we
shall behold in the form of images.

Because they arrive with sound, at home, in the car, the elevator, or the 6
waiting room, today's images are capable of attracting our attention during
much of the day. We may ignore most of them most of the time, take issue
with them or shrug them off (or think we are shrugging them off), but we
must do the work of dispelling them—and even then, we know we can usher
them into our presence whenever we like. Iconic plenitude is the contemporary condition, and it is taken for granted. To grow up in this culture is to
grow into an expectation that images and sounds will be there for us on command, and that the stories they compose will be succeeded by still other stories, all bidding for our attention, all striving to make sense, all, in some sense,
ours. Raymond Williams, the first analyst to pay attention to the fact that television is not just pictures but flow, and not just flow but drama upon drama,

pointed out more than a quarter century ago, long before hundred-channel cable TV and VCRs, that

> we have never as a society acted so much or watched so many others acting. . . . [W]hat is really new . . . is that drama . . . is built into the rhythms of everyday life. In earlier periods drama was important at a festival, in a season, or as a conscious journey to a theater; from honouring Dionysus or Christ to taking in a show. What we have now is drama as habitual experience: more in a week, in many cases, than most human beings would previously have seen in a lifetime.[4]

7   Around the time Vermeer painted *The Concert*, Blaise Pascal, who worried about the seductive power of distraction among the French royalty, wrote that "near the persons of kings there never fail to be a great number of people who see to it that amusement follows business, and who watch all the time of their leisure to supply them with delights and games, so that there is no blank in it."[5] In this one respect, today almost everyone—even the poor—in the rich countries resembles a king, attended by the courtiers of the media offering a divine right of choice.

Measures of Magnitude

8   Statistics begin—but barely—to convey the sheer magnitude of this in-touchness, access, exposure, plenitude, glut, however we want to think of it.

9   In 1999, a television set was on in the average American household more than seven hours a day, a figure that has remained fairly steady since 1983. According to the measurements of the A. C. Nielsen Company, the standard used by advertisers and the television business itself, the average individual watched television about four hours a day, not counting the time when the set was on but the individual in question was not watching. When Americans were asked to keep diaries of how they spend their time, the time spent actually watching dropped to a still striking three hours a day—probably an undercount. In 1995, of those who watched, the percentage who watched "whatever's on," as opposed to any specific program, was 43 percent, up from 29 percent in 1979.[6] Though cross-national comparisons are elusive because of differences in measurement systems, the numbers in other industrialized nations seem to be comparable—France, for example, averaging three and a half hours per person.[7]

---

[4]"Drama in a Dramatised Society," in Alan O'Connor, ed., *Raymond Williams on Television* (Toronto: Between the Lines, 1989 [1974]), pp. 3–5. *Flow* comes up in Williams's *Television: Technology and Cultural Form* (New York: Schocken, 1975), p. 86 ff.

[5]*Pensées*, trans. W. F. Trotter (www.eserver.org/philosophy/pascal-pensees.txt), sec. 2, par. 142.

[6]Robert D. Putnam, *Bowling Alone: The Collapse and Revival of American Community* (New York: Simon and Schuster, 2000), p. 222, citing John P. Robinson and Geoffrey Godbey, *Time for Life: The Surprising Ways Americans Use Their Time*, 2nd ed. (University Park: Pennsylvania State University Press, 1999), pp. 136–53, 340–41, 222.

[7]This April 2001 figure for individuals fifteen and older comes from Mediamat (Mediametrie www.mediametria.fr/television/mediamat_mensuel/2001/avril.html).

One survey of forty-three nations showed the United States ranking third in viewing hours, after Japan and Mexico. None of this counts time spent discussing programs, reading about their stars, or thinking about either.[8]

Overall, wrote one major researcher in 1990, "watching TV is the domi- 10 nant leisure activity of Americans, consuming 40 percent of the average person's free time as a primary activity [when people give television their undivided attention]. Television takes up more than half of our free time if you count . . . watching TV while doing something else like eating or reading . . . [or] when you have the set on but you aren't paying attention to it."[9] Sex, race, income, age, and marital status make surprisingly little difference in time spent.[10] Neither, at this writing, has the Internet diminished total media use, even if you don't count the Web as part of the media. While Internet users do watch 28 percent less television, they spend more time than nonusers playing video games and listening to the radio and recorded music—obviously a younger crowd. Long-term users (four or more years) say they go online for more than two hours a day, and boys and girls alike spend the bulk of their Internet time entertaining themselves with games, hobbies, and the like.[11] In other words, the Internet redistributes the flow of unlimited media but does not dry it up. When one considers the overlapping and additional hours of exposure to radio, magazines, newspapers, compact discs, movies (available via a range of technologies as well as in theaters), and comic books, as well as the accompanying articles, books, and chats about what's on or was on or is coming up via all these means, it is clear that the media flow into the home—not to mention outside—has swelled into a torrent of immense force and constancy, an accompaniment to life that has become a central experience *of* life.

The place of media in the lives of children is worth special attention—not 11 simply because children are uniquely impressionable but because their experience shapes everyone's future; if we today take a media-soaked environment for granted, surely one reason is that we grew up in it and can no longer see how remarkable it is. Here are some findings from a national survey of media conditions among American children aged two through eighteen. The average American child lives in a household with 2.9 televisions, 1.8 VCRs, 3.1 radios, 2.6 tape players, 2.1 CD players, 1.4 video game players, and 1 computer. Ninety-nine percent of these children live in homes with one or more TVs, 97 percent with a VCR, 97 percent with a radio, 94 percent with a tape player, 90 percent with a CD player, 70 percent with a video game player,

---

[8]Putnam, *Bowling Alone*, p. 480, citing Eurodata TV (*One Television Year in the World: Audience Report*, April 1999).
[9]John P. Robinson, "I Love My TV," *American Demographics*, September 1990, p. 24.
[10]Robert Kubey and Mihaly Csikszentmihalyi, *Television and the Quality of Life: How Viewing Shapes Everyday Experience* (Hillsdale, N.J.: Lawrence Erlbaum Associates, 1990), pp. 71–73.
[11]UCLA Center for Communication Policy, *The UCLA Internet Report: Surveying the Digital Future*, November 2000, pp. 10, 17, 18, 14 (www.ccp.ucla.edu).

69 percent with a computer. Eighty-eight percent live in homes with two or more TVs, 60 percent in homes with three or more. Of the 99 percent with a TV, 74 percent have cable or satellite service.[12] And so on, and on, and on.

12   The uniformity of this picture is no less astounding. A great deal about the lives of children depends on their race, sex, and social class, but access to major media does not. For TV, VCR, and radio ownership, rates do not vary significantly among white, black, and Hispanic children, or between girls and boys. For television and radio, rates do not vary significantly according to the income of the community.[13]

13   How accessible, then, is the media cavalcade at home? Of children eight to eighteen, 65 percent have a TV in their bedrooms, 86 percent a radio, 81 percent a tape player, 75 percent a CD player. Boys and girls are not significantly different in possessing this bounty, though the relative usages do vary by medium. Researchers also asked children whether the television was "on in their homes even if no one is watching 'most of the time,' 'some of the time,' 'a little of the time,' or 'never.'" Homes in which television is on "most of the time" are termed *constant television households.* By this measure, 42 percent of all American households with children are constant television households. Blacks are more likely than whites or Hispanics to experience TV in their lives: 56 percent of black children live in constant television households (and 69 percent have a TV in their bedrooms, compared to 48 percent of whites). The lower the family education and the median income of the community, the greater the chance that a household is a constant television household.[14]

14   As for time, the average child spent six hours and thirty-two minutes per day exposed to media of all kinds, of which the time spent reading books and magazines—not counting schoolwork—averaged about forty-five minutes. For ages two to seven, the average for total media was four hours and seventeen minutes; for ages eight to thirteen, eight hours and eight minutes, falling to seven hours and thirty-five minutes for ages fourteen to eighteen.[15] Here, race

[12]Donald F. Roberts, *Kids and Media @ the New Millennium* (Menlo Park, Calif.: Henry J. Kaiser Family Foundation, 1999), p. 9, table 1. There were 3,155 children in the sample, including over-samples of black and Hispanic children, to ensure that results in these minority populations would also be statistically significant. As best as a reader can discern, this was a reliable study, with a margin of error of no more than plus-or-minus five percentage points. Since the results for younger children, ages two to seven, come from parents' reports, they may well be conservative, since parents may be uninformed of the extent of their children's viewing or may be underplaying it in order not to feel ashamed before interviewers.

[13]Ibid., p. 11, tables 3-A, 3-B, 3-C.

[14]Ibid., pp. 13–15, tables 4, 5-A, 5-B, 6. In general, fewer western European or Israeli children than Americans have TVs in their bedrooms, but 70 percent in Great Britain do. Next highest in Europe is 64 percent in Denmark. The lows are 31 percent in Holland and 24 percent in Switzerland. Leen d'Haenens, "Old and New Media: Access and Ownership in the Home," in Sonia Livingstone and Moira Bovill, eds., *Children and Their Changing Media Environment: A European Comparative Study* (London: Lawrence Erlbaum Associates, 2001), p. 57.

[15]Roberts, *Kids and Media*, pp. 21–23, tables 8-C, 8-D.

and social class do count. Black children are most exposed, followed by Hispanics, then whites. At all age levels, the amount of exposure to all media varies inversely with class, from six hours and fifty-nine minutes a day for children in households where the median income for the zip code is under $25,000 to six hours and two minutes for children whose zip code median income is over $40,000. The discrepancy for TV exposure is especially pronounced, ranging from three hours and six minutes a day for children whose zip code incomes are under $25,000 to two hours and twenty-nine minutes for children whose zip code incomes are over $40,000.[16] Still, these differences are not vast. Given everything that divides the rich from the poor, the professional from the working class—differences in physical and mental health, infant mortality, longevity, safety, vulnerability to crime, prospects for stable employment, and so on—the class differences in media access and use are surprisingly slender. So are the differences between American and western European children, the latter averaging six hours a day total, though in Europe only two and a quarter of those hours are spent with TV.[17]

All such statistics are crude, of course. Most of them register the time that people *say* they spend. They are—thankfully—not checked by total surveillance. Moreover, the meaning of *exposure* is hard to assess, since the concept encompasses rapt attention, vague awareness, oblivious coexistence, and all possible shadings in between. As the images glide by and the voices come and go, how can we assess what goes on in people's heads? Still, the figures do convey some sense of the media saturation with which we live—and so far we have counted only what can be counted at home. These numbers don't take into account the billboards, the TVs at bars and on planes, the Muzak in restaurants and shops, the magazines in the doctor's waiting room, the digital displays at the gas pump and over the urinal, the ads, insignias, and logos whizzing by on the sides of buses and taxis, climbing the walls of buildings, making announcements from caps, bags, T-shirts, and sneakers. To vary our experience, we can pay to watch stories about individuals unfold across larger-than-life-size movie screens, or visit theme parks and troop from image to image, display to display. Whenever we like, on foot or in vehicles, we can

---

[16]The same point applies to differences in media use throughout the prosperous world. As the economist Adair Turner writes: "European Internet penetration lags the US by 18 to 24 months. When cars or television sets were first introduced, the lag was more like 15 years. . . . The shortness of the lag also suggests that social concern about a 'digital divide,' whether within or between nations, is largely misplaced. . . . Time lags between different income groups in the penetration of personal computers, Internet connections or mobile phones are much shorter, once again because all these products are cheap. . . . At the global level the same scepticism about a digital divide should prevail. Africa may lag 15 years or so behind US levels of PC and Internet penetration, but it lags more like a century behind in basic literacy and health care." Adair Turner, "Not the e-conomy," *Prospect* (London), April 2001 (www.prospect-magazine.co.uk/highlights/essay_turner_april01).

[17]Johannes W. J. Beentjes et al, "Children's Use of Different Media: For How Long and Why?" in Livingstone and Bovill, eds., *Children and Their Changing Media Environment*, p. 96.

convert ourselves into movable nodes of communication, thanks to car radios, tape, CD, and game players, cell phones, beepers, Walkmen, and the latest in "personal communication systems"—and even if we ourselves refrain, we find ourselves drawn willy-nilly into the soundscape that others broadcast around us.

16   Crucially, who we are is how we live our time—or *spend* it, to use the term that registers its intrinsic scarcity. What we believe, or say we believe, is less important. We vote for a way of life with our time. And increasingly, when we are not at work or asleep, we are in the media torrent. (Sometimes at work, we are also there, listening to the radio or checking out sports scores, pin-ups, or headlines on the Internet.) Steadily more inhabitants of the wealthy part of the world have the means, incentives, and opportunities to seek private electronic companionship. The more money we have to spend, the more personal space each household member gets. With personal space comes solitude, but this solitude is instantly crowded with images and soundtracks. To a degree that was unthinkable in the seventeenth century, life experience has become an experience in the presence of media.

COMPREHENSION

1. What does Gitlin's title mean? How are the concepts of "supersaturation" and "disposable feeling" reflected in the essay?
2. Summarize Gitlin's treatment of Vermeer. Who was Vermeer? How, according to the writer, would Vermeer's art be produced today?
3. List some of the facts and statistics that the writer presents to support his idea that we are caught in a "media torrent."

RHETORIC

1. What is Gitlin's argument? Where does he state his claim most clearly? What appeals to logic, ethics, and emotion does he make? Does he rely on his own opinions? Justify your answer.
2. How does the writer maintain unity between the two parts of this essay? Why, for example, does he open his essay with the story of Vermeer? How does Vermeer serve as a unifying element? What other unifying motifs can you find?
3. What varieties of evidence does the writer provide to bolster his argument? Does he rely on anecdotal or actual evidence? How do you know?
4. The writer employs a range of rhetorical strategies in this essay. Point to places where he uses description, comparison and contrast, classification, definition, and causal analysis.
5. Is the author's style personal, informal, or formal? How does this style explain Gitlin's relationship to his audience and the expectations he holds of his readers?
6. What strategy does the writer use in his conclusion? Is this strategy effective? Why or why not?
7. What do Gitlin's footnotes add to the essay? Why are they important?

WRITING

1. Write an essay in which you explain how one medium—television or the Internet, for example—has affected or changed your life. Make sure that you provide adequate detail or evidence.
2. **Writing an Argument:** Write an essay in which you either agree or disagree with Gitlin's claim that increasingly "we are in a media torrent." Use appeals to logic, ethics, and emotion to advance your claim. Make certain that you have adequate evidence to support your major and minor propositions.

NETWORKING
Applying 21st-Century Literacies

Comparing New and Old Media: Write a comparative essay in which you analyze the similarities and differences between an "old" and a "new" component of the media—actual books and e-books or audio books, or telephones and cell phones, for example. Use visuals to enhance and support your comparisons.

Escape from Wonderland: Disney and the Female Imagination

Deborah Ross

Deborah Ross is professor of English at Hawai'i Pacific University, where she teaches writing, literature, and humanities. She specializes in popular culture, especially from the perspective of gender. In the following research paper, published in a 2004 issue of Marvels & Tales: Journal of Fairy-Tale Studies, *Ross analyzes a series of Disney films, all based on children's books and fairy tales; she evaluates the Disney ideology as it affects the imaginative and actual lives of girls.*

In 1989, Disney's little mermaid first asked the musical question, "When's it my 1 turn?" She asked it again in 1996, when her movie was re-released in theaters, and she continues to ask it, frequently, in many of our living rooms. Never has a protagonist had so many turns to demand a turn: Yet, seemingly, she remains unsatisfied. If even the heroine in a Disney "girls' movie" does not enjoy being a girl, how must the girls watching her feel about it?

Behind this gender question lurks a larger political one. If Ariel's feminist 2 rhetoric is undercut by more conservative elements in her movie, so is the

environmentalism of *The Lion King*, the multiculturalism of *Pocahontas*, the valu-
ing of difference in *The Hunchback of Notre Dame*—in short, all the quasi-liberal
sentiments that focus groups have no doubt caused to grace the surface of the
last decade's Disney features. Ideology in Disney is a much vexed question, and
I will not attempt here to untangle a knot which began forming for critics when
Walt first denied having any politics back in the thirties, and which has only
grown in mass and complexity since his death, as his corporation's management style has evolved to cope with a burgeoning staff of artists and technicians, changing public tastes, and changing perceptions of those tastes.

3   One generalization I do suggest, however, is that Disney the man and the
corporation are known for a belief in control. The top-down management style
Disney epitomizes—Auschwitz (Giroux 55), or Mouschwitz (Lewis 88), is a frequent analogy—thrives on homogeneity and rigid adherence to rules. These are
features often decried in Disney production and product, both by critics of capitalism, such as Benjamin and Adorno,[1] and by far less radical proponents of
individualism and open debate, from early Disney biographer Richard Schickel
to educator Henry Giroux. Yet imagination, the company's major commodity,
does not easily lend itself to a program of control. To encourage imagination in
artists, and arouse it in viewers, is to invite unique self-expression rather than
homogeneity, and spontaneity rather than predictability. Link imagination to
the animated cartoon, an art form with roots in dada, surrealism, and radical
politics, and matters could well get out of hand.[2]

4   I believe that this conflict between control and imaginative freedom is visible in the animated features that have come out of the Disney studios, from
Snow White and the Seven Dwarfs to *Lilo and Stitch*. Of course, ambiguity is rarely
viewed now as either a moral or an aesthetic flaw, and the presence of elements
that contradict each other may well be preferable to consistent, monologic disapproval of imagination. Neither, however, do conflict and contradiction in
themselves necessarily create a space for viewers to question values and exercise judgment. Much depends on how the elements relate to each other, or how
an audience is likely to relate them. An audience even partially looking for
guides to behavior along with entertainment will have to resolve apparent am-
biguities into one suggested course of action. Giroux's attack on Disney rests on
the contention that for children, these movies, however apparently bland, do
have a didactic effect (18). For them, ambiguity at its best ultimately resolves
into a connected but complex world view that embraces difference and spontaneity; at its worst, it can produce confusion and anxiety.

---

[1]Miriam Hansen discusses Benjamin's and Adorno's objections to Disney in some detail. Jack
Zipes's critique of Disney also occurs within a larger argument about the "freezing" of fairy tales
into myths to perpetuate bourgeois, patriarchal values (see his Introduction and Chapter 3).
[2]Janet Wasko notes that Disney deliberately avoided the more "anarchistic and inventive" styles
of animation employed at other studios (115). My own belief, on which my approach to Disney is
based, is that where there is animation, anarchy can never be wholly suppressed. For discussion
of the roots of animation in surrealism and dada, see Inez Hedges.

I wish to explore the overall impressions these films may give children about 5
the value of their own imaginations, and thus about their own value as unique
individuals able to envision, and eventually to enact, change. In particular, to get
back to Ariel, I am concerned about what girls may learn about this potentially
explosive aspect of their characters that could so easily burst the bounds of traditional femininity. To help answer this question, I have chosen to examine the way
various elements of image, story, and dialogue interact to influence the valuation
of imagination in three of Disney's girls' movies: *Alice in Wonderland* (1951), *The
Little Mermaid* (1989), and *Beauty and the Beast* (1991, re-released 2001).

I have chosen these three because, although one might be called "prefemi- 6
nist" and the other two "post-," all specifically concern young women who fantasize about a life more vivid and exciting than their reality. I will suggest that
some of these films' discomfort with female imagination has roots far back in
didactic narrative for girls by looking at Charlotte Lennox's 1759 novel, *The
Female Quixote*, which concerns the fortunes of a young woman who might be
considered the great-grandmother, or prototype, of the Disney heroine. Then,
comparing the three Disney movies with their written fairy-tale sources, I will
show how much more confusing a many-tongued message can become when it
is told in pictures as well as words.

Girls have been learning from stories where to draw the line between fantasy and 7
reality probably since the first story was told, but one sees this didactic purpose
especially clearly beginning in the seventeenth century, when romances and literary fairy tales were first written specifically for, about, and even by women.
Samuel Johnson was greatly concerned about the effects of fiction on "the young,
the ignorant, and the idle," and Paul Hunter has shown that there was indeed a
class of new readers early in the eighteenth century who were socially displaced
and looking to novels for moral and social guidance as well as entertainment
(Hunter 271–72). From that time till the present, conservative authors have used
romances and novels to teach girls that their dreams are dangerous and of little
relevance to their daily lives. Progressive or feminist authors, on the other hand,
have encouraged young women readers' belief in fantasy to help them visualize
what they want, perhaps as a first step toward going after it. For example, it can
be argued (as I have done elsewhere) that European women's experience with
romantic fiction gradually gained them the right, first, to refuse to cooperate in
arranged marriages, and eventually, to choose husbands for themselves.[3]

Charlotte Lennox's *The Female Quixote* illustrates both these conservative 8
and progressive plot patterns, for it both draws upon and criticizes earlier romances, which themselves often both celebrated and punished female imagination

---

[3] I develop this argument in *The Excellence of Falsehood*. Marina Warner (169, 277–78) and Jack Zipes
(21–23, 28) discuss the seventeenth-century *précieuses'* preoccupation with the issue of forced
marriage.
[4] Warner discusses ambivalence about the old woman or "Mother Goose" figure who narrates
fairy tales throughout the first half of *From the Beast to the Blonde,* and more specifically the power
of the female voice in her discussion of "The Little Mermaid" (394).

and expressiveness.[4] Therefore, like Disney's movies today, which also use material from the romance and fairy-tale tradition, Lennox's novel can be more muddling than enlightening to young people seeking instruction on the conduct of real life. As the title suggests, the premise is that a young girl is at least as likely to have her head turned by reading romances as Cervantes's knight-errant had been over a century before. Appropriately, the romances devoured by this quixote, Arabella, are the largely female-centered French romances of d'Urfé and Scudéry, which focus more on love than on questing, and in which males are present mainly either to carry off or rescue heroines. A reader who takes too literally stories in which women wield such power, albeit of a limited kind, will not adjust well to woman's lot: being ignored, submitting always to others' convenience, like Jane Austen in her letters, perpetually waiting to be "fetched" by a male relative (Austen 9–10). Thus Arabella's reading sets her up to make many ridiculous mistakes, and ultimately to be humbled, or humiliated, when she learns her own real unimportance.

9   The novel shows its author's ambivalence about Arabella's fantasy in several ways. Overtly, she presents it as an adolescent error the heroine must grow out of in order to find happiness. Yet her very frank satire of the world to which Arabella's cure forces her to conform leaves readers wondering, along with the heroine, whether the world of romance might not be preferable. Romances also receive implicit support from the central "real" narrative's resemblance to romance: beautiful heroine, beloved by the perfect man, whom after trials and separations she marries, presumably to live happily ever after. If the novel presents a romantic story under the guise of realism, then perhaps Arabella is not so quixotic after all.

10   *The Female Quixote* thus presents contradictory impressions about the worthiness of the heroine's desires, the degree to which those desires are ultimately fulfilled or frustrated, and the amount of satisfaction with the outcome the tone directs the reader to feel. Critics of our own time naturally enjoy this ambivalence (the novel has had a comeback of sorts in the last decades and is available in paperback), which particularly lends itself to feminist approaches of the *Madwoman in the Attic,* conformist text–radical subtext variety. Yet the fact that this novel might well make a madwoman out of any young female reader looking for a framework for understanding life should also be part of our critical awareness. Critics may find it a useful model for highlighting similar constellations of ideological paradox in other stories about women's imagination, stories which also leave their audiences struggling to integrate contradictory messages.

11   Disney's female quixotes are at least as sorely beset by ambiguity as Arabella. The heroines' fantasies reveal desires for many things, including novelty, excitement, power, sex, and knowledge. Some of these desires are ridiculed, others respected; some are fulfilled, others surrendered. And the paradoxes in the plots are further complicated by words and images that seem at times to be telling stories of their own.

12 The presence of conservative elements in Disney's *Alice in Wonderland* is not surprising, considering that it was released in 1951, when "Hollywood's dark

prince" was still very much alive, fighting unions, castigating the League of Women Voters, and exerting strong control over the studio's output.[5] One would perhaps not expect, though, to find an American movie of the mid-twentieth century so much more stereotypically Victorian than its nineteenth-century British source.

Of course, Lewis Carroll's *Alice's Adventures in Wonderland* and *Through the* 13 *Looking Glass* are not typical of Victorian children's literature. In particular, most girls' stories of this era promoted humility, devotion, punctuality, and tidiness, implying that adventure (as a countess once told Lennox's Arabella) is something a nice girl would be wise to avoid (Lennox 365). The Alice stories, on the other hand, present adventure as positive: Whether wondrous or frightening, it leads the heroine in the direction of personal growth and control over her surroundings. Alice learns how to manage her size, how to talk back to a queen, and, finally, how to wear the crown of adulthood. Carroll celebrates childhood as a brief, fleeting time in which even girls may follow talking rabbits before being overtaken by the "dull reality" (115) of womanhood.

The Disney movie begins with the same positive message about girls' fan- 14 tasies. In her opening conversation, Disney's Alice, like Carroll's, expresses the usual quixotic desires: to escape boredom (with lessons), to satisfy curiosity (about the white rabbit), and above all, to exert power. Things would be different "in my world," she notes, though her sister ridicules her ambition. Books, for one thing, would all have pictures—a remark given to Alice by Carroll in a way that almost invites someone to make an Alice movie. The first few minutes of the movie do seem to deliver what Alice wants by introducing such pictorial wonders as singing flowers and surrealistic insects.

Soon, however, the plot darkens, signaled by small but significant cuts and 15 alterations in the original dialogue. Speaking with the Cheshire Cat, who tells her everyone in the neighborhood is mad, Alice speaks Carroll's line, "But I don't want to go among mad people" (63). The cat responds that everyone in Wonderland is mad, but he does not go on to say that Alice too is mad, so that already Disney's Alice is presented as out of her element, the lone sane and rational creature among lunatics.

After the mad tea party, in a section of plot invented for the movie, Dis- 16 ney's Alice has had enough craziness and wants to go home. Overjoyed to find what looks like a path—symbolic of her now acknowledged need for order and direction—she is reduced to helpless tears when it is erased by a fanciful broom creature. She then passively sits down to wait to be rescued, all the while lecturing herself about the importance of reason and patience, and berating herself for the curiosity that once again has led her into trouble. The movie takes a line from early in the story, "She generally gave herself very good advice (though she very seldom followed it)" (23), puts it in the first person, and makes

---

[5]I refer here to the title of Marc Eliot's Disney biography. Holly Allen and Michael Denning discuss politics at the Disney studio during the 1940s. For a full discussion of Disney's rather complex politics, see Steven Watts.

it the center of a self-lacerating musical lament in which Alice abandons for good her fantasy of excitement and power to dwindle into a tiny, forlorn figure in the center of a large, dark frame. In the end of the movie, the defiance and assertiveness of the line, "You're only a pack of cards," are lost, as she utters it while fleeing for her life from the menacing gang of wonders she has created. She is saved, not by facing them down with dawning maturity and confidence, like the "real" Alice, but by waking up.[6]

17   British reviewers at the time of the movie's release, when the militantly innocuous Enid Blyton held sway over English children's imaginations, objected to Disney's "anarchic" alteration of what they saw as a serene and placid children's tale (Allan 137). But Carroll's story is in fact far more tolerant of anarchy, in the sense of irrationality, than the Disney version. The images used to tell the story further support this rationalist message. Despite Disney artist Claude Coats's comment that the staff had "let [them]selves go with some wild designs" (Allan 138), the visuals in fact are rather staid and restrained, mainly literal, representational renderings of the story done in the highly finished, realistic style for which the studio was famous. The fall down the rabbit hole, for example, which marks Alice's entry into the dream state, might have lent itself to surrealistic treatment like that of *Dumbo*'s "Pink Elephants on Parade" sequence, but instead it is simply a serial listing in images of the objects Carroll mentions that Alice sees on her way down.

18   Surrealism does appear, briefly, in the visual puns formed by the caterpillar's smoke (as he asks "why [k]not"), and in the wild proliferation of crockery at the tea party, the cups and saucers truly "animated" and seeming to breed like, well, rabbits. Yet the story-line ensures that just as this style reaches its climax, Alice is reaching the limits of her fear of imagination. What might have been delightful Daliesque creatures—telephone-ducks, drum-frogs—function rather to frighten the heroine at a point in the plot when she has rejected all this "nonsense" and is anxious to get home to write a book about it.[7] Writing a story, she has decided, is much safer than living one.

19   Thus all elements combine to entrap the unwary viewer: to entice her to fantasize—even to pay money for the privilege—and then to make her feel, like Alice, guilty and ashamed.

20   Contrasting Alice's defeated whining with Ariel's anthem of independence in *The Little Mermaid,* one is apt to feel girls have come a long way. Here, as Laura Sells and Marina Warner observe, the tale on which the movie is based is ostensibly more conservative than Disney's retelling (Sells 176, 177, 181; Warner 397, 403).[8] Hans Christian Andersen's story is a tragic celebration of feminine

---

[6]Donald Britton comments that in the Disney cartoon universe, "children don't become adults; rather, adults kill children" (120).
[7]Dali had been at the studio in 1946, and Robin Allan believes his influence was still apparent in Alice (137).
[8]See also Wasko 134.

self-sacrifice. His mermaid fantasizes about becoming human partly because, like Alice, she is curious about a world she has only glimpsed (here, from below rather than from above). But that world interests her mainly because in it dwells a man who resembles a handsome statue she already adores. Her love is partly sexual, of course, since she needs to be human from the waist down to win the hero. But her ultimate desire is spiritual, for only by marrying a human can a mermaid, who normally lives three hundred years and then turns into sea foam, gain a soul and eternal life.

In pursuit of this desire Andersen's mermaid is willing to spend all she has: 21 her voice, her health, and eventually her life. She buys her new legs, from which blood oozes with every agonizing step, by letting the sea witch cut out her tongue. The permanent loss of her voice means playing dumb in more ways than one, as she can only listen demurely as the prince lectures her about her own world, the sea (166).[9] Failing to bring the prince to a proposal, she could save her own life by killing him, but she chooses instead to die. Her many acts of self-torture earn her a slight reprieve as she is turned into a spirit of the air, instead of sea-foam, and given a chance to gain a soul by performing more self-less deeds. Andersen gives her this reward, not for having a dream, but for de-siring martyrdom. No real authorial punishment is needed for a female quixote so intent on punishing herself.

Naturally in the Disney version the mutilation and blood would have to go. 22 But much more would have to be altered to make this tragic story look and sound so convincingly like a triumph of adolescent self-will and entitlement, as befit the close of the "me decade." (Warner comments on how often, while she can speak, Ariel utters the verb "want" [403].) For example, instead of making the mermaid love the human world because she loves a human, the movie has Ariel love a human mainly because she is already curious enough about his world to have collected a cave full of human souvenirs (in Andersen's story this collection belongs to a mermaid sister). Like Alice before her initiation, Ariel imagines this other world as in a sense more her own than her actual world. She believes it to be a utopia of free movement: She dreams of legs first for "jumping" and "dancing" and "strolling," and only secondarily for marrying.

There is nothing masochistic about this mermaid's fantasy; nor is she will- 23 ing to sacrifice herself to fulfill it, though she is willing to gamble. Her voice, for example, is not permanently lost but poured into a shell, ready to be returned to her if she succeeds, and she has every intention of succeeding. Eighties heroine that she is, she means to have it all: voice, soul, legs, and husband.

For the most part, the movie seems to present this female quixote's fantasy 24 positively and reward her with her desire, as the older generation, in the person of her father, learns to abandon prejudice and let teenagers live their own lives. But there are undercurrents here, so to speak, that work against the theme of imaginative freedom. The odd thing about Ariel's quixotism—what makes the

---

[9]See Warner's discussion on the significance of this silence, and of the blood which in Andersen's tale connects pain with the dawning of female sexuality (387–408).

audience recognize it *as* quixotism—is that the exotic world of her fantasy is, to us, boring and commonplace. Even a two-year-old viewer knows, as the heroine does not, that forks are not used to comb hair, and that human fathers do indeed "reprimand their daughters," just like old King Triton. Thus we laugh at Ariel's naïve reveries, as Andersen's listeners must have laughed at his mermaid's amazed reaction to birds (150). In the end, it seems ludicrous that Ariel should put so much rebellious energy into becoming the girl next door.

25   The visual style of the movie makes Andersen's painful story seem oddly encouraging by comparison. Andersen shifts points of view back and forth between the mermaids, who see our world as exotic, and his own audience, who glamorize the unknown world below. He provides lavish descriptions of the shore as well as the sea in order to reawaken his listeners' sense of wonder at their own city lights, sunsets, forests, and hills (151–52). An outsider's desire to live here thus becomes quite understandable. The movie contains no such balance, for beauty and splendor are mainly found "Under the Sea," the title of the dizzying production number in which Sebastian the crab tries to convince Ariel that there's no place like home. Here creatures and objects are surrealistically combined and transformed into an underwater orchestra. Here in abundance are the magical bubbles that have signaled fun with physics in Disney movies from *Snow White* to *Dumbo* to *Cinderella*. The world of humans, in contrast, though picturesque, is static and finite. When Ariel takes a bath at Eric's palace, while mundane, gossiping laundresses wash her clothes, one is forced to notice that bubbles here just don't *do* anything. Similarly, Grimsby's pipe, which Ariel mistakes for a musical instrument, produces more soot than smoke—nothing approaching the punning puffs from the caterpillar's hookah in *Alice,* or even the smoky ink that billows about in the sea witch's cave. Clearly, Sebastian is right: It is "better down where it's wetter."

26   The images the movie uses to tell the story thus give its trendy feminism a reverse spin. Whatever Ariel might *say,* or sing, what we see her *do* is flee a world of infinite possibility to settle in the land of the banal. Her fantasy is a sort of anti-fantasy. Yes, she gets her legs, she makes her stand, she marches—but only down the aisle, to marry some guy named Eric.

27 Many fairy tales, and many more movies, end with a wedding, and for this reason they often draw censure from critics, such as Janet Wasko (116) and Elizabeth Bell (114, 155), who would like to see our daughters presented with other options. Without question there ought to be more than one girls' story out there, relentlessly repeated with minor variations. I would also argue, however, that just as in life there are marriages and marriages, so in fiction living happily ever after is not always a euphemism for dying. When the marriage seems to grant the heroine true personal fulfillment and possibilities for further growth, the ending may actually seem like the beginning of a new life. Such is the case with *Beauty and the Beast,* a tale endowed by ancient archetypes with a feminine power that resists the attempts of individual authors, such as Madame Leprince de Beaumont in 1757, to tie its heroine down to mediocrity. With *The Little Mermaid* behind us, we might

expect Disney's version to dole out a similarly dull and didactic message, clothed in mock-progressive nineties clichés of gender equality. But in Disney's *Beauty and the Beast*, thanks in part to the screenplay by Linda Woolverton (the first woman writer of a Disney animated feature), imagination flows freely in the words and the images, allowing the tale to work its magic.[10]

One problem with the plot that ends in marriage, of course, is its reduction 28 of the heroine to an object of desire, and therefore a heroine actually named Beauty would not, on the face of it, seem like a good role model. In this tale, however, with its roots penetrating beyond the Cupid and Psyche tale from Apuleius's *The Golden Ass* to very old stories about beast bridegrooms (Warner 275; Zipes 24–25), the heroine is more subject than object because her quest for a desirable mate drives the plot. (Apuleius intensifies the female point of view by having the tale narrated by an old woman [Warner 275].) Of course, the whole question of the story's sexual politics hinges on whether the heroine's desire can be consciously controlled, by herself or by others; whether, as is often said in Christian wedding ceremonies, love is an act of will rather than a feeling; whether, therefore, she can make herself love the one she "ought." Conservative versions of *Beauty and the Beast* do tend to assume such schooling of the will is possible, as Jack Zipes emphasizes (29–40). Nevertheless, an important feature even in such versions is that the beast, though he may be dutifully or even cheerfully endured, cannot become a handsome prince until the heroine actively wants him, truly chooses him for reasons of her own. The young female audience is thus reassured that sex in conjunction with love is pleasant rather than frightening (Bettelheim 306; Warner 312–13); in other words, the beast of one's choice is not a beast at all.

At about the same time Charlotte Lennox was composing *The Female Quixote*, 29 Madame Leprince de Beaumont, with similar concerns about young women's imaginations, was dressing this ancient tale in anti-romance, turning to her own purpose a Scudérian vocabulary of love that, to her readers, would be all too familiar. Beauty feels "esteem" for the Beast because of his "great service" to her, and eventually she comes to feel "tenderness" for him as she wants to care for him and ease his distress (Beaumont 37). Out of this tenderness comes a desire to marry him—including, one supposes, some sexual feeling. The romance code word for active sexual desire—"inclination"—never appears.[11] By telling her young readers that esteem and tenderness are the best basis for marriage, Beaumont warns them not to wait for the handsome, witty lover of their fantasies; in the closing words of the rewarding fairy: "You have preferred virtue before either wit or beauty, and you deserve to find one in whom all these are united" (47). In this way, the author joins the tradition of conservative writers who urge girls to face reality and, to the very limited extent they will be permitted to choose, to choose wisely.[12] Still, while schooling the reader in what she ought

[10]See Bell 114; Murphy 133–34; Warner 313.
[11]See the Map of Tender in Scudéry's *Clelia* (1:42).
[12]See Warner 292–94.

to desire, Beaumont cannot avoid conveying the importance of the heroine's will, for until Beauty desires the Beast, a beast he will remain.

30   The Disney movie reaches past Beaumont to draw upon older strains of the story. For example, here, as in some older versions, including that of Beaumont's immediate predecessor, Madame de Villeneuve (Warner 290–91), it is the Beast rather than Beauty who is supposed to learn self-control. The heroine is therefore permitted—even encouraged—to fantasize to her heart's content. Where Beaumont only noted that Beauty liked to read, Disney enlarges on Belle's taste in books, which turns out to be just like Arabella's: fairy tales and romances about swordfights, magic, a prince in disguise, and above all, a "she" at the center of the action. Nor is she content just to read about "adventure in the great wide somewhere." Given the chance to tour the Beast's library—ordinarily for Belle the greatest of temptations—she chooses instead to explore the forbidden west wing of his castle, as if somehow aware that she will find there the escape from "provincial life" she has been longing and singing for. For all her quixotism, however, Belle, unlike Arabella, is seen as "rather odd" only by her neighbors, not by her audience.

31   Certainly, as several commentators observe, the movie has its share of politically correct modern touches to underscore the heroine's self-determination (Warner 316–17; Zipes 46). Interestingly, however, each apparent innovation in fact draws on the French romance tradition that Belle and Arabella revere. Most notably, the movie makes contemporary-sounding statements about gender stereotypes by introducing a new character as foil to the Beast, the hypermasculine Gaston, who boasts in a Sigmund Romberg-ish aria, "I'm especially good at expectorating," "I use antlers in all of my decorating," and "every last inch of me's covered with hair." He is the real beast, of course, an animal who sneers at the Beast for being so openly in touch with his feminine side, "the Male Chauvinist Pig [. . .] that would turn the women of any primetime talkshow audience into beasts themselves" (Jeffords 170). But Gaston is not really new. He dates back, beyond the Cocteau movie often cited as his source, to the French romance villain who loves the heroine selfishly, determined to possess her by force: by winning her in a duel, carrying her off, or scheming to get her parents to give her to him. Gaston arranges to have Belle's eccentric father locked in a madhouse unless she agrees to marry him. Then he nearly kills the Beast under the illusion that the winner gets Belle as prize. The Beast, in contrast, is the romance hero who fights the villain to win the heroine's freedom, not her hand, which he will accept only as her gift. In fact, he would rather die than oppress her. By choosing the Beast over Gaston, Belle helps this ancient story confirm the value of a woman's equal right to a will of her own.

32   Gaston also helps this movie make another observation mistakenly thought of as modern: that men and women aren't nearly as different as some men would like them to be. This idea is found in women's romantic writing from the seventeenth century on,[13] and it reverberates in Belle's opening song as she

[13]See for example the pastoral lyrics of Aphra Behn.

wishes for someone who understands her and shares her interests. Naturally she chooses to marry the gentleman who gives her the key to his extensive library, not the "positively primeval" clod who throws her book in the mud with a warning about what happens to society when women are taught to read. And in the end, when the spell is broken and the Beast resumes his original shape, he markedly resembles Belle, unruly bangs and all. By marrying a man who can help her get what she wants, and who wants the same things, symbolically she is marrying an aspect of herself.[14]

The Beast's oddly familiar new face is not the only image in the movie that 33 makes one feel the heroine's fantasy is a worthy one. Much creativity was lavished on the look of the castle that provides the atmosphere of old romance. Although for most of the movie it resembles a Gothic ruin, and Belle comes here at first as a prisoner, it is really a house of magic in which every object is alive, or "animated"—most famously the dinnerware that dances and sings "Be Our Guest." And the enchantment does not quite end with the breaking of the spell, but is rather replaced with a different kind of magic as the castle comes into its original baroque splendor with a seeming infinity of detail, something new around every corner, and always a new corner, for the eye to explore. As Belle waltzes with her Prince around that gorgeous marble hall, the title tune welling up around them, one may see as well as feel that she's getting not just a husband, but more books than she can read in a lifetime, and a home as big and beautiful as her imagination.

Neither age, divorce, nor parenthood has yet made me cynical enough to see 34 the ending of this movie without a sob of satisfaction. But then Disney did begin training me to react in just that way from a very early age (the first movie I ever saw, at the age of five, was *Sleeping Beauty*). Critics have been warning the public for decades about the Disney program to bring about the complete "invasion and control of children's imaginations" (Schickel 18), as well as the silencing of fairy tales' originally female voice (Warner 416–17); no doubt I am a cipher in the company's success. How much more complete the Disney conquest will become for our children and grandchildren, with the constant replay made possible by video and DVD, is definitely cause for concern.

The market forces that drive Disney today are dangerous, to be sure, as is 35 the ideology of the market-place the movies promote, as Giroux and others warn. Fortunately, however, because the overriding goal is self-promotion—because Disney will absorb and use whatever works, or whatever sells the product—the movies lack the philosophical consistency of propaganda.[15] Thus

---

[14]See Clarissa Pinkola Estes for an interpretation of the Beast as an aspect of the heroine's own personality (272–73). Warner also discusses how the beast in modern versions of the tale, including Disney's, functions to help the heroine get in touch with her own inner beast, or sexuality (307–13).
[15]Giroux notes inconsistent values among elements in the films (5, 91). Wasko emphasizes consistent elements that make "classic Disney" a recognizable "brand" (3, 152), but does not explore tensions among the elements she lists as consistent, such as "work ethic" vs. "escape fantasy" (114).

films like *Beauty and the Beast,* which pays more than lip-service to the liberating potential of fantasy, can sometimes appear.

36   Nevertheless, the fact that many Disney movies implant seeds of guilt and fear to spring up along with children's developing imaginations is a serious problem. The mixed messages noticeable in *Alice* are present in earlier movies such as *Dumbo* and "The Sorcerer's Apprentice" in *Fantasia.* They continue in more recent examples such as *Hercules* and *The Hunchback of Notre Dame,* in which only evil and terrifying characters wield the transformative power that is, in essence, the animator's art; thus these movies almost identify themselves as products of black magic.[16] Some recent films seem almost to reject the notion of animation altogether, striking the eye most forcibly with stills such as the battlefield in *Mulan,* or the cathedral of Notre Dame—breathtaking, to be sure, but unlike the Beast's castle, completely static. Clearly the reluctance to embrace imagination with both arms is still present among the many and shifting ideas that make up the Disney ethos.

37   The inconsistencies found in these movies do not lighten either the parent's burden of guiding the young in their adventures with the media, or the critic's task of understanding the various manifestations of culture. On the contrary, they oblige us to do more than count the number of profane words or violent acts or exposed body parts; and also to do more than catalogue plots, count the numbers of males and females, and quantify relative levels of aggression. Instead, we must watch carefully the interplay of elements within the films and notice how many stories are going on at one time. Watching the faces of our children as they watch, we will often find that imagination, in these movies, is like Alice's garden—just beyond a little locked door, the key to which is tantalizingly, frustratingly out of reach.

[16]A notable exception is *The Emperor's New Groove,* in which magic transformative potions intended as evil by the villain turn positive and bring about both the narrative and visual climax of the movie.

Works Cited*

Alice in Wonderland. Dir. Clyde Geronimi, Hamilton Luske, and Wilfred Jackson. Walt Disney Company, 1951.

Allan, Robin. "Alice in Disneyland." *Sight and Sound* 54 (Spring 1985): 136–38.

Allen, Holly, and Michael Denning. "The Cartoonists' Front." *South Atlantic Quarterly* 92.1 (1993): 89–117.

Andersen, Hans Christian. "The Little Mermaid." *Hans Christian Andersen: His Classic Fairy Tales.* Trans. Erik Haugaard. Garden City, NY: Doubleday, 1978. 149–70.

Apuleius. *Transformations of Lucius Otherwise Known as the Golden Ass.* Trans. Robert Graves. New York: Noonday, 1998.

Austen, Jane. *Selected Letters.* Oxford: Oxford UP, 1985.

*As noted in the Networking question that follows, this Works Cited section does not follow the latest MLA style. The spacing has also been condensed.

Beaumont, Madame Leprince de. *Beauty and the Beast.* Trans. P. H. Muir. New York: Knopf, 1968.

Beauty and the Beast. Dir. Gary Trousdale and Kirk Wise. Walt Disney Company, 1991.

Behn, Aphra. *The Works of Aphra Behn: Poetry.* Ed. Janet Todd. Columbus: Ohio UP, 1992.

Bell, Elizabeth. "Somatexts at the Disney Shop." Bell, Haas, and Sells 107–24.

Bell, Elizabeth, Lynda Haas, and Laura Sells, eds. *From Mouse to Mermaid: The Politics of Film, Gender, and Culture.* Bloomington: Indiana UP, 1995.

Bettelheim, Bruno. *The Uses of Enchantment.* New York: Vintage, 1977.

Britton, Donald. "The Dark Side of Disneyland." *Mythomania: Fantasies, Fables, and Sheer Lies in Contemporary American Popular Art.* By Bernard Welt. Los Angeles: Art Issues, 1996. 113–26.

Carroll, Lewis. *Alice's Adventures in Wonderland and Through the Looking-Glass.* New York: New American Library, 1960.

Cinderella. Dir. Hamilton Luske and Wilfred Jackson. Walt Disney Company, 1950.

Dumbo. Dir. Ben Sharpsteen. Walt Disney Company, 1941.

Eliot, Marc. *Walt Disney: Hollywood's Dark Prince.* New York: Birch Lane, 1993.

The Emperor's New Groove. Dir. Mark Dindal. Walt Disney Company, 2000.

Estes, Clarissa Pinkola. *Women Who Run with the Wolves.* New York: Ballantine, 1992.

Fantasia. Dir. Ford Beebe and Bill Roberts. Walt Disney Company, 1942.

Gilbert, Sandra, and Susan Gubar. *The Madwoman in the Attic.* New Haven: Yale UP, 1979.

Giroux, Henry. *The Mouse That Roared: Disney and the End of Innocence.* Lanham, MD: Rowman, 1999.

Hansen, Miriam. "Of Mice and Ducks: Benjamin and Adorno on Disney." *South Atlantic Quarterly* 92.1 (1993): 27–61.

Hedges, Inez. *Languages of Revolt: Dada and Surrealist Literature and Film.* Durham: Duke UP, 1983.

Hercules. Dir. Ron Clements and John Musker. Walt Disney Company, 1997.

The Hunchback of Notre Dame. Dir. Gary Trousdale and Kirk Wise. Walt Disney Company, 1996.

Hunter, J. Paul. "'The Young, the Ignorant, and the Idle': Some Notes on Readers and the Beginnings of the English Novel." *Anticipations of the Enlightenment in England, France, and Germany.* Ed. Alan Charles Kors and Paul J. Korshin. Philadelphia: U of Pennsylvania P, 1987. 259–82.

Jeffords, Susan. "The Curse of Masculinity." Bell, Haas, and Sells 161–72.

Johnson, Samuel. *The Rambler.* Ed. W. J. Bate and Albrecht B. Strauss. New Haven: Yale UP, 1969.

Lennox, Charlotte. *The Female Quixote,* 1759. Boston: Pandora, 1986.

Lewis, Jon. "Disney after Disney." *Disney Discourse: Producing the Magic Kingdom.* Ed. Eric Smoodin. New York: Routledge, 1994.

Lilo and Stitch. Dir. Dean DeBlois and Chris Sanders (III). Walt Disney Company, 2002.

The Lion King. Dir. Rob Minkoff and Roger Allers. Walt Disney Company, 1994.

The Little Mermaid. Dir. John Musker and Ron Clements. Walt Disney Company, 1989.

Mulan. Dir. Tony Bancroft and Barry Cook. Walt Disney Company, 1998.

Murphy, Patrick D. "'The Whole Wide World Was Scrubbed Clean': The Androcentric Animation of Denatured Disney." Bell, Haas, and Sells 125–36.

Pocahontas. Dir. Mike Gabriel and Eric Goldberg. Walt Disney Company, 1995.

Ross, Deborah. *The Excellence of Falsehood.* Lexington: UP of Kentucky, 1991.

Schickel, Richard. *The Disney Version.* New York: Simon, 1968.

Scudéry, Madeleine de. *Clelia.* Trans. John Davies. London: Herringman, 1678.

Sells, Laura. "'Where Do the Mermaids Stand?' Voice and Body in *The Little Mermaid.*" Bell, Haas, and Sells 175–92.

The Sleeping Beauty. Dir. Clyde Geronimi. Walt Disney Company, 1959.

Snow White and the Seven Dwarfs. Dir. David Hand. Walt Disney Company, 1938.

Warner, Marina. *From the Beast to the Blonde: On Fairy Tales and Their Tellers.* New York: Noonday, 1994.

Wasko, Janet. *Understanding Disney.* Cambridge, UK: Polity, 2001.

Watts, Steven. "Walt Disney: Art and Politics in the American Century." *Journal of American History* 82.1 (June 1995): 84–110.

Zipes, Jack. *Fairy Tale as Myth/Myth as Fairy Tale.* Lexington: UP of Kentucky, 1994.

COMPREHENSION

1. How does Ross define the ideology inherent in Disney's films for girls?
2. Summarize the content of the three films that Ross discusses. What similarities and differences does Ross see among them?
3. According to the writer, what is a "female Quixote"? Where does she treat this concept directly and indirectly?

RHETORIC

1. This essay appeared in a specialized scholarly journal. What "scholarly" elements appear in the paper? How does Ross adjust her style to this specialized audience? What strategies does she use to make the essay accessible to a wider audience?
2. Where does Ross state her claim most clearly? Analyze the varieties of evidence that she uses to support her claim and the minor propositions.
3. How does the writer organize her essay? What are the main divisions, and how do they cohere?
4. Why does Ross cite other scholars and writers? How does this strategy affect the power of her argument?
5. Ross elaborates a definition of the Disney "program" or ideology. What rhetorical strategies does she use to create this extended definition?
6. How effective do you find the concluding paragraph? Justify your response.

WRITING

1. Select one Disney movie and write an analysis of its "program"—its ethical message or ideology.
2. In an expository essay, explain why children's stories or fairy tales have such a hold on young people's imaginations.
3. **Writing an Argument:** Write a persuasive essay on the benefits of children's literature and film—even the films that Walt Disney produced. Present at least three extended examples to support your claim.

NETWORKING
Applying 21st-Century Literacies

Updating Citations to Reflect Current MLA Style: Since this essay was published, the MLA has made some changes to their guidelines for documenting sources; one change includes noting the medium of each source. Refer to Chapter 4, pp. 196–206 to help update Ross's Works Cited page; beyond this book's coverage, consult the MLA's Web site (see the Chapter 10 Networking page at *www.mhhe.com/mhreader11e*), or the seventh edition of the *MLA Handbook*, published in 2009.

Synthesis: Connections for Critical Thinking

1. Examine the role of the media in society and the responsibilities or duties to humanity of individuals associated with the media. Use at least three essays from this chapter to illustrate or support your thesis.
2. Define *popular culture,* using the essays of Barry, Gates, Ross, and Steinem as reference points, along with any additional essays that you consider relevant.
3. Use the essays of Warshow, Goodlad, Ross, and Gitlin to explore the connections of media representations to American cultural experience. What strategies do these writers use? Are their goals similar?
4. Use the essays of Gates and Barry to explore the importance of both the causes and effects of the media promoting particular lifestyles to the public.
5. Gates refers to the African American "style" of communicating through music, and Barry presents beer commercials as communicating the traditional "patriotic symbols" of America. Do these authors have similar or differing points of view regarding the issues they address? Refer specifically to selections in each essay to support your view.
6. After reading the essays of Warshow, Gates, and King, research the issue of the difference between popular entertainment and art. On the basis of your research, discuss whether there are legitimate criteria that distinguish the two forms. Apply these criteria to gangster films, rap music, and horror films.

NETWORKING
Applying 21st-Century Literacies

1. Do an online search using the keywords *television* and *teenagers.* Select three or four sites, and write an expository paper describing the various ways the authors interpret any of the major themes.
2. Select several images of real "gangsters" or other "bad" men from magazines, or print out images of them from the Internet. Compare and contrast them with advertisements depicting gangsters from contemporary crime movies such as *Pulp Fiction.* What are the similarities and differences in the subjects' dress, demeanor, facial expression, and so on? What can you conclude from your comparisons?

CH 10   **www.mhhe.com/mhreader11e**

- *Image Gallery:* Chapter images in color
- *Media and Popular Culture:* Information on the authors in this chapter
- *Ch 10 Networking*

chapter *11*

Literature and the Arts
Why Do They Matter?

Imagine a world without fiction, poetry, or drama, without music, art, or other fine arts. We are so accustomed to taking the arts in their totality for granted that it is hard for us to conceive of contemporary culture without them. Our fondness for stories or paintings or any other creative form might help us understand our culture or might even move us to action. Yet the value of various artistic forms doesn't derive exclusively from their ability to tell us something about life. The arts can also take us into an imaginative realm offering perhaps more intense experiences than anything we encounter in the "real" world.

Think of literature and the arts as an exercise in imaginative freedom. You are free to select the books you read, the music that appeals to you, the exhibitions and concerts you attend, and the entertainment software with which you interact. Some of your decisions might be serious and consequential to your education. Other decisions, perhaps to watch a few soap operas on a rainy afternoon or to buy the latest potboiler, are less important. The way you view the arts—whether as a way to learn something about the temper of civilization or as a temporary escape from conventional reality—is entirely a matter of taste. Regardless of your purpose or intent, you approach literature and the arts initially for the sheer exhilaration and pleasure they provide. Art, as Plato observed, is a dream for awakened minds.

The arts awaken you to the power and intensity of the creative spirit. At the same time, you make judgments and evaluations of the nature of your creative encounter. When you assert that you like this painting or dislike that poem, you are assessing the work and the value of the artistic experience. Clearly, you develop taste and become more equipped to discern the more subtle elements of art the more you are exposed to it. Perhaps you prefer to keep your experience of literature and the other arts a pleasurable pastime or an escape from reality. Or you may wish to participate in them as a creative writer, musician, painter, or photographer. Ultimately, you may come to view literature and the arts as a transformational experience, a voyage of discovery in which you encounter diverse peoples and cultures, learn to see the world in creative terms, and begin to perceive your own creative potential in a new light.

PREVIEWING THE CHAPTER

As you read the essays in this chapter and respond to them in discussion and writing, consider the following questions:

- According to the author, what is the value of the art or literary form under discussion?
- What function does literature or art serve?
- Is the writer's perspective subjective or objective, and why?
- How does the author define his or her subject—whether it is poetry, fiction, art, or photography?
- Is the writer's experience of literature or art similar to or different from your own?
- In what ways do gender and race influence the writer's perspective on the subject?
- What is the main idea that the author wants to present about literature or the arts? Do you agree or disagree with this key concept?
- What have you learned about the importance of literature and the arts from reading these essays?

Classic and Contemporary Images

HOW DO WE EVALUATE A WORK OF ART?

Using a Critical Perspective   Although "greatness" in art and literature might be in the mind of the beholder, it could be argued that you need certain standards of excellence or judgment to determine the quality of any work. The artist's or writer's control of the medium, the projection of a unique vision, the evidence of a superlative style—all enter into the evaluation process. As you consider these sculptures by Auguste Rodin and Jeff Koons, try to evaluate their relative worth. Which work reflects greater artistic control? What makes the sculpture appealing, and why? Which work strikes you as "new" or original, or modern? Explain your response and criteria for evaluation.

Auguste Rodin (1840–1917), a French sculptor famous for his bronze and marble figures, is thought by some critics to be one of the greatest portraitists in the history of sculpture. Yet he was also criticized in his time for the excessive realism and sensuousness of his figures. *Walking Man* hints at some of the objections contemporary critics lodged against Rodin's work.

Jeff Koons (b. 1955) is an American artist who, like Rodin, has had his admirers and detractors. Koons studied at the Art Institute of Chicago and elsewhere before becoming a commodities trader in New York City, which helped fund the materials for his art. *Rabbit* reflects Koons's fondness for popular culture and the way in which he takes consumer goods and repositions them as art objects.

Classic and Contemporary Essays
WHAT IS THE VALUE OF LITERATURE?

Although Eudora Welty was born at the beginning of the 20th century in a small Mississippi town and Sherman Alexie half a century later on a tribal reservation in the state of Washington, half a continent away, these writers share a reverence for the importance of literature in their childhood. Of course, there are understandable differences in the types of literature that formed their young minds. Welty, you will discover, grew up in a loving, middle-class household where virtually every room contained books—a treasury of English and European novels, classic fairy tales, and famous works of literature in the Western tradition. Alexie, on the other hand, from a family that was "middle-class by reservation standards" but in actuality poor, had a father who was addicted to alcohol but also to pulp fiction—westerns, detective stories, spy thrillers, comic books featuring action heroes. And despite their disparate backgrounds, lives, and reading tastes, Welty and Alexie grew up to be writers. They might represent different regional, ethnic, and cultural backgrounds, and they speak as a woman and man of different forms of knowledge and experience, but both attest to the value of literature. As they recount their childhood, Welty and Alexie struggle to establish an identity that will last a lifetime. They succeed in convincing us that whether one child reads Dickens and the other Superman comic books, their ideas and insights into the world derive from the active reading of texts.

One Writer's Beginnings
Eudora Welty

Eudora Welty (1909–2001), a celebrated American writer, was born and died in Jackson, Mississippi. Raised in a close-knit bookish family, Welty attended the Mississippi State College for Women for two years and then the University of Wisconsin (BA, 1929). In the 1930s she returned to Mississippi and worked for the Works Progress Administration as a reporter and photographer, traveling the state and recording the lives of its citizens during the Depression years. She also began a career as a short-story writer and novelist. Welty's superb short fiction collections include A Curtain of Green *(1941),* The Wide Net *(1943), and* Collected Stories *(1980), which received an American Book Award. She received the Pulitzer Prize for her novel* The Optimist's Daughter *(1972). The recipient of the President's Medal of Freedom and numerous other major awards, Welty spent virtually her entire life writing about the South but in ways that transcend her region, radiating outward to embrace universal truths.*

In the selection that follows, one of three lectures delivered at Harvard University in 1983 and published in her memoir One Writer's Beginnings *(1984), Welty speaks of the value of literature and the arts in her life.*

I learned from the age of two or three that any room in our house, at any time of 1
day, was there to read in, or to be read to. My mother read to me. She'd read to me in the big bedroom in the mornings, when we were in her rocker together, which ticked in rhythm as we rocked, as though we had a cricket accompanying the story. She'd read to me in the diningroom on winter afternoons in front of the coal fire, with our cuckoo clock ending the story with "Cuckoo," and at night when I'd got in my own bed. I must have given her no peace. Sometimes she read to me in the kitchen while she sat churning, and the churning sobbed along with *any* story. It was my ambition to have her read to me while *I* churned; once she granted my wish, but she read off my story before I brought her butter. She was an expressive reader. When she was reading "Puss in Boots," for instance, it was impossible not to know that she distrusted *all* cats.

It had been startling and disappointing to me to find out that story books 2
had been written by *people,* that books were not natural wonders, coming up of themselves like grass. Yet regardless of where they came from, I cannot remember a time when I was not in love with them—with the books themselves, cover and binding and the paper they were printed on, with their smell and their weight and with their possession in my arms, captured and carried off to myself. Still illiterate, I was ready for them, committed to all the reading I could give them.

Neither of my parents had come from homes that could afford to buy many 3
books, but though it must have been something of a strain on his salary, as the youngest officer in a young insurance company, my father was all the while carefully selecting and ordering away for what he and Mother thought we children should grow up with. They bought first for the future.

Besides the bookcase in the livingroom, which was always called "the li- 4
brary," there were the encyclopedia tables and dictionary stand under windows in our diningroom. Here to help us grow up arguing around the diningroom table were the Unabridged Webster, the Columbia Encyclopedia, Compton's Pictured Encyclopedia, the Lincoln Library of Information, and later the Book of Knowledge. And the year we moved into our new house, there was room to celebrate it with the new 1925 edition of the Britannica, which my father, his face always deliberately turned toward the future, was of course disposed to think better than any previous edition.

In "the library," inside the mission-style bookcase with its three diamond- 5
latticed glass doors, with my father's Morris chair and the glass-shaded lamp on its table beside it, were books I could soon begin on—and I did, reading them all alike and as they came, straight down their rows, top shelf to bottom. There was the set of Stoddard's Lectures, in all its late nineteenth-century vocabulary and vignettes of peasant life and quaint beliefs and customs, with matching halftone illustrations: Vesuvius erupting, Venice by moonlight, gypsies

glimpsed by their campfires. I didn't know then the clue they were to my father's longing to see the rest of the world. I read straight through his other love-from-afar: the Victrola Book of the Opera, with opera after opera in synopsis, with portraits in costume of Melba, Caruso, Galli-Curci, and Geraldine Farrar, some of whose voices we could listen to on our Red Seal records.

6   My mother read secondarily for information; she sank as a hedonist into novels. She read Dickens in the spirit in which she would have eloped with him. The novels of her girlhood that had stayed on in her imagination, besides those of Dickens and Scott and Robert Louis Stevenson, were *Jane Eyre, Trilby, The Woman in White, Green Mansions, King Solomon's Mines.* Marie Corelli's name would crop up but I understood she had gone out of favor with my mother, who had only kept *Ardath* out of loyalty. In time she absorbed herself in Galsworthy, Edith Wharton, above all in Thomas Mann of the *Joseph* volumes.

7   *St. Elmo* was not in our house; I saw it often in other houses. This wildly popular Southern novel is where all the Edna Earles in our population started coming from. They're all named for the heroine, who succeeded in bringing a dissolute, sinning roué and atheist of a lover (St. Elmo) to his knees. My mother was able to forgo it. But she remembered the classic advice given to rose growers on how to water their bushes long enough: "Take a chair and *St. Elmo.*"

8   To both my parents I owe my early acquaintance with a beloved Mark Twain. There was a full set of Mark Twain and a short set of Ring Lardner in our bookcase, and those were the volumes that in time united us all, parents and children.

9   Reading everything that stood before me was how I came upon a worn old book without a back that had belonged to my father as a child. It was called *Sanford and Merton.* Is there anyone left who recognizes it, I wonder? It is the famous moral tale written by Thomas Day in the 1780s, but of him no mention is made on the title page of *this* book; here it is *Sanford and Merton in Words of One Syllable* by Mary Godolphin. Here are the rich boy and the poor boy and Mr. Barlow, their teacher and interlocutor, in long discourses alternating with dramatic scenes—danger and rescue allotted to the rich and the poor respectively. It may have only words of one syllable, but one of them is "quoth." It ends with not one but two morals, both engraved on rings: "Do what you ought, come what may," and "If we would be great, we must first learn to be good."

10   This book was lacking its front cover, the back held on by strips of pasted paper, now turned golden, in several layers, and the pages stained, flecked, and tattered around the edges; its garish illustrations had come unattached but were preserved, laid in. I had the feeling even in my heedless childhood that this was the only book my father as a little boy had of his own. He had held onto it, and might have gone to sleep on its coverless face: He had lost his mother when he was seven. My father had never made any mention to his own children of the book, but he had brought it along with him from Ohio to our house and shelved it in our bookcase.

My mother had brought from West Virginia that set of Dickens; those books 11
looked sad, too—they had been through fire and water before I was born, she
told me, and there they were, lined up—as I later realized, waiting for *me.*

I was presented, from as early as I can remember, with books of my own, 12
which appeared on my birthday and Christmas morning. Indeed, my parents
could not give me books enough. They must have sacrificed to give me on my
sixth or seventh birthday—it was after I became a reader for myself—the ten-
volume set of Our Wonder World. These were beautifully made, heavy books I
would lie down with on the floor in front of the diningroom hearth, and more
often than the rest volume 5, *Every Child's Story Book,* was under my eyes. There
were the fairy tales—Grimm, Andersen, the English, the French, "Ali Baba and
the Forty Thieves"; and there was Aesop and Reynard the Fox; there were the
myths and legends, Robin Hood, King Arthur, and St. George and the Dragon,
even the history of Joan of Arc; a whack of *Pilgrim's Progress* and a long piece of
Gulliver. They all carried their classic illustrations. I located myself in these
pages and could go straight to the stories and pictures I loved; very often "The
Yellow Dwarf" was first choice, with Walter Crane's Yellow Dwarf in full color
making his terrifying appearance flanked by turkeys. Now that volume is as
worn and backless and hanging apart as my father's poor *Sanford and Merton.*
The precious page with Edward Lear's "Jumblies" on it has been in danger of
slipping out for all these years. One measure of my love for Our Wonder World
was that for a long time I wondered if I would go through fire and water for it
as my mother had done for Charles Dickens; and the only comfort was to think
I could ask my mother to do it for me.

I believe I'm the only child I know of who grew up with this treasure in the 13
house. I used to ask others, "Did you have Our Wonder World?" I'd have to tell
them The Book of Knowledge could not hold a candle to it.

I live in gratitude to my parents for initiating me—and as early as I begged 14
for it, without keeping me waiting—into knowledge of the word, into reading
and spelling, by way of the alphabet. They taught it to me at home in time for me
to begin to read before starting to school. I believe the alphabet is no longer considered an essential piece of equipment for traveling through life. In my day it
was the keystone to knowledge. You learned the alphabet as you learned to count
to ten, as you learned "Now I lay me" and the Lord's Prayer and your father's
and mother's name and address and telephone number, all in case you were lost.

My love for the alphabet, which endures, grew out of reciting it but, before 15
that, out of seeing the letters on the page. In my own story books, before I could
read them for myself, I fell in love with various winding, enchanting-looking
initials drawn by Walter Crane at the heads of fairy tales. In "Once upon a
time," an "O" had a rabbit running it as a treadmill, his feet upon flowers.
When the day came, years later, for me to see the Book of Kells, all the wizardry
of letter, initial, and word swept over me a thousand times over, and the illumi-
nation, the gold, seemed a part of the word's beauty and holiness that had been
there from the start.

. . .

16   Learning stamps you with its moments. Childhood's learning is made up of
       moments. It isn't steady. It's a pulse.

17   In a children's art class, we sat in a ring on kindergarten chairs and drew
       three daffodils that had just been picked out of the yard; and while I was draw-
       ing, my sharpened pencil and the cup of the yellow daffodil gave off whiffs just
       alike. That the pencil doing the drawing should give off the same smell as the
       flower it drew seemed a part of the art lesson—as shouldn't it be? Children, like
       animals, use all their senses to discover the world. Then artists come along and
       discover it the same way, all over again. Here and there, it's the same world. Or
       now and then we'll hear from an artist who's never lost it.

18   In my sensory education I include my physical awareness of the *word*. Of a
       certain word, that is; the connection it has with what it stands for. At around age
       six, perhaps, I was standing by myself in our front yard waiting for supper, just
       at that hour in a late summer day when the sun is already below the horizon and
       the risen full moon in the visible sky stops being chalky and begins to take on
       light. There comes the moment, and I saw it then, when the moon goes from flat
       to round. For the first time it met my eyes as a globe. The word "moon" came
       into my mouth as though fed to me out of a silver spoon. Held in my mouth the
       moon became a word. It had the roundness of a Concord grape Grandpa took off
       his vine and gave me to suck out of its skin and swallow whole, in Ohio.

19   This love did not prevent me from living for years in foolish error about the
       moon. The new moon just appearing in the west was the rising moon to me.
       The new should be rising. And in early childhood the sun and moon, those op-
       posite reigning powers, I just as easily assumed rose in east and west respec-
       tively in their opposite sides of the sky, and like partners in a reel they advanced,
       sun from the east, moon from the west, crossed over (when I wasn't looking)
       and went down on the other side. My father couldn't have known I believed
       that when, bending behind me and guiding my shoulder, he positioned me at
       our telescope in the front yard and, with careful adjustment of the focus,
       brought the moon close to me.

20   The night sky over my childhood Jackson was velvety black. I could see the
       full constellations in it and call their names; when I could read, I knew their myths.
       Though I was always waked for eclipses, and indeed carried to the window as an
       infant in arms and shown Halley's Comet in my sleep, and though I'd been taught
       at our diningroom table about the solar system and knew the earth revolved
       around the sun, and our moon around us, I never found out the moon didn't come
       up in the west until I was a writer and Herschel Brickell, the literary critic, told me
       after I misplaced it in a story. He said valuable words to me about my new profes-
       sion: "Always be sure you get your moon in the right part of the sky."

                                                    . . .

21   My mother always sang to her children. Her voice came out just a little bit in
       the minor key. "Wee Willie Winkie's" song was wonderfully sad when she sang
       the lullabies.

22   "Oh, but now there's a record. She could have her own record to listen to,"
       my father would have said. For there came a Victrola record of "Bobby Shafftoe"

and "Rock-a-Bye Baby," all of Mother's lullabies, which could be played to take her place. Soon I was able to play her my own lullabies all day long.

Our Victrola stood in the diningroom. I was allowed to climb onto the seat of 23 a diningroom chair to wind it, start the record turning, and set the needle playing. In a second I'd jumped to the floor, to spin or march around the table as the music called for—now there were all the other records I could play too. I skinned back onto the chair just in time to lift the needle at the end, stop the record and turn it over, then change the needle. That brass receptacle with a hole in the lid gave off a metallic smell like human sweat, from all the hot needles that were fed it. Winding up, dancing, being cocked to start and stop the record, was of course all in one the act of *listening*—to "Overture to *Daughter of the Regiment*," "Selections from *The Fortune Teller*," "Kiss Me Again," "Gypsy Dance from *Carmen*," "Stars and Stripes Forever," "When the Midnight Choo-Choo Leaves for Alabam," or whatever came next. Movement must be at the very heart of listening.

Ever since I was first read to, then started reading to myself, there has never 24 been a line read that I didn't *hear*. As my eyes followed the sentence, a voice was saying it silently to me. It isn't my mother's voice, or the voice of any person I can identify, certainly not my own. It is human, but inward, and it is inwardly that I listen to it. It is to me the voice of the story or the poem itself. The cadence, whatever it is that asks you to believe, the feeling that resides in the printed word, reaches me through the reader-voice. I have supposed, but never found out, that this is the case with all readers—to read as listeners—and with all writers, to write as listeners. It may be part of the desire to write. The sound of what falls on the page begins the process of testing it for truth, for me. Whether I am right to trust so far I don't know. By now I don't know whether I could do either one, reading or writing, without the other.

My own words, when I am at work on a story, I hear too as they go, in the same 25 voice that I hear when I read in books. When I write and the sound of it comes back to my ears, then I act to make my changes. I have always trusted this voice.

COMPREHENSION

1. What is the significance of the essay's title? Does Welty write about one continuous "beginning" or a series of beginnings? Explain.
2. What does Welty mean when she says that her mother was a "hedonist" (paragraph 6)? Does Welty also become a hedonist? Why or why not?
3. Explain the nature of Welty's "sensory" education.

RHETORIC

1. Welty alludes to dozens of works of literature. What does she assume about her audience's knowledge of these works? Can you appreciate the essay even if you are not familiar with most of this literature? Justify your response.
2. What is Welty's thesis, and how does she develop it?

3. What determines the order in which Welty organizes her essay, which she divides into three parts?
4. Welty includes several descriptive passages in this essay. Where are these passages, and what do they contribute to the overall meaning of the selection?
5. How do the last two paragraphs of the essay echo the first two paragraphs?

WRITING

1. Write a description of a scene or series of events from your childhood in which you were reading (or being read to), engaged in an art project, or listening to music. In your essay, explain the impact of this memory or activity on your current life.
2. Write an essay explaining the importance of providing children with sensory stimuli involving reading, artwork, and music.
3. **Writing an Argument:** Argue for or against the proposition that children today read less than those of previous generations—and suffer the consequences.

NETWORKING
Applying 21st-Century Literacies

Can e-Readers Save Reading? It's looking likely that children will soon be reading most texts—from textbooks to novels to comics—electronically. How might an electronic format make reading *more* engaging for today's kids? How might this new form enhance, rather than detract from, reading as a sensory experience?

Superman and Me

Sherman Alexie

Sherman Alexie (b. 1966) grew up and still lives on the Spokane Indian Reservation in Wellpinit, Washington. A Spokane/Coeur d'Alene tribal member, Alexie contended with a life-threatening illness when he was young, but managed to attend Gonzaga University before transferring to Washington State University (BA, 1991). Alexie writes and creates in many modes, and is also a performer. As many of the titles of his works suggest, the Native American experience informs his short stories, novels, poetry, songs, and films. Alexie's fiction includes Reservation Blues *(1995),* Ten Little Indians: Stories *(2003), and* Flight, A Novel *(2007); his poetry has been collected in* First Indian on the Moon *(1993),* The Man Who Loves Salmon *(1998), and other volumes. In the following essay, Alexie attests to the importance of literature—all kinds of literature—in his life.*

I learned to read with a Superman comic book. Simple enough, I suppose. I can- 1
not recall which particular Superman comic book I read, nor can I remember
which villain he fought in that issue. I cannot remember the plot, nor the means
by which I obtained the comic book. What I can remember is this: I was 3 years
old, a Spokane Indian boy living with his family on the Spokane Indian Reservation in eastern Washington state. We were poor by most standards, but one of
my parents usually managed to find some minimum-wage job or another,
which made us middle-class by reservation standards. I had a brother and three
sisters. We lived on a combination of irregular paychecks, hope, fear, and government surplus food.

My father, who is one of the few Indians who went to Catholic school on 2
purpose, was an avid reader of westerns, spy thrillers, murder mysteries, gangster epics, basketball player biographies, and anything else he could find. He
bought his books by the pound at Dutch's Pawn Shop, Goodwill, Salvation
Army, and Value Village. When he had extra money, he bought new novels at
supermarkets, convenience stores, and hospital gift shops. Our house was filled
with books. They were stacked in crazy piles in the bathroom, bedrooms, and
living room. In a fit of unemployment-inspired creative energy, my father built
a set of bookshelves and soon filled them with a random assortment of books
about the Kennedy assassination, Watergate, the Vietnam War, and the entire
23-book series of the Apache westerns. My father loved books, and since I loved
my father with an aching devotion, I decided to love books as well.

I can remember picking up my father's books before I could read. The words 3
themselves were mostly foreign, but I still remember the exact moment when I
first understood, with a sudden clarity, the purpose of a paragraph. I didn't have
the vocabulary to say "paragraph," but I realized that a paragraph was a fence
that held words. The words inside a paragraph worked together for a common
purpose. They had some specific reason for being inside the same fence. This
knowledge delighted me. I began to think of everything in terms of paragraphs.
Our reservation was a small paragraph within the United States. My family's
house was a paragraph, distinct from the other paragraphs of the LeBrets to the
north, the Fords to our south, and the Tribal School to the west. Inside our house,
each family member existed as a separate paragraph but still had genetics and
common experiences to link us. Now, using this logic, I can see my changed family as an essay of seven paragraphs: mother, father, older brother, the deceased
sister, my younger twin sisters, and our adopted little brother.

At the same time I was seeing the world in paragraphs, I also picked up 4
that Superman comic book. Each panel, complete with picture, dialogue, and
narrative was a three-dimensional paragraph. In one panel, Superman breaks
through a door. His suit is red, blue, and yellow. The brown door shatters into
many pieces. I look at the narrative above the picture. I cannot read the words,
but I assume it tells me that "Superman is breaking down the door." Aloud, I
pretend to read the words and say, "Superman is breaking down the door."
Words, dialogue, also float out of Superman's mouth. Because he is breaking
down the door, I assume he says, "I am breaking down the door." Once again,

I pretend to read the words and say aloud, "I am breaking down the door." In this way, I learned to read.

5   This might be an interesting story all by itself. A little Indian boy teaches himself to read at an early age and advances quickly. He reads "Grapes of Wrath" in kindergarten when other children are struggling through "Dick and Jane." If he'd been anything but an Indian boy living on the reservation, he might have been called a prodigy. But he is an Indian boy living on the reservation and is simply an oddity. He grows into a man who often speaks of his childhood in the third person, as if it will somehow dull the pain and make him sound more modest about his talents.

6 A smart Indian is a dangerous person, widely feared and ridiculed by Indians and non-Indians alike. I fought with my classmates on a daily basis. They wanted me to stay quiet when the non-Indian teacher asked for answers, for volunteers, for help. We were Indian children who were expected to be stupid. Most lived up to those expectations inside the classroom but subverted them on the outside. They struggled with basic reading in school but could remember how to sing a few dozen powwow songs. They were monosyllabic in front of their non-Indian teachers but could tell complicated stories and jokes at the dinner table. They submissively ducked their heads when confronted by a non-Indian adult but would slug it out with the Indian bully who was 10 years older. As Indian children, we were expected to fail in the non-Indian world. Those who failed were ceremonially accepted by other Indians and appropriately pitied by non-Indians.

7   I refused to fail. I was smart. I was arrogant. I was lucky. I read books late into the night, until I could barely keep my eyes open. I read books at recess, then during lunch, and in the few minutes left after I had finished my classroom assignments. I read books in the car when my family traveled to powwows or basketball games. In shopping malls, I ran to the bookstores and read bits and pieces of as many books as I could. I read the books my father brought home from the pawnshops and secondhand. I read the books I borrowed from the library. I read the backs of cereal boxes. I read the newspaper. I read the bulletins posted on the walls of the school, the clinic, the tribal offices, the post office. I read junk mail. I read auto-repair manuals. I read magazines. I read anything that had words and paragraphs. I read with equal parts joy and desperation. I loved those books, but I also knew that love had only one purpose. I was trying to save my life.

8   Despite all the books I read, I am still surprised I became a writer. I was going to be a pediatrician. These days, I write novels, short stories, and poems. I visit schools and teach creative writing to Indian kids. In all my years in the reservation school system, I was never taught how to write poetry, short stories, or novels. I was certainly never taught that Indians wrote poetry, short stories, and novels. Writing was something beyond Indians. I cannot recall a single time that a guest teacher visited the reservation. There must have been visiting teachers. Who were they? Where are they now? Do they exist? I visit the schools as often as possible. The Indian kids crowd the classroom. Many are writing their own poems, short stories, and novels. They have read my books. They

have read many other books. They look at me with bright eyes and arrogant wonder. They are trying to save their lives. Then there are the sullen and already defeated Indian kids who sit in the back rows and ignore me with theatrical precision. The pages of their notebooks are empty. They carry neither pencil nor pen. They stare out the window. They refuse and resist. "Books," I say to them. "Books," I say. I throw my weight against their locked doors. The door holds. I am smart. I am arrogant. I am lucky. I am trying to save our lives.

COMPREHENSION

1. Do you find it paradoxical that Alexie learned to read with a Superman comic book? Why or why not? What does Alexie learn from reading the Superman comic?
2. What connections do you see between Alexie and his father?
3. What does Alexie mean when he writes, "A smart Indian is a dangerous person . . . " (paragraph 6)?

RHETORIC

1. Does Alexie state or imply his thesis? State his thesis in your own words.
2. What is Alexie's purpose in writing this essay?
3. Why does Alexie divide his essay into two parts? Do you find this organizational scheme effective? Why or why not?
4. Explain the importance of comparison and contrast in this essay.
5. Alexie's concluding paragraph is quite long. Does it serve as an effective ending? Why or why not?

WRITING

1. Write a personal essay about the types of popular literature that you liked to read as a child.
2. **Writing an Argument:** Do you agree or disagree with Alexie's claim that a literate person—especially a member of any group that has experienced discrimination—is necessarily a dangerous individual? Write an argumentative essay in response to this question.

NETWORKING
Applying 21st-Century Literacies

Comparing Reading and Viewing Habits: Write a comparative essay in which you discuss the reading and viewing habits of your parents and your own tastes. Which media do each of you prefer for popular entertainment, and which do you prefer to get the news? Do you tend to *learn* more from watching a program, reading a print text, or reading an online hyperlinked text? Explore why.

Synthesis: Classic and Contemporary Essays for Comparison

1. Summarize and critique these two writers' agendas, explaining where their ideas overlap and where they diverge.
2. According to both writers, reading in childhood is important. How do Welty and Alexie support this claim? What types of evidence do they present?
3. Compare and contrast the style of each essay. Which essay seems more accessible to you, and why?
4. Imagine what Alexie might say about Welty's essay. What would he see in it that might inform his own writing?

NETWORKING
Applying 21st-Century Literacies

Go online and find out more about these two writers. Focus on Welty's life in Jackson, Mississippi, and Alexie's life on the Spokane Indian Reservation. Then write a brief essay summarizing the importance of place in their writing.

Moving Along

John Updike

John Updike (1932–2009), a major American novelist, short-story writer, poet, and critic, was born in Shillington, Pennsylvania. He graduated from Harvard University (AB, 1954) and attended the Ruskin School of Drawing and Fine Art at Oxford University. Associated for decades with the New Yorker, *where his short fiction, poetry, reviews, and criticism frequently appeared, Updike carved for himself a rare reputation as a master of several literary genres. He published more than 40 books during his career. Focusing in his fiction on suburban middle-class life, Updike received two Pulitzer prizes and many other major awards, including a National Book Award for his novel* The Centaur *(1963). His fiction includes the much-admired "Rabbit" quintet, five novels that track one central character, first introduced in* Rabbit, Run *(1960), through the passages in his life. Updike's poetry collections include* The Carpentered Hen and Other Tame Creatures *(1958) and* Americana: And Other Poems *(2001). Updike included the following essay in* Just Looking *(1981), a collection of his art criticism.*

1   In dreams, one is frequently travelling, and the more hallucinatory moments of our waking life, many of them, are spent in cars, trains, and airplanes. For millennia, Man has walked or run to where he wanted to go; the first naked ape

Artist unknown, *Baz Bahadur and Rupmati Riding by Moonlight*, c. 1780. Pahari miniature in Kangra style, 8¾ × 6¼". The British Museum, Department of Oriental Antiquities, London.

who had the mad idea of mounting a horse (or was it a *Camelops?*) launched a series of subtle internal dislocations of which jet lag is a vivid modern form. When men come to fly through space at near the speed of light, they will return to earth a century later but only a few years older. Now, driving (say) from Boston to Pittsburgh in a day, we arrive feeling greatly aged by the engine's innumerable explosive heartbeats, by the monotony of the highway surface and the constant windy press of unnatural speed. Beside the highway, a clamorous parasitic life signals for attention and halt; localities where generations have lived, bred, labored, and died are flung through the windshield and out through the rearview mirror. Men on the move brutalize themselves and render the world they arrow through phantasmal.

Our two artists, separated by two centuries, capture well the eeriness of travel. 2 In the Punjab Hills painting, Baz Bahadur, prince of Malwa, has eloped with the lovely Rupmati; in order to keep him faithful to her, the legend goes, she takes him riding by moonlight. The moon appears to exist not only in the sky but behind a grove of trees. Deer almost blend into the mauve-gray hills. A little citadel basks in

Roy de Forest, *Canoe of Fate*, 1974. Polymer on canvas, 66¾ × 90¼". Philadelphia Museum of Art, The Adele Haas Turner and Beatrice Pastorius Turner Fund.

starlight on a hilltop. In this soft night, nothing is brighter than the scarlet pasterns of the horses. Baz Bahadur's steed bears on his hide a paler version of the starry sky, and in his violet genitals carries a hint of this nocturnal ride's sexual undercurrent. To judge from the delicacy of their gestures and glances, the riders are being borne along as smoothly as on a merry-go-round. Though these lovers and their panoply are formalized to static perfection, if we cover them, a surprising depth appears in the top third of the painting, and carries the eye away.

3   The riders in Roy de Forest's contemporary painting move through a forest as crowded, garish, and menacing as the neon-lit main drag of a city. A throng of sinister bystanders, one built of brick and another with eyes that are paste gems, witness the passage of this *Canoe of Fate*, which with the coarseness of its stitching and the bulk of its passengers would make slow headway even on a less crowded canvas. Beyond the mountains, heavenly medallions and balloons of stippled color pre-empt space. Only the gesture of the black brave, echoing that of George Washington in another fabulous American crossing, gives a sense of direction and promises to open a path. Two exotic birds, a slavering wolf, and what may be a fair captive (gazing backward toward settlements where other red-haired bluefaces mourn her) freight the canoe with a suggestion of allegory, of myths to which we have lost the key. The personnel of the

aboriginal New World, at any rate, are here deep-dyed but not extinguished by the glitter and jazz of an urban-feeling wilderness.

In both representations, the movement is from right to left, like that of writ-   4 ing in the Semitic languages, like the motion of a mother when she instinctively shifts her baby to her left arm, to hold it closer to her heart. It feels natural, this direction, and slightly uphill. We gaze at these dreamlike tapestries of travel confident that no progress will be made—we will awaken in our beds.

COMPREHENSION

1. According to Updike, why does the idea of travel have such a hold on the collective imagination? What is the relationship of the travel motif to art?
2. Describe the two paintings that Updike analyzes in this essay. What other famous painting does he allude to in paragraph 3?
3. Why does Updike emphasize the "eeriness" of the two paintings? What is he saying about the human psyche?

RHETORIC

1. How does Updike design his introductory paragraph? What is his purpose?
2. What is Updike's thesis? Does he state or imply it? Explain.
3. Identify specific passages that highlight Updike's descriptive style. What types of figurative language does he employ?
4. Explain Updike's comparative method. What do the reproductions of the two paintings contribute to the overall comparative effect? Would this brief essay be as effective without these images? Why or why not?
5. Why is Updike's concluding paragraph relatively brief when compared with the preceding paragraphs? Is this end paragraph effective? Justify your response.

WRITING

1. Consider the two paintings that Updike reproduces, and write your own comparative essay based on them.
2. **Writing an Argument:** Argue for or against the proposition that when viewing a work of art, it is not necessary to relate it—as Updike does—to human behavior.

NETWORKING
Applying 21st-Century Literacies

Analyzing Themes in Fine Art: Select two paintings that reflect what you consider to be a common theme, and write a comparative essay about them. Provide images of these paintings in your essay. Recommended sites for viewing paintings are linked to on the Chapter 11 Networking page (at *www.mhhe.com/mhreader11e*).

Finding Neverland

David Gates

David Gates (b. 1947) is an American journalist and fiction writer. Gates attended Bard College and the University of Connecticut in the mid-1960s, subsequently work-ing as a cab driver and in other capacities while refining his literary craft. His first novel, Jernigan *(1991), was nominated for a Pulitzer prize. Both his second novel,* Preston Falls *(1998), and the collection* The Wonders of the Invisible World: Sto-ries *(1999), were finalists for the National Book Critics Circle Award. Gates is a senior editor and writer at* Newsweek, *covering books, music, and the arts. He also teaches in the graduate writing programs at Bennington College and New School University. In this essay from the July 13, 2009, issue of* Newsweek, *Gates surveys the life, death, and career of music legend Michael Jackson.*

1   True, for a while he was the king of pop—a term apparently originated by his friend Elizabeth Taylor—and he's the last we're ever likely to have. Before Michael Jackson came Frank Sinatra, Elvis Presley, and the Beatles; after him has come absolutely no one, however brilliant or however popular, who couldn't be ignored by vast segments of an ever-more-fragmented audience. Not Kurt Cobain, not Puffy, not Mariah Carey, not Céline Dion, not Beyoncé, not Radiohead—not even Madonna, his closest competitor. When the news of his death broke, the traffic on Twitter caused the site to crash, even though he hadn't had a hit song for years. But starting long before and continuing long after he lorded over the world of entertainment in the 1980s—his 1982 *Thriller* remains the bestselling album of all time—Jackson was the Prince of Artifice. As the prepubescent frontboy of the Jackson 5, he sang in a cherubic mezzo-soprano of sexual longing he could not yet have fully felt. As a young man, however ac-complished and even impassioned his singing was, he never had the sexual credibility of a James Brown or a Wilson Pickett, in part because of his still-high-pitched voice, in part because he seemed never to fully inhabit himself—whoever that self was. In middle age, he consciously took on the role of Peter Pan, with his Neverland Ranch and its amusement-park rides, with his lost-boy "friends" and with what he seemed to believe was an ageless, androgynous physical appearance—let's hope he believed it—thanks to straightened hair and plastic surgery. (No one—least of all Jackson himself—would have wanted to see the Dorian Gray portrait in his attic.) He did his best to construct an alter-nate reality on top of what must have been an initially miserable life: Imagine

589

Gypsy with—as Jackson claimed in interviews—a physically abusive father in place of Mama Rose, set among Jehovah's Witnesses. Which was the more imaginative creation: his music or his persona?

In retrospect, so much of what Jackson achieved seems baldly symbolic. This was the black kid from Gary, Ind., who ended up marrying Elvis's daughter, setting up Neverland in place of Graceland, and buying the Beatles' song catalog—bold acts of appropriation and mastery, if not outright aggression. (Of course, Elvis and the Beatles had come out of obscurity, too, but that was a long, long time ago, in a galaxy far away.) He made trademarks of the very emblems of his remoteness: his moonwalk dance and his jeweled glove—*noli me tangere*, and vice versa. He morphed relentlessly from the most adorable of kiddie performers (his 1972 movie-soundtrack hit, "Ben," was a love song to a pet rat) to the most sinister of superstars: not by adopting a campy persona, like those of his older contemporaries Alice Cooper or Ozzy Osbourne, but in real life, dodging accusations of child molestation, one of which led to a trial and acquittal in 2005. (One shrink concluded at the time that he was not a pedophile, but merely a case of arrested development.) The 2002 episode in which he briefly dangled his son Prince Michael II (a.k.a. Blanket) over a balcony in Berlin, above horrified, fascinated fans, seemed like a ritualized attempt to dispose of his own

590

...l surgeries, a skin ailment, serious
...ade him look like both a vampire and
...wins. That is, like the skeletal, pale-faced
...ndis's 14-minute "Thriller" video. When you
... a whole stage full of Michael Jacksons, the real
younger ...oking, the most unreal of all.

weight]personal traumas Jackson may have reenacted and
a mun re-reenacted—he performed his dance of death as a
zom'rica's long racial horror show. He was, quintessentially,
we products of America," who, as William Carlos Williams
...o crazy." To take the uplifting view, enunciated after his death
...[3] the Rev. Al Sharpton, he was a transracial icon, a black person
...e Americans took to their hearts and whose blackness came to seem
...l. In this he resembles such figures as Nat (King) Cole, Sammy Davis
...ney Poitier, Harry Belafonte, Sam Cooke, Jimi Hendrix, Arthur Ashe,
...ael Jordan, Oprah Winfrey, Tiger Woods, and, inevitably, Barack Obama. As
...singer-dancer, he clearly belongs not just in the tradition of Jackie Wilson, James
Brown, and the Temptations—who seem to have been among his immediate in-
spirations—but also in the tradition of such dancing entertainers as Fred Astaire
and Gene Kelly, who, in turn, drew from such black performers as Bill (Bojan-
gles) Robinson. In the 1978 film version of *The Wiz*, Jackson even seemed to appropriate and reinvent Ray Bolger's role as the Scarecrow in *The Wizard of Oz*.
And as a messianic global superstar, he resembles no one so much as his father-
in-law, Elvis Presley (who died long before Jackson married his daughter), a
transracial figure from the other side of the color line. When Presley's first records
were played on the radio in Memphis, DJs made a point of noting that he graduated from the city's all-white Humes High School, lest listeners mistake him for
black. Given the ubiquity of television, nobody mistook the wispy-voiced young
Michael Jackson for white, but it seemed, superficially, not to matter.

4   Yet Jackson, always the artificer, surely knew that part of his own appeal to
white audiences—who contributed substantially to the $50 million to $75 million a year he earned in his prime—lay initially in his precocious cuteness, and
when he was a grown man, in his apparent lack of adult sexuality. He was energetic, charismatic, and supremely gifted, but sexually unassertive—unlike
swaggeringly heterosexual black male performers from Big Joe Turner ("Shake,
Rattle, and Roll") to Jay-Z ("Big Pimpin'"). He neutered himself racially, too:
his hair went from kinky to straight, his lips from full to thin, his nose from
broad to pinched, his skin from dark to a ghastly pallor. You can't miss the connection between these forms of neutering if you know the history of white
America's atavistic dread of black male sexuality; the 1955 murder of 14-year-
old Emmett Till, for supposedly flirting with a white woman, is just one *locus
classicus*. That happened only three years before Jackson was born; when he
was 13, he was singing "Ben." No wonder Jackson chose—with whatever degree of calculation—to remake himself as an American Dream of innocence
and belovedness.

No wonder, either, that the artifice eventually turned scary, and the face of 5
the icon came to look more and more corpselike. Readers of Toni Morrison's latest novel, *A Mercy,* might recall the passage in which an African woman tells
about her first sight of white slavers: "There we see men we believe are ill or
dead. We soon learn they are neither. Their skin is confusing." That's the middle-
aged Michael Jackson to a T. Jackson arguably looked his "blackest" on the
original cover of 1979's *Off the Wall;* by *Thriller,* the transformation had begun.
Off the Wall was his declaration of manhood: It came out the year he turned 21,
and you could make the case that it was his greatest purely musical moment.
Why did he feel so deeply uncomfortable with himself? The hopeless task of
sculpting and bleaching yourself into a simulacrum of a white man suggests a
profound loathing of blackness. If Michael Jackson couldn't be denounced as a
race traitor, who could? Somehow, though, black America overlooked it, and
continued to buy his records, perhaps because some African-Americans, with
their hair relaxers and skin-lightening creams, understood why Jackson was
remaking himself, even if they couldn't condone it.

As with Ernest Hemingway—another case of deeply confused identity and 6
(who knew?) androgynous sexuality—we need to look past the deliberate creation of an image and a persona to appreciate the artistry. A more masterly en-
tertainer never took the stage. In 1988, the *New York Times* dance critic Anna
Kisselgoff called him "a virtuoso . . . who uses movement for its own sake. Yes,
Michael Jackson is an avant-garde dancer, and his dances could be called abstract. Like Merce Cunningham, he shows us that movement has a value of its
own." Better yet, Astaire himself once called Jackson to offer his compliments.
As a singer, Jackson was too much of a chameleon—from the tenderness of "I'll
Be There" to the rawness of "The Way You Make Me Feel" to the silken sorrow
of "She's Out of My Life"—to stamp every song with his distinct personality, as
Sinatra did, or Ray Charles, or Hank Williams. But these are demigods—Jackson
was merely a giant. (And how'd you like *their* dancing?) As a musical conceptu-
alizer, probably only James Brown has had a comparable influence: Jackson and
his visionary producer, Quincy Jones, fused disco, soul, and pop in a manner
that can still be heard every hour of every day on every top-40 radio station—
only not as well. Tommy Mottola, former head of Sony Music, called Jackson
"the corner-stone to the entire music business." The best recordings by Jackson
and Jones—"Don't Stop 'Til You Get Enough," "Billie Jean"—belong identifiably
to their time, as do Sinatra's 1950s recordings with the arranger Nelson Riddle.
Yet like Sinatra's "I've Got the World on a String" or "In the Wee Small Hours of
the Morning," they're so perfect of their kind that they'll never sound dated.

The night before he died, Jackson was rehearsing at the Staples Center in 7
Los Angeles for an epic comeback—a series of 50 concerts, beginning in July,
at London's O2 Arena. If that sounds impossibly grandiose, consider that all
50 shows had already sold out. People around him had been wondering if he
was really up to it, and the opening had already been put off by a week. He
was 50 years old, after all: long in the tooth for a *puer aeternus*—eight years
older than Elvis when he left the building, and a quarter century past his peak.

Jackson had had health problems for years. Drug problems, too, apparently: In 2007, according to the Associated Press, an L.A. pharmacy sued him, claiming he owed $100,000 for two years' worth of prescription meds. And money problems: In 2008, the ranch nearly went into foreclosure—he defaulted on a $24.5 million debt—and even the $50 million he stood to realize from his potentially grueling London concerts might not have helped that much. And of course, just problems: His very existence—as a son, as a black man—was problematic. In his last days, did the prospect of a comeback, of remythologizing himself one more time, excite him as much as it excited his fans? Did his magical moments in performance have an incandescent density that outweighed what must often have been burdensome hours and days? Ask him sometime, if you see him. Whatever his life felt like from inside, from outside it was manifestly a work of genius, whether you want to call it a triumph or a freak show—those are just words. We'd never seen anyone like this before, either in his artistic inventiveness or his equally artistic self-invention, and we won't forget him—until the big Neverland swallows us all.

COMPREHENSION

1. Summarize Gates's perception of Michael Jackson. How do you interpret the title? Why does Gates call Jackson an "artificer"? What does Gates mean by Jackson's "androgynous sexuality"?
2. Gates alludes to many stars from the world of music, dance, literature, and the arts. Which celebrities can you identify? What is Gates's purpose in listing so many of them?
3. What, in Gates's opinion, is Michael Jackson's legacy?

RHETORIC

1. Does this essay have an explicitly stated thesis? If so, where is it? If the thesis is implied, paraphrase it.
2. The first paragraph of this essay is quite long. What is Gates's strategy and purpose here? Does this lengthy opening paragraph weaken or strengthen the body of the essay? Explain.
3. Identify and comment on Gates's use of figurative language in this essay. How does figurative language—and Gates's overall style—influence the essay's tone?
4. What comparative points does Gates make about Jackson and other artists? How does the comparative method serve to organize the essay?
5. Explain the effect of the last paragraph, which resembles the introductory paragraph in length. Do you think this resemblance was intentional? Why or why not?

WRITING

1. Write your own evaluation of Michael Jackson or another celebrity from the world of music, explaining why you think this artist's achievement is important.

2. Write a comparative essay in which you discuss two artists from the world of music, film, or television.
3. **Writing an Argument:** Argue for or against the proposition that the media make too much of the deaths of prominent celebrities.

NETWORKING
Applying 21st-Century Literacies

Creating a Photo Biography: Strengthen your position in question 1 under Writing by adding a photo biography of Michael Jackson (or another musician-celebrity whose career you've chosen to evaluate). This biography would consist of 12 to 15 images that help tell the story of the celebrity's career; use succinct but compelling captions to supply narration that informs your evaluation.

George Orwell:
Some Personal Connections

Margaret Atwood

Margaret Atwood (b. 1939) is arguably Canada's most famous contemporary writer—a poet, novelist, short-story writer, and essayist who explores the role of personal consciousness in a troubled world. Atwood received degrees from the University of Toronto (BA, 1961) and Radcliffe College (AM, 1962). Her second collection of poetry, The Circle Game *(1966), brought her critical recognition. Atwood is even better known as a novelist; her fiction includes* Surfacing *(1973),* Life before Man *(1979),* The Handmaid's Tale *(1985),* Cat's Eye *(1988),* The Blind Assassin *(2000),* The Tent *(2006), and* The Year of the Flood *(2008). In the following selection, published in the* Manchester Guardian *in 2003, Atwood explains the relevance of one English writer for the post-9/11 world.*

I grew up with George Orwell. I was born in 1939, and *Animal Farm* was published in 1945. Thus, I was able to read it at the age of nine. It was lying around the house, and I mistook it for a book about talking animals, sort of like *Wind in the Willows*. I knew nothing about the kind of politics in the book—the child's version of politics then, just after the war, consisted of the simple notion that Hitler was bad but dead. So I gobbled up the adventures of Napoleon and Snowball, the smart, greedy, upwardly mobile pigs, and Squealer the spin-doctor, and Boxer the noble but thick-witted horse, and the easily led, slogan-chanting sheep, without making any connection with historical events.

    To say that I was horrified by this book is an understatement. The fate of the farm animals was so grim, the pigs so mean and mendacious and treacherous, 2 the sheep so stupid. Children have a keen sense of injustice, and this was the thing that upset me the most: The pigs were so unjust. I cried my eyes out when Boxer the horse had an accident and was carted off to be made into dog food, instead of being given the quiet corner of the pasture he'd been promised.

3   The whole experience was deeply disturbing to me, but I am forever grateful to Orwell for alerting me early to the danger flags I've tried to watch out for since. In the world of *Animal Farm*, most speechifying and public palaver is bullshit and instigated lying, and though many characters are good-hearted and mean well, they can be frightened into closing their eyes to what's really going on. The pigs browbeat the others with ideology, then twist that ideology to suit their own purposes: Their language games were evident to me even at that age. As Orwell taught, it isn't the labels—Christianity, Socialism, Islam, Democracy, Two Legs Bad, Four Legs Good, the works—that are definitive, but the acts done in their name.

4   I could see, too, how easily those who have toppled an oppressive power take on its trappings and habits. Jean-Jacques Rousseau was right to warn us that democracy is the hardest form of government to maintain; Orwell knew that to the marrow of his bones, because he had seen it in action. How quickly the precept "All Animals Are Equal" is changed into "All Animals Are Equal, but Some Are More Equal Than Others." What oily concern the pigs show for the welfare of the other animals, a concern that disguises their contempt for those they are manipulating. With what alacrity do they put on the once-despised uniforms of the tyrannous humans they have overthrown, and learn to use their whips. How self-righteously they justify their actions, helped by the verbal web-spinning of Squealer, their nimble-tongued press agent, until all power is in their trotters, pretence is no longer necessary, and they rule by naked force. A revolution often means only that: a revolving, a turn of the wheel of fortune, by which those who were at the bottom mount to the top, and assume the choice positions, crushing the former power-holders beneath them. We should beware of all those who plaster the landscape with large portraits of themselves, like the evil pig, Napoleon.

5   *Animal Farm* is one of the most spectacular Emperor-Has-No-Clothes books of the 20th century, and it got George Orwell into trouble. People who run counter to the current popular wisdom, who point out the uncomfortably obvious, are likely to be strenuously baa-ed at by herds of angry sheep. I didn't have all that figured out at the age of nine, of course—not in any conscious way. But we learn the patterns of stories before we learn their meanings, and *Animal Farm* has a very clear pattern.

6   Then along came *Nineteen Eighty-Four*, which was published in 1949. Thus, I read it in paperback a couple of years later, when I was in high school. Then I read it again, and again: It was right up there among my favourite books, along with *Wuthering Heights*. At the same time, I absorbed its two companions, Arthur Koestler's *Darkness at Noon* and Aldous Huxley's *Brave New World*. I was keen on all three of them, but I understood *Darkness at Noon* to be a tragedy about events that had already happened, and *Brave New World* to be a satirical comedy, with

events that were unlikely to unfold in exactly that way. (Orgy-Porgy, indeed.) *Nineteen Eighty-Four* struck me as more realistic, probably because Winston Smith was more like me—a skinny person who got tired a lot and was subjected to physical education under chilly conditions (this was a feature of my school)—and who was silently at odds with the ideas and the manner of life proposed for him. (This may be one of the reasons *Nineteen Eighty-Four* is best read when you are an adolescent: most adolescents feel like that.) I sympathised particularly with Winston's desire to write his forbidden thoughts down in a deliciously tempting, secret blank book: I had not yet started to write, but I could see the attractions of it. I could also see the dangers, because it's this scribbling of his—along with illicit sex, another item with considerable allure for a teenager of the 50s—that gets Winston into such a mess.

Animal Farm charts the progress of an idealistic movement of liberation to- 7 wards a totalitarian dictatorship headed by a despotic tyrant; *Nineteen Eighty-Four* describes what it's like to live entirely within such a system. Its hero, Winston, has only fragmentary memories of what life was like before the present dreadful regime set in: He's an orphan, a child of the collectivity. His father died in the war that has ushered in the repression, and his mother has disappeared, leaving him with only the reproachful glance she gave him as he betrayed her over a chocolate bar—a small betrayal that acts both as the key to Winston's character and as a precursor to the many other betrayals in the book.

The government of Airstrip One, Winston's "country," is brutal. The constant 8 surveillance, the impossibility of speaking frankly to anyone, the looming, ominous figure of Big Brother, the regime's need for enemies and wars—fictitious though both may be—which are used to terrify the people and unite them in hatred, the mind-numbing slogans, the distortions of language, the destruction of what has really happened by stuffing any record of it down the Memory Hole—these made a deep impression on me. Let me re-state that: They frightened the stuffing out of me. Orwell was writing a satire about Stalin's Soviet Union, a place about which I knew very little at the age of 14, but he did it so well that I could imagine such things happening anywhere.

There is no love interest in *Animal Farm* but there is in *Nineteen Eighty-Four.* 9 Winston finds a soulmate in Julia; outwardly a devoted Party fanatic, secretly a girl who enjoys sex and makeup and other spots of decadence. But the two lovers are discovered, and Winston is tortured for thought-crime—inner disloyalty to the regime. He feels that if he can only remain faithful in his heart to Julia, his soul will be saved—a romantic concept, though one we are likely to endorse. But like all absolutist governments and religions, the Party demands that every personal loyalty be sacrificed to it, and replaced with an absolute loyalty to Big Brother. Confronted with his worst fear in the dreaded Room 101, where a nasty device involving a cage-full of starving rats can be fitted to the eyes, Winston breaks: "Don't do it to me," he pleads, "do it to Julia." (This sentence has become shorthand in our household for the avoidance of onerous duties. Poor Julia—how hard we would make her life if she actually existed. She'd have to be on a lot of panel discussions, for instance.)

10   After his betrayal of Julia, Winston becomes a handful of malleable goo. He truly believes that two and two make five, and that he loves Big Brother. Our last glimpse of him is sitting drink-sodden at an outdoor cafe, knowing he's a dead man walking and having learned that Julia has betrayed him, too, while he listens to a popular refrain: "Under the spreading chestnut tree/I sold you and you sold me . . ."

11   Orwell has been accused of bitterness and pessimism—of leaving us with a vision of the future in which the individual has no chance, and where the brutal, totalitarian boot of the all-controlling Party will grind into the human face, forever. But this view of Orwell is contradicted by the last chapter in the book, an essay on Newspeak—the doublethink language concocted by the regime. By expurgating all words that might be troublesome—"bad" is no longer permitted, but becomes "double-plus-ungood"—and by making other words mean the opposite of what they used to mean—the place where people get tortured is the Ministry of Love, the building where the past is destroyed is the Ministry of Information—the rulers of Airstrip One wish to make it literally impossible for people to think straight. However, the essay on Newspeak is written in standard English, in the third person, and in the past tense, which can only mean that the regime has fallen, and that language and individuality have survived. For whoever has written the essay on Newspeak, the world of *Nineteen Eighty-Four* is over. Thus, it's my view that Orwell had much more faith in the resilience of the human spirit than he's usually been given credit for.

12   Orwell became a direct model for me much later in my life—in the real 1984, the year in which I began writing a somewhat different dystopia, *The Handmaid's Tale.* By that time I was 44, and I had learned enough about real despotisms—through the reading of history, travel, and my membership of Amnesty International—so that I didn't need to rely on Orwell alone.

13   The majority of dystopias—Orwell's included—have been written by men, and the point of view has been male. When women have appeared in them, they have been either sexless automatons or rebels who have defied the sex rules of the regime. They have acted as the temptresses of the male protagonists, however welcome this temptation may be to the men themselves. Thus Julia; thus the cami-knicker-wearing, orgy-porgy seducer of the Savage in *Brave New World*; thus the subversive femme fatale of Yevgeny Zamyatin's 1924 seminal classic, *We.* I wanted to try a dystopia from the female point of view—the world according to Julia, as it were. However, this does not make *The Handmaid's Tale* a "feminist dystopia," except insofar as giving a woman a voice and an inner life will always be considered "feminist" by those who think women ought not to have these things.

14   The 20th century could be seen as a race between two versions of manmade hell—the jackbooted state totalitarianism of Orwell's *Nineteen Eighty-Four* and the hedonistic ersatz paradise of *Brave New World*, where absolutely everything is a consumer good and human beings are engineered to be happy. With the fall of the Berlin Wall in 1989, it seemed for a time that *Brave New World* had won—from henceforth, state control would be minimal, and all we would have

to do was go shopping and smile a lot, and wallow in pleasures, popping a pill or two when depression set in.

But with 9/11, all that changed. Now it appears we face the prospect of two 15 contradictory dystopias at once—open markets, closed minds—because state surveillance is back again with a vengeance. The torturer's dreaded Room 101 has been with us for millennia. The dungeons of Rome, the Inquisition, the Star Chamber, the Bastille, the proceedings of General Pinochet and of the junta in Argentina—all have depended on secrecy and on the abuse of power. Lots of countries have had their versions of it—their ways of silencing troublesome dissent. Democracies have traditionally defined themselves by, among other things, openness and the rule of law. But now it seems that we in the west are tacitly legitimising the methods of the darker human past, upgraded technologically and sanctified to our own uses, of course. For the sake of freedom, freedom must be renounced. To move us towards the improved world—the utopia we're promised—dystopia must first hold sway.

It's a concept worthy of doublethink. It's also, in its ordering of events, 16 strangely Marxist. First the dictatorship of the proletariat, in which lots of heads must roll; then the pie-in-the-sky classless society, which oddly enough never materialises. Instead, we just get pigs with whips.

I often ask myself: What would George Orwell have to say about it?   17
Quite a lot.   18

COMPREHENSION

1. This article is an edited extract of a talk that Atwood gave on BBC Radio. Why do you think her talk would be of interest to a radio audience?
2. Summarize what you learn from Atwood's essay about George Orwell and his novels *Animal Farm* and *Nineteen Eighty-Four*.
3. What does Atwood learn from Orwell? What does she think all of us should learn from him today in our "post-9/11 world"?

RHETORIC

1. Why does Atwood begin on a personal note: "I grew up with George Orwell"? What do we learn about her as a person? How does this personal element influence the tone and development of the essay?
2. What is Atwood's main claim? What premises or warrants does she establish, and how sound is the logic? Justify your response.
3. Atwood seems to speak from a position of authority. How does she establish this sense of authority in the essay?
4. Why does Atwood summarize Orwell's two novels at considerable length? How does she use comparison and contrast to frame her discussion of the novels?
5. What causes and effects does Atwood analyze in this essay? What is her purpose here?

6. How does Atwood conclude her discussion of Orwell? How successful do you find the ending, and why?

WRITING

1. Read *Animal Farm* or view the film version. Then write your own analysis of Orwell's work.
2. In a comparative essay, relate Atwood's article to Orwell's "Politics and the English Language" (see pages 106–117).

NETWORKING
Applying 21st-Century Literacies

Persuading in Multiple Media: Atwood raises the question of whether writers and artists should warn us about dangers confronting society. Write a persuasive essay in which you take a clear stand on this issue. Provide examples drawn from literature, art, and the media.

Regarding the Torture of Others

Susan Sontag

Susan Sontag (1933–2004), one of the most influential critics of her generation, was born in New York City and grew up in Tucson, Arizona, and Los Angeles. After grad- uating from high school at the age of 15, she started studies at the University of Califor- nia at Berkeley; subsequently, she received degrees from the University of Chicago and Harvard University. As an art critic as well as a political and cultural commentator, Sontag brought intellectual rigor to her subjects. The main body of her work in prose consists of two collections of essays, Against Interpretation *(1966) and* Where the Stress Falls *(2001), as well as* Trip to Hanoi *(1968),* Illness as Metaphor *(1978), and* AIDS and Its Metaphors *(1988). In addition, Sontag wrote fiction, including* Volcano Lover *(1992) and* In America: A Novel *(2001), and several films and plays. In this essay, published in the* New York Times Magazine *in 2004, Sontag offers a meditation on the photographs of torture taken by American troops at Abu Ghraib prison in Baghdad.*

I.

1 For a long time—at least six decades—photographs have laid down the tracks of how important conflicts are judged and remembered. The Western memory museum is now mostly a visual one. Photographs have an insuperable power

An Iraqi detainee at Abu Ghraib: The horror of what is shown in the photographs cannot be separated from the horror that the photographs were taken.

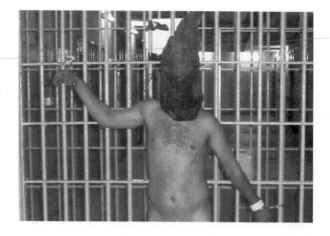

to determine what we recall of events, and it now seems probable that the defining association of people everywhere with the war that the United States launched pre-emptively in Iraq last year will be photographs of the torture of Iraqi prisoners by Americans in the most infamous of Saddam Hussein's prisons, Abu Ghraib.

The Bush administration and its defenders have chiefly sought to limit a public-relations disaster—the dissemination of the photographs—rather than deal with the complex crimes of leadership and of policy revealed by the pictures. There was, first of all, the displacement of the reality onto the photographs themselves. The administration's initial response was to say that the president was shocked and disgusted by the photographs—as if the fault or horror lay in the images, not in what they depict. There was also the avoidance of the word "torture." The prisoners had possibly been the objects of "abuse," eventually of "humiliation"—that was the most to be admitted. "My impression is that what has been charged thus far is abuse, which I believe technically is different from torture," Secretary of Defense Donald Rumsfeld said at a press conference. "And therefore I'm not going to address the 'torture' word."

Words alter, words add, words subtract. It was the strenuous avoidance of the word "genocide" while some 800,000 Tutsis in Rwanda were being slaughtered, over a few weeks' time, by their Hutu neighbors 10 years ago that indicated the American government had no intention of doing anything. To refuse to call what took place in Abu Ghraib—and what has taken place elsewhere in Iraq and in Afghanistan and at Guantánamo Bay—by its true name, torture, is as outrageous as the refusal to call the Rwandan genocide a genocide. Here is one of the definitions of torture contained in a convention to which the United States is a signatory: *"any act by which severe pain or suffering, whether physical or mental, is intentionally inflicted on a person for such purposes as obtaining from him or a third person information or a confession."* (The definition comes from the 1984

Convention Against Torture and Other Cruel, Inhuman or Degrading Treatment or Punishment. Similar definitions have existed for some time in customary law and in treaties, starting with Article 3—common to the four Geneva conventions of 1949—and many recent human rights conventions.) The 1984 convention declares, *"No exceptional circumstances whatsoever, whether a state of war or a threat of war, internal political instability or any other public emergency may be invoked as a justification of torture."* And all covenants on torture specify that it includes treatment intended to humiliate the victim, like leaving prisoners naked in cells and corridors.

4   Whatever actions this administration undertakes to limit the damage of the widening revelations of the torture of prisoners in Abu Ghraib and elsewhere—trials, courts-martial, dishonorable discharges, resignation of senior military figures and responsible administration officials and substantial compensation to the victims—it is probable that the "torture" word will continue to be banned. To acknowledge that Americans torture their prisoners would contradict everything this administration has invited the public to believe about the virtue of American intentions and America's right, flowing from that virtue, to undertake unilateral action on the world stage.

5   Even when the president was finally compelled, as the damage to America's reputation everywhere in the world widened and deepened, to use the "sorry" word, the focus of regret still seemed the damage to America's claim to moral superiority. Yes, President Bush said in Washington on May 6, standing alongside King Abdullah II of Jordan, he was "sorry for the humiliation suffered by the Iraqi prisoners and the humiliation suffered by their families." But, he went on, he was "equally sorry that people seeing these pictures didn't understand the true nature and heart of America."

6   To have the American effort in Iraq summed up by these images must seem, to those who saw some justification in a war that did overthrow one of the monster tyrants of modern times, "unfair." A war, an occupation, is inevitably a huge tapestry of actions. What makes some actions representative and others not? The issue is not whether the torture was done by individuals (i.e., "not by everybody")—but whether it was systematic. Authorized. Condoned. All acts are done by individuals. The issue is not whether a majority or a minority of Americans performs such acts but whether the nature of the policies prosecuted by this administration and the hierarchies deployed to carry them out makes such acts likely.

II.

7   Considered in this light, the photographs are us. That is, they are representative of the fundamental corruptions of any foreign occupation together with the Bush adminstration's distinctive policies. The Belgians in the Congo, the French in Algeria, practiced torture and sexual humiliation on despised recalcitrant natives. Add to this generic corruption the mystifying, near-total unpreparedness of the American rulers of Iraq to deal with the complex realities of the country

after its "liberation." And add to that the overarching, distinctive doctrines of the Bush administration, namely that the United States has embarked on an endless war and that those detained in this war are, if the president so decides, "unlawful combatants"—a policy enunciated by Donald Rumsfeld for Taliban and Qaeda prisoners as early as January 2002—and thus, as Rumsfeld said, "technically" they "do not have any rights under the Geneva Convention," and you have a perfect recipe for the cruelties and crimes committed against the thousands incarcerated without charges or access to lawyers in American-run prisons that have been set up since the attacks of Sept. 11, 2001.

So, then, is the real issue not the photographs themselves but what the pho- 8 tographs reveal to have happened to "suspects" in American custody? No: the horror of what is shown in the photographs cannot be separated from the horror that the photographs were taken—with the perpetrators posing, gloating, over their helpless captives. German soldiers in the Second World War took photographs of the atrocities they were committing in Poland and Russia, but snapshots in which the executioners placed themselves among their victims are exceedingly rare, as may be seen in a book just published, "Photographing the Holocaust," by Janina Struk. If there is something comparable to what these pictures show it would be some of the photographs of black victims of lynching taken between the 1880's and 1930's, which show Americans grinning beneath the naked mutilated body of a black man or woman hanging behind them from a tree. The lynching photographs were souvenirs of a collective action whose participants felt perfectly justified in what they had done. So are the pictures from Abu Ghraib.

The lynching pictures were in the nature of photographs as trophies—taken 9 by a photographer in order to be collected, stored in albums, displayed. The pictures taken by American soldiers in Abu Ghraib, however, reflect a shift in the use made of pictures—less objects to be saved than messages to be disseminated, circulated. A digital camera is a common possession among soldiers. Where once photographing war was the province of photojournalists, now the soldiers themselves are all photographers—recording their war, their fun, their observations of what they find picturesque, their atrocities—and swapping images among themselves and e-mailing them around the globe.

There is more and more recording of what people do, by themselves. At least 10 or especially in America, Andy Warhol's ideal of filming real events in real time—life isn't edited, why should its record be edited?—has become a norm for countless Webcasts, in which people record their day, each in his or her own reality show. Here I am—waking and yawning and stretching, brushing my teeth, making breakfast, getting the kids off to school. People record all aspects of their lives, store them in computer files and send the files around. Family life goes with the recording of family life—even when, or especially when, the family is in the throes of crisis and disgrace. Surely the dedicated, incessant home-videoing of one another, in conversation and monologue, over many years was the most astonishing material in "Capturing the Friedmans," the recent documentary by Andrew Jarecki about a Long Island family embroiled in pedophilia charges.

Most of the pictures, like this one of a young woman with a naked man on a leash, seem to depict part of a larger confluence of torture and pornography.

11   An erotic life is, for more and more people, that which can be captured in digital photographs and on video. And perhaps the torture is more attractive, as something to record, when it has a sexual component. It is surely revealing, as more Abu Ghraib photographs enter public view, that torture photographs are interleaved with pornographic images of American soldiers having sex with one another. In fact, most of the torture photographs have a sexual theme, as in those showing the coercing of prisoners to perform, or simulate, sexual acts among themselves. One exception, already canonical, is the photograph of the man made to stand on a box, hooded and sprouting wires, reportedly told he would be electrocuted if he fell off. Yet pictures of prisoners bound in painful positions, or made to stand with outstretched arms, are infrequent. That they count as torture cannot be doubted. You have only to look at the terror on the victim's face, although such "stress" fell within the Pentagon's limits of the acceptable. But most of the pictures seem part of a larger confluence of torture and pornography: A young woman leading a naked man around on a leash is classic dominatrix imagery. And you wonder how much of the sexual tortures inflicted on the inmates of Abu Ghraib was inspired by the vast repertory of pornographic imagery available on the Internet—and which ordinary people, by sending out Webcasts of themselves, try to emulate.

III.

12 To live is to be photographed, to have a record of one's life, and therefore to go on with one's life oblivious, or claiming to be oblivious, to the camera's nonstop attentions. But to live is also to pose. To act is to share in the community of actions recorded as images. The expression of satisfaction at the acts of torture being inflicted on helpless, trussed, naked victims is only part of the story.

There is the deep satisfaction of being photographed, to which one is now more inclined to respond not with a stiff, direct gaze (as in former times) but with glee. The events are in part designed to be photographed. The grin is a grin for the camera. There would be something missing if, after stacking the naked men, you couldn't take a picture of them.

Looking at these photographs, you ask yourself, How can someone grin at 13 the sufferings and humiliation of another human being? Set guard dogs at the genitals and legs of cowering naked prisoners? Force shackled, hooded prisoners to masturbate or simulate oral sex with one another? And you feel naïve for asking, since the answer is, self-evidently, People do these things to other people. Rape and pain inflicted on the genitals are among the most common forms of torture. Not just in Nazi concentration camps and in Abu Ghraib when it was run by Saddam Hussein. Americans, too, have done and do them when they are told, or made to feel, that those over whom they have absolute power deserve to be humiliated, tormented. They do them when they are led to believe that the people they are torturing belong to an inferior race or religion. For the meaning of these pictures is not just that these acts were performed, but that their perpetrators apparently had no sense that there was anything wrong in what the pictures show.

Even more appalling, since the pictures were meant to be circulated and 14 seen by many people: it was all fun. And this idea of fun is, alas, more and more—contrary to what President Bush is telling the world—part of "the true nature and heart of America." It is hard to measure the increasing acceptance of brutality in American life, but its evidence is everywhere, starting with the video games of killing that are a principal entertainment of boys—can the video game "Interrogating the Terrorists" really be far behind?—and on to the violence that has become endemic in the group rites of youth on an exuberant kick. Violent crime is down, yet the easy delight taken in violence seems to have grown. From the harsh torments inflicted on incoming students in many American suburban high schools—depicted in Richard Linklater's 1993 film, "Dazed and Confused"—to the hazing rituals of physical brutality and sexual humiliation in college fraternities and on sports teams, America has become a country in which the fantasies and the practice of violence are seen as good entertainment, fun.

What formerly was segregated as pornography, as the exercise of extreme 15 sadomasochistic longings—as in Pier Paolo Pasolini's last, near-unwatchable film, "Salò" (1975), depicting orgies of torture in the Fascist redoubt in northern Italy at the end of the Mussolini era—is now being normalized, by some, as high-spirited play or venting. To "stack naked men" is like a college fraternity prank, said a caller to Rush Limbaugh and the many millions of Americans who listen to his radio show. Had the caller, one wonders, seen the photographs? No matter. The observation—or is it the fantasy?—was on the mark. What may still be capable of shocking some Americans was Limbaugh's response: "Exactly!" he exclaimed. "Exactly my point. This is no different than what happens at the Skull and Bones initiation, and we're going to ruin people's

What formerly was segregated as pornography, as the exercise of extreme sadomasochistic longings, is being normalized, by some, as high-spirited play or venting.

lives over it, and we're going to hamper our military effort, and then we are going to really hammer them because they had a good time." "They" are the American soldiers, the torturers. And Limbaugh went on: "You know, these people are being fired at every day. I'm talking about people having a good time, these people. You ever heard of emotional release?"

16   Shock and awe were what our military promised the Iraqis. And shock and the awful are what these photographs announce to the world that the Americans have delivered: a pattern of criminal behavior in open contempt of international humanitarian conventions. Soldiers now pose, thumbs up, before the atrocities they commit, and send off the pictures to their buddies. Secrets of private life that, formerly, you would have given nearly anything to conceal, you now clamor to be invited on a television show to reveal. What is illustrated by these photographs is as much the culture of shamelessness as the reigning admiration for unapologetic brutality.

IV.

17 The notion that apologies or professions of "disgust" by the president and the secretary of defense are a sufficient response is an insult to one's historical and moral sense. The torture of prisoners is not an aberration. It is a direct consequence of the with-us-or-against-us doctrines of world struggle with which the Bush administration has sought to change, change radically, the international stance of the United States and to recast many domestic institutions and prerogatives. The Bush administration has committed the country to a pseudo-religious doctrine of war, endless war—for "the war on terror" is nothing less than that. Endless war is taken to justify endless incarcerations. Those held in

the extralegal American penal empire are "detainees"; "prisoners," a newly obsolete word, might suggest that they have the rights accorded by international law and the laws of all civilized countries. This endless "global war on terrorism"—into which both the quite justified invasion of Afghanistan and the unwinnable folly in Iraq have been folded by Pentagon decree—inevitably leads to the demonizing and dehumanizing of anyone declared by the Bush administration to be a possible terrorist: a definition that is not up for debate and is, in fact, usually made in secret.

The charges against most of the people detained in the prisons in Iraq and 18 Afghanistan being nonexistent—the Red Cross reports that 70 to 90 percent of those being held seem to have committed no crime other than simply being in the wrong place at the wrong time, caught up in some sweep of "suspects"—the principal justification for holding them is "interrogation." Interrogation about what? About anything. Whatever the detainee might know. If interrogation is the point of detaining prisoners indefinitely, then physical coercion, humiliation and torture become inevitable.

Remember: We are not talking about that rarest of cases, the "ticking time 19 bomb" situation, which is sometimes used as a limiting case that justifies torture of prisoners who have knowledge of an imminent attack. This is general or nonspecific information-gathering, authorized by American military and civilian administrators to learn more of a shadowy empire of evildoers about whom Americans know virtually nothing, in countries about which they are singularly ignorant: In principle, any information at all might be useful. An interrogation that produced no information (whatever information might consist of) would count as a failure. All the more justification for preparing prisoners to talk. Softening them up, stressing them out—these are the euphemisms for the bestial practices in American prisons where suspected terrorists are being held. Unfortunately, as Staff Sgt. Ivan (Chip) Frederick noted in his diary, a prisoner can get too stressed out and die. The picture of a man in a body bag with ice on his chest may well be of the man Frederick was describing.

The pictures will not go away. That is the nature of the digital world in 20 which we live. Indeed, it seems they were necessary to get our leaders to acknowledge that they had a problem on their hands. After all, the conclusions of reports compiled by the International Committee of the Red Cross, and other reports by journalists and protests by humanitarian organizations about the atrocious punishments inflicted on "detainees" and "suspected terrorists" in prisons run by the American military, first in Afghanistan and later in Iraq, have been circulating for more than a year. It seems doubtful that such reports were read by President Bush or Vice President Dick Cheney or Condoleezza Rice or Rumsfeld. Apparently it took the photographs to get their attention, when it became clear they could not be suppressed; it was the photographs that made all this "real" to Bush and his associates. Up to then, there had been only words, which are easier to cover up in our age of infinite digital self-reproduction and self-dissemination, and so much easier to forget.

21   So now the pictures will continue to "assault" us—as many Americans are bound to feel. Will people get used to them? Some Americans are already saying they have seen enough. Not, however, the rest of the world. Endless war: endless stream of photographs. Will editors now debate whether showing more of them, or showing them uncropped (which, with some of the best-known images, like that of a hooded man on a box, gives a different and in some instances more appalling view), would be in "bad taste" or too implicitly political? By "political," read: critical of the Bush administration's imperial project. For there can be no doubt that the photographs damage, as Rumsfeld testified, "the reputation of the honorable men and women of the armed forces who are courageously and responsibly and professionally defending our freedom across the globe." This damage—to our reputation, our image, our success as the lone superpower—is what the Bush administration principally deplores. How the protection of "our freedom"—the freedom of 5 percent of humanity—came to require having American soldiers "across the globe" is hardly debated by our elected officials.

22   Already the backlash has begun. Americans are being warned against indulging in an orgy of self-condemnation. The continuing publication of the pictures is being taken by many Americans as suggesting that we do not have the right to defend ourselves: After all, they (the terrorists) started it. They—Osama bin Laden? Saddam Hussein? what's the difference?—attacked us first. Senator James Inhofe of Oklahoma, a Republican member of the Senate Armed Services Committee, before which Secretary Rumsfeld testified, avowed that he was sure he was not the only member of the committee "more outraged by the outrage" over the photographs than by what the photographs show. "These prisoners," Senator Inhofe explained, "you know they're not there for traffic violations. If they're in Cellblock 1-A or 1-B, these prisoners, they're murderers, they're terrorists, they're insurgents. Many of them probably have American blood on their hands, and here we're so concerned about the treatment of those individuals." It's the fault of "the media" which are provoking, and will continue to provoke, further violence against Americans around the world. More Americans will die. Because of these photos.

23   There is an answer to this charge, of course. Americans are dying not because of the photographs but because of what the photographs reveal to be happening, happening with the complicity of a chain of command—so Maj. Gen. Antonio Taguba implied, and Pfc. Lynndie England said, and (among others) Senator Lindsey Graham of South Carolina, a Republican, suggested, after he saw the Pentagon's full range of images on May 12. "Some of it has an elaborate nature to it that makes me very suspicious of whether or not others were directing or encouraging," Senator Graham said. Senator Bill Nelson, a Florida Democrat, said that viewing an uncropped version of one photo showing a stack of naked men in a hallway—a version that revealed how many other soldiers were at the scene, some not even paying attention—contradicted the Pentagon's assertion that only rogue soldiers were involved. "Somewhere along the line," Senator Nelson said of the torturers, "they were

In this photograph, Specialist Charles Graner Jr., who identified men in another Abu Ghraib photo, poses over handcuffed detainees lying on the floor.

either told or winked at." An attorney for Specialist Charles Graner Jr., who is in the picture, has had his client identify the men in the uncropped version; according to the *Wall Street Journal,* Graner said that four of the men were military intelligence and one a civilian contractor working with military intelligence.

V.

But the distinction between photograph and reality—as between spin and policy—can easily evaporate. And that is what the administration wishes to happen. "There are a lot more photographs and videos that exist," Rumsfeld acknowledged in his testimony. "If these are released to the public, obviously, it's going to make matters worse." Worse for the administration and its programs, presumably, not for those who are the actual—and potential?—victims of torture. 24

The media may self-censor but, as Rumsfeld acknowledged, it's hard to censor soldiers overseas, who don't write letters home, as in the old days, that can be opened by military censors who ink out unacceptable lines. Today's soldiers instead function like tourists, as Rumsfeld put it, "running around with digital cameras and taking these unbelievable photographs and then passing them off, against the law, to the media, to our surprise." The administration's effort to withhold pictures is proceeding along several fronts. Currently, the argument is taking a legalistic turn: now the photographs are classified as evidence in future criminal cases, whose outcome may be prejudiced if they are made public. The Republican chairman of the Senate Armed Services Committee, John Warner of Virginia, after the May 12 slide show of image after image of sexual humiliation and violence against Iraqi prisoners, said he felt "very strongly" that the newer photos "should not be made public. I feel that it could 25 possibly endanger the men and women of the armed forces as they are serving and at great risk."

26   But the real push to limit the accessibility of the photographs will come from the continuing effort to protect the administration and cover up our misrule in Iraq—to identify "outrage" over the photographs with a campaign to undermine American military might and the purposes it currently serves. Just as it was regarded by many as an implicit criticism of the war to show on television photographs of American soldiers who have been killed in the course of the invasion and occupation of Iraq, it will increasingly be thought unpatriotic to disseminate the new photographs and further tarnish the image of America.

27   After all, we're at war. Endless war. And war is hell, more so than any of the people who got us into this rotten war seem to have expected. In our digital hall of mirrors, the pictures aren't going to go away. Yes, it seems that one picture is worth a thousand words. And even if our leaders choose not to look at them, there will be thousands more snapshots and videos. Unstoppable.

COMPREHENSION

1. Summarize Sontag's harsh condemnation of the Bush administration's prosecution of the Iraq war.
2. Sontag writes that the photographs coming out of Abu Ghraib "are us" (paragraph 7). What does she mean? Would you agree or disagree with the implications of her statement? Why?
3. Explain what Sontag finds to be uniquely powerful about photography as an art form.

RHETORIC

1. Sontag structures her essay around the dual subjects of photography and the American involvement in Iraq. Explain what her purpose is and how she links these two subjects.
2. What is Sontag's claim and in what place(s) does she state it? Where does she make logical, ethical, and emotional appeals? Are you persuaded by her argument? Why or why not?
3. Sontag includes six illustrations in the essay similar to the four we have included here. What is her objective? Does she mention additional photographs? How do the photographs enhance the message?
4. Sontag divides her essay into five numbered sections. How does each section serve to advance her argument?
5. How does Sontag's use of connotation and definition—of *torture, enemy combatants, the erotic life*, and so forth—serve her purpose?
6. What conclusions does Sontag draw "regarding the torture of others"?

WRITING

1. Sontag alludes to the popular radio commentator Rush Limbaugh. Find out more about this personality, and in an expository essay explain why Limbaugh would disagree with Sontag's argument.
2. **Writing an Argument:** Conduct your own research on Abu Ghraib, and then stake out an argumentative position on it. Develop logical, ethical, and emotional appeals to support your position.

NETWORKING
Applying 21st-Century Literacies

Using Visuals and Hyperlinks to Enhance a Definition Essay: Write your own extended definition of torture, linking it to a specific situation like Abu Ghraib. Add visuals and hyperlinks to support your definition.

The Boston Photographs

Nora Ephron

Nora Ephron (b. 1941) was born in New York City and grew up in Los Angeles, where her parents were involved in the film industry. She graduated from Wellesley College (BA, 1962) and began a career as a journalist, writing for the New York Post, *the* New York Times Magazine, Esquire, *and* New York *magazine. Her essays have been collected in* Wallflower at the Orgy *(1970),* Crazy Salad *(1975),* Scribble, Scribble: Notes on the Media *(1978), and* I Feel Bad about My Neck *(2006). Ephron has had a celebrated second career as a screenwriter and film director. Three of her screenplays—*Silkwood *(1983),* When Harry Met Sally *(1989), and* Sleepless in Seattle *(1993)—were nominated for Academy Awards. Among the films Ephron has directed are* You've Got Mail *(1998) and* Bewitched *(2006). In this essay, which appeared in* Esquire *in 1975 and subsequently in* Scribble Scribble, *Ephron analyzes public and editorial responses to the publication of three harrowing photographs in several American newspapers.*

"I made all kinds of pictures because I thought it would be a good rescue shot 1 over the ladder . . . never dreamed it would be anything else. . . . I kept having to move around because of the light set. The sky was bright and they were in deep shadow. I was making pictures with a motor drive and he, the fire fighter, was reaching up and, I don't know, everything started falling. I followed the girl down taking pictures . . . I made three or four frames. I realized

The Boston fire, July 22, 1975. Photograph by Stanley Forman.

what was going on and I completely turned around, because I didn't want to see her hit."

2   You probably saw the photographs. In most newspapers, there were three of them. The first showed some people on a fire escape—a fireman, a woman and a child. The fireman had a nice strong jaw and looked very brave. The woman was holding the child. Smoke was pouring from the building behind them. A rescue ladder was approaching, just a few feet away, and the fireman had one arm around the woman and one arm reaching out toward the ladder. The second picture showed the fire escape slipping off the building. The child had fallen on the escape and seemed about to slide off the edge. The woman was grasping desperately at the legs of the fireman, who had managed to grab the ladder. The third picture showed the woman and child in midair, falling to the ground. Their arms and legs were outstretched, horribly distended. A potted plant was falling too. The caption said that the woman, Diana Bryant, nineteen, died in the fall. The child landed on the woman's body and lived.

3   The pictures were taken by Stanley Forman, thirty, of the *Boston Herald American*. He used a motor-driven Nikon F set at 1/250, f 5.6–8. Because of the

motor, the camera can click off three frames a second. More than four hundred newspapers in the United States alone carried the photographs; the tear sheets from overseas are still coming in. The *New York Times* ran them on the first page of its second section; a paper in south Georgia gave them nineteen columns; the *Chicago Tribune,* the *Washington Post* and the *Washington Star* filled almost half their front pages, the *Star* under a somewhat redundant headline that read: SEN-SATIONAL PHOTOS OF RESCUE ATTEMPT THAT FAILED.

The photographs are indeed sensational. They are pictures of death in ac- 4 tion, of that split second when luck runs out, and it is impossible to look at them without feeling their extraordinary impact and remembering, in an almost subconscious way, the morbid fantasy of falling, falling off a building, falling to one's death. Beyond that, the pictures are classics, old-fashioned but perfect examples of photo-journalism at its most spectacular. They're throwbacks, really, fire pictures, 1930s tabloid shots; at the same time they're technically superb and thoroughly modern—the sequence could not have been taken at all until the development of the motor-driven camera some sixteen years ago.

Most newspaper editors anticipate some reader reaction to photographs 5 like Forman's; even so, the response around the country was enormous, and almost all of it was negative. I have read hundreds of the letters that were printed in letters-to-the-editor sections, and they repeat the same points. "Invading the privacy of death." "Cheap sensationalism." "I thought I was reading the *National Enquirer.*" "Assigning the agony of a human being in terror of imminent death to the status of a side-show act." "A tawdry way to sell newspapers." The *Seattle Times* received sixty letters and calls; its managing editor even got a couple of them at home. A reader wrote the *Philadelphia Inquirer: "Jaws* and *Towering Inferno* are playing downtown; don't take business away from people who pay good money to advertise in your own paper." Another reader wrote the *Chicago Sun-Times:* "I shall try to hide my disappointment that Miss Bryant wasn't wearing a skirt when she fell to her death. You could have had some award-winning photographs of her underpants as her skirt billowed over her head, you voyeurs." Several newspaper editors wrote columns defending the pictures: Thomas Keevil of the *Costa Mesa* (California) *Daily Pilot* printed a ballot for readers to vote on whether they would have printed the pictures; Marshall L. Stone of Maine's *Bangor Daily News,* which refused to print the famous assassination picture of the Vietcong prisoner in Saigon, claimed that the Boston pictures showed the dangers of fire escapes and raised questions about slumlords. (The burning building was a five-story brick apartment house on Marlborough Street in the Back Bay section of Boston.)

For the last five years, the *Washington Post* has employed various journal- 6 ists as ombudsmen, whose job is to monitor the paper on behalf of the public. The *Post's* current ombudsman is Charles Seib, former managing editor of the *Washington Star;* the day the Boston photographs appeared, the paper received over seventy calls in protest. As Seib later wrote in a column about the pictures, it was "the largest reaction to a published item that I have experienced in eight months as the *Post's* ombudsman. . . .

7   "In the *Post*'s newsroom, on the other hand, I found no doubts, no second thoughts . . . the question was not whether they should be printed but how they should be displayed. When I talked to editors . . . they used words like 'interesting' and 'riveting' and 'gripping' to describe them. The pictures told something about life in the ghetto, they said (although the neighborhood where the tragedy occurred is not a ghetto, I am told). They dramatized the need to check on the safety of fire escapes. They dramatically conveyed something that had happened, and that is the business we're in. They were news. . . .

8   "Was publication of that [third] picture a bow to the same taste for the morbidly sensational that makes gold mines of disaster movies? Most papers will not print the picture of a dead body except in the most unusual circumstances. Does the fact that the final picture was taken a millisecond before the young woman died make a difference? Most papers will not print a picture of a bare female breast. Is that a more inappropriate subject for display than the picture of a human being's last agonized instant of life?" Seib offered no answers to the questions he raised, but he went on to say that although as an editor he would probably have run the pictures, as a reader he was revolted by them.

9   In conclusion, Seib wrote: "Any editor who decided to print those pictures without giving at least a moment's thought to what purpose they served and what their effect was likely to be on the reader should ask another question: Have I become so preoccupied with manufacturing a product according to professional traditions and standards that I have forgotten about the consumer, the reader?"

10   It should be clear that the phone calls and letters and Seib's own reaction were occasioned by one factor alone: the death of the woman. Obviously, had she survived the fall, no one would have protested; the pictures would have had a completely different impact. Equally obviously, had the child died as well—or instead—Seib would undoubtedly have received ten times the phone calls he did. In each case, the pictures would have been exactly the same—only the captions, and thus the responses, would have been different.

11   But the questions Seib raises are worth discussing—though not exactly for the reasons he mentions. For it may be that the real lesson of the Boston photographs is not the danger that editors will be forgetful of reader reaction, but that they will continue to censor pictures of death precisely because of that reaction. The protests Seib fielded were really a variation on an old theme—and we saw plenty of it during the Nixon-Agnew years—the "Why doesn't the press print the good news?" argument. In this case, of course, the objections were all dressed up and cleverly disguised as righteous indignation about the privacy of death. This is a form of puritanism that is often justifiable; just as often it is merely puritanical.

12   Seib takes it for granted that the widespread though fairly recent newspaper policy against printing pictures of dead bodies is a sound one; I don't know that it makes any sense at all. I recognize that printing pictures of corpses raises all sorts of problems about taste and titillation and sensationalism; the fact is, however, that people die. Death happens to be one of life's main events. And it

is irresponsible—and more than that, inaccurate—for newspapers to fail to show it, or to show it only when an astonishing set of photos comes in over the Associated Press wire. Most papers covering fatal automobile accidents will print pictures of mangled cars. But the significance of fatal automobile accidents is not that a great deal of steel is twisted but that people die. Why not show it? That's what accidents are about. Throughout the Vietnam war, editors were reluctant to print atrocity pictures. Why *not* print them? That's what that war was about. Murder victims are almost never photographed; they are granted their privacy. But their relatives are relentlessly pictured on their way in and out of hospitals and morgues and funerals.

I'm not advocating that newspapers print these things in order to teach 13 their readers a lesson. The *Post* editors justified their printing of the Boston pictures with several arguments in that direction; every one of them is irrelevant. The pictures don't show anything about slum life; the incident could have happened anywhere, and it did. It is extremely unlikely that anyone who saw them rushed out and had his fire escape strengthened. And the pictures were not news—at least they were not national news. It is not news in Washington, or New York, or Los Angeles that a woman was killed in a Boston fire. The only newsworthy thing about the pictures is that they were taken. They deserve to be printed because they are great pictures, breathtaking pictures of something that happened. That they disturb readers is exactly as it should be: that's why photojournalism is often more powerful than written journalism.

COMPREHENSION

1. What does the photograph depict? If you did not have this photograph before you, would you be able to infer its content from Ephron's writing? Why or why not?
2. How does Ephron explain the public's response—and editorial reaction—to the publication of Forman's photographs?
3. Why and in what ways does Ephron defend the publication of the photographs? What is her overall position on photojournalism? How do you know?

RHETORIC

1. Why does Ephron begin her essay with an extended quotation from the photographer? Do you find this strategy to be acceptable and effective? Why or why not?
2. What is Ephron's claim? What support does she provide for her argument? How does she deal with opposing viewpoints?
3. How does Ephron weave causal analysis into the essay? Why is this strategy useful?
4. Examine the arrangement of details in this essay. What ordering principle does Ephron follow, and why?
5. What is the purpose of Ephron's concluding paragraph?

WRITING

1. Write your own response to the photograph included with Ephron's essay.
2. Write a cause-and-effect essay in which you analyze the reasons why the American public no longer seems to be shocked by even the most horrible or startling images from current events.

NETWORKING
Applying 21st-Century Literacies

Considering Ethics and the Use of Images: Compose an essay in which you argue for or against the need for ethical guidelines when reproducing images in newspapers and elsewhere on the Internet.

Saving the Life That Is Your Own: The Importance of Models in the Artist's Life

Alice Walker

Alice Walker (b. 1941) was born in Eatonton, Georgia, and now lives in San Francisco and Mendocino County, California. She attended Spelman College and graduated from Sarah Lawrence College. A celebrated and prolific novelist, short-story writer, poet, and essayist, she has also been active in the civil rights movement. Walker often draws on both her personal experience and historical records to reflect on the African American experience. Her books include The Color Purple *(1976), which won the American Book Award and the Pulitzer prize;* You Can't Keep a Good Woman Down *(1981);* Living in the World: Selected Essays, 1973–1987 *(1987);* The Temple of My Familiar *(1989);* By the Light of My Father's Smile *(1999);* The Way Forward Is with a Broken Heart *(2001) and* Devil's My Enemy *(2008). The following essay, from* In Search of Our Mothers' Gardens *(1983), offers a highly personalized and perceptive analysis of the importance of influence on both art and life.*

1 There is a letter Vincent van Gogh wrote to Emile Bernard that is very meaningful to me. A year before he wrote the letter, van Gogh had had a fight with his domineering friend Gauguin, left his company, and cut off, in desperation and anguish, his own ear. The letter was written in Saint-Remy, in the South of France, from a mental institution to which van Gogh had voluntarily committed himself.

I imagine van Gogh sitting at a rough desk too small for him, looking out at ₂
the lovely Southern light, and occasionally glancing critically next to him at his
own paintings of the landscape he loved so much. The date of the letter is December 1889. Van Gogh wrote:

> However hateful painting may be, and however cumbersome in the times we
> are living in, if anyone who has chosen this handicraft pursues it zealously, he
> is a man of duty, sound and faithful.
>
> Society makes our existence wretchedly difficult at times, hence our impo-
> tence and the imperfection of our work.
>
> . . . I myself am suffering under an absolute lack of models.
>
> But on the other hand, there are beautiful spots here. I have just done five
> size 30 canvasses, olive trees. And the reason I am staying on here is that my
> health is improving a great deal.
>
> What I am doing is hard, dry, but that is because I am trying to gather new
> strength by doing some rough work, and I'm afraid abstractions would make
> me soft.

Six months later, van Gogh—whose health was "improving a great deal"— ₃
committed suicide. He had sold one painting during his lifetime. Three times
was his work noticed in the press. But these are just details.

The real Vincent van Gogh is the man who has "just done five size 30 can- ₄
vasses, olive trees." To me, in context, one of the most moving and revealing
descriptions of how a real artist thinks. And the knowledge that when he spoke
of "suffering under an absolute lack of models" he spoke of that lack in terms of
both the intensity of his commitment and the quality and singularity of his
work, which was frequently ridiculed in his day.

The absence of models, in literature as in life, to say nothing of painting, is ₅
an occupational hazard for the artist, simply because models in art, in behavior, in growth of spirit and intellects—even if rejected—enrich and enlarge
one's view of existence. Deadlier still, to the artist who lacks models, is the
curse of ridicule, the bringing to bear on an artist's best work, especially his or
her most original, most strikingly deviant, only a fund of ignorance and the
presumption that, as an artist's critic, one's judgment is free of the restrictions
imposed by prejudice, and is well informed, indeed, about all the art in the
world that really matters.

What is always needed in the appreciation of art, or life, is the larger per- ₆
spective. Connections made, or at least attempted, where none existed before,
the straining to encompass in one's glance at the varied world the common
thread, the unifying theme through immense diversity, a fearlessness of
growth, of search, of looking, that enlarges the private and the public world.
And yet, in our particular society, it is the narrowed and narrowing view of life
that often wins.

Recently, I read at a college and was asked by one of the audience what I ₇
considered the major difference between the literature written by black and by
white Americans. I had not spent a lot of time considering this question, since it
is not the difference between them that interests me, but, rather, the way black

writers and white writers seem to me to be writing one immense story—the same story, for the most part—with different parts of this immense story coming from a multitude of different perspectives. Until this is generally recognized, literature will always be broken into bits, black and white, and there will always be questions, wanting neat answers, such as this.

8   Still, I answered that I thought, for the most part, white American writers tended to end their books and their characters' lives as if there were no better existence for which to struggle. The gloom of defeat is thick.

9   By comparison, black writers seem always involved in a moral and/or physical struggle, the result of which is expected to be some kind of larger freedom. Perhaps this is because our literary tradition is based on the slave narratives, where escape for the body and freedom for the soul went together, or perhaps this is because black people have never felt themselves guilty of global, cosmic sins.

10   This comparison does not hold up in every case, of course, and perhaps does not really hold up at all. I am not a gatherer of statistics, only a curious reader, and this has been my impression from reading many books by black and white writers.

11   There are, however, two books by American women that illustrate what I am talking about: *The Awakening,* by Kate Chopin, and *Their Eyes Were Watching God,* by Zora Neale Hurston.

12   The plight of Mme Pontellier is quite similar to that of Janie Crawford. Each woman is married to a dull, society-conscious husband and living in a dull, propriety-conscious community. Each woman desires a life of her own and a man who loves her and makes her feel alive. Each woman finds such a man.

13   Mme Pontellier, overcome by the strictures of society and the existence of her children (along with the cowardice of her lover), kills herself rather than defy the one and abandon the other. Janie Crawford, on the other hand, refuses to allow society to dictate behavior to her, enjoys the love of a much younger, freedom-loving man, and lives to tell others of her experience.

14   When I mentioned these two books to my audience, I was not surprised to learn that only one person, a young black poet in the first row, had ever heard of *Their Eyes Were Watching God* (*The Awakening* they had fortunately read in their "Women in Literature" class), primarily because it was written by a black woman, whose experience—in love and life—was apparently assumed to be unimportant to the students (and the teachers) of a predominantly white school.

15   Certainly, as a student, I was not directed toward this book, which would have urged me more toward freedom and experience than toward comfort and security, but was directed instead toward a plethora of books by mainly white male writers who thought most women worthless if they didn't enjoy bullfighting or hadn't volunteered for the trenches in World War I.

16   Loving both these books, knowing each to be indispensable to my own growth, my own life, I choose the model, the example, of Janie Crawford. And

yet this book, as necessary to me and to other women as air and water, is again out of print. But I have distilled as much as I could of its wisdom in this poem about its heroine, Janie Crawford:

> I love the way Janie Crawford
> left her husbands
> the one who wanted to change her
> into a mule
> and the other who tried to interest her
> in being a queen.
> A woman, unless she submits,
> is neither a mule
> nor a queen
> though like a mule she may suffer
> and like a queen pace the floor.

It has been said that someone asked Toni Morrison why she writes the kind 17 of books she writes, and that she replied: Because they are the kind of books I want to read.

This remains my favorite reply to that kind of question. As if anyone read- 18 ing the magnificent, mysterious *Sula* or the grim, poetic *The Bluest Eye* would require more of a reason for their existence than for the brooding, haunting *Wuthering Heights,* for example, or the melancholy, triumphant *Jane Eyre.* (I am not speaking here of the most famous short line of that book, "Reader, I married him," as the triumph, but, rather, of the triumph of Jane Eyre's control over her own sense of morality and her own stout will, which are but reflections of her creator's, Charlotte Brontë, who no doubt wished to write the sort of books *she* wished to read.)

Flannery O'Connor has written that more and more the serious novelist 19 will write, not what other people want, and certainly not what other people expect, but whatever interests her or him. And that the direction taken, there-fore, will be away from sociology, away from the "writing of explanation," of statistics, and further into mystery, into poetry, and into prophecy. I believe this is true, *fortunately true;* especially for "Third World Writers"; Morrison, Marquez, Ahmadi, Camara Laye make good examples. And not only do I be-lieve it is true for serious writers in general, but I believe, as firmly as did O'Connor, that this is our only hope—in a culture so in love with flash, with trendiness, with superficiality, as ours—of acquiring a sense of essence, of time-lessness, and of vision. Therefore, to write the books one wants to read is both to point in the direction of vision and, at the same time, to follow it.

When Toni Morrison said she writes the kind of books she wants to read, 20 she was acknowledging the fact that in a society in which "accepted literature" is so often sexist and racist and otherwise irrelevant or offensive to so many lives, she must do the work of two. She must be her own model as well as the artist attending, creating, learning from, realizing the model, which is to say, herself.

21   (It should be remembered that, as a black person, one cannot completely identify with a Jane Eyre, or with her creator, no matter how much one admires them. And certainly, if one allows history to impinge on one's reading pleasure, one must cringe at the thought of how Heathcliff, in the New World far from Wuthering Heights, amassed his Cathy-dazzling fortune.) I have often been asked why, in my own life and work, I have felt such a desperate need to know and assimilate the experiences of earlier black women writers, most of them unheard of by you and by me, until quite recently; why I felt a need to study them and to teach them.

22   I don't recall the exact moment I set out to explore the works of black women, mainly those in the past, and certainly, in the beginning, I had no desire to teach them. Teaching being for me, at that time, less rewarding than stargazing on a frigid night. My discovery of them—most of them out of print, abandoned, discredited, maligned, nearly lost—came about, as many things of value do, almost by accident. As it turned out—and this should not have surprised me—I found I was in need of something that only one of them could provide.

23   Mindful that throughout my four years at a prestigious black and then a prestigious white college I had heard not one word about early black women writers, one of my first tasks was simply to determine whether they had existed. After this, I could breathe easier, with more assurance about the profession I myself had chosen.

24   But the incident that started my search began several years ago: I sat down at my desk one day, in a room of my own, with key and lock, and began preparations for a story about voodoo, a subject that had always fascinated me. Many of the elements of this story I had gathered from a story my mother several times told me. She had gone, during the Depression, into town to apply for some government surplus food at the local commissary, and had been turned down, in a particularly humiliating way, by the white woman in charge.

25   My mother always told this story with a most curious expression on her face. She automatically raised her head higher than ever—it was always high— and there was a look of righteousness, a kind of holy *heat* coming from her eyes. She said she had lived to see this same white woman grow old and senile and so badly crippled she had to get about on *two* sticks.

26   To her, this was clearly the working of God, who, as in the old spiritual, ". . . may not come when you want him, but he's right on time!" To me, hearing the story for about the fiftieth time, something else was discernible: the possibilities of the story, for fiction.

27   What, I asked myself, would have happened if, after the crippled old lady died, it was discovered that someone, my mother perhaps (who would have been mortified at the thought, Christian that she is), had voodooed her?

28   Then, my thoughts sweeping me away into the world of hexes and conjurings of centuries past, I wondered how a larger story could be created out of my mother's story; one that would be true to the magnitude of her humiliation and grief, and to the white woman's lack of sensitivity and compassion.

My third quandary was: How could I find out all I needed to know in order ²⁹
to write a story that used *authentic* black witchcraft?

Which brings me back, almost, to the day I became really interested in black ³⁰
women writers. I say "almost" because one other thing, from my childhood,
made the choice of black magic a logical and irresistible one for my story. Aside
from my mother's several stories about root doctors she had heard of or known,
there was the story I had often heard about my "crazy" Walker aunt.

Many years ago, when my aunt was a meek and obedient girl growing up ³¹
in a strict, conventionally religious house in the rural South, she had suddenly
thrown off her meekness and had run away from home, escorted by a rogue of
a man permanently attached elsewhere.

When she was returned home by her father, she was declared quite mad. ³²
In the backwoods South at the turn of the century, "madness" of this sort was
cured not by psychiatry but by powders and by spells. (One can see Scott
Joplin's *Treemonisha* to understand the role voodoo played among black people
of that period.) My aunt's madness was treated by the community conjurer,
who promised, and delivered, the desired results. His treatment was a bag of
white powder, bought for fifty cents, and sprinkled on the ground around her
house, with some of it sewed, I believe, into the bodice of her nightgown.

So when I sat down to write my story about voodoo, my crazy Walker aunt ³³
was definitely on my mind.

But she had experienced her temporary craziness so long ago that her story ³⁴
had all the excitement of a might-have-been. I needed, instead of family memories, some hard facts about the *craft* of voodoo, as practiced by Southern blacks
in the nineteenth century. (It never once, fortunately, occurred to me that voodoo was not worthy of the interest I had in it, or was too ridiculous to study
seriously.)

I began reading all I could find on the subject of "The Negro and His Folk- ³⁵
ways and Superstitions." There were Botkin and Puckett and others, all white,
most racist. How was I to believe anything they wrote, since at least one of
them, Puckett, was capable of wondering, in his book, if "The Negro" had a
large enough brain?

Well, I thought, where are the *black* collectors of folklore? Where is the *black* ³⁶
anthropologist? Where is the *black* person who took the time to travel the back
roads of the South and collect the information I need: how to cure heat trouble,
treat dropsy, hex somebody to death, lock bowels, cause joints to swell, eyes to
fall out, and so on. Where was this black person?

And that is when I first saw, in a *footnote* to the white voices of authority, the ³⁷
name Zora Neale Hurston.

Folklorist, novelist, anthropologist, serious student of voodoo, also all- ³⁸
around black woman, with guts enough to take a slide rule and measure random black heads in Harlem; not to prove their inferiority, but to prove that
whatever their size, shape, or present condition of servitude, those heads contained all the intelligence anyone could use to get through this world.

39   Zora Hurston, who went to Barnard to learn how to study what she really wanted to learn: the ways of her own people, and what ancient rituals, customs, and beliefs had made them unique.

40   Zora, of the sandy-colored hair and the daredevil eyes, a girl who escaped poverty and parental neglect by hard work and a sharp eye for the main chance.

41   Zora, who left the South only to return to look at it again. Who went to root doctors from Florida to Louisiana and said, "Here I am. I want to learn your trade."

42   Zora, who had collected all the black folklore I could ever use.

43   *That Zora.*

44   And having found *that Zora* (like a golden key to a storehouse of varied treasure), I was hooked.

45   What I had discovered, of course, was a model. A model, who, as it happened, provided more than voodoo for my story, more than one of the greatest novels America had produced—though, being America, it did not realize this. She had provided, as if she knew someday I would come along wandering in the wilderness, a nearly complete record of her life. And though her life sprouted an occasional wart, I am eternally grateful for that life, warts and all.

46   It is not irrelevant, nor is it bragging (except perhaps to gloat a little on the happy relatedness of Zora, my mother and me), to mention here that the story I wrote, called "The Revenge of Hannah Kemhuff," based on my mother's experiences during the Depression, and on Zora Hurston's folklore collection of the 1920s, and on my own response to both out of a contemporary existence, was immediately published and was later selected, by a reputable collector of short stories, as one of the *Best Short Stories of 1974.*

47   I mention it because this story might never have been written, because the very bases of its structure, authentic black folklore, viewed from a black perspective, might have been lost.

48   Had it been lost, my mother's story would have had no historical underpinning, none I could trust, anyway. I would not have written the story, which I enjoyed writing as much as I've enjoyed writing anything in my life, had I not known that Zora had already done a thorough job of preparing the ground over which I was then moving.

49   In that story I gathered up the historical and psychological threads of the life my ancestors lived, and in the writing of it I felt joy and strength and my own continuity. I had that wonderful feeling writers get sometimes, not very often, of being *with* a great many people, ancient spirits, all very happy to see me consulting and acknowledging them, and eager to let me know, through the joy of their presence, that, indeed, I am not alone.

50   To take Toni Morrison's statement further, if that is possible, in my own work I write not only what I want to read—understanding fully and indelibly that if I don't do it no one else is so vitally interested, or capable of doing it to my satisfaction—I write all the things *I should have been able to read.* Consulting, as belatedly discovered models, those writers—most of whom, not surprisingly, are women—who understood that their experience as ordinary

human beings was also valuable, and in danger of being misrepresented, distorted, or lost:

> Zora Hurston—novelist, essayist, anthropologist, autobiographer;
>
> Jean Toomer—novelist, poet, philosopher, visionary, a man who cared what women felt;
>
> Colette—whose crinkly hair enhances her French, part-black face; novelist, playwright, dancer, essayist, newspaperwoman, lover of women, men, small dogs; fortunate not to have been born in America;
>
> Anaïs Nin—recorder of everything, no matter how minute;
>
> Tillie Olson—a writer of such generosity and honesty, she literally saves lives;
>
> Virginia Woolf—who has saved so many of us.

It is, in the end, the saving of lives that we writers are about. Whether we are "minority" writers or "majority." It is simply in our power to do this.   51

We do it because we care. We care that Vincent van Gogh mutilated his ear.   52
We care that behind a pile of manure in the yard he destroyed his life. We care that Scott Joplin's music *lives!* We care because we know this: *The life we save is our own.*

COMPREHENSION

1. Explain the significance of Walker's title. How does it serve her purpose and guide readers to her thesis? What is her thesis?
2. According to the author, what is the importance of models in art? What is the relationship of models to life? List the models in Walker's life. Which of them stand out?
3. Paraphrase Walker's remarks on the relationship between black American and white American writing.

RHETORIC

1. Walker uses many allusions in this essay. Identify as many as you can. What is the allusion in the title? Comment on the general effectiveness of her allusions.
2. Is the author's style and choice of diction suitable to her subject matter and to her audience? Why or why not?
3. Why does the author personalize her treatment of the topic? What does she gain? Is there anything lost?
4. Walker employs several unique structuring devices in this essay. Cite at least three, and analyze their utility.
5. Explain Walker's use of examples to reinforce her generalizations and to organize the essay.
6. Which paragraphs constitute Walker's conclusion? What is their effect?

WRITING

1. Write an essay expanding the meaning of Walker's remark "What is always needed in the appreciation of art, or life, is the larger perspective" (paragraph 6).
2. If you were planning on a career as a writer, artist, actor, or musician, who would your models be, and why?
3. **Writing an Argument:** Argue for or against Walker's proposition that the absence of models in art and life is an "occupational hazard" (paragraph 5).

NETWORKING
Applying 21st-Century Literacies

Keeping an "Importance of Models" Blog: Consider the importance of models in your life as a student (and as whatever else you are becoming or hope to become: a dancer, a basketball player, a social worker, a business executive, a nurse). Start and maintain a blog where you devote entries to individuals whom you've either studied from afar or studied with, who inform and influence your intellectual, artistic, athletic, professional, and/or personal growth. In each entry, describe this person and explain, with examples, what he or she has done or said that inspires you; record what you've learned and are continuing to learn from this person.

Synthesis: Connections for Critical Thinking

1. Write an essay comparing and contrasting literature and any other art form. What merits does each form have? Are there any limitations in either form? Which do you find more satisfying? Which form is more accessible? Use at least three essays in this chapter to illustrate or support your thesis.
2. Write an essay exploring the importance of role models in art and literature. Refer to the essays by Walker, Welty, and Gates to address the issue.
3. Analyze the illustrations that appear in the essays by Updike, Gates, Sontag, and Ephron. What is the purpose of these illustrations? What do the images contribute to the text?
4. Welty, Atwood, Alexie, Walker, and other writers in this chapter provide extended examples of art and artists. How do they develop these examples? What strategies do they use? Are their goals similar or not? Explain your response.
5. Use the essays by Welty, Updike, and Gates to explore the question of excellence in the arts. Answer this question: How do you know the work of art is good?
6. Examine the role of the artist in society and the artist's purpose in or duty to society. How would the writers in this chapter address this issue?

NETWORKING
Applying 21st-Century Literacies

1. Working as a group, discuss the two works by Orwell that appear in Atwood's essay. Go online to find out more about Orwell, and report your findings in group discussion.
2. After visiting several news Web sites, write an essay in which you explain the importance of photography and photojournalism. Connect your findings to the ideas presented by Ephron and Sontag in their essays.

CH 11   **www.mhhe.com/mhreader11e**

- *Image Gallery:* Chapter images in color
- *Literature and the Arts:* Information on the authors in this chapter
- *Ch. 11 Networking*

chapter *12*

Philosophy, Ethics, and Religion
What Do We Believe?

You do not have to be an academician in an ivory tower to think about religion and the destiny of humankind or about questions of right and wrong. All of us possess beliefs about human nature and conduct, about "rival conceptions of God" (to use C. S. Lewis's phrase), about standards of behavior and moral duty. In fact, as Robert Coles argues in an essay appearing in this chapter, even children make ethical choices every day and are attuned to the "moral currents and issues in the large society."

Most of us have a system of ethical and religious beliefs, a philosophy of sorts, although it may not be a fully logical and systematic philosophy, and we may not be conscious that it determines what we do in everyday life. This system of beliefs and values is transmitted to us by family members, friends, educators, religious figures, and representatives of social groups. Such a philosophical system is not unyielding or un-changing, because our typical conflicts and dilemmas often force us to test our ethical assumptions and our values. For example, you may believe in nonviolence, but what would you do if someone threatened physical harm to you or a loved one? Or you may oppose the death penalty but encounter an essay that causes you to reassess your posi-tion. Our beliefs about nonviolence, capital punishment, abortion, cheating, equality, and so on are often paradoxical and place us in a universe of ethical dilemmas.

Your ability to resolve such dilemmas and make complex ethical decisions depends on your storehouse of knowledge and experience and on how well formulated your philosophy or system of beliefs is. When you know what is truly important in your life, you can make choices and decisions carefully and responsibly. Growing up in a world with competing views on morality often makes these choices that much harder, for con-stellations of cultures, beliefs, and influences contribute to our own personal develop-ment. As Plato observes in his classic "The Allegory of the Cave," the idea of what is truly good and correct never appears without wisdom and effort.

In this context, religion is also intrinsically connected to our sense of morality and ethics. Our personal code of ethics often has a religious grounding. Our religion often determines the way in which we apply our ethics—for instance, it may determine our attitudes toward contraception, equality of the races or the sexes, and evolution. In all instances, competing religious and secular values may force us to make hard decisions about our positions on significant cultural issues. All authors in this chapter seek the es-sence of the values and ideas that we develop during our brief time on this planet and that lend meaning and vitality to our lives.

624

PREVIEWING THE CHAPTER

As you read the essays in this chapter and respond to them in discussion and writing, consider the following questions:

- On what ethical or religious problem or conflict does the author focus?
- Is the author's view of life optimistic or pessimistic? Why?
- Do you agree or disagree with the philosophical or religious perspective that the author adopts?
- Is there a clear solution to the issue the author investigates?
- Does the author present rational arguments or engage in emotional appeals and weak reasoning?
- Does the author approach ethical, theological, and philosophical issues in an objective or in a subjective way?
- How significant is the ethical or philosophical subject addressed by the author?
- What social, political, or racial issues are raised by the author?
- Are there religious dimensions to the essay? If so, how does religion reinforce the author's philosophical inquiry?
- How do these essays encourage you to examine your attitudes and values? In reading them, what do you discover about your system of beliefs and the beliefs of society at large?

Classic and Contemporary Images

DO WE BELIEVE IN GOOD AND EVIL?

Using a Critical Perspective   Comment on the composition of each of these works of art. How does each artist present the supernatural beings depicted? What do you notice about the organization of the images? From what angle does the artist approach the depiction? What do the artists have in common? Is the overall impression or effect of each illustration the same or different? Explain.

Angels, supernatural beings who serve as messengers from God, are found in the literature and imagery of Judaism, Christianity, and Islam from ancient times to the present, as in the Islamic painting from India shown here.

In more recent times, the sculptor Jacob Epstein (1880–1959) created a bronze statue of St. Michael for Coventry Cathedral in England. The ancient cathedral at Coventry was destroyed by German bombs in 1940. During the 1950s, a new cathedral was built near the ruins of the old one. With his spear in hand and his wings outstretched, St. Michael stands in triumph over the prone, chained figure of the devil.

Classic and Contemporary Essays
IS SUPERSTITION A FORM OF BELIEF?

Although most contemporary individuals who consider themselves "educated" deny any strong influence of superstition in their lives, both Margaret Mead and Letty Cottin Pogrebin suggest in their respective essays that neither contemporary ideas, with their reliance on science, nor higher education, with its focus on rational thinking, insulate us from at least a small amount of superstition in our lives. Mead discounts the notion that superstition is relegated to "primitive" societies or to the uneducated who have not been enlightened by a firm grounding in empiricism. The famed anthropologist suggests that we need superstition to provide coherence to our lives when other forms of belief and thought are not competent to satisfy us. In fact, in facing the unknown, we may turn to superstition as a welcome friend. How many of your fellow schoolmates, for example, will cross their fingers before an exam or keep a good-luck charm attached to their computer? Simply put, very few of us are so secure that we can rely on our own inner fortitude to ward off occasional fears or feelings of helplessness. Superstition, therefore, provides a framework to maintain a private sanctuary against the unknown. Pogrebin admits to being a "very rational person" who also "happen[s] to be superstitious." Although the particular rituals that inform her superstition were learned from her mother, who used them as a means of "imposing order," the function of superstition in her own life, Pogrebin claims, is to maintain coherence with the past: to feel the connection between herself and her mother. In other words, like Mead, Pogrebin contends that superstition helps us maintain a sense of security in an environment where we do not have complete control. By keeping the same rituals as her mother, Pogrebin senses her mother's protection. Does this mean that humans are flawed, weak creatures? If we consider the vicissitudes and uncertainties of modern life, perhaps the tendency of humans to have a bit of superstition in their worldview is a sign of intelligence.

New Superstitions for Old

Margaret Mead

Margaret Mead (1901–1979), famed American anthropologist, was curator of ethnology at the American Museum of Natural History and a professor at Columbia University. Her field expeditions to Samoa, New Guinea, and Bali in the 1920s and 1930s produced several major studies, notably Coming of Age in Samoa *(1928),* Growing Up in New Guinea *(1930), and* Sex and Temperament in Three Primitive Societies *(1935). In this essay, first published in* A Way of Seeing *(1970), Mead discusses the role that superstition plays in our daily life.*

Once in a while there is a day when everything seems to run smoothly and   1
even the riskiest venture comes out exactly right. You exclaim, "This is my
lucky day!" Then as an afterthought you say, "Knock on wood!" Of course, you
do not really believe that knocking on wood will ward off danger. Still, boasting
about your own good luck gives you a slightly uneasy feeling—and you carry
out the little protective ritual. If someone challenged you at that moment, you
would probably say, "Oh, that's nothing. Just an old superstition."

But when you come to think about it, what is superstition?   2

In the contemporary world most people treat old folk beliefs as superstitions—   3
the belief, for instance, that there are lucky and unlucky days or numbers, that
future events can be read from omens, that there are protective charms or that
what happens can be influenced by casting spells. We have excluded magic from
our current world view, for we know that natural events have natural causes.

In a religious context, where truths cannot be demonstrated, we accept   4
them as a matter of faith. Superstitions, however, belong to the category of beliefs, practices and ways of thinking that have been discarded because they are
inconsistent with scientific knowledge. It is easy to say that other people are
superstitious because they believe what we regard to be untrue. "Superstition"
used in that sense is a derogatory term for the beliefs of other people that we do
not share. But there is more to it than that. For superstitions lead a kind of half
life in a twilight world where, sometimes, we partly suspend our disbelief and
act as if magic worked.

Actually, almost every day, even in the most sophisticated home, some-   5
thing is likely to happen that evokes the memory of some old folk belief. The
salt spills. A knife falls to the floor. Your nose tickles. Then perhaps, with a
slightly embarrassed smile, the person who spilled the salt tosses a pinch over
his left shoulder. Or someone recites the old rhyme, "Knife falls, gentleman
calls." Or as you rub your nose you think, That means a letter. I wonder who's
writing? No one takes these small responses very seriously or gives them more
than a passing thought. Sometimes people will preface one of these ritual
acts—walking around instead of under a ladder or hastily closing an umbrella
that has been opened inside a house—with such remarks as "I remember my
great-aunt used to . . . " or "Germans used to say you ought not . . . " And then,
having placed the belief at some distance away in time or space, they carry out
the ritual.

Everyone also remembers a few of the observances of childhood—wishing   6
on the first star; looking at the new moon over the right shoulder; avoiding the
cracks in the sidewalk on the way to school while chanting, "Step on a crack,
break your mother's back"; wishing on white horses, on loads of hay, on covered bridges, on red cars; saying quickly, "Bread-and-butter" when a post or a
tree separated you from the friend you were walking with. The adult may not
actually recite the formula "Star light, star bright . . . " and may not quite turn to
look at the new moon, but his mood is tempered by a little of the old thrill that
came when the observance was still freighted with magic.

Superstition can also be used with another meaning. When I discuss the   7
religious beliefs of other peoples, especially primitive peoples, I am often asked,

"Do they really have a religion, or is it all just superstition?" The point of contrast here is not between a scientific and a magical view of the world but between the clear, theologically defensible religious beliefs of members of civilized societies and what we regard as the false and childish views of the heathen who "bow down to wood and stone." Within the civilized religions, however, where membership includes believers who are educated and urbane and others who are ignorant and simple, one always finds traditions and practices that the more sophisticated will dismiss offhand as "just superstition" but that guide the steps of those who live by older ways. Mostly these are very ancient beliefs, some handed on from one religion to another and carried from country to country around the world.

8   Very commonly, people associate superstition with the past, with very old ways of thinking that have been supplanted by modern knowledge. But new superstitions are continually coming into being and flourishing in our society. Listening to mothers in the park in the 1930s, one heard them say, "Now, don't you run out into the sun, or Polio will get you." In the 1940s elderly people explained to one another in tones of resignation, "It was the Virus that got him down." And every year the cosmetics industry offers us new magic—cures for baldness, lotions that will give every woman radiant skin, hair coloring that will restore to the middle-aged the charm and romance of youth—results that are promised if we will just follow the simple directions. Families and individuals also have their cherished, private superstitions. You must leave by the back door when you are going on a journey, or you must wear a green dress when you are taking an examination. It is a kind of joke, of course, but it makes you feel safe.

9   These old half-beliefs and new half-beliefs reflect the keenness of our wish to have something come true or to prevent something bad from happening. We do not always recognize new superstitions for what they are, and we still follow the old ones because someone's faith long ago matches our contemporary hopes and fears. In the past people "knew" that a black cat crossing one's path was a bad omen, and they turned back home. Today we are fearful of taking a journey and would give anything to turn back—and then we notice a black cat running across the road in front of us.

10   Child psychologists recognize the value of the toy a child holds in his hand at bedtime. It is different from his thumb, with which he can close himself in from the rest of the world, and it is different from the real world to which he is learning to relate himself. Psychologists call these toys—these furry animals and old, cozy baby blankets—"transitional objects"; that is, objects that help the child move back and forth between the exactions of everyday life and the world of wish and dream.

11   Superstitions have some of the qualities of these transitional objects. They help people pass between the areas of life where what happens has to be accepted without proof and the areas where sequences of events are explicable in terms of cause and effect, based on knowledge. Bacteria and viruses that cause sickness have been identified; the cause of symptoms can be diagnosed and a

rational course of treatment prescribed. Magical charms no longer are needed to treat the sick; modern medicine has brought the whole sequence of events into the secular world. But people often act as if this change had not taken place. Laymen still treat germs as if they were invisible, malign spirits, and physicians sometimes prescribe antibiotics as if they were magic substances.

Over time, more and more of life has become subject to the controls of   12
knowledge. However, this is never a one-way process. Scientific investigation is continually increasing our knowledge. But if we are to make good use of this knowledge, we must not only rid our minds of old, superseded beliefs and fragments of magical practice, but also recognize new superstitions for what they are. Both are generated by our wishes, our fears and our feeling of helplessness in difficult situations.

Civilized peoples are not alone in having grasped the idea of super-   13
stitions—beliefs and practices that are superseded but that still may evoke compliance. The idea is one that is familiar to every people, however primitive, that I have ever known. Every society has a core of transcendent beliefs—beliefs about the nature of the universe, the world and man—that no one doubts or questions. Every society also has a fund of knowledge related to practical life— about the succession of day and night and of the seasons; about correct ways of planting seeds so that they will germinate and grow; about the processes involved in making dyes or the steps necessary to remove the deadly poison from manioc roots so they become edible. Island peoples know how the winds shift and they know the star toward which they must point the prow of the canoe exactly so that as the sun rises they will see the first fringing palms on the shore toward which they are sailing.

This knowledge, based on repeated observations of reliable sequences,   14
leads to ideas and hypotheses of the kind that underlie scientific thinking. And gradually as scientific knowledge, once developed without conscious plan, has become a great self-corrective system and the foundation for rational planning and action, old magical beliefs and observances have had to be discarded.

But it takes time for new ways of thinking to take hold, and often the transi-   15
tion is only partial. Older, more direct beliefs live on in the hearts and minds of elderly people. And they are learned by children who, generation after generation, start out life as hopefully and fearfully as their forebears did. Taking their first steps away from home, children use the old rituals and invent new ones to protect themselves against the strangeness of the world into which they are venturing.

So whatever has been rejected as no longer true, as limited, provincial and   16
idolatrous, still leads a half life. People may say, "It's just a superstition," but they continue to invoke the ritual's protection or potency. In this transitional, twilight state such beliefs come to resemble dreaming. In the dream world a thing can be either good or bad; a cause can be an effect and an effect can be a cause. Do warts come from touching toads, or does touching a toad cure the wart? Is sneezing a good omen or a bad omen? You can have it either way—or

both ways at once. In the same sense, the half-acceptance and half-denial accorded superstitions give us the best of both worlds.

17   Superstitions are sometimes smiled at and sometimes frowned upon as observances characteristic of the old-fashioned, the unenlightened, children, peasants, servants, immigrants, foreigners or backwoods people. Nevertheless, they give all of us ways of moving back and forth among the different worlds in which we live—the sacred, the secular and the scientific. They allow us to keep a private world also, where, smiling a little, we can banish danger with a gesture and summon luck with a rhyme, make the sun shine in spite of storm clouds, force the stranger to do our bidding, keep an enemy at bay and straighten the paths of those we love.

COMPREHENSION

1. Explain in your own words the religious context for this essay.
2. What point is Mead making about superstition in modern life? Where does she state her main idea?
3. Where does Mead define *superstition?* How does it differ from folk beliefs?

RHETORIC

1. Explain what Mead means by "transitional objects" (paragraph 10). Why does she mention them?
2. Discuss the author's use of the pronouns *we* and *us* in the conclusion. Why does she state the conclusion in personal terms?
3. How does Mead use definition to differentiate *superstition* from *faith?* Explain the logic behind her distinction.
4. How does Mead use classification to describe the "worlds in which we live" (paragraph 17)? What are these worlds? What examples does she give of superstition in each of these worlds?
5. Look at paragraph 10. What is the purpose of this example? How does it figure in the context of Mead's essay?
6. Discuss the term *theologically defensible* as used in paragraph 7. Does Mead support this concept by example or evidence?

WRITING

1. Write an essay about beliefs you once held that you have since abandoned. Why did you abandon them? What was the practical result?
2. Select a saying or phrase based in superstition or folk belief that you or a friend are fond of. Analyze its appeal.
3. **Writing an Argument:** This article was published in 1966. Have we made any progress toward banishing superstition since then? Will we ever live in a culture free of superstition? Do we want to? Answer these questions in an argumentative essay.

NETWORKING
Applying 21st-Century Literacies

Reading a Podcast: From the Chapter 12 Networking page (at *www.mhhe.com/ mhreader11e*), link to a recent "60 Second Science" *Scientific American* podcast about superstition. First, compare and contrast the reading experiences of looking over the transcript of this program (shown on the screen) and listening to it. Then do some research of your own and craft a 60-second podcast response that questions or expands on "Superstitious Behavior Makes Evolutionary Sense." You don't actually have to record your podcast, but make sure it times out at exactly 60 seconds, too.

Superstitious Minds

Letty Cottin Pogrebin

Letty Cottin Pogrebin (b. 1939) is deeply committed to women's issues, family politics, and the nonsexist rearing and education of children. A native of New York, she graduated from Brandeis University and from 1971 to 1987 was the editor of Ms. *magazine, for which she remains a contributing editor. She has also contributed to such publications as the* New York Times *and the* Nation *and has written a number of books, including* Among Friends *(1986),* Debra Golda and Me: Being Female and Jewish in America *(1991), and* Getting Over Getting Older *(1996). Pogrebin lectures frequently and is a founder of the Women's Political Caucus as well as president of the Authors' Guild. She also contributes essays to the online* Huffington Post. *In the following essay, she reminisces about her fearful, superstitious mother, whom she understands much better since becoming a mother herself.*

I am a very rational person. I tend to trust reason more than feeling. But I also 1
happen to be superstitious—in my fashion. Black cats and rabbits' feet hold no power for me. My superstitions are my mother's superstitions, the amulets and incantations she learned from her mother and taught me.

I don't mean to suggest that I grew up in an occult atmosphere. On the con- 2
trary, my mother desperately wanted me to rise above her immigrant ways and become an educated American. She tried to hide her superstitions, but I came to know them all: Slap a girl's cheeks when she first gets her period. Never take a picture of a pregnant woman. Knock wood when speaking about your good fortune. Eat the ends of bread if you want to have a boy. Don't leave a bride alone on her wedding day.

3   When I was growing up, my mother often would tiptoe in after I seemed to be asleep and kiss my forehead three times, making odd noises that sounded like a cross between sucking and spitting. One night I opened my eyes and demanded an explanation. Embarrassed, she told me she was excising the "Evil Eye"—in case I had attracted its attention that day by being especially wonderful. She believed her kisses could suck out any envy or ill will that those less fortunate may have directed at her child.

4   By the time I was in my teens, I was almost on speaking terms with the Evil Eye, a jealous spirit that kept track of those who had "too much" happiness and zapped them with sickness and misery to even the score. To guard against his mischief, my mother practiced rituals of interference, evasion, deference, and above all, avoidance of situations where the Evil Eye might feel at home.

5   This is why I wasn't allowed to attend funerals. This is also why my mother hated to mend my clothes while I was wearing them. The only garment one should properly get sewn *into* is a shroud. To ensure that the Evil Eye did not confuse my pinafore with a burial outfit, my mother insisted that I chew a thread while she sewed, thus proving myself very much alive. Outwitting the Evil Eye also accounted for her closing the window shades above my bed whenever there was a full moon. The moon should only shine on cemeteries, you see; the living need protection from the spirits.

6   Because we were dealing with a deadly force, I also wasn't supposed to say any words associated with mortality. This was hard for a 12-year-old who punctuated every anecdote with the verb "to die," as in "You'll die when you hear this!" or "If I don't get home by ten, I'm dead." I managed to avoid using such expressions in the presence of my mother until the day my parents brought home a painting I hated and we were arguing about whether it should be displayed on our walls. Unthinking, I pressed my point with a melodramatic idiom: "That picture will hang over my dead body!" Without a word, my mother grabbed a knife and slashed the canvas to shreds.

7   I understand all this now. My mother emigrated in 1907 from a small Hungarian village. The oldest of seven children, she had to go out to work before she finished the eighth grade. Experience taught her that life was unpredictable and often incomprehensible. Just as an athlete keeps wearing the same T-shirt in every game to prolong a winning streak, my mother's superstitions gave her a means of imposing order on a chaotic system. Her desire to control the fates sprung from the same helplessness that makes the San Francisco 49ers' defensive more superstitious than its offensive team. Psychologists speculate this is because the defense has less control; they don't have the ball.

8   Women like my mother never had the ball. She died when I was 15, leaving me with deep regrets for what she might have been—and a growing understanding of who she was. *Superstitious* is one of the things she was. I wish I had a million sharp recollections of her, but when you don't expect someone to die, you don't store up enough memories. Ironically, her mystical practices are among the clearest impressions she left behind. In honor of this matrilineal

heritage—and to symbolize my mother's effort to control her life as I in my way try to find order in mine—I knock on wood and I do not let the moon shine on those I love. My children laugh at me, but they understand that these tiny rituals have helped keep my mother alive in my mind.

A year ago, I awoke in the night and realized that my son's window blinds 9 had been removed for repair. Smiling at my own compulsion, I got a bed sheet to tack up against the moonlight and I opened his bedroom door. What I saw brought tears to my eyes. There, hopelessly askew, was a blanket my son, then 18, had taped to his window like a curtain.

My mother never lived to know David, but he knew she would not want 10 the moon to shine upon him as he slept.

COMPREHENSION

1. What is the function of superstition in the writer's life? What purpose did it serve in her mother's life?
2. What was Pogrebin's reaction to her mother's behavior while she was growing up? How does the adult feel?
3. How does the writer use superstitions now as an adult? Has she passed on these beliefs to her children? Explain.

RHETORIC

1. Examine Pogrebin's first sentence. How does it prepare the reader for the content of the essay? How does its simplicity add to its force?
2. How do the accumulated examples in paragraph 2 illustrate the point of the paragraph?
3. What is the writer's tone? Justify your answer.
4. What is the point of paragraph 7? How does the comparison work to support Pogrebin's point?
5. What is the purpose of the essay? Where does it become apparent? How do the other paragraphs reinforce it?
6. Comment on the author's final sentence. What effect does it have on the reader? How does it help to hold the essay together?

WRITING

1. Write an essay in which you consider how your parents raised you—the values, opinions, and beliefs they instilled in you. Would you want to pass these on to your children? Why or why not?
2. **Writing an Argument:** Argue for or against the proposition that children need superstition—Santa Claus, the Tooth Fairy, and so forth—in their lives.

NETWORKING
Applying 21st-Century Literacies

Composing a Hyperlinked Essay: Write a hyperlinked essay about superstition. Consider the meaning of the word. What connection, if any, does it have with religion? How do superstitions affect the people who believe in them? Why do they believe? What is the role of superstition in your family? Provide examples of superstitions, and link to relevant sites for support and as possibilities for further exploration.

Synthesis: Classic and Contemporary Questions for Comparison

1. Mead presents her argument regarding the benefits of superstition through an anthropological analysis of the subject, whereas Pogrebin employs a more personal approach, focusing on the role of superstition in her own life. What are the merits of each approach? Do the two essays together contribute to a greater understanding of the nature of superstition than either one alone?
2. Both Mead and Pogrebin discuss the value of superstition in childhood. Why is childhood in particular a time in life when superstition can prove valuable? What is Mead's answer to this issue? How does it differ from Pogrebin's?
3. The tone of Mead's essay is objective, scientific, and critical. In addition, she never refers to personal experience, and we can assume she is writing from the perspective of someone who needs to maintain her professional status. Why would these factors influence her decision to contour her style so that she seems an observer of superstition rather than someone with superstitious leanings? On the other hand, why would Pogrebin choose to "personalize" her essay by referring to personal experience? Are these choices matters of style, audience, purpose, or a combination of these?
4. Mead seems more concerned with explicating her subject matter in academic terms. Note how she articulates the meaning of *folk beliefs, religion,* and *transitional objects*. How would you characterize the differences between an academically oriented argument such as Mead's and one intended for a more general audience such as Pogrebin's?

I Listen to My Parents and I Wonder What They Believe

Robert Coles

Robert Coles (b. 1929), author and psychologist, won the Pulitzer Prize in general nonfiction for volumes 1 and 2 of Children of Crisis, *in which he examines with compassion and intelligence the effects of the controversy over integration on children in the South. Walker Percy praised Coles because he "spends his time listening to people and trying to understand them." In its final form,* Children of Crisis *has five volumes, and Coles has widened its focus to include the children of the wealthy and the poor, the exploited and the exploiters. In collaboration with Jane Coles, he completed* Women in Crisis II *(1980). He has also written* The Secular Mind *(1999),* Lives of Moral Leadership *(2000), and* Bruce Springsteen's America *(2003). Below, Coles demonstrates his capacity to listen to and to understand children.*

Not so long ago children were looked upon in a sentimental fashion as "angels," 1 or as "innocents." Today, thanks to Freud and his followers, boys and girls are understood to have complicated inner lives; to feel love, hate, envy and rivalry in various and subtle mixtures; to be eager participants in the sexual and emotional politics of the home, neighborhood and school. Yet some of us parents still cling to the notion of childhood innocence in another way. We do not see that our children also make ethical decisions every day in their own lives, or realize how attuned they may be to moral currents and issues in the larger society.

In Appalachia I heard a girl of eight whose father owns coal fields (and gas 2 stations, a department store and much timberland) wonder about "life" one day: "I'll be walking to the school bus, and I'll ask myself why there's some who are poor and their daddies can't find a job, and there's some who are lucky like me. Last month there was an explosion in a mine my daddy owns, and everyone became upset. Two miners got killed. My daddy said it was their own fault, because they'll be working and they get careless. When my mother asked if there was anything wrong with the safety down in the mine, he told her no and she shouldn't ask questions like that. Then the Government people came and they said it was the owner's fault—Daddy's. But he has a lawyer and the lawyer is fighting the Government and the union. In school, kids ask me what I think, and I sure do feel sorry for the two miners and so does my mother—I know that. She told me it's just not a fair world and you have to remember that. Of course, there's no one who can be sure there won't be trouble; like my daddy says, the rain falls on the just and the unjust. My brother is only six and he asked Daddy awhile back who are the 'just' and the 'unjust,' and Daddy said there are people who work hard and they live good lives, and there are lazy people and they're always trying to sponge off others. But I guess you have to feel sorry for anyone who has a lot of trouble, because it's poured-down, heavy rain."

Listening, one begins to realize that an elementary-school child is no 3 stranger to moral reflection—and to ethical conflict. This girl was torn between her loyalty to her particular background, its values and assumptions, and to a larger affiliation—her membership in the nation, the world. As a human being whose parents were kind and decent to her, she was inclined to be thoughtful and sensitive with respect to others, no matter what their work or position in society. But her father was among other things a mineowner, and she had already learned to shape her concerns to suit that fact of life. The result: a moral oscillation of sorts, first toward nameless others all over the world and then toward her own family. As the girl put it later, when she was a year older: "You should try to have 'good thoughts' about everyone, the minister says, and our teacher says that too. But you should honor your father and mother most of all; that's why you should find out what they think and then sort of copy them. But sometimes you're not sure if you're on the right track."

4   *Sort of copy them.* There could be worse descriptions of how children acquire moral values. In fact, the girl understood how girls and boys all over the world "sort of" develop attitudes of what is right and wrong, ideas of who the just and the unjust are. And they also struggle hard and long, and not always with success, to find out where the "right track" starts and ends. Children need encouragement or assistance as they wage that struggle.

5   In home after home that I have visited, and in many classrooms, I have met children who not only are growing emotionally and intellectually but also are trying to make sense of the world morally. That is to say, they are asking themselves and others about issues of fair play, justice, liberty, equality. Those last words are abstractions, of course—the stuff of college term papers. And there are, one has to repeat, those in psychology and psychiatry who would deny elementary-school children access to that "higher level" of moral reflection. But any parent who has listened closely to his or her child knows that girls and boys are capable of wondering about matters of morality, and knows too that often it is their grown-up protectors (parents, relatives, teachers, neighbors) who are made uncomfortable by the so-called "innocent" nature of the questions children may ask or the statements they may make. Often enough the issue is not the moral capacity of children but the default of us parents who fail to respond to inquiries put to us by our daughters and sons—and fail to set moral standards for both ourselves and our children.

6   Do's and don't's are, of course, pressed upon many of our girls and boys. But a moral education is something more than a series of rules handed down, and in our time one cannot assume that every parent feels able—sure enough of her own or his own actual beliefs and values—to make even an initial explanatory and disciplinary effect toward a moral education. Furthermore, for many of us parents these days it is a child's emotional life that preoccupies us.

7   In 1963, when I was studying school desegregation in the South, I had extended conversations with Black and white elementary-school children caught up in a dramatic moment of historical change. For longer than I care to remember, I concentrated on possible psychiatric troubles, on how a given child was managing under circumstances of extreme stress, on how I could be of help—with "support," with reassurance, with a helpful psychological observation or interpretation. In many instances I was off the mark. These children weren't "patients"; they weren't even complaining. They were worried, all right, and often enough they had things to say that were substantive—that had to do not so much with troubled emotions as with questions of right and wrong in the real-life dramas taking place in their worlds.

8   Here is a nine-year-old white boy, the son of ardent segregationists, telling me about his sense of what desegregation meant to Louisiana in the 1960s: "They told us it wouldn't happen—never. My daddy said none of us white people would go into schools with the colored. But then it did happen, and

when I went to school the first day I didn't know what would go on. Would the school stay open or would it close up? We didn't know what to do; the teacher kept telling us that we should be good and obey the law, but my daddy said the law was wrong. Then my mother said she wanted me in school even if there were some colored kids there. She said if we all stayed home she'd be a 'nervous wreck.' So I went.

"After a while I saw that the colored weren't so bad. I saw that there are dif- 9 ferent kinds of colored people, just like with us whites. There was one of the colored who was nice, a boy who smiled, and he played real good. There was another one, a boy, who wouldn't talk with anyone. I don't know if it's right that we all be in the same school. Maybe it isn't right. My sister is starting school next year, and she says she doesn't care if there's 'mixing of the races.' She says they told her in Sunday school that everyone is a child of God, and then a kid asked if that goes for the colored too and the teacher said yes, she thought so. My daddy said that it's true, God made everyone—but that doesn't mean we all have to be living together under the same roof in the home or the school. But my mother said we'll never know what God wants of us but we have to try to read His mind, and that's why we pray. So when I say my prayers I ask God to tell me what's the right thing to do. In school I try to say hello to the colored, because they're kids, and you can't be mean or you'll be 'doing wrong,' like my grandmother says."

Children aren't usually long-winded in the moral discussions they have 10 with one another or with adults, and in quoting this boy I have pulled together comments he made to me in the course of several days. But everything he said was of interest to me. I was interested in the boy's changing racial attitudes. It was clear he was trying to find a coherent, sensible moral position too. It was also borne in on me that if one spends days, weeks in a given home, it is hard to escape a particular moral climate just as significant as the psychological one.

In many homes parents establish moral assumptions, mandates, priorities. 11 They teach children what to believe in, what not to believe in. They teach children what is permissible or not permissible—and why. They may summon up the Bible, the flag, history, novels, aphorisms, philosophical or political sayings, personal memories—all in an effort to teach children how to behave, what and whom to respect and for which reasons. Or they may neglect to do so, and in so doing teach their children *that*—a moral abdication, of sorts—and in this way fail their children. Children need and long for words of moral advice, instruction, warning, as much as they need words of affirmation or criticism from their parents about other matters. They must learn how to dress and what to wear, how to eat and what to eat; and they must also learn how to behave under X or Y or Z conditions, and why.

All the time, in 20 years of working with poor children and rich children, 12 Black children and white children, children from rural areas and urban areas and in every region of this country, I have heard questions—thoroughly intelligent and discerning questions—about social and historical matters, about personal behavior, and so on. But most striking is the fact that almost all those questions, in one way or another, are moral in nature: Why did the Pilgrims leave England? Why didn't they just stay and agree to do what the king wanted them to do? . . . Should you try to share all you've got or should you save a lot for yourself? . . . What do you do when you see others fighting—do you try to break up the fight, do you stand by and watch or do you leave as fast as you can? . . . Is it right that some people haven't got enough to eat? . . . I see other kids cheating and I wish I could copy the answers too; but I won't cheat, though sometimes I feel I'd like to and I get all mixed up. I go home and talk with my parents, and I ask them what should you do if you see kids cheating—pay no attention, or report the kids or do the same thing they are doing?

13   Those are examples of children's concerns—and surely millions of American parents have heard versions of them. Have the various "experts" on childhood stressed strongly enough the importance of such questions—and the importance of the hunger we all have, no matter what our age or background, to examine what we believe in, are willing to stand up for, and what we are determined to ask, likewise, of our children?

14   Children not only need our understanding of their complicated emotional lives; they also need a constant regard for the moral issues that come their way as soon as they are old enough to play with others and take part in the politics of the nursery, the back yard and the schoolroom. They need to be told what they must do and what they must not do. They need control over themselves and a sense of what others are entitled to from them—cooperation, thoughtfulness, an attentive ear and eye. They need discipline not only to tame their excesses of emotion but discipline also connected to stated and clarified moral values. They need, in other words, something to believe in that is larger than their own appetites and urges and, yes, bigger than their "psychological drives." They need a larger view of the world, a moral context, as it were—a faith that addresses itself to the meaning of this life we all live and, soon enough, let go of.

15   Yes, it is time for us parents to begin to look more closely at what ideas our children have about the world; and it would be well to do so before they become teenagers and young adults and begin to remind us, as often happens, of how little attention we did pay to their moral development. Perhaps a nine-year-old girl from a well-off suburban home in Texas put it better than anyone else I've met:

> I listen to my parents, and I wonder what they believe in more than anything else. I asked my mom and my daddy once: What's the thing that means most to you? They said they didn't know but I shouldn't worry my head too hard with questions like that. So I asked my best friend, and she said she wonders if there's a God and how do you know Him and what does He want you to do—I mean, when you're in school or out playing with your friends. They talk about God in church, but is it only in church that He's there and keeping an eye on you? I saw a kid steal in a store, and I know her father has a lot of money—because I hear my daddy talk. But stealing's wrong. My mother said she's a "sick girl," but it's still wrong what she did. Don't you think?

16   There was more—much more—in the course of the months I came to know that child and her parents and their neighbors. But those observations and

questions—a "mere child's"—reminded me unforgettably of the aching hunger for firm ethical principles that so many of us feel. Ought we not begin thinking about this need? Ought we not all be asking ourselves more intently what standards we live by—and how we can satisfy our children's hunger for moral values?

COMPREHENSION

1. How does Coles's title capture the substance of his essay? What is his thesis?
2. According to Coles, why do parents have difficulty explaining ethics to their children? On what aspects of their children's development do they tend to concentrate? Why?
3. There is an implied contrast between mothers' and fathers' attitudes toward morality in Coles's essay. Explain this contrast, and cite examples for your explanation.

RHETORIC

1. What point of view does Coles use here? How does that viewpoint affect the tone of the essay?
2. Compare Coles's sentence structure with the sentence structure of the children he quotes. How do they differ?
3. Does this essay present an inductive or a deductive argument? Give evidence for your answer.
4. How does paragraph 13 differ from paragraphs 3, 10, and 16? How do all four paragraphs contribute to the development of the essay?
5. Explain the line of reasoning in the first paragraph. Why does Coles allude to Freud? How is that allusion related to the final sentence of the paragraph?
6. What paragraphs constitute the conclusion of the essay? Why? How do they summarize Coles's argument?

WRITING

1. Write an essay describing conflict between your parents' ethical views and your own.
2. **Writing an Argument:** Coles asserts the need for clear ethical values. How have your parents provided such values? What kind of values will you give your children? Answer these questions in a brief argumentative essay.

NETWORKING
Applying 21st-Century Literacies

Conducting and Using Audio Interviews: Gather evidence, from conversations with friends and relatives, about an ethical issue such as poverty, world starvation, abortion, or capital punishment. With permission from all interviewees, record your conversations using your computer or another recording device. If your essay is an electronic/online document, include links to audio excerpts or even full interviews with some of your subjects.

Salvation

Langston Hughes

James Langston Hughes (1902–1967), poet, playwright, fiction writer, biographer, and essayist, was for more than 50 years one of the most productive and significant American authors. In The Weary Blues *(1926),* Simple Speaks His Mind *(1950),* The Ways of White Folks *(1940),* Selected Poems *(1959), and dozens of other books, he strove, in his own words, "to explain the Negro condition in America." This essay, from his 1940 autobiography* The Big Sea, *reflects the sharp, humorous, often bittersweet insights contained in Hughes's examination of human behavior.*

1   I was saved from sin when I was going on thirteen. But not really saved. It happened like this. There was a big revival at my Auntie Reed's church. Every night for weeks there had been much preaching, singing, praying, and shouting, and some very hardened sinners had been brought to Christ, and the membership of the church had grown by leaps and bounds. Then just before the revival ended, they held a special meeting for children, "to bring the young lambs to the fold." My aunt spoke of it for days ahead. That night I was escorted to the front row and placed on the mourners' bench with all the other young sinners, who had not yet been brought to Jesus.

2   My aunt told me that when you were saved you saw a light, and something happened to you inside! And Jesus came into your life! And God was with you from then on! She said you could see and hear and feel Jesus in your soul. I believed her. I had heard a great many old people say the same thing and it seemed to me they ought to know. So I sat there calmly in the hot, crowded church, waiting for Jesus to come to me.

3   The preacher preached a wonderful rhythmical sermon, all moans and shouts and lonely cries and dire pictures of hell, and then he sang a song about the ninety and nine safe in the fold, but one little lamb was left out in the cold. Then he said: "Won't you come? Won't you come to Jesus? Young lambs, won't you come?" And he held out his arms to all us young sinners there on the mourners' bench. And the little girls cried. And some of them jumped up and went to Jesus right away. But most of us just sat there.

4   A great many old people came and knelt around us and prayed, old women with jet-black faces and braided hair, old men with work-gnarled hands. And the church sang a song about the lower lights are burning, some poor sinners to be saved. And the whole building rocked with prayer and song.

5   Still I kept waiting to *see* Jesus.

6   Finally all the young people had gone to the altar and were saved, but one boy and me. He was a rounder's son named Westley. Westley and I were surrounded by sisters and deacons praying. It was very hot in the church, and

getting late now. Finally Westley said to me in a whisper: "God damn! I'm tired
o' sitting here. Let's get up and be saved." So he got up and was saved.

Then I was left all alone on the mourners' bench. My aunt came and knelt 7
at my knees and cried, while prayers and song swirled all around me in the
little church. The whole congregation prayed for me alone, in a mighty wail of
moans and voices. And I kept waiting serenely for Jesus, waiting, waiting—but
he didn't come. I wanted to see him, but nothing happened to me. Nothing! I
wanted something to happen to me, but nothing happened.

I heard the songs and the minister saying: "Why don't you come? My dear 8
child, why don't you come to Jesus? Jesus is waiting for you. He wants you.
Why don't you come? Sister Reed, what is this child's name?"

"Langston," my aunt sobbed.   9

"Langston, why don't you come? Why don't you come and be saved? Oh, 10
Lamb of God! Why don't you come?"

Now it was really getting late. I began to be ashamed of myself, holding every- 11
thing up so long. I began to wonder what God thought about Westley, who certainly
hadn't seen Jesus either, but who was now sitting proudly on the platform, swinging his knickerbockered legs and grinning down at me, surrounded by deacons and
old women on their knees praying. God had not struck Westley dead for taking his
name in vain or for lying in the temple. So I decided that maybe to save further
trouble, I'd better lie, too, and say that Jesus had come, and get up and be saved.

So I got up.   12

Suddenly the whole room broke into a sea of shouting, as they saw me rise. 13
Waves of rejoicing swept the place. Women leaped in the air. My aunt threw her
arms around me. The minister took me by the hand and led me to the platform.

When things quieted down, in a hushed silence, punctuated by a few ec- 14
static "Amens," all the new young lambs were blessed in the name of God.
Then joyous singing filled the room.

That night, for the last time in my life but one—for I was a big boy twelve 15
years old—I cried. I cried, in bed alone, and couldn't stop. I buried my head under the quilts, but my aunt heard me. She woke up and told my uncle I was crying because the Holy Ghost had come into my life, and because I had seen Jesus.
But I was really crying because I couldn't bear to tell her that I had lied, that I
had deceived everybody in the church, that I hadn't seen Jesus, and that now I
didn't believe there was a Jesus any more, since he didn't come to help me.

COMPREHENSION

1. What does the title tell you about the subject of this essay? How would you state, in
   your own words, the thesis that emerges from the title and the essay?
2. How does Hughes recount the revival meeting he attended? What is the dominant
   impression?
3. Explain Hughes's shifting attitude toward salvation in this essay. Why is he disap-
   pointed in the religious answers provided by his church? What does he say about
   salvation in the last paragraph?

RHETORIC

1. Key words and phrases in this essay relate to the religious experience. Locate five of these words and expressions, and explain their connotations.
2. Identify the level of language in the essay. How does Hughes employ language effectively?
3. Where is the thesis statement in the essay? Consider the following: the use of dialogue, the use of phrases familiar to you (idioms), and the sentence structure. Cite examples of these elements.
4. How much time elapses, and why is this important to the effect? How does the author achieve narrative coherence?
5. Locate details and examples in the essay that are especially vivid and interesting. Compare your list with what others have listed. What are the similarities? The differences?
6. What is the tone of the essay? What is the relationship between tone and point of view?

WRITING

1. Describe a time in your life when you suppressed your feelings about religion because you thought friends or adults would misunderstand.
2. Write a narrative account of the most intense religious experience in your life.
3. **Writing an Argument:** In an argumentative essay, explain why you think or do not think that politicians today often profess their religious beliefs simply to satisfy voters and not because of firmly held religious sentiments.

NETWORKING
Applying 21st-Century Literacies

Using Multiple Media as Support: Support your response to question 3 under Writing with citations from books and articles, but also with sources like TV news broadcasts, Webcasts, documentaries, photographs, maps, graphs, and/or podcasts. Incorporate sources from at least three different types of media—of which at least one of them is digital and one, print. Alternatively, respond to question 2 under Writing and incorporate, reference, or link to at least two different types of media to augment your narrative.

What's God Got to Do with It?

Karen Armstrong

Karen Armstrong (b. 1945), who was educated in an English convent and subsequently earned a doctorate from St. Anne's College, Oxford, is a renowned historian, public lecturer, and radio and television broadcaster. A former nun, Armstrong is the

author of more than a dozen books on religion, among them The Gospel according to
Woman *(1987),* A History of God *(1993), and* Muhammad: A Prophet for Our
Time *(2006). She also has written two autobiographies tracing her own spiritual jour-
ney:* Through the Narrow Gate *(1981) and* Beginning the World *(1983). Much of
Armstrong's work, as the next essay indicates, explores the world's religions from ethi-
cal and cross-cultural perspectives.*

The activity that we call religion is complex. Religious and non-religious people   1
alike often share the same misperceptions. Today in the West, it is often assumed that religion is all about the supernatural and that it is inseparable from
belief in an external, personalised deity. Critics claim that religion encourages
escapist fantasies that cannot be verified. The explosion of terrorism (which is
often given a religious justification) has convinced many people that religion is
incurably violent. I have lost count of the number of times a taxi driver has informed me that religion has been the cause of all the wars in history.

Yet we find something very different when we look back to the period that   2
the German philosopher Karl Jaspers called the "Axial Age" (c. 900 to 200 BCE)
because it proved to be pivotal to the spiritual development of humanity. In this
era, in four distinct regions of the world, the traditions that have continued to
nourish humanity either came into being or put down roots. Hinduism, Bud-
dhism and Jainism emerged in India; Confucianism and Taoism in China;
monotheism was born in Israel; and philosophical rationalism developed in
Greece. It was a period of astonishing creativity; we have never really succeeded in going beyond the insights of such sages as the Buddha, the mystics of
the Upanishads, Confucius, Lao-tzu, and the great Hebrew prophets. Rabbinic
Judaism, Christianity and Islam, for example, can be seen as a later flowering of
the religion that had developed in Israel during the Axial Age.

Despite interesting and revealing differences in emphasis, these traditions   3
all reached remarkably similar solutions. They can, perhaps, tell us something
important about the structure of our humanity. The God of Israel was an important symbol of transcendence, but in the other Axial faiths the gods were not
very important. Confucius discouraged speculation about spirits and the after-
life: How could you talk about other-worldly phenomena, when there was so
much that you did not understand about earthly matters?

During the Indian Axial Age, the ancient Vedic deities retreated from the   4
religious imagination. They were seen as unsatisfactory expressions of the sacred, and were either demoted to human status or seen as aspects of the psyche.
Many of the Axial sages were reaching beyond the gods to a more impersonal
transcendence—to Brahman, Nirvana or the Tao—that was also inseparable
from humanity. Yogins and Taoists did not believe that their ecstatic trances
represented an encounter with the supernatural, but regarded them as entirely
natural to humanity. Later, the more sophisticated theologians in all three of the
monotheistic religions would make similar claims about the experience of the
reality that they called God.

None of these sages was interested in dogma or metaphysics. A person's   5
theological opinions were a matter of total indifference to a teacher like the

Buddha. He insisted that nobody should ever take any religious teaching, from however august a source, on faith or at second hand. One of the Buddha's disciples pestered him continuously about metaphysics: Was there a God? Who created the world? He was so preoccupied with these matters that he neglected his yoga and ethical practice. The Buddha told him that he was like a man who had been shot with a poisoned arrow but refused to have any medical treatment until he discovered the name of his assailant and what village he came from: He would die before he got this perfectly useless information.

6   The Taoists were also wary of dogmatic conformity; they believed that the kind of certainty that many seek in religion was unrealistic and a sign of immaturity. Eventually, the Chinese preferred to synthesise the schools which had developed during their Axial Age, because no single tradition could have the monopoly of truth. In all four regions, when a sage started to insist upon strict orthodoxy, this was usually a sign that the Axial Age was drawing to a close.

7   The prophets of Israel were more like political commentators than theologians; they found the divine in analysis of current events rather than metaphysics. Jesus, as far as we know, spent no time discussing the trinity or original sin, which would later become so important to Christians; and the Koran dismisses theological dogmatism as *zannah,* self-indulgent guesswork that makes people stupidly quarrelsome and sectarian.

8   Religion was not about believing credal propositions, but about behaving in a way that changed you at a profound level. Human beings have always sought what the Greeks called *ekstasis,* a "stepping out" of the mundane, in moments when we feel deeply touched within and lifted momentarily beyond ourselves. The Axial sages all believed that if we stepped outside of our egotism and greed, we would transcend ourselves and achieve an enhanced humanity. Yoga, for instance, one of the great spiritual technologies of the Axial Age, was a formidable assault on the ego, designed to take the "I" out of the practitioner's thinking.

9 But the safest way to achieve this *ekstasis* was by the practice of compassion. Compassion—the ability to feel with another—was not simply the litmus test of any true religiosity, but the chief way of encountering the ineffable reality of Nirvana, Brahman, God and Tao. For the Buddha, compassion brought about *ceto-vimutti,* the "release of the mind" that was a synonym for the supreme enlightenment of Nirvana, a sacred realm of peace in the core of one's being.

10   All the Axial religions, in different ways, regarded what has been called the Golden Rule as the essence of religion: "Do not do to others what you would not like them to do to you." Confucius was the first to formulate this maxim. It was, he said, the thread that pulled all his teachings together and should be practised all day and every day. Five hundred years later, Rabbi Hillel was asked to sum up the whole of Jewish teaching while he stood on one leg. He replied: "That which is hateful to you, do not do to your neighbour. That is the Torah. The rest is commentary. Go and study it."

The Chinese sage Mo-tzu (c. 480–390) insisted that we had to have *jian ai,* 11
"concern for everybody." The priestly authors of Leviticus urged the Israel-
ites to love and honour the stranger; the Buddha taught layfolk and monks
alike a method of meditation called "the Immeasurables," in which they systematically extended benevolent thoughts to the four corners of the world.
Jesus told his disciples to love their enemies. This impartial sympathy would
break down the barricades of egotism, because it was offered with little hope
of any return.

If a ruler practised *jian ai,* Mo-tzu taught, war would be impossible. The 12
Axial religions all developed in regions that were convulsed by violence on an
unprecedented scale. Iron weaponry meant that warfare had become more
deadly; states had become more coercive; in the market place, merchants preyed
on each other aggressively. In every case, throughout the Axial Age, the catalyst
for religious change was always a disciplined revulsion towards this violence.

In the 9th century, the ritualists of India systematically extracted all the vio- 13
lence from the sacrificial ritual, and in seeking the cause of aggression in the
psyche, discovered the inner self. Renouncers, Buddhists and Jains all insisted
that *ahimsa,* "harmlessness," was an indispensable prerequisite to enlightenment. In the Tao Te Ching, Lao-tzu pointed out that violence could only elicit
more violence. The sage-ruler must always seek to bring a military campaign to
a speedy end: "Bring it to a conclusion, but do not intimidate." Some of the
gospels present Jesus as a man of *ahimsa* who taught his followers to turn the
other cheek.

Socrates, one of the greatest figures of the Axial Age, also condemned 14
retaliation as evil. In general, however, the Greeks did not eschew violence.
Ultimately, they did not have a religious Axial Age. Their great transformation was philosophical, scientific and mathematical, and pagan religion continued to flourish in Greece until it was forcibly replaced by Christianity in
the 5th century CE.

Compassion is an unpopular virtue. All too often, religious people have 15
preferred to be right rather than compassionate. They have shielded themselves
from the demands of empathy by making secondary and peripheral goals—
such as theological correctness or sexual orthodoxy—central to their faith. As
the Chinese sages pointed out, vehement professions of belief were essentially
egotistic, a pompous trumpeting of self, and, therefore, they impeded enlightenment. Denominational chauvinism, like nationalism, should also be seen as a
form of collective egotism or, in monotheistic terms, idolatry.

Nevertheless, in our torn, conflicted world, we need to revive the Axial 16
ethos. This does not require orthodox belief and need not involve the supernatural. In the Axial Age, individualism was beginning to supersede the older
tribal or communal expressions of identity. The sages were trying to moderate
the clash of competing egos and they were all concerned about the plight of
society. We are still rampant, chronic individualists, but our technology has created a global village, which is interconnected electronically, militarily, politically and economically. If we want to survive, it makes practical sense to

cultivate *jian ai*. We need to apply the Golden Rule politically, and learn that other nations, however remote from our own, are as important as ours.

COMPREHENSION

1. How does Armstrong answer the question posed by her title?
2. Identify the main religions mentioned by Armstrong. How are they alike and unlike? What idea or principle serves to unify them?
3. Armstrong writes of the Axial Age. Describe this period as she presents it. Why, according to Armstrong, is it important?

RHETORIC

1. What is Armstrong's claim? What is her persuasive purpose, and what techniques of argumentation does she employ to convince the reader? How convinced are you?
2. How do the first two paragraphs serve as an introduction to the essay?
3. Explain the writer's use of definition, classification and division, and comparison and contrast to organize her essay.
4. Does this essay reflect inductive or deductive reasoning? Justify your answer.
5. Why does the writer divide the essay into two sections? What relationships do you detect between the parts? What transitions does she use?
6. Armstrong's conclusion suggests a certain causality linking periods of history. How persuasive do you find her presentation of these historic interconnections, and how effective do you find the conclusion?

WRITING

1. Select a religion other than your own that Armstrong discusses, and write an explanatory essay in which you suggest ways in which this system of belief is relevant to some of today's most pressing global problems.
2. **Writing an Argument:** Answer the question posed by Armstrong in her title, relying on logical and ethical appeals.

NETWORKING
Applying 21st-Century Literacies

Using Your Library's Online Databases: Conduct research on the Axial Age using a subscription database, and write an extended definition of this period.

Our Mutual Joy: The Religious Case for Gay Marriage

Lisa Miller

Lisa Miller *is a senior writer and religion editor at* Newsweek. *She writes the magazine's Belief Watch column and also prepares longer articles on spirituality and belief. After graduating from Oberlin College (BA, 1984), Miller began her career at the* Harvard Business Review; *she also held positions at the* New Yorker *and the* Wall Street Journal *before joining* Newsweek *as the magazine's society editor in 2000. Miller's essay on gay marriage and Scripture, which appeared in* Newsweek's *December 15, 2008, issue, provoked thousands of responses, some supportive but others taking issue with her argument.*

Let's try for a minute to take the religious conservatives at their word and define 　1
marriage as the Bible does. Shall we look to Abraham, the great patriarch, who
slept with his servant when he discovered his beloved wife Sarah was infertile?
Or to Jacob, who fathered children with four different women (two sisters and
their servants)? Abraham, Jacob, David, Solomon and the kings of Judah and
Israel—all these fathers and heroes were polygamists. The New Testament
model of marriage is hardly better. Jesus himself was single and preached an
indifference to earthly attachments—especially family. The apostle Paul (also
single) regarded marriage as an act of last resort for those unable to contain their
animal lust. "It is better to marry than to burn with passion," says the apostle, in
one of the most lukewarm endorsements of a treasured institution ever uttered.
Would any contemporary heterosexual married couple—who likely woke up on
their wedding day harboring some optimistic and newfangled ideas about gender equality and romantic love—turn to the Bible as a how-to script?

　　Of course not, yet the religious opponents of gay marriage would have it 　2
be so.

　　The battle over gay marriage has been waged for more than a decade, but 　3
within the last six months—since California legalized gay marriage and then,
with a ballot initiative in November, amended its Constitution to prohibit it—the
debate has grown into a full-scale war, with religious-rhetoric slinging to match.
Not since 1860, when the country's pulpits were full of preachers pronouncing
on slavery, pro and con, has one of our basic social (and economic) institutions

been so subject to biblical scrutiny. But whereas in the Civil War the traditional-ists had their James Henley Thornwell—and the advocates for change, their Henry Ward Beecher—this time the sides are unevenly matched. All the reli-gious rhetoric, it seems, has been on the side of the gay-marriage opponents, who use Scripture as the foundation for their objections.

4   The argument goes something like this statement, which the Rev. Richard A. Hunter, a United Methodist minister, gave to the Atlanta *Journal-Constitution* in June: "The Bible and Jesus define marriage as between one man and one woman. The church cannot condone or bless same-sex marriages because this stands in opposition to Scripture and our tradition."

5   To which there are two obvious responses: First, while the Bible and Jesus say many important things about love and family, neither explicitly defines mar-riage as between one man and one woman. And second, as the examples above illustrate, no sensible modern person wants marriage—theirs or anyone else's—to look in its particulars anything like what the Bible describes. "Marriage" in America refers to two separate things, a religious institution and a civil one, though it is most often enacted as a messy conflation of the two. As a civil institu-tion, marriage offers practical benefits to both partners: contractual rights having to do with taxes; insurance; the care and custody of children; visitation rights; and inheritance. As a religious institution; marriage offers something else: a com-mitment of both partners before God to love, honor and cherish each other—in sickness and in health, for richer and poorer—in accordance with God's will. In a religious marriage, two people promise to take care of each other, profoundly,

the way they believe God cares for them. Biblical literalists will disagree, but the Bible is a living document, powerful for more than 2,000 years because its truths speak to us even as we change through history. In that light, Scripture gives us no good reason why gays and lesbians should not be (civilly and religiously) married—and a number of excellent reasons why they should.

In the Old Testament, the concept of family is fundamental, but examples of 6 what social conservatives would call "the traditional family" are scarcely to be found. Marriage was critical to the passing along of tradition and history, as well as to maintaining the Jews' precious and fragile monotheism. But as the Barnard University Bible scholar Alan Segal puts it, the arrangement was between "one man and as many women as he could pay for." Social conservatives point to Adam and Eve as evidence for their one man, one woman argument—in particular, this verse from Genesis: "Therefore shall a man leave his mother and father, and shall cleave unto his wife, and they shall be one flesh." But as Segal says, if you believe that the Bible was written by men and not handed down in its leather bindings by God, then that verse was written by people for whom polygamy was the way of the world. (The fact that homosexual couples cannot procreate has also been raised as a biblical objection, for didn't God say, "Be fruitful and multiply"? But the Bible authors could never have imagined the brave new world of international adoption and assisted reproductive technology—and besides, heterosexuals who are infertile or past the age of reproducing get married all the time.)

Ozzie and Harriet are nowhere in the New Testament either. The biblical 7 Jesus was—in spite of recent efforts of novelists to paint him otherwise—emphatically unmarried. He preached a radical kind of family, a caring community of believers, whose bond in God superseded all blood ties. Leave your families and follow me, Jesus says in the gospels. There will be no marriage in heaven, he says in Matthew. Jesus never mentions homosexuality, but he roundly condemns divorce (leaving a loophole in some cases for the husbands of unfaithful women).

The apostle Paul echoed the Christian Lord's lack of interest in matters of 8 the flesh. For him, celibacy was the Christian ideal, but family stability was the best alternative. Marry if you must, he told his audiences, but do not get divorced. "To the married I give this command (not I, but the Lord); a wife must not separate from her husband." It probably goes without saying that the phrase "gay marriage" does not appear in the Bible at all.

If the Bible doesn't give abundant examples of traditional marriage, then what 9 are the gay-marriage opponents really exercised about? Well, homosexuality, of course—specifically sex between men. Sex between women has never, even in biblical times, raised as much ire. In its entry on "Homosexual Practices," the Anchor Bible Dictionary notes that nowhere in the Bible do its authors refer to sex between women, "possibly because it did not result in true physical 'union' (by male entry)." The Bible does condemn gay male sex in a handful of passages. Twice Leviticus refers to sex between men as "an abomination" (King

James version), but these are throwaway lines in a peculiar text given over to codes for living in the ancient Jewish world, a text that devotes verse after verse to treatments for leprosy, cleanliness rituals for menstruating women and the correct way to sacrifice a goat—or a lamb or a turtle dove. Most of us no longer heed Leviticus on haircuts or blood sacrifices; our modern understanding of the world has surpassed its prescriptions. Why would we regard its condemnation of homosexuality with more seriousness than we regard its advice, which is far lengthier, on the best price to pay for a slave?

10   Paul was tough on homosexuality, though recently progressive scholars have argued that his condemnation of men who "were inflamed with lust for one another" (which he calls "a perversion") is really a critique of the worst kind of wickedness: self-delusion, violence, promiscuity and debauchery. In his book "The Arrogance of Nations," the scholar Neil Elliott argues that Paul is referring in this famous passage to the depravity of the Roman emperors, the craven habits of Nero and Caligula, a reference his audience would have grasped instantly. "Paul is not talking about what we call homosexuality at all," Elliott says. "He's talking about a certain group of people who have done everything in this list. We're not dealing with anything like gay love or gay marriage. We're talking about really, really violent people who meet their end and are judged by God." In any case, one might add, Paul argued more strenuously against divorce—and at least half of the Christians in America disregard that teaching.

11   Religious objections to gay marriage are rooted not in the Bible at all, then, but in custom and tradition (and, to talk turkey for a minute, a personal discomfort with gay sex that transcends theological argument). Common

prayers and rituals reflect our common practice: The Episcopal Book of Common Prayer describes the participants in a marriage as "the man and the woman." But common practice changes—and for the better; as the Rev. Martin Luther King Jr. said, "The arc of history is long, but it bends toward justice." The Bible endorses slavery, a practice that Americans now universally consider shameful and barbaric. It recommends the death penalty for adulterers (and in Leviticus, for men who have sex with men, for that matter). It provides conceptual shelter for anti-Semites. A mature view of scriptural authority requires us, as we have in the past, to move beyond literalism. The Bible was written for a world so unlike our own, it's impossible to apply its rules, at face value, to ours.

Marriage, specifically, has evolved so as to be unrecognizable to the wives 12 of Abraham and Jacob. Monogamy became the norm in the Christian world in the sixth century; husbands' frequent enjoyment of mistresses and prostitutes became taboo by the beginning of the 20th. (In the *Newsweek* Poll, 55 percent of respondents said that married heterosexuals who have sex with someone other than their spouses are more morally objectionable than a gay couple in a committed sexual relationship.) By the mid-19th century, U.S. courts were siding with wives who were the victims of domestic violence, and by the 1970s most states had gotten rid of their "head and master" laws, which gave husbands the right to decide where a family would live and whether a wife would be able to take a job. Today's vision of marriage as a union of equal partners, joined in a relationship both romantic and pragmatic, is, by very recent standards, radical, says Stephanie Coontz, author of "Marriage, a History."

Religious wedding ceremonies have already changed to reflect new concep- 13 tions of marriage. Remember when we used to say "man and wife" instead of "husband and wife"? Remember when we stopped using the word "obey"? Even Miss Manners, the voice of tradition and reason, approved in 1997 of that change. "It seems," she wrote, "that dropping 'obey' was a sensible editing of a service that made assumptions about marriage that the society no longer holds."

We cannot look to the Bible as a marriage manual, but we can read it for 14 universal truths as we struggle toward a more just future. The Bible offers inspiration and warning on the subjects of love, marriage, family and community. It speaks eloquently of the crucial role of families in a fair society and the risks we incur to ourselves and our children should we cease trying to bind ourselves together in loving pairs. Gay men like to point to the story of passionate King David and his friend Jonathan, with whom he was "one spirit" and whom he "loved as he loved himself." Conservatives say this is a story about a platonic friendship, but it is also a story about two men who stand up for each other in turbulent times, through violent war and the disapproval of a powerful parent. David rends his clothes at Jonathan's death and, in grieving, writes a song:

> I grieve for you, Jonathan my brother;
> You were very dear to me.
> Your love for me was wonderful,
> More wonderful than that of women.

15   Here, the Bible praises enduring love between men. What Jonathan and David did or did not do in privacy is perhaps best left to history and our own imaginations.

16   In addition to its praise of friendship and its condemnation of divorce, the Bible gives many examples of marriages that defy convention yet benefit the greater community. The Torah discouraged the ancient Hebrews from marrying outside the tribe, yet Moses himself is married to a foreigner, Zipporah. Queen Esther is married to a non-Jew and, according to legend, saves the Jewish people. Rabbi Arthur Waskow, of the Shalom Center in Philadelphia, believes that Judaism thrives through diversity and inclusion. "I don't think Judaism should or ought to want to leave any portion of the human population outside the religious process," he says. "We should not want to leave [homosexuals] outside the sacred tent." The marriage of Joseph and Mary is also unorthodox (to say the least), a case of an unconventional arrangement accepted by society for the common good. The boy needed two human parents, after all.

17   In the Christian story, the message of acceptance for all is codified. Jesus reaches out to everyone, especially those on the margins, and brings the whole Christian community into his embrace. The Rev. James Martin, a Jesuit priest and author, cites the story of Jesus revealing himself to the woman at the well— no matter that she had five former husbands and a current boyfriend—as evidence of Christ's all-encompassing love. The great Bible scholar Walter Brueggemann, emeritus professor at Columbia Theological Seminary, quotes the apostle Paul when he looks for biblical support of gay marriage: "There is neither Greek nor Jew, slave nor free, male nor female, for you are all one in Jesus Christ." The religious argument for gay marriage, he adds, "is not generally made with reference to particular texts, but with the general conviction that the Bible is bent toward inclusiveness."

18   The practice of inclusion, even in defiance of social convention, the reaching out to outcasts, the emphasis on togetherness and community over and against chaos, depravity, indifference—all these biblical values argue for gay marriage. If one is for racial equality and the common nature of humanity, then the values of stability, monogamy and family necessarily follow. Terry Davis is the pastor of First Presbyterian Church in Hartford, Conn., and has been presiding over "holy unions" since 1992. "I'm against promiscuity—love ought to be expressed in committed relationships, not through casual sex, and I think the church should recognize the validity of committed same-sex relationships," he says.

19   Still, very few Jewish or Christian denominations do officially endorse gay marriage, even in the states where it is legal. The practice varies by region, by church or synagogue, even by cleric. More progressive denominations—the United Church of Christ, for example—have agreed to support gay marriage. Other denominations and dioceses will do "holy union" or "blessing" ceremonies, but shy away from the word "marriage" because it is politically explosive. So the frustrating, semantic question remains: Should gay people be married in the same, sacramental sense that straight people are? I would argue that they should. If we are all God's children, made in his likeness and image, then to deny

access to any sacrament based on sexuality is exactly the same thing as denying it based on skin color—and no serious (or even semiserious) person would argue that. People get married "for their mutual joy," explains the Rev. Chloe Breyer, executive director of the Interfaith Center in New York, quoting the Episcopal marriage ceremony. That's what religious people do: care for each other in spite of difficulty, she adds. In marriage, couples grow closer to God: "Being with one another in community is how you love God. That's what marriage is about."

More basic than theology, though, is human need. We want, as Abraham 20 did, to grow old surrounded by friends and family and to be buried at last peacefully among them. We want, as Jesus taught, to love one another for our own good—and, not to be too grandiose about it, for the good of the world. We want our children to grow up in stable homes. What happens in the bedroom, really, has nothing to do with any of this. My friend the priest James Martin says his favorite Scripture relating to the question of homosexuality is Psalm 139, a song that praises the beauty and imperfection in all of us and that glorifies God's knowledge of our most secret selves: "I praise you because I am fearfully and wonderfully made." And then he adds that in his heart he believes that if Jesus were alive today, he would reach out especially to the gays and lesbians among us, for "Jesus does not want people to be lonely and sad." Let the priest's prayer be our own.

COMPREHENSION

1. What is important about the main title of Miller's essay, "Our Mutual Joy"? According to Miller, what does the Bible say about the traditional family, heterosexual love, and gay marriage?
2. What does Miller mean when she writes, "Ozzie and Harriet are nowhere in the New Testament . . ." (paragraph 7)?
3. What is Miller's purpose in relating the story of King David and his friend Jonathan? What other biblical tales does she recount, and why?

RHETORIC

1. How would you describe Miller's voice in paragraph 1? Does she sustain this voice and tone throughout the essay? Is her writing style subjective or objective? Justify your response.
2. What is Miller's claim, and where does she state it most clearly? What constitutes her primary and secondary support? What types of evidence does she present? How does she contend with opposing viewpoints?
3. What connections do you perceive among the three major parts of this essay? How do the beginning and ending paragraphs relate to each other? How does Miller's organizational strategy support the essay's content?
4. In what way might this essay be considered an extended comparative analysis? What is being compared or contrasted, and how is the comparison structured?
5. Miller is fond of recurring motifs. Identify some of these motifs, and explain how these repeated references help to support her claim.

WRITING

1. Write an essay in which you elaborate on Miller's statement, "Religious wedding ceremonies have already changed to reflect new conceptions of marriage."
2. Write a comparative essay explaining the two diverging ways in which the Bible— or another religious text with which you are familiar—can be used to support or reject gay marriage.
3. **Writing an Argument:** Using your own religious background as a foundation, argue for or against gay marriage.

NETWORKING
Applying 21st-Century Literacies

1. **Exploring Extra Features of an Online Article**: Through the Chapter 12 Networking page at *www.mhhe.com/mhreader11e*, visit *xtra.Newsweek.com* to read about the future of the gay rights movement and watch the magazine's video series on political/ideological divisions among lesbians of various ages and gay men. Write a synthesis of the videos and articles, including Miller's, discussing any larger conclusions they suggest, tensions they reveal, and further questions they raise.
2. **Using Visuals as Appeals:** How do the photographs support Miller's position? What type of appeal do they make, how effective are they in doing so, and why?

The Allegory of the Cave

Plato

Plato (427–347 BCE), pupil and friend of Socrates, was one of the greatest philosophers of the ancient world. Plato's surviving works are all dialogues and epistles, many of the dialogues purporting to be conversations of Socrates and his disciples. Two key aspects of his philosophy are the dialectical method—represented by the questioning and probing of the particular event to reveal the general truth—and the existence of Forms. Plato's best-known works include the Phaedo, Symposium, Phaedrus, *and* Timaeus. *The following selection, from the* Republic, *is an early description of the nature of Forms.*

1 And now, I said, let me show in a figure how far our nature is enlightened or unenlightened: Behold! human beings living in an underground den, which has a mouth open towards the light and reaching all along the den; here they have been from their childhood, and have their legs and necks chained so that they

cannot move, and can only see before them, being prevented by the chains from turning round their heads. Above and behind them a fire is blazing at a distance, and between the fire and the prisoners there is a raised way; and you will see, if you look, a low wall built along the way, like the screen which marionette players have in front of them, over which they show the puppets.

I see.   2

And do you see, I said, men passing along the wall carrying all sorts of ves-   3
sels, and statues and figures of animals made of wood and stone and various materials, which appear over the wall? Some of them are talking, others silent.

You have shown me a strange image, and they are strange prisoners.   4

Like ourselves, I replied; and they see only their own shadows, or the shad-   5
ows of one another, which the fire throws on the opposite wall of the cave?

True, he said; how could they see anything but the shadows if they were   6
never allowed to move their heads?

And of the objects which are being carried in like manner they would only   7
see the shadows?

Yes, he said.   8

And if they were able to converse with one another, would they not sup-   9
pose that they were naming what was actually before them?

Very true.   10

And suppose further that the prison had an echo which came from the   11
other side, would they not be sure to fancy when one of the passersby spoke that the voice which they heard came from the passing shadow?

No question, he replied.   12

To them, I said, the truth would be literally nothing but the shadows of the   13
images.

That is certain.   14

And now look again, and see what will naturally follow if the prisoners are   15
released and disabused of their error. At first, when any of them is liberated and compelled suddenly to stand up and turn his neck round and walk and look towards the light, he will suffer sharp pains; the glare will distress him and he will be unable to see the realities of which in his former state he had seen the shadows; and then conceive some one saying to him, that what he saw before was an illusion, but that now, when he is approaching nearer to being and his eye is turned towards more real existence, he has a clearer vision—what will be his reply? And you may further imagine that his instructor is pointing to the objects as they pass and requiring him to name them—will he not be perplexed? Will he not fancy that the shadows which he formerly saw are truer than the objects which are now shown to him?

Far truer.   16

And if he is compelled to look straight at the light, will he not have a pain   17
in his eyes which will make him turn away to take refuge in the objects of vision which he can see, and which he will conceive to be in reality clearer than the things which are now being shown to him?

True, he said.   18

19 And suppose once more, that he is reluctantly dragged up a steep and rugged ascent, and held fast until he is forced into the presence of the sun himself, is he not likely to be pained and irritated? When he approaches the light his eyes will be dazzled and he will not be able to see anything at all of what are now called realities.

20 Not all in a moment, he said.

21 He will require to grow accustomed to the sight of the upper world. And first he will see the shadows best, next the reflections of men and other objects in the water, and then the objects themselves; then he will gaze upon the light of the moon and the stars and the spangled heaven; and he will see the sky and the stars by night better than the sun or the light of the sun by day?

22 Certainly.

23 Last of all he will be able to see the sun, and not mere reflections of him in the water, but he will see him in his own proper place, and not in another; and he will contemplate him as he is.

24 Certainly.

25 He will then proceed to argue that this is he who gives the season and the years, and is the guardian of all that is in the visible world, and in a certain way the cause of all things which he and his fellows have been accustomed to behold?

26 Clearly, he said, he would first see the sun and then reason about him.

27 And when he remembered his old habitation, and the wisdom of the den and his fellow-prisoners, do you not suppose that he would felicitate himself on the change, and pity them?

28 Certainly, he would.

29 And if they were in the habit of conferring honors among themselves on those who were quickest to observe the passing shadows and to remark which of them went before, and which followed after, and which were together; and who were therefore best able to draw conclusions as to the future, do you think that he would care for such honors and glories, or envy the possessors of them? Would he not say with Homer, Better to be the poor servant of a poor master, and to endure anything, rather than think as they do and live after their manner?

30 Yes, he said, I think that he would rather suffer anything than entertain these false notions and live in this miserable manner.

31 Imagine once more, I said, such an one coming suddenly out of the sun to be replaced in his old situation; would he not be certain to have his eyes full of darkness?

32 To be sure, he said.

33 And if there were a contest, and he had to compete in measuring the shadows with the prisoners who had never moved out of the den, while his sight was still weak, and before his eyes had become steady (and the time which would be needed to acquire this new habit of sight might be very considerable) would he not be ridiculous? Men would say of him that up he went and down he came without his eyes; and that it was better not even to think of ascending;

and if any one tried to loose another and lead him up to the light, let them only catch the offender, and they would put him to death.

No question, he said.   34

This entire allegory, I said, you may now append, dear Glaucon, to the previ- 35 ous argument; the prison-house is the world of sight, the light of fire is the sun, and you will not misapprehend me if you interpret the journey upwards to be the ascent of the soul into the intellectual world according to my poor belief, which, at your desire, I have expressed—whether rightly or wrongly God knows. But, whether true or false, my opinion is that in the world of knowledge the idea of good appears last of all, and is seen only with an effort; and, when seen, is also inferred to be the universal author of all things beautiful and right, parent of light and of the lord of light in this visible world, and the immediate source of reason and truth in the intellectual; and that this is the power upon which he who would act rationally either in public or private life must have his eye fixed.

I agree, he said, as far as I am able to understand you.   36

Moreover, I said, you must not wonder that those who attain to this beauti- 37 ful vision are unwilling to descend to human affairs; for their souls are ever hastening into the upper world where they desire to dwell; which desire of theirs is very natural, if our allegory may be trusted.

Yes, very natural.   38

And is there anything surprising in one who passes from divine contempla- 39 tions to the evil state of man, misbehaving himself in a ridiculous manner; if, while his eyes are blinking and before he has become accustomed to the surrounding darkness, he is compelled to fight in courts of law, or in other places, about the images or the shadows of images of justice, and is endeavoring to meet the conceptions of those who have never yet seen absolute justice?

Anything but surprising, he replied.   40

Any one who has common sense will remember that the bewilderments of the 41 eyes are of two kinds, and arise from two causes, either from coming out of the light or from going into the light, which is true of the mind's eye, quite as much as of the bodily eye; and he who remembers this when he sees any one whose vision is perplexed and weak, will not be too ready to laugh; he will first ask whether that soul of man has come out of the brighter light, and is unable to see because unaccustomed to the dark, or having turned from darkness to the day is dazzled by excess of light. And he will count the one happy in his condition and state of being, and he will pity the other; or, if he have a mind to laugh at the soul which comes from below into the light, there will be more reason in this than in the laugh which greets him who returns from above out of the light into the den.

That, he said, is a very just distinction.   42

COMPREHENSION

1. What does Plato hope to convey to readers of his allegory?
2. According to Plato, do human beings typically perceive reality? To what does he compare the world?

3. According to Plato, what often happens to people who develop a true idea of reality? How well do they compete with others? Who is usually considered superior? Why?

RHETORIC

1. Is the conversation portrayed here realistic? How effective is this conversational style at conveying information?
2. How do you interpret such details of this allegory as the chains, the cave, and the fire? What connotations do such symbols have?
3. How does Plato use conversation to develop his argument? What is Glaucon's role in the conversation?
4. Note examples of transition words that mark contrasts between the real and the shadow world. How does Plato use contrast to develop his idea of the true real world?
5. Plato uses syllogistic reasoning to derive human behavior from his allegory. Trace his line of reasoning, noting transitional devices and the development of ideas in paragraphs 5–14. Find and describe a similar line of reasoning.
6. In what paragraph does Plato explain his allegory? Why do you think he locates his explanation where he does?

WRITING

1. Are Plato's ideas still influencing contemporary society? How do his ideas affect our evaluation of materialism, sensuality, sex, and love?
2. Write an allegory based on a sport, business, or space flight to explain how we act in the world.

NETWORKING
Applying 21st-Century Literacies

Adapting from the Cave to the Screen: In an extended essay, try to convince your audience that *The Matrix* films are based on Plato's essay.

Not about Islam?

Salman Rushdie

Salman Rushdie (b. 1947), a well-known novelist, essayist, and critic, was born in Bombay, India, into a middle-class Muslim family that relocated to Pakistan following the bloody Partition. He attended public school in Pakistan and England and graduated

*from Kings College at Cambridge University. Rushdie first received critical acclaim
for* Midnight's Children *(1981) and* Shame *(1983). With the publication of his controversial novel* Satanic Verses *(1989) and the subsequent* fatwa, *or religious edict,
issued by Ayatollah Khomeini ordering his death for blasphemy against Islam and his
depiction of Muhammad, Rushdie went into hiding for several years. In 1998, the
Islamic Republic of Iran announced that it would not carry out Rushdie's death sentence, but the* fatwa *remains in force. Rushdie's work includes* Imaginary Homelands: Essays and Criticism *(1991),* The Moor's Last Sigh *(1995),* Fury *(2001),*
Shalimar the Clown *(2005), and the* Enchantress of Florence *(2009). In the selection that follows, published in the* New York Times *in 2001, shortly after the 9/11
attacks, Rushdie confronts the issue of Islamic terrorism.*

"This isn't about Islam." The world's leaders have been repeating this mantra   1
for weeks, partly in the virtuous hope of deterring reprisal attacks on innocent
Muslims living in the West, partly because if the United States is to maintain its
coalition against terror it can't afford to allege that Islam and terrorism are in
any way related.

The trouble with this necessary disclaimer is that it isn't true. If this isn't   2
about Islam, why the worldwide Muslim demonstrations in support of Osama
bin Laden and Al-Qaida? Why did those ten thousand men armed with swords
and axes mass on the Pakistan-Afghanistan frontier, answering some mullah's
call to jihad? Why are the war's first British casualties three Muslim men who
died fighting on the Taliban side?

Why the routine anti-Semitism of the much-repeated Islamic slander that   3
"the Jews" arranged the hits on the World Trade Center and Pentagon, with
the oddly self-deprecating explanation offered by the Taliban leadership
among others; that Muslims could not have the technological know-how or
organizational sophistication to pull off such a feat? Why does Imran Khan, the
Pakistani ex–sports star turned politician, demand to be shown the evidence of
Al-Qaida's guilt while apparently turning a deaf ear to the self-incriminating
statements of Al-Qaida's own spokesmen (there will be a rain of aircraft from
the skies, Muslims in the West are warned not to live or work in tall buildings,
et cetera)? Why all the talk about U.S. military infidels desecrating the sacred
soil of Saudi Arabia, if some sort of definition of what is sacred is not at the
heart of the present discontents?

Let's start calling a spade a spade. Of course this is "about Islam." The ques-   4
tion is, what exactly does that mean? After all, most religious belief isn't very
theological. Most Muslims are not profound Quranic analysts. For a vast number of "believing" Muslim men, "Islam" stands, in a jumbled, half-examined
way, not only for the fear of God—the fear more than the love, one suspects—
but also for a cluster of customs, opinions, and prejudices that include their dietary practices; the sequestration or near-sequestration of "their" women; the
sermons delivered by their mullah of choice; a loathing of modern society in
general, riddled as it is with music, godlessness, and sex; and a more particularized loathing (and fear) of the prospect that their own immediate surroundings
could be taken over—"Westoxicated"—by the liberal Western-style way of life.

5   Highly motivated organizations of Muslim men (oh, for the voices of Muslim women to be heard) have been engaged, over the last thirty years or so, on growing radical political movements out of this mulch of "belief." These Islamists—we must get used to this word, "Islamists," meaning those who are engaged upon such political projects, and learn to distinguish it from the more general and politically neutral "Muslim"—include the Muslim Brotherhood in Egypt, the blood-soaked combatants of the FIS and GIA in Algeria, the Shia revolutionaries of Iran, and the Taliban. Poverty is their great helper, and the fruit of their efforts is paranoia. This paranoid Islam, which blames outsiders, "infidels," for all the ills of Muslim societies, and whose proposed remedy is the closing of those societies to the rival project of modernity, is presently the fastest-growing version of Islam in the world.

6   This is not really to go along with Samuel Huntington's thesis about the "clash of civilizations," for the simple reason that the Islamists' project is turned not only against the West and "the Jews" but also against their fellow Islamists. Whatever the public rhetoric, there's little love lost between the Taliban and Iranian regimes. Dissensions between Muslim nations run at least as deep as, if not deeper than, those nations' resentment of the West. Nevertheless, it would be absurd to deny that this self-exculpatory, paranoiac Islam is an ideology with widespread appeal.

7   Twenty years ago, when I was writing a novel about power struggles in a fictionalized Pakistan, it was already de rigueur in the Muslim world to blame all its troubles on the West and, in particular, the United States. Then as now, some of these criticisms were well-founded; no room here to rehearse the geopolitics of the Cold War, and America's frequently damaging foreign policy "tilts," to use the Kissinger term, toward (or away from) this or that temporarily useful (or disapproved-of) nation-state, or America's role in the installation and deposition of sundry unsavory leaders and regimes. But I wanted then to ask a question which is no less important now: Suppose we say that the ills of our societies are not primarily America's fault—that we are to blame for our own failings? How would we understand them then? Might we not, by accepting our own responsibility for our problems, begin to learn to solve them for ourselves?

8   It is interesting that many Muslims, as well as secularist analysts with roots in the Muslim world, are beginning to ask such questions now. In recent weeks Muslim voices have everywhere been raised against the obscurantist "hijack" of their religion. Yesterday's hotheads (among them Yusuf Islam, a.k.a. Cat Stevens) are improbably repackaging themselves as today's pussycats. An Iraqi writer quotes an earlier Iraqi satirist: "The disease that is in us, is from us." A British Muslim writes that "Islam has become its own enemy." A Lebanese writer friend, returning from Beirut, tells me that, in the aftermath of September 11, public criticism of Islamism has become much more outspoken. Many commentators have spoken of the need for a Reformation in the Muslim world. I'm reminded of the way non-communist socialists used to distance themselves from the tyrannous "actually existing" socialism of the Soviets; nevertheless, the first stirrings of this counterproject are of great significance. If Islam is to be

reconciled with modernity, these voices must be encouraged until they swell into a roar.

Many of them speak of another Islam, their personal, private faith, and the ₉ restoration of religion to the sphere of the personal, its de-politicization, is the nettle that all Muslim societies must grasp in order to become modern. The only aspect of modernity in which the terrorists are interested is technology, which they see as a weapon that can be turned against its makers. If terrorism is to be defeated, the world of Islam must take on board the secularist-humanist principles on which the modern is based, and without which their countries' freedom will remain a distant dream.

COMPREHENSION

1. What is Rushdie's response to statements that 9/11 was not "about Islam"?
2. What distinction does Rushdie draw between "Muslims" and "Islamists"? What, according to the writer, is the proper role of religion in the contemporary world?
3. Explain Rushdie's solution to some of the problems confronting Islamic nations today.

RHETORIC

1. How would you describe Rushdie's tone? Identify words, phrases, and sentences that capture his attitude toward his subject. How does the fact that he writes in the immediate aftermath of the events of September 11, 2001, affect the tone? How do his personal difficulties bear on his approach to the subject?
2. What is the key claim that the writer makes in this essay? Is it stated or implied?
3. Where does Rushdie engage in rebuttal of his opponents' points? Does he refute these points clearly and adequately? Why or why not?
4. What reasons and evidence does the writer offer to support his contention that if Muslim nations accepted responsibility for their internal conditions rather than blaming the West, they could solve their own problems?
5. Where does the writer apply the comparative method to advance his argument?
6. How does Rushdie support his premise that Islamic societies want to become modernized and can do so if their religion returns to "the sphere of the personal" (paragraph 9)?

WRITING

1. Write a personal essay in which you explain what you think the proper role of religion should be in the post–September 11 world.
2. Write a comparative essay in which you distinguish between "Islam" and "Islamists." Conduct research if necessary.
3. **Writing an Argument:** Take issue with Rushdie's claim that September 11, 2001, is "about Islam." Rebut his reasons, offering ideas and support for your alternative explanation.

NETWORKING
Applying 21st-Century Literacies

Creating an Interactive Argument: Condense your argument in question 3 under Writing into a 500-word blog post, complete with hyperlinks to sites that bolster support for your position. Encourage readers to post comments, which you should then respond to. Remember to keep the conversation civil and respectful, and the argument both rational and well supported; if comments get personal, rude, or worse, delete and do not respond to them.

The Rival Conceptions of God

C. S. Lewis

C(live) S(taples) Lewis (1898–1963) was born in Belfast, Ireland, but spent the most important years of his life as a lecturer in English at Oxford. His first book, Dymer, *was published in 1926, but it was not until the publication of* The Pilgrim's Regress *in 1933 that he addressed the central work of his life: a passionate defense of the Christian faith. Lewis's immense output embraces science fiction, fantasy, children's books, theology, and literary criticism. Among his best-known works are* The Screwtape Letters *(1942),* The Lion, the Witch, and the Wardrobe *(1950), along with the rest of* The Chronicles of Narnia *(1950–1956). In this essay, Lewis describes the reasoning that led to his conversion.*

1   I have been asked to tell you what Christians believe, and I am going to begin by telling you one thing that Christians do not need to believe. If you are a Christian you do not have to believe that all the other religions are simply wrong all through. If you are an atheist you do have to believe that the main point in all the religions of the whole world is simply one huge mistake. If you are a Christian, you are free to think that all these religions, even the queerest ones, contain at least some hint of the truth. When I was an atheist I had to try to persuade myself that most of the human race have always been wrong about the question that mattered to them most; when I became a Christian I was able to take a more liberal view. But, of course, being a Christian does mean thinking that where Christianity differs from other religions, Christianity is right and they are wrong. As in arithmetic—there is only one right answer to a sum, and all other answers are wrong: but some of the wrong answers are much nearer being right than others.

The first big division of humanity is into the majority, who believe in some 2
kind of God or gods, and the minority who do not. On this point, Christianity
lines up with the majority—lines up with ancient Greeks and Romans, modern
savages, Stoics, Platonists, Hindus, Mohammedans, etc., against the modern
Western European materialist.

Now I go on to the next big division. People who all believe in God can be 3
divided according to the sort of God they believe in. There are two very different ideas on this subject. One of them is the idea that He is beyond good and
evil. We humans call one thing good and another thing bad. But according to
some people that is merely our human point of view. These people would say
that the wiser you become the less you would want to call anything good or
bad, and the more clearly you would see that everything is good in one way
and bad in another, and that nothing could have been different. Consequently,
these people think that long before you got anywhere near the divine point of
view the distinction would have disappeared altogether. We call a cancer bad,
they would say, because it kills a man; but you might just as well call a successful surgeon bad because he kills a cancer. It all depends on the point of view.
The other and opposite idea is that God is quite definitely "good" or "righteous," a God who takes sides, who loves love and hates hatred, who wants us
to behave in one way and not in another. The first of these views—the one that
thinks God beyond good and evil—is called Pantheism. It was held by the great
Prussian philosopher Hegel and, as far as I can understand them, by the Hindus. The other view is held by Jews, Mohammedans and Christians.

And with this big difference between Pantheism and the Christian idea of 4
God, there usually goes another. Pantheists usually believe that God, so to
speak, animates the universe as you animate your body: that the universe almost *is* God, so that if it did not exist He would not exist either, and anything
you find in the universe is a part of God. The Christian idea is quite different.
They think God invented and made the universe—like a man making a picture
or composing a tune. A painter is not a picture, and he does not die if his picture
is destroyed. You may say, "He's put a lot of himself into it," but you only mean
that all its beauty and interest has come out of his head. His skill is not in the
picture in the same way that it is in his head, or even in his hands. I expect you
see how this difference between Pantheists and Christians hangs together with
the other one. If you do not take the distinction between good and bad very
seriously, then it is easy to say that anything you find in this world is a part of
God. But, of course, if you think some things really bad, and God really good,
then you cannot talk like that. You must believe that God is separate from the
world and that some of the things we see in it are contrary to His will. Confronted with a cancer or a slum the Pantheist can say, "If you could only see it
from the divine point of view, you would realize that this also is God." The
Christian replies, "Don't talk damned nonsense."[1] For Christianity is a fighting

---

[1] One listener complained of the word *damned* as frivolous swearing. But I mean exactly what I
say—nonsense that is *damned* is under God's curse, and will (apart from God's grace) lead those
who believe it to eternal death.

religion. It thinks God made the world—that space and time, heat and cold, and all the colors and tastes, and all the animals and vegetables, are things that God "made up out of His head" as a man makes up a story. But it also thinks that a great many things have gone wrong with the world that God made and that God insists, and insists very loudly, on our putting them right again.

5   And, of course, that raises a very big question. If a good God made the world why has it gone wrong? And for many years I simply refused to listen to the Christian answers to this question, because I kept on feeling "whatever you say, and however clever your arguments are, isn't it much simpler and easier to say that the world was not made by any intelligent power? Aren't all your arguments simply a complicated attempt to avoid the obvious?" But then that threw me back into another difficulty.

6   My argument against God was that the universe seemed so cruel and unjust. But how had I got this idea of *just* and *unjust*? A man does not call a line crooked unless he has some idea of a straight line. What was I comparing this universe with when I called it unjust? If the whole show was bad and senseless from A to Z, so to speak, why did I, who was supposed to be part of the show, find myself in such violent reaction against it? A man feels wet when he falls into water, because man is not a water animal: a fish would not feel wet. Of course I could have given up my idea of justice by saying it was nothing but a private idea of my own. But if I did that, then my argument against God collapsed too—for the argument depended on saying that the world was really unjust, not simply that it did not happen to please my private fancies. Thus in the very act of trying to prove that God did not exist—in other words, that the whole of reality was senseless—I found I was forced to assume that one part of reality—namely my idea of justice—was full of sense. Consequently atheism turns out to be too simple. If the whole universe has no meaning, we should never have found out that it has no meaning: just as, if there were no light in the universe and therefore no creature with eyes, we should never know it was dark. *Dark* would be without meaning.

COMPREHENSION

1. Who is Lewis's audience? What is his purpose? How do you know?
2. Lewis divides humanity into a number of distinct categories. Name them, and discuss his purpose in establishing these categories.
3. What is Lewis's purpose in likening Christianity to arithmetic? In what sense is this apt? Where does he use a similar image?

RHETORIC

1. Look up the following words from paragraph 2 in a dictionary or an encyclopedia: *Stoics, Platonists, Hindus,* and *Mohammedans.* What are the major tenets of their beliefs?

2. Explain Lewis's use of the word *damned* (paragraph 4). What is specific about his use of this word? Is it appropriate?
3. How does Lewis develop his argument? What line of reasoning does he follow? What transition markers does he use?
4. How does Lewis use definition to structure certain parts of his argument?
5. In which paragraph is Lewis making what he considers the one irrefutable argument in favor of the existence of God? Is this paragraph coherently reasoned in terms of the whole essay? Explain.
6. Why is Lewis's idea of justice critical to the evaluation of his thought? Is his use of the word *justice* idiosyncratic or objective? How does accepting his definition make an important difference in how a reader would respond to this piece?

WRITING

1. The Western tradition is based, in large part, on the belief that Christianity is right and other religions are wrong. Is this belief as strong today as it was in the past? Does it still cohere as an argument?
2. Write an essay describing your religious beliefs and how they originated.
3. **Writing an Argument:** Argue for or against atheism.

NETWORKING
Applying 21st-Century Literacies

Using Wikipedia as a Research Launch Pad: As a user-generated encyclopedia, *Wikipedia* may contain information that is unreliable or out of date; however, while it's not a source you'd want to cite in a paper, this resource can be a very useful place to *begin* your invention and online research processes—namely, to learn a little more about a topic and to identify other, more reliable, sources. Look up *Wikipedia*'s entry for "Atheism." Read the entry, and then consult the Notes, References, Further Reading, and External Links categories to help determine two things: First, how you would approach question 3 under Writing (what might your paper's thesis be?), and, second, which five sources listed on the page you might consult in your research.

The Culture of Disbelief

Stephen L. Carter

Stephen L. Carter (b. 1954) received a BA from Stanford University in 1976 and graduated from Yale University Law School in 1979. He served as a law clerk for the U.S. Supreme Court and as a lawyer in private practice before becoming a professor of law at Yale University Law School in 1982. An African American who is opposed to affirmative action, he has become a controversial figure among proponents of the policy. His first book, Reflections of an Affirmative Action Baby *(1991), outlines his views on the subject and draws on personal experience to show that, even though he was a beneficiary of affirmative action, such preference ultimately makes successful African Americans seem to have received preferential treatment. His second book,* The Culture of Disbelief: How American Law and Politics Trivialize Religious Devotion *(1993), addresses the ways he believes the law has recently operated against the spirit of American values in its effort to ban religion from political discourse and expression. Carter also writes novels, including* The Emperor of Ocean Park *(2002), and* Palace Council *(2008). The following essay succinctly sums up this argument.*

1   Contemporary American politics faces few greater dilemmas than deciding how to deal with the resurgence of religious belief. On the one hand, American ideology cherishes religion, as it does all matters of private conscience, which is why we justly celebrate a strong tradition against state interference with private religious choice. At the same time, many political leaders, commentators, scholars, and voters are coming to view any religious element in public moral discourse as a tool of the radical right for reshaping American society. But the effort to banish religion for politics' sake has led us astray: In our sensible zeal to keep religion from dominating our politics, we have created a political and legal culture that presses the religiously faithful to be other than themselves, to act publicly, and sometimes privately as well, as though their faith does not matter to them.

2   Recently, a national magazine devoted its cover story to an investigation of prayer: how many people pray, how often, why, how, and for what. A few weeks later came the inevitable letter from a disgruntled reader, wanting to know why so much space had been dedicated to such nonsense.[1]

3   Statistically, the letter writer was in the minority: By the magazine's figures, better than nine out of ten Americans believe in God and some four out of five pray regularly.[2] Politically and culturally, however, the writer was in the American mainstream, for those who do pray regularly—indeed, those who believe in God—are encouraged to keep it a secret, and often a shameful one at that. Aside from the ritual appeals to God that are expected of our politicians, for Americans to take their religions seriously, to treat them as ordained rather than chosen, is to risk assignment to the lunatic fringe.

4   Yet religion matters to people, and matters a lot. Surveys indicate that Americans are far more likely to believe in God and to attend worship services regularly than any other people in the Western world. True, nobody prays on prime-time television unless religion is a part of the plot, but strong majorities of citizens tell pollsters that their religious beliefs are of great importance to them

---

[1]"Talking to God," *Newsweek,* Jan. 6, 1992, p. 38; Letter to the Editor, *Newsweek,* Jan. 20, 1992, p. 10. The letter called the article a "theocratic text masquerading as a news article."
[2]"Talking to God," p. 39. The most recent Gallup data indicate that 96 percent of Americans say they believe in God, including 82 percent who describe themselves as Christians (56 percent Protestant, 25 percent Roman Catholic) and 2 percent who describe themselves as Jewish. (No other faith accounted for as much as 1 percent.) See Ari L. Goldman, "Religion Notes," *New York Times,* Feb. 27, 1993, p. 9.

in their daily lives. Even though some popular histories wrongly assert the contrary, the best evidence is that this deep religiosity has always been a facet of the American character and that it has grown consistently through the nation's history.[3] And today, to the frustration of many opinion leaders in both the legal and political cultures, religion, as a moral force and perhaps a political one too, is surging. Unfortunately, in our public life, we prefer to pretend that it is not.

Consider the following events: 5

- When Hillary Rodham Clinton was seen wearing a cross around her neck at some of the public events surrounding her husband's inauguration as President of the United States, many observers were aghast, and one television commentator asked whether it was appropriate for the First Lady to display so openly a religious symbol. But if the First Lady can't do it, then certainly the President can't do it, which would bar from ever holding the office an Orthodox Jew under a religious compulsion to wear a yarmulke.
- Back in the mid-1980s, the magazine *Sojourners*—published by politically liberal Christian evangelicals—found itself in the unaccustomed position of defending the conservative evangelist Pat Robertson against secular liberals who, a writer in the magazine sighed, "see[m] to consider Robertson a dangerous neanderthal because he happens to believe that God can heal diseases."[4] The point is that the editors of *Sojourners*, who are no great admirers of Robertson, also believe that God can heal diseases. So do tens of millions of Americans. But they are not supposed to say so.
- In the early 1980s, the state of New York adopted legislation that, in effect, requires an Orthodox Jewish husband seeking a divorce to give his wife a *get*—a religious divorce—without which she cannot remarry under Jewish law. Civil libertarians attacked the statute as unconstitutional. Said one critic, the "barriers to remarriage erected by religious law . . . only exist in the minds of those who believe in the religion."[5] If the barriers are religious, it seems, then they are not real barriers, they are "only" in the woman's mind—perhaps even a figment of the imagination.
- When the Supreme Court of the United States, ostensibly the final refuge of religious freedom, struck down a Connecticut statute requiring employers to make efforts to allow their employees to observe the sabbath, one Justice observed that the sabbath should not be singled out because all employees would like to have "the right to select the day of the week in which to refrain from labor."[6] Sounds good, except that, as one scholar has noted, "It would come as some surprise to a devout Jew to find that he has 'selected the day of the week in which to refrain from labor,' since the Jewish people

---

[3]See, for example, Jon Butler, *Awash in a Sea of Faith* (Cambridge: Harvard University Press, 1990).
[4]Collum, "The Kingdom and the Power," *Sojourners,* Nov. 1986, p. 4. Some 82 percent of Americans believe that God performs miracles today. George Gallup, Jr., and Jim Castelli, *The People's Religion: American Faith in the '90s* (New York: Macmillan, 1989), p. 58.
[5]Madeline Kochen, "Constitutional Implications of New York's 'Get' Statute," *New York Law Journal,* Oct. 27, 1983, p. 32.
[6]*Estate of Thornton v. Caldor, Inc.,* 472 U.S. 703, 711 (1985) (Justice Sandra Day O'Connor, concurring).

have been under the impression for some 3,000 years that this choice was made by God."[7] If the sabbath is just another day off, then religious choice is essentially arbitrary and unimportant; so if one sabbath day is inconvenient, the religiously devout employee can just choose another.

- When President Ronald Reagan told religious broadcasters in 1983 that all laws passed since biblical times "have not improved on the Ten Commandments one bit," which might once have been considered a pardonable piece of rhetorical license, he was excoriated by political pundits, including one who charged angrily that Reagan was giving "short shrift to the secular laws and institutions that a president is charged with protecting."[8] And as for the millions of Americans who consider the Ten Commandments the fundaments on which they build their lives, well, they are no doubt subversive of these same institutions.

6   These examples share a common rhetoric that refuses to accept the notion that rational, public-spirited people can take religion seriously. It might be argued that such cases as these involve threats to the separation of church and state, the durable and vital doctrine that shields our public institutions from religious domination and our religious institutions from government domination. I am a great supporter of the separation of church and state . . . but that is not what these examples are about.

7   What matters about these examples is the *language* chosen to make the points. In each example, as in many more that I shall discuss, one sees a trend in our political and legal cultures toward treating religious beliefs as arbitrary and unimportant, a trend supported by a rhetoric that implies that there is something wrong with religious devotion. More and more, our culture seems to take the position that believing deeply in the tenets of one's faith represents a kind of mystical irrationality, something that thoughtful, public-spirited American citizens would do better to avoid. If you must worship your God, the lesson runs, at least have the courtesy to disbelieve in the power of prayer; if you must observe your sabbath, have the good sense to understand that it is just like any other day off from work.

8   The rhetoric matters. A few years ago, my wife and I were startled by a teaser for a story on a network news program, which asked what was meant to be a provocative question: "When is a church more than just a place of worship?" For those to whom worship is significant, the subtle arrangement of words is arresting: *more than* suggests that what follows ("just a place of worship") is somewhere well down the scale of interesting or useful human activities, and certainly that whatever the story is about is *more than* worship; and *just*—suggests that what follows ("place of worship") is rather small potatoes.

9   A friend tells the story of how he showed his résumé to an executive search consultant—in the jargon, a corporate headhunter—who told him crisply that if

---

[7]Michael W. McConnell, "Religious Freedom at a Crossroads," *University of Chicago Law Review* 59 (1992):115.

[8]Robert G. Kaiser, "Hypocrisy: This Puffed-Up Piety Is Perfectly Preposterous," *Washington Post*, March 18,1984, p. C1.

he was serious about moving ahead in the business world, he should remove from the résumé any mention of his involvement with a social welfare organization that was connected with a church, but not one of the genteel mainstream denominations. Otherwise, she explained, a potential employer might think him a religious fanatic.

How did we reach this disturbing pass, when our culture teaches that religion is not to be taken seriously, even by those who profess to believe in it? Some observers suggest that the key moment was the Enlightenment, when the Western tradition sought to sever the link between religion and authority. One of the playwright Tom Stoppard's characters observes that there came "a calendar date—*a moment*—when the onus of proof passed from the atheist to the believer, when, quite suddenly, the noes had it."[9] To which the philosopher Jeffrey Stout appends the following comment: "If so, it was not a matter of majority rule."[10] Maybe not—but a strong undercurrent of contemporary American politics holds that religion must be kept in its proper place and, still more, in proper perspective. There are, we are taught by our opinion leaders, religious matters and important matters, and disaster arises when we confuse the two. Rationality, it seems, consists in getting one's priorities straight. (Ignore your religious law and marry at leisure.) Small wonder, then, that we have recently been treated to a book, coauthored by two therapists, one of them an ordained minister, arguing that those who would put aside, say, the needs of their families in order to serve their religions are suffering from a malady the authors called "toxic faith"—for no normal person, evidently, would sacrifice the things that most of us hold dear just because of a belief that God so intended it.[11] (One wonders how the authors would have judged the toxicity of the faith of Jesus, Moses, or Mohammed.)

We are trying, here in America, to strike an awkward but necessary balance, one that seems more and more difficult with each passing year. On the one hand, a magnificent respect for freedom of conscience, including the freedom of religious belief, runs deep in our political ideology. On the other hand, our understandable fear of religious domination of politics presses us, in our public personas, to be wary of those who take their religion too seriously. This public balance reflects our private selves. We are one of the most religious nations on earth, in the sense that we have a deeply religious citizenry; but we are also perhaps the most zealous in guarding our public institutions against explicit religious influences. One result is that we often ask our citizens to split their public and private selves, telling them in effect that it is fine to be religious in private, but there is something askew when those private beliefs become the basis for public action.

We teach college freshmen that the Protestant Reformation began the process of freeing the church from the state, thus creating the possibility of a powerful independent moral force in society. As defenders of the separation of

---

[9]Tom Stoppard, *Jumpers*, quoted in Jeffrey Stout, *The Flight from Authority: Religion, Morality and the Quest for Autonomy* (South Bend, Ind.: University of Notre Dame Press, 1981), p. 150.
[10]Ibid.
[11]Stephen Arterburn and Jack Felton, *Toxic Faith: Understanding and Overcoming Religious Addiction* (Nashville, Tenn.: Oliver Nelson Books, 1991).

church and state have argued for centuries, autonomous religions play a vital role as free critics of the institutions of secular society. But our public culture more and more prefers religion as something without political significance, less an independent moral force than a quietly irrelevant moralizer, never heard, rarely seen. "[T]he public sphere," writes the theologian Martin Marty, "does not welcome explicit Reformed witness—or any other particularized Christian witness."[12] Or, for that matter, any religious witness at all.

13   Religions that most need protection seem to receive it least. Contemporary America is not likely to enact legislation aimed at curbing the mainstream Protestant, Roman Catholic, or Jewish faiths. But Native Americans, having once been hounded from their lands, are now hounded from their religions, with the complicity of a Supreme Court untroubled when sacred lands are taken for road building or when Native Americans under a bona fide religious compulsion to use *peyote* in their rituals are punished under state antidrug regulations.[13] (Imagine the brouhaha if New York City were to try to take St. Patrick's Cathedral by eminent domain to build a new convention center, or if Kansas, a dry state, were to outlaw the religious use of wine.) And airports, backed by the Supreme Court, are happy to restrict solicitation by devotees of Krishna Consciousness, which travelers, including this one, find irritating.[14] (Picture the response should the airports try to regulate the wearing of crucifixes or yarmulkes on similar grounds of irritation.)

14   The problem goes well beyond our society's treatment of those who simply want freedom to worship in ways that most Americans find troubling. An analogous difficulty is posed by those whose religious convictions move them to action in the public arena. Too often, our rhetoric treats the religious impulse to public action as presumptively wicked—indeed, as necessarily oppressive. But this is historically bizarre. Every time people whose vision of God's will moves them to oppose abortion rights are excoriated for purportedly trying to impose their religious views on others, equal calumny is implicitly heaped upon the mass protest wing of the civil rights movement, which was openly and unashamedly religious in its appeals as it worked to impose its moral vision on, for example, those who would rather segregate their restaurants.

15   One result of this rhetoric is that we often end up fighting the wrong battles. Consider what must in our present day serve as the ultimate example of religion in the service of politics: the 1989 death sentence pronounced by the late Ayatollah Ruhollah Khomeini upon the writer Salman Rushdie for his authorship of *The Satanic Verses,* which was said to blaspheme against Islam. The death sentence is both terrifying and outrageous, and the Ayatollah deserved all the fury lavished upon him for imposing it. Unfortunately, for some critics the facts that the Ayatollah was a religious leader and that the "crime" was a religious one lends the sentence a particular monstrousness; evidently they are

[12]Martin E. Marty, "Reformed America and America Reformed," *Reformed Journal* (March 1989): 8, 10.
[13]*Employment Division, Department of Human Resources v. Smith,* 494 U.S. 872 (1990).
[14]*International Society for Krishna Consciousness v. Lee,* 112 S. Ct. 2701 (1992).

under the impression that writers who are murdered for their ideas are choosy about the motivations of their murderers, and that those whose writings led to their executions under, say, Stalin, thanked their lucky stars at the last instant of their lives that Communism was at least godless.

To do battle against the death sentence for Salman Rushdie—to battle [16] against the Ayatollah—one should properly fight against official censorship and intimidation, not against religion. We err when we presume that religious motives are likely to be illiberal, and we compound the error when we insist that the devout should keep their religious ideas—whether good or bad—to themselves. We do no credit to the ideal of religious freedom when we talk as though religious belief is something of which public-spirited adults should be ashamed.

The First Amendment to the Constitution, often cited as the place where this [17] difficulty is resolved, merely restates it. The First Amendment guarantees the "free exercise" of religion but also prohibits its "establishment" by the government. There may have been times in our history when we as a nation have tilted too far in one direction, allowing too much religious sway over politics. But in late-twentieth-century America, despite some loud fears about the influence of the weak and divided Christian right, we are upsetting the balance afresh by tilting too far in the other direction—and the courts are assisting in the effort. For example, when a group of Native Americans objected to the Forest Service's plans to allow logging and road building in a national forest area traditionally used by the tribes for sacred rituals, the Supreme Court offered the back of its hand. True, said the Justices, the logging "could have devastating effects on traditional Indian religious practices." But that was just too bad: "government simply could not operate if it were required to satisfy every citizen's religious needs and desires."[15]

A good point: but what, exactly, are the protesting Indians left to do? Pre- [18] sumably, now that their government has decided to destroy the land they use for their sacred rituals, they are free to choose new rituals. Evidently, a small matter like the potential destruction of a religion is no reason to halt a logging project. Moreover, had the government decided instead to prohibit logging in order to preserve the threatened rituals, it is entirely possible that the decision would be challenged as a forbidden entanglement of church and state. Far better for everyone, it seems, for the Native Americans to simply allow their rituals to go quietly into oblivion. Otherwise, they run the risk that somebody will think they actually take their rituals seriously.

The Price of Faith

When citizens do act in their public selves as though their faith matters, they risk [19] not only ridicule, but actual punishment. In Colorado, a public school teacher was ordered by his superiors, on pain of disciplinary action, to remove his personal Bible from his desk where students might see it. He was forbidden to read it silently when his students were involved in other activities. He was also told to take away books on Christianity he had added to the classroom library,

[15]*Lyng v. Northwest Indian Cemetery Protective Association,* 485 U.S. 439 (1988).

although books on Native American religious traditions, as well as on the occult, were allowed to remain. A federal appeals court upheld the instruction, explaining that the teacher could not be allowed to create a religious atmosphere in the classroom, which, it seems, might happen if the students knew he was a Christian.[16] One wonders what the school, and the courts, might do if, as many Christians do, the teacher came to school on Ash Wednesday with ashes in the shape of a cross imposed on his forehead—would he be required to wash them off? He just might. Early in 1993, a judge required a prosecutor arguing a case on Ash Wednesday to clean the ashes from his forehead, lest the jury be influenced by its knowledge of the prosecutor's religiosity.

20   Or suppose a Jewish teacher were to wear a yarmulke in the classroom. If the school district tried to stop him, it would apparently be acting within its authority. In 1986, after a Jewish Air Force officer was disciplined for wearing a yarmulke while on duty, in violation of a military rule against wearing headgear indoors, the Supreme Court shrugged: "The desirability of dress regulations in the military is decided by the appropriate military officials," the justices explained, "and they are under no constitutional mandate to abandon their considered professional judgment."[17] The Congress quickly enacted legislation permitting the wearing of religious apparel while in uniform as long as "the wearing of the item would [not] interfere with the performance of the member's military duties," and—interesting caveat—as long as the item is "neat and conservative."[18] Those whose faiths require them to wear dreadlocks and turbans, one supposes, need not apply to serve their country, unless they are prepared to change religions.

21   Consider the matter of religious holidays. One Connecticut town recently warned Jewish students in its public schools that they would be charged with *six* absences if they missed two days instead of the officially allocated one for Yom Kippur, the holiest observance in the Jewish calendar. And Alan Dershowitz of Harvard Law School, in his controversial book *Chutzpah,* castigates Harry Edwards, a Berkeley sociologist, for scheduling an examination on Yom Kippur, when most Jewish students would be absent. According to Dershowitz's account, Edwards answered criticism by saying: "That's how I'm going to operate. If the students don't like it, they can drop the class." For Dershowitz, this was evidence that "Jewish students [are] second-class citizens in Professor Edwards's classes."[19] Edwards has heatedly denied Dershowitz's description of events, but even if it is accurate, it is possible that Dershowitz has identified the right crime and the wrong villain. The attitude that Dershowitz describes, if it exists, might reflect less a personal prejudice against Jewish students than the society's broader prejudice against religious devotion, a prejudice that masquerades as "neutrality." If Edwards really dared his students to choose between their religion and their grade, and if that meant that he was treating them

[16]*Roberts v Madigan,* 921 F, 2d 1047 (10th Cir. 1990).
[17]*Goldman v Weinberger,* 475 U.S. 503 (1986)
[18]45 U.S.C. 774, as amended by Pub. L. No. 100-80, Dec. 4, 1987.
[19]Alan M. Dershowitz, *Chutzpah* (Boston: Little, Brown, 1991), pp. 329–30.

as second-class citizens, he was still doing no more than the courts have allowed all levels of government to do to one religious group after another—Jews, Christians, Muslims, Sikhs, it matters not at all. The consistent message of modern American society is that whenever the demands of one's religion conflict with what one has to do to get ahead, one is expected to ignore the religious demands and act . . . well . . . *rationally.*

Consider Jehovah's Witnesses, who believe that a blood transfusion from one human being to another violates the biblical prohibition on ingesting blood. To accept the transfusion, many Witnesses believe, is to lose, perhaps forever, the possibility of salvation. As the Witnesses understand God's law, moreover, the issue is not whether the blood transfusion is given against the recipient's will, but whether the recipient is, at the time of the transfusion, actively protesting. This is the reason that Jehovah's Witnesses sometimes try to impede the physical access of medical personnel to an unconscious Witness: Lack of consciousness is no defense. This is also the reason that Witnesses try to make the decisions on behalf of their children: A child cannot be trusted to protest adequately. 22

The machinery of law has not been particularly impressed with these arguments. There are many cases in which the courts have allowed or ordered transfusions to save the lives of unconscious Witnesses, even though the patient might have indicated a desire while conscious not to be transfused.[20] The machinery of modern medicine has not been impressed, either, except with the possibility that the Witnesses have gone off the deep end; at least one hospital's protocol apparently requires doctors to refer protesting Witnesses to psychiatrists.[21] Although the formal text of this requirement states as the reason the need to be sure that the Witness knows what he or she is doing, the subtext is a suspicion that the patient was not acting rationally in rejecting medical advice for religious reasons. After all, there is no protocol for packing *consenting* patients off to see the psychiatrist. But then, patients who consent to blood transfusions are presumably acting rationally. Perhaps, with a bit of gentle persuasion, the dissenting Witness can be made to act rationally too—even if it means giving up an important tenet of the religion. 23

And therein lies the trouble. In contemporary American culture, the religions are more and more treated as just passing beliefs—almost as fads, older, stuffier, less liberal versions of so-called New Age—rather than as the fundaments upon which the devout build their lives. (The noes have it!) And if religions *are* fundamental, well, too bad—at least if they're the *wrong* fundaments—if they're inconvenient, give them up! If you can't remarry because you have the wrong religious belief, well, hey, believe something else! If you can't take your exam because of a Holy Day, get a new Holy Day! If the government decides to destroy 24

---

[20]In every decided case that I have discovered involving efforts by Jehovah's Witness parents to prevent their children from receiving blood transfusions, the court has allowed the transfusion to proceed in the face of parental objection. I say more about transfusions of children of Witnesses, and about the rights of parents over their children's religious lives, in chapter 11 [of my book].

[21]See Ruth Macklin, "The Inner Workings of an Ethics Committee: Latest Battle over Jehovah's Witnesses," *Hastings Center Report* 18 (February/March 1988): 15.

your sacred lands, just make some other lands sacred! If you must go to work on your sabbath, it's no big deal! It's just a day off! Pick a different one! If you can't have a blood transfusion because you think God forbids it, no problem! Get a new God! And through all of this trivializing rhetoric runs the subtle but unmistakable message: Pray if you like, worship if you must, but whatever you do, do not on any account take your religion seriously.

COMPREHENSION

1. Where does Carter articulate the thesis of his essay?
2. The author cites the First Amendment as being a significant historical reference in raising the debate regarding the relationship between government and religion in the United States. What is the First Amendment to the Constitution? What does it mean that the Constitution was amended?
3. In your own words, what is the meaning of the essay's title?

RHETORIC

1. How does the opening line of the essay draw the reader into the concerns of the author?
2. What is the rhetorical function of the bulleted examples Carter uses in paragraph 5?
3. In paragraphs 8 and 9, the author introduces a personal tone to his essay. Does this add to or diminish his argument?
4. In paragraph 7, Carter places the word *language* in italics; while in other places, he refers to the use of rhetoric as a way of demeaning the religious impulse. For example, in paragraph 14, he states, "Too often, our rhetoric treats the religious impulse to public action as presumptively wicked." Why does Carter focus so much on the use of language as a tool in the attack on religion?
5. The author uses mainly anecdotal evidence to support his views, yet most social sciences claim that anecdotes are a poor form of evidence because they refer only to individual cases, and not to general trends. To what degree does Carter's strategy in using anecdotes strengthen or weaken his argument?
6. Carter devotes one section of his essay to "The Price of Faith." Why has he emphasized this religious issue by placing it in a separate category?
7. How does Carter use irony in his final paragraph? Why is this an effective way of both summing up his main points and drawing attention to them?

WRITING

1. In a research paper, compare and contrast court rulings regarding perceived governmental infringements on Christian rights of worship versus Native American rights of worship.
2. Assume the role of CEO of a corporation. Write a policy statement in which you provide guidelines for acceptable and unacceptable displays of religious behavior and symbols.
3. **Writing an Argument:** Argue for or against the view that the strength of religious toleration among the American people renders any specific legislation regarding religion merely an academic exercise, with no true social effect.

NETWORKING
Applying 21st-Century Literacies

Exploring Newsgroups: Join two religious or atheist newsgroups. Spend two weeks monitoring their messages. Compare and contrast their concerns, questions, perspectives, and beliefs.

Synthesis: Connections for Critical Thinking

1. Explore the connection between Plato, the philosopher, and Coles, the psychiatrist. How do their essays complement each other? How does Coles's attitude toward existence reflect Plato's philosophy of the cave?
2. What distinguishes a "true" religious belief from a superstition? What are their various functions? Is one more valid than the other? Explain your answer with reference to Mead, Pogrebin, Hughes, and Armstrong.
3. Coles argues that the moral education of children is essential to a well-functioning society. What function does superstition serve in the lives of children that a pure moral education may fail to provide?
4. Based on your reading of Lewis, explain whether you think he would agree or disagree with Rushdie's observations about Islam.
5. What is the difference between philosophy and religion? Is it merely a matter of belief? Address this question in an essay, using support from writers in this chapter.
6. Write an essay titled "The Purpose of Life." Using examples and evidence from their works, choose three writers in this chapter to develop this theme.

NETWORKING
Applying 21st-Century Literacies

---

1. Working with classmates, create your own interactive blog or Web site displaying an excerpt from Miller's essay. Ask for personal responses from all its visitors, and report your findings.
2. Research online the role of cults in American society, particularly among young people. Focus on finding specific superstitions they have that can inflict self-harm or harm on others. Using the essays by Mead and Pogrebin as sources, explore the differences between "good" and "bad" superstitions.

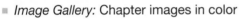

CH 12   **www.mhhe.com/mhreader11e**

- *Image Gallery:* Chapter images in color
- *Philosophy, Ethics, and Religion:* Information on the authors in this chapter
- *Ch. 12 Networking*

chapter 13

Health and Medicine
What Are the Challenges?

Today, medicine and the health sciences are recasting our lives and the world we know. From stem-cell research, to the abortion debate, to the AIDS epidemic, we are dealing with enormous medical challenges and controversies. At the same time, commonplace conditions ranging from starvation to the common cold continue to defy solutions. There are surely medical breakthroughs—new drugs, therapies, technologies, and delivery systems—that offer some cause for optimism. However, we must acknowledge the ongoing reality of illness, both physical and psychological, and the serious imbalance in individuals' access to health care.

It could be argued that medical science presents an unequal playing field to Americans and people worldwide, for health care clearly is a privilege rather than a right. For millions of people in the United States and billions around the world, health care is rudimentary or nonexistent. College students, of course, are among the privileged. They typically enjoy health insurance, access to campus clinics or affiliated hospitals, counseling and psychiatric intervention, and an entire network of other health care support systems. Health care at an American college or university is a model that we would wish for any culture, society, or nation.

Medicine and health care are also subjects for civic discourse, cultural argument, and political debate. Disputes over medicine—abortion, cloning, drug addiction, and more—are also part of everyday life. The subject was an integral part of the most recent U.S. presidential election and assuredly will resurface in future election cycles. And, of course, the media (as we discussed in an earlier chapter) exploit our fascination with health and medicine. Television shows feature extreme surgical makeovers and contests among oversized people competing to lose the most weight. Magazines and television promote potentially dangerous body images. On the Internet, people suffering from anorexia and other dietary disorders can find solace and support.

The writers in this chapter contend with some of the most pressing issues confronting medical science today. Some of the writers are physicians. Some authors personalize their subject; others offer objective analysis or compelling arguments. All raise moral and ethical issues as they deal with ways in which medicine is shaping our personalities and our lives.

PREVIEWING THE CHAPTER

As you read the essays in this chapter and respond to them in discussion and writing, consider the following questions:

- What is the writer's subject? What perspective on medicine or health does she or he take?
- What is the writer's purpose: to explain, narrate, argue, or persuade?
- Do you find the writer's tone to be subjective or objective? Does the author have a personal motive in addressing the topic in the way he or she does?
- What moral, ethical, or religious issues does the writer raise in connection with medicine or health science?
- What logical, emotional, and ethical appeals does the author make to his or her audience?
- Which level of specialized knowledge—history, science, medicine, or some other area—does the author bring to bear on the subject? What level of authority does she or he bring to the topic?
- What cultural, economic, or political problems does the author connect to the medical topic under consideration?
- Do you agree or disagree with the author's thesis or claim, and why?
- Which essays appear similar in subject, thesis, or perspective?
- Which essays did you find most compelling or convincing, and why?
- Which ones changed your opinion or altered your thinking on the subject?

Classic and Contemporary Images
WHAT DOES MEDICAL RESEARCH TELL US?

Using a Critical Perspective   The medical universe has changed radically since 1632, when Rembrandt painted *The Anatomy Lesson of Professor Nicolaes Tulp*. Flash forward to 2004 and move from Holland to New York City, where photographer Gary Bramnick captured the release of conjoined twins after successful surgery. As you consider these visual texts, answer these questions: What is the main purpose of the artist or the photographer? What elements in each image contribute to the overall effect? How is the human subject portrayed, and which scene evokes the strongest emotional reaction? How does the much earlier scene relate to the contemporary one?

Rembrandt van Rijn (1606–1669) was the most gifted painter, draftsman, and etcher of Holland's Golden Age. *The Anatomy Lesson* (1632) is a group portrait of the Amsterdam surgeon's guild, whose members, led by Dr. Nicolaes Tulp, were unsurpassed in the surgical techniques of the period.

Clarence and Carl Aguirre, formerly conjoined twins who were separated by surgery, are followed by their mother Arlene Aguirre, center left, and grandmother Evelyn, center right, as they leave Children's Hospital at Montefiore in New York, flanked by the doctors who performed the surgery, Dr. James T. Goodrich, left, and Dr. David A. Staffenberg. Nurses loaded the boys into separate ambulances, which took off with a police escort for Blythedale Children's Hospital in Valhalla, where they and their mother lived between operations at Montefiore.

Classic and Contemporary Essays
CAN WE AVOID EPIDEMICS?

We would like to think that the 21st century will avoid a plague like the one that swept through Asia and Europe during the 14th century. Yet the AIDS epidemic proves to be intractable and growing in sub-Saharan Africa, Asia, Russia, and the Indian subcontinent, while outbreaks of new potential epidemics like Ebola and SARS pose serious challenges for medical researchers and dangers for humankind. Plagues seem to be as old and persistent as civilization itself. Looking back to the 14th century, the noted historian Barbara Tuchman tells the story of the Black Death—the bubonic plague—that devastated Europe, resulting in the extinction of perhaps one-third of the population. With a historian's eye for narrative and detail, she describes the symptoms associated with plague, the process by which it spread inexorably from one nation to the next, and the religious, political, and cultural impact of the disease on the continent. Like Tuchman, Jill Lepore is a historian with wide-ranging research interests in American culture and civilization. However, Lepore in her essay deals with the 20th century while implying that we are facing new epidemics or plague years. Both writers trace the origins of emerging plagues and their consequences. Lepore also makes a pointed argument about the failure of the American health care system and the media to deal rationally with diseases that might or might not be of epidemic proportions. As you read these two essays, consider the rhetorical strategies that Tuchman and Lepore employ to render their respective vision of epidemics in vivid and compelling ways.

"This Is the End of the World": The Black Death

Barbara Tuchman

Barbara Tuchman (1912–1989) was born in New York City and graduated from Radcliffe College. A self-taught historian, she worked as a writer for the Nation *magazine and during World War II served as an editor at the U.S. Office of War Information. Her book* The Guns of August *(1960), a narrative history of the outbreak of World War I, won the Pulitzer prize. She won it again for her book* Stilwell and the American Experience in China: 1911–45 *(1971). Her other books include such best-sellers as* A Distant Mirror: The Calamitous 14th Century *(1978) and* The First Salute *(1989). In her later years, she was a lecturer at Harvard University and at the U.S. Naval War College. In this selection, excerpted from* A Distant Mirror, *Tuchman explains in her vivid narrative style the effects of the bubonic plague on Western Europe.*

In October 1347, two months after the fall of Calais, Genoese trading ships put 1
into the harbor of Messina in Sicily with dead and dying men at the oars. The
ships had come from the Black Sea port of Caffa (now Feodosiya) in the Crimea,
where the Genoese maintained a trading post. The diseased sailors showed
strange black swellings about the size of an egg or an apple in the armpits and
groin. The swellings oozed blood and pus and were followed by spreading boils
and black blotches on the skin from internal bleeding. The sick suffered severe
pain and died quickly within five days of the first symptoms. As the disease
spread, other symptoms of continuous fever and spitting of blood appeared instead of the swellings or buboes. These victims coughed and sweated heavily
and died even more quickly, within three days or less, sometimes in 24 hours. In
both types everything that issued from the body—breath, sweat, blood from the
buboes and lungs, bloody urine, and blood-blackened excrement—smelled foul.
Depression and despair accompanied the physical symptoms, and before the
end "death is seen seated on the face."

The disease was bubonic plague, present in two forms: one that infected the 2
bloodstream, causing the buboes and internal bleeding, and was spread by contact; and a second, more virulent pneumonic type that infected the lungs and was
spread by respiratory infection. The presence of both at once caused the high mortality and speed of contagion. So lethal was the disease that cases were known of
persons going to bed well and dying before they woke, of doctors catching the illness at a bedside and dying before the patient. So rapidly did it spread from one to
another that to a French physician, Simon de Covino, it seemed as if one sick person "could infect the whole world." The malignity of the pestilence appeared
more terrible because its victims knew no prevention and no remedy.

The physical suffering of the disease and its aspect of evil mystery were ex- 3
pressed in a strange Welsh lament which saw "death coming into our midst like
black smoke, a plague which cuts off the young, a rootless phantom which has no
mercy for fair countenance. Woe is me of the shilling in the armpit! It is seething,
terrible . . . a head that gives pain and causes a loud cry . . . a painful angry
knob . . . Great is its seething like a burning cinder . . . a grievous thing of ashy
color." Its eruption is ugly like the "seeds of black peas, broken fragments of brit-
tle sea-coal . . . the early ornaments of black death, cinders of the peelings of the
cockle weed, a mixed multitude, a black plague like halfpence, like berries. . . . "

Rumors of a terrible plague supposedly arising in China and spreading 4
through Tartary (Central Asia) to India and Persia, Mesopotamia, Syria, Egypt,
and all of Asia Minor had reached Europe in 1346. They told of a death toll so
devastating that all of India was said to be depopulated, whole territories covered by dead bodies, other areas with no one left alive. As added up by Pope
Clement VI at Avignon, the total of reported dead reached 23,840,000. In the
absence of a concept of contagion, no serious alarm was felt in Europe until the
trading ships brought their black burden of pestilence into Messina while other
infected ships from the Levant carried it to Genoa and Venice.

By January 1348 it penetrated France via Marseille, and North Africa via 5
Tunis. Shipborne along coasts and navigable rivers, it spread westward from
Marseille through the ports of Languedoc to Spain and northward up the Rhône

to Avignon, where it arrived in March. It reached Narbonne, Montpellier, Carcassonne, and Toulouse between February and May, and at the same time in Italy spread to Rome and Florence and their hinterlands. Between June and August it reached Bordeaux, Lyon, and Paris, spread to Burgundy and Normandy, and crossed the Channel from Normandy into southern England. From Italy during the same summer it crossed the Alps into Switzerland and reached eastward to Hungary.

6   In a given area the plague accomplished its kill within four to six months and then faded, except in the larger cities, where, rooting into the close-quartered population, it abated during the winter, only to reappear in spring and rage for another six months.

7   In 1349 it resumed in Paris, spread to Picardy, Flanders, and the Low Countries, and from England to Scotland and Ireland as well as to Norway, where a ghost ship with a cargo of wool and a dead crew drifted offshore until it ran aground near Bergen. From there the plague passed into Sweden, Denmark, Prussia, Iceland, and as far as Greenland. Leaving a strange pocket of immunity in Bohemia, and Russia unattacked until 1351, it had passed from most of Europe by mid-1350. Although the mortality rate was erratic, ranging from one fifth in some places to nine tenths or almost total elimination in others, the overall estimate of modern demographers has settled—for the area extending from India to Iceland—around the same figure expressed in Froissart's casual words: "a third of the world died." His estimate, the common one at the time, was not an inspired guess but a borrowing of St. John's figure for mortality from plague in Revelation, the favorite guide to human affairs of the Middle Ages.

8   A third of Europe would have meant about 20 million deaths. No one knows in truth how many died. Contemporary reports were an awed impression, not an accurate count. In crowded Avignon, it was said, 400 died daily; 7,000 houses emptied by death were shut up; a single graveyard received 11,000 corpses in six weeks; half the city's inhabitants reportedly died, including 9 cardinals or one third of the total, and 70 lesser prelates. Watching the endlessly passing death carts, chroniclers let normal exaggeration take wings and put the Avignon death toll at 62,000 and even at 120,000, although the city's total population was probably less than 50,000.

9   When graveyards filled up, bodies at Avignon were thrown into the Rhône until mass burial pits were dug for dumping the corpses. In London in such pits corpses piled up in layers until they overflowed. Everywhere reports speak of the sick dying too fast for the living to bury. Corpses were dragged out of homes and left in front of doorways. Morning light revealed new piles of bodies. In Florence the dead were gathered up by the Compagnia della Misericordia— founded in 1244 to care for the sick—whose members wore red robes and hoods masking the face except for the eyes. When their efforts failed, the dead lay putrid in the streets for days at a time. When no coffins were to be had, the bodies were laid on boards, two or three at once, to be carried to graveyards or common pits. Families dumped their own relatives into the pits, or buried them so hastily and thinly "that dogs dragged them forth and devoured their bodies."

Burial of the plague victims. From Annales de Gilles de Muisit.

Amid accumulating death and fear of contagion, people died without last 10
rites and were buried without prayers, a prospect that terrified the last hours of
the stricken. A bishop in England gave permission to laymen to make confession to each other as was done by the Apostles, "or if no man is present then
even to a woman," and if no priest could be found to administer extreme unc-
tion, "then faith must suffice." Clement VI found it necessary to grant remis-
sions of sin to all who died of the plague because so many were unattended by
priests. "And no bells tolled," wrote a chronicler of Siena, "and nobody wept no
matter what his loss because almost everyone expected death. . . . And people
said and believed, 'This is the end of the world.'"

In Paris, where the plague lasted through 1349, the reported death rate was 11
800 a day, in Pisa 500, in Vienna 500 to 600. The total dead in Paris numbered
50,000 or half the population. Florence, weakened by the famine of 1347, lost
three to four fifths of its citizens, Venice two thirds, Hamburg and Bremen,
though smaller in size, about the same proportion. Cities, as centers of transportation, were more likely to be affected than villages, although once a village
was infected, its death rate was equally high. At Givry, a prosperous village in
Burgundy of 1,200 to 1,500 people, the parish register records 615 deaths in the
space of fourteen weeks, compared to an average of thirty deaths a year in the
previous decade. In three villages of Cambridgeshire, manorial records show a
death rate of 47 percent, 57 percent, and in one case 70 percent. When the last
survivors, too few to carry on, moved away, a deserted village sank back into
the wilderness and disappeared from the map altogether, leaving only a grass-
covered ghostly outline to show where mortals once had lived.

12   In enclosed places such as monasteries and prisons, the infection of one
person usually meant that of all, as happened in the Franciscan convents of
Carcassonne and Marseille, where every inmate without exception died. Of the
140 Dominicans at Montpellier only seven survived. Petrarch's brother
Gherardo, member of a Carthusian monastery, buried the prior and 34 fellow
monks one by one, sometimes three a day, until he was left alone with his dog
and fled to look for a place that would take him in. Watching every comrade
die, men in such places could not but wonder whether the strange peril that
filled the air had not been sent to exterminate the human race. In Kilkenny,
Ireland, Brother John Clyn of the Friars Minor, another monk left alone among
dead men, kept a record of what had happened lest "things which should be
remembered perish with time and vanish from the memory of those who come
after us." Sensing "the whole world, as it were, placed within the grasp of the
Evil One," and waiting for death to visit him too, he wrote, "I leave parchment
to continue this work, if perchance any man survive and any of the race of
Adam escape this pestilence and carry on the work which I have begun."
Brother John, as noted by another hand, died of the pestilence, but he foiled
oblivion.

13   The largest cities of Europe, with populations of about 100,000, were Paris
and Florence, Venice and Genoa. At the next level, more than 50,000 were Ghent
and Bruges in Flanders, Milan, Bologna, Rome, Naples, and Palermo, and
Cologne. London hovered below 50,000, the only city in England except York
with more than 10,000. At the level of 20,000 to 50,000 were Bordeaux, Toulouse,
Montpellier, Marseille, and Lyon in France, Barcelona, Seville, and Toledo in
Spain, Siena, Pisa, and other secondary cities in Italy, and the Hanseatic trading
cities of the Empire. The plague raged through them all, killing anywhere from
one third to two thirds of their inhabitants. Italy, with a total population of 10 to
11 million, probably suffered the heaviest toll. Following the Florentine bankrupt-
cies, the crop failures and workers' riots of 1346–47, the revolt of Cola di Rienzi
that plunged Rome into anarchy, the plague came as the peak of successive calamities. As if the world were indeed in the grasp of the Evil One, its first appearance on the European mainland in January 1348 coincided with a fearsome
earthquake that carved a path of wreckage from Naples up to Venice. Houses
collapsed, church towers toppled, villages were crushed, and the destruction
reached as far as Germany and Greece. Emotional response, dulled by horrors,
underwent a kind of atrophy epitomized by the chronicler who wrote, "And in
these days was burying without sorrowe and wedding without friendschippe."

14   In Siena, where more than half the inhabitants died of the plague, work was
abandoned on the great cathedral, planned to be the largest in the world, and
never resumed, owing to loss of workers and master masons and "the melancholy and grief" of the survivors. The cathedral's truncated transept still stands
in permanent witness to the sweep of death's scythe. Angolo di Tura, a chronicler of Siena, recorded the fear of contagion that froze every other instinct.
"Father abandoned child, wife husband, one brother another," he wrote, "for
this plague seemed to strike through the breath and sight. And so they died.

And no one could be found to bury the dead for money or friendship. . . . And I, Angolo di Tura, called the Fat, buried my five children with my own hands, and so did many others likewise."

There were many to echo his account of inhumanity and few to balance it,   15
for the plague was not the kind of calamity that inspired mutual help. Its loathsomeness and deadliness did not herd people together in mutual distress, but only prompted their desire to escape each other. "Magistrates and notaries refused to come and make the wills of the dying," reported a Franciscan friar of Piazza in Sicily; what was worse, "even the priests did not come to hear their confessions." A clerk of the Archbishop of Canterbury reported the same of English priests who "turned away from the care of their benefices from fear of death." Cases of parents deserting children and children their parents were reported across Europe from Scotland to Russia. The calamity chilled the hearts of men, wrote Boccaccio in his famous account of the plague in Florence that serves as introduction to the *Decameron*. "One man shunned another . . . kinsfolk held aloof, brother was forsaken by brother, oftentimes husband by wife; nay, what is more, and scarcely to be believed, fathers and mothers were found to abandon their own children to their fate, untended, unvisited as if they had been strangers." Exaggeration and literary pessimism were common in the 14th century, but the Pope's physician, Guy de Chauliac, was a sober, careful observer who reported the same phenomenon: "A father did not visit his son, nor the son his father. Charity was dead."

Yet not entirely. In Paris, according to the chronicler Jean de Venette, the   16
nuns of the Hôtel Dieu or municipal hospital, "having no fear of death, tended the sick with all sweetness and humility." New nuns repeatedly took the places of those who died, until the majority "many times renewed by death now rest in peace with Christ as we may piously believe."

When the plague entered northern France in July 1348, it settled first in   17
Normandy and, checked by winter, gave Picardy a deceptive interim until the next summer. Either in mourning or warning, black flags were flown from church towers of the worst-stricken villages of Normandy. "And in that time," wrote a monk of the abbey of Fourcarment, "the mortality was so great among the people of Normandy that those of Picardy mocked them." The same unneighborly reaction was reported of the Scots, separated by a winter's immunity from the English. Delighted to hear of the disease that was scourging the "southrons," they gathered forces for an invasion, "laughing at their enemies." Before they could move, the savage mortality fell upon them too, scattering some in death and the rest in panic to spread the infection as they fled.

In Picardy in the summer of 1349 the pestilence penetrated the castle of   18
Coucy to kill Enguerrand's mother, Catherine, and her new husband. Whether her nine-year-old son escaped by chance or was perhaps living elsewhere with one of his guardians is unrecorded. In nearby Amiens, tannery workers, responding quickly to losses in the labor force, combined to bargain for higher wages. In another place villagers were seen dancing to drums and trumpets, and on being asked the reason, answered that, seeing their neighbors die day

by day while their village remained immune, they believed they could keep the plague from entering "by the jollity that is in us. That is why we dance." Further north in Tournai on the border of Flanders, Gilles li Muisis, Abbot of St. Martin's, kept one of the epidemic's most vivid accounts. The passing bells rang all day and all night, he recorded, because sextons were anxious to obtain their fees while they could. Filled with the sound of mourning, the city became oppressed by fear, so that the authorities forbade the tolling of bells and the wearing of black and restricted funeral services to two mourners. The silencing of funeral bells and of criers' announcements of deaths was ordained by most cities. Siena imposed a fine on the wearing of mourning clothes by all except widows.

19   Flight was the chief recourse of those who could afford it or arrange it. The rich fled to their country places like Boccaccio's young patricians of Florence, who settled in a pastoral palace "removed on every side from the roads" with "wells of cool water and vaults of rare wines." The urban poor died in their burrows, "and only the stench of their bodies informed neighbors of their death." That the poor were more heavily afflicted than the rich was clearly remarked at the time, in the north as in the south. A Scottish chronicler, John of Fordun, stated flatly that the pest "attacked especially the meaner sort and common people—seldom the magnates." Simon de Covino of Montpellier made the same observation. He ascribed it to the misery and want and hard lives that made the poor more susceptible, which was half the truth. Close contact and lack of sanitation was the unrecognized other half. It was noticed too that the young died in greater proportion than the old. Simon de Covino compared the disappearance of youth to the withering of flowers in the fields.

20   In the countryside peasants dropped dead on the roads, in the fields, in their houses. Survivors in growing helplessness fell into apathy, leaving ripe wheat uncut and livestock untended. Oxen and asses, sheep and goats, pigs and chickens ran wild and they too, according to local reports, succumbed to the pest. English sheep, bearers of the precious wool, died throughout the country. The chronicler Henry Knighton, canon of Leicester Abbey, reported 5,000 dead in one field alone, "their bodies so corrupted by the plague that neither beast nor bird would touch them," and spreading an appalling stench. In the Austrian Alps wolves came down to prey upon sheep and then, "as if alarmed by some invisible warning, turned and fled back into the wilderness." In remote Dalmatia bolder wolves descended upon a plague-stricken city and attacked human survivors. For want of herdsmen, cattle strayed from place to place and died in hedgerows and ditches. Dogs and cats fell like the rest.

21   The dearth of labor held a fearful prospect because the 14th century lived close to the annual harvest both for food and for next year's seed. "So few servants and laborers were left," wrote Knighton, "that no one knew where to turn for help." The sense of a vanishing future created a kind of dementia of despair. A Bavarian chronicler of Neuberg on the Danube recorded that "Men and women . . . wandered around as if mad" and let their cattle stray "because no one had any inclination to concern themselves about the future." Fields went

uncultivated, spring seed unsown. Second growth with nature's awful energy crept back over cleared land, dikes crumbled, salt water reinvaded and soured the lowlands. With so few hands remaining to restore the work of centuries, people felt, in Walsingham's words, that "the world could never again regain its former prosperity."

Though the death rate was higher among the anonymous poor, the known 22 and the great died too. King Alfonso XI of Castile was the only reigning monarch killed by the pest, but his neighbor King Pedro of Aragon lost his wife, Queen Leonora, his daughter Marie, and a niece in the space of six months. John Cantacuzene, Emperor of Byzantium, lost his son. In France the lame Queen Jeanne and her daughter-in-law Bonne de Luxemburg, wife of the Dauphin, both died in 1349 in the same phase that took the life of Enguerrand's mother. Jeanne, Queen of Navarre, daughter of Louis X, was another victim. Edward III's second daughter, Joanna, who was on her way to marry Pedro, the heir of Castile, died in Bordeaux. Women appear to have been more vulnerable than men, perhaps because, being more housebound, they were more exposed to fleas. Boccaccio's mistress Fiammetta, illegitimate daughter of the King of Naples, died, as did Laura, the beloved—whether real or fictional—of Petrarch. Reaching out to us in the future, Petrarch cried, "Oh happy posterity who will not experience such abysmal woe and will look upon our testimony as a fable."

In Florence Giovanni Villani, the great historian of his time, died at 68 in the 23 midst of an unfinished sentence: ". . . *e dure questo pistolenza fino a . . .* (in the midst of this pestilence there came to an end . . .)." Siena's master painters, the brothers Ambrogio and Pietro Lorenzetti, whose names never appear after 1348, presumably perished in the plague, as did Andrea Pisano, architect and sculptor of Florence. William of Ockham and the English mystic Richard Rolle of Hampole both disappear from mention after 1349. Francisco Datini, merchant of Prato, lost both his parents and two siblings. Curious sweeps of mortality afflicted certain bodies of merchants in London. All eight wardens of the Company of Cutters, all six wardens of the Hatters, and four wardens of the Goldsmiths died before July 1350. Sir John Pulteney, master draper and four times Mayor of London, was a victim, likewise Sir John Montgomery, Governor of Calais.

Among the clergy and doctors the mortality was naturally high because of 24 the nature of their professions. Out of 24 physicians in Venice, 20 were said to have lost their lives in the plague, although according to another account, some were believed to have fled or to have shut themselves up in their houses. At Montpellier, site of the leading medieval medical school, the physician Simon de Covino reported that, despite the great number of doctors, "hardly one of them escaped." In Avignon, Guy de Chauliac confessed that he performed his medical visits only because he dared not stay away for fear of infamy, but "I was in continual fear." He claimed to have contracted the disease but to have cured himself by his own treatment; if so, he was one of the few who recovered.

Clerical mortality varied with rank. Although the one-third toll of cardi- 25 nals reflects the same proportion as the whole, this was probably due to their concentration in Avignon. In England, in strange and almost sinister procession, the Archbishop of Canterbury, John Stratford, died in August 1348, his appointed successor died in May 1349, and the next appointee three months later, all three within a year. Despite such weird vagaries, prelates in general managed to sustain a higher survival rate than the lesser clergy. Among bishops the deaths have been estimated at about one in twenty. The loss of priests, even if many avoided their fearful duty of attending the dying, was about the same as among the population as a whole.

26   Government officials, whose loss contributed to the general chaos, found, on the whole, no special shelter. In Siena four of the nine members of the governing oligarchy died, in France one third of the royal notaries, in Bristol 15 out of the 52 members of the Town Council or almost one third. Tax-collecting obviously suffered, with the result that Philip VI was unable to collect more than a fraction of the subsidy granted him by the Estates in the winter of 1347–48.

27   Lawlessness and debauchery accompanied the plague as they had during the great plague of Athens of 430 B.C., when according to Thucydides, men grew bold in the indulgence of pleasure: "For seeing how the rich died in a moment and those who had nothing immediately inherited their property, they reflected that life and riches were alike transitory and they resolved to enjoy themselves while they could." Human behavior is timeless. When St. John had his vision of plague in Revelation, he knew from some experience or race memory that those who survived "repented not of the work of their hands. . . . Neither repented they of their murders, nor of their sorceries, nor of their fornication, nor of their thefts."

COMPREHENSION

1. The title of this essay suggests a religious theme. Why did intellectuals and religious leaders associate the bubonic plague with biblical prophecy?
2. Does this essay have a thesis, or does it merely record in detail a period in European history? If it does have a thesis, is it implied or expressed directly? Explain your answer.
3. Does Tuchman suggest that Europe was "fated" to endure the tragic consequences of the plague owing to a higher power, or does she attribute the disaster to a confluence of history and chance? Explain your answer.

RHETORIC

1. Tuchman begins her essay by describing in detail the physical symptoms of the plague. What strategy lies behind this rhetorical decision?
2. Tuchman has a reputation as a historian whose goal was to bring "history to life." What methods does she use to realize this goal? Is she successful? Why or why not? What does the illustration on page 685 contribute?
3. Contemporary authors and filmmakers often select morbid themes for their sensational value or for financial gain, or both. For example, there is a plethora of

"true-crime" stories, "re-creations" of natural disasters, and profiles of aberrant and murderous personalities such as Jeffrey Dahmer, Ted Bundy, and the "Hillside Strangler." Is this Tuchman's purpose? Explain why or why not.

4. Note the particular parts of speech Tuchman uses to begin paragraphs 5–7, 9, 11, 12, 14, 16–18, 20, 22, and 23. All begin with either conjunctions or prepositions. How do these grammatical devices help maintain the flow of Tuchman's narrative?

5. Tuchman makes references to a vast number of historical figures and specific locations in 14th-century Europe. What is her assumption about the educational level of her intended audience? About the specialization of her readership? Is it necessary to know something about the people and places she cites to appreciate the essay? Or is Tuchman writing a book of general interest, with the implicit supposition that different readers will extract their own level of appreciation from her narrative? Explain.

6. Tuchman uses direct quotations from the observers and chroniclers of the times. Examine the use of such sources in paragraphs 10, 13, 15–20, and 23, among others. How does Tuchman weave their observations into her own narrative so that the essay maintains unity and coherence? How does her use of these citations affect the strength of her writing?

WRITING

1. Write a 300-word summary of Tuchman's essay.

2. For a research project, study Tuchman's philosophy regarding how history should be reported. Apply your research to her treatment of the Black Death.

3. **Writing an Argument:** Argue for or against the proposition that an epidemic as severe as the one that Tuchman describes could not possibly occur in the 21st century.

NETWORKING *Applying 21st-Century Literacies*	
Using Visuals to Make Logical Appeals: In your response to question 3 under Writing, include at least one visual that supports your argument with hard data. If you use an existing chart or graph, be sure to document your source; and if you create a visual from data, be sure to cite the source that data came from.	

It's Spreading

Jill Lepore

Jill Lepore (b. 1966) is a prize-winning historian who teaches at Harvard University. She was born in Worcester, Massachusetts, and received degrees from Tufts University (BA, 1987), the University of Michigan (MA, 1990), and Yale University (1995) before embarking on her academic career. Among her several books are King Philip's War and the Origins of American Identity *(1998) and* New York Burning: Liberty and Slavery in an Eighteenth Century City *(2005). Lepore is also a staff writer at the* New Yorker, *in which the following essay on American epidemics appeared in 2009.*

1   On December 14, 1929, during a holiday shopping season darkened by the greatest stock-market crash in American history, Simon S. Martin bought a parrot for his wife, Lillian, at a pet shop on North Eutaw Street, in Baltimore. It was not, as it happened, a well parrot. Hoping to surprise his wife, Martin seems to have asked his daughter, Edith, and her husband, Lee Kalmey, the owner of an auto repair shop, to take care of the bird and bring it over to his house in Annapolis in ten days' time. By Christmas Eve, the parrot must have shown signs of illness: puffy eyes, a drooping head, and feathers as ruffled as if it had flown through a squall. Come Yuletide, the Martins had a dead parrot on their hands.

2   The pet-shop owner, who may have been wise to the fact that Simon Martin was secretary of the Annapolis Chamber of Commerce, at first offered a replacement, although by New Year's, when Lillian Martin and Edith and Lee Kalmey fell dangerously ill, he was backpedalling, denying that he had ever sold Martin a bird. Meanwhile, the Kalmeys were getting sicker and sicker, showing symptoms of both pneumonia and typhoid.

3   On January 6th, a local doctor examined the patients. He had just read a newspaper article about something called parrot fever: It had shown up in Argentina months earlier, when an actor playing a sailor had caught it from his stage parrot. The disease, also called psittacosis, had since spread through South America and Europe. No one seemed to know much about it except that it was deadly. The doctor sent a telegram to the U.S. Public Health Service, in Washington: "Can you place supply parrot fever serum our disposal immediately." Unfortunately, there was no serum, or any known treatment. The mayor alerted the governor. Within forty-eight hours, epidemiologists from the Baltimore City Health Department, the Maryland Department of Health, the United States Navy and Army, and the Public Health Service, including a team of men from the Hygienic Laboratory in Washington, arrived on the scene. Someone called the newspaper.

4   "'Parrot' Disease Baffles Experts" the Washington *Post* reported in an issue that went to press the night of January 8th, thrilling readers with a medical mystery that would capture the nation's attention with the prospect of a parrot-fever pandemic. Reports, cabled and wired and radioed across land and sea, were printed in the daily paper or broadcast, within minutes, on the radio: tallies, theories, postmortems, more to fear. Before it was over, an admiral in the U.S. Navy ordered sailors at sea to cast their pet parrots into the ocean. One city health commissioner urged everyone who owned a parrot to wring its neck. People abandoned their pet parrots on the streets. Every sneeze seemed a symptom. As the story grew, it took on certain familiar—and, as it turned out, durable—features, features that borrow as much from pulp fiction as from public health: super scientists fight super bugs in race to defeat foreign menace invading American homes, beneath the very Christmas tree.

Epidemics follow patterns because diseases follow patterns. Viruses spread; 5
they reproduce; they die. Epidemiologists study patterns in order to combat infection. Stories about epidemics follow patterns, too. Stories aren't often deadly
but they can be virulent: spreading fast, weakening resistance, wreaking havoc.
During the recent swine-flu panic, Joe Biden warned Americans not to ride the
subway or fly on an airplane, and pharmacies ran out of surgical masks. Why
was it so hard to tell, as the story was breaking, if a flu outbreak of pandemic
proportions was under way? The world is a far better place for the work epidemiologists do. Maybe, though, we could do with a few more narratologists.

The stories about epidemics that are told in the American press—their plots 6
and tropes—date to the nineteen-twenties, when modern research science, science journalism, and science fiction were born. The germ theory of disease
dates to the mid-eighteen-hundreds. Pasteur developed a rabies vaccine in
1885, launching a global battle against infectious illness. By the nineteen-twenties,
scientists had developed a vaccine for diphtheria; other vaccines, like the one
for polio, would take decades, but hopes ran high. In *The Conquest of Disease*
(1927), Thurman B. Rice, a professor of sanitary science, predicted the eradication of sickness itself.

Meanwhile, ordinary people learned to blame germs, not God, for catastro- 7
phes like the pandemic of 1918, when at least fifty million people, including
nearly seven hundred thousand Americans, died of influenza. Germ theory,
which secularized infectious disease, had a side effect: It sacralized epidemiology.
The nineteen-twenties witnessed the inauguration of what the historian of medicine Nancy Tomes has called the "epidemic exposé," the hair-raising account of a
disease that threatens to destroy the human race. The genre's master was a bacte-
riologist turned journalist named Paul de Kruif. He had taught at the University
of Michigan and worked for the U.S. Sanitary Corps, studying the gangrene ba-
cillus. After the war, he turned to writing. In 1925, his collaboration with Sinclair
Lewis led to the publication of *Arrowsmith,* a novel about a young doctor fighting
bubonic plague—an early medical thriller, for which de Kruif received twenty-
five percent of the royalties. In 1926, de Kruif turned to nonfiction, publishing
Microbe Hunters, a book of profiles of scientists, starting with Leeuwenhoek, who
can see tiny things the rest of us can't, things that are trying to kill us.

Microbe Hunters, which inspired a generation of young readers to pursue 8
careers in science, appeared a month before the first issue of Hugo Gernsback's
Amazing Stories, the first magazine of what is now called science fiction. Many
of its stories concern the work of laboratory scientists; the issue of July, 1929,
included "The Purple Death," the story of a young doctor who keeps a copy of
Microbe Hunters on his desk.

The coming plague was Paul de Kruif's bread and butter. Three months 9
before Simon Martin bought his wife a parrot for Christmas, de Kruif issued a
warning in the lead article of *Ladies' Home Journal:* "In American milk today
there lurks a terrible, wasting fever, that may keep you in bed for a couple of
weeks, that may fasten itself on you for one, or for two, or even for seven
years—that might culminate by killing you." What was this dread malady?
Undulant fever. "At least 50,000 people are sick with it at this very moment,"

their ailment virtually unknown to "their baffled doctors." De Kruif's article, titled "Before You Drink a Glass of Milk," scared a lot of people and sold a lot of magazines. Boasting of its success, the editor of *Ladies' Home Journal* explained, "Nobody had ever heard of undulant fever before."

10 The experts who descended on Annapolis in early January, 1930, weren't half as baffled as the Washington *Post* made them out to be, but the reading public must have been at least twice as confused. Was parrot fever really something to worry about? Reading the newspaper, it was hard to say. "Not Contagious in Man," the *Times* announced. "Highly contagious," the Washington *Post* said. Who knew? Nobody had ever heard of it before. It lurked in American homes. It came from afar. It was invisible. It might kill you. It made a very good story. In the late hours of January 8th, editors at the Los Angeles *Times* decided to put it on the front page: "Two Women and Man in Annapolis Believed to Have 'Parrot Fever.'"

11   The next day, in Toledo, Mrs. Percy Q. Williams, whose husband had just returned from Cuba with two parrots, died in Mercy Hospital; in Baltimore, Mrs. Louise Schaeffer succumbed to what had at first appeared to be pneumonia. (Women, many of them widows, constituted the majority of the outbreak's victims. There were suggestions that lonely old women had got the disease by feeding their parrots mouth to mouth. Some called the disease "old maid's pneumonia.") Those deaths would normally have been unremarkable: two older women fading away in the cold of winter. Not this week. On learning that Schaeffer "had been in contact with a parrot several days before she became ill," physicians suspected parrot fever and ordered an autopsy, whereupon the Surgeon General, Dr. Hugh Smith Cumming (a eugenicist best known to history for launching the Tuskegee syphilis experiment, that same year), warned Americans to stay away from recently imported parrots. He insisted that he "did not fear an epidemic," but that, of course, only got people talking about one. Although the results of Schaeffer's autopsy were not yet available, "Baltimore Woman Dies" made it onto the front page of the Chicago *Daily Tribune* on January 11th and "Parrot Fever Kills 2 in this Country" appeared on page 3 of the *Times*. That paper also reported on efforts to trace deadly Argentine parrots that had come to the United States through what were called, as if they were criminals, "two suspected New York dealers."

12   Some people were worried about more than parrots. On January 11th, after several clerks in the poultry department of a Toledo store started coughing, the city's Health Department launched an investigation into "incipient cases" of psittacosis. Two days later, in a story that appeared on the front page of William Randolph Hearst's San Francisco *Examiner,* the Associated Press announced that the country's scientists had declared war: "The disease-fighting armament of the nation today was directed against a new and mysterious enemy." The microbe hunters had taken out their microscopes.

13 In the years following the First World War, a great many American scientists were looking for sources to fund their vital research. The nation's scientific

organizations hired publicity firms. In 1926, a coalition of scientists launched a campaign to raise "A National Fund for the Support of Research in Pure Science." Half the battle, though, had to do with winning over the public, and de Kruif's work made clear that stories were powerful ammunition. Before the First World War, journalists didn't generally report on science, and they certainly didn't profile scientists. After the war, scientists tried writing for newspapers and magazines, attempting to explain the value of their work, but, year by year, the number of scientists writing for a popular audience fell while the number of journalists specializing in science writing rose. Perhaps the era's most effective pro-science publicity machine was the Science Service, a wire service founded in 1920 and edited by a chemist named Edwin E. Slosson. Its purpose was to promote scientific research by feeding stories to newspapers. The service, Slosson said, would not "indulge in propaganda unless it be propaganda to urge the value of research and the usefulness of science." Financed by the newspaper publisher E. W. Scripps, and later by the American Association for the Advancement of Science and the National Research Council, the Science Service reached a fifth of the American reading public by the mid-nineteen-thirties.

What a microbe hunter needed to do to get funding was to hunt and kill a 14 microbe, preferably a lethal one that nobody had ever heard of before. On January 6, 1930, when that family doctor sent his telegram to the U.S. Public Health Service, the message was sent on to the Hygienic Laboratory, where Dr. Charles Armstrong, a forty-five-year-old pathologist, was charged with heading the investigation. Armstrong wanted to contain the outbreak, urgently; he also wanted to develop a serum, to save the lives of people already infected. Doing so would require experiments; those experiments required infected parrots and infected people. To gather subjects, Armstrong needed to spread the word about psittacosis. What Armstrong needed was a parrot-fever panic.

As Armstrong arrived in Annapolis, a team of public-health officials was 15 sent to that North Eutaw Street pet shop in Baltimore—where four employees were now sick—to track down the purchasers of all the recently imported parrots. Not all those parrots had stayed in town. Mrs. Hugh Lett bought a parrot in Baltimore on December 18th; the bird died on New Year's Eve; Mrs. Lett took sick on January 7th, by which time she was in Cambridge. Armstrong wired messages to public-health officials across the country, asking them to be on the lookout for psittacosis. In city after city, parrot dealers handed over to investigators sick parrots and lists of the people who had bought parrots for Christmas. Dead birds, some of which were exhumed, were shipped to Washington. Cases of suspected psittacosis cropped up in Providence and Chicago, New Haven and Los Angeles. The home of an Ohio family was quarantined after yet another Christmas parrot died. Inevitably, there were cases merely "simulating psittacosis," like the parents of fifteen-year-old Lillian Muller, of the Bronx, who had bought their daughter a parrot, imported from Argentina, at a pet shop in Harlem. The *Times* offered reassurance: "The Mullers' parrot has been eating regularly and has exhibited no signs of drooping." (One constabulary note: The

A.P. reported from North Adams, Massachusetts, on January 13th, "A parrot in a local family, whose name was not given out, recently died." Polly?)

16   By January 15th, the *Times* reported fifty cases nationwide, including eleven in New York City, and seven deaths, including one in Queens and one in Yonkers. Doctors insisted, in vain, that "there was no occasion for general alarm," and "stressed the fact that in none of the cases reported so far in New York has the diagnosis been definitely established as psittacosis." Later that day—after the *Times* went to press with the death count—authorities revealed that blood tests on the New York dead had all come out negative. The *Times*, whose coverage of parrot fever was, all things considered, a model of restraint and clarity, made a point of announcing those negative tests. Elsewhere, though, autopsies and blood cultures that came out negative for psittacosis didn't make it into the papers. By now, Lillian Martin and Edith and Lee Kalmey were fast improving; this was not widely reported, either. People who got better simply fell out of the news.

17 The nationwide sweep for psittacosis soon supplied Armstrong with enough samples—parrots, healthy, sick, and dead; the blood from infected humans; and even the scrapings from Lillian Martin's birdcage—to begin his work, which he conducted in two basement rooms in the Hygienic Laboratory, aided by his technician, Henry (Shorty) Anderson. "Those parrots were sure mean bastards," Armstrong said. Armstrong and Anderson wore rubber gloves, put trays filled with cresol in the doorways, and covered the birds' cages with disinfectant-soaked curtains. They were not, however, especially fastidious. "The only thing hygienic about the Hygienic Laboratory was its name," one researcher there said. Armstrong explained, "If we'd got too careful, we'd have spent all our time being careful and how could we have found out anything about it?"

18   This was yet another hallmark of the swashbuckling microbe hunter, who lacked the fussiness of the housewife. "Germ" became a household word in the nineteen-teens. By the twenties, Americans, and especially housewives, lived in fear of germs. Not only did newspapers and magazines run almost daily stories about newly discovered germs like undulant fever but their pages were filled with advertisements for hygiene products, like Listerine (first sold over the counter in 1914 and, in many ways, the granddaddy of Purell), Lysol (marketed, in 1918, as an anti-flu measure), Kotex ("feminine hygiene," the first menstrual pad, introduced in 1920, a postwar conversion of a surgical dressing developed by Kimberly-Clark), Cellophane (1923), and Kleenex (1924; another Kimberly-Clark product, sold as a towel for removing makeup until a consumer survey revealed that people were using it to blow their noses). Perhaps because kitchens and laboratories have much in common, journalists like de Kruif strove to underscore the manliness of the microbe hunter. Armstrong, de Kruif wrote, "was definitely not the kind of man who would even own a parrot, let alone kiss it."

19   Armstrong and Anderson and other government scientists worked night and day. On January 13th, the Chicago *Daily Tribune* reported a landmark success: "Parrot Fever Germ Isolated."

The parrot-fever story made the malady out to be virulent, mysterious, and 20
exotic, despite these facts: The disease was not baffling; it had been identified in
the nineteenth century; it was known to infect members of the Psittacidae family, which includes parrots, parakeets, macaws, and cockatoos; in the nineteen-
thirties, the only birds likely to be contagious were those brought to the United
States during the last months of 1929; it is possible to catch the disease only
from an infected bird (people can't spread it); it infected then, and continues to
infect today, between one and two hundred Americans every year. There was a
danger, to be sure. Psittacosis is now easily treated with antibiotics like doxycy-
cline, but that wasn't the case in 1930, when one in five people infected with the
disease died. Nevertheless, the only people who had much to worry about were
people who had been in quite close contact with certain tropical birds very recently imported from South America.

Psittacosis incited, if briefly, a sizable panic among people who, by any rea- 21
sonable measure, had nothing to fear. That was dangerous. Even as the story
unfolded, what to make of parrot fever and just how much responsibility the
press or the scientific community bore for the panic proved matters of dispute.
But what happened next seems nearly as dangerous as the panic itself: People
suddenly started insisting that parrot fever didn't exist.

"U.S. Alarm Over Parrot Disease Not Warranted," the Chicago *Daily Tri-* 22
bune declared, on January 15th. Less than two weeks into the story, parrot fever
looked, suddenly, silly. Parrot fever became a national joke. A Washington correspondent for the *Times* filed a story about a parrot owned by Secretary of
State Henry Stimson. The parrot, named the Old Soak, had been locked in the
basement of the Pan-American Building, "not because he has psittacosis" but
because he had a habit of swearing. The *Wall Street Journal* ran this joke: What
did the janitor say when the professor at the Polytechnic Institute asked him
why he was cleaning the lab with carbolic acid? "'So none of de Poly students
gets dis new parrot fever.'" Even the straight stories weren't taken seriously. "A
parrot foundling made its appearance early yesterday morning when a green
bird with a chipped beak was discovered in the vestibule of John Schreyer's
home, 25–27 Humphreys Street, East Elmhurst, Queens," the *Times* reported,
whereupon jailbirds at Sing Sing offered asylum for all unwanted parrots; the
warden said, "The inmates here think this talk about parrot fever is nonsense."

A pro-parrot lobby formed. On January 17th, six of the country's leading 23
importers of winged pets, including the Odenwald Bird Company, the Imperial
Pet Shop, and the Dahle Bird Company of Philadelphia, gathered at the Hotel
Commodore in New York, where they founded the Bird Dealers' Association of
America. Prussia and Bavaria, suffering from their own outbreaks, had already
instituted parrot embargoes. The bird business was in a bad way. The Bird Dealers fought back by claiming that the disease did not exist, had never existed in
human beings, "and that the scare over 'parrot fever' had been chiefly brought
about by the active imagination of a Baltimore newspaper man."

Exaggeration breeds exaggeration. The counter-story spread as wildly as 24
the story had. And the Bird Dealers had a point about the imagination of

newspapermen. The first American doctor to believe he had seen psittacosis had read about it in the newspaper. The Martins' doctor probably read Hearst's Baltimore *American*. Every Sunday, Hearst produced for his papers a supplement called the *American Weekly*. Edited by Morrill Goddard, the *American Weekly* was something between *Parade* and the *National Enquirer*. Goddard knew how to sell a plague and knew, too, that selling plagues was good for his advertising accounts with hygiene-product manufacturers. In March, 1930, Goddard was interviewed by the staff of the J. Walter Thompson Company, one of the nation's most influential advertising agencies. "There is a lot of interest now in parrot fever," the interviewer observed, asking, "How far will the research on parrot fever have to go before you print something about it?" Goddard took umbrage at the suggestion that he had not already covered parrot fever—that he had not, in fact, *scooped* parrot fever. "We were the first newspaper to present it to the American public," he claimed, not quite accurately, "to warn them that parrots might be deadly in the home." As to how he had come by the story, Goddard explained that he spent his evenings reading obscure scientific journals, where he read about the outbreak in Buenos Aires:

> I sent down to our man there and he sent me a wretched story without details and I cabled him and he sent me a second story with further details and pictures and that story was printed about four or five weeks before the first case developed in New York. It gave all the details of what is known as "psittacosis." Now, it is a matter of dispute whether it is a germ or a virus but it is a matter of no consequence as far as making a feature out of it.

25   Goddard had no real interest in the science. He wanted to run a story about a danger lurking in American homes: "The fact that the parrot in the cage at your house may put you in the cemetery is enough for me."

26 On January 16th, just over one week after the Washington *Post* printed its first parrot-fever piece, the *Times* ran a story radioed in by a correspondent in Austria: A Viennese scientist believed that Americans were suffering from "mass suggestion." Dr. Julius Bauer said, "Psittacosis has been known to science since 1892. Now for some reason it has assumed in the public mind the dimensions of a plague." The next day, the Science Service, reporting on an article in the *Journal of the American Medical Association*, reminded Americans that "the possibility of unusual disorders must be ever present in the medical mind." Who knew what might infect us next? Parrot fever ought to serve as proof that "it is no longer possible for any person or any nation to live in isolation." The world, in short, was a dangerous place.

27   Or was it just a gullible one? "Every winter, America has to have a new malady, and this year it is Parrot Fever," a columnist for the *Post* wrote. "People are getting all worked up over this new 'parrot-fever,'" a writer for *Life* scoffed, "but Lord! it's been endemic at the Capitol since Polly was an egg." E. B. White figured that the country was suffering from nothing so much as a bad case of the heebie-jeebies, brought on by extended exposure to newspapers

that were forever issuing warnings about sharks infesting the beaches of New Jersey, anthrax spores contaminating unsterilized shaving brushes, and noxious gases escaping from iceboxes in the middle of the night. In an issue that went to press on January 20th, the *New Yorker*'s Talk of the Town included a piece by White calling parrot fever merely "the latest and most amusing example of the national hypochondria":

> There have been hundreds of national menaces, keeping us all on tenterhooks, keeping the populace feeling the national pulse and applying the national stethoscope. Psittacosis is one of the best, because one of the most picturesque. What will probably happen will be that some reporter will invent a disease traceable to something that happens to everybody: "Otis heart" from riding in elevators, maybe, or "corn-flakes itch" from eating breakfast food, and we'll all die of autosuggestion.

That hasn't happened quite yet, but we still can't tell whether we are all about to die or whether we are being sold a bill of goods. This condition is chronic. 28

On January 22, 1930, the *Post* reported that Lillian Martin and Edith and Lee Kalmey had recovered. Herbert Hoover prepared to sign an executive order banning the importation of parrots. The story seemed more or less wrapped up. But then, terribly, scientists starting dying. On January 23rd, Dr. Daniel S. Hatfield, the chief of the bureau of communicable diseases of the Baltimore City Health Department, succumbed to psittacosis. Hatfield's colleague Dr. William Stokes died on February 10th. Shorty Anderson died on February 8th. That same day, Charles Armstrong was admitted to the U.S. Naval Hospital with a fever of 104 degrees. 29

The director of the Hygienic Laboratory, George McCoy, insisted on taking over Armstrong's work himself. He took blood from a patient who had recovered from psittacosis and injected it into Armstrong's veins. Armstrong improved, and eventually recovered. Afterward, he wrote up his report, according to which there had been a total of a hundred and sixty-nine cases of psittacosis nationwide, and thirty-three fatalities. In his report, Armstrong credited the press, without which, he believed, "this outbreak would largely have escaped detection." Armstrong's work earned him a place in de Kruif's 1932 sequel to *Microbe Hunters*, a book titled *Men Against Death*. 30

In February and early March of 1930, while Armstrong was still recovering, nine other people at the Hygienic Laboratory became sick. Psittacosis seemed to have contaminated the whole building. On March 15th, McCoy ordered the building evacuated. Alone, he walked down the stairs to Armstrong's basement laboratory. He killed, with chloroform, every parrot, mouse, pigeon, guinea pig, rat, and monkey that had been used in the psittacosis experiments. "He murdered and murdered and made a slick and clean job of it," de Kruif wrote. He burned the bodies in the building's incinerator. He sealed all the windows. The fumigation squad arrived at 2 P.M. and began spraying the building with cyanide. Sparrows flying fifty feet over the building froze, mid-flight, and fell to earth. The 31 next day, the headline in the *Post* read, "Parrot Fever Panic Seizes Laboratory." Two months later, on May 26, 1930, Congress rewarded the Hygienic Laboratory by expanding it and granting it a new name: the National Institute of Health.

COMPREHENSION

1. Summarize the parrot fever epidemic that Lepore recounts. According to Lepore, what significance does this episode have for people today?
2. In paragraph 5, Lepore states, "Epidemics follow patterns because diseases follow patterns." What does she mean? What additional information in the essay supports this observation?
3. What does Lepore think about disease and epidemic "experts"? What is her opinion of media representatives who report on epidemics? Refer to the text to support your answer.

RHETORIC

1. How clearly does the essay's title express Lepore's thesis in this essay? How does she use the opening event in relation to her thesis? What sorts of materials does she use to develop her thesis?
2. Is Lepore's account objective or subjective? Explain your answer.
3. What primary organizational strategy does Lepore use to structure this essay? What other strategies are evident?
4. What transitional devices does Lepore use as she moves from section to section?
5. Explain the purpose of Lepore's concluding paragraph. What point is she trying to make?

WRITING

1. Select a current epidemic or pandemic, and write your own account of this disease.
2. Examine the proper role of the media in warning the public about epidemics.
3. **Writing an Argument:** Argue for or against the proposition that we are overly concerned about epidemics today.

NETWORKING
Applying 21st-Century Literacies

Conducting a Multimedia Research Project: Respond to question 1 under Writing with a research project that incorporates multiple media to inform your audience about a current epidemic or pandemic. Consider approaching this as a documentary that includes visuals like graphs, maps, and photographs—or as a hyperlinked paper that includes links to interviews, newscasts, etc. You could also do an oral presentation that incorporates audio, video, and even a print handout. Don't choose your project's components at random; figure out what genres and media would best suit your purpose: to educate your audience about this disease.

Synthesis: Classic and Contemporary Questions for Comparison

1. Discuss Tuchman's and Lepore's essays in terms of style, method, and tone. What level of language do they employ? What forms of authority do they bring to bear on their subject? What rhetorical strategies do they use? How does the fact that both writers are historians affect their approach to the subject? Does one argue and the other explain or do they both make similar assertions?
2. Compare Tuchman's view of the bubonic plague of the 14th century with Lepore's presentation of the parrot fever epidemic.
3. In groups of three or four, conduct research on epidemics throughout history not mentioned by either Tuchman or Lepore. How do these epidemics serve to reinforce the assertions that the two writers make?

The Masked Marvel's Last Toehold

Richard Selzer

Richard Selzer (b. 1928) is a surgeon who started writing for several hours each night after he had already established a successful medical career. He was born in Troy, New York, and received degrees from Union College (BS, 1948) and Albany Medical College (MD, 1953). For more than two decades Selzer was on the faculty of the Yale School of Medicine. His first collection, Mortal Essays: Notes on the Art of Surgery *(1974), established Selzer as an essayist specializing in the world of medicine and surgery. Selzer employs an elegant prose style in describing the painful and often tragic world of medical procedures and patients. His essays have been collected in several books, among them* Confessions of a Knife *(1979),* Letters to a Young Doctor *(1982),* Taking the World in for Repairs *(1997), and* The Exact Location of the Soul *(2001). Selzer has also written for numerous magazines and has compiled a book of stories,* Imagine a Woman *(1997). The following essay demonstrates Selzer's experience as a surgeon as well as his ability to describe the world of medicine in poetic and haunting terms.*

Morning rounds.

On the fifth floor of the hospital, in the west wing, I know that a man is sitting up in his bed, waiting for me. Elihu Koontz is seventy-five, and he is diabetic. It is two weeks since I amputated his left leg just below the knee. I walk down the corridor, but I do not go straight into his room. Instead, I pause in the doorway. He is not yet aware of my presence, but gazes down at the place in the bed where his leg used to be, and where now there is the collapsed leg of his pajamas. He is totally absorbed, like an athlete appraising the details of his body. What is he thinking, I wonder. Is he dreaming the outline of his toes? Does he see there his foot's incandescent ghost? Could he be angry? Feel that I have taken from him something for which he yearns now with all his heart? Has he forgotten so soon the pain? It was a pain so great as to set him apart from all other men, in a red-hot place where he had no kith or kin. What of those black gorilla toes and the soupy mess that was his heel? I watch him from the doorway. It is a kind of spying, I know.

2   Save for a white fringe open at the front, Elihu Koontz is bald. The hair has grown too long and is wilted. He wears it as one would wear a day-old laurel wreath. He is naked to the waist, so that I can see his breasts. They are the breasts of Buddha, inverted triangles from which the nipples swing, dark as garnets.

3   I have seen enough. I step into the room, and he sees that I am there.

4   "How did the night go, Elihu?"

5   He looks at me for a long moment. "Shut the door," he says.

6   I do, and move to the side of the bed. He takes my left hand in both of his, gazes at it, turns it over, then back, fondling, at last holding it up to his cheek. I do not withdraw from this loving. After a while he relinquishes my hand, and looks up at me.

7   "How is the pain?" I ask.

8   He does not answer, but continues to look at me in silence. I know at once that he has made a decision.

9   "Ever hear of The Masked Marvel?" He says this in a low voice, almost a whisper.

10   "What?"

11   "The Masked Marvel," he says. "You never heard of him?"

12   "No."

13   He clucks his tongue. He is exasperated.

14   All at once there is a recollection. It is dim, distant, but coming near.

15   "Do you mean the wrestler?"

16   Eagerly, he nods, and the breasts bob. How gnomish he looks, oval as the huge helpless egg of some outlandish lizard. He has very long arms, which, now and then, he unfurls to reach for things—a carafe of water, a get-well card. He gazes up at me, urging. He *wants* me to remember.

17   "Well . . . yes," I say. I am straining backward in time. "I saw him wrestle in Toronto long ago."

18   "Ha!" He smiles. "You saw *me*." And his index finger, held rigid and upright, bounces in the air.

19   The man has said something shocking, unacceptable. It must be challenged.

20   "You?" I am trying to smile.

21   Again that jab of the finger. "You saw *me*."

22   "No," I say. But even then, something about Elihu Koontz, those prolonged arms, the shape of his head, the sudden agility with which he leans from his bed to get a large brown envelope from his nightstand, something is forcing me toward a memory. He rummages through his papers, old newspaper clippings, photographs, and I remember . . .

It is almost forty years ago. I am ten years old. I have been sent to Toronto to 23
spend the summer with relatives. Uncle Max has bought two tickets to the
wrestling match. He is taking me that night.

"He isn't allowed," says Aunt Sarah to me. Uncle Max has angina.   24

"He gets too excited," she says.   25

"I wish you wouldn't go, Max," she says.   26

"You mind your own business," he says.   27

And we go. Out into the warm Canadian evening. I am not only abroad, I 28
am abroad in the *evening!* I have never been taken out in the evening. I am terribly excited. The trolleys, the lights, the horns. It is a bazaar. At the Maple Leaf
Gardens, we sit high and near the center. The vast arena is dark except for the
brilliance of the ring at the bottom.

It begins.   29

The wrestlers circle. They grapple. They are all haunch and paunch. I am 30
shocked by their ugliness, but I do not show it. Uncle Max is exhilarated. He
leans forward, his eyes unblinking, on his face a look of enormous happiness.
One after the other, a pair of wrestlers enter the ring. The two men join, twist,
jerk, tug, bend, yank, and throw. Then they leave and are replaced by another
pair. At last it is the main event. "The Angel vs. The Masked Marvel."

On the cover of the program notes, there is a picture of The Angel hanging 31
from the limb of a tree, a noose of thick rope around his neck. The Angel hangs
just so for an hour every day, it is explained, to strengthen his neck. The Masked
Marvel's trademark is a black stocking cap with holes for the eyes and mouth.
He is never seen without it, states the program. No one knows who The Masked
Marvel really is!

"Good," says Uncle Max. "Now you'll see something." He is fidgeting, 32
waiting for them to appear. They come down separate aisles, climb into the ring
from opposite sides. I have never seen anything like them. It is The Angel's
neck that first captures the eye. The shaved nape rises in twin columns to puff
into the white hood of a sloped and bosselated skull that is too small. As
though, strangled by the sinews of that neck, the skull had long since withered
and shrunk. The thing about The Angel is the absence of any mystery in his
body. It is simply *there*. A monosyllabic announcement. A grunt. One looks and
knows everything at once, the fat thighs, the gigantic buttocks, the great spine
from which hang knotted ropes and pale aprons of beef. And that prehistoric
head. He is all of a single hideous piece, The Angel is. No detachables.

The Masked Marvel seems dwarfish. His fingers dangle kneeward. His 33
short legs are slightly bowed as if under the weight of the cask they are forced
to heft about. He has breasts that swing when he moves! I have never seen such
breasts on a man before.

There is a sudden ungraceful movement, and they close upon one an- 34
other. The Angel stoops and hugs The Marvel about the waist, locking his
hands behind The Marvel's back. Now he straightens and lifts The Marvel as
though he were uprooting a tree. Thus he holds him, then stoops again, thrusts
one hand through The Marvel's crotch, and with the other grabs him by the
neck. He rears and . . . The Marvel is aloft! For a long moment, The Angel stands

as though deciding where to make the toss. Then throws. Was that board or bone that splintered there? Again and again, The Angel hurls himself upon the body of The Masked Marvel.

35   Now The Angel rises over the fallen Marvel, picks up one foot in both of his hands, and twists the toes downward. It is far beyond the tensile strength of mere ligament, mere cartilage. The Masked Marvel does not hide his agony, but pounds and slaps the floor with his hand, now and then reaching up toward The Angel in an attitude of supplication. I have never seen such suffering. And all the while his black mask rolls from side to side, the mouth pulled to a tight slit through which issues an endless hiss that I can hear from where I sit. All at once, I hear a shouting close by.

36   "Break it off! Tear off a leg and throw it up here!"

37   It is Uncle Max. Even in the darkness I can see that he is gray. A band of sweat stands upon his upper lip. He is on his feet now, panting, one fist pressed at his chest, the other raised warlike toward the ring. For the first time I begin to think that something terrible might happen here. Aunt Sarah was right.

38   "Sit down, Uncle Max," I say. "Take a pill, please."

39   He reaches for the pillbox, gropes, and swallows without taking his gaze from the wrestlers. I wait for him to sit down.

40   "That's not fair," I say, "twisting his toes like that."

41   "It's the toehold," he explains.

42   "But it's not *fair*," I say again. The whole of the evil is laid open for me to perceive. I am trembling.

43   And now The Angel does something unspeakable. Holding the foot of The Marvel at full twist with one hand, he bends and grasps the mask where it clings to the back of The Marvel's head. And he pulls. He is going to strip it off! Lay bare an ultimate carnal mystery! Suddenly it is beyond mere physical violence. Now I am on my feet, shouting into the Maple Leaf Gardens.

44   "Watch out," I scream. "Stop him. Please, somebody, stop him."

45   Next to me, Uncle Max is chuckling.

46   Yet The Masked Marvel hears me, I know it. And rallies from his bed of pain. Thrusting with his free heel, he strikes The Angel at the back of the knee. The Angel falls. The Masked Marvel is on top of him pinning his shoulders to the mat. One! Two! Three! And it is over. Uncle Max is strangely still. I am gasping for breath. All this I remember as I stand at the bedside of Elihu Koontz.

47   Once again, I am in the operating room. It is two years since I amputated the left leg of Elihu Koontz. Now it is his right leg which is gangrenous. I have already scrubbed. I stand to one side wearing my gown and gloves. And . . . *I am masked.* Upon the table lies Elihu Koontz, pinned in a fierce white light. Spinal anesthesia has been administered. One of his arms is taped to a board placed at a right angle to his body. Into this arm, a needle has been placed. Fluid drips here from a bottle overhead. With his other hand, Elihu Koontz beats feebly at the side of the operating table. His head rolls from side to side. His mouth is pulled into weeping. It seems to me that I have never seen such misery.

An orderly stands at the foot of the table, holding Elihu Koontz's leg aloft 48 by the toes so that the intern can scrub the limb with antiseptic solutions. The intern paints the foot, ankle, leg, and thigh, both front and back, three times. From a corner of the room where I wait, I look down as from an amphitheater. Then I think of Uncle Max yelling, "Tear off a leg. Throw it up here." And I think that forty years later I am making the catch.

"It's not fair," I say aloud. But no one hears me. I step forward to break The 49 Masked Marvel's last toehold.

COMPREHENSION

1. Who is (was) the Masked Marvel? What is Selzer's relation to this man? What are his personal feelings?
2. Is this essay strictly about an amputation? Why or why not?
3. Explain your understanding of the last bit of dialogue in this essay.

RHETORIC

1. Consider the importance of Selzer's title. What does it reveal about Selzer's purpose and thesis?
2. What aspects of narrative and descriptive technique stand out in this essay?
3. What stylistic shifts can you detect in this essay? For example, where does the writer use figurative language, and where does he use technical language? What is the effect?
4. Why does Selzer divide his essay into sections? How does each section function? Is this strategy effective? Justify your response.
5. Explain the atmosphere that Selzer evokes and the final tone of the piece.

WRITING

1. Analyze Selzer's essay as an example of effective narrative and descriptive technique.
2. Select a well-known athlete, and examine the ironies of a seemingly superbly conditioned individual whose career is compromised by injury, drug abuse, aging, or disease.
3. **Writing an Argument:** Argue for or against the proposition that a doctor should not let feelings interfere with his or her treatment of a patient.

NETWORKING
Applying 21st-Century Literacies

Using Images to Enhance a Descriptive/Narrative Essay: Supplement Selzer's essay with images in a meaningful way that contributes to this story's use of narrative and description.

I Worked Hard
for That Furrowed Brow

Ellen Goodman

Ellen Goodman (b. 1941) is an award-winning journalist and associate editor of the
Boston Globe. *She was born in Newton, Massachusetts, and educated at Radcliffe*
College. *She began working for the* Globe *in 1967 and started writing a weekly column
in 1971, which today is syndicated in more than 400 newspapers across the United
States. Starting with* Close to Home *(1979), Goodman has published six collections of
her columns, dealing with a broad range of topics, including the status of women,
health and reproductive issues, politics, and the family. In 1980 her columns were
awarded the Pulitzer Prize for Distinguished Commentary. Her most recent book is*
Paper Trail *(2004). Here, in a column that appeared in 2002, she dissents from the
current obsession with Botox and other forms of cosmetic surgery.*

1   Just because the FDA has approved of Botox doesn't mean that I have to. In fact,
since 835,000 people have already had their foreheads injected with the paralyzing fluid that keeps them from being able to frown, I figure that somebody
has to frown for them.

2   When I first read about Botox as a cosmetic, I thought there was something
vaguely charming about the idea. After all, the microbe created by the U.S. Army
to inflict botulism poisoning on our enemies was now being used for domestic
and aesthetic purposes. Talk about beating your swords into tweezers.

3   But even before the FDA gave the green light, we heard that Botox gather-
ings of women had become the Tupperware parties of the 21st century. Only
what's being preserved are the women, not the leftovers.

4   This is not, I promise you, a screed about the political incorrectness of plastic surgery or vanity. Nor is it about how beauty is only skin deep.

5   Over the years, my attitudes—like my jaw line—have softened toward
women who choose to change their faces rather than live with them. I know
there's a line between those who "need" to be "fixed" and those who don't,
between those who need surgery—think burn victim—and those who need
therapy—think Michael Jackson. But I'm less inclined to draw it for anyone else.

6   When 47-year-old Greta Van Susteren became the poster anchor for plastic
surgery, I thought the criticism was way over the top. As she said, "Having plastic

surgery isn't shoplifting." If it were, nearly every female-and-fifty face on TV would be behind bars. After all, most of us choose, um, some self-improvement. Where is the unacceptable point on the aesthetic slope between braces and face lifts? Aging gracefully does not mean that you have to age grayly. So, you tell me the cut-off between hair color and collagen.

Nevertheless.   7

As a woman of a certain age—the age targeted by the hefty $53 million ad 8 campaign being launched by Allergan, the maker of Botox—every time someone I know, or watch, has some "work" done, I have a vague feeling of being deserted. It's as if they'd left a threatened neighborhood, the endangered, natural species free range, and sided with the image-makers.

Remember back when Gloria Steinem turned 40? (If you do, it's probably 9 too late for Botox, anyway.) She said: "This is what 40 looks like." At that time it was a statement that said proudly: We are not your grandmother's 40-year-old.

Of course, 40 never did necessarily look like Gloria. But what happens 10 when 50 is supposed to look like 40? Does that mean the whole standard of aging has changed? Do we think 60 should look like 50? Does, say, a 70-year-old Barbara Walters actually change the future for older women on TV? Or is an older woman only accepted if she doesn't look her age?

Chemical peels. Endoscopic lifts. Microfat injections. Eyelid lifts. Face lifts. 11 Botox marketed to women the way Viagra is to men (never mind). How long is it before looking "your age" is regarded as a slatternly failure of effort? How long before any woman who doesn't try one of the above is dismissed as someone who is "letting herself go"?

I have always loved the expression, "letting yourself go." Where do you go, 12 when you let yourself? To the recycle bin or to freedom? On Oscar night, in a sea of nipped and tucked, siliconed and surgeried women, the only seamed faces over 50 belonged to the likes of Judi Dench, Maggie Smith, and Helen Mirren. They are all character actors. Is that where they let themselves go? Into character?

In the past few years, I have found myself looking at older women as har- 13 bingers of the future. I'm looking for energy and confidence, and yes, attractiveness. Who do I want to be when I grow up? I am sure there are young women searching for the same clues. But there's no way to find them on the Botox party masks. This is the real symbolism of Botox. It eliminates lines temporarily by paralyzing muscles. It offers an actual trade-off. You trade the ability, literally, to express your emotions—furrow that brow, crinkle that eye—for a flawless appearance. In the search for approval from others, you hide what you are feeling. Especially anger.

This seems to my cranky eye and creased eyebrow to be exactly the opposite 14 of my goal to become an outspoken, maybe even outrageous, laugh-out-loud, nothing-left-to-lose old lady. Spare me the Botox. I plan to remain the kind of character actor who wears her emotions, not on her sleeve or on her surgeon's bill, but on her face.

COMPREHENSION

1. What does Goodman think about Botox? What other forms of cosmetic surgery does she mention? What is her attitude toward them?
2. Why does the author mention Michael Jackson? Who are Greta Van Susteren and Gloria Steinem (see page 537), and how do they differ in their approach to beauty?
3. What, finally, is the author's attitude toward aging?

RHETORIC

1. A newspaper column places strict stylistic and formal demands on a writer. What journalistic elements do you find in this essay? What elements of style stand out?
2. Explain the tone of this essay. Where is Goodman serious? Where does she employ irony and satire? What is the overall effect?
3. What is the main idea of this essay? Which sentence serves as the thesis statement?
4. Analyze the essay as an argument and an attempt to persuade. What is the author's warrant, claim, and support? Does she engage in refutation? Why or why not?
5. What is the purpose and effect of the many questions that the author poses in this essay?
6. Where does Goodman use metaphors and other types of figurative language? What ideas do they convey?
7. How effective is the conclusion? Why?

WRITING

1. Have you had cosmetic surgery, or do you know someone who has? Write an essay telling about the procedure and the result.
2. Write an essay that compares and contrasts the ways that men and women view cosmetic surgery.
3. **Writing an Argument:** Compose an answer to Goodman in which you offer a humorous defense of cosmetic surgery.

NETWORKING
Applying 21st-Century Literacies

Using Images to Enhance a Comparison/Contrast Essay: Supplement assignment 2 under Writing with images in a meaningful way. Use images—whether tables, photographs, and/or cartoons—that help illustrate the similarities and differences between how men and women view cosmetic surgery. You might want to focus on a particular procedure in your response.

Between a Woman and Her Doctor

Martha Mendoza

Martha Mendoza (b. 1969) was born and raised in Los Angeles and attended college at the University of California at Santa Cruz (BA, 1988). Based in San Jose, Mendoza is a national investigative reporter for the Associated Press. Her work has appeared in the Los Angeles Times, Houston Chronicle, Newsday, *and elsewhere. Mendoza is also the co-author of* The Bridge at No Gun Ri: A Hidden Nightmare from the Korean War *(2001). In 2000, she won a pulitzer prize for investigative reporting. In this essay, which appeared in* Ms. *magazine in 2004, Mendoza tells of her abortion while at the same time exploring broader medical, social, and legal issues.*

I could see my baby's amazing and perfect spine, a precise, pebbled curl of ver- 1
tebrae. His little round skull. The curve of his nose. I could even see his small
leg floating slowly through my uterus.

My doctor came in a moment later, slid the ultrasound sensor around my 2
growing, round belly and put her hand on my shoulder. "It's not alive," she
said.

She turned her back to me and started taking notes. I looked at the wall, 3
breathing deeply, trying not to cry.

I can make it through this, I thought. I can handle this. 4

I didn't know I was about to become a pariah. 5

I was 19 weeks pregnant, strong, fit and happy, imagining our fourth child, 6
the newest member of our family. He would have dark hair and bright eyes.
He'd be intelligent and strong—really strong, judging by his early kicks.

And now this. Not alive? 7

I didn't realize that pressures well beyond my uterus, beyond the too- 8
bright, too-loud, too-small ultrasound room, extending all the way to board-
rooms of hospitals, administrative sessions at medical schools and committee
hearings in Congress, were going to deepen and expand my sorrow and
pain.

On November 6, 2003, President Bush signed what he called a "partial birth 9
abortion ban," prohibiting doctors from committing an "overt act" designed to
kill a partially delivered fetus. The law, which faces vigorous challenges, is the
most significant change to the nation's abortion laws since the U.S. Supreme
Court ruled abortion legal in *Roe v. Wade* in 1973. One of the unintended consequences of this new law is that it put people in my position, with a fetus that is
already dead, in a technical limbo.

Legally, a doctor can still surgically take a dead body out of a pregnant 10
woman. But in reality, the years of angry debate that led to the law's passage,

restrictive state laws and the violence targeting physicians have reduced the number of hospitals and doctors willing to do dilations and evacuations (D&Es) and dilations and extractions (intact D&Es), which involve removing a larger fetus, sometimes in pieces, from the womb.

11   At the same time, fewer medical schools are training doctors to do these procedures. After all, why spend time training for a surgery that's likely to be made illegal?

12   At this point, 74 percent of obstetrics and gynecology residency programs do *not* train all residents in abortion procedures, according to reproductive health researchers at the National Abortion Federation. Those that do usually teach only the first trimester abortion procedures such as dilation and curettage—D&C, the 15-minute uterine scraping. Fewer than 7 percent of obstetricians are trained to do D&Es, the procedure used on fetuses from about 13 to 19 weeks. Almost all the doctors doing them are over 50 years old.

13   "Finding a doctor who will do a D&E is getting very tough," says Ron Fitzsimmons, executive director of the National Coalition of Abortion Providers.

14   My doctor turned around and faced me. She told me that because dilation and evacuation is rarely offered in my community, I could opt instead to chemically induce labor over several days and then deliver the little body at my local maternity ward.

15   "It's up to you," she said.

16   I'd been through labor and delivery three times before, with great joy as well as pain, and the notion of going through that profound experience only to deliver a dead fetus (whose skin was already starting to slough off, whose skull might be collapsing) was horrifying.

17   I also did some research, spoke with friends who were obstetricians and gynecologists, and quickly learned this: Study after study shows D&Es are *safer* than labor and delivery. Women who had D&Es were far less likely to have bleeding requiring transfusion, infection requiring intravenous antibiotics, organ injuries requiring additional surgery or cervical laceration requiring repair and hospital readmission. A review of 300 second-trimester abortions published in 2002 in the *American Journal of Obstetrics & Gynecology* found that 29 percent of women who went through labor and delivery had complications, compared with just 4 percent of those who had D&Es.

18   The American Medical Association said D&Es, compared to labor and delivery, "may minimize trauma to the woman's uterus, cervix and other vital organs."

19   There was this fact, too: The intact D&E surgery makes less use of "grasping instruments," which could damage the body of the fetus. If the body were intact, doctors might be able to more easily figure out why my baby died in the womb.

20   I'm a healthy person. I run, swim and bike. I'm 37 years old and optimistic. Good things happen to me. I didn't want to rule out having more kids, but I did want to know what went wrong before I tried again.

We told our doctor we had chosen a dilation and evacuation.   21

"I can't do these myself," said my doctor. "I trained at a Catholic hospital."   22

My doctor recommended a specialist in a neighboring county, but when I   23
called for an appointment, they said they couldn't see me for almost a week.

I could feel my baby's dead body inside of mine. This baby had thrilled me   24
with kicks and flutters, those first soft tickles of life bringing a smile to my face
and my hand to my rounding belly. Now this baby floated, limp and heavy,
from one side to the other, as I rolled in my bed. And within a day, I started to
bleed. My body, with or without a doctor's help, was starting to expel the fetus.
Technically, I was threatening a spontaneous abortion, the least safe of the available options.

I did what any pregnant patient would do. I called my doctor. And she ad-   25
vised me to wait.

I lay in my bed, not sleeping day or night, trying not to lose this little baby's   26
body that my own womb was working to expel. Wait, I told myself. Just hold
on. Let a doctor take this out. I was scared. Was it going to fall out of my body
when I rose, in the middle of the night, to check on my toddler? Would it come
apart on its own and double me over, knock me to the floor, as I stood at the
stove scrambling eggs for my boys?

On my fourth morning, with the bleeding and cramping increasing, I   27
couldn't wait any more. I called my doctor and was told that since I wasn't
hemorrhaging, I should not come in. Her partner, on call, pedantically explained that women can safely lose a lot of blood, even during a routine period.

I began calling labor and delivery units at the top five medical centers in   28
my area. I told them I had been 19 weeks along. The baby is dead. I'm bleeding,
I said. I'm scheduled for a D&E in a few days. If I come in right now, what
could you do for me, I asked.

Don't come in, they told me again and again. "Go to your emergency room   29
if you are hemorrhaging to avoid bleeding to death. No one here can do a D&E
today, and unless you're really in active labor you're safer to wait."

More than 66,000 women each year in the U.S. undergo an abortion at some   30
point between 13 and 20 weeks, according to the Centers for Disease Control
and Prevention. The CDC doesn't specify the physical circumstances of the
women or their fetuses. Other CDC data shows that 4,000 women miscarry in
their second trimester. Again, the data doesn't clarify whether those 4,000
women have to go through surgery.

Here's what is clear: Most of those women face increasingly limited ac-   31
cess to care. One survey showed that half of the women who got abortions
after 15 weeks of gestation said they were delayed because of problems in af-
fording, finding or getting to abortion services. No surprise there; abortion is
not readily available in 86 percent of the counties in the U.S.

Although there are some new, early diagnostic tests available, the most   32
common prenatal screening for neural tube defects or Down syndrome is done
around the 16th week of pregnancy. When problems are found—some times

life-threatening problems—pregnant women face the same limited options that I did.

33   At last I found one university teaching hospital that, at least over the telephone, was willing to take me.

34   "We do have one doctor who can do a D&E," they said. "Come in to our emergency room if you want."

35   But when I arrived at the university's emergency room, the source of the tension was clear. After examining me and confirming I was bleeding but not hemorrhaging, the attending obstetrician, obviously pregnant herself, defensively explained that only one of their dozens of obstetricians and gynecologists still does D&Es, and he was simply not available. Not today. Not tomorrow. Not the next day. No, I couldn't have his name. She walked away from me and called my doctor.

36   "You can't just dump these patients on us," she shouted into the phone, her high-pitched voice floating through the heavy curtains surrounding my bed. "You should be dealing with this yourself."

37   Shivering on the narrow, white exam table, I wondered what I had done wrong. Then I pulled back on my loose maternity pants and stumbled into the sunny parking lot, blinking back tears in the dazzling spring day, trying to understand the directions they sent me out with: Find a hotel within a few blocks from a hospital. Rest, monitor the bleeding. Don't go home—the 45-minute drive might be too far.

38   The next few days were a blur of lumpy motel beds, telephone calls to doctors, cramps. The pre-examination for my D&E finally arrived. First, the hospital required me to sign a legal form consenting to terminate the pregnancy. Then they explained I could, at no cost, have the remains incinerated by the hospital pathology department as medical waste, or for a fee have them taken to a funeral home for burial or cremation.

39   They inserted sticks of seaweed into my cervix and told me to go home for the night. A few hours later—when the contractions were regular, strong and frequent—I knew we needed to get to the hospital.

40   "The patient appeared to be in active labor," say my charts, "and I explained this to the patient and offered her pain medication for vaginal delivery."

41   According to the charts, I was "adamant" in demanding a D&E. I remember that I definitely wanted the surgical procedure that was the safest option. One hour later, just as an anesthesiologist was slipping me into unconsciousness, I had the D&E and a little body, my little boy, slipped out. Around his neck, three times and very tight, was the umbilical cord, source of his life, cause of his death.

42   This past spring, as the wild flowers started blooming around the simple cross we built for this baby, the Justice Department began trying to enforce the Bush administration's ban and federal courts in three different cities heard arguments regarding the new law. Doctors explained that D&Es are the safest procedure in

many cases, and that the law is particularly cruel to mothers like me whose babies were already dead. In hopes of bolstering their case, prosecutors sent federal subpoenas to various medical centers, asking for records of D&Es. There's an attorney somewhere, someday, who may poke through the files of my loss.

I didn't watch the trial because I had another appointment to keep—another 43 ultrasound. Lying on the crisp white paper, watching the monitor, I saw new life, the incredible spine, tiny fingers waving slowly across my uterus, a perfect thigh. Best of all, there it was, a strong, four-chamber heart, beating steady and solid. A soft quiver, baby rolling, rippled across my belly.

"Everything looks wonderful," said my doctor. "This baby is doing great." 44

COMPREHENSION

1. Explain the nature and extent of Mendoza's "sorrow and pain" (paragraph 8).
2. What is "D&E"? What is Mendoza's understanding of the procedure, and how does she react to it?
3. What elements of government policy does Mendoza discuss, and why?

RHETORIC

1. Mendoza's title might contain more than one level of meaning. Would you agree or disagree? Explain.
2. Why does Mendoza begin with personal narrative and then switch to exposition? How does she sustain this back-and-forth movement between narration and exposition?
3. Do you think that Mendoza develops an argument in this essay or attempts to persuade readers to adopt a certain position regarding abortion? Or is she merely investigating, as a journalist, a procedure that she and many other women experience? Elaborate on your response.
4. Mendoza's essay appeared in a feminist magazine. Why would the article and the position that Mendoza stakes out appeal to *Ms.* readers?
5. What elements of investigative reporting do you find in this essay?
6. What is your response to the conclusion? What is Mendoza's purpose in using an emotional appeal at this end point in the essay?

WRITING

1. Investigate "partial birth abortion," and write an essay analyzing the process.
2. Write a personal essay recounting an illness or painful medical procedure that you or someone close to you experienced.
3. **Writing an Argument:** Argue for or against the proposition that abortion should be strictly a matter "between a woman and her doctor."

NETWORKING
Applying 21st-Century Literacies

Evaluating Web Sites about Abortion: On the Chapter 13 Networking page (at *www.mhhe.com/mhreader11e*), visit the listed sites about abortion and write a paragraph-long evaluation of each. In your assessment, note (1) what organization sponsors this Web site, (2) what that organization's agenda or purpose is, (3) what position the site/organization takes on abortion, (4) what they hope visitors will come away with from the site, and (5) how various features on the site—its design, use of visuals, use of interactive features, etc.—contribute to its goals.

The Terrifying Normalcy of AIDS

Stephen Jay Gould

Stephen Jay Gould (1941–2002), an acclaimed contemporary science writer, taught biology, geology, and the history of science at Harvard University, where he was Alexander Agassiz Professor of Zoology. Born in New York City, he was educated at Antioch College (BA, 1963) and Columbia University (PhD, 1967). He wrote a monthly column, "This View of Life," for Natural History *magazine and was the author of* Ever Since Darwin *(1977),* Ontogeny and Phylogeny *(1977),* The Panda's Thumb *(1980),* Wonderful Life *(1989),* Bully for Brontosaurus *(1991),* The Structure of Evolutionary Theory *(2002), and other books. In this 1987 essay, Gould explains in clear, precise language why AIDS is a "natural phenomenon" and warns against viewing it in moral terms.*

1   Disney's Epcot Center in Orlando, Fla., is a technological tour de force and a conceptual desert. In this permanent World's Fair, American industrial giants have built their versions of an unblemished future. These masterful entertainments convey but one message, brilliantly packaged and relentlessly expressed: Progress through technology is the solution to all human problems. G.E. proclaims from Horizons: "If we can dream it, we can do it." A.T.&T. speaks from on high within its giant golf ball: We are now "unbounded by space and time." United Technologies bubbles from the depths of Living Seas: "With the help of modern technology, we feel there's really no limit to what can be accomplished."

2   Yet several of these exhibits at the Experimental Prototype Community of Tomorrow, all predating last year's space disaster, belie their stated message from within by using the launch of the shuttle as a visual metaphor for technological triumph. The *Challenger* disaster may represent a general malaise, but it remains an incident. The AIDS pandemic, an issue that may rank with nuclear

weaponry as the greatest danger of our era, provides a more striking proof that mind and technology are not omnipotent and that we have not canceled our bond to nature.

In 1984, John Platt, a biophysicist who taught at the University of Chicago 3 for many years, wrote a short paper for private circulation. At a time when most of us were either ignoring AIDS, or viewing it as a contained and peculiar affliction of homosexual men, Platt recognized that the limited data on the origin of AIDS and its spread in America suggested a more frightening prospect: We are all susceptible to AIDS, and the disease has been spreading in a simple exponential manner.

Exponential growth is a geometric increase. Remember the old kiddy prob- 4 lem: If you place a penny on square one of a checkerboard and double the number of coins on each subsequent square—2, 4, 8, 16, 32 . . . —how big is the stack by the sixty-fourth square? The answer: about as high as the universe is wide. Nothing in the external environment inhibits this increase, thus giving to exponential processes their relentless character. In the real, noninfinite world, of course, some limit will eventually arise, and the process slows down, reaches a steady state, or destroys the entire system: The stack of pennies falls over, the bacterial cells exhaust their supply of nutrients.

Platt noticed that data for the initial spread of AIDS fell right on an expo- 5 nential curve. He then followed the simplest possible procedure of extrapolating the curve unabated into the 1990's. Most of us were incredulous, accusing Platt of the mathematical gamesmanship that scientists call "curve fitting." After all, aren't exponential models unrealistic? Surely we are not all susceptible to AIDS. Is it not spread only by odd practices to odd people? Will it not, therefore, quickly run its short course within a confined group?

Well, hello 1987—worldwide data still match Platt's extrapolated curve. 6 This will not, of course, go on forever. AIDS has probably already saturated the African areas where it probably originated, and where the sex ratio of afflicted people is 1-to-1, male-female. But AIDS still has far to spread, and may be moving exponentially, through the rest of the world. We have learned enough about the cause of AIDS to slow its spread, if we can make rapid and fundamental changes in our handling of that most powerful part of human biology—our own sexuality. But medicine, as yet, has nothing to offer as a cure and precious little even for palliation.

This exponential spread of AIDS not only illuminates its, and our, biology, but 7 also underscores the tragedy of our moralistic misperception. Exponential processes have a definite time and place of origin, an initial point of "inoculation"—in this case, Africa. We didn't notice the spread at first. In a population of billions, we pay little attention when one increases to two, or eight to sixteen, but when one million becomes two million, we panic, even though the *rate* of doubling has not increased.

The infection has to start somewhere, and its initial locus may be little 8 more than an accident of circumstance. For a while, it remains confined to those in close contact with the primary source, but only by accident of proximity, not by intrinsic susceptibility. Eventually, given the power and lability of human sexuality, it spreads outside the initial group and into the general population. And now AIDS has begun its march through our own heterosexual community.

9   What a tragedy that our moral stupidity caused us to lose precious time, the greatest enemy in fighting an exponential spread, by down-playing the danger because we thought that AIDS was a disease of three irregular groups of minorities: minorities of life style (needle users), of sexual preference (homosexuals) and of color (Haitians). If AIDS had first been imported from Africa into a Park Avenue apartment, we would not have dithered as the exponential march began.

10   The message of Orlando—the inevitability of technological solutions—is wrong, and we need to understand why.

11   Our species has not won its independence from nature, and we cannot do all that we can dream. Or at least we cannot do it at the rate required to avoid tragedy, for we are not unbounded from time. Viral diseases are preventable in principle, and I suspect that an AIDS vaccine will one day be produced. But how will this discovery avail us if it takes until the millennium, and by then AIDS has fully run its exponential course and saturated our population, killing a substantial percentage of the human race? A fight against an exponential enemy is primarily a race against time.

12   We must also grasp the perspective of ecology and evolutionary biology and recognize, once we reinsert ourselves properly into nature, that AIDS represents the ordinary workings of biology, not an irrational or diabolical plague with a moral meaning. Disease, including epidemic spread, is a natural phenomenon, part of human history from the beginning. An entire subdiscipline of my profession, paleopathology, studies the evidence of ancient diseases preserved in the fossil remains of organisms. Human history has been marked by episodic plagues. More native peoples died of imported disease than ever fell before the gun during the era of colonial expansion. Our memories are short, and we have had a respite, really, only since the influenza pandemic at the end of World War I, but AIDS must be viewed as a virulent expression of an ordinary natural phenomenon.

13   I do not say this to foster either comfort or complacency. The evolutionary perspective is correct, but utterly inappropriate for our human scale. Yes, AIDS is a natural phenomenon, one of a recurring class of pandemic diseases. Yes, AIDS may run through the entire population, and may carry off a quarter or more of us. Yes, it may make no *biological* difference to Homo sapiens in the long run: There will still be plenty of us left and we can start again. Evolution cares as little for its agents—organisms struggling for reproductive success—as physics cares for individual atoms of hydrogen in the sun. But we care. These atoms are our neighbors, our lovers, our children and ourselves. AIDS is both a natural phenomenon and, potentially, the greatest natural tragedy in human history.

The cardboard message of Epcot fosters the wrong attitudes: We must both re- 14 insert ourselves into nature and view AIDS as a natural phenomenon in order to fight properly. If we stand above nature and if technology is all-powerful, then AIDS is a horrifying anomaly that must be trying to tell us something. If so, we can adopt one of two attitudes, each potentially fatal. We can either become complacent, because we believe the message of Epcot and assume that medicine will soon generate a cure, or we can panic in confusion and seek a scapegoat for something so irregular that it must have been visited upon us to teach us a moral lesson.

But AIDS is not irregular. It is part of nature. So are we. This should galva- 15 nize us and give us hope, not prompt the worst of all responses: a kind of "new-age" negativism that equates natural with what we must accept and cannot, or even should not, change. When we view AIDS as natural, and when we recognize both the exponential property of its spread and the accidental character of its point of entry into America, we can break through our destructive tendencies to blame others and to free ourselves of concern.

If AIDS is natural, then there is no message in its spread. But by all that science 16 has learned and all that rationality proclaims, AIDS works by a *mechanism*—and we can discover it. Victory is not ordained by any principle of progress, or any slogan of technology, so we shall have to fight like hell, and be watchful. There is no message, but there is a mechanism.

COMPREHENSION

1. What does Gould mean when he defines AIDS as a "natural phenomenon" (paragraph 12)? How does the title support this definition?
2. What does Gould mean by "our moral stupidity" in paragraph 9?
3. What connection does Gould make between our reaction to the AIDS crisis and our alienation from nature?

RHETORIC

1. What is Gould's main idea? Where in the essay is it stated?
2. What is the purpose of paragraphs 1 and 2? How do they contribute to Gould's argument? How do they help establish the tone of the essay? What is the tone? What is the importance of Epcot Center to Gould's thesis?
3. Gould uses scientific terminology in his essay. Define the words *exponential* (paragraph 3) and *pandemic* and *phenomenon* (paragraph 13). Is this essay intended for a specialized audience? Justify your response.
4. Trace the progression of ideas in paragraphs 2–5. What transitions does Gould employ?
5. Does Gould use rhetorical strategies besides argument in his essay? Cite evidence of this varied rhetorical approach.
6. Explain the final sentence in Gould's conclusion. What is its relation to the paragraph as a whole?

WRITING

1. Gould states that we must "reinsert ourselves into nature" (paragraph 14). What does he mean by this? How would this affect the way in which we deal with disease and death in our society? Explore this issue in a brief essay.
2. Write an extended definition of HIV/AIDS, attempting to avoid moralizing about the subject. Conduct research if necessary.
3. **Writing an Argument:** Write an essay in which you expand on Gould's belief that our moral stupidity has not only hindered society's recognition of the AIDS threat but continues to impede AIDS research and treatment.

NETWORKING
Applying 21st-Century Literacies

Creating an Informational Web Page: After completing question 2 under Writing, write and design a single Web page that defines and provides important at-a-glance information about HIV/AIDS. Its purpose should be to inform the public by providing facts and dispelling harmful myths; it should *not* make an argument. Incorporate one image and provide a few select hyperlinks.

Full Moon Friday the Thirteenth

Atul Gawande

Atul Gawande (b. 1965), the son of two physicians, was born in Brooklyn, New York. After taking degrees at Stanford University (BA, BS, 1987), Gawande attended Balliol College, Oxford (MA, 1989) before enrolling in Harvard Medical School. He uses his experience as a medical resident in his critically acclaimed collection of essays on medical science in Complications: A Surgeon's Notes on an Imperfect Science *(2002) and* Better: A Surgeon's Notes on Performance *(2007). Gawande's most recent book is* The Checklist Manifesto: How to Get Things Right *(2009). Gawande is a staff writer for the* New Yorker. *He is also active in the public arena, serving first as an advisor to President Bill Clinton and then, starting in 1993, as a senior advisor for the U.S. Department of Health and Human Services. In this essay from* Complications, *Gawande offers a lighthearted assessment of the role of superstition in life and medical practice.*

1 Jack Nicklaus would not play a round of golf without three pennies in his pocket. Michael Jordan always had to wear University of North Carolina boxer shorts under his Chicago Bulls uniform. And Duke Ellington would not play a show, or allow his band members to play a show, wearing anything yellow. For

people who have to perform for a living, superstitions seem almost de rigueur. Baseball players, for example, are notoriously superstitious. Wade Boggs, the Boston Red Sox's former star third baseman, famously insisted on eating chicken before every game. Tommy Lasorda, on the other hand, when he was managing the Los Angeles Dodgers, always ate linguine—with either red clam sauce if his team was facing a right-handed pitcher, or white if up against a lefty. Even in this crowd, however, the New York Mets' pitcher Turk Wendell seems unusual. For luck during games, he used to wear an animal-fang necklace, refuse to wear socks, never step on the foul line, and brush his teeth between innings. When he signed his contract for the 1999 season, he insisted that his salary be $1,200,000.99. "Hey, I just like the number ninety-nine," he told the press.

I have yet to know, however, any doctors with such superstitions. Doctors 2 tend to have a fierce commitment to the rational—surgeons especially. For one of the main satisfactions of science, and operating on people in particular, is the success of logical planning and thinking. If there is a credo in practical medicine, it is that the important thing is to be sensible. And we who are in it are usually uncomfortable, if not outright contemptuous, of the mystical. At the most, you might find a surgeon with a favorite pair of operating shoes or a quirky way of dressing a wound after closing up. And even then we are always careful to account for our idiosyncracies with at least a plausible-sounding explanation: "Other shoes aren't as comfortable," the surgeon might say, or, "That dressing tape causes blisters" (though no one else seems to have trouble with it). As a rule, you will not find doctors saying that, actually, we just think a thing is unlucky.

So it struck me as odd to find, one afternoon when I and my fellow surgical 3 residents sat around a table divvying up the next month's schedule of nights on emergency room duty, that no one was volunteering to take Friday the thirteenth. We were taking turns making picks, and for the first few rounds, everything seemed normal. We left all the Fridays alone, weekend nights not being popular. But as the nights remaining dwindled to just a few, it became apparent that that one Friday was being conspicuously bypassed. C'mon, I thought, this is ridiculous. So when my turn came up again, I put my name down for duty that night. "Rest up," one resident said. "You're going to be in for a busy night." I laughed and dismissed the idea.

Looking at my calendar a few days later, however, I noticed that the moon 4 would also be full that Friday night. Then someone mentioned that a lunar eclipse would be occurring then, too. And for a moment—only a moment, mind you—I felt my confidence slip. Perhaps I really would be in for a miserable night, I began to think. But being a sober and well-trained doctor, I did not let myself succumb to such thoughts so easily. Surely, I thought, the evidence is against such preposterousness. And then, just to confirm it, I went to the library to check.

I managed to find exactly one scientific study assessing whether or not 5 luck actually does go bad on Friday the thirteenth. (I'm not sure which is more surprising, that people have in fact researched this question, or that I could only find one such example. This is, after all, a world with studies on almost anything you could think of. Once, poking around the library, I even found a report on how saliva distributes around the mouth when chewing gum.) The 1993 study, published in the *British Medical Journal,* compared hospital admissions for traffic accidents on a Friday the thirteenth with those on a Friday the sixth in a community outside London. Despite a lower highway traffic volume on the thirteenth than on the sixth, admissions for traffic accident victims increased 52 percent on the thirteenth. "Friday the thirteenth is unlucky for some," the authors concluded. "Staying at home is recommended." How you escape the bad luck at home they didn't explain.

6   Still, I told myself, you really can't make much of one study of one Friday the thirteenth in one town. Random variation could easily have accounted for the increase in crashes. You would need to see consistently bad results across a number of studies to be convinced. And that has yet to be shown.

7   By contrast, one thing that has been shown is that human beings commonly imagine patterns (whether good or bad) where really there are none. It's just how our brains work. Even totally random patterns will often appear non-random to us. The statistician William Feller described one now classic example. During the Germans' intensive bombing of South London in the Second World War, a few areas were hit many times over while some others were not hit at all. The places that were not hit seemed to have been deliberately spared, and people concluded that those places were where the Germans had their spies. When Feller analyzed the statistics of the bomb hits, however, he found that the distribution was purely random.

8   This propensity to see nonexistent patterns has been called the Texas-sharpshooter fallacy. Like a Texas sharpshooter who shoots at the side of a barn and then draws a bull's-eye around the bullet holes, we tend to notice unusual occurrences first—four bad things happening on one day, for example—and then define a pattern around them. It seems to me we could just as well have feared Thursday the thirteenth, or Friday the fifth, as Friday the thirteenth. Nonetheless, phobia about Friday the thirteenth is widespread. Based on surveys, Donald Dossey, a North Carolina behavioral scientist, estimates that between seventeen million and twenty-one million Americans suffer mild to severe anxiety or change their activities because of *paraskevidekatriaphobia* (which is Greek for "fear of Friday the thirteenth"). They perform rituals before leaving the house, call in sick to work, or postpone flights or major purchases, causing businesses to lose seven hundred and fifty million dollars annually.

9   Superstitions about the moon appear to be taken even more seriously. A 1995 poll found that 43 percent of Americans believed that the moon alters individual behavior. And, interestingly, mental health professionals were more likely to believe it than people in other lines of work. The full moon has been thought to be linked to madness for centuries—hence the term "lunatic"—and in disparate civilizations across the world. Certainly, the idea of lunar human cycles seems more plausible than a Friday-the-thirteenth effect. Scientists once

dismissed the idea of biological cycles, but now widely accept that season can affect mood and behavior and that we all have "circadian rhythms" in which time of day affects body temperature, alertness, memory, and mood.

In a computer search, I managed to find some one hundred studies that 10 attempted to identify "circalunidian" cycles. The most intriguing one I looked up was a five-year study of self-poisoning at a hospital in New South Wales, Australia, published in the *Medical Journal of Australia*. From 1988 to 1993, the hospital admitted 2,215 patients for overdosing on drugs or poisoning themselves with toxic substances. The researchers checked to see whether peaks in such events occurred not just according to the phase of the moon but also according to one's zodiac sign or numerological readings (as "calculated according to the formulas contained in *Zolar's Encyclopedia of Ancient and Forbidden Knowledge*," the authors reported). To no one's surprise, self-poisoning rates were not affected by whether a patient was born a Virgo or a Libra. Nor did Zolar's "Name Number," "Month Number," or "Birth Path Number" for a person make any difference. However, women (but not men) were about 25 percent *less* likely to overdose around the time of a full moon than around a new moon.

Strangely enough, this decrease in self-poisonings actually correlated with 11 the results of other studies. If any link between psychology and the full moon exists, it would seem to be protective. The authors of a 1996 study of ten years of suicides in the Dordogne region of France concluded, in charmingly ungrammatical English, that "the French dies less in Full Moon, and more in New Moon period." Studies in Cuyahoga County, Ohio, and Dade County, Florida, also found a drop in suicides at the full moon. These studies didn't quite clinch the full moon's happy effect, however. Far more studies failed to find any lunar correlation with suicide.

As for other forms of craziness, the moon seems to play no role. Research- 12 ers have reviewed logs for calls to police stations, consultations to psychiatrists, homicides, and other records of our daily burden of madness—including, I noticed, emergency room visits. They found no consistent relationship, one way or another, with the moon.

Reassured by this, I was finally able to leave the library convinced that nei- 13 ther the full moon nor the inauspicious date threatened my night on call. A couple of weeks later the appointed evening arrived. I walked into the ER at 6 P.M. sharp to take over from the daytime resident. To my dismay, he was already swamped with patients for me to see. Then, just as soon as I began to get caught up, a fresh trauma came in—a pale and bloodied twenty-eight-year-old knocked unconscious in a high-speed head-on collision. The police and paramedics said he had been stalking his girlfriend with a gun in hand. The cops then arrived and he fled in his car, leading them on a chase that ended in the massive crash.

The rest of the night went no better. I was, as we say, "slammed"—running 14 hard, unable to get two minutes to sit down, hardly able to keep the patients straight.

"It's full moon Friday the thirteenth," a nurse explained.   15

16   I was about to say that, actually, the studies show no connection. But my pager went off before I could get the words out of my mouth. I had a new trauma coming in.

COMPREHENSION

1. According to Gawande, are physicians typically susceptible to superstitious practices? Why or why not?
2. What is the "Texas-sharpshooter fallacy"? How does Gawande relate this concept to medical practice?
3. Why does Gawande insert himself into this essay as a participant? What is his purpose?

RHETORIC

1. How does Gawande develop his introductory paragraph? Why does he allude to figures from the sports world? What have these figures got to do with the world of medicine?
2. Explain the tone of Gawande's essay. Is he serious or humorous, subjective or objective? How does this tone influence the writer's thesis?
3. How does causal analysis function in this essay? What causes does Gawande establish, and which effects does he mention?
4. What types of evidence does Gawande cite to support his thesis?
5. Why does Gawande present himself as a medical authority on a subject—superstition—that does not easily lend itself to rational discussion? How does he go about researching his subject in order to establish an authoritative persona?

WRITING

1. Write an essay of causal analysis in which you explain why physicians or members of other professional groups might be susceptible to superstition.
2. Explain your own attitude toward superstition and whether you would permit it to influence your behavior if you were sick and in need of a physician. Would you submit to an operation on full moon Friday the thirteenth?
3. **Writing an Argument:** Argue for or against the proposition that superstition should play absolutely no role in medical practice.

NETWORKING
Applying 21st-Century Literacies

Using Images to Enhance a Causal Analysis Essay: Incorporate images in a meaningful way into assignment 1 under Writing. Be sure that these visuals help illustrate a causal relationship and that they do more than merely decorate the written text.

The Globalization
of Eating Disorders

Susan Bordo

Susan Bordo (b. 1947) was born in Newark, New Jersey, and was educated at Carleton University (BA, 1972) and the State University of New York at Stony Brook (PhD, 1982). She is the Singletary Chair in the Humanities and a professor of English and women's studies at the University of Kentucky. A feminist philosopher and interdisciplinary scholar who focuses on Western culture's attitudes toward gender and the body, Bordo has written The Flight to Objectivity: Essays on Cartesianism and Culture *(1987),* Unbearable Weight: Feminism, Western Culture, and the Body *(1993, 2004),* Twilight Zones: The Hidden Life of Cultural Images from Plato to O.J. *(1997), and* The Male Body: A New Look at Men in Public and in Private *(1999). In this selection, Bordo offers an overview of a new kind of epidemic, fueled by Western media images, that is affecting cultures around the world.*

The young girl stands in front of the mirror. Never fat to begin with, she's been 1 on a no-fat diet for a couple of weeks and has reached her goal weight: 115 lb., at 5'4"—exactly what she should weigh, according to her doctor's chart. But in her eyes she still looks dumpy. She can't shake her mind free of the "Lady Marmelade" video from Moulin Rouge. Christina Aguilera, Pink, L'il Kim, and Mya, each one perfect in her own way: every curve smooth and sleek, lean-sexy, nothing to spare. Self-hatred and shame start to burn in the girl, and envy tears at her stomach, enough to make her sick. She'll never look like them, no matter how much weight she loses. Look at that stomach of hers, see how it sticks out? Those thighs—they actually jiggle. Her butt is monstrous. She's fat, gross, a dough girl.

As you read the imaginary scenario above, whom did you picture standing 2 in front of the mirror? If your images of girls with eating and body image problems have been shaped by *People* magazine and Lifetime movies, she's probably white, North American, and economically secure. A child whose parents have never had to worry about putting food on the family table. A girl with money to spare for fashion magazines and trendy clothing, probably college-bound. If you're familiar with the classic psychological literature on eating disorders, you may also have read that she's an extreme "perfectionist" with a hyper-demanding mother, and that she suffers from "body-image distortion syndrome" and other severe perceptual and cognitive problems that "normal" girls don't share. You probably don't picture her as Black, Asian, or Latina.

Read the description again, but this time imagine twenty-something Tenisha 3 Williamson standing in front of the mirror. Tenisha is black, suffers from anorexia, and feels like a traitor to her race. "From an African-American standpoint," she writes, "we as a people are encouraged to embrace our big, voluptuous bodies. This makes me feel terrible because I don't want a big, voluptuous body! I don't ever want to be fat—ever, and I don't ever want to gain weight. I would rather die from starvation than gain a single pound."[1] Tenisha is no longer an anomaly. Eating and body image problems are now not only crossing racial and class lines, but gender lines. They have also become a global phenomenon.

4   Fiji is a striking example. Because of their remote location, the Fiji islands did not have access to television until 1995, when a single station was introduced. It broadcasts programs from the United States, Great Britain, and Australia. Until that time, Fiji had no reported cases of eating disorders, and a study conducted by anthropologist Anne Becker showed that most Fijian girls and women, no matter how large, were comfortable with their bodies. In 1998, just three years after the station began broadcasting, 11 percent of girls reported vomiting to control weight, and 62 percent of the girls surveyed reported dieting during the previous months.[2]

5   Becker was surprised by the change; she had thought that Fijian cultural traditions, which celebrate eating and favor voluptuous bodies, would "withstand" the influence of media images. Becker hadn't yet understood that we live in an empire of images, and that there are no protective borders.

6   In Central Africa, for example, traditional cultures still celebrate voluptuous women. In some regions, brides are sent to fattening farms, to be plumped and massaged into shape for their wedding night. In a country plagued by AIDS, the skinny body has meant—as it used to among Italian Jewish, and Black Americans—poverty, sickness, death. "An African girl must have hips," says dress designer Frank Osodi, "We have hips. We have bums. We like flesh in Africa." For years, Nigeria sent its local version of beautiful to the Miss World Competition. The contestants did very poorly. Then a savvy entrepreneur went against local ideals and entered Agbani Darego, a light-skinned, hyper-skinny beauty. (He got his inspiration from M-Net, the South African network seen across Africa on satellite television, which broadcasts mostly American movies and television shows.) Agbani Darego won the Miss World Pageant, the first Black African to do so. Now, Nigerian teenagers fast and exercise, trying to become "lepa"—a popular slang phrase for the thin "it" girls that are all the rage. Said one: "People have realized that slim is beautiful."[3]

7   How can mere images be so powerful? For one thing, they are never "just pictures," as the fashion magazines continually maintain (disingenuously) in their own defense. They speak to young people not just about how to be beautiful but also about how to become what the dominant culture admires, values,

---

[1]From the Colours of Ana website (http://coloursofana.com//ss8.asp).
[2]Reported in Nancy Snyderman, *The Girl in the Mirror* (New York: Hyperion, 2002), p. 84.
[3]Norimistsu Onishi, "Globalization of Beauty Makes Slimness Trendy," *The New York Times,* Oct. 3, 2002.

rewards. They tell them how to be cool, "get it together," overcome their shame. To girls who have been abused they may offer a fantasy of control and invulnerability, immunity from pain and hurt. For racial and ethnic groups whose bodies have been deemed "foreign," earthy, and primitive, and considered unattractive by Anglo-Saxon norms, they may cast the lure of being accepted as "normal" by the dominant culture.

In today's world, it is through images—much more than parents, teachers, 8 or clergy—that we are taught how to be. And it is images, too, that teach us how to see, that educate our vision in what's a defect and what is normal, that give us the models against which our own bodies and the bodies of others are measured. Perceptual pedagogy: "How To Interpret Your Body 101." It's become a global requirement.

I was intrigued, for example, when my articles on eating disorders began to 9 be translated, over the past few years, into Japanese and Chinese. Among the members of audiences at my talks, Asian women had been among the most insistent that eating and body image weren't problems for their people, and indeed, my initial research showed that eating disorders were virtually unknown in Asia. But when, this year, a Korean translation of *Unbearable Weight* was published, I felt I needed to revisit the situation. I discovered multiple reports on dramatic increases in eating disorders in China, South Korea, and Japan. "As many Asian countries become Westernized and infused with the Western aesthetic of a tall, thin, lean body, a virtual tsunami of eating disorders has swamped Asian countries," writes Eunice Park in *Asian Week* magazine. Older people can still remember when it was very different. In China, for example, where revolutionary ideals once condemned any focus on appearance and there have been several disastrous famines, "little fatty" was a term of endearment for children. Now, with fast food on every corner, childhood obesity is on the rise, and the cultural meaning of fat and thin has changed. "When I was young," says Li Xiaojing, who manages a fitness center in Beijing, "people admired and were even jealous of fat people since they thought they had a better life. . . . But now, most of us see a fat person and think 'He looks awful.'"[4]

Clearly, body insecurity can be exported, imported, and marketed—just 10 like any other profitable commodity. In this respect, what's happened with men and boys is illustrative. Ten years ago men tended, if anything, to see themselves as better looking than they (perhaps) actually were. And then (as I chronicle in detail in my book *The Male Body*) the menswear manufacturers, the diet industries, and the plastic surgeons "discovered" the male body. And now, young guys are looking in their mirrors, finding themselves soft and ill defined, no matter how muscular they are. Now they are developing the eating and body image disorders that we once thought only girls had. Now they are abusing steroids, measuring their own muscularity against the oiled and perfected images of professional athletes, body-builders, and *Men's Health* models. Now

[4]Reported in Elizabeth Rosenthal, "Beijing Journal: China's Chic Waistline: Convex to Concave," *The New York Times*, Dec. 9, 1999.

the industries in body-enhancement—cosmetic surgeons, manufacturers of anti-aging creams, spas and salons—are making huge bucks off men, too.

11   What is to be done? I have no easy answers. But I do know that we need to acknowledge, finally and decisively, that we are dealing here with a cultural problem. If eating disorders were biochemical, as some claim, how can we account for their gradual "spread" across race, gender, and nationality? And with mass media culture increasingly providing the dominant "public education" in our children's lives—and those of children around the globe—how can we blame families? Families matter, of course, and so do racial and ethnic traditions. But families exist in cultural time and space—and so do racial groups. In the empire of images, no one lives in a bubble of self-generated "dysfunction" or permanent immunity. The sooner we recognize that—and start paying attention to the culture around us and what it is teaching our children—the sooner we can begin developing some strategies for change.

COMPREHENSION

1. How does Bordo define the "body-image distortion syndrome" (paragraph 2)?
2. Why have body image and weight problems become a global phenomenon? What is the main cause of this phenomenon?
3. How, according to the author, should we deal with the globalization of eating disorders?

RHETORIC

1. How does the author establish herself as an authority on her subject? Do you think that she succeeds? Why or why not?
2. What is the writer's claim? Where does she place it, and why?
3. Bordo begins with an imaginary situation. Does this strategy enhance or detract from the validity of her argument? Justify your response.
4. The writer uses several rhetorical strategies to advance her argument. Identify places where she employs description, illustration, comparison and contrast, and causal analysis.
5. The writer has been praised for her readable or accessible style. Do you think that this essay is well written and thought provoking? Explain.
6. How does Bordo develop this selection as a problem-solution essay? Where does the solution appear, and how effective is its placement within the essay?

WRITING

1. Write a causal essay analyzing young Americans' fascination with body image and the consequences of this preoccupation.
2. Why are women in the United States and around the world more susceptible to eating disorders than men? Answer this question in an analytical essay.
3. **Writing an Argument:** Write an essay titled "Body Images, Eating Disorders, and Cultural Imperialism." In this essay, argue for or against the proposition that American media are exporting potentially unhealthy images of the human body.

NETWORKING
Applying 21st-Century Literacies

Critiquing a Web Site about Eating Disorders: On the Chapter 13 Networking page (at *www.mhhe.com/mhreader11e*), choose one of the listed Web sites and write a careful critique of both its purpose and its effectiveness at achieving that purpose. Depending on the site you choose and your opinions, your critique might be favorable, mixed, or denunciatory. Whatever your position, it should be carefully illustrated with examples from the Web site, and your points of agreement or contention should be supported by other sources.

Synthesis: Connections for Critical Thinking

1. Research the current status of public health in the United States and what is being done to prevent major outbreaks of disease. Refer to at least three essays in this chapter to support your findings and thesis.
2. Compare approaches to women's health issues as discussed by several writers in this chapter, notably Goodman, Mendoza, and Bordo.
3. Compare and contrast the strategies that Gawande, Goodman, and Bordo use to develop their arguments.
4. Referring to any three essays in this chapter, analyze some of the major moral, ethical, and religious issues raised by current medical research.
5. Compare and contrast the treatment of death in the essays by Tuchman, Lepore, and Selzer.
6. Compare and contrast the essays by Gawande and Bordo.
7. Research the subject of AIDS, and connect your findings to the essays by Tuchman and Gould.
8. Working with three other class members, develop a PowerPoint presentation informing your college about a health issue of campus concern.

NETWORKING
Applying 21st-Century Literacies

1. Compare and contrast two Web sites devoted to some aspect of medicine and health—for example, stem-cell research, abortion, funeral practices, cosmetic surgery, or dieting.
2. Explore the World Health Organization Web site (*www.who.int/en*), and summarize what you find about global pandemics.

CH 13   **www.mhhe.com/mhreader11e**

- *Image Gallery:* Chapter images in color
- *Health and Medicine:* Information on the authors in this chapter
- *Ch. 13 Networking*

chapter *14*

Nature and the Environment
How Do We Relate to the Natural World?

We are at a point in the history of civilization where consciousness of our fragile relationship with nature and the environment is high. Even as you spend an hour reading a few of the essays in this chapter, it is estimated that we are losing 3,000 acres of rain forest around the world and four species of plants or animals. From pollution, to the population explosion, to the depletion of the ozone layer, to global climate change, we seem to be confronted with ecological catastrophe. Nevertheless, as Rachel Carson reminds us, we have "an obligation to endure," to survive potential natural catastrophes by understanding and managing our relationship with the natural world.

Ecology, or the study of nature and the environment, as many of the essayists in this chapter attest, involves us in the conservation of the earth. It moves us to suppress our rapacious destruction of the planet. Clearly, the biological stability of the planet is increasingly precarious. More plants, insects, birds, and animals became extinct in the 20th century than in any era since the Cretaceous catastrophe more than 65 million years ago that led to the extinction of the dinosaurs. Within this ecological context, writers like Carson become our literary conscience, reminding us of how easily natural processes can break down unless we insist on a degree of ecological economy.

Of course, any modification of human behavior in an effort to conserve nature is a complex matter. To save the spotted owl in the Pacific Northwest, we must sacrifice the jobs of people in the timber industry. To reduce pollution, we must forsake gas and oil for alternate energy sources that are costly to develop. To reduce the waste stream, we must shift from a consumption to a conservation ethos. The ecological debate is complicated, but it is clear that the preservation of the myriad life cycles on earth is crucial, for we, too, could become an endangered species.

The language of nature is as enigmatic as the sounds of dolphins and whales communicating with their respective species. Writers like Barry Lopez and Rachel Carson and the vision expressed in the letter of Chief Seattle help us decipher the language of our environment. These writers encourage us to converse with nature, learn from it, and even revere it. All of us are guests on this planet; the natural world is our host. If we do not protect the earth, how can we guarantee the survival of civilization?

PREVIEWING THE CHAPTER

As you read the essays in this chapter and respond to them in discussion and writing, consider the following questions:

- According to the author, what should our relationship to the natural world be?
- What claims or arguments does the author make about the importance of nature? Do you agree or disagree with these claims and arguments?
- What specific ecological problem does the author investigate?
- How does the author think that nature influences human behavior?
- What cultural factors are involved in our approach to the environment?
- Is the writer optimistic, pessimistic, or neutral in the assessment of our ability to conserve nature?
- Do you find that the author is too idealistic or sentimental in the depiction of nature? Why?
- Based on the author's essay, how does he or she qualify as a nature writer?
- How have you been challenged or changed by the essays in this chapter?

Classic and Contemporary Images
ARE WE DESTROYING OUR NATURAL WORLD?

Using a Critical Perspective   Imagine yourself to be part of each of the scenes depicted in these two illustrations. How do you feel, and why? Now examine the purpose of each image. What details do the artists emphasize to convey their feelings about our relationship to the natural world? What images does each artist create to capture your attention and direct your viewing and thinking toward a specific, dominant impression?

The painters of the Hudson River School such as John Frederick Kensett (1816–1872) celebrated American landscapes in their art, painting breathtaking scenes in meticulous detail. In *Along the Hudson* (1852), the beauty of the river is unspoiled.

Vehicles travel on the 405 Freeway where it intersects with the 10 West Freeway in Los Angeles. California could take the lead in the international effort to reduce global warming after the state's Air Resources Board gave approval to a package of regulations that would cut vehicle emissions by as much as 25 percent.

Classic and Contemporary Essays
Do We Own Nature?

The simple yet passionate reflections of Chief Seattle regarding the destruction of a worldview are complemented by the more scholarly and learned meditations, nearly a century and a half later, of the esteemed naturalist and writer Barry Lopez. Chief Seattle mourns the death of a way of life, a way of thinking, and a way of being as he accepts that the cultural world of his people is doomed to disappear with the encroachment of "civilization." The white man exploits nature, uses nature, and perhaps most radically of all, perceives himself as apart from nature. This is in profound contrast to the ways of Chief Seattle's people, who saw themselves as in harmony with nature or, more specifically, as inseparable from it—as inseparable perhaps as from a part of their own bodies. Chief Seattle's address is simple. And so perhaps is his message, although one should not confuse simplicity with lack of profundity. Barry Lopez has a similar message. Writing from the perspective of a 21st-century naturalist and teacher, Lopez speaks of "a sense of responsibility toward children." He urges adults to both teach and learn from children about the wonders of nature and how the natural world can inform us about our human condition. With a personal touch, Lopez recounts key encounters with children and nature, finding evidence of that union with nature that Chief Seattle spoke of so eloquently. Although Chief Seattle and Barry Lopez speak in different levels of discourse and from different perspectives, they share an awe of nature and a desire to inform their respective audiences of the sacredness of all life.

Letter to President Pierce, 1855

Chief Seattle

Chief Seattle (1786–1866) was the leader of the Dewamish and other Pacific Northwest tribes. The city of Seattle, Washington, bears his name. In 1854, Chief Seattle reluctantly agreed to sell tribal lands to the U.S. government and move to the government-established reservations. The authenticity of the following speech has been challenged by many scholars. However, most specialists agree that it contains the substance and perspective of Chief Seattle's attitude toward nature and the white race.

1   We know that the white man does not understand our ways. One portion of the land is the same to him as the next, for he is a stranger who comes in the night and takes from the land whatever he needs. The earth is not his brother, but his enemy, and when he has conquered it, he moves on. He leaves his fathers'

graves, and his children's birthright is forgotten. The sight of your cities pains the eyes of the red man. But perhaps it is because the red man is a savage and does not understand.

There is no quiet place in the white man's cities. No place to hear the leaves 2 of spring or the rustle of insect's wings. But perhaps because I am a savage and do not understand, the clatter only seems to insult the ears. The Indian prefers the soft sound of the wind darting over the face of the pond, the smell of the wind itself cleansed by a mid-day rain, or scented with the piñon pine. The air is precious to the red man. For all things share the same breath—the beasts, the trees, the man. Like a man dying for many days, he is numb to the stench.

What is man without the beasts? If all the beasts were gone, men would die 3 from great loneliness of spirit, for whatever happens to the beasts also happens to man. All things are connected. Whatever befalls the earth befalls the sons of the earth.

It matters little where we pass the rest of our days; they are not many. A few 4 more hours, a few more winters, and none of the children of the great tribes that once lived on this earth, or that roamed in small bands in the woods, will be left to mourn the graves of a people once as powerful and hopeful as yours.

The whites, too, shall pass—perhaps sooner than other tribes. Continue to 5 contaminate your bed, and you will one night suffocate in your own waste. When the buffalo are all slaughtered, the wild horses all tamed, the secret corners of the forest heavy with the scent of many men, and the view of the ripe hills blotted by talking wires, where is the thicket? Gone. Where is the eagle? Gone. And what is it to say goodbye to the swift and the hunt, the end of living and the beginning of survival? We might understand if we knew what it was that the white man dreams, what he describes to his children on the long winter nights, what visions he burns into their minds, so they will wish for tomorrow. But we are savages. The white man's dreams are hidden from us.

COMPREHENSION

1. What does Chief Seattle suggest is the major difference between the white man's relationship with nature and that of the red man?
2. Chief Seattle claims that perhaps the red man would understand the white man better if he understood better the "dreams" and "visions" of the white man. What does Chief Seattle suggest by these terms?
3. Chief Seattle refers to Native Americans as "savages." Why?

RHETORIC

1. The author uses a number of sensory details in describing both nature and the white man's crimes against nature. How does the eliciting of sensations help determine the relationship between writer, text, and reader?
2. The letter is written simply, with simply constructed paragraphs and sentences. What does this style suggest about the writer's voice?

3. There is a noted absence of transitional expressions in the writing, that is, such linking words as *in addition, furthermore, nevertheless,* and *moreover.* How does this absence contribute to the directness of the writing?

4. The author uses the convention of the series, as in the following examples: "For all things share the same breath—the beasts, the trees, the man" (paragraph 2) and "When the buffalo are all slaughtered, the wild horses all tamed, the secret corners of the forest heavy with the scent of many men, and the view of the ripe hills blotted by talking wires" (paragraph 5). What is the rhetorical effect of this device?

5. Note the opening and closing sentences of the letter. How do they frame the letter? What do they suggest about one of its major themes?

6. Some scholars dispute the authenticity of the letter, attributing it to a white man who was attempting to articulate the essence of Chief Seattle's oratory in an effort to champion Native American causes. What elements of the letter resemble the rhetorical elements of a speech?

WRITING

1. Write a 250-word summary in which you compare and contrast the major differences between the white man's and the red man's perception of and relationship to nature as conceived by Chief Seattle.

2. For a research project, trace the use of the word *savage* as it has been used to describe Native Americans.

3. **Writing an Argument:** Argue for or against the view that the charge by Chief Seattle that the white man is contemptuous of nature is still valid today. Use at least three points to support your thesis.

NETWORKING
Applying 21st-Century Literacies

Writing a Radio PSA: Public service announcements, or PSAs, which you've likely heard on your campus radio station or NPR, are advertisements designed to raise awareness about issues, not sell products or services. Draft a PSA that informs or educates the public about an environmental issue.

Children in the Woods

Barry Lopez

Barry Lopez (b. 1945) was born in New York City but grew up in southern California's San Fernando Valley, which at the time was still largely rural. He attended the University of Notre Dame (BA, 1966) and the University of Oregon (MA, 1968), and he pursued additional graduate work before starting a career as a full-time writer. Lopez's early essays in such periodicals as National Geographic, Wilderness, Science, *and* Harper's *established him as an authoritative voice in the environmental movement. His first major nonfiction work,* Of Wolves and Men *(1978), brought him national acclaim, an American Book Award nomination, and the John Burroughs medal for nature writing. His venture into fiction with* River Notes: The Dance of Herons *(1979) and* Winter Count *(1980) were also well received. Among Lopez's other books are* Arctic Dreams: Imagination and Desire in a Northern Landscape *(1986),* Crossing Open Ground *(1988),* The Rediscovery of North America *(1991),* Crow and Weasel *(1999), the autobiography* About This Life *(1999), and a short-story collection,* Resistance *(2004). Lopez sees himself as a storyteller, someone who has the responsibility to create an atmosphere in which the wisdom of the work can reveal itself and, as he has written, "make the reader feel part of something." In this essay from his collection* Crossing Open Ground, *Lopez sets himself and other children in the natural world in order to discover their own part of something.*

When I was a child growing up in the San Fernando Valley in California, a trip 1 into Los Angeles was special. The sensation of movement from a rural area into an urban one was sharp. On one of these charged occasions, walking down a sidewalk with my mother, I stopped suddenly, caught by a pattern of sunlight trapped in a spiraling imperfection in a windowpane. A stranger, an elderly woman in a cloth coat and a dark hat, spoke out spontaneously, saying how remarkable it is that children notice these things.

I have never forgotten the texture of this incident. Whenever I recall it I am 2 moved not so much by any sense of my young self but by a sense of responsibility toward children, knowing how acutely I was affected in that moment by that woman's words. The effect, for all I know, has lasted a lifetime.

Now, years later, I live in a rain forest in western Oregon, on the banks of a 3 mountain river in relatively undisturbed country, surrounded by 150-foot-tall Douglas firs, delicate deer-head orchids, and clearings where wild berries grow. White-footed mice and mule deer, mink and coyote move through here. My wife and I do not have children, but children we know, or children whose parents we are close to, are often here. They always want to go into the woods. And I wonder what to tell them.

In the beginning, years ago, I think I said too much. I spoke with an ency- 4 clopedic knowledge of the names of plants or the names of birds passing through in season. Gradually I came to say less. After a while the only words I spoke, beyond answering a question or calling attention quickly to the slight difference between a sprig of red cedar and a sprig of incense cedar, were to elucidate single objects.

I remember once finding a fragment of a raccoon's jaw in an alder thicket. I 5 sat down alongside the two children with me and encouraged them to find out who this was—with only the three teeth still intact in a piece of the animal's maxilla to guide them. The teeth told by their shape and placement what this animal ate. By a kind of visual extrapolation its size became clear. There were other clues, immediately present, which told, with what I could add of climate and terrain, how this animal lived, how its broken jaw came to be lying here. Raccoon, they surmised. And tiny tooth marks along the bone's broken edge told of a mouse's hunger for calcium.

6   We set the jaw back and went on.

7   If I had known more about raccoons, finer points of osteology, we might have guessed more: say, whether it was male or female. But what we deduced was all we needed. Hours later, the maxilla, lost behind us in the detritus of the forest floor, continued to effervesce. It was tied faintly to all else we spoke of that afternoon.

8   In speaking with children who might one day take a permanent interest in natural history—as writers, as scientists, as filmmakers, as anthropologists—I have sensed that an extrapolation from a single fragment of the whole is the most invigorating experience I can share with them. I think children know that nearly anyone can learn the names of things; the impression made on them at this level is fleeting. What takes a lifetime to learn, they comprehend, is the existence and substance of myriad relationships: It is these relationships, not the things themselves, that ultimately hold the human imagination.

9   The brightest children, it has often struck me, are fascinated by metaphor—with what is shown in the set of relationships bearing on the raccoon, for example, to lie quite beyond the raccoon. In the end, you are trying to make clear to them that everything found at the edge of one's senses—the high note of the winter wren, the thick perfume of propolis that drifts downwind from spring willows, the brightness of wood chips scattered by beaver—that all this fits together. The indestructibility of these associations conveys a sense of permanence that nurtures the heart, that cripples one of the most insidious of human anxieties, the one that says, you do not belong here, you are unnecessary.

10   Whenever I walk with a child, I think how much I have seen disappear in my own life. What will there be for this person when he is my age? If he senses something ineffable in the landscape, will I know enough to encourage it?—to somehow show him that, yes, when people talk about violent death, spiritual exhilaration, compassion, futility, final causes, they are drawing on forty thousand years of human meditation on *this*—as we embrace Douglas firs, or stand by a river across whose undulating back we skip stones, or dig out a camas bulb, biting down into a taste so much wilder than last night's potatoes.

11   The most moving look I ever saw from a child in the woods was on a mud bar by the footprints of a heron. We were on our knees, making handprints beside the footprints. You could feel the creek vibrating in the silt and sand. The sun beat down heavily on our hair. Our shoes were soaking wet. The look said: I did not know until now that I needed someone much older to confirm this, the feeling I have of life here. I can now grow older, knowing it need never be lost.

12   The quickest door to open in the woods for a child is the one that leads to the smallest room, by knowing the name each thing is called. The door that leads to the cathedral is marked by a hesitancy to speak at all, rather to encourage by

example a sharpness of the senses. If one speaks it should only be to say, as well as one can, how wonderfully all this fits together, to indicate what a long, fierce peace can derive from this knowledge.

COMPREHENSION

1. What is Lopez's primary purpose in this essay? How does the title relate to the purpose?
2. Does Lopez assume his audience has the same value position as he does? Why or why not?
3. What, ultimately, does Lopez want children to learn about the natural world? How does he teach them?

RHETORIC

1. Does Lopez state his thesis or imply it? Justify your response.
2. Why does Lopez use a personal tone or voice at the start of this essay? How does his opening paragraph connect to the body of the essay?
3. Cite instances where Lopez moves from vivid description to response and reflection.
4. Where does Lopez employ the comparative method, and toward what objective?
5. What extended metaphor does Lopez establish in the final paragraph? Is this an appropriate and effective metaphor to end the essay? Why or why not?

WRITING

1. Write a narrative and descriptive essay in which you recount a childhood experience that taught you something about the natural world.
2. How would you speak to children if you were taking them on a nature walk? Write a reflective essay addressing this question.
3. **Writing an Argument:** Argue for or against the proposition that you can learn profound truths about yourself and the world by immersing yourself in nature.

NETWORKING
Applying 21st-Century Literacies

Promoting the Natural World from the Virtual One: Create a blog or the home page of a Web site, the purpose of which is to get visitors excited about a natural space—a nearby national park, a reservoir, the Everglades—or an environmental issue—an endangered species, the effects of global climate change, ways to be more "green" around campus, etc. Think of creative ways to use text, visuals, videos, sound, and even music to appeal to your readers.

Synthesis: Classic and Contemporary Questions for Comparison

1. Chief Seattle and Barry Lopez ponder the destruction of nature as a physical and spiritual presence. In what ways are their stakes in this destruction the same? In what ways are they different? Does either writer have the power to effect a transformation in our attitude toward nature? Explain.

2. It has often been said that intellectual knowledge changes one's relationship with the world environment. In what ways has Lopez's "book learning" and erudition made him a different person from Chief Seattle? Base your response on the style and tone of each author.

3. Chief Seattle is literally the leader and spokesperson of a defeated nation. How does he preserve his dignity in the face of being conquered? How does he indicate to the white man that his "victory" is temporary? Lopez, on the other hand, is a successful member of his society: esteemed naturalist, award-winning writer, popular lecturer. What is his relationship to society and to America? Explain by referring to the text.

A City beyond the Reach of Empathy

Richard Ford

Richard Ford (b. 1944) was born in Jackson, Mississippi, and grew up there and in Little Rock, Arkansas. Ford left the South to study at Michigan State University. He started law school but left after one year to prepare for a career as a writer, studying with E. L. Doctorow at the University of California at Irvine (MFA, 1970). His early novels include A Piece of My Heart *(1976),* The Ultimate Good Luck *(1981),* The Sportswriter *(1986), and* Wildlife *(1990). Ford's novel,* Independence Day *(1995) won both the Pulitzer prize and the Pen/Faulkner Award, and subsequently was made into a film. His latest novel is* The Lay of the Land *(2006). Ford's collected short fiction appears in* Vintage Ford *(2003). In this essay, published in the* New York Times *on September 4, 2005, a week after Hurricane Katrina, which devastated New Orleans and large swaths of the Gulf Coast, Ford offers a meditation on the enormity of the catastrophe.*

1 Who can write about New Orleans now? Tell us what it's like there. Bring us near to what people are experiencing, to their loss, to what will survive. People

who are close should write that. Only they're in the city, or they're on a bus, or they're seeking shelter. We don't know where they are.

It's just a keyhole, and a small one, onto this great civic tragedy. The people 2 who should be writing of it can't be found. An attempt to set out a vocabulary for empathy and for reckoning is frustrated in a moment of sorest need by the plain terms of the tragedy that wants telling. There are many such keyholes.

In America, even with our incommensurable memories of 9/11, we still 3 do not have an exact human vocabulary for the loss of a city—our great iconic city, so graceful, livable, insular, self-delighted, eccentric, the one New Orleanians always said, with a wink, that care forgot and that sometimes, it might seem, forgot to care. Other peoples have experienced their cities' losses. Some bombed away (sometimes by us). Others gone in the flood. Here now is one more tragedy that we thought, by some divinity's grace that didn't arrive, we'd miss. But not. And our inept attempts at words run only to lists, costs, to assessing blame. It's like Hiroshima, a public official said. But no. It's not like anything. It's what it is. That's the hard part. He, with all of us, lacked the words.

For those away from New Orleans—most all of us—in this week of tears 4 and wrenching, words fail. Somehow our hearts' reach comes short and we've been left with an aching, pointless inwardness. "All memory resolves itself in gaze," the poet Richard Hugo wrote once about another town that died.

Empathy is what we long for—not sadness for a house we own, or owned 5 once—now swept away. Not even for the felt miracle of two wide-eyed children whirled upward into a helicopter as if into clouds. And we want more than that, even at this painful long distance: We want to project our sympathies straight into the life of a woman standing waist-deep in a glistening toxic current with a whole city's possessions all floating about, her own belongings in a white plastic bag, and who has no particular reason for hope, and so is just staring up. We would all give her hope. Comfort. A part of ourselves. Perform an act of renewal. It's hard to make sense of this, we say. But it makes sense. Making sense just doesn't help.

Tell me what you feel, a woman in Los Angeles said to me today by tele- 6 phone. (I have a telephone, of course.) Tell me what you think of when you think of New Orleans. There must be special things you feel the loss of. Memories. And I realized, by her voice, that she had made a firm decision already about this loss.

Oh, yes, I said, though not always the memories you'd think. I have a pic- 7 ture of my parents on V-J Day, in City Park, holding a baby, staring at the camera and the sun. They are all dressed up and happy. The baby is me. So, I wonder, how is that park faring tonight.

I have a memory of my father and mother drunk as loons on New Year's 8 Eve, in front of Antoine's. It was nearly midnight, 1951. There was no place to leave me, so they had their fight (only an argument, really) in front of me. My father held my mother against a wall on St. Louis Street and shouted at her. About what I don't know. Later, when we were in bed in the Hotel Monteleone, with me between them and the ceiling fan turning, they both cried. So. What of Antoine's now? What of the waiters who a week ago stood out on the street in tuxedos aprons and smoked? What of St. Louis Street?

9   I have a memory of a hot and breathless summer. It is many summers joined into one. My mother took me onto the Algiers Ferry, an open boat with cars driven onto the deck. Out on the great sliding brown river there was the only hint of breeze you could find anywhere. Back and across to the foot of Canal Street. Back and across, we went. She bought me pralines. I held her hand during it all, until the sun finally fell and the hot night rose. So, now, what of that river? And the Algiers Ferry? And Algiers? All memory resolves itself in gaze.

10   And a last one, more up to date. My wife and I are walking home from a friend's house down tree-shrouded Coliseum Street. It is 2003, and 11 o'clock on a warm January night. We are only steps from our door, just in a cone of street light, when a boy hops out of a car and says he will definitely kill us if we don't hand it over right away. He has a little silver pistol to persuade us. Let's say he's 16. And he is serious. But he laughs when we tell him we don't have a penny. And it's true. I pull my pockets out like a bum. "You people," he says, almost happily, his gun become an afterthought. "You shouldn't be out here this way." He shakes his head, looks at the pavement, then gets in his car and drives away. He, that boy—he'd be 19—I hope he's safe somewhere.

11   It is—New Orleans is—a city foremost for special projections, for the things you can't do, see, think, consume, feel, forget up in Jackson or Little Rock or home in Topeka. "We're at the jumping-off place," Eudora Welty wrote. This was about Plaquemines, just across the river. It is—New Orleans—the place where the firm ground ceases and the unsound footing begins. A certain kind of person likes such a place. A certain kind of person wants to go there and never leave.

12   And there are the streetcars (or there were). And there are the oak trees and the lovely French boulevards and the stately rich men's houses. And Buddy Bolden was born there and Satchmo grew up in Storyville. Huey Long lived in the Roosevelt Hotel, where he really had a "de-duct box." His brother, Uncle Earl, was crazy as a betsy-bug. If you knew a waiter you could get a table anywhere. You couldn't get divorced or married or sell your house on Fat Tuesday. And while they didn't let Jews and blacks in the Boston Club, the races still mingled and often people danced in the streets. They subscribed to the Napoleonic Code.

13   But so much for memory now. It charms, but it confuses and possibly holds us back. It's hard enough to take things in. When I think of my friends in the city this morning, I think of them as high and dry, as being where they belong, being themselves in their normal life that was. I turn off the TV, as I did four years ago next week, just to think my own sorrowing and prospective thoughts of them.

14   From the ruins it's not easy to know what's best to think. Even the president may have felt this way in his low pass over that wide sheet of onyx water, the bobbing roofs peeking above the surfaces, the vast collapse, the wind-riddled

buildings, that little figure (could he see who she was?) staring skyward. Something will be there when the flood recedes. We know that. It will be those people now standing in the water, and on those rooftops—many black, many poor. Homeless. Overlooked. And it will be New Orleans—though its memory may be shortened, its self-gaze and eccentricity scoured out so that what's left is a city more like other cities, less insular, less self-regarding, but possibly more self-knowing after today. A city on firmer ground.

I write in the place of others, today, for the ones who can't be found. And 15 there is a blunt ending now, one we always feared, never wished for, and do not deserve. Don't get me wrong. We would all turn the days back if we could, have those old problems, those old eccentricities again. But today is a beginning. There's no better way to think of it now. Those others surely will be writing soon.

COMPREHENSION

1. Why does Ford call Hurricane Katrina a "great civic tragedy"? Does he explain what he means by this phrase? Justify your response.
2. Ford speaks of "the vocabulary for empathy and for reckoning." How does he explain and amplify this idea throughout the essay?
3. According to Ford, is the devastation wreaked on New Orleans a tragedy caused by nature, human vanity, political failure, or a combination of these? Explain. Does Ford finally "make sense" of the tragedy? Why or why not?

RHETORIC

1. Why does Ford open his essay with a question? Where else does he pose questions? What is the effect?
2. Explain the tone and atmosphere that Ford creates in this essay. What do his allusions to New Orleans culture—Satchmo, Fat Tuesday, the Napoleonic Code, and more—contribute to these elements?
3. How might this essay be considered an extended definition or a series of definitions?
4. How does Ford develop the metaphor of the "keyhole" that he introduces in paragraph 2?
5. Ford begins several paragraphs with the phrase "I have a memory" or variants of this phrase. How does this compositional strategy serve as an organizing principle for the essay?

WRITING

1. Write an essay in which you explain why it is necessary to empathize with the victims of natural disasters.
2. **Writing an Argument:** Establish a claim about the federal government's response to Hurricane Katrina, develop at least three minor propositions supporting this claim, and provide adequate evidence to bolster your argument.

NETWORKING
Applying 21st-Century Literacies

Researching Post-Katrina Reconstruction: Go online and research the status of renovation efforts in New Orleans today. Summarize your findings in a short informative essay.

Why I Hunt

Rick Bass

Rick Bass (b. 1958) was born in Fort Worth, Texas, and grew up in the Texas hill country where his grandfather taught him how to hunt. His collection of essays, The Deer Pasture *(1985), recounts his Texas years, the ethos of hunting, and the allure of the outdoors. Bass studied at Utah State University (BS, 1979) and worked as an oil and gas geologist in Mississippi for eight years. His time working in the oil fields of the deep South is documented in* Oil Notes *(1979). Bass has written more than a dozen works of nonfiction and fiction, many of them reflecting environmental issues and people's search for balance in the natural world. An environmental advocate and land conservationist, Bass lives in the remote Yaak Valley on the Montana–Canada border, a region depicted in books such as* Winter: Notes from Montana *(1991),* Brown Dog of the Yaak: Essays on Art and Activism *(1999), and* The Roadless Yaak: Reflections and Observations about One of Our Last Great Wild Places *(2002). His most recent book of fiction is* Why I Came West *(2008). Bass wrote this vivid and provocative essay on the allure of the hunt for* Sierra *magazine in 2001.*

1   I was a hunter before I came far up into northwest Montana, but not to the degree I am now. It astounds me sometimes to step back particularly at the end of autumn, the end of the hunting season, and take both mental and physical inventory of all that was hunted and all that was gathered from this life in the mountains. The woodshed groaning tight, full of firewood. The fruits and herbs and vegetables from the garden, canned or dried or frozen; the wild mushrooms, huckleberries, thimbleberries, and strawberries. And most precious of all, the flesh of the wild things that share with us these mountains and the plains to the east—the elk, the whitetail and mule deer; the ducks and geese, grouse and pheasant and Hungarian partridge and dove and chukar and wild turkey; the trout and whitefish. Each year the cumulative bounty seems unbelievable. What heaven is this into which we've fallen?

2   How my wife and I got to this valley—the Yaak—15 years ago is a mystery, a move that I've only recently come to accept as having been inevitable. We got in the truck one day feeling strangely restless in Mississippi, and we drove.

What did I know? Only that I missed the West's terrain of space. Young and healthy, and not coincidentally new-in-love, we hit that huge and rugged landscape in full stride. We drove north until we ran out of country—until the road ended, and we reached Canada's thick blue woods—and then we turned west and traveled until we ran almost out of mountains: the backside of the Rockies, to the wet, west-slope rainforest.

We came over a little mountain pass—it was August and winter was already fast approaching—and looked down on the soft hills, the dense purples of the spruce and fir forests, the ivory crests of the ice-capped peaks, and the slender ribbons of gray thread rising from the chimneys of the few cabins nudged close to the winding river below, and we fell in love with the Yaak Valley and the hard-logged Kootenai National Forest—the way people in movies fall with each other, star and starlet, as if a trap door has been pulled out from beneath them: tumbling through the air, arms windmilling furiously, and suddenly no other world but each other, no other world but this one and eyes for no one, or no place, else.

Right from the beginning, I could see that there was extraordinary bounty in this low-elevation forest, resting as it does in a magical seam between the Pacific Northwest and the northern Rockies. Some landscapes these days have been reduced to nothing but dandelions and fire ants, knapweed and thistle, where the only remaining wildlife are sparrows, squirrels, and starlings. In the blessed Yaak, however, not a single mammal has gone extinct since the end of the Ice Age. This forest sustains more types of hunters—carnivores—than any valley in North America. It is a predator's showcase, home not just to wolves and grizzlies, but wolverines, lynx, bobcat, marten, fisher, black bear, mountain lion, golden eagle, bald eagle, coyote, fox, weasel. In the Yaak, everything is in motion, either seeking its quarry, or seeking to avoid becoming quarry.

The people who have chosen to live in this remote valley—few phones, very little electricity, and long, dark winters—possess a hardness and a dreaminess both. They—we—can live a life of deprivation, and yet are willing to enter the comfort of daydreams and imagination. There is something mysterious happening here between the landscape and the people, a thing that stimulates our imagination, and causes many of us to set off deep into the woods in search of the unknown, and sustenance—not just metaphorical or spiritual sustenance, but the real thing.

Only about 5 percent of the nation and 15 to 20 percent of Montanans are hunters. But in this one valley, almost everyone is a hunter. It is not the peer pressure of the local culture that recruits us into hunting, nor even necessarily the economic boon of a few hundred pounds of meat in a cash-poor society. Rather, it is the terrain itself, and one's gradual integration into it, that summons the hunter. Nearly everyone who has lived here for any length of time has ended up—sometimes almost against one's conscious wishes—becoming a hunter. This wild and powerful landscape sculpts us like clay. I don't find such sculpting an affront to the human spirit, but instead, wonderful testimony to our pliability, our ability to adapt to a place.

7   I myself love to hunt the deer, the elk, and the grouse—to follow them into the mouth of the forest, to disappear in their pursuit—to get lost following their snowy tracks up one mountain and down the next. One sets out after one's quarry with senses fully engaged, wildly alert: entranced, nearly hypnotized. The tiniest of factors can possess the largest significance—the crack of a twig, the shift of a breeze, a single stray hair caught on a piece of bark, a fresh-bent blade of grass.

8   Each year during such pursuits, I am struck more and more by the conceit that people in a hunter-gatherer culture might have richer imaginations than those who dwell more fully in an agricultural or even post-agricultural environment. What else is the hunt but a stirring of the imagination, with the quarry, or goal, or treasure lying just around the corner or over the next rise? A hunter's imagination has no choice but to become deeply engaged, for it is never the hunter who is in control, but always the hunted, in that the prey directs the predator's movements.

9   The hunted shapes the hunter; the pursuit and evasion of predator and prey are but shadows of the same desire. The thrush wants to remain a thrush. The goshawk wants to consume the thrush and in doing so, partly become the thrush—to take its flesh into its flesh. They weave through the tangled branches of the forest, zigging and zagging, the goshawk right on the thrush's tail, like a shadow. Or perhaps it is the thrush that is the shadow thrown by the light of the goshawk's fiery desire.

10   Either way, the escape maneuvers of the thrush help carve and shape and direct the muscles of the goshawk. Even when you are walking through the woods seeing nothing but trees, you can feel the unseen passage of pursuits that might have occurred earlier that morning, precisely where you are standing— pursuits that will doubtless, after you are gone, sweep right back across that same spot again and again.

11   As does the goshawk, so too do human hunters imagine where their prey might be, or where it might go. They follow tracks hinting at not only distance

and direction traveled, but also pace and gait and the general state of mind of the animal that is evading them. They plead to the mountain to deliver to them a deer, an elk. They imagine and hope that they are moving toward their goal of obtaining game.

When you plant a row of corn, there is not so much unknown. You can be 12 fairly sure that, if the rains come, the corn is going to sprout. The corn is not seeking to elude you. But when you step into the woods, looking for a deer—well, there's nothing in your mind, or in your blood, or in the world, but imagination.

Most Americans neither hunt nor gather nor even grow their own food, 13 nor make, with their own hands, any of their other necessities. In this postagricultural society, too often we confuse anticipation with imagination. When we wander down the aisle of the supermarket searching for a chunk of frozen chicken, or cruise into Dillard's department store looking for a sweater, we can be fairly confident that grayish wad of chicken or that sweater is going to be there, thanks to the vigor and efficiency of a supply-and-demand marketplace. The imagination never quite hits second gear. Does the imagination atrophy, from such chronic inactivity? I suspect that it does.

All I know is that hunting—beyond being a thing I like to do—helps keep 14 my imagination vital. I would hope never to be so blind as to offer it as prescription; I offer it only as testimony to my love of the landscape where I live—a place that is still, against all odds, its own place, quite unlike any other. I don't think I would be able to sustain myself as a dreamer in this strange landscape if I did not take off three months each year to wander the mountains in search of game; to hunt, stretching and exercising not just my imagination, but my spirit. And to wander the mountains, too, in all the other seasons. And to be nourished by the river of spirit that flows, shifting and winding, between me and the land.

COMPREHENSION

1. Why did Bass and his wife fall in love with the Yaak Valley? What does this fondness for wild places tell us about his character and interests?
2. Explain the relationship between the people residing in the Yaak Valley and their fondness for hunting.
3. Does Bass apologize for his fondness for hunting? Explain your response.

RHETORIC

1. Bass wrote this essay for the official magazine of the Sierra Club, of which he is an active member. Why would an organization whose goal is the preservation of wilderness and wildlife agree to publish an article expressing love for hunting? How does Bass anticipate objections to his argument?
2. What is Bass's claim and where does he state it? Does he rely on logical, ethical, or emotional appeal—or a combination—to advance his argument, and why?

3. What causal connection does Bass establish between landscape and human behavior? Where does he use comparison and contrast to distinguish this place and its people from other places and other Americans?
4. Cite examples of Bass's descriptive skills. How does description enhance the appeal of the writer's argument?
5. What is the dominant impression that Bass creates of the Yaak Valley region?
6. Evaluate Bass's conclusion. How does it serve as a writer's justification for hunting?

WRITING

1. Select a natural landscape that you know well and, including description as one rhetorical strategy, explain how this site affects the behavior of people and their ethical values.
2. **Writing an Argument:** What is the difference between killing the game that you consume and buying meat in a grocery store or supermarket? Is one act more ethical than the other? Compose an argumentative essay dealing with this issue.

NETWORKING
Applying 21st-Century Literacies

Interpreting an Organization's Web Site: Go online and locate the Web Site for the Sierra Club. Summarize the organization's goals, and then evaluate whether Bass's essay conforms to these objectives.

The Environmental Issue from Hell

Bill McKibben

Bill McKibben (b. 1960) was born in Palo Alto, California. After receiving a BA from Harvard University (1982), McKibben became a staff writer for the New Yorker. *McKibben's chief concern is the impact of humans on the environment and the ways in which consumerism affects the global ecosystem. A prominent writer for the environmental movement, he has published several books, among them* The End of Nature *(1989),* The Age of Missing Information *(1992),* Long Distance: A Year of Living Strenuously *(2000),* Enough: Staying Human in an Engineered Age *(2003), and* The Bill McKibben Reader: Pieces from an Active Life *(2009). In the essay that follows, which was published in* These Times *in 2001, McKibben argues for a new approach to global warming.*

1　When global warming first emerged as a potential crisis in the late 1980s, one academic analyst called it "the public policy problem from hell." The years since have only proven him more astute: Fifteen years into our understanding of climate change, we have yet to figure out how we're going to tackle it. And environmentalists are just as clueless as anyone else: Do we need to work on lifestyle or on lobbying, on photovoltaics or on politics? And is there a difference? How well we handle global warming will determine what kind of century we inhabit—and indeed what kind of planet we leave behind. The issue cuts close to home and also floats off easily into the abstract. So far it has been the ultimate "can't get there from here" problem, but the time has come to draw a road map—one that may help us deal with the handful of other issues on the list of real, world-shattering problems.

Typically, when you're mounting a campaign, you look for self-interest, you 2 scare people by saying what will happen to us if we don't do something: All the birds will die, the canyon will disappear beneath a reservoir, we will choke to death on smog. But in the case of global warming, that doesn't exactly do the trick, at least in the time frame we're discussing. In temperate latitudes, climate change will creep up on us. Severe storms already have grown more frequent and more damaging. The progression of seasons is less steady. Some agriculture is less reliable. But face it: Our economy is so enormous that it takes those changes in stride. Economists who work on this stuff talk about how it will shave a percentage or two off the GNP over the next few decades. And most of us live lives so divorced from the natural world that we hardly notice the changes anyway. Hotter? Turn up the air-conditioning. Stormier? Well, an enormous percentage of Americans commute from remote-controlled garage to office parking garage—it may have been some time since they got good and wet in a rainstorm. By the time the magnitude of the change is truly in our faces, it will be too late to do much about it: There's such a lag time to increased levels of carbon dioxide in the atmosphere that we need to be making the switch to solar and wind and hydrogen power right now to prevent disaster decades away. Yesterday, in fact.

So maybe we should think of global warming in a different way—as the 3 great moral crisis of our time, the equivalent of the civil rights movement of the 1960s.

Why a moral question? In the first place, no one's ever figured out a more 4 effective way to screw the marginalized and poor of this planet than climate change. Having taken their dignity, their resources, and their freedom under a variety of other schemes, we now are taking the very physical stability on which their already difficult lives depend.

Our economy can absorb these changes for a while, but consider Bangla- 5 desh for a moment. In 1998 the sea level in the Bay of Bengal was higher than normal, just the sort of thing we can expect to become more frequent and severe. The waters sweeping down the Ganges and the Brahmaputra rivers from the Himalayas could not drain easily into the ocean—they backed up across the country, forcing most of its inhabitants to spend three months in thigh-deep water. The fall rice crop didn't get planted. We've seen this same kind of disaster over the past few years in Mozambique and Honduras and Venezuela and other places.

6   And global warming is a moral crisis, too, if you place any value on the rest of creation. Coral reef researchers indicate that these spectacularly intricate ecosystems are also spectacularly vulnerable. Rising water temperatures are likely to bleach them to extinction by mid-century. In the Arctic, polar bears are 20 percent scrawnier than they were a decade ago: As pack ice melts, so does the opportunity for hunting seals. All in all, the 21st century seems poised to see extinctions at a rate not observed since the last big asteroid slammed into the planet. But this time the asteroid is us.

7   It's a moral question, finally, if you think we owe any debt to the future. No one ever has figured out a more thoroughgoing way to strip-mine the present and degrade what comes after—all the people who will ever be related to you. Ever. No generation yet to come will ever forget us—we are the ones present at the moment when the temperature starts to spike, and so far we have not reacted. If it had been done to us, we would loathe the generation that did it, precisely as we will one day be loathed.

8   But trying to launch a moral campaign is no easy task. In most moral crises, there is a villain—some person or class or institution that must be overcome. Once the villain is identified, the battle can commence. But you can't really get angry at carbon dioxide, and the people responsible for its production are, well, us. So perhaps we need some symbols to get us started, some places to sharpen the debate and rally ourselves to action. There are plenty to choose from: our taste for ever bigger houses and the heating and cooling bills that come with them, our penchant for jumping on airplanes at the drop of a hat. But if you wanted one glaring example of our lack of balance, you could do worse than point the finger at sport utility vehicles.

9   SUVs are more than mere symbols. They are a major part of the problem—we emit so much more carbon dioxide now than we did a decade ago in part because our fleet of cars and trucks actually has gotten steadily less fuel efficient for the past 10 years. If you switched today from the average American car to a big SUV, and drove it for just one year, the difference in carbon dioxide that you produced would be the equivalent of opening your refrigerator door and then forgetting to close it for six years. SUVs essentially are machines for burning fossil fuel that just happen to also move you and your stuff around.

10   But what makes them such a perfect symbol is the brute fact that they are simply unnecessary. Go to the parking lot of the nearest suburban supermarket and look around: The only conclusion you can draw is that to reach the grocery, people must drive through three or four raging rivers and up the side of a canyon. These are semi-military machines, armored trucks on a slight diet. While they do not keep their occupants appreciably safer, they do wreck whatever they plow into, making them the perfect metaphor for a heedless, super-sized society.

11   That's why we need a much broader politics than the Washington lobbying that's occupied the big environmental groups for the past decade. We need to take all the brilliant and energetic strategies of local grassroots groups fighting dumps and cleaning up rivers and apply those tactics in the national and

international arenas. That's why some pastors are starting to talk with their congregations about what cars to buy, and why some college seniors are passing around petitions pledging to stay away from the Ford Explorers and Excursions, and why some auto dealers have begun to notice informational picketers outside their showrooms on Saturday mornings urging customers to think about gas mileage when they look at cars.

The point is not that such actions by themselves—any individual actions— 12 will make any real dent in the levels of carbon dioxide pouring into our atmosphere. Even if you got 10 percent of Americans really committed to changing their energy use, their solar homes wouldn't make much of a difference in our national totals. But 10 percent would be enough to change the politics around the issue, enough to pressure politicians to pass laws that would cause us all to shift our habits. And so we need to begin to take an issue that is now the province of technicians and turn it into a political issue, just as bus boycotts began to make public the issue of race, forcing the system to respond. That response is likely to be ugly—there are huge companies with a lot to lose, and many people so tied in to their current ways of life that advocating change smacks of subversion. But this has to become a political issue—and fast. The only way that may happen, short of a hideous drought or monster flood, is if it becomes a personal issue first.

COMPREHENSION

1. According to McKibben, what are the causes of global warming?
2. What instances of ecological disaster does the writer say will occur if we do not change our habits?
3. Why is a new approach to the problem of global warming needed? What approach does McKibben suggest?

RHETORIC

1. How does McKibben's title capture the tone of the essay? What is his purpose in writing the essay? Does he see his readers as hostile or sympathetic to his position? How do you know?
2. How does McKibben develop his introduction? Why does he pose questions? Where does he state his claim?
3. Does McKibben make his argument through appeals to reason, emotion, ethics—or a combination of these elements? Justify your response.
4. How does the writer contend with possible objections to his position on global warming?
5. Explain the pattern of cause and effect that McKibben uses to structure his essay.
6. What varieties of evidence does the writer present to support his claim? What extended illustration does he provide? How effective is it, and why?
7. In the concluding paragraph, McKibben issues a call to action. How does the body of the essay prepare the reader for this persuasive appeal?

WRITING

1. Write an essay in which you explain your own sense of the causes and effects of global warming.
2. Research your state's policy toward global warming. Present your findings in a summary essay.
3. **Writing an Argument:** McKibben argues that SUVs are a primary cause of wastefulness and global warming and that both moral persuasion and political activism are required to change consumers' habits. Do you agree or disagree with his assertions? Write an argumentative essay responding to this issue.

NETWORKING
Applying 21st-Century Literacies

Delivering an Oral Presentation: Reshape your response to any of the three assignments under Writing to function as an oral presentation; incorporate visual aids (digital or hard copy) and one carefully designed and written handout for your listeners.

The Obligation to Endure

Rachel Carson

Rachel Carson (1907–1964) was a seminal figure in the environmental movement. Born in Pennsylvania, she awakened public consciousness to environmental issues through her writing. Her style was both literary and scientific as she described nature's riches in such books as The Sea around Us *(1951) and* The Edge of the Sea *(1954). Her last book,* Silent Spring *(1962), aroused controversy and concern with its indictment of insecticides. In the following excerpt from that important book, Carson provides compelling evidence of the damage caused by indiscriminate use of insecticides and the danger of disturbing the earth's delicate balance.*

1 The history of life on earth has been a history of interaction between living things and their surroundings. To a large extent, the physical form and the habits of the earth's vegetation and its animal life have been molded by the environment. Considering the whole span of earthly time, the opposite effect, in which life actually modifies its surroundings, has been relatively slight. Only within the moment of time represented by the present century has one species—man—acquired significant power to alter the nature of his world.

2   During the past quarter century this power has not only increased to one of disturbing magnitude but it has changed in character. The most alarming of all

man's assaults upon the environment is the contamination of air, earth, rivers, and sea with dangerous and even lethal materials. This pollution is for the most part irrecoverable; the chain of evil it initiates not only in the world that must support life but in living tissues is for the most part irreversible. In this now universal contamination of the environment, chemicals are the sinister and little-recognized partners of radiation in changing the very nature of the world—the very nature of its life. Strontium 90, released through nuclear explosions into the air, comes to earth in rain or drifts down as fallout, lodges in soil, enters into the grass or corn or wheat grown there, and in time takes up its abode in the bones of a human being, there to remain until his death. Similarly, chemicals sprayed on croplands or forests or gardens lie long in soil, entering into living organisms, passing from one to another in a chain of poisoning and death. Or they pass mysteriously by underground streams until they emerge and, through the alchemy of air and sunlight, combine into new forms that kill vegetation, sicken cattle, and work unknown harm on those who drink from once pure wells. As Albert Schweitzer has said, "Man can hardly even recognize the devils of his own creation."

It took hundreds of millions of years to produce the life that now inhabits 3 the earth—eons of time in which that developing and evolving and diversifying life reached a state of adjustment and balance with its surroundings. The environment, rigorously shaping and directing the life it supported, contained elements that were hostile as well as supporting. Certain rocks gave out dangerous radiation; even within the light of the sun, from which all life draws its energy, there were shortwave radiations with power to injure. Given time—time not in years but in millennia—life adjusts, and a balance has been reached. For time is the essential ingredient; but in the modern world there is no time.

The rapidity of change and the speed with which new situations are created 4 follow the impetuous and heedless pace of man rather than the deliberate pace of nature. Radiation is no longer merely the background radiation of rocks, the bombardment of cosmic rays, the ultraviolet of the sun that have existed before there was any life on earth; radiation is now the unnatural creation of man's tampering with the atom. The chemicals to which life is asked to make its adjustment are no longer merely the calcium and silica and copper and all the rest of the minerals washed out of the rocks and carried in rivers to the sea; they are the synthetic creations of man's inventive mind, brewed in his laboratories, and having no counterparts in nature.

To adjust to these chemicals would require time on the scale that is nature's; 5 it would require not merely the years of a man's life but the life of generations. And even this, were it by some miracle possible, would be futile, for the new chemicals come from our laboratories in an endless stream; almost five hundred annually find their way into actual use in the United States alone. The figure is staggering and its implications are not easily grasped—500 new chemicals to which the bodies of men and animals are required somehow to adapt each year, chemicals totally outside the limits of biologic experience.

6   Among them are many that are used in man's war against nature. Since the mid-1940s over 200 basic chemicals have been created for use in killing insects, weeds, rodents, and other organisms described in the modern vernacular as "pests"; and they are sold under several thousand different brand names.

7   These sprays, dusts, and aerosols are now applied almost universally to farms, gardens, forests, and homes—nonselective chemicals that have the power to kill every insect, the "good" and the "bad," to still the song of birds and the leaping of fish in the streams, to coat the leaves with a deadly film, and to linger on in soil—all this though the intended target may be only a few weeds or insects. Can anyone believe it is possible to lay down such a barrage of poisons on the surface of the earth without making it unfit for all life? They should not be called "insecticides," but "biocides."

8   The whole process of spraying seems caught up in an endless spiral. Since DDT was released for civilian use, a process of escalation has been going on in which ever more toxic materials must be found. This has happened because insects, in a triumphant vindication of Darwin's principle of the survival of the fittest, have evolved super races immune to the particular insecticide used, hence a deadlier one has always to be developed—and then a deadlier one than that. It has happened also because, for reasons to be described later, destructive insects often undergo a "flareback," or resurgence, after spraying in numbers greater than before. Thus the chemical war is never won, and all life is caught in its violent crossfire.

9   Along with the possibility of the extinction of mankind by nuclear war, the central problem of our age has therefore become the contamination of man's total environment with such substances of incredible potential for harm—substances that accumulate in the tissues of plants and animals and even penetrate the germ cells to shatter or alter the very material of heredity upon which the shape of the future depends.

10   Some would-be architects of our future look toward a time when it will be possible to alter the human germ plasm by design. But we may easily be doing so now by inadvertence, for many chemicals, like radiation, bring about gene mutations. It is ironic to think that man might determine his own future by something so seemingly trivial as the choice of an insect spray.

11   All this has been risked—for what? Future historians may well be amazed by our distorted sense of proportion. How could intelligent beings seek to control a few unwanted species by a method that contaminated the entire environment and brought the threat of disease and death even to their own kind? Yet this is precisely what we have done. We have done it, moreover, for reasons that collapse the moment we examine them. We are told that the enormous and expanding use of pesticides is necessary to maintain farm production. Yet is our real problem not one of *overproduction?* Our farms, despite measures to remove acreages from production and to pay farmers *not* to produce, have yielded such a staggering excess of crops that the American taxpayer in 1962 is paying out more than one billion dollars a year as the total carrying cost of the surplus-food storage program. And is the situation helped when one branch of

the Agriculture Department tries to reduce production while another states, as it did in 1958, "It is believed generally that reduction of crop acreages under provisions of the Soil Bank will stimulate interest in use of chemicals to obtain maximum production on the land retained in crops."

All this is not to say there is no insect problem and no need of control. I am 12 saying, rather, that control must be geared to realities, not to mythical situations, and that the methods employed must be such that they do not destroy us along with the insects.

The problem whose attempted solution has brought such a train of disaster in 13 its wake is an accompaniment of our modern way of life. Long before the age of man, insects inhabited the earth—a group of extraordinarily varied and adaptable beings. Over the course of time since man's advent, a small percentage of the more than half a million species of insects have come into conflict with human welfare in two principal ways: as competitors for the food supply and as carriers of human disease.

Disease-carrying insects become important where human beings are 14 crowded together, especially under conditions where sanitation is poor, as in times of natural disaster or war or in situations of extreme poverty and deprivation. Then control of some sort becomes necessary. It is a sobering fact, however, as we shall presently see, that the method of massive chemical control has had only limited success, and also threatens to worsen the very conditions it is intended to curb.

Under primitive agricultural conditions the farmer had few insect prob- 15 lems. These arose with the intensification of agriculture—the devotion of immense acreages to a single crop. Such a system set the stage for explosive increases in specific insect populations. Single-crop farming does not take advantage of the principles by which nature works; it is agriculture as an engineer might conceive it to be. Nature has introduced great variety into the landscape, but man has displayed a passion for simplifying it. Thus he undoes the built-in checks and balances by which nature holds the species within bounds. One important natural check is a limit on the amount of suitable habitat for each species. Obviously then, an insect that lives on wheat can build up its population to much higher levels on a farm devoted to wheat than on one in which wheat is intermingled with other crops to which the insect is not adapted.

The same thing happens in other situations. A generation or more ago, the 16 towns of large areas of the United States lined their streets with the noble elm tree. Now the beauty they hopefully created is threatened with complete destruction as disease sweeps through the elms, carried by a beetle that would have only limited chance to build up large populations and to spread from tree to tree if the elms were only occasional trees in a richly diversified planting.

Another factor in the modern insect problem is one that must be viewed 17 against a background of geologic and human history: the spreading of thousands of different kinds of organisms from their native homes to invade new territories. This worldwide migration has been studied and graphically described by the

British ecologist Charles Elton in his recent book *The Ecology of Invasions.* During the Cretaceous Period, some hundred million years ago, flooding seas cut many land bridges between continents and living things found themselves confined in what Elton calls "colossal separate nature reserves." There, isolated from others of their kind, they developed many new species. When some of the land masses were joined again, about 15 million years ago, these species began to move out into new territories—a movement that is not only still in progress but is now receiving considerable assistance from man.

18   The importation of plants is the primary agent in the modern spread of species, for animals have almost invariably gone along with the plants, quarantine being a comparatively recent and not completely effective innovation. The United States Office of Plant Introduction alone has introduced almost 200,000 species and varieties of plants from all over the world. Nearly half of the 180 or so major insect enemies of plants in the United States are accidental imports from abroad, and most of them have come as hitchhikers on plants.

19   In new territory, out of reach of the restraining hand of the natural enemies that kept down its numbers in its native land, an invading plant or animal is able to become enormously abundant. Thus it is no accident that our most troublesome insects are introduced species.

20   These invasions, both the naturally occurring and those dependent on human assistance, are likely to continue indefinitely. Quarantine and massive chemical campaigns are only extremely expensive ways of buying time. We are faced, according to Dr. Elton, "with a life-and-death need not just to find new technological means of suppressing this plant or that animal"; instead we need the basic knowledge of animal populations and their relations to their surroundings that will "promote an even balance and damp down the explosive power of outbreaks and new invasions."

21   Much of the necessary knowledge is now available but we do not use it. We train ecologists in our universities and even employ them in our governmental agencies but we seldom take their advice. We allow the chemical death rain to fall as though there were no alternative, whereas in fact there are many, and our ingenuity could soon discover many more if given opportunity.

22   Have we fallen into a mesmerized state that makes us accept as inevitable that which is inferior or detrimental, as though having lost the will or the vision to demand that which is good? Such thinking, in the words of the ecologist Paul Shepard, "idealizes life with only its head out of water, inches above the limits of toleration of the corruption of its own environment. . . . Why should we tolerate a diet of weak poisons, a home in insipid surroundings, a circle of acquaintances who are not quite our enemies, the noise of motors with just enough relief to prevent insanity? Who would want to live in a world which is just not quite fatal?"

23   Yet such a world is pressed upon us. The crusade to create a chemically sterile, insect-free world seems to have engendered a fanatic zeal on the part of many specialists and most of the so-called control agencies. On every hand there is evidence that those engaged in spraying operations exercise a ruthless power. "The regulatory entomologists . . . function as prosecutor, judge and

jury, tax assessor and collector and sheriff to enforce their own orders," said Connecticut entomologist Neely Turner. The most flagrant abuses go unchecked in both state and federal agencies.

It is not my contention that chemical insecticides must never be used. I do 24 contend that we have put poisonous and biologically potent chemicals indiscriminately into the hands of persons largely or wholly ignorant of their potentials for harm. We have subjected enormous numbers of people to contact with these poisons, without their consent and often without their knowledge. If the Bill of Rights contains no guarantee that a citizen shall be secure against lethal poisons distributed either by private individuals or by public officials, it is surely only because our forefathers, despite their considerable wisdom and foresight, could conceive of no such problem.

I contend, furthermore, that we have allowed these chemicals to be used 25 with little or no advance investigation of their effect on soil, water, wildlife, and man himself. Future generations are unlikely to condone our lack of prudent concern for the integrity of the natural world that supports all life.

There is still very limited awareness of the nature of the threat. This is an era 26 of specialists, each of whom sees his own problem and is unaware of or intolerant of the larger frame into which it fits. It is also an era dominated by industry, in which the right to make a dollar at whatever cost is seldom challenged. When the public protests, confronted with some obvious evidence of damaging results of pesticide applications, it is fed little tranquilizing pills of half truth. We urgently need an end to these false assurances, to the sugar coating of unpalatable facts. It is the public that is being asked to assume the risks that the insect controllers calculate. The public must decide whether it wishes to continue on the present road, and it can do so only when in full possession of the facts. In the words of Jean Rostand, "The obligation to endure gives us the right to know."

COMPREHENSION

1. What does Carson mean by "the obligation to endure"?
2. What reasons does the author cite for the overpopulation of insects?
3. What remedies does Carson propose?

RHETORIC

1. What tone does Carson use in her essay? Does she seem to be a subjective or an objective writer? Give specific support for your response.
2. How does the use of words such as *dangerous, evil, irrevocable,* and *sinister* help shape the reader's reaction to the piece? What emotional and ethical appeals do such words indicate?
3. Examine the ordering of ideas in paragraph 4, and consider how such an order serves to reinforce Carson's argument.
4. Paragraph 9 consists of only one (long) sentence. What is its function in the essay's scheme?

5. Examine Carson's use of expert testimony. How does it help strengthen her thesis?
6. How effectively does the essay's conclusion help tie up Carson's points? What is the writer's intent in this final paragraph? How does she accomplish this aim?

WRITING

1. Write an essay in which you suggest solutions to the problems brought up in Carson's piece. You may want to suggest measures that the average citizen can take to eliminate the casual use of insecticides to control the insect population.
2. Write a biographical research paper on Carson that focuses on her involvement with nature and environmental issues.
3. **Writing an Argument:** Write an essay titled "Insects Are Not the Problem; Humanity Is." In this essay, argue that it is humanity's greed that has caused such an imbalance in nature as to threaten the planet's survival.

NETWORKING
Applying 21st-Century Literacies

Composing an Interactive Argument Essay: Create question 1 or 3 under Writing as an electronic document, one that readers can interact with by clicking on links that take them to other essays and articles that both support *and* refute your position. Post the essay on a Web site or blog and enable comments so your classmates (or other readers) can actively engage with your topic. Respond to at least two comments, being sure to keep dialogue civil and arguments well supported. Make your Works Cited page interactive as well, documenting all sources and linking to any that are available on the Web.

Am I Blue?

Alice Walker

Alice Walker (b. 1944) was born in Eatonton, Georgia; attended Spelman College; and graduated from Sarah Lawrence College. Besides being a prolific novelist, short-story writer, poet, and essayist, she has also been active in the civil rights movement. She often draws on both her own history and historical records to reflect on the African American experience. Some of her well-known books are The Color Purple *(1976),* You Can't Keep a Good Woman Down *(1981),* Living in the World: Selected Writings, 1973–1987 *(1987),* The Temple of My Familiar *(1989),* By the Light of My Father's Smile *(1999),* The Way Forward Is with a Broken Heart *(2001), and* Why War Is Never a Good Idea *(2007). In the following essay from* Living in the World, *Walker questions the distinctions commonly made between human and animal.*

For about three years my companion and I rented a small house in the country 1
that stood on the edge of a large meadow that appeared to run from the end of
our deck straight into the mountains. The mountains, however, were quite far
away, and between us and them there was, in fact, a town. It was one of the
many pleasant aspects of the house that you never really were aware of this.

It was a house of many windows, low, wide, nearly floor to ceiling in the 2
living room, which faced the meadow, and it was from one of these that I first
saw our closest neighbor, a large white horse, cropping grass, flipping its mane,
and ambling about—not over the entire meadow, which stretched well out of
sight of the house, but over the five or so fenced-in acres that were next to the
twenty-odd that we had rented. I soon learned that the horse, whose name was
Blue, belonged to a man who lived in another town, but was boarded by our
neighbors next door. Occasionally, one of the children, usually a stocky teenager, but sometimes a much younger girl or boy, could be seen riding Blue.
They would appear in the meadow, climb up on his back, ride furiously for ten
or fifteen minutes, then get off, slap Blue on the flanks, and not be seen again
for a month or more.

There were many apple trees in our yard, and one by the fence that Blue 3
could almost reach. We were soon in the habit of feeding him apples, which he
relished, especially because by the middle of summer the meadow grasses—so
green and succulent since January—had dried out from lack of rain, and Blue
stumbled about munching the dried stalks half-heartedly. Sometimes he would
stand very still just by the apple tree, and when one of us came out he would
whinny, snort loudly, or stamp the ground. This meant, of course: I want an apple.

It was quite wonderful to pick a few apples, or collect those that had fallen 4
to the ground overnight, and patiently hold them, one by one, up to his large,
toothy mouth. I remained as thrilled as a child by his flexible dark lips, huge,
cubelike teeth that crunched the apples, core and all, with such finality, and his
high, broad-breasted *enormity*; beside which, I felt small indeed. When I was a
child, I used to ride horses, and was especially friendly with one named Nan
until the day I was riding and my brother deliberately spooked her and I was
thrown, head first, against the trunk of a tree. When I came to, I was in bed and
my mother was bending worriedly over me; we silently agreed that perhaps
horseback riding was not the safest sport for me. Since then I have walked, and
prefer walking to horseback riding—but I had forgotten the depth of feeling
one could see in horses' eyes.

I was therefore unprepared for the expression in Blue's. Blue was lonely. 5
Blue was horribly lonely and bored. I was not shocked that this should be the
case; five acres to tramp by yourself, endlessly, even in the most beautiful of
meadows—and his was—cannot provide many interesting events, and once the
rainy season turned to dry that was about it. No, I was shocked that I had forgotten that human animals and nonhuman animals can communicate quite
well; if we are brought up around animals as children we take this for granted.
By the time we are adults we no longer remember. However, the animals have
not changed. They are in fact *completed* creations (at least they seem to be, so

much more than we) who are not likely *to* change; it is their nature to express themselves. What else are they going to express? And they do. And, generally speaking, they are ignored.

6   After giving Blue the apples, I would wander back to the house, aware that he was observing me. Were more apples not forthcoming then? Was that to be his sole entertainment for the day? My partner's small son had decided he wanted to learn how to piece a quilt; we worked in silence on our respective squares as I thought . . .

7   Well, about slavery: about white children, who were raised by black people, who knew their first all-accepting love from black women, and then, when they were twelve or so, were told they must "forget" the deep levels of communication between themselves and "mammy" that they knew. Later they would be able to relate quite calmly, "My old mammy was sold to another good family." "My old mammy was _____." Fill in the blank. Many more years later a white woman would say: "I can't understand these Negroes, these blacks. What do they want? They're so different from us."

8   And about the Indians, considered to be "like animals" by the "settlers" (a very benign euphemism for what they actually were), who did not understand their description as a compliment.

9   And about the thousands of American men who marry Japanese, Korean, Filipina, and other non-English-speaking women and of how happy they report they are, *"blissfully,"* until their brides learn to speak English, at which point the marriages tend to fall apart. What then did the men see, when they looked into the eyes of the women they married, before they could speak English? Apparently only their own reflections.

10   I thought of society's impatience with the young. "Why are they playing the music so loud?" Perhaps the children have listened to much of the music of oppressed people their parents danced to before they were born, with its passionate but soft cries for acceptance and love, and they have wondered why their parents failed to hear.

11   I do not know how long Blue had inhabited his five beautiful, boring acres before we moved into our house; a year after we had arrived—and had also traveled to other valleys, other cities, other worlds—he was still there.

12   But then, in our second year at the house, something happened in Blue's life. One morning, looking out the window at the fog that lay like a ribbon over the meadow, I saw another horse, a brown one, at the other end of Blue's field. Blue appeared to be afraid of it, and for several days made no attempt to go near. We went away for a week. When we returned, Blue had decided to make friends and the two horses ambled or galloped along together, and Blue did not come nearly as often to the fence underneath the apple tree.

13   When he did, bringing his new friend with him, there was a different look in his eyes. A look of independence, of self-possession, of inalienable *horse*ness. His friend eventually became pregnant. For months and months there was, it seemed to me, a mutual feeling between me and the horses of justice, of peace. I fed apples to them both. The look in Blue's eyes was one of unabashed "this is *it*ness."

It did not, however, last forever. One day, after a visit to the city, I went out 14
to give Blue some apples. He stood waiting, or so I thought, though not beneath
the tree. When I shook the tree and jumped back from the shower of apples, he
made no move. I carried some over to him. He managed to half-crunch one.
The rest he let fall to the ground. I dreaded looking into his eyes—because I had
of course noticed that Brown, his partner, had gone—but I did look. If I had
been born into slavery, and my partner had been sold or killed, my eyes would
have looked like that. The children next door explained that Blue's partner had
been "put with him" (the same expression that old people used, I had noticed,
when speaking of an ancestor during slavery who had been impregnated by
her owner) so that they could mate and she conceive. Since that was accomplished, she had been taken back by her owner, who lived somewhere else.

Will she be back? I asked. 15

They didn't know. 16

Blue was like a crazed person. Blue *was*, to me, a crazed person. He galloped 17
furiously, as if he were being ridden, around and around his five beautiful
acres. He whinnied until he couldn't. He tore at the ground with his hooves. He
butted himself against his single shade tree. He looked always and always toward the road down which his partner had gone. And then, occasionally, when
he came up for apples, or I took apples to him, he looked at me. It was a look so
piercing, so full of grief, a look so *human*, I almost laughed (I felt too sad to cry)
to think there are people who do not know that animals suffer. People like me
who have forgotten, and daily forget, all that animals try to tell us. "Everything
you do to us will happen to you; we are your teachers, as you are ours. We are
one lesson" is essentially it, I think. There are those who never once have even
considered animals' rights: those who have been taught that animals actually
want to be used and abused by us, as small children "love" to be frightened, or
women "love" to be mutilated and raped. . . . They are the great-grandchildren
of those who honestly thought, because someone taught them this: "Woman
can't think" and "niggers can't faint." But most disturbing of all, in Blue's
large brown eyes was a new look, more painful than the look of despair: the
look of disgust with human beings, with life; the look of hatred. And it was
odd what the look of hatred did. It gave him, for the first time, the look of a
beast. And what that meant was that he had put up a barrier within to protect
himself from further violence; all the apples in the world wouldn't change
that fact.

And so Blue remained, a beautiful part of our landscape, very peaceful to 18
look at from the window, white against the grass. Once a friend came to visit
and said, looking out on the soothing view: "And it *would* have to be a *white*
horse; the very image of freedom." And I thought, yes, the animals are forced to
become for us merely "images" of what they once so beautifully expressed.
And we are used to drinking milk from containers showing "contented" cows,
whose real lives we want to hear nothing about, eating eggs and drumsticks
from "happy" hens, and munching hamburgers advertised by bulls of integrity
who seem to command their fate.

19   As we talked of freedom and justice one day for all, we sat down to steaks. I am eating misery, I thought, as I took the first bite. And spit it out.

COMPREHENSION

1. What is the major thesis of the essay? Is it stated explicitly in the text, or does one have to infer it? Explain.
2. In paragraph 5, Walker states that animals are *"completed* creations (at least they seem to be, so much more than we) who are not likely to change." What does she mean by making this distinction between animals and humans?
3. What is the significance of the title of the essay? Does it have more than one meaning? Explain your answer.

RHETORIC

1. In paragraph 4, Walker creates a vivid description of Blue. How does she achieve this?
2. In paragraph 7, Walker makes a cognitive association between the relationship between humans and animals and the relationship between whites and blacks during slavery. Does this transition seem too abrupt, or is there a rhetorical reason for the immediate comparison? Explain.
3. Explore the other analogies Walker makes in paragraphs 8 and 9. Are they pertinent? What is the rhetorical effect of juxtaposing seemingly different realms to convey one central idea?
4. Walker often breaks the conventions of "college English." For example, paragraphs 8 and 9 both begin with the coordinating conjunction *and.* Paragraph 12 begins with the coordinating conjunction *but.* Paragraphs 15 and 16 are only one short sentence each. Explain the effect of each of these rhetorical devices. Find three other unusual rhetorical strategies—either on the paragraph or sentence level—and explain their effects.
5. In paragraphs 17 and 18, Walker speeds up the tempo of her writing by beginning many of the sentences with the conjunction *and.* What is the purpose and rhetorical effect of this strategy, and how does it mimic—in linguistic terms—Blue's altered emotional state?
6. Walker seems to have a profound empathy for animals, yet it is only at the end that she is repulsed by the thought of eating meat. What rhetorical strategy is she employing in the conclusion that helps bring closure to her meditation on Blue? Does it matter whether the culminating event actually occurred in her experience, or is it all right for an essayist to use poetic license for stylistic purposes?

WRITING

1. Write a personal essay in which you describe your relationship with a favorite pet. Include your observations of, responses to, and attitude toward your pet. Compare and contrast this relationship to those you have with humans.

2. Some writers have argued that it matters little if certain "nonessential" endangered species become extinct if they interfere with "human progress." Argue for or against this proposition.
3. **Writing an Argument:** Argue for or against one of the following practices: (**a**) hunting for the sake of the hunt, (**b**) eating meat, or (**c**) keeping animals in zoos.

NETWORKING
Applying 21st-Century Literacies

Exploring Multiple Sides to an Issue: Approach question 3 under Writing as an exploratory, rather than an argumentative, essay. Use online research to examine at least three different ways of approaching one of the possible issues, such as eating meat, and arrive at a thesis only in your conclusion.

The Greenest Campuses: An Idiosyncratic Guide

Noel Perrin

Noel Perrin *(1927–2004) was born in New York City and worked as an editor before starting a career as a college instructor at the University of North Carolina and then Dartmouth College, where he taught beginning in 1959. He was awarded two Guggenheim Fellowships, contributed to numerous periodicals, and authored more than 10 books. His subject matter ranges from the scholarly, such as* Dr. Bowdler's Legacy *(1969)* and Giving Up the Gun: Japan's Reversion to the Sword, 1543–1879 (1979), *to his experiences as a part-time farmer. Among the latter are* First Person Plural *(1978),* Second Person Plural *(1980),* Third Person Plural *(1983),* Last Person Plural *(1991), and* A Child's Delight *(1998). His concerns about the environment made him a popular speaker on ecological issues. In the following essay, first published in the* Chronicle of Higher Education *in April 2001, Perrin creates his own "best" college guide by ranking institutions of higher learning according to their environmental awareness.*

About 1,100 American colleges and universities run at least a token environmental- 1
studies program, and many hundreds of those programs offer well-designed and useful courses. But only a drastically smaller number practice even a portion of what they teach. The one exception is recycling. Nearly every institution

that has so much as one lonely environmental-studies course also does a little halfhearted recycling. Paper and glass, usually.

2   There are some glorious exceptions to those rather churlish observations, I'm glad to say. How many? Nobody knows. No one has yet done the necessary research (though the National Wildlife Federation's Campus Ecology program is planning a survey).

3   Certainly *U.S. News & World Report* hasn't. Look at the rankings in their annual college issue. The magazine uses a complex formula something like this: Institution's reputation, 25 percent; student-retention rate, 20 percent; faculty resources, 20 percent; and so on, down to alumni giving, 5 percent. The lead criterion may help explain why Harvard, Yale, and Princeton Universities so frequently do a little dance at the top of the list.

4   But *U.S. News* has nothing at all to say about the degree to which a college or university attempts to behave sustainably—that is, to manage its campus and activities in ways that promote the long-term health of the planet. The magazine is equally mum about which of the institutions it is ranking can serve as models to society in a threatened world.

5   And, of course, the world is threatened. When the Royal Society in London and the National Academy of Sciences in Washington issued their first-ever joint statement, it ended like this: "The future of our planet is in the balance. Sustainable development can be achieved, but only if irreversible degradation of the environment can be halted in time. The next 30 years may be crucial." They said that in 1992. If all those top scientists are right, we have a little more than 20 years left in which to make major changes in how we live.

6 All this affects colleges. I have one environmentalist friend who loves to point out to the deans and trustees she meets that if we don't make such changes, and if the irreversible degradation of earth does occur, Harvard's huge endowment and Yale's lofty reputation will count for nothing.

7   But though *U.S. News* has nothing to say, fortunately there is a fairly good grapevine in the green world. I have spent considerable time in the past two years using it like an organic cell phone. By that means I have come up with a short, idiosyncratic list of green colleges, consisting of six that are a healthy green, two that are greener still, and three that I believe are the greenest in the United States.

8   Which approved surveying techniques have I used? None at all. Some of my evidence is anecdotal, and some of my conclusions are affected by my personal beliefs, such as that electric and hybrid cars are not just a good idea, but instruments of salvation.

9   Obviously I did not examine, even casually, all 1,100 institutions. I'm sure I have missed some outstanding performers. I hope I have missed a great many.

10   Now, here are the 11, starting with **Brown University.**

11   It is generally harder for a large urban university to move toward sustainable behavior than it is for a small-town college with maybe a thousand students. But it's not impossible. Both Brown, in the heart of Providence, R.I., and Yale University (by no means an environmental leader in other respects), in the

heart of New Haven, Conn., have found a country way of dealing with food waste. Pigs. Both rely on pigs.

For the past 10 years, Brown has been shipping nearly all of its food waste 12 to a Rhode Island piggery. Actually, not shipping it—just leaving it out at dawn each morning. The farmer comes to the campus and gets it. Not since Ralph Waldo Emerson took food scraps out to the family pig have these creatures enjoyed such a high intellectual connection.

But there is a big difference in scale. Where Emerson might have one pail of 13 slops now and then, Brown generates 700 tons of edible garbage each year. Haulage fee: $0. Tipping fee: $0. (That's the cost of dumping the garbage into huge cookers, where it is heated for the pigs.) Annual savings to Brown: about $50,000. Addition to the American food supply: many tons of ham and bacon each year.

Of course, Brown does far more than feed a balanced diet to a lot of pigs. 14 That's just the most exotic (for an urban institution) of its green actions. "Brown is Green" became the official motto of the university in August 1990. It was accurate then, and it remains accurate now.

Yale is the only other urban institution I'm aware of that supports a pig 15 population. Much of the credit goes to Cyril May, the university's environmental coordinator, just as much of the credit at Brown goes to its environmental coordinator, Kurt Teichert.

May has managed to locate two Connecticut piggeries. The one to which he 16 sends garbage presents problems. The farmer has demanded—and received—a collection fee. And he has developed an antagonistic relationship with some of Yale's food-service people. (There are a lot of them: The campus has 16 dining facilities.) May is working on an arrangement with the second piggery. But if it falls through, he says, "I may go back on semibended knee to the other."

Yale does not make the list as a green college, for reasons you will learn 17 later in this essay. But it might in a few more years

Carleton College is an interesting example of an institution turning green 18 almost overnight. No pig slops here; the dining halls are catered by Marriott. But change is coming fast.

In the summer of 1999, Carleton appointed its first-ever environmental 19 coordinator, a brand-new graduate named Rachel Smit. The one-year appointment was an experiment, with a cobbled-together salary and the humble title of "fifth-year intern." The experiment worked beyond anyone's expectation.

Smit began publishing an environmental newsletter called *The Green Bean* 20 and organized a small committee of undergraduates to explore the feasibility of composting the college's food waste, an effort that will soon begin. A surprised Marriott has already found itself serving organic dinners on Earth Day.

Better yet, the college set up an environmental-advisory committee of three 21 administrators, three faculty members, and three students to review all campus projects from a green perspective. Naturally, many of those projects will be buildings, and to evaluate them, Carleton is using the *Minnesota Sustainable Design Guide*, itself cowritten by Richard Strong, director of facilities.

22   The position of fifth-year intern is now a permanent one-year position, and its salary is a regular part of the budget.

23   What's next? If Carleton gets a grant it has applied for, there will be a massive increase in environmental-studies courses and faculty seminars and, says the dean of budgets, "a whole range of green campus projects under the rubric of 'participatory learning.'"

24   And if Carleton doesn't get the grant? Same plans, slower pace.

25   Twenty years ago, **Dartmouth College** would have been a contender for the title of greenest college in America, had such a title existed. It's still fairly green. It has a large and distinguished group of faculty members who teach environmental studies, good recycling, an organic farm that was used last summer in six courses, years of experience with solar panels, and a fair number of midlevel administrators (including three in the purchasing office) who are ardent believers in sustainability.

26   But the college has lost ground. Most troubling is its new $50-million library, which has an actual anti-environmental twist: A portion of the roof requires steam from the power plant to melt snow off of it. The architect, Robert Venturi, may be famous, but he's no environmentalist.

27   Dartmouth is a striking example of what I shall modestly call Perrin's Law: No college or university can move far toward sustainability without the active support of at least two senior administrators. Dartmouth has no such committed senior administrators at all. It used to. James Hornig, a former dean of sciences, and Frank Smallwood, a former provost, were instrumental in creating the environmental-studies program, back in 1970. They are now emeriti. The current senior administrators are not in the least hostile to sustainability; they just give a very low priority to the college's practicing what it preaches.

28   **Emory University** is probably further into the use of nonpolluting and low-polluting motor vehicles than any other college in the country. According to Eric Gaither, senior associate vice president for business affairs, 60 percent of Emory's fleet is powered by alternative fuels. The facilities-management office has 40 electric carts, which maintenance workers use for getting around campus. The community-service office (security and parking) has its own electric carts and an electric patrol vehicle. There are five electric shuttle buses and 14 compressed–natural-gas buses on order, plus one natural-gas bus in service.

29   Bill Chace, Emory's president, has a battery-charging station for electric cars in his garage, and until recently an electric car to charge. Georgia Power, which lent the car, has recalled it, but Chace hopes to get it back. Meanwhile, he rides his bike to work most of the time.

30   How has Emory made such giant strides? "It's easy to do," says Gaither, "when your president wants you to."

31   If Carleton is a model of how a small college turns green, the **University of Michigan at Ann Arbor** is a model of how a big university does. Carleton is changing pretty much as an entity, while Michigan is more like the Electoral College—50 separate entities. The School of Natural Resources casts its 6 votes

for sustainability, the English department casts its 12 for humanistic studies, the recycling coordinator casts her 1, the electric-vehicle program casts its 2, and so on. An institution of Michigan's size changes in bits and pieces.

Some of the bits show true leadership. For example, the university is within 32 weeks of buying a modest amount of green power. It makes about half of its own electricity (at its heating plant) and buys the other half. Five percent of that other half soon will come from renewable sources: hydro (water power) and biomass (so-called fuel crops, which are grown specifically to be burned for power).

The supporters of sustainability at Michigan would like to see the university 33 adopt a version of what is known as the Kyoto Protocol. The agreement, which the United States so far has refused to sign, requires that by 2012 each nation reduce its emission of greenhouse gases to 7 percent below its 1990 figure. Michigan's version of the protocol, at present a pipe dream, would require the university to do what the government won't—accept that reduction as a goal.

The immediate goal of "sustainabilists" at Ann Arbor is the creation of a 34 universitywide environmental coordinator, who would work either in the president's or the provost's office.

Giants are slow, but they are also strong.   35

Tulane University has the usual programs, among green institutions, in 36 recycling, composting, and energy efficiency. But what sets it apart is the Tulane Environmental Law Clinic, which is staffed by third-year law students. The director is a faculty member, and there are three law "fellows," all lawyers, who work with the students. The clinic does legal work for environmental organizations across Louisiana and "most likely has had a greater environmental impact than all our other efforts combined," says Elizabeth Davey, Tulane's first-ever environmental coordinator.

At least two campuses of the **University of California** (Berkeley is not among 37 them) have taken a first and even a second step toward sustainable behavior. First step: symbolic action, like installing a few solar panels, to produce clean energy and to help educate students. With luck, one of those little solar arrays might produce as much as a 20th of a percent of the electricity the university uses. It's a start.

The two campuses are Davis and Santa Cruz, and I think Davis nudges 38 ahead of Santa Cruz. That is primarily because Davis the city and Davis the university have done something almost miraculous. They have brought car culture at least partially under control, greatly reducing air pollution as a result.

The city has a population of about 58,000, which includes 24,000 students. 39 According to reliable estimates, there are something over 50,000 bikes in town or on the campus, all but a few hundred owned by their riders. Most of the bikes are used regularly on the city's 45 miles of bike paths (closed to cars) and the 47 miles of bike lanes (cars permitted in the other lanes). The university maintains an additional 14 miles of bike paths on its large campus

40   What happens on rainy days? "A surprising number continue to bike," says David Takemoto-Weerts, coordinator of Davis's bicycle program.

41   If every American college in a suitable climate were to behave like Davis, we could close a medium-sized oil refinery. Maybe we could even get rid of one coal-fired power plant, and thus seriously improve air quality.

42   The **University of New Hampshire** is trying to jump straight from symbolic gestures, like installing a handful of solar panels, to the hardest task of all for an institution trying to become green—establishing a completely new mind-set among students, administrators, and faculty and staff members. It may well succeed.

43   Campuses that have managed to change attitudes are rare. Prescott College, in Prescott, Ariz., and Sterling College, in Craftsbury Common, Vt., are rumored to have done so, and there may be two or three others. They're not on my list—because they're so small, because their students tend to be bright green even before they arrive, and because I have limited space.

44   New Hampshire has several token green projects, including a tiny solar array, able to produce one kilowatt at noon on a good day. And last April it inaugurated the Yellow Bike Cooperative. It is much smaller than anything that happens at Davis, where a bike rack might be a hundred yards long. But it's also more original and more communitarian. Anyone in Durham—student, burger flipper, associate dean—can join the Yellow Bike program by paying a $5 fee.

45   What you get right away is a key that unlocks all 50 bikes owned by the cooperative. (They are repaired and painted by student volunteers.) Want to cross campus? Just go to the nearest bike rack, unlock a Yellow, and pedal off. The goal, says Julie Newman, of the Office of Sustainability Programs, is "to greatly decrease one-person car trips on campus."

46   But the main thrust at New Hampshire is consciousness-raising. When the subject of composting food waste came up, the university held a seminar for its food workers.

47   New Hampshire's striking vigor is partly the result of a special endowment—about $12.8 million—exclusively for the sustainability office. Tom Kelly, the director, refuses to equate sustainability with greenness. Being green, in the sense of avoiding pollution and promoting reuse, is just one aspect of living sustainably, which involves "the balancing of economic viability with ecological health and human well-being," he says.

48   **Oberlin College** is an exception to Perrin's Law. The college has gotten deeply into environmental behavior without the active support of two or, indeed, any senior administrators. As at Dartmouth, the top people are not hostile; they just have other priorities.

49   Apparently, until this year, Oberlin's environmental-studies program was housed in a dreary cellar. Now it's in the $8.2-million Adam Joseph Lewis Environmental Studies Center, which is one of the most environmentally benign college buildings in the world. The money for it was raised as a result of a deal that the department chairman, David Orr, made with the administration:

He could raise money for his own program, provided that he approached only people and foundations that had never shown the faintest interest in Oberlin.

It's too soon for a full report on the building. It is loaded with solar panels— 50 690 of them, covering the roof (for a diagram of the building, see www.oberlin .edu/newserv/esc/escabout.html). In about a year, data will be available on how much energy the panels have saved and whether, as Orr hopes, the center will not only make all its own power, but even export some.

Northland College, in Wisconsin, also goes way beyond tokenism. Its 51 McLean Environmental Living and Learning Center, a two-year-old residence hall for 114 students, is topped by a 120-foot wind tower that, with a good breeze coming off Lake Superior, can generate 20 kilowatts of electricity. The building also includes three arrays of solar panels. They are only token-size, generating a total of 3.2 kilowatts at most. But one array does heat most of the water for one wing of McLean, while the other three form a test project.

One test array is fixed in place—it can't be aimed. Another is like that 52 sunflower in Blake's poem—it countest the steps of the sun. Put more prosaically, it tracks the sun across the sky each day. The third array does that and can also be tilted to get the best angle for each season of the year.

Inside the dorm is a pair of composting toilets—an experiment, to see if 53 students will use them. Because no one is forced to try the new ones if they don't want to—plenty of conventional toilets are close by—it means something when James Miller, vice president and dean of student development and enrollment, reports, "Students almost always choose the composting bathrooms."

From the start, the college's goal has been to have McLean operate so effi- 54 ciently that it consumes 40 percent less outside energy than would a conventional dormitory of the same dimensions. The building didn't reach that goal in its first year; energy use dropped only 34.2 percent. But anyone dealing with a new system knows to expect bugs at the beginning. There were some at Northland, including the wind generator's being down for three months. (As I write, it's turning busily.) Dean Miller is confident that the building will meet or exceed the college's energy-efficiency goal.

There is no room here to talk about the octagonal classroom structure made 55 of bales of straw, built largely by students. Or about the fact that Northland's grounds are pesticide- and herbicide-free.

If Oberlin is a flagrant exception to Perrin's Law, **Middlebury College** is 56 a strong confirmation. Middlebury is unique, as far as I know, in having not only senior administrators who strongly back environmentalism, but one senior administrator right inside the program. What Michigan wants, Middlebury has.

Nan Jenks-Jay, director of environmental affairs, reports directly to the 57 provost. She is responsible for both the teaching side and the living-sustainably side of environmentalism. Under her are an environmental coordinator, Amy Self, and an academic-program coordinator, Janet Wiseman.

58   The program has powerful backers, including the president, John M. McCardell Jr.; the provost and executive vice president, Ronald D. Liebowitz; and the executive vice president for facilities planning, David W. Ginevan. But everyone I talked with at Middlebury, except for the occasional student who didn't want to trouble his mind with things like returnable bottles—to say nothing of acid rain—seemed at least somewhat committed to sustainable living.

59   Middlebury has what I think is the oldest environmental-studies program in the country; it began back in 1965. It has the best composting program I've ever seen. And, like Northland, it is pesticide- and herbicide-free.

60   Let me end as I began, with Harvard, Yale, and Princeton. And with *U.S. News*'s consistently ranking them in the top five, accompanied from time to time by the California Institute of Technology, Stanford University, and the Massachusetts Institute of Technology.

61   What if *U.S. News* did a green ranking? What if it based the listings on one of the few bits of hard data that can be widely compared: the percentage of waste that a college recycles?

62   Harvard would come out okay, though hardly at the top. The university recycled 24 percent of its waste last year, thanks in considerable part to the presence of Rob Gogan, the waste manager. He hopes to achieve 28 percent this year. That's feeble compared with Brown's 35 percent, and downright puny against Middlebury's 64 percent.

63   But compared with Yale and Princeton, it's magnificent. Most of the information I could get from Princeton is sadly dated. It comes from the 1995 report of the Princeton Environmental Reform Committee, whose primary recommendation was that the university hire a full-time waste manager. The university has not yet done so. And if any administrators on the campus know the current recycling percentage, they're not telling.

64   And Yale—poor Yale! It does have a figure. Among the performances of the 20 or so other colleges and universities whose percentages I'm aware of, only Carnegie Mellon's is worse. Yale: 19 percent. Carnegie Mellon: 11 percent.

65   What should universities—and society—be shooting for? How can you ask? One-hundred-percent retrieval of everything retrievable, of course.

COMPREHENSION

1. Why does Perrin call his essay an "idiosyncratic guide" when environmentalism has become a major issue in most municipalities, regions, and countries?
2. Is Perrin's purpose to inform, argue, or both? Does he have a clear-cut thesis, or does he leave it up to the reader to infer the thesis? Explain.
3. What information is Perrin's informal guide providing that is not offered in more conventional college rankings? Is he suggesting that parents and students consider "green rankings" in choosing which college to apply to? Explain.

RHETORIC

1. What purpose might Perrin have for choosing to create a "green guide" for colleges when there are so many other institutions or items he could have selected for review, such as corporations, towns, cities, automobiles, and numerous household products? What makes colleges and universities a particularly apt target?
2. Usually, Ivy League colleges are at the top of college guide lists as most desirable. Where do they rank on Perrin's list? What ironic statement is Perrin making by providing their rankings on the "green scale"? What is he implying about American values, particularly as they pertain to education?
3. Colleges and universities often pride themselves on the renown of their faculties. Who are the people Perrin cites as models of academic worth? Why has he chosen them?
4. What is the ironic purpose behind the author mentioning "Perrin's Law" (paragraph 27)? Is it a true "law," like the law of gravity? What body of knowledge is the author satirizing by invoking such a law?
5. Perrin is not didactic, since he does not recommend that other colleges adopt the environmental measures his model colleges have chosen. Would more direct advocacy on his part have strengthened his argument or weakened it, or not have had any effect? Explain.
6. In Perrin's conclusion, he changes his purpose from providing a purely informational assessment to offering a strong reprimand and recommendation. Why does he wait until the concluding paragraph to do so?

WRITING

1. Describe an environmentally friendly practice conducted at your college or university. Is it truly helpful for the environment, or is it largely symbolic?
2. Compare and contrast the academically oriented courses and programs offered at your school with what your institution actually does in the way of helping the environment. Discuss which of the two priorities is more prominent, and why.
3. **Writing an Argument:** Argue for or against the proposition that a magazine such as *U.S. News & World Report* should include environmental awareness and practice in its formula for assessing the rankings of colleges.

NETWORKING
Applying 21st-Century Literacies

Creating a Facebook Group for a Cause: With several of your classmates, create a Facebook group that calls for action or raises awareness about an environmental issue or natural space that is relevant to your campus or local community. Consider carefully what you'll call the group (names are important!), and in a mission statement, articulate what you hope to accomplish by organizing it.

The Last Americans: Environmental Collapse and the End of Civilization

Jared Diamond

Jared Diamond (b. 1937), who was born in Boston, is a physiologist, ecologist, and prolific writer who has published hundreds of popular and scientific articles. He has a BA from Harvard University (1958) and a PhD from Cambridge University (1961). Currently a professor of geography at UCLA and formerly professor of physiology at UCLA's School of Medicine, Diamond has conducted research in ecology and evolutionary biology in New Guinea and other southwest Pacific islands. As a field researcher and director of the World Wildlife Fund, Diamond helped to establish New Guinea's national park system. He received the Pulitzer prize for Guns, Germs, and Steel: The Fates of Human Societies *(1997). Another well-received book of Diamonds's is* Collapse: How Societies Choose to Fail or Succeed *(2004). In the following essay, which appeared in the June 2003 issue of* Harper's, *Diamond examines the environmental crises and failures of previous societies and civilizations, and how we might be able to learn lessons from these lost worlds.*

I met a traveler from an antique land
Who said: Two vast and trunkless legs of stone
Stand in the desert. . . . Near them, on the sand,
Half sunk, a shattered visage lies, whose frown,
And wrinkled lip, and sneer of cold command,
Tell that its sculptor well those passions read
Which yet survive, stamped on these lifeless things,
The hand that mocked them, and the heart that fed:
And on the pedestal these words appear:
"My name is Ozymandias, king of kings:
Look on my works, ye Mighty, and despair!"
Nothing beside remains. Round the decay
Of that colossal wreck, boundless and bare
The lone and level sands stretch far away.
                              —*"Ozymandias," Percy Bysshe Shelley*

1   One of the disturbing facts of history is that so many civilizations collapse. Few people, however, least of all our politicians, realize that a primary cause of the collapse of those societies has been the destruction of the environmental resources on which they depended. Fewer still appreciate that many of those civilizations share a sharp curve of decline. Indeed, a society's demise may begin only a decade or two after it reaches its peak population, wealth, and power.

Recent archaeological discoveries have revealed similar courses of collapse 2 in such otherwise dissimilar ancient societies as the Maya in the Yucatán, the Anasazi in the American Southwest, the Cahokia mound builders outside St. Louis, the Greenland Norse, the statue builders of Easter Island, ancient Mesopotamia in the Fertile Crescent, Great Zimbabwe in Africa, and Angkor Wat in Cambodia. These civilizations, and many others, succumbed to various combinations of environmental degradation and climate change, aggression from enemies taking advantage of their resulting weakness, and declining trade with neighbors who faced their own environmental problems. Because peak population, wealth, resource consumption, and waste production are accompanied by peak environmental impact—approaching the limit at which impact outstrips resources—we can now understand why declines of societies tend to follow swiftly on their peaks.

These combinations of undermining factors were compounded by cultural 3 attitudes preventing those in power from perceiving or resolving the crisis. That's a familiar problem today. Some of us are inclined to dismiss the importance of a healthy environment, or at least to suggest that it's just one of many problems facing us—an "issue." That dismissal is based on three dangerous misconceptions.

Foremost among these misconceptions is that we must balance the environ- 4 ment against human needs. That reasoning is exactly upside-down. Human needs and a healthy environment are not opposing claims that must be balanced; instead, they are inexorably linked by chains of cause and effect. We need a healthy environment because we need clean water, clean air, wood, and food from the ocean, plus soil and sunlight to grow crops. We need functioning natural ecosystems, with their native species of earthworms, bees, plants, and microbes, to generate and aerate our soils, pollinate our crops, decompose our wastes, and produce our oxygen. We need to prevent toxic substances from accumulating in our water and air and soil. We need to prevent weeds, germs, and other pest species from becoming established in places where they aren't native and where they cause economic damage. Our strongest arguments for a healthy environment are selfish: We want it for ourselves, not for threatened species like snail darters, spotted owls, and Furbish louseworts.

5   Another popular misconception is that we can trust in technology to solve our problems. Whatever environmental problem you name, you can also name some hoped-for technological solution under discussion. Some of us have faith that we shall solve our dependence on fossil fuels by developing new technologies for hydrogen engines, wind energy, or solar energy. Some of us have faith that we shall solve our food problems with new or soon-to-be-developed genetically modified crops. Some of us have faith that new technologies will succeed in cleaning up the toxic materials in our air, water, soil, and foods without the horrendous cleanup expenses that we now incur.

6   Those with such faith assume that the new technologies will ultimately succeed, but in fact some of them may succeed and others may not. They assume that the new technologies will succeed quickly enough to make a big difference soon, but all of these major technological changes will actually take five to thirty years to develop and implement—if they catch on at all. Most of all, those with faith assume that new technology won't cause any new problems. In fact, technology merely constitutes increased power, which produces changes that can be either for the better or for the worse. All of our current environmental problems are unanticipated harmful consequences of our existing technology. There is no basis for believing that technology will miraculously stop causing new and unanticipated problems while it is solving the problems that it previously produced.

7   The final misconception holds that environmentalists are fear-mongering, overreacting extremists whose predictions of impending disaster have been proved wrong before and will be proved wrong again. Behold, say the optimists: Water still flows from our faucets, the grass is still green, and the supermarkets are full of food. We are more prosperous than ever before, and that's the final proof that our system works.

8   Well, for a few billion of the world's people who are causing us increasing trouble, there isn't any clean water, there is less and less green grass, and there are no supermarkets full of food. To appreciate what the environmental problems of those billions of people mean for us Americans, compare the following two lists of countries. First ask some ivory-tower academic ecologist who knows a lot about the environment but never reads a newspaper and has no interest in politics to list the overseas countries facing some of the worst problems of environmental stress, overpopulation, or both. The ecologist would answer, "That's a no-brainer, it's obvious. Your list of environmentally stressed or overpopulated countries should surely include Afghanistan, Bangladesh, Burundi, Haiti, Indonesia, Iraq, Nepal, Pakistan, the Philippines, Rwanda, the Solomon Islands, and Somalia, plus others." Then ask a First World politician who knows nothing, and cares less, about the environment and population problems to list the world's worst trouble spots: countries where state government has already been overwhelmed and has collapsed, or is now at risk of collapsing, or has been wracked by recent civil wars; and countries that, as a result of their problems, are also creating problems for us rich First World countries, which may be deluged by illegal immigrants, or have to provide foreign aid to those countries, or

may decide to provide them with military assistance to deal with rebellions and terrorists, or may even (God forbid) have to send in our own troops. The politician would answer, "That's a no-brainer, it's obvious. Your list of political trouble spots should surely include Afghanistan, Bangladesh, Burundi, Haiti, Indonesia, Iraq, Nepal, Pakistan, the Philippines, Rwanda, the Soloman Islands, and Somalia, plus others."

The connection between the two lists is transparent. Today, just as in the 9 past, countries that are environmentally stressed, overpopulated or both are at risk of becoming politically stressed, and of seeing their governments collapse. When people are desperate and undernourished, they blame their government, which they see as responsible for failing to solve their problems. They try to emigrate at any cost. They start civil wars. They kill one another. They figure that they have nothing to lose, so they become terrorists, or they support or tolerate terrorism. The results are genocides such as the ones that already have exploded in Burundi, Indonesia, and Rwanda; civil wars, as in Afghanistan, Indonesia, Nepal, the Philippines, and the Solomon Islands; calls for the dispatch of First World troops, as to Afghanistan, Indonesia, Iraq, the Philippines, Rwanda, the Solomon Islands, and Somalia; the collapse of central government, as has already happened in Somalia; and overwhelming poverty, as in all of the countries on these lists.

But what about the United States? Some might argue that the environmen- 10 tal collapse of ancient societies is relevant to the modern decline of weak, far-off, overpopulated Rwanda and environmentally devastated Somalia, but isn't it ridiculous to suggest any possible relevance to the fate of our own society?

After all, we might reason, those ancients didn't enjoy the wonders of modern environment-friendly technologies. Those ancients had the misfortune to suffer from the effects of climate change. They behaved stupidly and ruined their own environment by doing obviously dumb things, like cutting down their forests, watching their topsoil erode, and building cities in dry areas likely to run short of water. They had foolish leaders who didn't have books and so couldn't learn from history, and who embroiled them in destabilizing wars and didn't pay attention to problems at home. They were overwhelmed by desperate immigrants, as one society after another collapsed, sending floods of economic refugees to tax the resources of the societies that weren't collapsing. In all those respects, we modern Americans are fundamentally different from those primitive ancients, and there is nothing that we could learn from them.

11   Or so the argument goes. It's an argument so ingrained both in our subconscious and in public discourse that it has assumed the status of objective reality. We think we are different. In fact, of course, all of those powerful societies of the past thought that they too were unique, right up to the moment of their collapse. It's sobering to consider the swift decline of the ancient Maya, who 1,200 years ago were themselves the most advanced society in the Western Hemisphere, and who, like us now, were then at the apex of their own power and numbers. Two excellent recent books, David Webster's *The Fall of the Ancient Maya* and Richardson Gill's *The Great Maya Droughts,* help bring the trajectory of Maya civilization back to life for us. Their studies illustrate how even sophisticated societies like that of the Maya (and ours) can be undermined by details of rainfall, farming methods, and motives of leaders.

12 By now, millions of modern Americans have visited Maya ruins. To do so, one need only take a direct flight from the United States to the Yucatán capital of Mérida, jump into a rental car or minibus, and drive an hour on a paved highway. Most Maya ruins, with their great temples and monuments, lie surrounded by jungles (seasonal tropical forests), far from current human settlement. They are "pure" archaeological sites. That is, their locations became depopulated, so they were not covered up by later buildings as were so many other ancient cities, like the Aztec capital of Tenochtitlán—now buried under modern Mexico City—and Rome.

13   One of the reasons few people live there now is that the Maya homeland poses serious environmental challenges to would-be farmers. Although it has a somewhat unpredictable rainy season from May to October, it also has a dry season from January through April. Indeed, if one focuses on the dry months, one could describe the Yucatán as a "seasonal desert."

14   Complicating things, from a farmer's perspective, is that the part of the Yucatán with the most rain, the south, is also the part at the highest elevation above the water table. Most of the Yucatán consists of karst—a porous, sponge-like, limestone terrain—and so rain runs straight into the ground, leaving little or no surface water. The Maya in the lower-elevation regions of the north were able to reach the water table by way of deep sinkholes called cenotes, and the

Maya in low coastal areas without sinkholes could reach it by digging wells up to 75 feet deep. Most Maya, however, lived in the south. How did they deal with their resulting water problem?

Technology provided an answer. The Maya plugged up leaks on karst 15 promontories by plastering the bottoms of depressions to create reservoirs, which collected rain and stored it for use in the dry season. The reservoirs at the Maya city of Tikal, for example, held enough water to meet the needs of about 10,000 people for eighteen months. If a drought lasted longer than that, though, the inhabitants of Tikal were in deep trouble.

Maya farmers grew mostly corn, which constituted the astonishingly high 16 proportion of about 70 percent of their diet, as deduced from isotope analyses of ancient Maya skeletons. They grew corn by means of a modified version of swidden slash-and-burn agriculture, in which forest is cleared, crops are grown in the resulting clearing for a few years until the soil is exhausted, and then the field is abandoned for fifteen to twenty years until regrowth of wild vegetation restores the soil's fertility. Because most of the land under a swidden agricultural system is fallow at any given time, it can support only modest population densities. Thus, it was a surprise for archaeologists to discover that ancient Maya population densities, judging from numbers of stone foundations of farmhouses, were often far higher than what unmodified swidden agriculture could support: often 250 to 750 people per square mile. The Maya probably achieved those high populations by such means as shortening the fallow period and tilling the soil to restore soil fertility, or omitting the fallow period entirely and growing crops every year, or, in especially moist areas, growing two crops per year.

Socially stratified societies, ours included, consist of farmers who produce 17 food, plus nonfarmers such as bureaucrats and soldiers who do not produce food and are in effect parasites on farmers. The farmers must grow enough food to meet not only their own needs but also those of everybody else. The number of nonproducing consumers who can be supported depends on the society's agricultural productivity. In the United States today, with its highly efficient agriculture, farmers make up only 2 percent of our population, and each farmer can feed, on the average, 129 other people. Ancient Egyptian agriculture was efficient enough for an Egyptian peasant to produce five times the food required for himself and his family. But a Maya peasant could produce only twice the needs of himself and his family.

18   Fully 80 percent of Maya society consisted of peasants. Their inability to support many nonfarmers resulted from several limitations of their agriculture. It produced little protein, because corn has much lower protein content than wheat, and because the few edible domestic animals kept by the Maya (turkeys, ducks, and dogs) included no large animals like our cows and sheep. There was little use of terracing or irrigation to increase production. In the Maya area's humid climate, stored corn would rot or become infested after a year, so the Maya couldn't get through a longer drought by eating surplus corn accumulated in good years. And unlike Old World peoples with their horses, oxen, donkeys, and camels, the Maya had no animal-powered transport. Indeed, the Maya lacked not only pack animals and animal-drawn plows but also metal tools, wheels, and boats with sails. All of those great Maya temples were built by stone and wooden tools and human muscle power alone, and all overland transport went on the backs of human porters.

19   Those limitations on food supply and food transport may in part explain why Maya society remained politically organized in small kingdoms that were perpetually at war with one another and that never became unified into large empires like the Aztec empire of the Valley of Mexico (fed by highly productive agriculture) or the Inca empire of the Andes (fed by diverse crops carried on llamas). Maya armies were small and unable to mount lengthy campaigns over long distances. The typical Maya kingdom held a population of only up to 50,000 people, within a radius of two or three days' walk from the king's palace. From the top of the temple of some Maya kingdoms, one could see the tops of the temples of other kingdoms.

20   Presiding over the temple was the king himself, who functioned both as head priest and as political leader. It was his responsibility to pray to the gods, to perform astronomical and calendrical rituals, to ensure the timely arrival of the rains on which agriculture depended, and thereby to bring prosperity. The king claimed to have the supernatural power to deliver those good things because of his asserted family relationship to the gods. Of course, that exposed him to the risk that his subjects would become disillusioned if he couldn't fulfill his boast of being able to deliver rains and prosperity.

21   Those are the basic outlines of Classic Maya society, which for all its limitations lasted more than 500 years. Indeed, the Maya themselves believed that it had lasted for much longer. Their remarkable Long Count calendar had its starting date (analogous to January 1, A.D. 1 of our calendar) backdated into the remote

preliterate past, at August 11, 3114 B.C. The first physical evidence of civilization within the Maya area, in the form of villagers and pottery, appeared around 1400 B.C., substantial buildings around 500 B.C., and writing around 400 B.C. The so-called Classic period of Maya history arose around A.D. 250, when evidence for the first kings and dynasties emerged. From then, the Maya population increased almost exponentially, to reach peak numbers in the eighth century A.D. The largest monuments were erected toward the end of that century. All the indicators of a complex society declined throughout the ninth century, until the last date on any monument was A.D. 909. This decline of Maya population and architecture constitutes what is known as the Classic Maya collapse.

What happened? Let's consider in more detail a city whose ruins now lie in 22 western Honduras at the world-famous site of Copán. The most fertile ground in the Copán area consists of five pockets of flat land along a river valley with a total area of only one square mile; the largest of those five pockets, known as the Copán pocket, has an area of half a square mile. Much of the land around Copán consists of steep hills with poor soil. Today, corn yields from valley-bottom fields are two or three times those of fields on hill slopes, which suffer rapid erosion and lose most of their productivity within a decade of farming.

To judge by the number of house sites, population growth in the Copán 23 valley rose steeply from the fifth century up to a peak estimated at around 27,000 people between A.D. 750 and 900. Construction of royal monuments glorifying kings became especially massive from A.D. 650 onward. After A.D. 700, nobles other than kings got into the act and began erecting their own palaces, increasing the burden that the king and his own court already imposed on the peasants. The last big buildings at Copán were put up around A.D. 800; the last date on an incomplete altar possibly bearing a king's name is A.D. 822.

Archaeological surveys of different types of habitats in the Copán valley 24 show that they were occupied in a regular sequence. The first area farmed was the large Copán pocket of bottomland, followed by occupation of the other four bottomland pockets. During that time the human population was growing, but the hills remained uninhabited. Hence that increased population must have been accommodated by intensifying production in the bottomland pockets: probably some combination of shorter fallow periods and double-cropping. By A.D. 500, people had started to settle the hill slopes, but those sites were occupied only briefly. The percentage of Copán's total population that was in the hills, rather than in the valleys, peaked in the year 575 and then declined, as the population again became concentrated in the pockets.

What caused that pullback of population from the hills? From excavation of 25 building foundations on the valley floor we know that they became covered with sediment during the eighth century, meaning that the hill slopes were becoming eroded and probably also leached of nutrients. The acidic hill soils being carried down into the valley would have reduced agricultural yields. The reason for that erosion of the hillsides is clear: the forests that formerly covered them and protected their soil were being cut down. Dated pollen samples show that the pine forests originally covering the hilltops were eventually all cleared, to be burned for fuel. Besides causing sediment accumulation in the valleys and depriving valley inhabitants of wood supplies, that deforestation may have begun to cause a "man-made drought" in the valley bottom, because forests play a major role in water cycling, such that massive deforestation tends to result in lowered rainfall.

26   Hundreds of skeletons recovered from Copán archaeological sites have been studied for signs of disease and poor nutrition, such as porous bones and stress lines in the teeth. Those skeletal signs show that the health of Copán's inhabitants deteriorated from A.D. 650 to 850, among both the elite and commoners, though the health of commoners was worse.

27   Recall that Copán's population was growing rapidly while the hills were being occupied. The subsequent abandonment of all of those hill fields meant that the burden of feeding the extra population formerly dependent on the hills now fell increasingly on the valley floor, and that more and more people were competing for the food grown on that one square mile of bottomland. That would have led to fighting among the farmers themselves for the best land, or for any land, just as in modern Rwanda. Because the king was failing to deliver on his promises of rain and prosperity, he would have been the scapegoat for this agricultural failure, which explains why the last that we hear of any king is A.D. 822, and why the royal palace was burned around A.D. 850.

28   Datable pieces of obsidian, the sharp rock from which the Maya made their stone tools, suggest that Copán's total population decreased more gradually than did its signs of kings and nobles. The estimated population in the year A.D. 950 was still around 15,000, or 55 percent of the peak population of 27,000. That population continued to dwindle, until there are few signs of anyone in the Copán valley after around A.D. 1235. The reappearance of pollen from forest trees thereafter provides independent evidence that the valley became virtually empty of people.

29   The Maya history that I have just related, and Copán's history in particular, illustrate why we talk about "the Maya collapse." But the story grows more complicated, for at least five reasons. There was not only that enormous Classic collapse but also at least two smaller pre-Classic collapses, around A.D. 150 and 600, as well as some post-Classic collapses. The Classic collapse was obviously not complete, because hundreds of thousands of Maya survived, in areas with stable water supplies, to meet and fight the Spaniards. The collapse of population (as gauged by numbers of house sites and of obsidian tools) was in some cases much slower than the decline in numbers of Long Count dates. Many apparent collapses of cities were nothing more than "power cycling"; i.e., particular cities becoming more powerful at the expense of neighboring cities, then declining or getting conquered by neighbors, without changes in the whole population. Finally, cities in different parts of the Maya area rose and fell on different trajectories.

30   Some archaeologists focus on these complications and don't want to recognize a Classic Maya collapse at all. But this overlooks the obvious fact that cries

out for explanation: the disappearance of between 90 and 99 percent of the Maya population after A.D. 800, and of the institution of the kingship, Long Count calendars, and other complex political and cultural institutions. Before we can understand those disappearances, however, we need first to understand the roles of warfare and of drought.

Archaeologists for a long time believed the ancient Maya to be gentle and 31 peaceful people. We now know that Maya warfare was intense, chronic, and unresolvable, because limitations of food supply and transportation made it impossible for any Maya principality to unite the whole region in an empire. The archaeological record shows that wars became more intense and frequent toward the time of the Classic collapse. That evidence comes from discoveries of several types since the Second World War: archaeological excavations of massive fortifications surrounding many Maya sites; vivid depictions of warfare and captives on stone monuments and on the famous painted murals discovered in 1946 at Bonampak; and the decipherment of Maya writing, much of which proved to consist of royal inscriptions boasting of conquests. Maya kings fought to capture and torture one another; an unfortunate loser was a Copán king with the to us unforgettable name of King 18 Rabbit.

Maya warfare involved well-documented types of violence: wars among 32 separate kingdoms; attempts of cities within a kingdom to secede by revolting against the capital; and civil wars resulting from frequent violent attempts by would-be kings to usurp the throne. All of these events were described or depicted on monuments, because they involved kings and nobles. Not considered worthy of description, but probably even more frequent, were fights between commoners over land, as overpopulation became excessive and land became scarce.

The other phenomenon important to understanding all of these collapses is 33 the repeated occurrence of droughts, as inferred by climatologists from evidence of lake evaporation preserved in lake sediments, and as summarized by Gill in *The Great Maya Droughts*. The rise of Maya civilization may have been facilitated by a rainy period beginning around 250 B.C., until a temporary drought after A.D. 125 was associated with a pre-Classic collapse at some sites. That collapse was followed by the resumption of rainy conditions and the buildup of Classic Maya cities, briefly interrupted by another drought around 600 corresponding to a decline at Tikal and some other sites. Finally, around A.D. 750 there began the worst drought in the past 7,000 years, peaking around the year A.D. 800, and suspiciously associated with the Classic collapse.

The area most affected by the Classic collapse was the southern highlands, 34 probably for the two reasons already mentioned: It was the area with the densest population, and it also had the most severe water problems because it lay too high above the water table for cenotes or wells to provide water. The southern highlands lost more than 99 percent of its population in the course of the Classic collapse. When Cortés and his Spanish army marched in 1524 and 1525 through an area formerly inhabited by millions of Maya, he nearly starved because he encountered so few villagers from whom to acquire corn. The Spaniards passed

within only a few miles of the abandoned ruins of the great Classic cities of Tikal and Palenque, but still they heard or saw nothing of them.

35 We can identify increasingly familiar strands in the Classic Maya collapse. One consisted of population growth outstripping available resources: the dilemma foreseen by Thomas Malthus in 1798. As Webster succinctly puts it in *The Fall of the Ancient Maya*, "Too many farmers grew too many crops on too much of the landscape." While population was increasing, the area of usable farmland paradoxically was decreasing from the effects of deforestation and hillside erosion.

36   The next strand consisted of increased fighting as more and more people fought over fewer resources. Maya warfare, already endemic, peaked just before the collapse. That is not surprising when one reflects that at least 5 million people, most of them farmers, were crammed into an area smaller than the state of Colorado. That's a high population by the standards of ancient farming societies, even if it wouldn't strike modern Manhattan-dwellers as crowded.

37   Bringing matters to a head was a drought that, although not the first one the Maya had been through, was the most severe. At the time of previous droughts, there were still uninhabited parts of the Maya landscape, and people in a drought area or dust bowl could save themselves by moving to another site. By the time of the Classic collapse, however, there was no useful unoccupied land in the vicinity on which to begin anew, and the whole population could not be accommodated in the few areas that continued to have reliable water supplies.

38   The final strand is political. Why did the kings and nobles not recognize and solve these problems? A major reason was that their attention was evidently focused on the short-term concerns of enriching themselves, waging wars, erecting monuments, competing with one another, and extracting enough food from the peasants to support all those activities. Like most leaders

throughout human history, the Maya kings and nobles did not have the leisure to focus on long-term problems, insofar as they perceived them.

What about those same strands today? The United States is also at the peak of 39 its power, and it is also suffering from many environmental problems. Most of us have become aware of more crowding and stress. Most of us living in large American cities are encountering increased commuting delays, because the number of people and hence of cars is increasing faster than the number of freeway lanes. I know plenty of people who in the abstract doubt that the world has a population problem, but almost all of those same people complain to me about crowding, space issues, and traffic experienced in their personal lives.

Many parts of the United States face locally severe problems of water re- 40 striction (especially southern California, Arizona, the Everglades, and, increasingly, the Northeast); forest fires resulting from logging and forest-management practices throughout the intermontane West; and losses of farmlands to salinization, drought, and climate change in the northern Great Plains. Many of us frequently experience problems of air quality, and some of us also experience problems of water quality and taste. We are losing economically valuable natural resources. We have already lost American chestnut trees, the Grand Banks cod fishery, and the Monterey sardine fishery; we are in the process of losing swordfish and tuna and Chesapeake Bay oysters and elm trees; and we are losing topsoil.

The list goes on: All of us are experiencing personal consequences of our 41 national dependence on imported energy, which affects us not only through higher gas prices but also through the current contraction of the national economy, itself the partial result of political problems associated with our oil dependence. We are saddled with expensive toxic cleanups at many locations, most notoriously near Montana mines, on the Hudson River, and in the Chesapeake Bay. We also face expensive eradication problems resulting from hundreds of introduced pest species—including zebra mussels, Mediterranean fruit flies, Asian longhorn beetles, water hyacinth, and spotted knapweed—that now affect our agriculture, forests, waterways, and pastures.

These particular environmental problems, and many others, are enor- 42 mously expensive in terms of resources lost, cleanup and restoration costs, and the cost of finding substitutes for lost resources: a billion dollars here, 10 billion there, in dozens and dozens of cases. Some of the problems, especially those of air quality and toxic substances, also exact health costs that are large, whether measured in dollars or in lost years or in quality of life. The cost of our home-grown environmental problems adds up to a large fraction of our gross national product, even without mentioning the costs that we incur from environmental problems overseas, such as the military operations that they inspire. Even the mildest of bad scenarios for our future include a gradual economic decline, as happened to the Roman and British empires. Actually, in case you didn't notice it, our economic decline is already well under way. Just check the numbers for

our national debt, yearly government budget deficit, unemployment statistics, and the value of your investment and pension funds.

43   The environmental problems of the United States are still modest compared with those of the rest of the world. But the problems of environmentally devastated, overpopulated, distant countries are now our problems as well. We are accustomed to thinking of globalization in terms of us rich, advanced First Worlders sending our good things, such as the Internet and Coca-Cola, to those poor backward Third Worlders. Globalization, however, means nothing more than improved worldwide communication and transportation, which can convey many things in either direction; it is not restricted to good things carried only from the First to the Third World. They in the Third World can now, intentionally or unintentionally, send us their bad things: terrorists; diseases such as AIDS, SARS, cholera, and West Nile fever, carried inadvertently by passengers on transcontinental airplanes; unstoppable numbers of immigrants, both legal and illegal, arriving by boat, truck, train, plane, and on foot; and other consequences of their Third World problems. We in the United States are no longer the isolated Fortress America to which some of us aspired in the 1930s; instead, we are tightly and irreversibly connected to overseas countries. The United States is the world's leading importer, and it is also the world's leading exporter. Our own society opted long ago to become interlocked with the rest of the world.

44   That's why political stability anywhere in the world now affects us, our trade routes, and our overseas markets and suppliers. We are so dependent on the rest of the world that if a decade ago you had asked a politician to name the

countries most geopolitically irrelevant to U.S. interests because of their being so remote, poor, and weak, the list would have begun with Afghanistan and Somalia, yet these countries were subsequently considered important enough to warrant our dispatching U.S. troops. The Maya were "globalized" only within the Yucatán: the southern Yucatán Maya affected the northern Yucatán Maya and may have had some effects on the Valley of Mexico, but they had no contact with Somalia. That's because Maya transportation was slow, short-distance, on foot or else in canoes, and had low cargo capacity. Our transport today is much more rapid and has much higher cargo capacity. The Maya lived in a globalized Yucatán; we live in a globalized world.

If all of this reasoning seems straightforward when expressed so bluntly, one 45 has to wonder: Why don't those in power today get the message? Why didn't the leaders of the Maya, Anasazi, and those other societies also recognize and solve their problems? What were the Maya thinking while they watched loggers clearing the last pine forests on the hills above Copán? Here, the past really is a useful guide to the present. It turns out that there are at least a dozen reasons why past societies failed to *anticipate* some problems before they developed, or failed to *perceive* problems that had already developed, or failed even to try to solve problems that they did perceive. All of those dozen reasons still can be seen operating today. Let me mention just three of them.

First, it's difficult to recognize a slow trend in some quantity that fluctuates 46 widely up and down anyway, such as seasonal temperature, annual rainfall, or economic indicators. That's surely why the Maya didn't recognize the oncoming drought until it was too late, given that rainfall in the Yucatán varies several-fold from year to year. Natural fluctuations also explain why it's only within the last few years that all climatologists have become convinced of the reality of climate change, and why our president still isn't convinced but thinks that we need more research to test for it.

Second, when a problem *is* recognized, those in power may not attempt to 47 solve it because of a clash between their short-term interests and the interests of the rest of us. Pumping that oil, cutting down those trees, and catching those fish may benefit the elite by bringing them money or prestige and yet be bad for society as a whole (including the children of the elite) in the long run. Maya kings were consumed by immediate concerns for their prestige (requiring more and bigger temples) and their success in the next war (requiring more followers), rather than for the happiness of commoners or of the next generation. Those people with the greatest power to make decisions in our own society today regularly make money from activities that may be bad for society as a whole and for their own children; those decision-makers include Enron executives, many land developers, and advocates of tax cuts for the rich.

Finally, it's difficult for us to acknowledge the wisdom of policies that clash 48 with strongly held values. For example, a belief in individual freedom and a distrust of big government are deeply ingrained in Americans, and they make sense under some circumstances and up to a certain point. But they also make it hard for us to accept big government's legitimate role in ensuring that each individual's freedom to maximize the value of his or her land holdings doesn't decrease the value of the collective land of all Americans.

49   Not all societies make fatal mistakes. There are parts of the world where societies have unfolded for thousands of years without any collapse, such as Java, Tonga, and (until 1945) Japan. Today, Germany and Japan are successfully managing their forests, which are even expanding in area rather than shrinking. The Alaskan salmon fishery and the Australian lobster fishery are being managed sustainably. The Dominican Republic, hardly a rich country, nevertheless has set aside a comprehensive system of protected areas encompassing most of the country's natural habitats.

50   Is there any secret to explain why some societies acquire good environmental sense while others don't? Naturally, part of the answer depends on accidents of individual leaders' wisdom (or lack thereof). But part also depends upon whether a society is organized so as to minimize built-in clashes of interest between its decision-making elites and its masses. Given how our society is organized, the executives of Enron, Tyco, and Adelphi correctly calculated that their own interests would be best promoted by looting the company coffers, and that they would probably get away with most of their loot. A good example of a society that minimizes such clashes of interest is the Netherlands, whose citizens have perhaps the world's highest level of environmental awareness and of membership in environmental organizations. I never understood why, until on a recent trip to the Netherlands I posed the question to three of my Dutch friends while driving through their countryside.

51   Just look around you, they said. All of this farmland that you see lies below sea level. One fifth of the total area of the Netherlands is below sea level, as much as 22 feet below, because it used to be shallow bays, and we reclaimed it from the sea by surrounding the bays with dikes and then gradually pumping out the water. We call these reclaimed lands "polders." We began draining our polders nearly a thousand years ago. Today, we still have to keep pumping out the water that gradually seeps in. That's what our windmills used to be for, to drive the pumps to pump out the polders. Now we use steam, diesel, and electric pumps instead. In each polder there are lines of them, starting with those farthest from the sea, pumping the water in sequence until the last pump finally deposits it into a river or the ocean. And all of us, rich or poor, live down in the polders. It's not the case that rich people live safely up on top of the dikes while poor people live in the polder bottoms below sea level. If the dikes and pumps fail, we'll all drown together.

52   Throughout human history, all peoples have been connected to some other peoples, living together in virtual polders. For the ancient Maya, their polder consisted of most of the Yucatán and neighboring areas. When the Classic Maya cities collapsed in the southern Yucatán, refugees may have reached the northern Yucatán, but probably not the Valley of Mexico, and certainly not Florida. Today, our whole world has become one polder, such that events in even Afghanistan and Somalia affect Americans. We do indeed differ from the Maya, but not in

ways we might like: We have a much larger population, we have more potent destructive technology, and we face the risk of a worldwide rather than a local decline. Fortunately, we also differ from the Maya in that we know their fate, and they did not. Perhaps we can learn.

COMPREHENSION

1. Explain the significance of Shelley's poem "Ozymandias" for Diamond's essay.
2. What are the "three dangerous misconceptions" (paragraph 3) about the environment that Diamond discusses?
3. List all the civilizations that Diamond mentions in this essay. Which civilization does he emphasize? According to Diamond, why did previous civilizations fail, and how do these collapses provide guides to the state of contemporary American civilization?

RHETORIC

1. State Diamond's argument or major proposition. Where does his claim appear most clearly? What minor propositions does he develop? How does he deal with opposing viewpoints?
2. What types of evidence does the writer provide to support his claim?
3. Why does Diamond divide his essay into so many sections? What relationships do you detect between and among these sections?
4. Where does Diamond use comparison and contrast and causal analysis to organize parts of his essay?
5. How does classification operate as a rhetorical element in this article?
6. Assess the relative effectiveness of Diamond's conclusion. How does the ending serve as a coda for the entire essay?

WRITING

1. Write an essay focusing on a local environmental problem. Analyze the ways in which this environmental problem affects the lives of nearby residents.
2. Select one civilization that Diamond mentions. Conduct research on this civilization, and then write a report on the environmental factors that led to the decline of that society.
3. **Writing an Argument:** Write a persuasive essay in which you warn readers about three environmental dangers confronting the United States today.

NETWORKING
Applying 21st-Century Literacies

Analyzing the Use of Images: How do the illustrations in this essay interact with Diamond's written text? What is their rhetorical purpose, and how do they influence the text's tone?

Synthesis: Connections
for Critical Thinking

1. Using support from the works of Lopez, Carson, Chief Seattle, and others, write a causal-analysis essay tracing our relationship to the land. To what extent have history, greed, and fear helped shape our attitude? Can this attitude be changed? How?

2. Consider the empathy and sensitivity Walker has toward animals. How do her attitude and perceptions coincide with the views expressed by Bass and Chief Seattle concerning the natural world?

3. Write a letter to the op-ed page of a newspaper objecting to a governmental ruling harmful to the environment. State the nature of the policy, its possible dangers, and your reasons for opposing it. Use support from Ford, McKibben, Diamond, and any other writers in this chapter. Extra reading or research may be necessary.

4. Consider why we fear nature. Why do we consider it an enemy, an alien, something to be destroyed? How would Walker, Lopez, and Chief Seattle respond to this question? Do you agree or disagree with them?

5. Both Lopez and Diamond use narration and description to explore our relationship to the land. How do they approach their subject in terms of language, attitude, and style?

6. Choose an author in this chapter whose essay, in your opinion, romanticizes nature. Compare his or her attitude with that of a writer with a more pragmatic approach to the subject. Compare the two views, and specify the elements in their writing that contribute to the overall strength of their arguments.

7. Perrin uses enumeration and illustration to structure his essay. What are some of the strengths and weaknesses of employing traditional and orderly means of presenting one's thoughts?

8. Write an essay titled "Nature's Revenge" in which you examine the consequences of environmental abuse. Consider the short- as well as the long-term effects on the quality of life. Use support from any three writers in this chapter to defend your opinion.

9. Write specifically about our relationship to other living creatures on our planet. Is it one of exploitation, cooperation, or tyranny? How does this relationship influence how we treat each other? Explore the answers to these questions in an essay. Use the works of Lopez, Walker, and Chief Seattle to support your thesis.

NETWORKING
Applying 21st-Century Literacies

1. Join an online newsgroup devoted to addressing a specific environmental issue—for example, atomic waste, overdevelopment, or environmental regulations and deregulations. Follow the conversation of the newsgroup for one month. Write an essay describing what the chief concerns of the newsgroup members are, how they address issues regarding the environment, and what specific actions they recommend or take over the course of your membership.
2. Visit the Web site of the Environmental Protection Agency. Write a report describing the agency's announcements, speeches, activities, and proposals.
3. Create your own interactive Web site focusing on the environment. Present, in its headline, this request: "In a statement of 100 words, please explain whether we are doing enough to reverse the destruction to our environment." Check back in a month, and write a report summarizing the responses.

CH 14   **www.mhhe.com/mhreader11e**

- *Image Gallery:* Chapter images in color
- *Nature and the Environment:* Information on the authors in this chapter
- *Ch. 14 Networking*

chapter *15*

Science and Technology
What Can Science Teach Us?

Contrary to popular assumptions, contemporary science and technology are not dry subjects but rather are bodies of specialized knowledge concerned with the great how and why questions of our time. In fact, we are currently in the midst of a whole series of scientific revolutions that will radically transform our lives in the 21st century. The essential problem for humankind is to make sense of all this revolutionary scientific and technological knowledge, invest it with value, use it ethically, and make it serve our cultural and global needs.

As you will see in the essays in this chapter, human beings are always the ultimate subject of scientific investigation. Science and mathematics attempt to understand the physical, biological, and chemical events that shape our lives. Whenever we switch on a light or turn on a computer, take an aspirin or start the car, we see that science and technology have intervened effectively in our lives. Often the specialized knowledge of science forces us to make painful decisions, and the misuse of science can have disastrous results. As Terry Tempest Williams demonstrates in her highly personal essay "The Clan of One-Breasted Women," science can have dire, unforeseen ethical implications.

The technology that arises from science affects everyday decisions as well as the larger culture. Nowhere is the impact of science more apparent than in the field of biotechnology. As Dinesh D'Souza observes in his essay on the biotech revolution, science is intended to serve us, to help us with our common dilemmas. At the same time, biotechnology reminds us that despite advances, we are still mortals confronting ethical dilemmas. Even as knowledge flows from research laboratories, these mortal paradoxes tend to perplex and goad us as we seek scientific solutions to the complex problems of our era.

Science and technology as specialized bodies of knowledge can send contradictory messages because science and technology are socially constructed and reflect the contours of culture. How we manage the revolution in science—how we harness nuclear power or battle the ravages of AIDS—will determine the health of civilization in our century.

PREVIEWING THE CHAPTER

As you read the essays in this chapter and respond to them in discussion and writing, consider the following questions:

- Does the author take a personal or an objective approach to the subject? What is the effect?
- What area of scientific or technological inquiry does the writer focus on?
- What scientific conflicts arise in the course of the essay?
- Is the writer a specialist, a layperson, a journalist, or a commentator? How does the background of the writer affect the tone of the essay?
- What assumptions does the author make about his or her audience? How much specialized knowledge must you bring to the essay?
- How do social issues enter into the author's presentation?
- What gender issues are raised by the author?
- How have your perceptions of the author's topic been changed or enhanced? What new knowledge have you gained? Does the writer contradict any of your assumptions or beliefs?
- Is the writer optimistic or pessimistic about the state of technology or science? How do you know?

Classic and Contemporary Images
WHERE IS SCIENCE TAKING US?

Using a Critical Perspective   Make a series of observations about each of these images. Where does your eye rest in each one? How many objects and details do you see? What reasonable inferences can you draw about the relationship of the artist who created the 15th-century image to the culture and historical period? What purpose did the scientists who created and control the Hubble Space Telescope have? What purposes do the 15th-century artist and 20th-century scientist have in common? Argue for or against the proposition that art can actually capture the advances in science, technology, and humanity that we have experienced over time.

During the Renaissance in Europe, scientists such as Nicolaus Copernicus (1473–1543) and Galileo Galilei (1564–1642) revolutionized the way Europeans viewed the universe and their place in it by proving that the earth and the planets revolve around the sun, thus changing forever the worldview exemplified by the 15th-century Flemish depiction of the movements of the sun and moon shown here.

Galileo's primitive telescope was a distant forerunner of the powerful
Hubble Space Telescope, launched in 1990, which is able to take
photographs of extremely distant stars and other phenomena,
such as the gaseous pillars shown here, as it orbits the earth.

Classic and Contemporary Essays
HOW HAS NATURE EVOLVED?

Evolution seems to be more highly and hotly debated each year, insinuating itself into educational, political, scientific, and religious debates. Unfortunately, extreme positions on evolution tend to obscure what is valuable about the concept. The idea or theory of evolution is rooted in scientific creativity and the scientific method. Scientists are observers and collectors of information, and they use facts to build an explanation of the natural world and our place in it. Darwin looked carefully at nature and the physical world, as the following reading on natural selection illustrates. In his autobiography, Darwin observed that he "collected facts on a wholesale scale" before arriving at his theory of natural selection, and this inductive approach, at the heart of *On the Origin of Species* (1859), typifies his method of inquiry. But does evolutionary theory explain all the facts—all of humankind's problems? Does evolution mark the progress of human civilization, or are dimensions needed to explain our relationship to the world and the world's events? Verlyn Klinkenborg, who writes editorials and vignettes on science and nature for the *New York Times*, touches on these questions in an essay he composed celebrating the bicentennial of Darwin's birth. But Klinkenborg broadens his inquiry to touch on the scientific ideas of Mendel, the structure of DNA, and the broader issue of "our failure to come to terms with science and the teaching of science." Darwin's great idea, as Klinkenborg suggests, helps to explain our struggle for existence and meaning in the modern world.

Natural Selection

Charles Darwin

Charles Darwin (1809–1882) was born in England and studied medicine at Edinburgh. He also studied for the ministry at Cambridge but soon turned his interest to natural history. Through his friendship with a well-known botanist, he was given the opportunity to take a five-year cruise around the world (1831–1836) aboard the H.M.S. Beagle, *serving as a naturalist. This started Darwin on a career of accumulating and assimilating data that resulted in the formulation of his concept of evolution. He spent the remainder of his life carefully and methodically working over the information from his copious notes. He first published his findings in 1858 and a year later published his influential* On the Origin of Species. *This seminal work was supplemented and elaborated on in many later books, including* The Descent of Man *(1871). The following selection demonstrates the methodical and meticulous method Darwin used in developing his concepts.*

In order to make it clear how, as I believe, natural selection acts, I must beg permission to give one or two imaginary illustrations. Let us take the case of a wolf, which preys on various animals, securing some by craft, some by strength, and some by fleetness; and let us suppose that the fleetest prey, a deer for instance, had from any change in the country increased in numbers, or that other prey had decreased in numbers, during that season of the year when the wolf is hardest pressed for food. I can under such circumstances see no reason to doubt that the swiftest and slimmest wolves would have the best chance of surviving, and so be preserved or selected, provided always that they retained strength to master their prey at this or at some other period of the year, when they might be compelled to prey on other animals. I can see no more reason to doubt this, than that man can improve the fleetness of his greyhounds by careful and methodical selection, or by that unconscious selection which results from each man trying to keep the best dogs without any thought of modifying the breed.

Even without any change in the proportional numbers of the animals on which our wolf preyed, a cub might be born with an innate tendency to pursue certain kinds of prey. Nor can this be thought very improbable; for we often observe great differences in the natural tendencies of our domestic animals; one cat, for instance, taking to catch rats, another mice; one cat, according to Mr. St. John, bringing home winged game, another hares or rabbits, and another hunting on marshy ground and almost nightly catching woodcocks or snipes. The tendency to catch rats rather than mice is known to be inherited. Now, if any slight innate change of habit or of structure benefited an individual wolf, it would have the best chance of surviving and of leaving offspring. Some of its young would probably inherit the same habits or structure, and by the repetition of this process, a new variety might be formed which would either supplant or coexist with the parent-form of wolf. Or, again, the wolves inhabiting a mountainous district, and those frequenting the lowlands, would naturally be forced to hunt different prey; and from the continued preservation of the individuals best fitted for the two sites, two varieties might slowly be formed. These varieties would cross and blend where they met; but to this subject of intercrossing we shall soon have to return. I may add, that, according to Mr. Pierce, there are two varieties of the wolf inhabiting the Catskill Mountains in the United States, one with a light greyhound-like form, which pursues deer, and the other more bulky, with shorter legs, which more frequently attacks the shepherd's flocks.

Let us now take a more complex case. Certain plants excrete a sweet juice, apparently for the sake of eliminating something injurious from their sap; this is effected by glands at the base of the stipules in some Leguminosae, and at the back of the leaf of the common laurel. This juice, though small in quantity, is greedily sought by insects. Let us now suppose a little sweet juice or nectar to be excreted by the inner bases of the petals of a flower. In this case insects in seeking the nectar would get dusted with pollen, and would certainly often transport the pollen from one flower to the stigma of another flower. The flowers of two distinct individuals of the same species would thus get crossed; and the act of crossing, we have good reason to believe (as will hereafter be more fully alluded to), would produce very vigorous seedlings, which consequently would have the best chance of flourishing and surviving. Some of these seedlings would probably inherit the nectar-excreting power. Those individual flowers which had the largest glands or nectaries, and which excreted most nectar, would be oftenest visited by insects, and would be oftenest crossed; and so in the long-run would gain the upper hand. Those flowers, also, which had their stamens and pistils placed, in relation to the size and habits of the particular insects which visited them, so as to favor in any degree the transportal of their pollen from flower to flower, would likewise be favored or selected. We might have taken the case of insects visiting flowers for the sake of collecting pollen instead of nectar; and as pollen is formed for the sole object of fertilization, its destruction appears a simple loss to the plant; yet if a little pollen were carried, at first occasionally and then habitually, by the pollen-devouring insects from flower to flower, and a cross thus effected, although nine-tenths of the pollen were destroyed, it might still be a great gain to the plant; and those individuals which produced more and more pollen, and had larger and larger anthers, would be selected.

4   When our plant, by this process of the continued preservation or natural selection of more and more attractive flowers, had been rendered highly attractive to insects, they would, unintentionally on their part, regularly carry pollen from flower to flower; and that they can most effectually do this, I could easily show by many striking instances. I will give only one—not as a very striking case, but as likewise illustrating one step in the separation of the sexes of plants, presently to be alluded to. Some holly-trees bear only male flowers, which have four stamens producing rather a small quantity of pollen, and a rudimentary pistil; other holly-trees bear only female flowers; these have a full-sized pistil, and four stamens with shriveled anthers, in which not a grain of pollen can be detected. Having found a female tree exactly sixty yards from a male tree, I put the stigmas of twenty flowers, taken from different branches, under the microscope, and on all, without exception, there were pollen-grains, and on some a profusion of pollen. As the wind had set for several days from the female to the male tree, the pollen could not thus have been carried. The weather had been cold and boisterous, and therefore not favorable to bees; nevertheless every female flower which I examined had been effectually fertilized by the bees, accidentally dusted with pollen, having flown from tree to tree in search of nectar. But to return to our imaginary case: As soon as the plant had been rendered so highly attractive to insects that pollen was regularly carried from flower to flower, another process might commence. No naturalist doubts the advantage of what has been called the "physiological division of labor"; hence we may believe that it would be advantageous to a plant to produce stamens alone in one flower or on one whole plant, and pistils alone in another flower or on another plant. In plants under culture and placed under new conditions of life, sometimes the male organs and sometimes the female organs become more or less impotent; now if we suppose this to occur in ever so slight a degree under

nature, then as pollen is already carried regularly from flower to flower, and as a more complete separation of the sexes of our plant would be advantageous on the principle of the division of labor, individuals with this tendency more and more increased, would be continually favored or selected, until at last a complete separation of the sexes would be effected.

Let us now turn to the nectar-feeding insects in our imaginary case: We may suppose the plant of which we have been slowly increasing the nectar by continued selection, to be a common plant; and that certain insects depended in main part on its nectar for food. I could give many facts, showing how anxious bees are to save time; for instance, their habit of cutting holes and sucking the nectar at the bases of certain flowers, which they can, with a very little more trouble, enter by the mouth. Bearing such facts in mind, I can see no reason to doubt that an accidental deviation in the size and form of the body, or in the curvature and length of the proboscis, etc., far too slight to be appreciated by us, might profit a bee or other insect, so that an individual so characterized would be able to obtain its food more quickly, and so have a better chance of living and leaving descendants. Its descendants would probably inherit a tendency to a similar slight deviation of structure. The tubes of the corollas of the common red and incarnate clovers (Trifolium pratense and incarnatum) do not on a hasty glance appear to differ in length; yet the hive-bee can easily suck the nectar out of the incarnate clover, but not out of the common red clover, which is visited by humble-bees alone; so that the whole fields of the red clover offer in vain an abundant supply of precious nectar to the hive-bee. Thus it might be a great advantage to the hive-bee to have a slightly longer or differently constructed proboscis. On the other hand, I have found by experiment that the fertility of clover greatly depends on bees visiting and moving parts of the corolla, so as to push the pollen on to the stigmatic surface. Hence, again, if humble-bees were to become rare in any country, it might be a great advantage to the red clover to have a shorter or more deeply divided tube to its corolla, so that the hive-bee could visit its flowers. Thus I can understand how a flower and a bee might slowly become, either simultaneously or one after the other, modified and adapted in the most perfect manner to each other, by the continued preservation of individuals presenting mutual and slightly favorable deviations of structure.

I am well aware that this doctrine of natural selection, exemplified in the above imaginary instances, is open to the same objections which were at first urged against Sir Charles Lyell's noble views on "the modern changes of the earth, as illustrative of geology"; but we now very seldom hear the action, for instance, of the coast-waves, called a trifling and insignificant cause, when applied to the excavation of gigantic valleys or to the formation of the longest lines of inland cliffs. Natural selection can act only by the preservation and accumulation of infinitesimally small inherited modifications, each profitable to the preserved being; and as modern geology has almost banished such views as the excavation of a great valley by a single diluvial wave, so will natural selection, if it be a true principle, banish the belief of the continued creation of new organic beings, or of any great and sudden modification in their structure.

COMPREHENSION

1. What does Darwin mean by the term *natural selection?*
2. What is Darwin attempting to refute by his concept of natural selection? Where in the essay is this refutation articulated?
3. Explain what Darwin means by the "physiological division of labor" (paragraph 4).
4. Define the following terms: *innate* (paragraph 2), *stamens* and *pistils* (paragraph 3), *rudimentary* (paragraph 4), *incarnate* (paragraph 5), and *doctrine* (paragraph 6).

RHETORIC

1. In the introduction, Darwin makes an analogy between the needs of humans and those of nature. What is this analogy, and why is it important in devising his argument?
2. What is the tone of the essay? Consider such phrases as "beg permission" (paragraph 1) and "Let us now" (paragraph 3).
3. Darwin uses two "imaginary illustrations" in an attempt to prove his point. What are they, and why are these hypothetical illustrations more effective than real-life ones for his purpose?
4. Darwin tends to use extremely long sentences when he wishes to illustrate a process. For example, the sentence in paragraph 3 that begins "We might have taken" is 101 words long. Deconstruct this sentence by paying special attention to its punctuation, its logical succession of clauses, and its effect on the reader of describing so many processes within its boundaries. What is the relationship between its rhetorical style and purpose?
5. Who is the implied audience for the essay? Cite specific aspects of the rhetoric that led you to your conclusion.
6. What gives Darwin his authority? Specifically, how is his authority linked to the specialized vocabulary of the essay and to the way Darwin uses language to articulate natural processes?
7. Darwin uses the argumentative technique of disarming potential critics in the final paragraph. What is the rhetorical function of this device? Does it strengthen or weaken his argument? Explain your view.

WRITING

1. Write a précis of the essay, focusing on the major points Darwin is trying to assert in his theory of natural selection.
2. **Writing an Argument:** In an essay, argue for or against the proposition that in order to agree with or refute Darwin's ideas of natural selection, one would have to have at least as much experience in observing nature as Darwin obviously had.
3. **Writing an Argument:** Argue for or against the view that Darwin's theory can have disastrous consequences for the human species if applied to politics, sociology, or economics.

NETWORKING

Applying 21st-Century Literacies

Exploring a Museum's Online Exhibit: On the Chapter 15 Networking page (at *www.mhhe.com/mhreader11e*), click on the link to visit the American Museum of Natural History's Web site and virtual exhibit about Charles Darwin, including an informational video. Which aspect of this exhibit do you find the most interesting, and why? How many types of media does the site make use of? What are your thoughts on the site's navigability? What about its design? How do all of these aspects contribute to its purpose?

Darwin at 200: The Ongoing Force of His Unconventional Idea

Verlyn Klinkenborg

Verlyn Klinkenborg (b. 1952) was born in Colorado and raised on an Iowa farm until he was 14, at which time his family moved to the San Francisco Bay Area. Klinkenborg studied at Pomona College (BA, 1974) and Princeton University (PhD, 1982); he has taught at Princeton, Pomona, Harvard University, Fordham University, Bard College, and elsewhere. His books include Making Hay *(1986),* The Last Fine Time *(1991),* The Rural Life *(2003), and* Timothy: Or, Notes on an Abject Reptile *(2006). Klinkenborg, who now lives on a farm in upstate New York, joined the editorial board of the* New York Times *in 1997, and his essays on rural life are a regular feature of the newspaper's editorial page. In this essay, published in the* Times *in 2009, Klinkenborg celebrates the bicentennial of Charles Darwin.*

I can't help wondering what Charles Darwin would think if he could survey the   1 state of his intellectual achievement today, 200 years after his birth and 150 years after the publication of *On the Origin of Species*, the book that changed everything. His central idea—evolution by means of natural selection—was in some sense the product of his time, as Darwin well knew. He was the grandson of Erasmus Darwin, who grasped that there was something wrong with the conventional notion of fixed species. And his theory was hastened into print and into joint presentation by the independent discoveries of Alfred Russel Wallace half a world away.

2   But Darwin's theory was the product of years of patient observation. We love to believe in science by epiphany, but the work of real scientists is to rigorously test their epiphanies after they have been boiled down to working hypotheses. Most of Darwin's life was devoted to gathering evidence for just such tests. He writes with an air of incompleteness because he was aware that it would take the work of many scientists to confirm his theory in detail.

3   I doubt that much in the subsequent history of Darwin's idea would have surprised him. The most important discoveries—Mendel's genetics and the structure of DNA—would almost certainly have gratified him because they reveal the physical basis for the variation underlying evolution. It would have gratified him to see his ideas so thoroughly tested and to see so many of them confirmed. He could hardly have expected to be right so often.

4   Perhaps one day we will not call evolution "Darwinism." After all, we do not call classical mechanics "Newtonism." But that raises the question of whether a biological Einstein is possible, someone who demonstrates that Darwin's theory is a limited case. What Darwin proposed was not a set of immutable mathematical formulas. It was a theory of biological history that was itself set in history. That the details have changed does not invalidate his accomplishment. If anything, it enhances it. His writings were not intended to be scriptural. They were meant to be tested.

5   As for the other fate of so-called Darwinism—the reductionist controversy fostered by religious conservatives—well, Darwin knew plenty about that, too. The cultural opposition to evolution was then, as now, scientifically irrelevant. Perhaps the persistence of opposition to evolution is a reminder that culture is not biological, or else we might have evolved past such a gnashing of sensibilities. In a way, our peculiarly American failure to come to terms with Darwin's theory and what it's become since 1859 is a sign of something broader: our failure to come to terms with science and the teaching of science.

6   Darwin does not fit our image of a scientist. From the 21st century, he seems at first to bear a closer resemblance to an amateur naturalist like Gilbert White in the 18th century. But that is an illusion. Darwin's funding was private, his habit was retiring and he lacked the kind of institutional support that we associate with science because it did not exist. But Darwin's extensive scientific correspondence makes it clear that he was not the least bit reclusive intellectually and that he understood the character of science as it was practiced in his day as well as anyone.

7   We expect these days that a boy or girl obsessed with beetles may eventually find a home in a university or a laboratory or a museum. But Darwin's life was his museum, and he was its curator. In June 1833, still early in the five-year voyage of the *Beagle,* he wrote about rounding Cape Horn: "It is a grand spectacle to see all nature thus raging; but Heaven knows every one in the *Beagle* has seen enough in this one summer to last them their natural lives." (In this same letter, he celebrates the parliamentary attack on slavery in England.)

8   The rest of Darwin's life did in fact revolve around that voyage. As you sift through the notes and letters and publications that stemmed from his years on

the *Beagle*, you begin to understand how careful, how inquisitive and how various his mind was. The voyage of the *Beagle*—and of a young naturalist who was 22 at its outset—is still one of the most compelling stories in science.

Darwin recedes, but his idea does not. It is absorbed, with adaptations, into the foundation of the biological sciences. In a very real sense, it is the cornerstone of what we know about life on earth. Darwin's version of that great idea was very much of its time, and yet the whole weight of his time was set against it. From one perspective, Darwin looks completely conventional—white, male, well born, leisured, patrician. But from another, he turned the fortune of his circumstances into the most unconventional idea of all: the one that showed humans their true ancestry in nature. 9

COMPREHENSION

1. According to Klinkenborg, why was Darwin's idea "unconventional"?
2. How does Darwin's theory reflect the scientific method?
3. What is Klinkenborg's opinion concerning "Darwinism" and "so-called Darwinism"? Would he be happy to see both terms disappear? Why or why not?

RHETORIC

1. Does Klinkenborg establish a claim in this essay, or does he simply want to celebrate the bicentennial of Darwin's birth? Justify your answer.
2. How does Klinkenborg use exemplification as a compositional strategy? What examples does he provide, and why?
3. Klinkenborg alludes to Erasmus Darwin, Alfred Russel Wallace, Mendel, Newton, and Gilbert White. Who were they, and what is the writer's purpose in referring to them?
4. Explain the way that definition serves to structure parts of this essay.
5. Do you find Klinkenborg's conclusion effective? Why or why not?

WRITING

1. Compose your own brief celebration of Charles Darwin.
2. Write an extended definition of evolutionary theory.
3. **Writing an Argument:** Argue for or against the proposition that "Darwinism" is no longer a useful term to describe evolutionary theory.

NETWORKING
Applying 21st-Century Literacies

Creating a Hyperlinked Extended Definition: Format question 2 under Writing as an electronic text, using hyperlinks to clarify and expand on your definition of evolutionary theory.

Synthesis: Classic and Contemporary Questions for Comparison

1. How do Darwin and Klinkenborg approach the subject of evolution? Do they have the same or different priorities, and why? Are they writing for the same audience? Use examples from both selections to support your response.
2. Analyze the language used in the two essays. What is similar or different about the style and diction of the two pieces? How does each use details? Is one essay more accessible to the modern reader? Why or why not?
3. How do both essays treat the scientific method? Is one selection more "scientific" in its approach than the other? Explain your response.

Nutcracker.com

David Sedaris

David Sedaris (b. 1957), who was born in Johnson City, New York, and grew up in Raleigh, North Carolina, is a well-known humorist, essayist, diarist, short-story writer, and radio commentator. After graduating from the Art Institute of Chicago in 1987, Sedaris held several temporary jobs, ranging from a cleaner of apartments to an elf in SantaLand at Macy's. His stint on National Public Radio's Morning Edition *established Sedaris as a popular if quirky humorist and led to his first collection of essays,* Barrel Fever *(2000). Termed by* Entertainment Weekly *"a crackpot in the best sense of the word," Sedaris has also written* Naked *(1997),* Me Talk Pretty One Day *(2000),* Dress Your Family in Corduroy and Denim *(2004),* When You're Engulfed in Flames *(2008), and other works. In this essay, Sedaris humorously explains why he is a technophobe.*

1 It was my father's dream that one day the people of the world would be connected to one another through a network of blocky, refrigerator-size computers, much like those he was helping develop at IBM. He envisioned families of the future gathered around their mammoth terminals, ordering groceries and paying their taxes from the comfort of their own homes. A person could compose music, design a doghouse, and . . . something more, something even better. "A person could . . . he could . . . "

2 When predicting this utopia, he would eventually reach a point where words failed him. His eyes would widen and sparkle at the thought of this indescribable something more. "I mean, my God," he'd say, "just think about it."

3 My sisters and I preferred not to. I didn't know about them, but I was hoping the people of the world might be united by something more interesting, like drugs or an armed struggle against the undead. Unfortunately, my father's

team won, so computers it is. My only regret is that this had to happen during my lifetime.

Somewhere in the back of my mind is a dim memory of standing in some line 4 holding a perforated card. I remember the cheap, slightly clinical feeling it gave me, and recall thinking that the computer would never advance much further than this. Call me naive, but I seem to have underestimated the universal desire to sit in a hard plastic chair and stare at a screen until your eyes cross. My father saw it coming, but this was a future that took me completely by surprise. There were no computers in my high school, and the first two times I attempted college, people were still counting on their fingers and removing their shoes when the numbers got above ten. I wasn't really aware of computers until the mid-1980s. For some reason, I seemed to know quite a few graphic designers whose homes and offices pleasantly stank of Spray Mount. Their floors were always collaged with stray bits of paper, and trapped flies waved for help from the gummy killing fields of their tabletops. I had always counted on these friends to loan me the adhesive of my choice, but then, seemingly overnight, their Scotch tape and rubber cement were gone, replaced with odorless computers and spongy mouse pads. They had nothing left that I wanted to borrow, and so I dropped them and fell in with a group of typesetters who ultimately betrayed me as well.

Thanks to my complete lack of office skills, I found it fairly easy to avoid 5 direct contact with the new technology. The indirect contact was disturbing enough. I was still living in Chicago when I began to receive creepy Christmas newsletters designed to look like tabloids and annual reports. Word processors made writing fun. They did not, however, make reading fun, a point made painfully evident by such publications as *The Herald Family Tribune* and *Wassup with the Wexlers!*

Friends who had previously expressed no interest in torture began sending 6 letters composed to resemble Chinese take-out menus and the Dead Sea Scrolls. Everybody had a font, and I was told that I should get one, too. The authors of these letters shared an enthusiasm with the sort of people who now arrived at dinner parties hoisting expensive new video cameras and suggesting that, after dessert, we all sit down and replay the evening on TV. We, the regular people of the world, now had access to the means of production, but still I failed to see what all the fuss was about. A dopey letter is still a dopey letter, no matter how you dress it up; and there's a reason regular people don't appear on TV: We're boring.

By the early 1990s I was living in New York and working for a houseclean- 7 ing company. My job taught me that regardless of their purported virtues, computers are a pain in the ass to keep clean. The pebbled surface is a magnet for grease and dirt, and you can pretty much forget about reaming out the gaps in the keyboard. More than once I accidentally pushed a button and recoiled in terror as the blank screen came to life with exotic tropical fish or swarms of flying toasters. Equally distressing was the way people used the slanted roofs of their terminals to display framed photographs and great populations of plush and plastic creatures, which would fall behind the desk the moment I began cleaning the screen. There was never any place to plug in the vacuum, as every outlet was occupied by some member of the computer family. Cords ran wild, and everyone seemed to own one of those ominous foot-long power strips with the blinking red light that sends the message YOU MUST LEAVE US ALONE. I was more than happy to comply, and the complaints came rolling in.

8   Due to my general aversion to machines and a few pronounced episodes of screaming, I was labeled a technophobe, a term that ranks fairly low on my scale of fightin' words. The word *phobic* has its place when properly used, but lately it's been declawed by the pompous insistence that most animosity is based upon fear rather than loathing. No credit is given for distinguishing between these two very different emotions. I fear snakes. I hate computers. My hatred is entrenched, and I nourish it daily. I'm comfortable with it, and no community outreach program will change my mind.

9   I hate computers for getting their own section in the *New York Times* and for lengthening commercials with the mention of a Web site address. Who really wants to find out more about Procter & Gamble? Just buy the toothpaste or laundry detergent, and get on with it. I hate them for creating the word *org* and I hate them for e-mail, which isn't real mail but a variation of the pointless notes people used to pass in class. I hate computers for replacing the card catalog in the New York Public Library and I hate the way they've invaded the movies. I'm not talking about their contribution to the world of special effects. I have nothing against a well-defined mutant or full-scale alien invasion—that's *good* technology. I'm talking about their actual presence *in* any given movie. They've become like horses in a western—they may not be the main focus, but everybody seems to have one. Each tiresome new thriller includes a scene in which the hero, trapped by some version of the enemy, runs for his desk in a desperate race against time. Music swells and droplets of sweat rain down onto the keyboard as he sits at his laptop, frantically pawing for answers. It might be different if he were flagging down a passing car or trying to phone for help, but typing, in and of itself, is not an inherently dramatic activity.

10   I hate computers for any number of reasons, but I despise them most for what they've done to my friend the typewriter. In a democratic country you'd think there would be room for both of them, but computers won't rest until I'm making my ribbons from torn shirts and brewing Wite-Out in my bathtub. Their goal is to place the IBM Selectric II beside the feather quill and chisel in the museum of antiquated writing implements. They're power hungry, and someone needs to stop them.

11   When told I'm like the guy still pining for his eight-track tapes, I say, "You have eight-tracks? Where?" In reality I know nothing about them, yet I feel it's important to express some solidarity with others who have had the rug pulled out from beneath them. I don't care if it can count words or rearrange paragraphs at the push of a button, I don't want a computer. Unlike the faint scurry raised by fingers against a plastic computer keyboard, the smack and clatter of a typewriter suggests that you're actually building something. At the end of a miserable day, instead of grieving my virtual nothing, I can always look at my loaded wastepaper basket and tell myself that if I failed, at least I took a few trees down with me.

When forced to leave my house for an extended period of time, I take my 12 typewriter with me, and together we endure the wretchedness of passing through the X-ray scanner. The laptops roll merrily down the belt, while I'm instructed to stand aside and open my bag. To me it seems like a normal enough thing to be carrying, but the typewriter's declining popularity arouses suspicion and I wind up eliciting the sort of reaction one might expect when traveling with a cannon.

"It's a typewriter," I say. "You use it to write angry letters to airport 13 authorities."

The keys are then slapped and pounded, and I'm forced to explain that if you 14 want the words to appear, you first have to plug it in and insert a sheet of paper.

The goons shake their heads and tell me I really should be using a computer. 15 That's their job, to stand around in an ill-fitting uniform and tell you how you should lead your life. I'm told the exact same thing later in the evening when the bellhop knocks on my hotel door. The people whose televisions I can hear have complained about my typing, and he has come to make me stop. To hear him talk, you'd think I'd been playing the kettledrum. In the great scheme of things, the typewriter is not nearly as loud as he makes it out to be, but there's no use arguing with him. "You know," he says, "you really should be using a computer."

You have to wonder where you've gone wrong when twice a day you're 16 offered writing advice from men in funny hats. The harder I'm pressured to use a computer, the harder I resist. One by one, all of my friends have deserted me and fled to the dark side. "How can I write you if you don't have an e-mail address?" they ask. They talk of their B-trees and Disk Doctors and then have the nerve to complain when I discuss bowel obstructions at the dinner table.

Who needs them? I think. I figured I'd always have my family and was 17 devastated when my sister Amy brought home a candy-colored laptop. "I only use it for e-mail," she said. Coming from her, these words made me physically ill. "It's fun," she said. "People send you things. Look at this." She pushed a button, and there, on the screen, was a naked man lying facedown on a carpet. His hair was graying and his hands were cuffed behind his doughy back. A woman entered the room. You couldn't see her face, just her legs and feet, which were big and mean-looking, forced into sharp-toed shoes with high, pencil-thin heels. The man on the carpet shifted position, and when his testicles came into view, the woman reacted as if she had seen an old balding mouse, one that she had been trying to kill for a long time. She stomped on the man's testicles with the toes of her shoes and then she turned around and stomped on them with the heels. She kicked them mercilessly and, just when I thought she'd finished, she got her second wind and started all over again.

I'd never realized that a computer could act so much like a TV set. No one 18 had ever told me that the picture could be so clear, that the cries of pain could be heard so distinctly. This, I thought, was what my father had been envisioning all those years ago when words had failed him, not necessarily this scene, but something equally capable of provoking such wonder.

"Again?" Amy pushed a button and, our faces bathed in the glow of the 19 screen, we watched the future a second time.

COMPREHENSION

1. What distinguishes the author from his father and his sister Amy?
2. Why does Sedaris hate computers? Does he actually enjoy being a "technophobe"? How do you know?
3. What sort of writer is Sedaris? Why doesn't he want to use computers to help him in the writing process?

RHETORIC

1. How do you interpret the title? How does the title prepare us for the tone of this selection?
2. Sedaris employs a personal voice in this essay. What does the "I" point of view contribute to the selection?
3. What comic strategies does the author develop? What details stand out? Does comedy serve to support or undercut his claim?
4. How does Sedaris argue his case? Does he actually have a case, or a cause, or is his purpose simply to amuse the reader? How do you know?
5. What principle of classification appears in the essay, and how does this rhetorical strategy serve the author's purpose?
6. How does the writer use comparison and contrast, narration, and description to develop the essay?
7. Explain the impact and significance of the concluding scene. How does the tone alter here? What is the final effect? What is the writer's parting message to his readers?

WRITING

1. In a personal essay employing narration and description as well as analysis, describe the impact of computers on your family life. Use a comic approach to the subject.
2. Write an analysis of the elements of humor that appear in Sedaris's essay. Why is comedy an appropriate strategy for dealing with the subject of computer technology?
3. **Writing an Argument:** Write an essay about why you love or hate computers. Use ironic humor to undercut your argument—to convince readers that your opinions are actually the opposite of what you proclaim.

NETWORKING
Applying 21st-Century Literacies

Using Technology (and Humor) to Critique Technology: Make your response to question 3 under Writing even more humorous by employing specific aspects of technology just as you are declaring your dislike for or frustration with them. For instance, you might create a blog that complains about bloggers, or bemoan the lack of focus in hyperlinked texts in an essay that is rife with linkage. Have a little fun with this one.

How Computers Change the Way We Think

Sherry Turkle

Sherry Turkle (b. 1948), born and raised in New York City, attended Harvard University where she received her BA (1970), MA (1973), and PhD (1976). A professor in the Program in Science, Technology, and Society at the Massachusetts Institute of Technology, Turkle observes: "I study the sociology of sciences of mind, a study of the interactions among technical, literary, and popular discourses about the self as they develop in specific social contexts." The results of Turkle's research appear in Psychoanalytic Politics: Freud's French Revolution *(1992),* The Second Self: Computers and the Human Spirit *(1984),* Life on the Screen: Identity in the Age of the Internet *(1995) and* Simulation and Its Discontents *(2009). "My work on computation," Turkle states, "begins with the premise that we live in a nascent computer culture that will exert an analogous influence on the way we think"—an idea she explores in the following essay, which appeared in a 2004 issue of the* Chronicle of Higher Education.

The tools we use to think change the ways in which we think. The invention of written language brought about a radical shift in how we process, organize, store, and transmit representations of the world. Although writing remains our primary information technology, today when we think about the impact of technology on our habits of mind, we think primarily of the computer.

My first encounters with how computers change the way we think came soon after I joined the faculty at the Massachusetts Institute of Technology in the late 1970s, at the end of the era of the slide rule and the beginning of the era of the personal computer. At a lunch for new faculty members, several senior professors in engineering complained that the transition from slide rules to calculators had affected their students' ability to deal with issues of scale. When students used slide rules, they had to insert decimal points themselves. The professors insisted that that required students to maintain a mental sense of scale, whereas those who relied on calculators made frequent errors in orders of magnitude. Additionally, the students with calculators had lost their ability to do "back of the envelope" calculations, and with that, an intuitive feel for the material.

That same semester, I taught a course in the history of psychology. There, I experienced the impact of computational objects on students' ideas about their emotional lives. My class had read Freud's essay on slips of the tongue, with its famous first example: The chairman of a parliamentary session opens a meeting by declaring it closed. The students discussed how Freud interpreted such errors as revealing a person's mixed emotions. A computer-science major disagreed with Freud's approach. The mind, she argued, is a computer. And in a computational dictionary—like we have in the human mind—"closed" and "open" are designated by the same symbol, separated by a sign for opposition. "Closed" equals "minus open." To substitute "closed" for "open" does not require the notion of ambivalence or conflict.

4   "When the chairman made that substitution," she declared, "a bit was dropped; a minus sign was lost. There was a power surge. No problem."

5   The young woman turned a Freudian slip into an information-processing error. An explanation in terms of meaning had become an explanation in terms of mechanism.

6   Such encounters turned me to the study of both the instrumental and the subjective sides of the nascent computer culture. As an ethnographer and psychologist, I began to study not only what the computer was doing for us, but what it was doing to us, including how it was changing the way we see ourselves, our sense of human identity.

7   In the 1980s, I surveyed the psychological effects of computational objects in everyday life—largely the unintended side effects of people's tendency to project thoughts and feelings onto their machines. In the 20 years since, computational objects have become more explicitly designed to have emotional and cognitive effects. And those "effects by design" will become even stronger in the decade to come. Machines are being designed to serve explicitly as companions, pets, and tutors. And they are introduced in school settings for the youngest children.

8   Today, starting in elementary school, students use e-mail, word processing, computer simulations, virtual communities, and PowerPoint software. In the process, they are absorbing more than the content of what appears on their screens. They are learning new ways to think about what it means to know and understand.

9   What follows is a short and certainly not comprehensive list of areas where I see information technology encouraging changes in thinking. There can be no simple way of cataloging whether any particular change is good or bad. That is contested terrain. At every step we have to ask, as educators and citizens, whether current technology is leading us in directions that serve our human purposes. Such questions are not technical; they are social, moral, and political. For me, addressing that subjective side of computation is one of the more significant challenges for the next decade of information technology in higher education. Technology does not determine change, but it encourages us to take certain directions. If we make those directions clear, we can more easily exert human choice.

10   **Thinking about privacy.** Today's college students are habituated to a world of online blogging, instant messaging, and Web browsing that leaves electronic traces. Yet they have had little experience with the right to privacy. Unlike past generations of Americans, who grew up with the notion that the privacy of their mail was sacrosanct, our children are accustomed to electronic surveillance as part of their daily lives.

11   I have colleagues who feel that the increased incursions on privacy have put the topic more in the news, and that this is a positive change. But middle-school

and high-school students tend to be willing to provide personal information on-line with no safeguards, and college students seem uninterested in violations of privacy and in increased governmental and commercial surveillance. Professors find that students do not understand that in a democracy, privacy is a right, not merely a privilege. In 10 years, ideas about the relationship of privacy and gov-ernment will require even more active pedagogy. (One might also hope that in-creased education about the kinds of silent surveillance that technology makes possible may inspire more active political engagement with the issue.)

Avatars or a self? Chat rooms, role-playing games, and other technological 12 venues offer us many different contexts for presenting ourselves online. Those possibilities are particularly important for adolescents because they offer what Erik Erikson described as a moratorium, a time out or safe space for the per-sonal experimentation that is so crucial for adolescent development. Our dan-gerous world—with crime, terrorism, drugs, and AIDS—offers little in the way of safe spaces. Online worlds can provide valuable spaces for identity play.

But some people who gain fluency in expressing multiple aspects of self 13 may find it harder to develop authentic selves. Some children who write narra-tives for their screen avatars may grow up with too little experience of how to share their real feelings with other people. For those who are lonely yet afraid of intimacy, information technology has made it possible to have the illusion of companionship without the demands of friendship.

From powerful ideas to PowerPoint. In the 1970s and early 1980s, some 14 educators wanted to make programming part of the regular curriculum for K–12 education. They argued that because information technology carries ideas, it might as well carry the most powerful ideas that computer science has to offer. It is ironic that in most elementary schools today, the ideas being carried by information technology are not ideas from computer science like proce-dural thinking, but more likely to be those embedded in productivity tools like PowerPoint presentation software.

PowerPoint does more than provide a way of transmitting content. It carries 15 its own way of thinking, its own aesthetic—which not surprisingly shows up in the aesthetic of college freshmen. In that aesthetic, presentation becomes its own powerful idea.

To be sure, the software cannot be blamed for lower intellectual standards. 16 Misuse of the former is as much a symptom as a cause of the latter. Indeed, the culture in which our children are raised is increasingly a culture of presentation, a corporate culture in which appearance is often more important than reality. In contemporary political discourse, the bar has also been lowered. Use of rhetorical devices at the expense of cogent argument regularly goes without notice. But it is precisely because standards of intellectual rigor outside the educational sphere have fallen that educators must attend to how we use, and when we introduce, software that has been designed to simplify the organization and processing of information.

In *The Cognitive Style of PowerPoint* (Graphics Press, 2003), Edward R. Tufts 17 suggests that PowerPoint equates bulleting with clear thinking. It does not teach students to begin a discussion or construct a narrative. It encourages presentation, not conversation. Of course, in the hands of a master teacher, a PowerPoint presentation with few words and powerful images can serve as the jumping-off point for a brilliant lecture. But in the hands of elementary-school students, often introduced to PowerPoint in the third grade, and often infatuated with its swooshing sounds, animated icons, and flashing text, a slide show is more likely to close down debate than open it up.

18   Developed to serve the needs of the corporate boardroom, the software is designed to convey absolute authority. Teachers used to tell students that clear exposition depended on clear outlining, but presentation software has fetishized the outline at the expense of the content.

19   Narrative, the exposition of content, takes time. PowerPoint, like so much in the computer culture, speeds up the pace.

20   **Word processing vs. thinking.** The catalog for the Vermont Country Store advertises a manual typewriter, which the advertising copy says "moves at a pace that allows time to compose your thoughts." As many of us know, it is possible to manipulate text on a computer screen and see how it looks faster than we can think about what the words mean.

21   Word processing has its own complex psychology. From a pedagogical point of view, it can make dedicated students into better writers because it allows them to revise text, rearrange paragraphs, and experiment with the tone and shape of an essay. Few professional writers would part with their computers; some claim that they simply cannot think without their hands on the keyboard. Yet the ability to quickly fill the page, to see it before you can think it, can make bad writers even worse.

22   A seventh grader once told me that the typewriter she found in her mother's attic is "cool because you have to type each letter by itself. You have to know what you are doing in advance or it comes out a mess." The idea of thinking ahead has become exotic.

23   **Taking things at interface value.** We expect software to be easy to use, and we assume that we don't have to know how a computer works. In the early 1980s, most computer users who spoke of transparency meant that, as with any other machine, you could "open the hood" and poke around. But only a few years later, Macintosh users began to use the term when they talked about seeing their documents and programs represented by attractive and easy-to-interpret icons. They were referring to an ability to make things work without needing to go below the screen surface. Paradoxically, it was the screen's opacity that permitted that kind of transparency. Today, when people say that something is transparent, they mean that they can see how to make it work, not that they know how it works. In other words, transparency means epistemic opacity.

24   The people who built or bought the first generation of personal computers understood them down to the bits and bytes. The next generation of operating systems were more complex, but they still invited that old-time reductive understanding. Contemporary information technology encourages different habits of mind. Today's college students are already used to taking things at

(inter) face value; their successors in 2014 will be even less accustomed to probing below the surface.

Simulation and its discontents. Some thinkers argue that the new opacity ²⁵ is empowering, enabling anyone to use the most sophisticated technological tools and to experiment with simulation in complex and creative ways. But it is also true that our tools carry the message that they are beyond our understanding. It is possible that in daily life, epistemic opacity can lead to passivity.

I first became aware of that possibility in the early 1990s, when the first ²⁶ generation of complex simulation games were introduced and immediately became popular for home as well as school use. SimLife teaches the principles of evolution by getting children involved in the development of complex ecosystems; in that sense it is an extraordinary learning tool. During one session in which I played SimLife with Tim, a 13-year-old, the screen before us flashed a message: "Your orgot is being eaten up." "What's an orgot?" I asked. Tim didn't know. "I just ignore that," he said confidently. "You don't need to know that kind of stuff to play."

For me, that story serves as a cautionary tale. Computer simulations enable ²⁷ their users to think about complex phenomena as dynamic, evolving systems. But they also accustom us to manipulating systems whose core assumptions we may not understand and that may not be true.

We live in a culture of simulation. Our games, our economic and political sys- ²⁸ tems, and the ways architects design buildings, chemists envisage molecules, and surgeons perform operations all use simulation technology. In 10 years the degree to which simulations are embedded in every area of life will have increased exponentially. We need to develop a new form of media literacy: readership for the culture of simulation.

We come to written text with habits of readership based on centuries of ²⁹ civilization. At the very least, we have learned to begin with the journalist's traditional questions: who, what, when, where, why, and how. Who wrote these words, what is their message, why were they written, and how are they situated in time and place, politically and socially? A central project for higher education during the next 10 years should be creating programs in information-technology literacy, with the goal of teaching students to interrogate simulations in much the same spirit, challenging their built-in assumptions.

Despite the ever-increasing complexity of software, most computer envi- ³⁰ ronments put users in worlds based on constrained choices. In other words, immersion in programmed worlds puts us in reassuring environments where the rules are clear. For example, when you play a video game, you often go through a series of frightening situations that you escape by mastering the rules—you experience life as a reassuring dichotomy of scary and safe. Children grow up in a culture of video games, action films, fantasy epics, and computer programs that all rely on that familiar scenario of almost losing but then regaining total mastery: There is danger. It is mastered. A still-more-powerful monster appears. It is subdued. Scary. Safe.

Yet in the real world, we have never had a greater need to work our way ³¹ out of binary assumptions. In the decade ahead, we need to rebuild the culture around information technology. In that new sociotechnical culture, assumptions about the nature of mastery would be less absolute. The new culture would make it easier, not more difficult, to consider life in shades of gray, to see moral dilemmas in terms other than a battle between Good and Evil. For never has our world been more complex, hybridized, and global. Never have we so needed to have many contradictory thoughts and feelings at the same time. Our tools must help us accomplish that, not fight against us.

32   Information technology is identity technology. Embedding it in a culture that supports democracy, freedom of expression, tolerance, diversity, and complexity of opinion is one of the next decade's greatest challenges. We cannot afford to fail.

33   When I first began studying the computer culture, a small breed of highly trained technologists thought of themselves as "computer people." That is no longer the case. If we take the computer as a carrier of a way of knowing, a way of seeing the world and our place in it, we are all computer people now.

COMPREHENSION

1. According to Turkle, in what ways do computers change the ways we think?
2. What does Turkle mean by "the instrumental and subjective sides of nascent computer culture" (paragraph 6)? What examples of these two sides does she offer?
3. What are some of the challenges facing the "sociotechnical culture" Turkle says we are entering?

RHETORIC

1. Turkle published this essay in a weekly newspaper designed for people in higher education. What stylistic elements suggest that she gears her writing to this specialized audience? How does she make the article accessible to a broader, secondary audience?
2. What is Turkle's thesis, and where does she state it?
3. How does Turkle use classification to advance her thesis and organize the essay? Where does she employ process and causal analysis?
4. What comparative points does the writer draw between actual and virtual reality?
5. Turkle's paragraphs are relatively brief, some no more than two or three sentences. Why does she employ this method? Does this strategy ruin the coherence of the essay or weaken the emphasis on certain ideas? Why or why not?
6. In the final analysis, does Turkle prove the point made in the final paragraph, that "we are all computer people now"?

WRITING

1. Using Turkle's essay as a model, write a classification essay on the ways that computers are changing the way we think.
2. Select one area where information technology is changing our processes and habits of thought, and write an essay explaining this phenomenon.

3. **Writing an Argument:** Do you agree or disagree with Turkle's assertion that information technology can foster democracy? Write a persuasive essay that articulates your position on the issue.

NETWORKING
Applying 21st-Century Literacies

Using Images to Strengthen a Classification Essay: Enhance question 1 under Writing by incorporating four or five images that help illustrate the classifications you put forth in the essay. Take care to use images purposefully, not merely for decoration.

Can We Know the Universe? Reflections on a Grain of Salt

Carl Sagan

Carl Edward Sagan (1931–1996) received BA, BS, MA, and PhD degrees from the University of Chicago. Probably the most popular scientist in America in the 1970s and 1980s, he was the host of several television series on science and wrote a number of best-selling books on science, including The Dragons of Eden *(1977) and* Broca's Brain *(1979). The former earned him a Pulitzer prize for general nonfiction in 1978. He also contributed hundreds of papers to scientific journals. Besides writing, Sagan served as a full-time professor at Cornell University and a visiting professor at dozens of other institutions of higher learning in the United States and abroad. He was also an activist for many philanthropic causes and served as an advisor to groups such as the Council for a Livable World Education Fund, the Children's Health Fund, and the American Committee on U.S.– Soviet Relations. Despite controversies surrounding the speculative nature of his work, Carl Sagan was one of modern science's most popular spokespersons. Sagan's philosophy may be summed up in a statement he made in a* Time *interview: "We make our world significant by the courage of our questions and by the depth of our answers."*

Nothing is rich but the inexhaustible wealth of nature. She shows us only surfaces, but she is a million fathoms deep.

—Ralph Waldo Emerson

Science is a way of thinking much more than it is a body of knowledge. Its goal 1 is to find out how the world works, to seek what regularities there may be, to penetrate to the connections of things—from subnuclear particles, which may be the constituents of all matter, to living organisms, the human social community, and thence to the cosmos as a whole. Our intuition is by no means an infallible guide. Our perceptions may be distorted by training and prejudice or merely because of the limitations of our sense organs, which, of course, perceive directly but a small fraction of the phenomena of the world. Even so straightforward a question as whether in the absence of friction a pound of lead falls faster than a gram of fluff was answered incorrectly by Aristotle and almost everyone else before the time of Galileo. Science is based on experiment, on a willingness to challenge old dogma, on an openness to see the universe as it really is. Accordingly, science sometimes requires courage—at the very least the courage to question the conventional wisdom.

2   Beyond this the main trick of science is to *really* think of something: the shape of clouds and their occasional sharp bottom edges at the same altitude everywhere in the sky; the formation of a dewdrop on a leaf; the origin of a name or a word—Shakespeare, say, or "philanthropic"; the reason for human social customs—the incest taboo, for example; how it is that a lens in sunlight can make paper burn; how a "walking stick" got to look so much like a twig; why the Moon seems to follow us as we walk; what prevents us from digging a hole down to the center of the Earth; what the definition is of "down" on a spherical Earth; how it is possible for the body to convert yesterday's lunch into today's muscle and sinew; or how far is up—does the universe go on forever, or if it does not, is there any meaning to the question of what lies on the other side? Some of these questions are pretty easy. Others, especially the last, are mysteries to which no one even today knows the answer. They are natural questions to ask. Every culture has posed such questions in one way or another. Almost always the proposed answers are in the nature of "Just So Stories," attempted explanations divorced from experiment, or even from careful comparative observations.

3   But the scientific cast of mind examines the world critically as if many alternative worlds might exist, as if other things might be here which are not. Then we are forced to ask why what we see is present and not something else. Why are the Sun and the Moon and the planets spheres? Why not pyramids, or cubes, or dodecahedra? Why not irregular, jumbly shapes? Why so symmetrical worlds? If you spend any time spinning hypotheses, checking to see whether they make sense, whether they conform to what else we know, thinking of tests you can pose to substantiate or deflate your hypotheses, you will find yourself doing science. And as you come to practice this habit of thought more and more you will get better and better at it. To penetrate into the heart of the thing—even a little thing, a blade of grass, as Walt Whitman said—is to experience a kind of exhilaration that, it may be, only human beings of all the beings on this planet can feel. We are an intelligent species and the use of our intelligence quite properly gives us pleasure. In this respect the brain is like a muscle. When we think well, we feel good. Understanding is a kind of ecstasy.

4   But to what extent can we *really* know the universe around us? Sometimes this question is posed by people who hope the answer will be in the negative, who are fearful of a universe in which everything might one day be known. And sometimes we hear pronouncements from scientists who confidently state that everything worth knowing will soon be known—or even is already

known—and who paint pictures of a Dionysian or Polynesian age in which the zest for intellectual discovery has withered, to be replaced by a kind of subdued languor, the lotus eaters drinking fermented coconut milk or some other mild hallucinogen. In addition to maligning both the Polynesians, who were intrepid explorers (and whose brief respite in paradise is now sadly ending), as well as the inducements to intellectual discovery provided by some hallucinogens, this contention turns out to be trivially mistaken.

Let us approach a much more modest question: not whether we can know   5 the universe or the Milky Way Galaxy or a star or a world. Can we know, ultimately and in detail, a grain of salt? Consider one microgram of table salt, a speck just barely large enough for someone with keen eyesight to make out without a microscope. In that grain of salt there are about 10^{16} sodium and chlorine atoms. This is a 1 followed by 16 zeros, 10 million billion atoms. If we wish to know a grain of salt, we must know at least the three-dimensional positions of each of these atoms. (In fact, there is much more to be known—for example, the nature of the forces between the atoms—but we are making only a modest calculation.) Now, is this number more or less than the number of things which the brain can know?

How much *can* the brain know? There are perhaps 10^{11} neurons in the brain,   6 the circuit elements and switches that are responsible in their electrical and chemical activity for the functioning of our minds. A typical brain neuron has perhaps a thousand little wires, called dendrites, which connect it with its fellows. If, as seems likely, every bit of information in the brain corresponds to one of these connections, the total number of things knowable by the brain is no more than 10^{14}, one hundred trillion. But this number is only one percent of the number of atoms in our speck of salt.

So in this sense the universe is intractable, astonishingly immune to any   7 human attempt at full knowledge. We cannot on this level understand a grain of salt, much less the universe.

But let us look a little more deeply at our microgram of salt. Salt happens to   8 be a crystal in which, except for defects in the structure of the crystal lattice, the position of every sodium and chlorine atom is predetermined. If we could shrink ourselves into this crystalline world, we would see rank upon rank of atoms in an ordered array, a regularly alternating structure—sodium, chlorine, sodium, chlorine, specifying the sheet of atoms we are standing on and all the sheets above us and below us. An absolutely pure crystal of salt could have the position of every atom specified by something like 10 bits of information.[1] This would not strain the information-carrying capacity of the brain.

If the universe had natural laws that governed its behavior to the same de-   9 gree of regularity that determines a crystal of salt, then, of course, the universe

[1]Chlorine is a deadly poison gas employed on European battlefields in World War I. Sodium is a corrosive metal which burns upon contact with water. Together they make a placid and unpoisonous material, table salt. Why each of these substances has the properties it does is a subject called chemistry, which requires more than 10 bits of information to understand.

would be knowable. Even if there were many such laws, each of considerable complexity, human beings might have the capability to understand them all. Even if such knowledge exceeded the information-carrying capacity of the brain, we might store the additional information outside our bodies—in books, for example, or in computer memories—and still, in some sense, know the universe.

10   Human beings are, understandably, highly motivated to find regularities, natural laws. The search for rules, the only possible way to understand such a vast and complex universe, is called science. The universe forces those who live in it to understand it. Those creatures who find everyday experience a muddled jumble of events with no predictability, no regularity, are in grave peril. The universe belongs to those who, at least to some degree, have figured it out.

11   It is an astonishing fact that there *are* laws of nature, rules that summarize conveniently—not just qualitatively but quantitatively—how the world works. We might imagine a universe in which there are no such laws, in which the 10^{80} elementary particles that make up a universe like our own behave with utter and uncompromising abandon. To understand such a universe we would need a brain at least as massive as the universe. It seems unlikely that such a universe could have life and intelligence, because beings and brains require some degree of internal stability and order. But even if in a much more random universe there were such beings with an intelligence much greater than our own, there could not be much knowledge, passion or joy.

12   Fortunately for us, we live in a universe that has at least important parts that are knowable. Our common-sense experience and our evolutionary history have prepared us to understand something of the workaday world. When we go into other realms, however, common sense and ordinary intuition turn out to be highly unreliable guides. It is stunning that as we go close to the speed of light our mass increases indefinitely, we shrink toward zero thickness in the direction of motion, and time for us comes as near to stopping as we would like. Many people think that this is silly, and every week or two I get a letter from someone who complains to me about it. But it is a virtually certain consequence not just of experiment but also of Albert Einstein's brilliant analysis of space and time called the Special Theory of Relativity. It does not matter that these effects seem unreasonable to us. We are not in the habit of traveling close to the speed of light. The testimony of our common sense is suspect at high velocities.

13   Or consider an isolated molecule composed of two atoms shaped something like a dumbbell—a molecule of salt, it might be. Such a molecule rotates about an axis through the line connecting the two atoms. But in the world of quantum mechanics, the realm of the very small, not all orientations of our dumbbell molecule are possible. It might be that the molecule could be oriented in a horizontal position, say, or in a vertical position, but not at many angles in between. Some rotational positions are forbidden. Forbidden by what? By the laws of nature. The universe is built in such a way as to limit, or quantize, rotation. We do not experience this directly in everyday life; we would find it startling as well as awkward in sitting-up exercises, to find arms outstretched from the sides or pointed up to the skies permitted but

many intermediate positions forbidden. We do not live in the world of the small, on the scale of 10^{-13} centimeters, in the realm where there are twelve zeros between the decimal place and the one. Our common-sense intuitions do not count. What does count is experiment—in this case observations from the far infrared spectra of molecules. They show molecular rotation to be quantized.

The idea that the world places restrictions on what humans might do is 14
frustrating. Why *shouldn't* we be able to have intermediate rotational positions? Why *can't* we travel faster than the speed of light? But so far as we can tell, this is the way the universe is constructed. Such prohibitions not only press us toward a little humility; they also make the world more knowable. Every restriction corresponds to a law of nature, a regularization of the universe. The more restrictions there are on what matter and energy can do, the more knowledge human beings can attain. Whether in some sense the universe is ultimately knowable depends not only on how many natural laws there are that encompass widely divergent phenomena, but also on whether we have the openness and the intellectual capacity to understand such laws. Our formulations of the regularities of nature are surely dependent on how the brain is built, but also, and to a significant degree, on how the universe is built.

For myself, I like a universe that includes much that is unknown and, at the 15
same time, much that is knowable. A universe in which everything is known would be static and dull, as boring as the heaven of some weak-minded theologians. A universe that is unknowable is no fit place for a thinking being. The ideal universe for us is one very much like the universe we inhabit. And I would guess that this is not really much of a coincidence.

COMPREHENSION

1. What is the thesis of the essay? In what paragraph is this thesis most clearly expressed?
2. Why does Sagan say, in paragraph 12, that in many circumstances, "common sense and ordinary intuition turn out to be highly unreliable guides"?
3. Why does Sagan say, in his conclusion, that "the ideal universe for us is one very much like the universe we inhabit"?

RHETORIC

1. What is the function of the epigram by Emerson? How does it relate to the essay proper?
2. Many of the paragraphs in the essay begin with coordinating conjunctions (a structure frowned on by many high school English teachers). What is Sagan's rhetorical purpose in using them as connecting devices?
3. What specific clues are there in the essay that Sagan's tone is one of excitement and celebration regarding science?
4. Sagan refers often to what he calls "a law of nature." Where and how in the essay does he explain, describe, or define this term?

5. The essay begins abruptly with an explanation of the concept of science. What purpose is served by diving into the subject so dramatically?
6. What is the intended effect of combining the terms *universe* and *grain of salt* in the title and subtitle? How does the author exploit this juxtaposition in his essay?
7. Examine the italicized words in the essay. Why has Sagan chosen to italicize these words? Explain.

WRITING

1. Write a personal essay in which you describe how you felt when you suddenly understood a particular topic in school that had previously eluded you.
2. For a research paper, select one of the items Sagan enumerates in paragraph 2, such as "the formation of a dewdrop on a leaf," the origin of the name *Shakespeare* or the word *philanthropic*, "the incest taboo," or "how a 'walking stick' got to look so much like a twig." Write an expository essay on your topic.
3. **Writing an Argument:** Argue for or against the proposition that scientific knowledge takes the mystery out of life.

NETWORKING
Applying 21st-Century Literacies

Using a Blog Entry as Prewriting for a Larger Assignment: Before you begin either question 1, 2, or 3 under Writing, get your thoughts (and maybe even some preliminary research) down by posting a blog entry that responds to the prompt. Depending on your work style, articulating your initial thoughts in a public forum might jump-start your essay even more than private prewriting would.

Staying Human

Dinesh D'Souza

Dinesh D'Souza, a leading conservative thinker, was born in Bombay, India, and came to the United States for his high school education. He graduated from Dartmouth College (BA, 1983) and subsequently wrote for several magazines, notably the National Review, *before becoming a policy analyst for the Reagan administration. His books include* Illiberal Education: The Politics of Race and Sex on Campus *(1991),* The End of Racism: Principles for a Multicultural Society *(1995),* The Virtue of Prosperity: Finding Values in an Age of Techno-Affluence *(2001),* What's So Great about America *(2002),* What's So Great about Christianity *(2007), and* The Enemy at Home: The Cultural Left and Its Responsibility for 9/11 *(2007). D'Souza has been a visiting scholar at the Hoover Institution and a research scholar at the American Enterprise Institute. In the following essay, written for the* National Review *in 2001, D'Souza offers a wide-ranging assessment of our emerging "techno-utopia."*

We are as gods, and we might as well get good at it.
—Kevin Kelly, author and techno-utopian

The most important technological advance of recent times is not the Internet, but rather the biotech revolution—which promises to give us unprecedented power to transform human nature. How should we use that power? A group of cutting-edge scientists, entrepreneurs, and intellectuals has a bold answer. This group—I call them the techno-utopians—argues that science will soon give us the means to straighten the crooked timber of humanity, and even to remake our species into something "post-human." 1

One of the leading techno-utopians is Lee Silver, who teaches molecular biology at Princeton University. Silver reports that biotechnology is moving beyond cloning to offer us a momentous possibility: designer children. He envisions that, in the not too distant future, couples who want to have a child will review a long list of traits on a computer screen, put together combinations of "virtual children," decide on the one they want, click on the appropriate selection, and thus—in effect—design their own offspring. "Parents are going to be able to give their children . . . genes that increase athletic ability, genes that increase musical talents . . . and ultimately genes that affect cognitive abilities." 2

But even this, the techno-utopians say, is a relatively small step: People living today can determine the genetic destiny of all future generations. Some writers, including physicist Stephen Hawking, have suggested that genetic engineering could be used to reduce human aggression, thus solving the crime problem and making war less likely. James Watson, co-discoverer of the structure of DNA, argues that if biological interventions could be used to "cure what I feel is a very serious disease—that is, stupidity—it would be a great thing for people." Silver himself forecasts a general elevation of intellectual, athletic, temperamental, and artistic abilities so that we can over time create "a special group of mental beings" who will "trace their ancestry back to Homo sapiens," but who will be "as different from humans as humans are from the primitive worms with tiny brains that first crawled along the earth's surface." 3

These ideas might seem implausible, but they are taken very seriously by some of the best minds in the scientific community. The confidence of the techno-utopians is based on stunning advances that have made cloning and genetic engineering feasible. In theoretical terms, biotechnology crossed a major threshold with James Watson and Francis Crick's 1953 discovery of the structure of DNA, but practical applications were slow in coming. In 1997, an obscure animal-husbandry laboratory in Scotland cloned a sheep named Dolly; today, the knowledge and the means of cloning human beings already exist, and the only question is whether we are going to do it. And why stop there? As the scientific journal *Nature* editorialized shortly after the emergence of Dolly, 4

"The growing power of molecular genetics confronts us with future prospects of being able to change the nature of our species."

5   In 1999, neurobiologist Joe Tsien boosted the intelligence of mice by inserting extra copies of a gene that enhances memory and learning; these mouse genes are virtually identical to those found in human beings. Gene therapy has already been successfully carried out in people, and now that the Human Genome Project has made possible a comprehensive understanding of the human genetic code, scientists will possess a new kind of power: the power to design our children, and even to redesign humanity itself.

The Hitler Scenario

6 The fact that these things are possible does not, of course, mean that they should be done. As one might expect, cloning and genetic engineering are attracting criticism. The techno-utopians have not yet made their products and services available to consumers; but one can reasonably expect that a society that is anxious about eating genetically modified tomatoes is going to be vastly more anxious about a scheme to engineer our offspring and our species.

7   A recent book communicating that sense of outrage is Jeremy Rifkin's *The Biotech Century*. Rifkin alleges that we are heading for a nightmarish future "where babies are genetically designed and customized in the womb, and where people are identified, stereotyped and discriminated against on the basis of their genotype." How can living beings be considered sacred, Rifkin asks, if they are treated as nothing more than "bundles of genetic information"? Biotechnology, he charges, is launching us into a new age of eugenics. In Rifkin's view, the Nazi idea of the superman is very much alive, but now in a different form: the illusion of the "perfect child."

8   Although Rifkin has a propensity for inflammatory rhetoric, he is raising some important concerns: The new technology is unprecedented, so we should be very cautious in developing it. It poses grave risks to human health. Cloning and genetic engineering are unnatural; human beings have no right to do this to nature and to ourselves.

9   These criticisms meet with derision on the part of the techno-utopians. Every time a major new technology is developed, they say, there are people who forecast the apocalypse. The techno-utopians point out that the new technology will deliver amazing medical benefits, including cures for genetic diseases. How can it be ethical, they ask, to withhold these technologies from people who need and want them?

10   Lee Silver, the biologist, is annoyed at critics such as Rifkin who keep raising the specter of Hitler and eugenics. "It is individuals and couples, not governments, who will seize control of these new technologies," Silver writes. The premise of the techno-utopians is that if the market produces a result, it is good. In this view, what is wrong with the old eugenics is not that it sought to eliminate defective types and produce a superior kind of being, but that it sought to do so in a coercive and collectivist way. The new advocates of biotechnology speak approvingly of what they term "free-market eugenics."

The champions of biotechnology concede that cloning and genetic 11 engineering should not be permitted in human beings until they are safe. But "safe," they say, does not mean "error-free"; it means safe compared with existing forms of reproduction. And they are confident that the new forms of reproduction will soon be as safe as giving birth the natural way.

The techno-utopians are also not very concerned that the availability of en- 12 hancement technologies will create two classes in society, the genetically advantaged and the genetically disadvantaged. They correctly point to the fact that two such classes exist now, even in the absence of new therapies. Physicist Freeman Dyson says that genetic enhancement might be costly at first, but won't remain permanently expensive: "Most of our socially important technologies, such as telephones, automobiles, television, and computers, began as expensive toys for the rich and afterwards became cheap enough for ordinary people."

Dyson is right that time will make genetic enhancements more widely avail- 13 able, just as cars and TV sets are now. But the poor family still drives a second-hand Plymouth while the rich family can afford a new Porsche. This may not be highly significant when it comes to cars, because both groups can still get around fairly well. What about when it comes to genetic advantages conferred at birth? Democratic societies can live with inequalities conferred by the lottery of nature, but can they countenance the deliberate introduction of biological alterations that give some citizens a better chance to succeed than others?

The techno-utopians have not, to my knowledge, addressed this concern. 14 They emphasize instead that it is well established in law, and widely recognized in society, that parents have a right to determine what is best for their children. "There are already plenty of ways in which we design our children," remarks biologist Gregory Stock. "One of them is called piano lessons. Another is called private school." Stock's point is that engineering their children's genes is simply one more way in which parents can make their children better people.

Some people might find it weird and unnatural to fix their child in the same 15 way they fix their car—but, say the techno-utopians, this is purely a function of habit. We're not used to genetic engineering, so it seems "unnatural" to us. But think about how unnatural driving a car seemed for people who previously got around on horses and in carriages. "The smallpox virus was part of the natural order," Silver wryly observes, "until it was forced into extinction by human intervention." Diseases and death are natural; life-saving surgery is unnatural.

Not Sacred after All?

Nor are the techno-utopians worried about diminishing the sanctity of human 16 life because, they say, it isn't intrinsically sacred. "This is not an ethical argument but a religious one," says Silver. "There is no logic to it." Biologist David Baltimore, a Nobel laureate, argues that "statements about morally and ethically unacceptable practices" have no place in the biotechnology debate "because those are subjective grounds and therefore provide no basis for discussion." Silver and Baltimore's shared assumption is that the moralists are talking about values while they, the hard scientists, are dealing in facts.

17   In this view, the subjective preferences of those who seek to mystify human life do not square with the truths about human biology taught by science. The cells of human beings, Silver points out, are not different in their chemical makeup from the cells of horses and bacteria. If there is such a thing as human dignity, Silver argues, it derives exclusively from consciousness, from our ability to perceive and apprehend our environment. "The human mind," Silver writes, "is much more than the genes that brought it into existence." Somehow the electrochemical reactions in our brain produce consciousness, and it is this consciousness, Silver contends, that is the source of man's autonomy and power. While genes fully control the activity of all life forms, Silver writes that in human beings "master and slave have switched positions." Consciousness enables man to complete his dominance over nature by prevailing over his human nature. Silver concludes that, in a bold assertion of will, we can defeat the program of our genes, we can take over the reins of evolution, we can choose the genetic code we want for our children, and we can collectively determine the future of our species.

18   This triumphant note is echoed by many techno-utopians. Biotech, writes journalist Ronald Bailey, "will liberate future generations from today's limitations and offer them a much wider scope of freedom." Physicist Gregory Benford is even more enthusiastic: "It is as though prodigious, bountiful Nature for billions of years has tossed off variations on its themes like a careless, prolific Picasso. Now Nature finds that one of its casual creations has come back with a piercing, searching vision, and its own pictures to paint."

19   These are ringing statements. But do they make sense? Clearly there are many problems with Silver's definition of human dignity as based in consciousness. Animals are conscious; do they deserve the same dignity as human beings? Moreover, are human beings entitled to dignity only when they are conscious? Do we lose our right to be respected, and become legitimate subjects for discarding medical experiments, when we fall asleep, or into a coma? Surely Silver would disavow these conclusions. They do, however, flow directly from his definition, which is, in fact, just as heavily freighted with values as are the statements of his opponents.

20   There is, behind the proclamations of scientific neutrality, an ideology that needs to be spelled out, a techno-Nietzschean doctrine that proclaims: We are molecules, but molecules that know how to rebel. Our values do not derive from nature or nature's God; rather, they arise from the arbitrary force of our wills. And now our wills can make the most momentous choice ever exercised on behalf of our species: the choice to reject our human nature. Why should we remain subject to the constraints of our mortality and destiny? Wealth and technology have given us the keys to unlimited, indeed godlike, power: the dawn of the post-human era.

21   What is one to make of all this? In many respects, we should celebrate the advent of technologies that enable us to alleviate suffering and extend life. I have no problem with genetic therapy to cure disease; I am even willing to endorse therapy that not only cures illness in patients but also prevents it from being transmitted to the next generation. Under certain circumstances, I can see the benefits of cloning. The cloning of animals can provide organs for transplant as

well as animals with medicinal properties ("drugstores on the hoof"). Even human cloning seems defensible when it offers the prospect of a biological child to married couples who might not otherwise be able to have one.

Creating the Perfect Child

But there is a seduction contained in these exercises in humanitarianism: They urge us to keep going, to take the next step. And when we take that step, when we start designing our children, when we start remaking human beings, I think we will have crossed a perilous frontier. Even cloning does not cross this frontier, because it merely replicates an existing genetic palate. It is unconvincing to argue, as some techno-utopians do, that giving a child a heightened genetic capacity for music or athletics or intelligence is no different from giving a child piano, swimming, or math lessons. In fact, there is a big difference. It is one thing to take a person's given nature and given capacity, and seek to develop it, and quite another to shape that person's nature in accordance with one's will.

There is no reason to object to people's attempting brain implants and somatic gene enhancements on themselves. Perhaps, in some cases, these will do some good; others may end up doing injury. But at least these people have, through their free choices, done it to themselves. The problem arises when people seek to use enhancement technologies to shape the destiny of others, and especially their children.

But, argues Lee Silver, we have the right to terminate pregnancy and control our children's lives in every other way; why shouldn't parents be permitted to alter their child's genetic constitution? In the single instance of gene therapy to cure disease, I'd agree—because, in this one limited case, we can trust the parents to make a decision that there is every rational reason to believe their offspring would decide in the identical manner, were they in a position to make the choice. No child would say, "I can't believe my parents did that to me. I would have chosen to have Parkinson's disease."

But I would contend that in no other case do people have the right to bend the genetic constitution of their children—or anyone else—to their will. But they might, in good conscience, be tempted to do so; and this temptation must be resisted. Indeed, it must be outlawed—because what the techno-utopians want does, in fact, represent a fundamental attack on the value of human life, and the core principle of America.

Rescuing Humanity and the American Idea

The scientific-capitalist project at the heart of the American experiment was an attempted "conquest of nature." Never did the early philosophers of science, like Francis Bacon, or the American Founders conceive that this enterprise would eventually seek to conquer human nature. Their goal was to take human nature as a given, as something less elevated than the angels, and thus requiring a government characterized by separation of offices, checks and balances, limited power. At the same time, the Founders saw human nature as more elevated than that of other animals. They held that human beings have claims to dignity and rights that do not extend to animals: Human beings cannot be killed for sport or rightfully governed without their consent.

27   The principles of the Founders were extremely far-reaching. They called into question the legitimacy of every existing government, because at the time of the American founding, no government in the world was entirely based on the consent of the governed. The ideals of the Founders even called into question their own practices, such as slavery. It took the genius of Abraham Lincoln, and the tragedy of the Civil War, to compel the enforcement of the central principle of the Declaration of Independence: that we each have an inalienable right to life, liberty, and the pursuit of happiness, and that these rights shall not be abridged without our consent.

28   The attempt to enhance and redesign other human beings represents a flagrant denial of this principle that is the basis of our dignity and rights. Indeed, it is a restoration of the principle underlying slavery, and the argument between the defenders and critics of genetic enhancement is identical in principle, and very nearly in form, to the argument between Stephen Douglas and Abraham Lincoln on the issue of human enslavement.

29   In that tempestuous exchange, which laid the groundwork for the Civil War, Douglas argued for the pro-choice position. He wanted to let each new territory decide for itself whether it wanted slavery. He wanted the American people to agree to disagree on the issue. He advocated for each community a very high value: the right to self-determination.

30   Lincoln challenged him on the grounds that choice cannot be exercised without reference to the content of the choice. How can it make sense to permit people to choose to enslave another human being? How can self-determination be invoked to deny others the same? A free people can disagree on many things, but it cannot disagree on the distinction between freedom and despotism. Lincoln summarized Douglas's argument as follows: "If any one man choose to enslave another, no third man shall be allowed to object."

31   Lincoln's argument was based on a simple premise: "As I would not be a slave, so I would not be a master." Lincoln rejects in principle the subordination implied in the master-slave relationship. Those who want freedom for themselves, he insists, must also show themselves willing to extend it to others. At its deepest level, Lincoln's argument is that the legitimacy of popular consent is itself dependent on a doctrine of natural rights that arises out of a specific understanding of human nature and human dignity. "Slavery," he said, "is founded in the selfishness of man's nature-opposition to it, in his love of justice. These principles are in eternal antagonism; and when brought into collision so fiercely . . . convulsions must ceaselessly follow." What Lincoln is saying is that self-interest by itself is too base a foundation for the new experiment called America. Selfishness is part of our nature, but it is not the best part of our nature. It should be subordinated to a nobler ideal. Lincoln seeks to dedicate America to a higher proposition: the proposition that all men are created equal. It is the denial of this truth, Lincoln warns, that will bring on the cataclysm.

Let me restate Lincoln's position for our current context. We speak of "our 32
children," but they are not really ours; we do not own them. At most, we own
ourselves. It is true that *Roe v. Wade* gives us the right to kill our unborn in the
womb. The right to abortion has been defended, both by its advocates and by
the Supreme Court, as the right of a woman to control her own body. This is not
the same as saying the woman has ownership of the fetus, that the fetus is the
woman's property. The Supreme Court has said that as long as the fetus is
occupying her womb, she can treat it as an unwelcome intruder, and get rid of
it. (Even here, technology is changing the shape of the debate by moving up
the period when the fetus can survive outside the womb.) But once a woman
decides to carry the pregnancy to term, she has already exercised her choice.
She has chosen to give birth to the child, which is in the process of becoming
an independent human being with its own dignity and rights.

No Place for Parental Tyranny

As parents, we have been entrusted with our children, and it is our privilege 33
and responsibility to raise them as best we can. Undoubtedly we will infuse
them with our values and expectations, but even so, the good parent will respect the child's right to follow his own path. There is something perversely
restrictive about parents who apply relentless pressure on their children to
conform to their will—to follow the same professional paths that they did, or to
become the "first doctor in the family." These efforts, however well intentioned,
are a betrayal of the true meaning of parenthood. Indeed, American culture
encourages a certain measure of adolescent rebellion against parental expectations, precisely so that young people making the transition to independence
can "find themselves" and discover their own identity.

Consequently, parents have no right to treat their children as chattels; but 34
this is precisely the enterprise that is being championed by the techno-utopians.
Some of these people profess to be libertarians, but they are in fact totalitarians.
They speak about freedom and choice, although what they advocate is despotism and human bondage. The power they seek to exercise is not over "nature"
but over other human beings.

Parents who try to design their children are in some ways more tyrannical 35
than slaveowners, who merely sought to steal the labor of their slaves. Undoubtedly some will protest that they only wish the best for their children, that
they are only doing this for their own good. But the slaveowners made similar
arguments, saying that they ruled the Negroes in the Negroes' own interest.
The argument was as self-serving then as it is now. What makes us think that in
designing our children it will be their objective good—rather than our desires
and preferences—that will predominate?

The argument against slavery is that you may not tyrannize over the life and 36
freedom of another person for any reason whatsoever. Even that individual's
consent cannot overturn "inalienable" rights: One does not have the right to sell
oneself into slavery. This is the clear meaning of the American proposition. The

object of the American Revolution that is now spreading throughout the world has always been the affirmation, not the repudiation, of human nature. The Founders envisioned technology and capitalism as providing the framework and the tools for human beings to live richer, fuller lives. They would have scorned, as we should, the preposterous view that we are the servants of our technology. They would have strenuously opposed, as we should, the effort on the part of the techno-utopians to design their offspring; to alter, improve, and perfect human nature; or to relinquish our humanity in pursuit of some post-human ideal.

37   Mary Shelley's 1818 novel *Frankenstein* describes a monster that is the laboratory creation of a doctor who refuses to accept the natural limits of humanity. He wants to appropriate to himself the traditional prerogatives of the deity, such as control over human mortality. He even talks about making "a new species" with "me as its creator and source." In his rhetoric, Frankenstein sounds very much like today's techno-utopians. And, contrary to what most people think, the real monster in the novel isn't the lumbering, tragic creature; it is the doctor who creates him. This is the prophetic message of Shelley's work: In seeking to become gods, we are going to make monsters of ourselves.

COMPREHENSION

1. What is the meaning of D'Souza's title? According to the writer, what are the dangers we face in our effort to "stay human"? What must we do to retain our essential humanity?
2. What aspects of the biotech revolution does the author treat? What is his opinion of each?
3. What does the writer mean by the "Hitler Scenario" and the "American Idea"?

RHETORIC

1. What is D'Souza's purpose? What is his tone? Does he seem reasonable or unnecessarily argumentative? Objective or biased? How do you know? For what type of audience does he seem to be writing?
2. D'Souza begins his essay by introducing the ideas of such "leading techno-utopians" as Lee Silver, Stephen Hawking, James Watson and Francis Crick, and Joe Tsien. It this an effective opening strategy? Why or why not?
3. Explain the author's claim. What minor propositions does he provide? Where does he advance logical, ethical, and emotional appeals? Cite instances in which he employs refutation to advance his argument. What faults does he find with the techno-utopians?
4. Consider the essay's section headings. How do they serve to focus the content of each section? What characterizes the progression of ideas from section to section? How does the author's decision to divide the essay into sections help him to construct his argument?
5. Does D'Souza reveal any of his own biases in this essay? Explain.
6. In the concluding paragraph, D'Souza alludes to Mary Shelley's novel *Frankenstein*. Does this allusion flow naturally from the introduction and body? Why or why not?

WRITING

1. Write a 300-word summary of this essay, transcribing all of the main aspects of D'Souza's argument.
2. Write your own survey of the biotech revolution. Refer to some of the topics and ideas mentioned by D'Souza in his essay.
3. **Writing an Argument:** Select one aspect of the biotech revolution—for instance, cloning or stem-cell research—and write an argumentative essay supporting or opposing developments in the field.

NETWORKING
Applying 21st-Century Literacies

Debating the Ethics behind Cloning: Work in groups of three to prepare for and engage in a debate about some aspect of cloning or stem-cell research. Two of you will be debaters, each doing research to inform your assigned position: one for and one against a proposed development. Come to the debate with notes and solid arguments and counterarguments prepared. The third person will serve as the moderator, who will come prepared with questions and possible follow-up questions, as well as with a one- or two-page informative, unbiased introduction to the issues. He or she will open the debate by reading this document. If possible, videotape the debate, and watch it later to determine if there was a clear "winner." Discuss each of your strengths and weaknesses as public speakers/debaters, providing constructive criticism and praise.

Anybody Out There?

Oliver Sacks

Oliver Sacks (b. 1933), a well-known neurologist, was born in London and immigrated to the United States in 1960. He was educated at Queens College, Oxford, where he received a BA (1954) and subsequent degrees in chemistry and medicine. Sacks has practiced and taught medicine, surgery, and neurology at several institutions, including Albert Einstein College of Medicine, Bronx Psychiatric Hospital, and New York University Medical Center. An award-winning physician and science writer, Sacks has written numerous books, including Awakenings *(1973), which was made into a film starring Robin Williams and Robert De Niro;* The Man Who Mistook His Wife for a Hat, and Other Clinical Tales *(1985);* An Anthropologist on Mars *(1995);* Uncle Tungsten: Memories of a Chemical Boyhood *(2001);* Vintage Sacks *(2004), and* Musicophilia: Tales of Music and the Brain *(2007). In this essay, published in* Natural History *in 2002, Sacks speculates about the existence of life-forms in the universe.*

1   One of the first books I read as a boy was H. G. Wells's 1901 fable, *The First Men in the Moon*. The two men, Cavor and Bedford, land in a crater, apparently barren and lifeless, just before the lunar dawn; then, as the sun rises, they realize there is an atmosphere. They spot small pools and eddies of water, and then little round objects scattered on the ground. One of them, as it is warmed by the sun, bursts open and reveals a sliver of green. ("'A seed,' said Cavor . . . And then . . . very softly, 'Life!'") They light a piece of paper and throw it onto the surface of the Moon. It glows and sends up a thread of smoke, indicating that the atmosphere, though thin, is rich in oxygen and will support life as they know it.

2   Here, then, was how Wells conceived the prerequisites of life: water, sunlight (a source of energy), and oxygen. "A Lunar Morning," the eighth chapter in his book, was my first introduction to astrobiology.

3   It was apparent, even in Wells's day, that most of the planets in our solar system were not possible homes for life. The only reasonable surrogate for the Earth was Mars, which was known to be a solid planet of reasonable size, in stable orbit, not too distant from the sun, and so, it was thought, having a range of surface temperatures compatible with the presence of liquid water.

4   But free oxygen gas—how could that occur in a planet's atmosphere? What would keep it from being mopped up by ferrous iron and other oxygen-hungry chemicals on the surface unless, somehow, it was continuously pumped out in huge quantities, enough to oxidize all the surface minerals and keep the atmosphere charged as well?

5   It was the blue-green algae, or cyanobacteria, that infused the Earth's atmosphere with oxygen, a process that took between a billion and two billion years. The fossil record shows that cyanobacteria go back three and a half billion years. Yet, amazingly, some of them still thrive today in odd corners of the world, forming strange, cushion-shaped colonies called stromatolites. It is an extraordinary experience to go to Shark Bay in western Australia, where stromatolites flourish in the hypersaline waters, to watch them slowly bubbling oxygen, and to reflect that, three billion years ago, this was how the Earth was transformed. The cyanobacteria invented photosynthesis: by capturing the energy of the sun, they were able to combine carbon dioxide (massively present in the Earth's early atmosphere) with water to create complex molecules—sugars, carbohydrates—which the bacteria could then store and tap for energy as needed. This process generated free oxygen as a by-product—a waste product that was to determine the future course of evolution.

6   Although free oxygen in a planet's atmosphere would be an infallible marker of life, and one that, if present, should be readily detected in the spectra of extra-solar planets, it is not a prerequisite for life. Planets, after all, get started without free oxygen, and may remain without it all their lives. Anaerobic organisms swarmed before oxygen was available, perfectly at home in the atmosphere of the early Earth, converting nitrogen to ammonia, sulfur to hydrogen sulfide, carbon dioxide to formaldehyde, and so forth. (From formaldehyde and ammonia the bacteria could make every organic compound they needed.)

7   There may be planets in our solar system and elsewhere that lack an atmosphere of oxygen but are nonetheless teeming with anaerobes. And such anaerobes

need not live on the surface of the planet; they could occur well below the surface, in boiling vents and sulfurous hot pots, as they do on Earth today, to say nothing of subterranean oceans and lakes. (There is thought to be such a subsurface ocean on Jupiter's moon Europa, locked beneath a shell of ice several miles thick, and its exploration is one of the astrobiological priorities of this century. Curiously, Wells, in *The First Men in the Moon,* imagines life originating in a central sea in the middle of the Moon and then spreading outward to its inhospitable periphery.)

It is not clear whether life has to "advance"—whether evolution must take 8 place—if there is a satisfactory status quo. Brachiopods—lampshells—for instance, have remained virtually unchanged since they first appeared in the Cambrian Period, more than 500 million years ago. But there does seem to be a drive for organisms to become more highly organized and more efficient in retaining energy, at least when environmental conditions are changing rapidly, as they were before the Cambrian. The evidence indicates that the first primitive anaerobes on Earth were prokaryotes: small, simple cells—just cytoplasm, usually bounded by a cell wall, but with little if any internal structure.

By degrees, however—and the process took place with glacial slowness— 9 prokaryotes became more complex, acquiring internal structure, nuclei, mitochondria, and so on. The microbiologist Lynn Margulis of the University of Massachusetts, Amherst, has convincingly suggested that these complex so-called eukaryotes arose when prokaryotes began incorporating other prokaryotes within their own cells. The incorporated organisms at first became symbiotic and later came to function as essential organelles of their hosts, enabling the resultant organisms to use what was originally a noxious poison: oxygen.

Primitive as they are, prokaryotes are still highly sophisticated organisms 10 with formidable genetic and metabolic machinery. Even the simplest ones manufacture more than five hundred proteins, and their DNA includes at least half a million base pairs. Hence it is certain that still more primitive life forms must have preceded the prokaryotes.

Perhaps, as the physicist Freeman Dyson of the Institute for Advanced 11 Study in Princeton has suggested, there were "pro-genotes" capable of metabolizing, growing, and dividing but lacking any genetic mechanism for precise replication. And before them there must have been millions of years of purely chemical, prebiotic evolution—the synthesis, over eons, of formaldehyde and cyanide, of amino acids and peptides, of proteins and self-replicating molecules. Perhaps that chemistry took place in the minute vesicles, or globules, that develop when fluids at very different temperatures meet, as may well have happened around the boiling midocean vents of the Archaean sea.

Life as we know it is not imaginable without proteins, and proteins are built 12 from peptides, and ultimately from amino acids. It is easy to imagine that amino acids were abundant in the early Earth, either formed as a result of lightning discharges or brought to the planet by comets and meteors.

The real problem is to get from amino acids and other simple compounds 13 to peptides, nucleotides, proteins, and so on. It is unlikely that such delicate chemical syntheses would occur in "some warm little pond," as Darwin imagined, or on the surface of a primordial sea. Instead, they would probably require unusual conditions of heat and concentration, as well as the presence of special catalysts and energy-rich compounds to make them proceed. The biochemist Christian de Duve of Rockefeller University suggests that complex organic sulfur compounds played a crucial role in providing chemical energy, and that these compounds may have formed spontaneously early in Earth's history, perhaps in the hot, acidic, sulfurous depths of the seafloor vents (where, it is increasingly believed, life probably originated). De Duve imagines this purely chemical world as the precursor of an "RNA world," believed by many to represent the first form of self-replicating life. He thinks that the movement from one to the other was both inevitable and fast.

14 The two preeminent evolutionary changes in the early history of life on Earth—from prokaryote to eukaryote, from anaerobe to aerobe—took the better part of two billion years. And there then had to pass another 1,200 or 1,300 million years before life rose above the microscopic forms, and the first "higher," multicellular organisms appeared. So if the Earth's history is anything to go by, we should not expect to find any higher life on a planet that is still young. Even if extraterrestrial life has appeared, and all goes well, it could take billions of years for evolutionary processes to move it along to the multicellular stage.

15   Moreover, all those "stages" of evolution—including the evolution of intelligent, conscious beings from the first multicellular forms—may have happened against daunting odds. Stephen Jay Gould spoke of life as "a glorious accident"; Richard Dawkins of Oxford University likens evolution to "climbing Mount Improbable." And life, once started, is subject to vicissitudes of all kinds: from meteors and volcanic eruptions to global overheating and cooling; from dead ends in evolution to mysterious mass extinctions; and finally (if things get that far) the fateful proclivities of a species like ourselves.

16   We know there are microfossils in some of the Earth's most ancient rocks, rocks more than three and a half billion years old. So life must have appeared within 100 or 200 million years after the Earth had cooled off sufficiently for water to become liquid. That astonishingly rapid transformation makes one think that life may develop readily, perhaps inevitably, as soon as the right physical and chemical conditions appear.

17   But can one argue from a single example? Can one speak confidently of "earthlike" planets, or is the Earth physically, chemically, and geologically unique? And even if there are other "habitable" planets, what are the chances that life, with its thousands of physical and chemical coincidences and contingencies, will emerge? Life may be a one-off event.

18   Opinion here varies as widely as it can. The French biochemist Jacques Monod regarded life as a fantastically improbable accident, unlikely to have arisen anywhere else in the universe. In his book *Chance and Necessity*, he writes, "The universe was not pregnant with life." De Duve takes issue with this, and sees the origin of life as determined by a large number of steps, most of which must have

had a "high likelihood of taking place under the prevailing conditions." Indeed, de Duve believes that there is not merely unicellular life throughout the universe but complex, intelligent life, too, on trillions of planets. How are we to align ourselves between these utterly opposite but theoretically defensible positions?

What we need, what we must have, is hard evidence of life on another 19 planet or heavenly body. Mars is the obvious candidate: It was wet and warm there once, with lakes and hydrothermal vents and perhaps deposits of clay and iron ore. It is especially in such places that we should look, suggests Malcolm Walter, an expert on fossil bacteria that date from the Earth's earliest epochs. If the evidence shows that life once existed on Mars, we will then need to know, crucially, whether it originated there or was transported (as would have been readily possible) from the young, teeming, volcanic Earth. If we can determine that life originated independently on Mars (if Mars, for instance, once harbored DNA nucleotides different from our own), we will have made an incredible discovery—one that will alter our view of the universe and enable us to perceive it, in the words of the physicist Paul Davies, as a "biofriendly" one. It would help us to gauge the probability of finding life elsewhere instead of bombinating in a vacuum of data, caught between the poles of inevitability and uniqueness.

In just the past twenty years life has been discovered in previously unexpected 20 places on our own planet, such as the life-rich black smokers of the ocean depths, where organisms thrive in conditions biologists would once have dismissed as utterly deadly. Life is much tougher, much more resilient, than we once thought. It now seems to me quite possible that microorganisms or their remains will be found on Mars and perhaps on some of the satellites of Jupiter and Saturn.

It seems far less likely, many orders of magnitude less likely, that we will find 21 any evidence of higher-order, intelligent life forms, at least in our own solar system. But who knows? Given the vastness and age of the universe at large, the innumerable stars and planets it must contain, and our radical uncertainties about life's origin and evolution, the possibility cannot be ruled out. And though the rate of evolutionary and geochemical processes is incredibly slow, that of technological progress is incredibly fast. Who is to say (if humanity survives) what we may not be capable of, or discover, in the next thousand years?

For myself, since I cannot wait, I turn to science fiction on occasion—and, 22 not least, back to my favorite Wells. Although it was written a hundred years ago, "A Lunar Morning" has the freshness of a new dawn, and it remains for me, as when I first read it, the most poetic evocation of how it may be when, finally, we encounter alien life.

COMPREHENSION

1. What is Sacks's answer to the question he poses in the title?
2. Explain the connection between the writer's boyhood reading and his interest in life elsewhere in the universe.

3. List and define some of the scientific evidence and scientific principles Sacks mentions in his essay.

RHETORIC

1. Why does Sacks begin with an anecdote about his boyhood? How might this strategy appeal to readers of *Natural History,* where the essay first appeared?
2. In what ways does Sacks demonstrate his expertise and authority as a scientist in this essay? What tone does he take in presenting this information?
3. What is Sacks's thesis? What types of evidence does he offer to support his main idea?
4. Identify the main sections in this essay and the transitions Sacks uses to link them.
5. Where does Sacks use definition, comparison and contrast, process analysis, and causal analysis? Does he mix patterns successfully? Why or why not?
6. Examine the conclusion. Why does Sacks ask questions, and why does he end on a provisional note?

WRITING

1. In an expository essay, examine the popularity of science fiction in literature and/ or film. How does science fiction present the notion of life in the universe? Be certain to develop examples to support your thesis.
2. Conduct research on H. G. Wells, and then write an evaluative paper in which you highlight the ways in which he predicted the future.
3. **Writing an Argument:** Do you think that extraterrestrial life exists? Answer this question in an argumentative essay.

NETWORKING
Applying 21st-Century Literacies

Creating an Online Literature Review: For question 1, 2, or 3 under Writing, compile a review of the literature you would use to research this topic and help write an essay about it. For each source, provide a Works Cited entry and a paragraph-long summary of the source and how it relates to your topic; for online sources, also provide a direct link to the source. If you work with question 1, be sure to include the science fiction novels you would like to discuss.

The Clan of One-Breasted Women

Terry Tempest Williams

Terry Tempest Williams (b. 1955) is the author of many books of nonfiction, including A Journey to Navajoland *(1984),* Coyote's Canyon *(1989),* Refuge: An Unnatural History of Family and Place *(1991),* An Unspoken Hunger *(1994),*

Desert Quartet *(1995), and* Finding Beauty in a Broken World *(2009). Williams was identified by* Newsweek *magazine as someone who will have "a considerable impact on the political, economic and environmental issues facing the western states in this decade." She is the recipient of a Lannan Fellowship in creative nonfiction and was chosen by the* UTNE Reader *as a "visionary," one of the UTNE 100 "who could change your life." She is the Annie Clark Tanner Scholar in Environmental Humanities at the University of Utah. The following essay—published in 1989 in* Witness— *describes the pernicious intergenerational effects of nuclear testing.*

I belong to a Clan of One-Breasted Women. My mother, my grandmothers, and 1 six aunts have all had mastectomies. Seven are dead. The two who survive have just completed rounds of chemotherapy and radiation.

I've had my own problems: two biopsies for breast cancer and a small tumor 2 between my ribs diagnosed as "a border-line malignancy."

This is my family history. 3

Most statistics tell us breast cancer is genetic, hereditary, with rising per- 4 centages attached to fatty diets, childlessness, or becoming pregnant after thirty. What they don't say is living in Utah may be the greatest hazard of all.

We are a Mormon family with roots in Utah since 1847. The word-of-wisdom, 5 a religious doctrine of health, kept the women in my family aligned with good foods: no coffee, no tea, tobacco, or alcohol. For the most part, these women were finished having their babies by the time they were thirty. And only one faced breast cancer prior to 1960. Traditionally, as a group of people, Mormons have a low rate of cancer.

Is our family a cultural anomaly? The truth is we didn't think about it. 6 Those who did, usually the men, simply said, "bad genes." The women's attitude was stoic. Cancer was part of life. On February 16, 1971, the eve before my mother's surgery, I accidentally picked up the telephone and overheard her ask my grandmother what she could expect.

"Diane, it is one of the most spiritual experiences you will ever encounter." 7

I quietly put down the receiver. 8

Two days later, my father took my three brothers and me to the hospital to 9 visit her. She met us in the lobby in a wheelchair. No bandages were visible. I'll never forget her radiance, the way she held herself in a purple velour robe and how she gathered us around her.

"Children, I am fine. I want you to know I felt the arms of God around me." 10

We believed her. My father cried. Our mother, his wife, was thirty-eight 11 years old.

Two years ago, after my mother's death from cancer, my father and I were 12 having dinner together. He had just returned from St. George where his construction company was putting in natural gas lines for towns in southern Utah. He spoke of his love for the country: the sandstoned landscape, bare-boned and beautiful. He had just finished hiking the Kolob trail in Zion National Park. We got caught up in reminiscing, recalling with fondness our walk up Angel's Landing on his fiftieth birthday and the years our family had vacationed there. This was a remembered landscape where we had been raised.

13   Over dessert, I shared a recurring dream of mine. I told my father that for years, as long as I could remember, I saw this flash of light in the night in the desert. That this image had so permeated my being, I could not venture south without seeing it again, on the horizon, illuminating buttes and mesas.

14   "You did see it," he said.

15   "Saw what?" I asked, a bit tentative.

16   "The bomb. The cloud. We were driving home from Riverside, California. You were sitting on your mother's lap. She was pregnant. In fact, I remember the date, September 7, 1957. We had just gotten out of the Service. We were driving north, past Las Vegas. It was an hour or so before dawn, when this explosion went off. We not only heard it, but felt it. I thought the oil tanker in front of us had blown up. We pulled over and suddenly, rising from the desert floor, we saw it, clearly, this golden-stemmed cloud, the mushroom. The sky seemed to vibrate with an eerie pink glow. Within a few minutes, a light ash was raining on the car."

17   I stared at my father. This was new information to me.

18   "I thought you knew that," my father said. "It was a common occurrence in the fifties."

19   It was at this moment I realized the deceit I had been living under. Children growing up in the American Southwest, drinking contaminated milk from contaminated cows, even from the contaminated breasts of their mother, my mother—members, years later, of the Clan of One-Breasted Women.

20   It is a well-known story in the Desert West, "The Day We Bombed Utah," or perhaps, "The Years We Bombed Utah."[1] Above ground atomic testing in Nevada took place from January 27, 1951, through July 11, 1962. Not only were the winds blowing north, covering "low use segments of the population" with fallout and leaving sheep dead in their tracks, but the climate was right.[2] The United States of the 1950s was red, white, and blue. The Korean War was raging. McCarthyism was rampant. Ike was in and the Cold War was hot. If you were against nuclear testing, you were for a Communist regime.

21   Much has been written about this "American nuclear tragedy." Public health was secondary to national security. The Atomic Energy Commissioner, Thomas Murray said, "Gentlemen, we must not let anything interfere with this series of tests, nothing."[3]

22   Again and again, the American public was told by its government, in spite of burns, blisters, and nausea, "It has been found that the tests may be conducted with adequate assurance of safety under conditions prevailing at the bombing reservations."[4] Assuaging public fears was simply a matter of public relations. "Your best action," an Atomic Energy Commission booklet read, "is not to be

[1]Fuller, John G., *The Day We Bombed Utah* (New York: New American Library, 1984). [This and subsequent notes in the selection are the author's.]
[2]Discussion on March 14, 1988, with Carole Gallagher, photographer and author, *Nuclear Towns: The Secret War in the American Southwest*, published by Doubleday, Spring, 1990.
[3]Szasz, Ferenc M., "Downwind from the Bomb," *Nevada Historical Society Quarterly*, Fall 1987, Vol. XXX, No. 3, p. 185.
[4]Fradkin, Philip L., *Fallout* (Tucson: University of Arizona Press, 1989), 98.

worried about fallout." A news release typical of the times stated, "We find no basis for concluding that harm to any individual has resulted from radioactive fallout."[5]

On August 30, 1979, during Jimmy Carter's presidency, a suit was filed 23 entitled "Irene Allen vs. the United States of America." Mrs. Allen was the first to be alphabetically listed with twenty-four test cases, representative of nearly 1200 plaintiffs seeking compensation from the United States government for cancers caused from nuclear testing in Nevada.

Irene Allen lived in Hurricane, Utah. She was the mother of five children 24 and had been widowed twice. Her first husband with their two oldest boys had watched the tests from the roof of the local high school. He died of leukemia in 1956. Her second husband died of pancreatic cancer in 1978.

In a town meeting conducted by Utah Senator Orrin Hatch, shortly before 25 the suit was filed, Mrs. Allen said, "I am not blaming the government, I want you to know that, Senator Hatch. But I thought if my testimony could help in any way so this wouldn't happen again to any of the generations coming up after us . . . I am really happy to be here this day to bear testimony of this."[6]

God-fearing people. This is just one story in an anthology of thousands. 26

On May 10, 1984, Judge Bruce S. Jenkins handed down his opinion. Ten of 27 the plaintiffs were awarded damages. It was the first time a federal court had determined that nuclear tests had been the cause of cancers. For the remaining fourteen test cases, the proof of causation was not sufficient. In spite of the split decision, it was considered a landmark ruling.[7] It was not to remain so for long.

In April 1987, the 10th Circuit Court of Appeals overturned Judge Jenkins' 28 ruling on the basis that the United States was protected from suit by the legal doctrine of sovereign immunity, the centuries-old idea from England in the days of absolute monarchs.[8]

In January 1988, the Supreme Court refused to review the Appeals Court 29 decision. To our court system, it does not matter whether the United States Government was irresponsible, whether it lied to its citizens or even that citizens died from the fallout of nuclear testing. What matters is that our government is immune. "The King can do no wrong."

In Mormon culture, authority is respected, obedience is revered, and indepen- 30 dent thinking is not. I was taught as a young girl not to "make waves" or "rock the boat."

"Just let it go—" my mother would say. "You know how you feel, that's 31 what counts."

For many years, I did just that—listened, observed, and quietly formed my 32 own opinions within a culture that rarely asked questions because they had all

[5]Ibid., 109.
[6]Town meeting held by Senator Orrin Hatch in St. George, Utah, April 17, 1979, transcript, 26–28.
[7]Fradkin, Op. cit., 228.
[8]*U.S. vs. Allen*, 816 Federal Reporter, 2d/1417 (10th Circuit Court 1987), cert. denied, 108 S. CT. 694 (1988).

the answers. But one by one, I watched the women in my family die common, heroic deaths. We sat in waiting rooms hoping for good news, always receiving the bad. I cared for them, bathed their scarred bodies and kept their secrets. I watched beautiful women become bald as cytoxan, cisplatin and adriamycin were injected into their veins. I held their foreheads as they vomited green-black bile and I shot them with morphine when the pain became inhuman. In the end, I witnessed their last peaceful breaths, becoming a midwife to the re-birth of their souls. But the price of obedience became too high.

33   The fear and inability to question authority that ultimately killed rural communities in Utah during atmospheric testing of atomic weapons was the same fear I saw being held in my mother's body. Sheep. Dead sheep. The evidence is buried.

34   I cannot prove that my mother, Diane Dixon Tempest, or my grandmothers, Lettie Romney Dixon and Kathryn Blackett Tempest, along with my aunts contracted cancer from nuclear fallout in Utah. But I can't prove they didn't.

35   My father's memory was correct, the September blast we drove through in 1957 was part of Operation Plumbbob, one of the most intensive series of bomb tests to be initiated. The flash of light in the night in the desert I had always thought was a dream developed into a family nightmare. It took fourteen years, from 1957 to 1971, for cancer to show up in my mother—the same time, Howard L. Andrews, an authority on radioactive fallout at the National Institutes of Health, says radiation cancer requires to become evident.[9] The more I learn about what it means to be a "downwinder," the more questions I drown in.

36   What I do know, however, is that as a Mormon woman of the fifth generation of Latter-day Saints. I must question everything, even if it means losing my faith, even if it means becoming a member of a border tribe among my own people. Tolerating blind obedience in the name of patriotism or religion ultimately takes our lives.

37   When the Atomic Energy Commission described the country north of the Nevada Test Site as "virtually uninhabited desert terrain," my family members were some of the "virtual uninhabitants."

38   One night, I dreamed women from all over the world were circling a blazing fire in the desert. They spoke of change, of how they hold the moon in their bellies and wax and wane with its phases. They mocked at the presumption of even- tempered beings and made promises that they would never fear the witch inside themselves. The women danced wildly as sparks broke away from the flames and entered the night sky as stars.

39   And they sang a song given to them by Shoshoni grandmothers:

Ah ne nah, nahn
in nah nah—
Ah ne nah, nah,
nin nah nah—

[9]Fradkin, Op. cit. 116.

Nyaga mutzi
oh ne nay—
Nyaga mutzi
oh ne nay—[10]

The women danced and drummed and sang for weeks, preparing them- 40
selves for what was to come. They would reclaim the desert for the sake of their
children, for the sake of the land.

A few miles downwind from the fire circle, bombs were being tested. 41
Rabbits felt the tremors. Their soft leather pads on paws and feet recognized the
shaking sands while the roots of mesquite and sage were smoldering. Rocks
were hot from the inside out and dust devils hummed unnaturally. And each
time there was another nuclear test, ravens watched the desert heave. Stretch
marks appeared. The land was losing its muscle.

The women couldn't bear it any longer. They were mothers. They had suffered 42
labor pains but always under the promise of birth. The red hot pains beneath the
desert promised death only as each bomb became a stillborn. A contract had been
broken between human beings and the land. A new contract was being drawn by
the women who understood the fate of the earth as their own.

Under the cover of darkness, ten women slipped under the barbed wire 43
fence and entered the contaminated country. They were trespassing. They
walked toward the town of Mercury in moonlight, taking their cues from coyote, kit fox, antelope squirrel, and quail. They moved quietly and deliberately
through the maze of Joshua trees. When a hint of daylight appeared they rested,
drinking tea and sharing their rations of food. The women closed their eyes.
The time had come to protest with the heart, that to deny one's genealogy with
the earth was to commit treason against one's soul.

At dawn, the women draped themselves in mylar, wrapping long stream- 44
ers of silver plastic around their arms to blow in the breeze. They wore clear
masks that became the faces of humanity. And when they arrived on the edge
of Mercury, they carried all the butterflies of a summer day in their wombs.
They paused to allow their courage to settle.

The town which forbids pregnant women and children to enter because of 45
radiation risks to their health was asleep. The women moved through the
streets as winged messengers, twirling around each other in slow motion, peeking inside homes and watching the easy sleep of men and women. They were
astonished by such stillness and periodically would utter a shrill note or low
cry just to verify life.

The residents finally awoke to what appeared as strange apparitions. 46
Some simply stared. Others called authorities, and in time, the women were

---

[10]This song was sung by the Western Shoshone women as they crossed the line at the Nevada Test
Site on March 18, 1988, as part of their "Reclaim the Land" action. The translation they gave was:
"Consider the rabbits how gently they walk on the earth. Consider the rabbits how gently they
walk on the earth. We remember them. We can walk gently also. We remember them. We can
walk gently also."

apprehended by wary soldiers dressed in desert fatigues. They were taken to a white, square building on the other edge of Mercury. When asked who they were and why they were there, the women replied, "We are mothers and we have come to reclaim the desert for our children."

47   The soldiers arrested them. As the ten women were blindfolded and hand-cuffed, they began singing:

> You can't forbid us everything
> You can't forbid us to think—
> You can't forbid our tears to flow
> And you can't stop the songs that we sing.

48   The women continued to sing louder and louder, until they heard the voices of their sisters moving across the mesa.

> Ah ne nah, nah
> nin nah nah—
> Ah ne nah, nah
> nin nah nah—
> Nyaga mutzi
> oh ne nay—
> Nyaga mutzi
> oh ne nay—

49   "Call for re-enforcement," one soldier said.

50   "We have," interrupted one woman. "We have—and you have no idea of our numbers."

51   On March 18, 1988, I crossed the line at the Nevada Test Site and was arrested with nine other Utahns for trespassing on military lands. They are still conducting nuclear tests in the desert. Ours was an act of civil disobedience. But as I walked toward the town of Mercury, it was more than a gesture of peace. It was a gesture on behalf of the Clan of One-Breasted Women.

52   As one officer cinched the handcuffs around my wrists, another frisked my body. She found a pen and a pad of paper tucked inside my left boot.

53   "And these?" she asked sternly.

54   "Weapons," I replied.

55   Our eyes met. I smiled. She pulled the leg of my trousers back over my boot.

56   "Step forward, please," she said as she took my arm.

57   We were booked under an afternoon sun and bussed to Tonapah, Nevada. It was a two-hour ride. This was familiar country to me. The Joshua trees standing their ground had been named by my ancestors who believed they looked like prophets pointing west to the promised land. These were the same trees that bloomed each spring, flowers appearing like white flames in the Mojave. And I recalled a full moon in May when my mother and I had walked among them, flushing out mourning doves and owls.

58   The bus stopped short of town. We were released. The officials thought it was a cruel joke to leave us stranded in the desert with no way to get home.

What they didn't realize is that we were home, soul-centered and strong, women who recognized the sweet smell of sage as fuel for our spirits.

COMPREHENSION

1. What is the subject of the essay? How did you arrive at your answer?
2. The credo of the United States promotes "life, liberty, and the pursuit of happiness." In her essay, what does Williams imply is the major antagonist to this philosophy?
3. Define the following words and terms: *doctrine* (paragraph 5), *anomaly* (paragraph 6), *buttes* and *mesas* (paragraph 13), *plaintiffs* (paragraph 23), and *sovereign* (paragraph 28).

RHETORIC

1. Williams often uses quotation marks to signal irony in her writing. What is the perverse irony in the following expressions: "low use segments of the population" (paragraph 20), "downwinder" (paragraph 35), and "virtually uninhabited desert terrain" (paragraph 37)?
2. Although this is a highly personal essay and reveals a profound and emotional personal experience, Williams also relies on evidence from secondary source material to support her thesis. What is the effect of using such sources in terms of the author's authority and believability?
3. The essay is divided into four segments. What is the main subject of each one?
4. Williams uses extended metaphor, personification, and comparison and contrast in paragraphs 41 and 42. Explain how she incorporates these three rhetorical devices and what their relevance is to the overarching theme of the essay.
5. Williams provides a revelation to the reader in paragraph 16 that determines to a large degree the focus of her essay. What was the rhetorical purpose in waiting so long to reveal it?
6. Literary critics often state that one of the essential elements of powerful drama is some profound change that the main protagonist undergoes. What change in perspective did Williams undergo, and what was its implication for her attitudes and actions toward society?
7. Despite profound tragedy and continuous frustration in her life, Williams ends her essay on a positive note. Where is this change in tone most evident? What images reflect her ultimate triumph?

WRITING

1. In an expository essay, analyze the dangers that nuclear proliferation poses for humanity.
2. For a research project, study public policy in the 1950s and 1960s regarding aboveground nuclear testing, and report on whether the American government foresaw that some individuals likely would suffer dire physical infirmities as a result of such procedures.
3. **Writing an Argument:** Argue for or against the proposition that technology is never value-free.

NETWORKING
Applying 21st-Century Literacies

Uploading an Original Video: Work with two or three classmates and respond to question 1 or 2 under Writing with a short, scripted film. Incorporate or even act out a brief story, using a specific piece of narration to strengthen your claim. Upload the video to YouTube, or to a password-protected site, for evaluation.

Synthesis: Connections for Critical Thinking

1. Using the essays of D'Souza and Williams, discuss the need for strict ethics among scientists in regards to their concern over the well-being of the general populace.
2. Imagine a conversation between Sedaris and Turkle. What would they say to each other?
3. Compare the process of natural selection as advanced by Darwin with the concept of evolution as defined by Sacks and Klinkenborg.
4. Rent the DVD version of the television series *Cosmos,* which was based on a novel by Carl Sagan. Compare the ideas set forth in the film with those in Sagan's essay "Can We Know the Universe? Reflections on a Grain of Salt."
5. Compare and contrast the expository methods Darwin uses to explain the process of natural selection and the narrative technique Sedaris uses to describe his technophobia.
6. Using Williams's essay on the pernicious effects of technology and Klinkenborg's presentation of Darwin, explore how science can be either a friend or a foe of humankind.

NETWORKING
Applying 21st-Century Literacies

1. Search the Web for two sites: one promoting the idea of evolution, the other promoting the idea of creationism. Compare and contrast the approach of each site as well as responses by the visitors to each site.
2. Have your class create a private chat room or password-protected blog with user names that do not divulge the gender of the participants. Discuss the pros and cons of computers as described by Sedaris. Have a host tally the nature of the responses, reveal the gender of the students who participated, and discuss any differences between the responses of the male and female students.
3. Do an online search using the keywords *cloning* and *children.* Analyze three hits to demonstrate the ethical and religious controversies raised by the subject.

CH 15   **www.mhhe.com/mhreader11e**

- *Image Gallery:* Chapter images in color
- *Science and Technology:* Information on the authors in this chapter
- *Ch. 15 Networking*

We Are the World

William Ecenbarger

William Ecenbarger, who graduated from Susquehanna University (BA, 1961) and lives in Lancaster, Pennsylvania, has had a distinguished career as a freelance writer and journalist, contributing to the Philadelphia Inquirer, Reader's Digest, Smithsonian, *and many other publications. He received a Pulitzer Prize in 1979 for his role in covering the Three Mile Island nuclear accident for the* Inquirer. *An inveterate traveler who has visited more than 40 countries and written about many of them, Ecenbarger is the author of* Walkin' the Line: A Journey from Past to Present Along the Mason-Dixon *(2000). He received the Travel Journalist of the Year award from the Society of American Travel Writers in 1996. In the following essay, which appeared in the* Times-Picayune *of New Orleans in 2003, Ecenbarger offers snapshots from his travels that reveal the impact of American popular culture on even the most remote parts of the world.*

1   At 5 A.M. I am awakened by the voice of the pilot, who delivers his words as though they were oracular. The gist is that the No. 3 engine is leaking oil, we're going out to sea to dump most of our fuel, and then we're going to make an emergency landing in Asuncion, Paraguay. I have an appointment at 10 A.M. in Buenos Aires, but that doesn't seem important now.

2   The cabin is prickly with tension, but we land without incident. Shaken passengers on the DC-10 begin filing off the plane. The heat slams into me as I step down to the runway and think that Paraguay brings to my mind a Banana Republic dictatorship peopled by unrepentant Nazis. I will learn later that the nation recently became democratized, but right now I'm looking at a line of khaki-clad soldiers with slung carbines, standing as though glued to the tarmac by their shadows, glowering like sullen watchdogs.

3   The leader of these carabineros, a balding man with a face like a pallbearer, is checking passports and furrowing his brow with self-importance. He returns mine with a look Patton might direct toward a deserter. I am wondering whether anyone ever tries to sneak IN to Paraguay.

4   There are vintage DC-3s parked all over the airport, their tails low to the ground and their fuselages tilted at 30 degrees, just like in Terry and the Pirates or Steve Canyon. The airport access road is lined with billboards for Coca Cola and Kent cigarettes. The latter shows two tanned Americans, Ken and Barbie, smoking as they lean on a white convertible parked at a palm-fringed lagoon in which is moored a yacht flying Old Glory.

There are a few places on Earth where an American can get away from America, 5
but I haven't been to any of them recently.

Most of the world has literally become a Mickey Mouse operation. The USA 6
reigns supreme as the exporter of music, film, television, sports, food and hundreds of consumer products ranging form Levis to Pampers to Barbie dolls.

American travelers are discovering that the sun never sets on the U.S. pop- 7
ular culture empire. Madonna writhes and jiggles and kisses Britney Spears on
MTV from Rangoon to Rio de Janeiro. I visited a Burger King in Kuala Lumpur,
a Pizza Hut on Fiji and a McDonald's in Buenos Aires. I turned on my hotel
television in Taipei to find Geraldo interviewing Elvis impersonators.

In Hanoi, I saw former Viet Cong soldiers standing in line wearing New 8
York Yankee baseball caps waiting to see movies such as "Platoon" and "Apocalypse Now." From my hotel room in Manila, I watched protesters against
American policies burning the Stars and Stripes while wearing Nikes and Levis,
righteously indignant right down to their Calvin Klein underwear . . .

In many Asian and Latin American cities, hanging out at the local American 9
fast-food restaurant is part of the trendy youth lifestyle. Conspicuous
consumption takes on a new meaning in Bangkok, where the McDonald's
restaurants have floor-to-ceiling windows. The better, I was advised by a local
doctor, to be seen.

Unlike their U.S. counterparts, Dunkin' Donut stores in Asia do the bulk of 10
their business at night. They are a gathering place for young professional men
to impress their dates. Meanwhile, Coke and Pepsi are slugging it out on the
Serengeti Plain and in the tin-roofed kampungs of Malaysia.

I was in a cab whiz-banging from the airport into downtown Bangkok, and 11
it was a real white-knuckler. I peeked at the speedometer and tried to convert
127 kilometers into miles per hour. The driver didn't speak English, but nevertheless he lip-synched along with Ray Charles, whose voice was coming from a
speaker inches behind my right ear . . . "just an old sweet song keeps Georgia
on my mind."

We stopped for a red light and I saw two young Thai boys, wearing 12
Mohawk haircuts and Guns N' Roses T-shirts, standing in front of a Pizza Hut,
bartering with tourists in English over pirated music cassettes. Paula Abdul
was going for $1. The driver pointed across the street to a long line waiting to
get into the latest Sylvester Stallone epic. He shrugged philosophically, lit a
Marlboro and hooked up with Simon and Garfunkel, "What's that you say,
Mrs. Robinson . . . ?"

MTV, with all its nymphets in underwear, screaming guitars, and guys with 13
earrings and gold chains, is wrapped around the globe like an extension cord,
and it is nothing less than the defining influence of a new international youth
culture. These days a 17-year-old Malaysian has more in common with a
17-year-old Chilean than with a 40-year-old Malaysian.

14   The emphasis on American music can turn wretched at times. In Suva, capital of Fiji, I watched four perfectly talented local doctors make fools of themselves trying to play light jazz for the Americans in the audience; I've heard various versions of "Feelings" played in Manila, Bangkok and Nairobi—and heard it sung over and over at a karaoke bar in Santiago.

15   From Togo to Tegucigalpa, people are doing the same thing: sitting in front of their televisions watching American programs and American commercials. Couch potatoes are sprouting up along the Amazon, the Nile and the Ganges.

16   Even local TV takes its cues form the Americans. The local news in Taipei is delivered by blow-dried mannequins who confuse the substantive with the merely photogenic. Just like the Americans on action news, they exchange quips, give the temperature at the airport (the last place anyone needs to know the temperature) and at the sign-off, pound their stack of 8-by-11-inch papers endlessly into the table.

17   In Taipei, I had some time on my hands and felt like a bit of the National Pastime. So I plunked down and watched the Weichuan Dragons battle the Brother Hotel Elephants in an important Taiwan Professional Baseball League contest.

18   "Play ball" is now a global cry, and they're tying on the spikes from Australia to Zaire. About 100 million people are playing organized baseball—and only about one in every five is an American. Baseball is now the International Pastime.

19   Baseball isn't the only American game gone global. Some 300 million Chinese watched the 1992 Super Bowl, and National Basketball Association games are telecast to 90 nations, including Reykjavik, Iceland, where they love the Boston Celtics.

20 Some American advertisers don't even bother to dub their spots in the local language, figuring that English is understood in many places, and even if it's not, it carries a certain snob appeal. In fact, the sun never sets on the English language.

21   English has long been spoken in cockpits and control towers the world over, and now it is becoming a language for universal communication, because of the dominance of American popular culture.

22   With 700 million people using it, English ranks second only to Chinese in number of speakers, but it is spoken commonly in more countries than any other language. Indeed, the number of non-native users of the English language now outnumber those who were born into it.

23   Perhaps *New York Times* columnist Thomas Friedman summed it up best in his book, "The Lexus and the Olive Tree: Understanding Globalization." He wrote, "On top of it all, globalization has a distinctly American face. It wears Mickey Mouse ears, it eats Big Macs, it drinks Coke or Pepsi and it does its computing on an IBM or Apple laptop, using Windows 98. . . . In most societies, most people cannot distinguish anymore between American power, American exports, American cultural assaults, American cultural exports and plain vanilla globalization. They are now all wrapped into one."

I have just flown over the Rift Valley, where Darwinists believe mankind began 24
at least 2.7 million years ago, and now I sit in an outdoor restaurant in a small
market town near Nairobi, sampling grilled wildebeest and smoked impala
with my Kenyan host.

Around us the market throbs like a helicopter. It is a thicket of humanity, 25
and everyone is talking earnestly, rapidly, as though if they stop for an instant
they will crumble to dust in the red clay ground. The cacophony is like an overpopulated marsh. We are interrupted by a young boy, who seems to have
stepped off a page of National Geographic. He extends toward me a wood-
carving of a tribal mask.

"He wants to trade you," says my companion.   26
"What does he want?"   27
He talks to the boy in Swahili and then answers. "He wants anything from 28
America. A T-shirt, a cassette, a baseball cap. As long as it's from America." In
my bag I find a gray sweatshirt that says "New York Giants."

The boy's eyes widen in appreciation, and we make a deal. Later the boy 29
comes back and takes my picture with a Polaroid camera. And then he offers to
come to the United States and work as my "assistant."

"Our young people are absolutely daft about America," says my host, a 30
Kenyan of English ancestry. "It is said that Kenyan children hope for two
things—to go to heaven, and to go to America . . ."

COMPREHENSION

1. What are the major popular culture references that Ecenbarger mentions in
   his essay? What is his attitude toward these manifestations of American
   culture?
2. What does Ecenbarger mean when he writes, "Most of the world has
   literally become a Mickey Mouse operation" (paragraph 6)? What common
   saying does he seems to be invoking, and why?
3. What nations, regions, and continents does Ecenbarger touch on? What is
   his purpose in creating this panorama of places?

RHETORIC

1. How does Ecenbarger's introductory section (paragraphs 1–4) help to
   establish his claim? What is his claim, and where does he state it?
2. What tone does Ecenbarger establish in this essay? What aspects of his style
   reinforce this tone?
3. What grounds or types of support does Ecenbarger provide to reinforce his
   claim?
4. How does Ecenbarger employ narration and description to support his
   argument? How effective do you find these strategies, and why?

5. Why does Ecenbarger divide this essay into sections? Do you sense a progression, or could these units be reorganized without damaging the essay's unity and coherence? Justify your response.

WRITING

1. Write as essay analyzing the reasons why American popular culture is so popular overseas. Refer to at least varieties of popular culture to develop your thesis.
2. Write an extended definition of *cultural imperialism,* and explain the role of the United States in perpetuating his phenomenon.
3. **Writing an Argument:** Compose an argumentative essay in which you attempt to persuade readers that American popular culture is actually good for people around the world.

NETWORKING

Applying 21st-Century Literacies

Composing a Hyperlinked Essay: Format your essay for question 3 under Writing as an electronic or online text: use hyperlinks to enhance your content and take readers to relevant sites that support your argument or help refute specific counterarguments to your case for American popular culture. Use at least six hyperlinks in your essay.

The Death of Horatio Alger

Paul Krugman

Paul Krugman (b. 1953), who teaches at Princeton University, received the Nobel Prize for Economics in 2008 for his analysis of trade patterns and economic activity. Raised in the suburbs of New York City, Krugman attended Yale University for two years before transferring to Massachusetts Institute of Technology, where he received his PhD in economics in 1977. Krugman has published many highly specialized texts in economic theory, but also more popular works like Peddling Prosperity *(1994),* The Accidental Theorist: And Other Dispatches from the Dismal Science *(1998), and* The Return of Depression Economics and the Crisis of 2008 *(2008). A frequent contributor to such newspapers and magazines as the* New Republic, Financial Times, *and* Mother Jones, *Krugman currently is an op-ed columnist for the* New York Times. *Known for his trenchant style and oppositional viewpoints, Krugman attempts to make*

complex economic trends comprehensible to a broad audience. In this essay from the
Nation, *published in 2004, Krugman looks into the causes of economic inequality.*

The other day I found myself reading a leftist rag that made outrageous claims 1
about America. It said that we are becoming a society in which the poor tend to
stay poor, no matter how hard they work; in which sons are much more likely to
inherit the socioeconomic status of their father than they were a generation ago.

The name of the leftist rag? *Business Week,* which published an article titled 2
"Waking Up from the American Dream." The article summarizes recent
research showing that social mobility in the United States (which was never as
high as legend had it) has declined considerable over the past few decades. If
you put that research together with other research that shows a drastic increase
in income and wealth inequality, you reach an uncomfortable conclusion:
America looks more and more like a class-ridden society.

And guess what? Our political leaders are doing everything they can to 3
fortify class inequality, while denouncing anyone who complains—or even
points out what is happening—as a practitioner of "class warfare."

Let's talk first about the facts on income distribution. Thirty years ago we 4
were a relatively middle-class nation. It had not always been thus: Gilded Age
America was a highly unequal society, and it stayed that way through the
1920s. During the 1930s and '40s, however, America experienced what
the economic historians Claudia Goldin and Robert Margo have dubbed the
Great Compression: a drastic narrowing of income gaps, probably as a result of
New Deal policies. And the new economic order persisted for more than a
generation: Strong unions; taxes on inherited wealth, corporate profits and high
incomes; close public scrutiny of corporate management—all helped to keep
income gaps relatively small. The economy was hardly egalitarian, but a
generation ago the gross inequalities of the 1920s seemed very distant.

Now they're back. According to estimates by the economists Thomas 5
Piketty and Emmanuel Saez—confirmed by data from the Congressional
Budget Office—between 1973 and 2000 the average real income of the bottom
90 percent of American taxpayers actually fell by 7 percent. Meanwhile, the
income of the top 1 percent rose by 148 percent, the income of the top 0.1 percent
rose by 343 percent and the income of the top 0.01 percent rose 599 percent.
(Those numbers exclude capital gains, so they're not an artifact of the stock-
market bubble.) The distribution of income in the United States has gone right
back to Gilded Age levels of inequality.

Never mind, say the apologists, who churn out papers with titles like that 6
of a 2001 Heritage Foundation piece, "Income Mobility and the Fallacy of Class-
Warfare Arguments." America, they say, isn't a caste society—people with high
incomes this year may have low incomes next year and vice versa, and the route
to wealth is open to all. That's where those commies at *Business Week* come in:
As they point out (and as economists and sociologists have been pointing out
for some time), America actually is more of a caste society than we like to think.
And the caste lines have lately become a lot more rigid.

7   The myth of income mobility has always exceeded the reality: As a general rule, once they've reached their 30s, people don't move up and down the income ladder very much. Conservatives often cite studies like a 1992 report by Glenn Hubbard, a Treasury official under the elder Bush who later became chief economic adviser to the younger Bush, that purport to show large numbers of Americans moving from low-wage to high-wage jobs during their working lives. But what these studies measure, as the economist Kevin Murphy put it, is mainly "the guy who works in the college bookstore and has a real job by his early 30s." Serious studies that exclude this sort of pseudo-mobility show that inequality in average incomes over long periods isn't much smaller than inequality in annual incomes.

8   It is true, however, that America was once a place of substantial intergenerational mobility: Sons often did much better than their fathers. A classic 1978 survey found that among adult men whose fathers were in the bottom 25 percent of the population as ranked by social and economic status, 23 percent had made it into the top 25 percent. In other words, during the first thirty years or so after World War II, the American dream of upward mobility was a real experience for many people.

9   Now for the shocker: The *Business Week* piece cites a new survey of today's adult men, which finds that this number has dropped to only 10 percent. That is, over the past generation upward mobility has fallen drastically. Very few children of the lower class are making their way to even moderate affluence. This goes along with other studies indicating that rags-to-riches stories have become vanishingly rare, and that the correlation between fathers' and sons' incomes has risen in recent decades. In modern America, it seems, you're quite likely to stay in the social and economic class into which you were born.

10   *Business Week* attributes this to the "Wal-Martization" of the economy, the proliferation of dead-end, low-wage jobs and the disappearance of jobs that provide entry to the middle class. That's surely part of the explanation. But public policy plays a role—and will, if present trends continue, play an even bigger role in the future.

11   Put it this way: Suppose that you actually liked a caste society, and you were seeking ways to use your control of the government to further entrench the advantages of the haves against the have-nots. What would you do?

12   One thing you would definitely do is get rid of the estate tax, so that large fortunes can be passed on the next generation. More broadly, you would seek to reduce tax rates both on corporate profits and on unearned income such as dividends and capital gains, so that those with large accumulated or inherited wealth could more easily accumulate even more. You'd also try to create tax shelters mainly useful for the rich. And more broadly still, you'd try to reduce tax rates on people with high incomes, shifting the burden to the payroll tax and other revenue sources that bear most heavily on people with lower incomes.

13   Meanwhile, on the spending side, you'd cut back on healthcare for the poor, on the quality of public education and on state aid for higher education.

This would make it more difficult for people with low incomes to climb out of their difficulties and acquire the education essential to upward mobility in the modern economy.

And just to close off as many routes to upward mobility as possible, you'd 14 do everything possible to break the power of unions, and you'd privatize government functions so that well-paid civil servants could be replaced with poorly paid private employees.

It all sounds sort of familiar, doesn't it?   15

Where is this taking us? Thomas Piketty, whose work with Saez has trans- 16 formed our understanding of income distribution, warns that current policies will eventually create "a class of rentiers in the U.S., whereby a small group of wealthy but untalented children controls vast segments of the US economy and penniless, talented children simply can't compete." If he's right—and I fear that he is—we will end up suffering not only from injustice, but from a vast waste of human potential.

Goodbye, Horatio Alger. And goodbye, American Dream.   17

COMPREHENSION

1. What reasons does Krugman give for the creation of a caste society in the United States?
2. Who is Horatio Alger? Why doesn't Krugman explain who he is in his essay?
3. Krugman alludes to the "leftist rag" *Business Week*. What can you infer about the contents and political opinions of this publication?

RHETORIC

1. What is Krugman's claim, and where does he state it most clearly?
2. Comment on the types of evidence that Krugman uses to support his argument. Do you find this evidence to be sufficient and convincing? Why or why not?
3. Krugman's style is quite impersonal. Locate examples of this style, and explain the overall effect.
4. Much of this essay involves comparative analysis. What subjects and ideas does Krugman compare and contrast?
5. Krugman's conclusion is very brief. Do you find it effective? Explain.

WRITING

1. Do you think that your life will be better economically than that of your parents? Write a personal essay in response to this question.
2. Write your own analysis of class inequality in the United States or in another nation that you are familiar with.

3. Writing an Argument: Write a rebuttal to Krugman, arguing that the American Dream is still alive and well.

NETWORKING

Applying 21st-Century Literacies

Making a Brochure: Create a brochure titled either "The American Dream Is Live and Well" or "The Myth of Upward Mobility." Avoiding propaganda or other fallacious forms of argument, make a solid, convincing case. Consider creating or finding visuals to use in this project.

Why We Love "Mad Men"

Lauren M. E. Goodlad

Lauren M. E. Goodlad has degrees from Cornell University (BS), New York University (MA), and Columbia University (PhD). She is an associate professor of English at the University of Illinois at Urbana-Champaign, where she teaches Victorian literature and directs the Unit for Criticism and Interpretative Theory. Goodlad has published Victorian Literature and the Victorian State *(2003) and most recently is a co-editor of* Goth: Undead Subculture *(2007). She worked in the 1980s as a cosmetics and fragrance copywriter in New York City. In the following essay, which was published in the* Chronicle of Higher Education *in 2009, Goodlad combines her personal response to* Mad Men *with unique feminist critical inquiry.*

1   Like most women who call themselves feminists, I've spent my life avoiding men like Don Draper, the incorrigible ladies' man at the center of *Mad Men*, a show about a Madison Avenue advertising agency in the early 1960s. I took a pass on the show during its first season, catching up with it on DVD when the mounting enthusiasm of friends and co-workers piqued my curiosity.

2   By the time the season-three premier was promoted this month, my friends (men and women in their 30s and 40s) had taken to posting Madmenized avatars of themselves on their Facebook pages. And I was one of them, styling myself on madmenyourself.com in a chic red dress, gloves, and cat's-eye glasses. What had happened to make these politically progressive adults in the last days of their youth identify with characters from their parents' generation?

I have been intrigued by the mysteries of culture before. In the 1990s, I was 3
writing on gothic subculture and the phenomenon of "men who feel and cry"—
men like Anne Rice's vampires, Tim Burton's Edward Scissorhands, and Nine
Inch Nails' Trent Reznor, all of whom beckoned young men to dramatize emotion in ways that previous generations had scorned as unmasculine. Alongside
those men in black were harsher specimens of masculinity in crisis: men like
Tyler Durden, the split personality who launches an underground subculture
called Fight Club.

While superficially different, both kinds of men were desperate to feel, 4
through catharsis or brutal violence. Yet most of these tales focused on men's
relationships with one another, like Tyler's two halves, or Lestat and Louis in
Rice's *Interview With the Vampire.* They were men searching for their feelings in
the company of other men.

And now comes Don Draper, icon of masculinity-in-crisis for the 21st 5
century. Don is in pain, yes, and hurting himself, too (for all his spectacular
emotional reserve). But he is also different. No tears or blood on that impeccably
pressed suit. No close ties to other men. What is it that makes this odd blend of
Jay Gatsby, American Gigolo, and the Man in the Gray Flannel Suit so
captivating a figure for today?

When I asked a sample of folks close to hand what they thought of the 6
show, strangely enough, the first three said virtually the same thing—all
references to Don: *"The guy is hot."* (OK, my mother, a veteran of the *Mad Men*
era, said "very handsome," not "hot"). To be sure, the show need not be
experienced as the story of a "hot" guy in crisis. A close female colleague,
indifferent to Don's eros, tunes in mostly for the Peggy Olson narrative. And
there is my husband, who enjoys the show for its complexity and period detail,
but hates Don Draper for his selfishness and lies. Like Don, my husband is a
hard-working professional father of two in his late 30s. Unlike Don . . . well,
you could call him the anti-Don.

Although Don Draper is the show's center of gravity, a constellation of 7
intriguing personalities surrounds him. Several of those characters suggest
series that might have been: *Mad Women,* in which Joan Holloway and Peggy
Olson take different paths in the struggle for integrity in a man's world; *Mad
Closet,* the story of Salvatore Romano's slow-motion sexual awakening; *Bad
Men,* a close study of Pete Campbell's toxic cocktail of ambition and insecurity;
Race Men, in which Paul Kinsey strives to be a hero in the civil-rights movement
without exposing himself as an insufferable honkie; *Sad Men,* a nighttime soap
in which Roger Sterling deludes himself about his impending mortality; and of
course *Mod Men,* a show about style.

And then there is Don's beautiful wife, Betty, who, though clearly his better 8
half, is not his patsy. A kind of Donna Reed on steroids, she is much, much more
than the first woman on television to have a passionate affair with a household
appliance. Her vigorous horsemanship, her facility with a shotgun: These are
the signs that though raised to follow the grooves, Betty cannot be underestimated.

Jon Hamm as Don Draper in the AMC series *Mad Men*.

Witness the end of the first season when, opening the phone bill, she learns that Don has been checking up on her with her psychoanalyst. We think she is in the dark about Don's infidelity; but then, as she lies on the couch, we learn that she has known all along. Betty's decision to tell the good doctor wasn't Freud's talking cure but a savvy move on the chess board that is the Draper marriage. She knows that the shrink will tell Don, so that Don will learn, with a minimum of confrontation, that his fooling around isn't fooling anyone.

9   Conventional wisdom says that women are irresistibly attracted to power. And yet, professionally speaking, Don's position is precarious. Less Gordon Gekko in *Wall Street* than Montgomery Clift's character in *A Place in the Sun*, he is vulnerable to corporate management, professional rivals, and the whims of clients. With no family connections to buttress him, Don has nothing to sell but himself. If he is powerful, it's because the particular commodity he has to offer is selling itself: the trick of making selling seem magical in a consumer society. That is why Don's "hotness" is not the garden-variety sort—not the televised equivalent of an Abercrombie & Fitch ad—but the aspect of his character that connects his existential crisis to ours.

Don's sexual tensions bespeak his brilliance as an ad man. His genius for 10
spinning fantasies works in boardroom and bedroom alike. Though superficially
a "man's man," he does not long for intimacy with other men. Women are his
métier; their desire is the complement to the seductive powers his clients pay
him to wield. This is not to say that "sex sells"—a crude logic that Don despises.
It is to a say that in a consumer society, the fine art of selling is a lot like sex.

While his milieu is fundamentally misogynistic, Don himself is far less so. 11
At home he is a possessive, philandering husband, but at work he is the least
sexist of the lot, respecting the feelings of middle-age women and promoting
his talented secretary.

If Betty is stuck playing Don's Madonna—the angelic mother he never 12
had—the other women in his life are more like female variations on Don. There
is Midge, the independent bohemian who doesn't make breakfast; Bobbie
Barrett, the shrewd businesswoman whose frank sexual hunger ignites Don's
kinky side; and Rachel, also a businesswoman, but memorable as the one who
got away. Her Jewishness stands for a kind of depth that might cut through
Don's mad world if only his desire to connect could trump his need to seduce.
In one of many grace notes, Don, in need of a pseudonym, calls himself Tilden
Katz—the man Rachel marries after she ends their affair. It is Don imagining
himself as an anti-Don.

In the title poem of *Meditations in an Emergency*, a collection by Frank 13
O'Hara that Don reads, the speaker writes, "no one trusts me" because "I am
always looking away." As we eventually learn, Don sends this book to the
widow of the man whose identity he stole. But Don's past is really window
dressing for a more systemic crisis. There are lots of men with Don's issues who
aren't orphans and didn't change their names. If there is anyone who trusts
Don it is Peggy, a woman whose loyalty he values too much to throw away—
perhaps because he knows that she is like him: Her talent for selling will take
her places.

For some viewers, the secret of *Mad Men*'s success is the pleasure of 14
watching characters who don't know, as we do, that "change is gonna come." If
that's true, we have more reason to be anxious voyeurs than smug ones. We
may know more than Don, Roger, and Betty about the dangers of booze and
cigarettes—but we still die as they do (and die increasingly of cancer). And
while we have made real gains in sexual and racial equality, the price we have
paid is the reactionary anger that haunts every aspect of our social being.

The open secret of our time is that we are less secure than were our 15
precursors in the *Mad Men* era. If we know them to be in the grips of a cold war
that finally came to an end, we know ourselves to be losing wars of our own
making—a boundless "war on terror" and the destruction of our own
environment. We do not watch *Mad Men* because we imagine ourselves as free
of vice and illusions; we watch it because we know that our lives, too, are one
long meditation in an emergency.

16   In the dwindling prosperity that is capitalism in the 21st century, every one of us knows that we must sell ourselves, make our pitch, compete for our place in the sun. Though Don has a nice house and car, like most of us, he will never join the big leagues. Among us today, he would not be a Wall Street banker or CEO, for he is not cut from that cloth. His golden parachute is the dream of another life in a California that, if it ever existed, exists no more.

17   *"The guy is hot."* If we feast our eyes on Don, wanting him and wanting to be like him, it is perhaps because we, too, want to make it look that good. As Frank O'Hara wrote, "It is easy to be beautiful; it is difficult to appear so." Don gratifies the illusion that a life lived as a commodity can somehow be meaningful; that if we close our eyes, the art of selling will be like the best sex we ever had.

COMPREHENSION

1. Why does Goodlad identify herself as a feminist? What bearing does her feminism have on her interpretation of *Mad Men?* Provide examples from the essay to support your response.
2. According to Goodlad, the main character in *Mad Men*, Don Draper, is an "icon of masculinity-in-crisis" (paragraph 5). What does she mean by this phrase? Where in the essay does she explore this idea? Why would a self-styled feminist defend a character like Don Draper? How does this defense of Don work in Goodlad's feminist interpretation of *Mad Men?*
3. What observations does Goodlad make about American culture in this essay?

RHETORIC

1. Goodlad summarizes various plot lines and introduces primary characters in *Mad Men*. Why does she devote so much space to this overview? What assumptions is she making about her primary audience, who typically would be college teachers and administrators? (Recall that this essay appeared in the *Chronicle of Higher Education.*) What information does she convey that the average viewer might not know or find interesting?
2. What is Goodlad's thesis? Does she state or imply her main idea? Explain.
3. Identify the allusions that Goodlad uses in this essay. What is her purpose in referring to other characters and works, ranging from Anne Rice's vampires to Frank O'Hara? (Who *was* Frank O'Hara?)

4. Goodlad makes a number of assertions regarding the cultural significance of *Mad Men*. What are they, and do they effectively support her thesis? Are these assertions facts or opinions? Explain your viewpoint.
5. Which paragraphs constitute what we might consider to be Goodlad's conclusion? Is this conclusion effective? Why or why not?

WRITING

1. Watch one episode of *Mad Men*, and then write your own critical response to it.
2. **Writing an Argument:** It could be argued that television series like *Mad Men*, *The Sopranos*, and *Breaking Bad* engage in negative stereotyping. Which side of the debate do you take? Write an argumentative essay on this topic. State your claim, offer evidence, and structure the argument carefully in a series of key reasons in support of your claim.

NETWORKING

Applying 21st-Century Literacies

Critically Interpreting a Television Series: Write a feminist interpretation of a television series that you watch regularly or are familiar with.

Synthesis: Classic and Contemporary Questions for Comparison

1. Warshow critiques the function and role of the gangster in popular media, whereas Goodlad focuses on an analysis of one television series in which the life of an ad man is articulated. How do these different focuses determine the theses of each essay? What are the positive and negative consequences of addressing a broad issue in "The Gangster as Tragic Hero" without using one extended example, as opposed to the detailed analysis of one TV series by Goodlad?
2. Goodlad writes an admittedly feminist critique of *Mad Men*. How would you categorize Warshow's critical approach? Is he interested in theory? Why or why not?
3. Compare and contrast Warshow's and Goodlad's observations about American culture in their respective essays. In which of these essays do you find these cultural insights to be most convincing, and why?

Once Upon a Quinceañera

Julia Alvarez

Julia Alvarez (b. 1950), a novelist, poet, and nonfiction writer, was born in New York City but raised until the age of 10 in the Dominican Republic. She was forced to flee with her family after her father, a physician, was implicated in a plot to overthrow the dictator Rafael Trujillo, an event alluded to in her semiautobiographical novel, How the Garcia Girls Lost Their Accents *(1991). (A second novel,* Yo!, *which continues the Garcia/Alvarez family saga, appeared in 1997.) Alvarez attended Middlebury College (BA, 1971) and Syracuse University (MFA, 1975), and she is currently on the English faculty at Middlebury. In addition to her fiction, Alvarez has published several volumes of poetry, books for children, a collection of essays, and numerous articles for major magazines. One of her latest books is* Saving the World *(2006), in which Alvarez examines the global attempt to eradicate smallpox. In this selection from* Once Upon a Quinceañera *(2007), Alvarez provides readers with insight into one of the most common and compelling rituals that frame the lives of young Latinas.*

1   I'm sitting in my room at the Pan American Hotel feeling pretty much like Cinderella before her fairy godmother shows up. I drove down from Vermont early this morning, a five-hour drive that had taken me six hours since I'm not used to finding my way through the urban labyrinths of parkways and expressways with exits popping up out of nowhere to this multicultural, multilingual, multimulti area of Queens where forty years ago my own immigrant adolescence was spent.

2   I've driven down here to attend Monica Ramos's quinceañera. The plan was that I would phone the Ramoses as soon as I arrived and they would come and get me so I could follow the quinceañera in the last few hours of her preparations. But I've been calling the family home number and Monica's father's cell number for the last half hour and nobody answers. Maybe it's the busy floral pattern of the hotel bedspread or the scented air freshener recently sprayed in the room, but I'm beginning to feel lightheaded with misgivings. Did I come this far just to spend a night in my overpriced room at the Pan American, only to have to turn around tomorrow morning and drive back to Vermont without even a glimpse of this Queens quinceañera?

3   Like many USA-born Latinas, Monica, whose parents were both born in the Dominican Republic, is actually celebrating her quinceañera on her sixteenth birthday. This is just one more adaptation of the old-country tradition which has now survived more than four decades on American soil. But with a persistence unique to this immigrant group that seems to retain at least some of its Spanish and its feeling that "home" is still south of the Rio Grande even into a second and third generation, Monica calls her sweet sixteen a "quinceañera sort of."

Monica's quinceañera had sounded great over the phone. It was going to be 4 so special, she told me during several long-distance conversations. Open, friendly, easy to talk to, Monica was one of the most verbal and forthcoming quinceañeras I interviewed. She didn't want a party at first, but she was finally won over by two things: the chance to dress up in a beautiful princess gown and the opportunity to give a speech in front of her whole family and all her friends. Monica's party will include the lighting of seventeen candles, each one dedicated to a special person with a little speech about why this person is so special to her.

"There's always an added candle, dedicated to someone absent," Monica 5 explains about the extra candle. "Mine's going to be dedicated to God for giving me such a special life."

Monica has told me that she is a devoted Catholic. I have to bite my tongue 6 so as not to point out that a candle meant for someone absent is perhaps not the best category for a God who I'm sure Monica believes is everywhere. But it's hard enough to get these young ladies to confide in a virtual stranger without peppering them with prickly questions. As one young lady told me when I pursued a line of questioning about how exactly she thought she was going to go from being a girl to being a woman by having a quinceañera, "This is becoming annoying."

Instead I asked Monica if her quinceañera was going to have a 7 theme. Themes are popular: the quinceañera is a butterfly, emerging from a flower. The quinceañera is a princess, sitting on a throne. The quinceañera is a cowgirl, with a court of boys sporting lassos. The quinceañera, like a magician's trick, rises up out of a trapdoor in a puff of smoke.

"Mine is all based on Disney characters," Monica announced excitedly. The 8 girlfriends in her court were going to be Sleeping Beauty, Snow White, Jasmine, Belle . . . "We're going to do like little play where my prince is going to find my heels on the dance floor and bring them to my dad to put on my feet," Monica gushed on.

Before hanging up, I asked Monica what her quinceañera meant to her. 9 Although she had been quite garrulous about the party details, Monica seemed stumped by the question. Every quinceañera I've asked has given me the same pat answer. Claudia in Lawrence, Massachusetts, a short, stocky girl in sweat pants, pressured by her mami to have a quince party; Ashley in San Antonio, a popular, petite girl with a string of girlfriends who had celebrated or were in line to celebrate their quinces; Leticia in East L.A., who ran off with her chambelán seven months later—all of them echoed Monica as if reciting the mantra of quinceañeras: "I'm going from being a girl to being a woman." When I pressed Monica about what this meant, she answered vaguely: "It's like part of my culture."

"So, did your mother have a quinceañera back in the D.R.?" I wondered.   10

Monica wasn't sure. "Mami!" she called out from her end of the phone. 11 "Did you have a quinceañera?" The answer came back, "A quinceañera quinceañera, no, mi'ja."

12   I found out about Monica's quinceañera only four days ago in that word-of-mouth way so reminiscent of our home cultures. A Dominican student's Co-lombian friend has a mother who owns a flower shop in Queens that does a lot of quinceañeras, and she (the mother) was doing Monica's flowers and also providing some of the props, and she told the Ramoses about me. By the time I got word back that the Ramoses would be happy to have me attend Monica's party and, phone number in hand, I called them, they were into that forty-eight-hour countdown usually associated with weddings in which everyone is racing around, hyperventilating, arguing, bursting into tears, and the bride is threatening to call the whole thing off. In fact, Monica's party is taking place soon after the headline story about the runaway bride, Jennifer Wilbanks, who disappeared days before her wedding in Duluth, Georgia. As I sit in my hotel room, waiting to get through to the Ramoses, I wonder if no one is answering because Monica has run off. Perhaps she will be the first runaway quinceañera to get national media attention.

13   On the phone, a very generous Mr. Ramos ("José, por favor!") had offered to pick me up at the airport should I come by plane. "I wouldn't think of it with as much as you have to do," I declined. In part, I thought it wise to have a way to get from the church, where a Mass or blessing would precede the party, to the Dance Club, where the ceremony, supper, and dance would take place, and back to the hotel at a reasonable hour, as these parties tend to go on past the Cinderella stroke of midnight. Bringing my own wheels will turn out to be an inspired decision in more ways than I would ever have anticipated. But at the moment, I am wondering if the long drive has been in vain as none of the messages I've left on Mr. Ramos's cell phone or home phone have been returned. Foolishly, I have no address, no other way to contact the family. I look out the grimy picture window of the Pan American past the back parking lot toward street after street of fenced-in row houses, and I know, with a sinking heart, that this is not the kind of neighborhood where everyone knows everybody else.

14   An hour goes by. It's Friday, so back in Vermont, my husband is still at work. I had suggested we both fly down, wimpy city driver that I am, and make a weekend of it, but before I could finish outlining the fun of two nights at the Pan American Hotel, my husband was shaking his head. He'd had enough of quinceañeras, thank you. "You've only been to a few," I argued, feeling vaguely wounded at his obvious disenchantment with one of *my* cultural traditions. "I've been to four and that's three too many," he countered. I don't know if it's his thrifty German-Lutheran roots, but from the beginning he has looked askance at these over the top celebrations, many of them costing much more than working-class families can afford.

15   His skepticism about this tradition is also my own. The incredible expense; a girl encouraged in the dubious fantasy of being a princess as if news of feminism had never reached her mami; the marketing of a young lady as attractive, marriageable goods. Why not save the money for education? I've snuck in that question in all of my interviews. Why not have coming-of-age celebrations for boys as well as girls? But still, every time the young lady makes an entrance

through her archway, or curtains part and there she is, sitting on her swing or a throne or a carousel horse, while the whole familia and roomful of friends applaud her, my eyes tear up and my throat catches. The tradition, whatever its trappings, is homing in on a need to acknowledge and celebrate these new arrivals in the field of time. From my spot in the crowd I am torn between optimism for this tender, young being emerging from the cocoon of her childhood and a sense of dread that the world she is entering, unlike the fantasy she is enjoying this one night, will not allow for such winged flight.

COMPREHENSION

1. Why does Alvarez inject herself into this story? What is her purpose?
2. Why, according to Alvarez, is quinceañera so important in Latino/Hispanic culture? Do you think she makes a convincing case for its importance? Why or why not?
3. What, ultimately, is Alvarez's attitude toward quinceañera? How do you know? Why doesn't Alvarez's husband want to accompany her as she attends the Ramos's quinceañera?

RHETORIC

1. Although she writes in various literary modes, Alvarez is best known as a novelist. What elements of fiction do you detect in this essay? Identify specific passages to support your analysis. How effective are these strategies, and why?
2. How would you describe Alvarez's audience for this essay? How successful is she in tailoring the tone and content of the selection to this audience? Does she present herself as an authority on the subject or an investigator, and what is the importance of this stance?
3. Does Alvarez establish a thesis or claim about quinceañeras? Why or why not?
4. Alvarez gradually establishes an extended or working definition of quinceañera. Locate passages where the reader receives information about this custom or ritual.
5. How does Alvarez link her introductory and concluding paragraphs? How do these two paragraphs serve as a framing device for the body of the selection?

WRITING

1. Write a narrative essay in which you tell about a ritual, custom, or celebration that is important to your family or culture.
2. Compose a comparative essay on quinceañeras and sweet sixteen celebrations, bar/bat mitzvahs, or other coming-of-age celebrations.

3. **Writing an Argument:** Argue for or against the proposition that coming-of-age celebrations have become too expensive and ostentatious in contemporary American culture.

NETWORKING

Applying 21st-Century Literacies

Shooting a Video Essay or Documentary: Approach question 1 under Writing as a video essay/documentary. If you don't own camera equipment of your own, borrow some from the school. Shoot and narrate a video documenting a ritual, custom, holiday, or other type of celebration important to your family or culture. To make your video especially engaging, before you begin the actual shooting, think of questions to ask participants, and write yourself at least the outline of a script. You can also edit sound in later for the main narration. You might focus on something specific, like the preparation of a particular type of dish, or show a broader overview of the events that make up the tradition.

NETWORKING
Applying 21st-Century Literacies

Listening and Synthesizing: On the Chapter 2 Networking page (at *www.mhhe .com/mhreader11e*), listen to the podcast of student newspaper *InsideVandy*'s interview with Chancellor Nicholas Zeppos of Vanderbilt University. Expanding on assignment 3 under "Writing," synthesize his positions into your argument, providing solid reasons why you agree, agree with qualifications, or disagree with his position on an "English-Only" referendum in Davidson County, Tennessee.

Freewriting

Peter Elbow

Peter Elbow (b. 1935) was born in New York and received degrees from Williams College, Exeter College, Oxford, and Brandeis University. He has taught at the University of Massachusetts at Amherst, the State University of New York at Stony Brook, the Massachusetts Institute of Technology, Franconia College, and Evergreen State College. He is considered by some writing teachers to have revolutionized the teaching of writing through his popularization of the concept and practice called "freewriting." He is the author or editor of more than 15 books on writing, including Writing without Teachers, Writing with Power, Embracing Contraries, What Is English? *and, most recently,* Everyone Can Write: Essays toward a Hopeful Theory of Writing and Teaching Writing *(2000). In "Freewriting," taken from* Writing without Teachers, *Elbow explains an exercise for writing students that he helped popularize in American colleges, universities, and writing workshops.*

1   The most effective way I know to improve your writing is to do freewriting exercises regularly. At least three times a week. They are sometimes called "automatic writing," "babbling," or "jabbering" exercises. The idea is simply to write for ten minutes (later on, perhaps fifteen or twenty). Don't stop for anything. Go quickly without rushing. Never stop to look back, to cross something out, to wonder how to spell something, to wonder what word or thought to use, or to think about what you are doing. If you can't think of a word or a spelling, just use a squiggle or else write, "I can't think of it." Just put down something. The easiest thing is just to put down whatever is in your mind. If you get stuck it's fine to write "I can't think what to say, I can't think

what to say" as many times as you want; or repeat the last word you wrote over and over again; or anything else. The only requirement is that you *never* stop.

What happens to a freewriting exercise is important. It must be a piece of ₂ writing which, even if someone reads it, doesn't send any ripples back to you. It is like writing something and putting it in a bottle in the sea. The teacherless class helps your writing by providing maximum feedback. Freewritings help you by providing no feedback at all. When I assign one, I invite the writer to let me read it. But also tell him to keep it if he prefers. I read it quickly and make no comments at all and I do not speak with him about it. The main thing is that a freewriting must never be evaluated in any way; in fact there must be no discussion or comment at all.

Here is an example of a fairly coherent exercise (sometimes they are very ₃ incoherent, which is fine):

> I think I'll write what's on my mind, but the only thing on my mind right now is what to write for ten minutes. I've never done this before and I'm not prepared in any way—the sky is cloudy today, how's that? now I'm afraid I won't be able to think of what to write when I get to the end of the sentence—well, here I am at the end of the sentence—here I am again, again, again, again, at least I'm still writing—Now I ask is there some reason to be happy that I'm still writing—ah yes! Here comes the question again—What am I getting out of this? What point is there in it? It's almost obscene to always ask it but I seem to question everything that way and I was gonna say something else pertaining to that but I got so busy writing down the first part that I forgot what I was leading into. This is kind of fun oh don't stop writing—cars and trucks speeding by somewhere out the window, pens clittering across people's papers. The sky is cloudy—is it symbolic that I should be mentioning it? Huh? I dunno. Maybe I should try colors, blue, red, dirty words—wait a minute—no can't do that, orange, yellow, arm tired, green pink violet magenta lavender red brown black green—now that I can't think of any more colors—just about done—relief? maybe.

Freewriting may seem crazy but actually it makes simple sense. Think of the difference between speaking and writing. Writing has the advantage of permitting more editing. But that's its downfall too. Almost everybody interposes a massive and complicated series of editings between the time words start to be born into consciousness and when they finally come off the end of the pencil or typewriter onto the page. This is partly because schooling makes us obsessed with the "mistakes" we make in writing. Many people are constantly thinking about spelling and grammar as they try to write. I am always thinking about the awkwardness, wordiness, and general mushiness of my natural verbal product as I try to write down words.

But it's not just "mistakes" or "bad writing" we edit as we write. We also ₄ edit unacceptable thoughts and feelings, as we do in speaking. In writing there is more time to do it so the editing is heavier: when speaking, there's someone right there waiting for a reply and he'll get bored or think we're crazy if we don't come out with *something*. Most of the time in speaking, we settle for the catch-as-catch-can way in which the words tumble out. In writing, however, there's a chance to try to get them right. But the opportunity to get them right is a terrible burden: you can work for two hours trying to get a paragraph "right" and discover it's not right at all. And then give up.

5   Editing, *in itself,* is not the problem. Editing is usually necessary if we want to end up with something satisfactory. The problem is that editing goes on *at the same time* as producing. The editor is, as it were, constantly looking over the shoulder of the producer and constantly fiddling with what he's doing while he's in the middle of trying to do it. No wonder the producer gets nervous, jumpy, inhibited, and finally can't be coherent. It's an unnecessary burden to try to think of words and also worry at the same time whether they're the right words.

6   The main thing about freewriting is that it is *nonediting.* It is an exercise in bringing together the process of producing words and putting them down on the page. Practiced regularly, it undoes the ingrained habit of editing at the same time you are trying to produce. It will make writing less blocked because words will come more easily. You will use up more paper, but chew up fewer pencils.

7   Next time you write, notice how often you stop yourself from writing down something you were going to write down. Or else cross it out after it's written. "Naturally," you say, "it wasn't any good." But think for a moment about the occasions when you spoke well. Seldom was it because you first got the beginning just right. Usually it was a matter of a halting or even garbled beginning, but you kept going and your speech finally became coherent and even powerful. There is a lesson here for writing: trying to get the beginning just right is a formula for failure—and probably a secret tactic to make your-self give up writing. Make some words, whatever they are, and then grab hold of that line and reel in as hard as you can. Afterwards you can throw away lousy beginnings and make new ones. This is the quickest way to get into good writing.

8   The habit of compulsive, premature editing doesn't just make writing hard. It also makes writing dead. Your voice is damped out by all the inter-ruptions, changes, and hesitations between the consciousness and the page. In your natural way of producing words there is a sound, a texture, a rhythm—a voice—which is the main source of power in your writing. I don't know how it works, but this voice is the force that will make a reader listen to you, the energy that drives the meanings through his thick skull. Maybe you don't *like* your voice; maybe people have made fun of it. But it's the only voice you've got. It's your only source of power. You better get back into it, no mat-ter what you think of it. If you keep writing in it, it may change into some-thing you like better. But if you abandon it, you'll likely never have a voice and never be heard.

9   Freewritings are vacuums. Gradually you will begin to carry over into your regular writing some of the voice, force, and connectedness that creep into those vacuums.

COMPREHENSION

1. What is the thesis of the essay? Is it implied or stated directly in the text?
2. In paragraph 5, Elbow refers to the "producer" and the "editor." Who are they? Where are they located? How did they develop?
3. In paragraph 8, the author makes a connection between one's personal "voice" and the idea of "power." Why does Elbow focus so strongly on this connection?

RHETORIC

1. Elbow frequently uses the "imperative" (or command) sentence form in the opening paragraph. Why? What would have been the effect had he used the simple declarative form?
2. Writers often use examples to help illustrate their point. Does the example of a freewriting exercise Elbow provides in paragraph 3 help you to understand the method? Why or why not?
3. The author uses colloquial terms such as "squiggle" (paragraph 1), "crazy" and "mushiness" (paragraph 3), and "lousy" (paragraph 7). How does his use of such words affect the tone of the essay?
4. Are there any elements in Elbow's own style that suggest his essay may have started as a freewriting exercise? Consider the reasons he provides for the importance of freewriting—for example, generating ideas, discovering one's own voice, or expressing oneself succinctly and naturally.
5. Elbow is himself a college writing teacher. Based on your assessment of the tone of the essay, whom do you think is his intended audience? Is it broad or narrow? Specialized or general? Or could he have in mind more than one type of audience? Explain your answer.
6. Note the number of times Elbow begins his sentences with coordinating conjunctions ("but," "and," "or"). For example, in paragraph 4, he does it three times. Many writing teachers frown on this method of structuring sentences. Why does Elbow employ it?
7. Compare the essay's introduction to its conclusion. Note how the introduction is rather long and the conclusion is quite short (two sentences, in fact). How do these two elements contribute to the overall "pace" of the essay?

WRITING

1. During one week, complete three freewriting exercises. Wait one week, and then review what you have written. Explore any insights your freewriting gives you into your writer's "voice"— your concerns, interests, style, and "power."
2. Write an expository paper explaining the difficulties you have when writing an essay homework assignment or writing an essay-length response during an exam.
3. Write a comparison and contrast essay wherein you examine the similarities and differences of speaking and writing.
4. **Writing an Argument:** Write an essay in which you support or discourage the act of freewriting.

NETWORKING
Applying 21st-Century Literacies

Paper vs. Screen: When freewriting, do you prefer to do so on paper or on your computer? In a paragraph, discuss what you see as two or three key advantages to your preferred way of freewriting, acknowledging (and rebutting) at least one anticipated counterargument.

The Maker's Eye: Revising Your Own Manuscripts

Donald M. Murray

Donald M. Murray (1917–2006) has combined a career as teacher, journalist, fiction writer, poet, and author of several important textbooks on writing. He has worked as a teacher, journalist, and editor for Time *magazine. His books include* A Writer Teaches Writing, Write to Learn, Read to Write, *and more recently* Shoptalk: Learning to Write with Writers *(1991),* Crafting a Life in Essay, Story, Poem *(1996), and* The Craft of Revision *(1997). In this essay, originally published in the magazine* The Writer, *Murray argues for the absolute importance of the revision process to the writer. As he presents the stages of the revision process, Murray illustrates their usefulness to any writer—whether beginner or experienced—and offers his personal views and those of other authors.*

1   When students complete a first draft, they consider the job of writing done— and their teachers too often agree. When professional writers complete a first draft, they usually feel that they are at the start of the writing process. When a draft is completed, the job of writing can begin.

2   That difference in attitude is the difference between amateur and professional, inexperience and experience, journeyman and craftsman. Peter F. Drucker, the prolific business writer, calls his first draft "the zero draft"—after that he can start counting. Most writers share the feeling that the first draft, and all of those which follow, are opportunities to discover what they have to say and how best they can say it.

3   To produce a progression of drafts, each of which says more and says it more clearly, the writer has to develop a special kind of reading skill. In school we are taught to decode what appears on the page as finished writing. Writers, however, face a different category of possibility and responsibility when they read their own drafts. To them the words on the page are never finished. Each

can be changed and rearranged, can set off a chain reaction of confusion or clarified meaning. This is a different kind of reading, which is possibly more difficult and certainly more exciting.

Writers must learn to be their own best enemy. They must accept the criti- 4 cism of others and be suspicious of it; they must accept the praise of others and be even more suspicious of it. Writers cannot depend on others. They must detach themselves from their own pages so that they can apply both their caring and their craft to their own work.

Such detachment is not easy. Science fiction writer Ray Bradbury suppos- 5 edly puts each manuscript away for a year to the day and then rereads it as a stranger. Not many writers have the discipline or the time to do this. We must read when our judgment may be at its worst, when we are close to the euphoric moment of creation.

Then the writer, counsels novelist Nancy Hale, "should be critical of every- 6 thing that seems to him most delightful in his style. He should excise what he most admires, because he wouldn't thus admire it if he weren't . . . in a sense protecting it from criticism." John Ciardi, the poet, adds, "The last act of the writing must be to become one's own reader. It is, I suppose, a schizophrenic process, to begin passionately and to end critically, to begin hot and to end cold; and, more important, to be passion-hot and critic-cold at the same time."

Most people think that the principal problem is that writers are too proud 7 of what they have written. Actually, a greater problem for most professional writers is one shared by the majority of students. They are overly critical, think everything is dreadful, tear up page after page, never complete a draft, see the task as hopeless.

The writer must learn to read critically but constructively, to cut what is 8 bad, to reveal what is good. Eleanor Estes, the children's book author, explains: "The writer must survey his work critically, coolly, as though he were a stranger to it. He must be willing to prune, expertly and hard-heartedly. At the end of each revision, a manuscript may look . . . worked over, torn apart, pinned together, added to, deleted from, words changed and words changed back. Yet the book must maintain its original freshness and spontaneity."

Most readers underestimate the amount of rewriting it usually takes to pro- 9 duce spontaneous reading. This is a great disadvantage to the student writer, who sees only a finished product and never watches the craftsman who takes the necessary step back, studies the work carefully, returns to the task, steps back, returns, steps back, again and again. Anthony Burgess, one of the most prolific writers in the English-speaking world, admits, "I might revise a page twenty times." Roald Dahl, the popular children's writer, states, "By the time I'm nearing the end of a story, the first part will have been reread and altered and corrected at least 150 times. . . . Good writing is essentially rewriting. I am positive of this."

Rewriting isn't virtuous. It isn't something that ought to be done. It is sim- 10 ply something that most writers find they have to do to discover what they have to say and how to say it. It is a condition of the writer's life.

11   There are, however, a few writers who do little formal rewriting, primarily because they have the capacity and experience to create and review a large number of invisible drafts in their minds before they approach the page. And some writers slowly produce finished pages, performing all the tasks of revision simultaneously, page by page, rather than draft by draft. But it is still possible to see the sequence followed by most writers most of the time in rereading their own work.

12   Most writers scan their drafts first, reading as quickly as possible to catch the larger problems of subject and form, then move in closer and closer as they read and write, reread and rewrite.

13   The first thing writers look for in their drafts is *information.* They know that a good piece of writing is built from specific, accurate, and interesting information. The writer must have an abundance of information from which to construct a readable piece of writing.

14   Next writers look for *meaning* in the information. The specifics must build a pattern of significance. Each piece of specific information must carry the reader toward meaning.

15   Writers reading their own drafts are aware of *audience.* They put themselves in the reader's situation and make sure that they deliver information which a reader wants to know or needs to know in a manner which is easily digested. Writers try to be sure that they anticipate and answer the questions a critical reader will ask when reading the piece of writing.

16   Writers make sure that the *form* is appropriate to the subject and the audience. Form, or genre, is the vehicle which carries meaning to the reader, but form cannot be selected until the writer has adequate information to discover its significance and an audience which needs or wants that meaning.

17   Once writers are sure the form is appropriate, they must then look at the *structure,* the order of what they have written. Good writing is built on a solid framework of logic, argument, narrative, or motivation which runs through the entire piece of writing and holds it together. This is the time when many writers find it most effective to outline as a way of visualizing the hidden spine by which the piece of writing is supported.

18   The element on which writers may spend a majority of their time is *development.* Each section of a piece of writing must be adequately developed. It must give readers enough information so that they are satisfied. How much information is enough? That's as difficult as asking how much garlic belongs in a salad. It must be done to taste, but most beginning writers underdevelop, underestimating the reader's hunger for information.

19   As writers solve development problems, they often have to consider questions of *dimension.* There must be a pleasing and effective proportion among all the parts of the piece of writing. There is a continual process of subtracting and adding to keep the piece of writing in balance.

20   Finally, writers have to listen to their own voices. *Voice* is the force which drives a piece of writing forward. It is an expression of the writer's authority and concern. It is what is between the words on the page, what glues the piece

of writing together. A good piece of writing is always marked by a consistent, individual voice.

As writers read and reread, write and rewrite, they move closer and closer 21 to the page until they are doing line-by-line editing. Writers read their own pages with infinite care. Each sentence, each line, each clause, each phrase, each word, each mark of punctuation, each section of white space between the type has to contribute to the clarification of meaning.

Slowly the writer moves from word to word, looking through language to 22 see the subject. As a word is changed, cut, or added, as a construction is rearranged, all the words used before that moment and all those that follow that moment must be considered and reconsidered.

Writers often read aloud at this stage of the editing process, muttering or 23 whispering to themselves, calling on the ear's experience with language. Does this sound right—or that? Writers edit, shifting back and forth from eye to page to ear to page. I find I must do this careful editing in short runs, no more than fifteen or twenty minutes at a stretch, or I become too kind with myself. I begin to see what I hope is on the page, not what actually is on the page.

This sounds tedious if you haven't done it, but actually it is fun. Making 24 something right is immensely satisfying, for writers begin to learn what they are writing about by writing. Language leads them to meaning, and there is the joy of discovery, of understanding, of making meaning clear as the writer employs the technical skills of language.

Words have double meanings, even triple and quadruple meanings. Each 25 word has its own potential for connotation and denotation. And when writers rub one word against the other, they are often rewarded with a sudden insight, an unexpected clarification.

The maker's eye moves back and forth from word to phrase to sentence to 26 paragraph to sentence to phrase to word. The maker's eye sees the need for variety and balance, for a firmer structure, for a more appropriate form. It peers into the interior of the paragraph, looking for coherence, unity, and emphasis, which make meaning clear.

I learned something about this process when my first bifocals were pre- 27 scribed. I had ordered a larger section of the reading portion of the glass because of my work, but even so, I could not contain my eyes within this new limit of vision. And I still find myself taking off my glasses and bending my nose towards the page, for my eyes unconsciously flick back and forth across the page, back to another page, forward to still another, as I try to see each evolving line in relation to every other line.

When does this process end? Most writers agree with the great Russian 28 writer Tolstoy, who said, "I scarcely ever reread my published writings, if by chance I come across a page, it always strikes me: all this must be rewritten; this is how I should have written it."

The maker's eye is never satisfied, for each word has the potential to ignite 29 new meaning. This article has been twice written all the way through the writing process, and it was published four years ago. Now it is to be republished in a book. The editors make a few small suggestions, and then I read it with my maker's eye. Now it has been re-edited, re-revised, re-read, re-re-edited, for each piece of writing to the writer is full of potential and alternatives.

30   A piece of writing is never finished. It is delivered to a deadline, torn out of the typewriter on demand, sent off with a sense of accomplishment and shame and pride and frustration. If only there were a couple more days, time for just another run at it, perhaps then . . .

COMPREHENSION

1. In paragraph 1, what does Murray mean by the statement "When a draft is completed, the job of writing can begin"? Isn't a draft a form of writing?
2. According to Murray, what are the major differences between student and professional writers? Why do the differences help make the "professional" more accomplished at his or her work?
3. What are the differences between the reading styles of novice and experienced writers? How do the differences affect their own writings?

RHETORIC

1. Compare the introduction of this essay to that of Elbow's "Freewriting." How do they differ in tone and structure?
2. Murray begins to classify various aspects of the writer's concern in paragraph 13. Why does he wait so long to begin this analysis? Why are certain key words in paragraphs 13–20 italicized?
3. Murray uses analogy, comparing one thing with another, very different thing, to make the writing process concrete and familiar. Identify some of these analogies. Why are they models of clarity?
4. Murray refers to a writer as "the maker" several times in the essay. What does he imply by this usage? What other professions might be included in this category?
5. What is the purpose of the essay? Is it to inform? To persuade? To serve as a model? Anything else? Explain your response.
6. Murray ends the essay with an ellipses. Why?
7. Notice the sentence in paragraph 29 that has four consecutive words with the prefix "re-." What is the purpose and effect of this rhetorical device?

WRITING

1. Murray focuses on the process, craft, and purpose of the writer, but he does not define "writer." Write an extended definition explaining what he means by this occupation or profession.
2. Write an essay explaining your own writing process. Do not be intimidated if it is not like the one described by Murray. Compare and contrast your method with that of one or more of your classmates.
3. **Writing an Argument:** Murray suggests that revision is actually "fun" (paragraph 24). Do you agree or disagree? Write an essay defending your position.

Glossary

Abstract/concrete patterns of language reflect an author's word choice. Abstract words (for example, *wisdom, power,* and *beauty*) refer to general ideas, qualities, or conditions. Concrete words name material objects and items associated with the five senses—words like *rock, pizza,* and *basketball.* Both abstract and concrete language are useful in communicating ideas. Generally, you should not be too abstract in writing. It is best to employ concrete words, naming things that can be seen, touched, smelled, heard, or tasted in order to support generalizations, topic sentences, or more abstract ideas.

Acronym is a word formed from the first or first few letters of several words, as in OPEC (Organization of Petroleum Exporting Countries).

Action in narrative writing is the sequence of happenings or events. This movement of events may occupy just a few minutes or extend over a period of years or centuries.

Alliteration is the repetition of initial consonant sounds in words placed closely next to each other, as in "what a tale of terror now their turbulency tells." Prose that is highly rhythmical or "poetic" often makes use of this method.

Allusion is a literary, biographical, or historical reference, whether real or imaginary. It is a "figure of speech" (a fresh, useful comparison) employed to illuminate an idea. A writer's prose style can be made richer through this economical method of evoking an idea or emotion, as in E. M. Forster's biblical allusion in this sentence: "Property produces men of weight, and it was a man of weight who failed to get into the Kingdom of Heaven."

Analogy is a form of comparison that uses a clear illustration to explain a difficult idea or function. It is unlike a formal comparison in that its subjects of comparison are from different categories or areas. For example, an analogy likening "division of labor" to the activity of bees in a hive makes the first concept more concrete by showing it to the reader through the figurative comparison with the bees. Analogy in exposition can involve a few sentences, a paragraph or set of paragraphs, or an entire essay. Analogies can also be used in argumentation to heighten an appeal to emotion, but they cannot actually *prove* anything.

Analysis is a method of exposition in which a subject is broken up into its parts to explain their nature, function, proportion, or relationship. Analysis thus explores connections and processes within the context of a given subject. (See *causal analysis* and *process analysis.*)

Anecdote is a brief, engaging account of some happening, often historical, biographical, or personal. As a technique in writing, anecdote is especially effective in creating interesting essay introductions and also in illuminating abstract concepts in the body of the essay.

Antecedent   in grammar refers to the word, phrase, or clause to which a pronoun refers. In writing, antecedent also refers to any happening or thing that is prior to another or to anything that logically precedes a subject.

Antithesis   is the balancing of one idea or term against another for emphasis.

Antonym   is a word whose meaning is opposite to that of another word.

Aphorism   is a short, pointed statement expressing a general truism or an idea in an original or imaginative way. Marshall McLuhan's statement that "the medium is the message" is a well-known contemporary aphorism.

Archaic   language is vocabulary or usage that belongs to an earlier period and is old-fashioned today. The word *thee* for *you* is an archaism still in use in certain situations.

Archetypes   are special images or symbols that, according to Carl Jung, appeal to the total racial or cultural understanding of a people. Such images or symbols as the mother archetype, the cowboy in American film, a sacred mountain, or spring as a time of renewal tend to trigger the "collective unconscious" of the human race.

Argumentation   is a formal variety of writing that offers reasons for or against something. Its goal is to persuade or convince the reader through logical reasoning and carefully controlled emotional appeal. Argumentation as a formal mode of writing contains many properties that distinguish it from exposition. (See *assumption, deduction, evidence, induction, logic, persuasion, proposition,* and *refutation.*)

Assonance   is defined generally as likeness or rough similarity of sound. Its specific definition is a partial rhyme in which the stressed vowel sounds are alike but the consonant sounds are unlike, as in *late* and *make.* Although more common to poetry, assonance can also be detected in highly rhythmic prose.

Assumption   in argumentation is anything taken for granted or presumed to be accepted by the audience and therefore unstated. Assumptions in argumentative writing can be dangerous because the audience might not always accept the idea implicit in them. (See *begging the question.*)

Audience   is that readership toward which an author directs his or her essay. In composing essays, writers must acknowledge the nature of their expected readers—whether specialized or general, minimally educated or highly educated, sympathetic or unsympathetic toward the writer's opinions, and so forth. Failure to focus on the writer's true audience can lead to confusion in language and usage, presentation of inappropriate content, and failure to appeal to the expected reader.

Balance   in sentence structure refers to the assignment of equal treatment in the arrangement of coordinate ideas. It is often used to heighten a contrast of ideas.

Begging the question   is an error or a fallacy in reasoning and argumentation in which the writer assumes as a truth something for which evidence or proof is actually needed.

Causal analysis   is a form of writing that examines causes and effects of events or conditions as they relate to a specific subject. Writers can investigate the causes of a particular effect or the effects of a particular cause or combine both methods. Basically, however, causal analysis looks for connections between things and reasons behind them.

Characterization   is the creation of people involved in the action. It is used especially in narrative or descriptive writing. Authors use techniques of dialogue, description, reportage, and observation in attempting to present vivid and distinctive characters.

Chronology or chronological order   is the arrangement of events in the order in which they happened. Chronological order can be used in such diverse narrative situations as history, biography, scientific process, and personal account. Essays that are ordered by chronology move from one step or point to the next in time.

Cinematic technique   in narration, description, and occasionally exposition is the conscious application of film art to the development of the contemporary essay. Modern writers often are aware of such film techniques as montage (the process of cutting and arranging film so that short scenes are presented in rapid succession), zoom (intense enlargement of subject), and various forms of juxtaposition, and use these methods to enhance the quality of their essays.

Classification   is a form of exposition in which the writer divides a subject into categories and then groups elements in each of those categories according to their relationships with one another. Thus a writer using classification takes a topic, divides it into several major groups, and then often subdivides those groups, moving always from larger categories to smaller ones.

Cliché   is an expression that once was fresh and original but that has lost much of its vitality through overuse. Because expressions like "as quick as a wink" and "blew her stack" are trite or common today, they should be avoided in writing.

Climactic ordering   is the arrangement of a paragraph or essay so that the most important items are saved for last. The effect is to build slowly through a sequence of events or ideas to the most critical part of the composition.

Coherence   is a quality in effective writing that results from the careful ordering of each sentence in a paragraph and each paragraph in the essay. If an essay is coherent, each part will grow naturally and logically from those parts that come before it. Following careful chronological, logical, spatial, or sequential order is the most natural way to achieve coherence in writing. The main devices used in achieving coherence are transitions, which help connect one thought with another.

Colloquial language   is conversational language used in certain types of informal and narrative writing but rarely in essays, business writing, or research writing. Expressions like "cool," "pal," or "I can dig it" often have a place in conversational settings. However, they should be used sparingly in essay writing for special effects.

Comparison/contrast   as an essay pattern treats similarities and differences between two subjects. Any useful comparison involves two items from the same class. Moreover, there must be a clear reason for the comparison or contrast. Finally, there must be a balanced treatment of the various comparative or contrasting points between the two subjects.

Conclusions   are the endings of essays. Without a conclusion, an essay would be incomplete, leaving the reader with the feeling that something important has been left out. There are numerous strategies for conclusions available to writers: summarizing main points in the essay, restating the main idea, using an effective quotation, offering the reader the climax to a series of events, returning to the beginning and echoing it, offering a solution to a problem, emphasizing the topic's significance, or setting a new frame of reference by generalizing from the main the-sis. A conclusion should end the essay in a clear, convincing, emphatic way.

Concrete   (See *abstract/concrete*.)

Conflict   in narrative writing is the clash or opposition of events, characters, or ideas that makes the resolution of action necessary.

Connotation/denotation   are terms specifying the way a word has meaning. Connota-tion refers to the "shades of meaning" that a word might have because of various emotional associations it calls up for writers and readers alike. Words like *patrio-tism, pig,* and *rose* have strong connotative overtones to them. Denotation refers to the "dictionary" definition of a word—its exact meaning. Good writers understand the connotative and denotative value of words and control the shades of meaning that many words possess.

Context   is the situation surrounding a word, group of words, or sentence. Often the elements coming before or after a certain confusing or difficult construction will provide insight into the meaning or importance of that item.

Coordination   in sentence structure refers to the grammatical arrangement of parts of the same order or equality in rank.

Declarative sentences   make a statement or assertion.

Deduction   is a form of logic that begins with a generally stated truth or principle and then offers details, examples, and reasoning to support the generalization. In other words, deduction is based on reasoning from a known principle to an unknown principle, from the general to the specific, or from a premise to a logical conclusion. (See *syllogism*.)

Definition   in exposition is the extension of a word's meaning through a paragraph or an entire essay. As an extended method of explaining a word, this type of definition relies on other rhetorical methods, including detail, illustration, comparison and contrast, and anecdote.

Denotation   (See *connotation/denotation*.)

Description   in the prose essay is a variety of writing that uses details of sight, sound, color, smell, taste, and touch to create a word picture and to explain or illustrate an idea.

Development   refers to the way a paragraph or an essay elaborates or builds upon a topic or theme. Typical development proceeds either from general illustrations to specific ones or from one generalization to another. (See *horizontal/vertical*.)

Dialogue   is the reproduction of speech or conversation between two or more persons in writing. Dialogue can add concreteness and vividness to an essay and can also help reveal character. A writer who reproduces dialogue in an essay must use it for a purpose and not simply as a decorative device.

Diction   is the manner of expression in words, choice of words, or wording. Writers must choose vocabulary carefully and precisely to communicate a message and also to address an intended audience effectively; this is good diction.

Digression   is a temporary departure from the main subject in writing. Any digression in the essay must serve a purpose or be intended for a specific effect.

Discourse (forms of)   relates conventionally to the main categories of writing—narration, description, exposition, and argumentation. In practice, these forms of discourse often blend or overlap. Essayists seek the ideal fusion of forms of discourse in the treatment of their subject.

Division is that aspect of classification in which the writer divides some large subject into categories. Division helps writers split large and potentially complicated subjects into parts for orderly presentation and discussion.

Dominant impression in description is the main impression or effect that writers attempt to create for their subject. It arises from an author's focus on a single subject and from the feelings the writer brings to that subject.

Editorializing is to express personal opinions about the subject of the essay. An editorial tone can have a useful effect in writing, but at other times an author might want to reduce editorializing in favor of a better balanced or more objective tone.

Effect is a term used in causal analysis to describe the outcome or expected result of a chain of happenings.

Emphasis indicates the placement of the most important ideas in key positions in the essay. As a major principle, emphasis relates to phrases, sentences, and paragraphs—the construction of the entire essay. Emphasis can be achieved by repetition, subordination, careful positioning of thesis and topic sentences, climactic ordering, comparison and contrast, and a variety of other methods.

Episodic relates to that variety of narrative writing that develops through a series of incidents or events.

Essay is the name given to a short prose work on a limited topic. Essays take many forms, ranging from personal narratives to critical or argumentative treatments of a subject. Normally, an essay will convey the writer's personal ideas about the subject.

Etymology is the origin and development of a word—tracing a word back as far as possible.

Evidence is material offered to support an argument or a proposition. Typical forms of evidence are facts, details, and expert testimony.

Example is a method of exposition in which the writer offers illustrations in order to explain a generalization or a whole thesis. (See *illustration*.)

Exclamatory sentences in writing express surprise or strong emotion.

Expert testimony as employed in argumentative essays and in expository essays is the use of statements by authorities to support a writer's position or idea. This method often requires careful quotation and acknowledgment of sources.

Exposition is a major form of discourse that informs or explains. Exposition is the form of expression required in much college writing, for it provides facts and information, clarifies ideas, and establishes meaning. The primary methods of exposition are *illustration, comparison and contrast, analogy, definition, classification, causal analysis,* and *process analysis* (see entries).

Extended metaphor is a figurative comparison that is used to structure a significant part of the composition or the whole essay. (See *figurative language* and *metaphor*.)

Fable is a form of narrative containing a moral that normally appears clearly at the end.

Fallacy in argumentation is an error in logic or in the reasoning process. Fallacies occur because of vague development of ideas, lack of awareness on the part of writers of the requirements of logical reasoning, or faulty assumptions about the proposition.

Figurative language   as opposed to literal language is a special approach to writing that departs from what is typically a concrete, straightforward style. It is the use of vivid, imaginative statements to illuminate or illustrate an idea. Figurative language adds freshness, meaning, and originality to a writer's style. Major figures of speech include *allusion, hyperbole, metaphor, personification,* and *simile* (see entries).

Flashback   is a narrative technique in which the writer begins at some point in the action and then moves into the past in order to provide crucial information about characters and events.

Foreshadow   is a technique that indicates beforehand what is to occur at a later point in the essay.

Frame   in narration and description is the use of a key object or pattern—typically at the start and end of the essay—that serves as a border or structure for the substance of the composition.

General/specific words   are the basis of writing, although it is wise in college composition to keep vocabulary as specific as possible. General words refer to broad categories and groups, whereas specific words capture with force and clarity the nature of the term. General words refer to large classes, concepts, groups, and emotions; specific words are more particular in providing meanings. The distinction between general and specific language is always a matter of degree.

Generalization   is a broad idea or statement. All generalizations require particulars and illustrations to support them.

Genre   is a type or form of literature—for example, short fiction, novel, poetry, or drama.

Grammatical structure   is a systematic description of language as it relates to the grammatical nature of a sentence.

Horizontal/vertical   paragraph and essay development refers to the basic way a writer moves either from one generalization to another in a carefully related series of generalizations (horizontal) or from a generalization to a series of specific supporting examples (vertical).

Hortatory style   is a variety of writing designed to encourage, give advice, or urge to good deeds.

Hyperbole   is a form of figurative language that uses exaggeration to overstate a position.

Hypothesis   is an unproven theory or proposition that is tentatively accepted to explain certain facts. A working hypothesis provides the basis for further investigation or argumentation.

Hypothetical examples   are illustrations in the form of assumptions that are based on the hypothesis. As such, they are conditional rather than absolute or certain facts.

Identification   as a method of exposition refers to focusing on the main subject of the essay. It involves the clear location of the subject within the context or situation of the composition.

Idiomatic language   is the language or dialect of a people, region, or class—the individual nature of a language.

Ignoring the question   in argumentation is a fallacy that involves the avoidance of the main issue by developing an entirely different one.

Illustration is the use of one or more examples to support an idea. Illustration permits the writer to support a generalization through particulars or specifics.

Imagery is clear, vivid description that appeals to the sense of sight, smell, touch, sound, or taste. Much imagery exists for its own sake, adding descriptive flavor to an essay. However, imagery (especially when it involves a larger pattern) can also add meaning to an essay.

Induction is a method of logic consisting of the presentation of a series of facts, pieces of information, or instances in order to formulate or build a likely generalization. The key is to provide prior examples before reaching a logical conclusion. Consequently, as a pattern of organization in essay writing, the inductive method requires the careful presentation of relevant data and information before the conclusion is reached at the end of the paper.

Inference involves arriving at a decision or opinion by reasoning from known facts or evidence.

Interrogative sentences are sentences that ask or pose a question.

Introduction is the beginning or opening of an essay. The introduction should alert the reader to the subject by identifying it, set the limits of the essay, and indicate what the thesis (or main idea) will be. Moreover, it should arouse the reader's interest in the subject. Among the devices available in the creation of good introductions are making a simple statement of thesis; giving a clear, vivid description of an important setting; posing a question or series of questions; referring to a relevant historical event; telling an anecdote; using comparison and contrast to frame the subject; using several examples to reinforce the statement of the subject; and presenting a personal attitude about a controversial issue.

Irony is the use of language to suggest the opposite of what is stated. Writers use irony to reveal unpleasant or troublesome realities that exist in life or to poke fun at human weaknesses and foolish attitudes. In an essay there may be verbal irony, in which the result of a sequence of ideas or events is the opposite of what normally would be expected. A key to the identification of irony in an essay is our ability to detect where the author is stating the opposite of what he or she actually believes.

Issue is the main question upon which an entire argument rests. It is the idea that the writer attempts to prove.

Jargon is special words associated with a specific area of knowledge or a particular profession. Writers who employ jargon either assume that readers know specialized terms or take care to define terms for the benefit of the audience.

Juxtaposition as a technique in writing or essay organization is the placing of elements—either similar or contrasting—close together, positioning them side by side in order to illuminate the subject.

Levels of language refer to the kinds of language used in speaking and writing. Basically, there are three main levels of language—formal, informal, and colloquial. Formal English, used in writing or speech, is the type of English employed to address special groups and professional people. Informal English is the sort of writing found in newspapers, magazines, books, and essays. It is popular English for an educated audience but still more formal than colloquial (conversational) English. Colloquial English is spoken (and occasionally written) English used in conversations with friends, employees, and peer group members; it is characterized by the use of slang, idioms, ordinary language, and loose sentence structure.

Linear order   in paragraph development means the clear line of movement from one point to another.

Listing   is a simple technique of illustration in which facts or examples are used to support a topic or generalization.

Logic   as applied to essay writing is correct reasoning based on induction or deduction. The logical basis of an essay must offer reasonable criteria or principles of thought, present these principles in an orderly manner, avoid faults in reasoning, and result in a complete and satisfactory outcome in the reasoning process.

Metaphor   is a type of figurative language in which an item from one category is compared briefly and imaginatively with an item from another category. Writers use such implied comparisons to assign meaning in a fresh, vivid, and concrete way.

Metonymy   is a figure of language in which a thing is not designated by its own name but by another associated with or suggested by it, as in "The Supreme Court has decided" (meaning the judges of the Supreme Court have decided).

Mood   is the creation of atmosphere in descriptive writing.

Motif   in an essay is any series of components that can be detected as a pattern. For example, a particular detail, idea, or image can be elaborated upon or designed to form a pattern or motif in the essay.

Myth   in literature is a traditional story or series of events explaining some basic phenomenon of nature; the origin of humanity; or the customs, institutions, and religious rites of a people. Myth often relates to the exploits of gods, goddesses, and heroes.

Narration   as a form of essay writing is the presentation of a story in order to illustrate an idea.

Non sequitur   in argumentation is a conclusion or inference that does not follow from the premises or evidence on which it is based. The non sequitur thus is a type of logical fallacy.

Objective/subjective   writing refers to the attitude that writers take toward their subject. When writers are objective, they try not to report their personal feelings about the subject; they attempt to be detached, impersonal, and unbiased. Conversely, subjective writing reveals an author's personal attitudes and emotions. For many varieties of college writing, such as business or laboratory reports, term papers, and literary analyses, it is best to be as objective as possible. But for many personal essays in composition courses, the subjective touch is fine. In the hands of skilled writers, the objective and subjective tones often blend.

Onomatopoeia   is the formation of a word by imitating the natural sound associated with the object or action, as in *buzz* or *click*.

Order   is the arrangement of information or materials in an essay. The most common ordering techniques are *chronological order* (time in sequence), *spatial order* (the arrangement of descriptive details), *process order* (a step-by-step approach to an activity), *deductive order* (a thesis followed by information to support it), and *inductive order* (evidence and examples first, followed by the thesis in the form of a conclusion). Some rhetorical patterns, such as comparison and contrast, classification, and argumentation, require other ordering methods. Writers should select those ordering principles that permit them to present materials clearly.

Overstatement is an extravagant or exaggerated claim or statement.

Paradox is a statement that seems to be contradictory but actually contains an element of truth.

Paragraph is a unit in an essay that serves to present and examine one aspect of a topic. Composed normally of a group of sentences (one-sentence paragraphs can be used for emphasis or special effect), the paragraph elaborates an idea within the larger framework of the essay and the thesis unifying it.

Parallelism is a variety of sentence structure in which there is balance or coordination in the presentation of elements. "I came, I saw, I conquered" is a standard example of parallelism, presenting both pronouns and verbs in a coordinated manner. Parallelism can appear in a sentence, a group of sentences, or an entire paragraph.

Paraphrase as a literary method is the process of rewording the thought or meaning expressed in something that has been said or written before.

Parenthetical refers to giving qualifying information or explanation. This information normally is marked off or placed within parentheses.

Parody is ridiculing the language or style of another writer or composer. In parody, a serious subject tends to be treated in a nonsensical manner.

Periphrasis is the use of many words where one or a few would do; it is a roundabout way of speaking or writing.

Persona is the role or characterization that writers occasionally create for themselves in a personal narrative.

Personification is giving an object, a thing, or an idea lifelike or human characteristics, as in the common reference to a car as "she." Like all forms of figurative language, personification adds freshness to description and makes ideas vivid by setting up striking comparisons.

Persuasion is the form of discourse, related to argumentation, that attempts to move a person to action or to influence an audience toward a particular belief.

Point of view is the angle from which a writer tells a story. Many personal and informal essays take the *first-person* (or "I") point of view, which is natural and fitting for essays in which the author wants to speak in a familiar way to the reader. On the other hand, the *third-person* point of view ("he," "she," "it," "they") distances the reader somewhat from the writer. The third-person point of view is useful in essays in which the writers are not talking exclusively about themselves, but about other people, ideas, and events.

Post hoc, ergo propter hoc in logic is the fallacy of thinking that a happening that follows another must be its result. It arises from a confusion about the logical causal relationship.

Process analysis is a pattern of writing that explains in a step-by-step way how something is done, how it is put together, how it works, or how it occurs. The subject can be a mechanical device, a product, an idea, a natural phenomenon, or a historical sequence. However, in all varieties of process analysis, the writer traces all important steps, from beginning to end.

Progression   is the forward movement or succession of acts, events, or ideas presented in an essay.

Proportion   refers to the relative emphasis and length given to an event, an idea, a time, or a topic within the whole essay. Basically, in terms of proportion, the writer gives more emphasis to a major element than to a minor one.

Proposition   is the main point of an argumentative essay—the statement to be defended, proved, or upheld. It is like a *thesis* (see entry) except that it presents an idea that is debatable or can be disputed. The *major proposition* is the main argumentative point; *minor propositions* are the reasons given to support or prove the issue.

Purpose   is what the writer wants to accomplish in an essay. Writers having a clear purpose will know the proper style, language, tone, and materials to utilize in designing an effective essay.

Refutation   in argumentation is a method by which writers recognize and deal effectively with the arguments of their opponents. Their own argument will be stronger if they refute—prove false or wrong—all opposing arguments.

Repetition   is a simple method of achieving emphasis by repeating a word, a phrase, or an idea.

Rhetoric   is the art of using words effectively in speaking or writing. It is also the art of literary composition, particularly in prose, including both figures of speech and such strategies as *comparison and contrast, definition,* and *analysis.*

Rhetorical question   is a question asked only to emphasize a point, introduce a topic, or provoke thought, but not to elicit an answer.

Rhythm   in prose writing is a regular recurrence of elements or features in sentences, creating a patterned emphasis, balance, or contrast.

Sarcasm   is a sneering or taunting attitude in writing, designed to hurt by evaluating or criticizing. Basically, sarcasm is a heavy-handed form of *irony* (see entry). Writers should try to avoid sarcastic writing and to use more acceptable varieties of irony and satire to criticize their subject.

Satire   is the humorous or critical treatment of a subject in order to expose the subject's vices, follies, stupidities, and so forth. The intention of such satire is to reform by exposing the subject to comedy or ridicule.

Sensory language   is language that appeals to any of the five senses—sight, sound, touch, taste, or smell.

Sentimentality   in prose writing is the excessive display of emotion, whether intended or unintended. Because sentimentality can distort the true nature of a situation or an idea, writers should use it cautiously, or not at all.

Series   as a technique in prose is the presentation of several items, often concrete details or similar parts of grammar such as verbs or adjectives, in rapid sequence.

Setting   in narrative and descriptive writing is the time, place, environment, background, or surroundings established by an author.

Simile   is a figurative comparison using *like* or *as.*

Slang   is a kind of language that uses racy or colorful expressions associated more often with speech than with writing. It is colloquial English and should be used in essay writing only to reproduce dialogue or to create a special effect.

Spatial order   in descriptive writing is the careful arrangement of details or materials in space—for example, from left to right, top to bottom, or near to far.

Specific words   (See *general/specific words.*)

Statistics   are facts or data of a numerical kind, assembled and tabulated to present significant information about a given subject. As a technique of illustration, statistics can be useful in analysis and argumentation.

Style   is the specific or characteristic manner of expression, execution, construction, or design of an author. As a manner or mode of expression in language, it is the unique way each writer handles ideas. There are numerous stylistic categories—such as literary, formal, argumentative, and satiric—but ultimately, no two writers have the same style.

Subjective   (See *objective/subjective.*)

Subordination   in sentence structure is the placing of a relatively less important idea in an inferior grammatical position to the main idea. It is the designation of a minor clause that is dependent upon a major clause.

Syllogism   is an argument or form of reasoning in which two statements or premises are made and a logical conclusion is drawn from them. As such, it is a form of deductive logic—reasoning from the general to the particular. The *major premise* presents a quality of class ("All writers are mortal"). The *minor premise* states that a particular subject is a member of that class ("Ernest Hemingway was a writer"). The conclusion states that the qualities of the class and the member of the class are the same ("Hemingway was mortal").

Symbol   is something—normally a concrete image—that exists in itself but also stands for something else or has greater meaning. As a variety of figurative language, the symbol can be a strong feature in an essay, operating to add depth of meaning and even to unify the composition.

Synonym   is a word that means roughly the same as another word. In practice, few words are exactly alike in meaning. Careful writers use synonyms to vary word choice without ever moving too far from the shade of meaning intended.

Theme   is the central idea in an essay; it is also termed the *thesis.* Everything in an essay should support the theme in one way or another.

Thesis   is the main idea in an essay. The *thesis sentence,* appearing early in the essay (normally somewhere in the first paragraph) serves to convey the main idea to the reader in a clear and emphatic manner.

Tone   is the writer's attitude toward his or her subject or material. An essay writer's tone may be objective, subjective, comic, ironic, nostalgic, critical, or a reflection of numerous other attitudes. Tone is the voice that writers give to an essay.

Topic sentence   is the main idea that a paragraph develops. Not all paragraphs contain topic sentences; often the topic is implied.

Transition   is the linking of ideas in sentences, paragraphs, and larger segments of an essay in order to achieve *coherence* (see entry). Among the most common techniques to achieve smooth transitions are (1) repeating a key word or phrase, (2) using a pronoun to refer to a key word or phrase, (3) relying on traditional connectives such as *thus, however, moreover, for example, therefore, finally,* or *in conclusion,* (4) using parallel structure (see *parallelism*), and (5) creating a sentence or paragraph that serves as a bridge from one part of an essay to another. Transition is best achieved when a writer presents ideas and details carefully and in logical order.

Understatement   is a method of making a weaker statement than is warranted by truth, accuracy, or importance.

Unity   is a feature in an essay whereby all material relates to a central concept and contributes to the meaning of the whole. To achieve a unified effect in an essay, the writer must design an effective introduction and conclusion, maintain consistent tone or point of view, develop middle paragraphs in a coherent manner, and above all stick to the subject, never permitting unimportant or irrelevant elements to enter.

Usage   is the way in which a word, phrase, or sentence is used to express a particular idea; it is the customary manner of using a given language in speaking or writing.

Vertical   (See *horizontal/vertical.*)

Voice   is the way you express your ideas to the reader, the tone you take in addressing your audience. Voice reflects your attitude toward both your subject and your readers. (See *tone.*)

Credits

Photos and Illustrations

Page 40: © Joe Rosenthal/AP/Wide World Photos; **41:** © Thomas E. Franklin; **42:** © 2010, The National Campaign to Prevent Teen and Unplanned Pregnancy. Reprinted with permission; **46:** Library of Congress; **47:** Courtesy of Heather Vogel Frederick; **52:** InfoQube graphic reprinted by permission of NeoTech Systems; **67:** © Lars A. Niki; **68:** © Mike Theiler/Reuters/Corbis; **122:** Goya y Lucientes, Francisco de (1746–1828), *The Third of May, 1808*. Painted in 1814. Oil on canvas, 266 × 345 cm. Museo del Prado, Madrid, Spain. Photo © Erich Lessing/Art Resource, NY; **123:** © Eddie Adams/AP/ Wide World Photos; **130:** Figure from Lydia Saad, "Tolerance for Gay Rights at High-Water Mark," Gallup News Service, May 29, 2007. Copyright © 2007 Gallup, Inc. Reprinted with permission; **131:** © Kimberly White/Corbis; **132:** © Getty Images; **174:** © 2010 The Ohio State University Libraries. Reprinted with permission; **175:** © 2009 EBSCO Publishing, Inc. All rights reserved. Abstract from Martha Wörsching, "Gender and images of nature and sport in British and German news magazines: the global and the national in images of advertising," *International Journal of Media & Cultural Politics*, vol. 5, issue 3 (Oct. 2009), p. 217. Reprinted by permission of Intellect; **222:** Courtesy of Rutgers University Press; **226 (Web page):** SPLICEDwire.com © Rob Blackwelder/ SPLICEDwire. Reprinted with permission; **226 (film still):** Courtesy of Photofest, Inc.; **227, 233:** *Donnie Brasco* © 1997 Mandalay Entertainment. All Rights Reserved. Courtesy of Columbia Pictures; **234:** © Mandalay Ent/Baltimore Pics/The Kobal Collection; **236:** © The Everett Collection; **256:** © Oberlin College Archives, Oberlin, Ohio; **257:** © Tom Stewart/Corbis/Stock Market; **296:** © Museum of Fine Art, Ghent, Belgium/The Bridgeman Art Library; **297:** © AP/Wide World Photos; **343:** © Xinhua/Landov; **350:** © National Park Service: Statue of Liberty National Monument; **351:** © Reforma Archivo/ AP/Wide World Photos; **398:** © The Granger Collection, New York; **399:** © Chris Fitzgerald/Candidate Photos/The Image Works ; **426:** © Christine Car; **454:** © Detroit Institute of Arts/The Bridgeman Art Library; **455:** © Digital Vision/PunchStock; **510:** © Photofest; **511:** © HBO/The Kobal Collection; **519:** © AMC/Courtesy: Everett Collection; **572:** © Musée Rodin/Bridgeman Art collection; **573:** *Rabbit*, 1986, Stainless Steel, 41" × 19" × 11 7/8" © Jeff Koons; **585:** © The Trustees of the British Museum; **586:** Roy De Forest, *Canoe of Fate*. 1974. Polymer on canvas. 1975-83-1. Philadelphia Museum of Art: Purchased with the Adele Haas Turner and Beatrice Pastorius Turner Memorial Fund, 1975. Courtesy of The Philadelphia Museum of Art and the Allan Frumkin Gallery; **589:** © Redferns/Getty Images; **599, 602, 604, 607:** © AP/Wide World Photos; **610:** © Stanley Forman; **626:** With kind permission of the University of Edinburgh/ The Bridgeman Art Library; **627:** © Gillian Darley/EDIFICE; **650:** © Angela Wyant/ Getty Images; **652:** © Gene Blevins/LA Daily News/Corbis; **680:** © Corbis; **681:** © Gary

Bramnick/AP/Wide World Photos; **685:** © Bibliotheque Royal, Brussels/The Bridgeman Art Library; **730:** Kensett, John Frederick (1816–1872), *Along the Hudson.* 1852. Smithsonian American Art Museum, Washington, DC, U.S.A. Photo © Smithsonian American Art Museum, Washington, DC/Art Resource, NY; **731:** © Damian Dovarganes/AP/Wide World Photos; **744:** © image100/PunchStock; **790:** © Musee Condée, Chantilly, France/The Bridgeman Art Library; **791:** © Corbis RF

Color Insert

Page 1: © AP/Wide World Photos; **2:** Image courtesy of The Advertising Archives; **3 (top):** Courtesy of Photofest, Inc.; **3 (bottom):** © AMC/Photofest, Inc.; **4:** © AP/Wide World Photos; **5 (top):** © Kaveh Kazemi/Getty Images; **5 (bottom):** © Tim Graham/Getty Images; **6: (top):** *Protect Insurance Companies PSA.* Reprinted by permission of MoveOn .org Political Action; **6 (bottom):** *We Can't Afford to Wait.* Reprinted by permission of MoveOn.org Political Action. YouTube is a trademark of Google Inc.; **7:** © 2010 United States Conference of Catholic Bishops; **8:** © Irwin Thompson/The Dallas Morning News/AP/Wide World Photos

Text

Adler, Mortimer J. "How to Mark a Book," *The Saturday Review of Literature*, July 6, 1941. Reprinted by permission of the author.

Alexie, Sherman. "Superman and Me," *Los Angeles Times*, April 19, 1998. Copyright © 1998 by Sherman Alexie. All rights reserved.

Allen, Woody. "Tails of Manhattan." © 2009 Woody Allen. All Rights Reserved. Originally published in *The New Yorker*, March 30, 2009.

Alvarez, Julia. "Once upon a quinceañera." From *Once Upon a Quinceañera: Coming of Age in the USA.* Copyright © 2007 by Julia Alvarez. Published by Plume, a member of The Penguin Group (USA), Inc., and originally in hardcover by Viking. By permission of Susan Bergholz Literary Services, New York, NY and Lamy, NM. All rights reserved.

Armstrong, Karen. "What's God Got to Do with It?" by Karen Armstrong. Reprinted by permission of *The New Statesman.* Copyright © 2006. All rights reserved.

Atwood, Margaret. "George Orwell: Some Personal Connections" from *Moving Targets: Writing with Intent 1982–2004* by Margaret Atwood, copyright © 2004 O.W. Toad Ltd. Reprinted with the permission of House of Anansi Press.

Baldwin, James. "Stranger in the Village" from *Notes of a Native Son* by James Baldwin. Copyright © 1955, renewed 1983, by James Baldwin. Reprinted by permission of Beacon Press, Boston.

Barry, Dave. "Red, White, and Beer" from *Dave Barry's Greatest Hits* by Dave Barry. Copyright © 1988 by Dave Barry. Reprinted by permission of the author.

Bass, Rick. "Why I Hunt" by Rick Bass. Copyright © 2001 by Rick Bass. First appeared in *Sierra.* Reprinted by permission of the author.

Bordo, Susan. "The Globalization of Eating Disorders" by Susan Bordo. Copyright © Susan Bordo, Otis A. Singletary Professor of the Humanities, University of Kentucky. Reprinted by permission of the author.

Carson, Clayborne. "Two Cheers for *Brown v. Board of Education*" by Clayborne Carson from *Journal of American History*, June 2004: pp. 26–31. Copyright © Organization of American Historians.

Carson, Rachel. "The Obligation to Endure" from *Silent Spring* by Rachel Carson. Copyright © 1962 by Rachel L. Carson, renewed 1990 by Roger Christie. Reprinted by permission of Houghton Mifflin Harcourt Publishing Company. All rights reserved.

Carter, Stephen L. Excerpt from Chapter 1: "The Culture of Disbelief" from *The Culture of Disbelief: How American Law and Politics Trivialize Religious Devotion*, pp. 3–15. Copyright © 1993 Stephen L. Carter. Reprinted by permission of Basic Books, a member of the Perseus Books Group.

Catton, Bruce. "Grant and Lee: A Study in Contrasts" by Bruce Catton from *The American Story* edited by Earl Schenck Miers. Reprinted with permission of William Catton.

Chaudhry, Lakshmi. "Mirror, Mirror On the Web." Reprinted with permission from the January 29, 2007 issue of *The Nation*. For subscription information, call 1-800-333-8536. Portions of each week's *Nation* magazine can be accessed at http://www.thenation.com.

Coles, Robert. "I Listen to My Parents and I Wonder What They Believe" by Robert Coles. Originally published in *Redbook* Magazine, February 1980. Reprinted by permission of the author.

Diamond, Jared. "The Last Americans: Environmental Collapse and the End of Civilization." Copyright © 2003 by Harper's Magazine. All rights reserved. Reproduced from the June issue by special permission. Illustrations by Stan Fellows. Copyright © Stan Fellows. Reprinted by permission of the illustrator, c/o Joanie Bernstein, art rep.

Dillard, Annie. Excerpt from pp. 110–17 from *An American Childhood* by Annie Dillard. Copyright © 1987 by Annie Dillard. Reprinted by permission of HarperCollins Publishers.

D'Souza, Dinesh. "Staying Human" by Dinesh D'Souza from *National Review*, January 22, 2001. Reprinted with permission from the author.

Dyson, Esther. "Cyberspace: If You Don't Love It, Leave It," *The New York Times*, July 16, 1995. Copyright © 1995 by Esther Dyson. Reprinted by permission.

Ecenbarger, William. "We Are the World," *Times-Picayune* (New Orleans), October 12, 2003. Copyright © 2003 by William Ecenbarger. Reprinted by permission of the author.

Ehrenreich, Barbara. Excerpt from "Scrubbing in Maine" from *Nickel and Dimed: On (Not) Getting By in America* by Barbara Ehrenreich. Copyright © 2001 by Barbara Ehrenreich. Reprinted by arrangement with Henry Holt and Company, LLC.

Elbow, Peter. From *Writing without Teachers*, 2nd ed., pp. 3–7. Copyright © 1973, 1998 by Oxford University Press, Inc. By permission of Oxford University Press, Inc.

Ephron, Nora. "The Boston Photographs" from *Scribble Scribble: Notes on the Media*. New York: Knopf, 1978. Reprinted by permission of International Creative Management, Inc. Copyright © 1975 by Nora Ephron. Originally appeared in *Esquire*, November 1975.

Friedman, Thomas L. "Prologue: The Super-Story" from *Longitudes and Attitudes* by Thomas L. Friedman. Copyright © 2002 by Thomas L. Friedman. Reprinted by permission of Farrar, Straus and Giroux, LLC.

Gates, Henry Louis Jr. "Delusions of Grandeur" by Henry Louis Gates Jr. Copyright © 1991 by Henry Louis Gates Jr. Originally published in *Sports Illustrated*. Reprinted by permission of the author.

Kingsolver, Barbara. "Stone Soup" (pp. 135–45) from *High Tide in Tucson: Essays from Now or Never* by Barbara Kingsolver. Copyright © 1995 by Barbara Kingsolver. Reprinted by permission of HarperCollins Publishers.

Krugman, Paul. "The Death of Horatio Alger." Reprinted with permission from the January 5, 2004 issue of *The Nation*. For subscription information, call 1-800-333-8536. Portions of each week's *Nation* magazine can be accessed at http://www.thenation.com.

Lepore, Jill. "It's Spreading." Copyright © 2009 by Jill Lepore. Originally Published in *The New Yorker*. Reprinted by permission of the author.

Lopez, Barry. "Children in the Woods" from *Crossing Open Ground*. Scribner's, 1988. Reprinted by permission of SLL/Sterling Lord Literistic, Inc. Copyright by Barry Holstun Lopez.

Martin, Steve. "Writing Is Easy!" *The New Yorker*, June 24, 1996. Reprinted by permission of International Creative Management, Inc. Copyright © 1996 by Steve Martin for *The New Yorker*.

McKibben, Bill. "The Environmental Issue from Hell" by Bill McKibben from *In These Times*, April 30, 2001. This article is reprinted with permission from *In These Times* magazine (www.inthesetimes.com).

Mead, Margaret. "New Superstitions for Old" (pp. 263–67) from *A Way of Seeing* by Margaret Mead and Rhoda Metraux. Copyright © 1970, 1969, 1968, 1967, 1966, 1965, 1964, 1963, 1962, 1961 by Margaret Mead and Rhoda Metraux. Reprinted by permission of HarperCollins Publishers.

Mendoza, Martha. "Between a Woman and Her Doctor," *Ms.* magazine, Summer 2004. Reprinted by permission of *Ms.* magazine, © 2004.

Mernissi, Fatema. "Digital Scheherazades in the Arab World." Reprinted with permission from *Current History* magazine (March, 2006). © 2006 Current History, Inc.

Mukherjee, Bharati. "American Dreamer." Copyright © 1997 by Bharati Mukherjee. Originally Published in *Mother Jones*. Reprinted by permission of the author.

Murray, Donald M. "The Maker's Eye: Revising Your Own Manuscripts" by Donald Murray from *The Writer*, 1973. Copyright © 1973 by Donald M. Murray. Reprinted by permission of the Rosenberg Group.

Orwell, George. "Politics and the English Language" by George Orwell, copyright 1946 by Sonia Brownell Orwell and renewed 1974 by Sonia Orwell, reproduced from his volume *Shooting an Elephant and Other Essays* by permission of Houghton Mifflin Harcourt Publishing Company.

Perrin, Noel. "The Greenest Campuses: An Idiosyncratic Guide" by Noel Perrin. Copyright © 2001 by Noel Perrin. Originally appeared in *Chronicle of Higher Education*, April 6, 2001. Reprinted by permission of the author.

Pogrebin, Letty Cottin. "Superstitious Minds," *Ms.* Magazine (1988). Reprinted by permission of *Ms.* magazine, © 1988.

Priestley, J. B. "Wrong Ism." Extract by J. B. Priestley from *Essays of Five Decades* (© J. B. Priestley, 1968) is reproduced by permission of PFD (www.pfd.co.uk) on behalf of The Estate of J. B. Priestley.

Quindlen, Anna. "Sex Ed" from *Living Out Loud* by Anna Quindlen, copyright © 1987 by Anna Quindlen. Used by permission of Random House, Inc.

Reed, Ishmael. "America: The Multinational Society" from *Writin' Is Fightin': Forty-Three Years of Boxing on Paper* by Ishmael Reed. Copyright © Ishmael Reed. Reprinted by permission of Lowenstein Associates.

Index